INSIDERS' GUIDE® TO

NASHVILLE

HELP US KEEP THIS GUIDE UP TO DATE

Every effort has been made by the author and editors to make this guide as accurate and useful as possible. However, many changes can occur after a guide is published—establishments close, phone numbers change, facilities come under new management, etc.

We would love to hear from you concerning your experiences with this guide and how you feel it could be improved and be kept up to date. While we may not be able to respond to all comments and suggestions, we'll take them to heart, and we'll make certain to share them with the author. Please send your comments and suggestions to the following address:

The Globe Pequot Press
Reader Response/Editorial Department
P.O. Box 480
Guilford, CT 06437

Or you may e-mail us at: editorial@GlobePequot.com

Thanks for your input, and happy travels!

INSIDERS' GUIDE® SERIES

INSIDERS' GUIDE® TO

NASHVILLE

SEVENTH EDITION

JACKIE SHECKLER FINCH

INSIDERS' GUIDE®

GUILFORD, CONNECTICUT
AN IMPRINT OF THE GLOBE PEQUOT PRESS

The prices and rates in this guidebook were confirmed at press time. We recommend, however, that you call establishments before traveling to obtain current information.

INSIDERS' GUIDE®

Copyright © 2003, 2005, 2007, 2009 by Morris Book Publishing, LLC

Text design by Sheryl Kober
Maps by XNR Productions, Inc. © Morris Book Publishing, LLC

ISSN 1525-8157
ISBN 978-0-7627-4867-9

Printed in the United States of America
10 9 8 7 6 5 4 3 2 1

CONTENTS

Directory of Maps

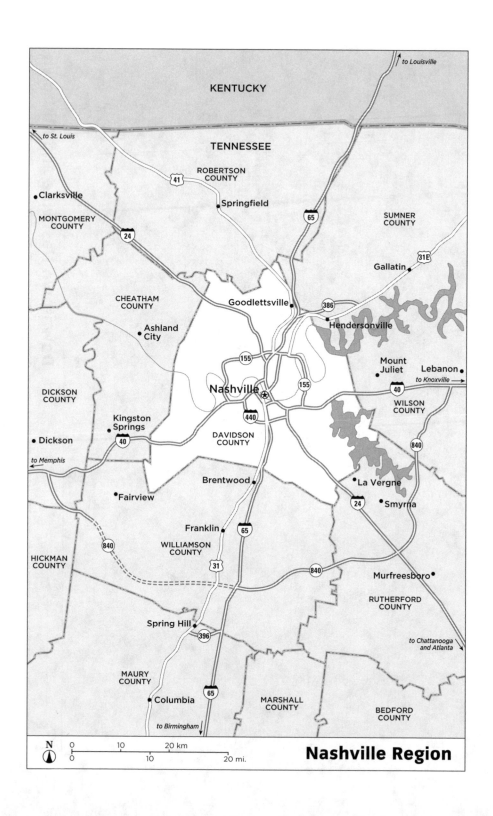

Nashville Region

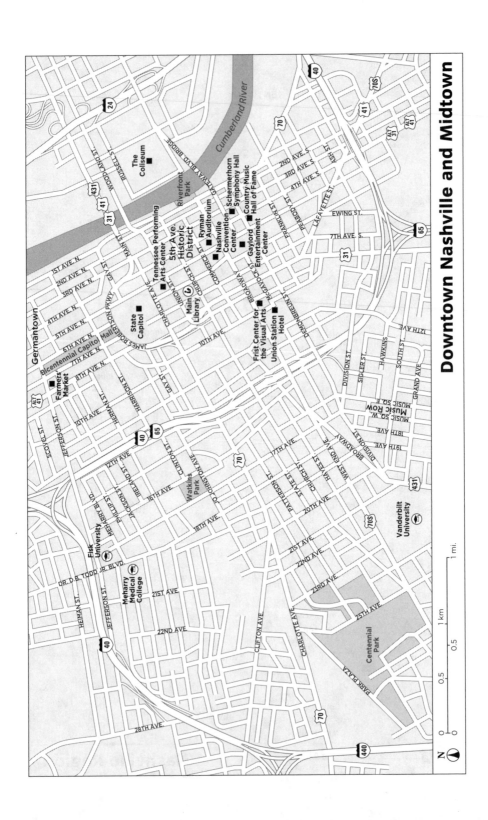

Downtown Nashville and Midtown

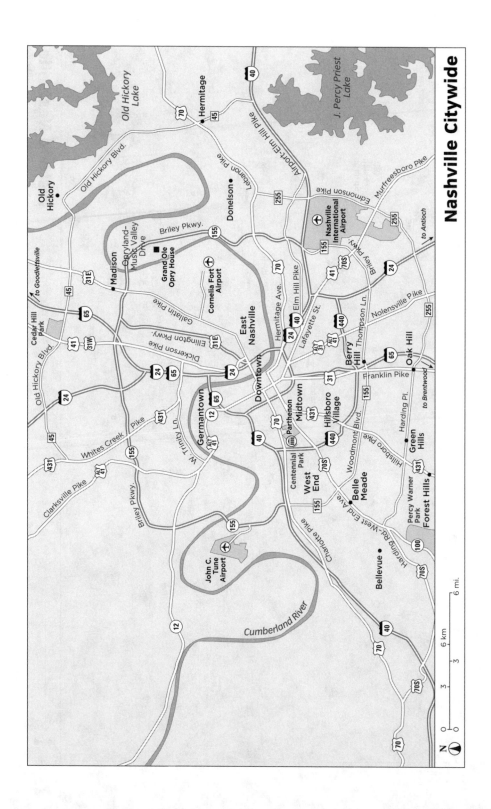

Nashville Citywide

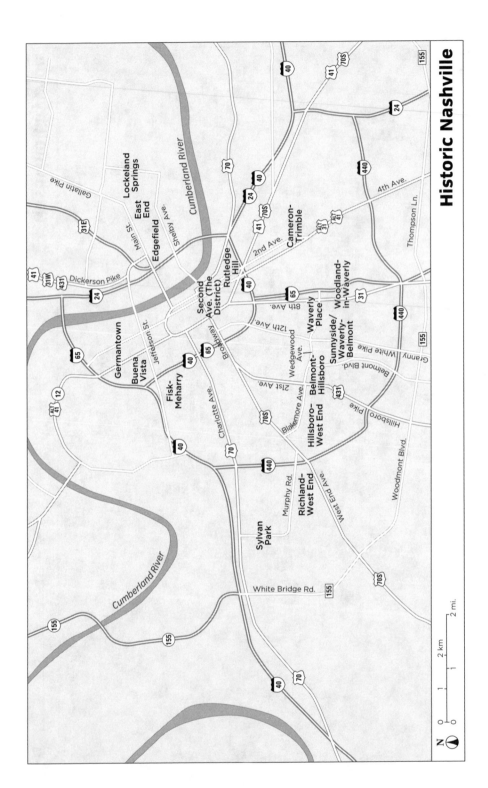

Historic Nashville

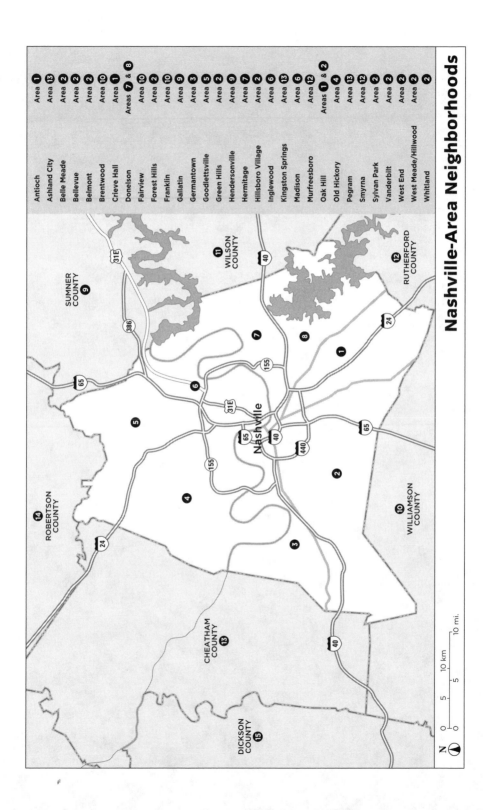

Nashville-Area Neighborhoods

Antioch	Area ❶
Ashland City	Area ⓭
Belle Meade	Area ❷
Bellevue	Area ❷
Belmont	Area ❷
Brentwood	Area ❿
Crieve Hall	Area ❶
Donelson	Areas ❼ & ❽
Fairview	Area ❿
Forest Hills	Area ❷
Franklin	Area ❿
Gallatin	Area ❾
Germantown	Area ❸
Goodlettsville	Area ❺
Green Hills	Area ❷
Hendersonville	Area ❾
Hermitage	Area ❼
Hillsboro Village	Area ❷
Inglewood	Area ❻
Kingston Springs	Area ⓭
Madison	Area ❻
Murfreesboro	Area ⓬
Oak Hill	Areas ❶ & ❷
Old Hickory	Area ❹
Pegram	Area ⓭
Smyrna	Area ⓬
Sylvan Park	Area ❷
Vanderbilt	Area ❷
West End	Area ❷
West Meade/Hillwood	Area ❷
Whitland	Area ❷

PREFACE

Nashville!

If you're reading this, it's likely to be because you are either visiting or planning to visit Nashville or are a new resident. Or perhaps you are a Nashville native or well-entrenched transplant who wants to learn more about this great city. Whatever the case may be, you have come to the right place. The book is loaded with information about Nashville—from its interesting history to its restaurants and neighborhoods, and from its recreation opportunities to its colleges and universities. The pages are packed with helpful Insiders' tips, too (look for the [i]).

If you have a previous edition of the *Insiders' Guide to Nashville,* you'll definitely want to add this one to your collection. Nashville is ever-changing and growing. With that in mind, we've made many, many updates in every chapter of this book. Throughout the following pages you'll find new information on restaurants, nightspots, events, attractions, recreation, education, and much more. We have expanded our neighborhoods and real estate coverage into a more comprehensive, and rather hefty, chapter titled Relocation. This chapter should be especially helpful for newcomers as well as for those who want to learn more about neighborhoods and real estate in Nashville and the surrounding areas.

If it's Nashville's music that interests you, know that you won't find any guidebook with a more comprehensive Insiders' overview of our city's music scene than *Insiders' Guide to Nashville.*

Nashville is known worldwide as Music City. This is the home of country music and the *Grand Ole Opry.* We are proud of our musical heritage and the role the city and its people have played in creating what has become one of the most loved and most listened-to genres of music. In this book you'll find page after page of information about Nashville's music culture. We'll tell you all about the Opry and other music attractions, the best places to hear live music, and our favorite music events and festivals.

The spotlight is always on Nashville's music, but as you'll see when you flip through the pages of this book, there is much more to Nashville than music. Nashville is a leader in education, publishing, and health care. Our population continues to grow because the word is getting out that Nashville is a wonderful place to call home—it has the just-right combination of big-city and small-town qualities that makes it appealing to longtime residents, former big-city dwellers, relocating companies, and other newcomers.

In writing *Insiders' Guide to Nashville,* we've tried to cover just about every topic we could think of, from a real Insider's viewpoint. We haven't attempted to cover every place in Nashville, but if you explore the many chapters in this book, we guarantee you'll make some new discoveries. We encourage you to use this book as a guide to learning more about Nashville and its surrounding area. We hope to spark your interest in the city and perhaps lead you to some new experiences.

Tell your friends about *Insiders' Guide to Nashville.* Before long, you and everyone you know will be Nashville Insiders!

ACKNOWLEDGMENTS

Many thanks to Nashville residents, public-relations officials, and business owners who took the time to help me update this book. Thanks especially to Heather Middleton of the Nashville Convention & Visitors Bureau for her patience and answers to my endless questions, and to Cindy Dupree of Tennessee Tourism for her valuable assistance. My gratitude to my daughter, Kelly Rose, for helping carry the load, and to my grandchildren, Logan Peters, Stefanie Rose, and Sean Rose, for their encouragement.

This book is dedicated to my parents, Jack and Margaret Poynter, for instilling in me the desire to travel. And to my first traveling buddies—my sisters, Elaine Emmich, Jennifer Davenport Boyer, Juliette Maples, and Jeanine Clifford; and my brothers, Jim and Joe Poynter. And to our "second family"—Aunt Daisy and my cousins, Jean Abbott, Gary Norris, Georgianna Fultz, and Peggy Jones.

A special remembrance to my husband, Bill Finch, whose spirit goes with me every mile and step of the way through life's journey.

—Jackie Sheckler Finch

HOW TO USE THIS BOOK

Insiders' Guide to Nashville is meant to be used, and used often. It is not a coffee-table book (even though we believe it will add a certain grace and elegance to your table—and when friends ask about it, you can tell them where to get one of their own). Just be sure to take it with you whenever you go out, so you can avoid potentially unpleasant conversations like this:

"Honey, what was the name of that little barbecue place that sounded so appetizing?"

"It's in our *Insiders' Guide*. Didn't you bring it?"

"I thought you had it."

"Aarrgghh!"

Obviously, how you use the book is not nearly as important as that you use it. That said, we'd like to make a few suggestions that will help you make the most of this book, so you soon will feel like an Insider yourself.

First of all, feel free to experience the book on your own terms. Obviously, if you and the family are hungry right now, you'll want to go immediately to the Restaurants chapter. If you're looking for something exciting to do, turn to Attractions or Kidstuff or Recreation or Nightlife. In the mood to discover why Nashville is known worldwide as "Music City"? We've devoted a hefty chapter to that subject, too, and you may be surprised at the diversity of sounds you can find here. Need a way to get from point A to point B? Then you may want to go first to the Getting Here, Getting Around chapter. Or you might choose to take the casual approach and simply flip through the book, skimming the pages to see what catches your eye. Throughout the book we've given you Insiders' tips (indicated by 🛈) for quick insights, and more lengthy Close-Ups with information that is particularly interesting or helpful.

We've designed *Insiders' Guide to Nashville* to be self-contained. That means each chapter essentially stands on its own, so wherever you start reading, you'll find the information you need to enjoy that aspect of Nashville life. And there are lots of cross-references.

While our primary focus is Nashville and Davidson County, we'll also take you through parts of the 13-county Metropolitan Statistical Area—Cannon, Cheatham, Dickson, Hickman, Macon, Robertson, Rutherford, Smith, Sumner, Trousdale, Williamson, and Wilson Counties. You'll visit towns and communities such as Hermitage, Old Hickory, Brentwood, Franklin, Hendersonville, Goodlettsville, Murfreesboro, Lebanon, Springfield, Smyrna, and Madison, to name a few. And our Day Trips and Weekend Getaways chapter will take you to some great places a little farther away but still within easy driving distance.

Don't hesitate to personalize this book—make it your own! Scribble notes in the margins, circle places you have visited, underline points of interest. There's even a chance that, somewhere along the way, you might disagree with something we've said. That is to be expected in any forum where someone dares to make subjective judgments. Go ahead, write something like "They're way off base on this one!"

You might also discover some diner or nightclub that has escaped our notice. Make a note of it and, if you would be so kind, share it with us so we can include it in our next edition.

Please remember that, in a rapidly growing metropolitan area such as Nashville, things are bound to change. By the time you read this book, there will be new places to visit and experiences to savor—and, unfortunately, some old favorites that might have bid us farewell. Menus will be revised and schedules altered. It's always a good idea to call before visiting an attraction or restaurant. And, again, feel free to share your experiences with us, so we can keep *Insiders' Guide to Nashville* as accurate and up-to-date as possible.

Address all correspondence (complaints as well as information and compliments) to:

The Globe Pequot Press

Reader Response/Editorial Department

P.O. Box 480

Guilford, CT 06437-0480

Or e-mail us at editorial@GlobePequot.com.

A final thought: If you enjoy *Insiders' Guide to Nashville,* you might be interested to know that Insiders' Guides are also available for many other American cities. Be sure to visit Insiders' Guide online at www.insiders.com.

We're pleased that, whether you're a visitor, a newcomer, or perhaps even a longtime resident wanting to see whether you've been missing anything, you have chosen us to be your companion here in Nashville. We sincerely hope we're able to make your experience a pleasant one.

AREA OVERVIEW

Welcome to Nashville! In the more than 200 years since its founding in 1779, the community now known worldwide as Nashville, Tennessee, has earned fame and prestige in many areas and, in the process, earned a proportionate number of nicknames. "Music City"… "Athens of the South"…"Wall Street of the South"… "The Buckle of the Bible Belt"…"City of Parks"—those are just a few of the names Nashville has been given throughout its history.

The problem we have with such nicknames is that each is severely limited, generally paying tribute to only one facet of what is truly a multifaceted metropolitan area. At the same time, we appreciate that each of these names, in its own way, serves as a tribute to some of the accomplishments that have made our city great. In other words, it is significant that Nashville has inspired so many terms of endearment, and so we'll look at these nicknames in greater detail later in this chapter. But first, we'd like to take time to point out something that, although you probably already know it, can occasionally get obscured by all the hype. And that is: Nashville is a *wonderful* place to live or to visit.

You might say that Nashville is the embodiment of Southern hospitality. Waitresses call you "honey" while serving you down-home delicacies such as fried chicken, made-from-scratch biscuits, grits, and country ham. People smile and speak to you on the street and are generally willing to give you the time of day or directions if you need them. Adding to the laid-back hospitable atmosphere are a few antebellum mansions, some of which could have been used as sets for *Gone with the Wind;* elegant Victorian homes; and lush flowering gardens. Nashville is a casual place, and many businesspeople wear cowboy boots with their suits. If you're thinking now that we're merely catering to stereotypes, rest assured that these scenes are all very real, although they're only a part of the big picture. There are, of course, plenty of Nashvillians who wouldn't be caught dead in cowboy boots, for example, and many who prefer to dine on continental cuisine and live in modern condominiums. Such is the diversity that characterizes this town.

This is a place where, fortunately, quality of life and cost of living don't go hand in hand. According to the ACCRA Cost of Living Index for the first quarter of 2008 Nashville's cost of living was 97.6 percent of the national average. (In comparison, the cost of living for Richmond, Virginia—a comparable-size city—was 107.6 percent.) In Tennessee you pay no state income tax—although this may someday change.

Of course, with attractions like the *Grand Ole Opry,* the Country Music Hall of Fame & Museum, the Ryman Auditorium, historic Belle Meade Plantation, the Hermitage estate of Andrew Jackson, and countless museums, art galleries, and outdoor recreational activities, Nashville remains a top tourist destination among Americans as well as visitors from other countries.

Whether you're here on vacation or you're planning to make a home here, you'll find a wealth of opportunities in practically any area that interests you, from education to recreation, from child care to retirement.

Nashville Vital Statistics

Founded: 1779 as Fort Nashborough; established as town of Nashville by North Carolina Legislature in 1784

Mayor/governor: Mayor Bill Purcell and Governor Phil Bredesen

Population:

• Nashville-Davidson County: 569,891

• Nashville-Davidson-Murfreesboro Metropolitan Statistical Area: 1,311,789

• Tennessee: 5,689,283

Area:

• Nashville: 533 square miles

• Nashville Economic Market: 5,225 square miles

Counties in the Nashville area (with major cities and county seats):

• Davidson County (Nashville is the capital)

• Cannon County (county seat Woodbury)

• Cheatham County (county seat Ashland City)

• Dickson County (Dickson, county seat Charlotte)

• Hickman County (county seat Centerville)

• Macon County (county seat Lafayette)

• Maury County (county seat Columbia)

• Montgomery County (county seat Clarksville)

• Robertson County (county seat Springfield)

• Rutherford County (Smyrna, county seat Murfreesboro)

• Smith County (county seat Carthage)

• Sumner County (Hendersonville, Portland, county seat Gallatin)

• Trousdale County (county seat Hartsville)

• Williamson County (Brentwood, county seat Franklin)

• Wilson County (county seat Lebanon)

Major airport/major interstates:

• Nashville International Airport; I-24, I-40, and I-65 converge in Nashville

Nickname: "Music City"

Average temperatures:

• Winter: High 39°F, low 30°F, mean 39°F

• Summer: High 88°F, low 67°F, mean 78°F

• Annual: High 70°F, low 48°F, mean 59°F

Average annual precipitation: Rainfall: 47.3 inches; snowfall: 11.0 inches

Major colleges and universities:

• Nashville: Vanderbilt University, Belmont University, Fisk University, David Lipscomb University, Meharry Medical College, Tennessee State University, Trevecca Nazarene College

• Nashville area: Austin Peay State University, Cumberland University, Middle Tennessee State University

Notable events in Nashville history:

December 25, 1779: Fort Nashborough is founded.

1784: North Carolina Legislature establishes town of Nashville, population 600.

June 1, 1796: Tennessee becomes the 16th state in the Union. Also, Nashville's first church is built.

1806: Nashville is incorporated as a city.

1850: Nashville's population tops 10,000. The Adelphi Theater opens.

1854: Nashville & Chattanooga Railroad is completed.

June 8, 1861: Tennessee becomes 11th and final state to join the Confederacy.

February 24, 1862: Nashville is captured by Union troops.

December 2, 1865: Battle of Nashville, the last major conflict of the Civil War, is fought.

April 15, 1865: President Lincoln dies; Andrew Johnson becomes the 17th U.S. president.

July 24, 1866: Tennessee is first state to be readmitted into the Union.

1866: Fisk School (now known as Fisk University), a free school for African Americans, opens.

1873: Vanderbilt University is founded, opening its doors in 1875.

1876: Meharry Medical College, now the country's largest private medical school for African Americans, opens.

1892: Union Gospel Tabernacle, later renamed Ryman Auditorium, opens.

November 28, 1925: The WSM Barn Dance (later named the *Grand Ole Opry*) makes its radio premiere.

1943: Roy Acuff and Fred Rose establish Acuff-Rose Publishing, a leader in the publishing of country songs.

1952: Owen Bradley opens a studio on 16th Avenue S., the beginning of Music Row.

1957: Chet Atkins and Owen Bradley begin developing the "Nashville Sound."

1957: Nashville public schools are desegregated.

1958: The Country Music Association is founded.

May 10, 1960: Nashville becomes Tennessee's first major city to desegregate public facilities.

1962: Voters approve the merger of Nashville and Davidson County governments.

1972: Opryland USA theme park, the start of the Opryland complex, opens.

March 16, 1974: *Grand Ole Opry* leaves the historic Ryman Auditorium and moves into the *Grand Ole Opry* House at Opryland. President Richard Nixon participates.

1993: The renovated Ryman Auditorium reopens.

1996: Nashville Arena opens (it is renamed Gaylord Entertainment Center in August 1999).

1997: Opryland theme park closes. NFL's Houston Oilers (later the Tennessee Titans) relocate to Nashville, becoming Tennessee's first NFL team.

April 16, 1998: Tornadoes strike downtown and east Nashville.

May 11, 2000: Opry Mills opens on the site of the former Opryland theme park.

2000: Native son Al Gore becomes the Democratic nominee for president and loses to George W. Bush in the closest presidential race in U.S. history.

May 17, 2001: The new Country Music Hall of Fame Museum opens downtown.

June 9, 2001: The new downtown library opens.

June 2006: The Musicians Hall of Fame and Museum opens.

October 2006: The Schermerhorn Symphony Center opens.

September 2007: The Barbershop Harmony Society opens it headquarters.

Major area employers: Vanderbilt University and Medical Center, Saturn Corporation, Dell Computer Corporation, HCA Inc., Gaylord Entertainment, Nissan North America, Kroger Company, United Parcel Service, AmSouth Bank, Saint Thomas Hospital, Tennessee state government

Famous sons and daughters: Andrew Jackson, James K. Polk, Andrew Johnson, Wilma Rudolph, Kitty Wells, Pat Boone, Oprah Winfrey, Al Gore, Reese Witherspoon (see more "Nashville Notables" later in this chapter)

Public transportation: Metropolitan Transit Authority operates intercity bus lines, downtown trolleys, and two downtown landports.

Military base: Fort Campbell, on the Tennessee-Kentucky state line at Clarksville, Tennessee, and Fort Campbell, Kentucky

Driving laws:
• General speed limits: 70 mph on interstates in rural areas, 55 mph in urban areas, 30–35 mph in residential and business areas
• When it's raining or snowing, the law requires use of headlights as well as windshield wipers.
• HOV lanes (marked with a diamond): Two or more people must be in your vehicle for use from 7:00 to 9:00 a.m. Monday through Friday (inbound), and 4:00 to 6:00 p.m. Monday through Friday (outbound).

Alcohol laws:
• You must be 21 to legally purchase or consume alcoholic beverages.
• The blood alcohol level at which one is legally presumed to be intoxicated is 0.08.
• Beer can be purchased in grocery and convenience markets on Sunday, but liquor stores are closed.
• Liquor-by-the-drink is available in restaurants on Sunday after 10:00 a.m.
• Bars can remain open until 3:00 a.m.

Daily newspapers: *The Tennessean, The City Paper*

Weekly newspaper: *The Nashville Scene*

Taxes:
• State sales tax is 5.5 percent for food and grocery items and 7 percent for all other items; prepared meals are taxed at 7 percent. With a local option tax of 2.25 percent; combined 9.25 percent tax applies in most counties to almost all purchases.
• Hotel-motel occupancy tax is 14.25 percent (9.25 percent sales tax plus 5 percent) in Nashville-Davidson County.

Chamber of commerce:

Nashville Area Chamber of Commerce
211 Commerce Street, Suite 100, Nashville, TN 37201
(615) 743-3000
(615) 256-3074 (fax)
www.nashvillechamber.com

Visitor center:

Nashville Convention and Visitors Bureau
161 Fourth Avenue N., Nashville, TN 37219
(615) 259-4700
www.nashvillecvb.com

Time/weather:

WSIX Time & Temperature Service: (615) 259-2222
National Weather Service: www.srh.noaa.gov/bna

SOME BASIC FACTS

Nashville, the capital of Tennessee, is the center of a 13-county metropolitan statistical area (MSA) with a population of some 1.3 million, which makes it the most populated MSA in the state. The Nashville-Davidson-Murfreesboro MSA covers the counties of Davidson, Cheatham, Dickson, Robertson, Rutherford, Sumner, Wilson, and Williamson, as well as five counties that were added when the area's MSA was expanded in 2003: Cannon, Hickman, Macon, Smith, and Trousdale.

In addition, two other counties—Maury, with its county seat of Columbia; and Montgomery, with its county seat of Clarksville—are considered part of the "Nashville Economic Market."

Nashville-Davidson County has a combined metropolitan government. According to the 2000 U.S. census, the population of Nashville-Davidson County is 569,891. That population makes Nashville the second largest city in Tennessee, after Memphis, and Nashville's 533 square miles make it one of the United States' largest cities in area.

Nashville is one of the fastest-growing large cities in the nation, with vigorous population growth that has continued for more than three decades. What brings so many people here is a strong economy that even in times of economic slowdown has bucked national trends,

i Close to 40 historical markers decorate the roadsides and neighborhoods of west Nashville. They commemorate significant sites in the Battle of Nashville, the last major battle of the Civil War.

maintaining below-average unemployment rates and luring big corporate employers such as Dell Computer. That has helped land Nashville on some impressive national lists: BusinessWeek .com and *Sperling's Best Places* named Nashville, in 2007, one of the best places for artists in the United States.

Nashville itself has a diverse ethnic makeup, with African Americans comprising about 16 percent of the population according to the 2000 U.S. census, and other ethnic groups such as Asians and Hispanics also present in growing numbers. That diversity was honored nationwide in 2007 when Nashville was ranked No. 5 in *Black Enterprise* magazine's Top 10 Best Cities for African Americans.

i Tennessee ties Missouri as the most neighborly state in the nation. Eight states border Tennessee: Arkansas, Alabama, Georgia, Kentucky, Mississippi, Missouri, North Carolina, and Virginia.

A PROGRESSIVE AND SOPHISTICATED CITY

When Nashville and Davidson County formed their combined city-county metropolitan government in 1962, it was one of the first of its kind. The act served a dual purpose: increasing a tax base that had been dwindling because of numbers of people moving from the city to the suburbs, and eliminating much duplication of services, thus resulting in a more efficient form of government. Still, several cities located within the boundaries of Metro Nashville opted to remain separate from the new metropolitan government. These include the cities of Belle Meade, Berry Hill, Goodlettsville, and Forest Hills. While located within the Nashville city limits, they maintain their own city governments and provide different levels of service to their residents.

Nashville has proven to be a progressive and sophisticated city in other ways, such as race relations and urban development. During the turbulence of the civil rights movement, the city made great strides without much of the violence that marked other southern cities at this time. Desegregation of public schools began in 1957 in response to a class-action suit filed by a black man named A. Z. Kelley, who wanted his son to attend a neighborhood school rather than be bused across town. In 1960, after several peaceful sit-ins at downtown lunch counters, desegregation also began taking effect in public facilities, a process that was largely complete by the summer of 1963. And in 1967 Vanderbilt University's Perry Wallace became the Southeastern Conference's first African-American basketball player.

i | **Nashville is one of the largest cities in the United States in terms of area. It occupies 533 square miles. In comparison, Los Angeles covers 468 square miles.**

The early 1950s witnessed the Capitol Hill Redevelopment Project, one of the nation's first federal urban renewal projects. Through this and other similar undertakings, the city has largely demonstrated that it understands the challenge of balancing the sometimes conflicting goals of progress and preservation. During the late 1970s a commission studying Nashville's long-term development adopted the motto "Celebrating the Past While Looking into the Future." Now, more than two decades later, those words still serve to describe Nashville's philosophy.

Downtown Nashville today is a vibrant, thriving area that is a blend of old and new. While many of the old buildings that line Broadway have changed little since the turn of the 20th century, steel-and-glass skyscrapers loom nearby. Just down the street from the legendary honky-tonks where many of yesterday's country singers and songwriters first plied their trade, you'll also find newer attractions such as the Hard Rock Cafe. The Ryman Auditorium, a true landmark since its completion in 1892, has served as a tabernacle, assembly hall, and theater as well as onetime home of the *Grand Ole Opry*. The beautifully restored building still plays host to a variety of entertainers, including modern-day legends such as Bruce Springsteen and Bob Dylan.

Another example of Nashville's ingenuity in forging onward while honoring its illustrious past is the Bicentennial Capitol Mall State Park (see our Parks chapter), which opened in 1996. This Tennessee state park, just north of the State Capitol downtown, was built on land that had long been considered too swampy for development. As the town's skyline grew during the building boom of the 1950s and '60s, the State Capitol disappeared from view on three of its four sides—east, west, and south. The north side is now a 19-acre commemoration of Tennessee's first 200 years, highlighted by such features as a 200-foot granite map of the state embedded in a concrete plaza, a visitor center, 31 fountains representing Tennessee's major rivers, a Walk of Counties with a time capsule from each of the state's 95 counties, a Wall of Tennessee History, and an outdoor amphitheater. Looming proudly over the park from atop downtown's tallest hill is the beautiful State Capitol.

Nashville's inventiveness will be further tested into the 21st century. As with any metropolitan

The Nashville skyline reflects the city's variety. JACKIE SHECKLER FINCH

area, Nashville must find creative and progressive ways to answer questions related to such vital issues as continued growth and modernization, race relations, education, crime, poverty, and homelessness. Obviously, many of these issues are related. Like our counterparts nationwide, we must find better ways for people from various backgrounds to live together in harmony, while equipping themselves with the knowledge and skills they need to build better lives.

Now, about those nicknames…

"MUSIC CITY"

From Roy Acuff, Minnie Pearl, Ernest Tubb, and Hank Williams to Garth Brooks, Faith Hill, Alan Jackson, and Shania Twain, Nashville has long been known as the world's capital of country music. But while country music remains Nashville's signature sound, other styles of music call Nashville home as well. Music City is headquarters for the growing contemporary Christian and gospel music industry, and stars of the genre—such as Amy Grant, Michael W. Smith, Jars of Clay, and dc Talk—all live or spend large amounts of time here. Premier jazz and classical label Naxos USA moved its U.S. headquarters from New Jersey to Nashville in 1998.

Nashville has also seen an explosion in the number of independent labels opening their doors. Fueled in part by a decline in country music sales, several increasingly frustrated artists and music executives who decry what they call a restrictive climate at country radio have launched their own labels. This renewed energy has yielded positive results, as such alt-country artists as Gillian Welch, Lucinda Williams, Kim Richey, Todd Snider, and Ryan Adams burn up the critics' polls and the cash registers.

> **i** Nashville was ranked No. 4 in the Top 10 destinations for motorcoach travel in 2007 *ByWays* magazine. Tennessee was named No. 4 out of the Top 10 motorcoach states. Nashville's *Grand Ole Opry* was No. 2 in the "man-made" attractions category, behind Disney World.

Record labels, recording studios, music publishers, video production firms, booking agencies, management companies, and more support all this activity; in turn, these industries increase the city's appeal to artists, musicians, songwriters, and executives from around the world.

Since 1943 when Roy Acuff and Fred Rose launched Nashville's first music-publishing company, *Nashville* has been synonymous with *songwriting*. Today Nashville serves as the worldwide headquarters for Sony/ATV Tree, one of the world's largest music publishers, as well as a host of smaller publishing houses, many of which operate out of cozy foursquare cottages. Music licensing organizations BMI and SESAC make their headquarters in Nashville as well, while ASCAP's glittering Nashville office complex is the unofficial gateway to Music Row.

Some of pop music's biggest hits were written by Nashville tunesmiths. Bette Midler has Nashville songwriters to thank for two of her biggest successes, "Wind Beneath My Wings" and "From a Distance." And Eric Clapton's Grammywinning smash "Change the World" was penned by three local songwriters who frequently appear at various clubs around town.

Recent years have also seen a new phenomenon whereby a hit country ballad is remixed (cynics would say "de-twanged") and sent out to pop radio, where it takes up permanent residence in the No. 1 slot on the pop charts. As a result, decountrified pop songs like "Amazed," "I Hope You Dance," "One More Day," and "I Swear" have become a part of virtually every senior prom, wedding celebration, and high school graduation ceremony from coast to coast.

All this and country music, too. It's a heady mix that truly makes Nashville, in every respect, Music City.

> **i** Union soldiers brought baseball to Nashville during the Civil War, playing in the area where the Bicentennial Capitol Mall State Park now stands. In the early 1900s Nashville had a Southern Association team that played at Sulphur Dell Park, in the same area, and won championships in 1901, 1902, and 1908.

Close-up

Nashville Notables

Not surprisingly, perhaps, the renowned musicians and music industry giants who hang their hats in Nashville make up a veritable Who's Who list. But Music City has long been home to many notable nonmusicians. Other famous Nashvillians outside country music include:

- James Robertson and John Donelson, who led Nashville's first settlers to the area.

- Andrew "Old Hickory" Jackson, hero of the Battle of New Orleans and seventh president of the United States.

- James K. Polk, 11th president of the United States.

- Andrew Johnson, 17th president of the United States.

- Sam Houston, who led the Texas army to victory over Santa Ana after the defeat at the Alamo.

- Civil rights leader Julian Bond.

- John Bell, U.S. congressman, Speaker of the House, and senator who ran unsuccessfully for president in 1860 against Abraham Lincoln.

- Thomas Hart Benton, U.S. senator and onetime friend of Andrew Jackson, who later shot Jackson during a brawl in Nashville.

- William Walker, a soldier of fortune who became president of Nicaragua but was executed by a Honduran firing squad four years later when he tried to become Honduran president.

- Mickey Kantor, former U.S. secretary of commerce and advisor to President Bill Clinton.

- Felix Grundy, prominent lawyer, congressman, senator, and U.S. attorney general.

- Wilma Rudolph, who ran for three gold medals at the 1960 Summer Olympics in Rome.

- Former Vice President Al Gore.

- Fred Thompson, Watergate investigator, U.S. senator, and actor.

- Grantland Rice, the sportswriter who first wrote of the University of Notre Dame's "Four Horsemen of the Apocalypse."

- Outlaws Jesse and Frank James, who lived here under assumed names during the 1870s.

- *Designing Women* actress Annie Potts.

- Frank Andrews, successor of Gen. Dwight D. Eisenhower as army commander of the European Theater and namesake of Andrews Air Force Base in Maryland.

- Robert Penn Warren, Vanderbilt University alumnus and Pulitzer Prize–winning author of *All the King's Men*.

- Ron Mercer, former University of Kentucky basketball star and current NBA star.

- Dinah Shore, singer and Emmy-winning television entertainer.

- Oprah Winfrey, actress and TV talk-show host.

- Reese Witherspoon, actress.

- Actress Ashley Judd and her husband, race car driver Dario Franchitti.

- Capt. William Driver, credited with dubbing the American flag "Old Glory."

"ATHENS OF THE SOUTH"

It's easy, we confess, to be a little skeptical about titles like this. After all, Lexington, Kentucky, about a three-hour drive northeast, has long perpetuated its claim to the title "Athens of the West," which was bestowed back when it was still a thriving frontier town. How many Athenses can you have in one region? But we have to say that Nashville is worthy of the title. The city is brimming with arts, culture, learning institutions, and classical Greek architecture, and by the late 1800s, people were calling it "Athens of the South" (we're not sure who said it first, though Jesse C. Burt, in his 1959 book *Nashville: Its Life and Times*, attributes it to Philip Lindsley, a highly influential educator). In 1897 Nashville made the title tangible by celebrating its 100th birthday around a full-size replica of the Parthenon in the middle of Centennial Park (see our History and Parks chapters for details).

In Nashville and the rest of Middle Tennessee, education for all ages is a priority. We particularly realize the importance of higher education, as our 19 colleges, universities, technical schools, and other postsecondary programs, with a total enrollment of more than 85,000 students, will attest. In the Nashville metropolitan statistical area, more than 55 percent of adults 25 and older have at least one year of college education; more than 69,000 people have graduate or professional degrees. Each year more than 10,000 new college graduates enter the workforce.

Vanderbilt University has been ranked among the nation's best; its schools of education, medicine, business, and law have also been ranked near the top. Vanderbilt University Medical Center is the largest private employer in Middle Tennessee, with a workforce of some 13,600.

Meharry Medical College is the largest private, African-American institution dedicated solely to educating health-care professionals and scientists in the United States. Nearly 15 percent of all African-American physicians and dentists practicing in the United States are Meharry graduates.

Founded in 1866, Fisk University, like Meharry, is renowned for its contributions to minority higher education. One out of every six of the nation's African-American doctors, dentists, and lawyers is a Fisk graduate. The school has also gained nationwide attention for its Fisk Jubilee Singers and its collection of modern and African-American art.

Nashville has also made substantial contributions to primary education. In 1855 it became the first southern city to establish a public school system. In 1963 Susan Gray, an educational researcher at the city's Peabody College, introduced a program for disadvantaged preschoolers that became the prototype for Head Start. Peabody College, which became a part of Vanderbilt in 1979, remains a leading center for training teachers.

For more information on education in Nashville, see our Education and Child Care chapter.

As for the arts and culture, Nashville has a ballet, a symphony orchestra, a Broadway Series, an opera company, several theater groups, numerous art galleries, and the Frist Center for the Visual Arts. For more information see The Arts chapter.

Incidentally, the Athens comparison even extends to food. As you'll discover in our Restaurants chapter, you can dine on falafel, tabbouleh, or a Greek salad in Nashville.

i The renovated Downtown Presbyterian Church is one of the few examples of Egyptian Revival architecture in the entire country. It was built in 1851 by William Strickland, a prominent architect who came to Nashville to build the State Capitol.

"WALL STREET OF THE SOUTH"

Music and entertainment are just a part of Nashville's economy—and not even the largest part at that. The same creative flair, innovation, and energy that go into making great music have also made the area a leader in such industries as health care, publishing, tourism, and insurance. The diversity of the local marketplace has given us the ability to weather economic downturns.

The nicknames "Wall Street of the South" and "Financial Center of the Southeast," while no longer as accurate as they once were, are reflections of the influence that banking has had in contributing to the area's growth. Even today, finance, insurance, and real estate are responsible for more than 35,000 jobs. Government, education, automotive and other manufacturing, and communications are responsible for hundreds of thousands more.

But the field that Nashville is really dominating is health-care management. As noted previously, Vanderbilt University Medical Center employs some 13,600 people. HCA Inc., the nation's largest for-profit health-care company, has its headquarters in Nashville and employs more than 10,000 here. There are more than 250 health-care management companies in the area as well as about 70 other health-related firms. One of the largest is St. Thomas Health Services, which employs more than 5,000 people. See our Health Care and Wellness chapter for more details about Nashville's offerings in this area.

For years Nashville has been the largest publishing and printing center in the South. Much of this is attributable to the city's status as "The Buckle of the Bible Belt" (see subsequent section), but now a number of national secular publications are printed here as well.

Today it might be appropriate to bestow a new nickname: "The New Motor City." We made that one up, but it's not that much of an exaggeration. The nearby Nissan plant in Smyrna and the Saturn plant in Spring Hill are helping the region make a name for itself in the automotive industry. In addition to employing about 15,000 people, these plants have also attracted suppliers and related businesses to the region.

Nashville's central location makes it a great distribution center by land, by air, and by water. The three major interstates—Interstate 24, Interstate 40, and Intertstate 65—that converge here are ideal for trucking. Nashville is home of the largest CSX rail yard in the Southeast; Nashville International Airport, in addition to transporting passengers, handles tons of cargo; and the Cumberland River remains a viable option for some types of shipping.

Publicly held firms based in Nashville include O'Charley's and Cracker Barrel—see what we mean by Southern hospitality?—as well as Tractor Supply Co., Dollar General, and Thomas Nelson Publishers.

"THE BUCKLE OF THE BIBLE BELT"

Nashville is said to have more churches per capita than any other U.S. city. Today there are more than 800 houses of worship in Nashville, spanning a wide array of faiths. The vast majority of area worshipers remain Protestants, however, and some have gone so far as to dub Nashville the "Protestant Vatican."

LifeWay Christian Resources (formerly known as the Baptist Sunday School Board), the publishing arm of the Southern Baptist Convention, employs about 1,650 people at its Nashville business and publishing facilities. The National Baptist Publishing Board, established here in 1896, is the nation's oldest and largest religious publishing and printing corporation owned and operated by African Americans. Although the United Methodist Publishing House, the largest agency of the United Methodist Church, was not formed in Nashville until 1968, several of its predecessors were based here as early as the 1830s. Thomas Nelson Publishers, also based in Nashville, is the world's largest publisher of Bibles and other religious literature.

Opportunities for a religious education abound in Nashville, too, from the collegiate level down to the primary. Church-affiliated colleges and universities include David Lipscomb University, founded by the Church of Christ; Belmont University, which is affiliated with the Tennessee Baptist Convention; Free Will Baptist Bible College; and Trevecca Nazarene University.

For more information about the religion scene in Nashville, see our Worship chapter.

i *American Baby* magazine named Nashville among their Top 10 Family-Friendly Cities in 2007.

"CITY OF PARKS"

If you equate "quality of life" with recreational opportunities, Nashville is just the place for you. With several thousand acres of municipal parks and state parks, two large recreational lakes, and miles of undeveloped land, you can find practically any activity you can imagine. Whether you prefer peaceful nature walks replete with flora and fauna or more physical activities such as swimming, tennis, golf, or ice skating, Nashville's parks are sure to have what you're looking for.

Percy Warner Park is the city's largest, at more than 2,000 acres. Together, Percy Warner Park and the adjacent Edwin Warner Park make up one of the nation's largest municipal parks. J. Percy Priest and Old Hickory Lakes add a wealth of water activities to the mix. Eight state parks in the metropolitan statistical area offer even more outdoor opportunities, including bird-watching, hiking, camping, and learning about the state's history.

i **Artist Georgia O'Keeffe donated the collection of her husband, noted photographer Alfred Stieglitz, to Fisk University in 1949. Today visitors can see world-class works by such artists as Picasso, Renoir, and Cezanne, as well as O'Keeffe and Stieglitz, at Fisk's Carl Van Vechten Gallery.**

The beauty of Nashville's gardens, such as Cheekwood Botanical Garden and Museum of Art (see our Attractions chapter) is renowned among lovers of flowering plants. Elsewhere there are seemingly countless playgrounds and ball fields.

If you like to watch sports as much as play them, you're also in luck. Nashville has become a mecca for professional athletics. Football fans rejoiced when, after a long period of debate, it was announced that the National Football League's Houston Oilers would relocate to Nashville. After an interim season in Memphis, the Tennessee Oilers moved to Nashville in 1998, changing their name to the Tennessee Titans at the end of the 1998–1999 season. They began the 1999–2000 season in their new stadium, the Coliseum, on the east bank of the Cumberland River and finished it with a trip to the Super Bowl, literally coming within inches of victory against the St. Louis Rams.

Nashville is also home to an expansion National Hockey League franchise, the Predators, who began play here in the 1998–1999 season. Sports fans can also go to Greer Stadium to root for the Nashville Sounds, the AAA affiliate of major-league baseball's Pittsburgh Pirates.

The college athletics scene is thriving as well. For more information see our Spectator Sports chapter.

As you can see, Nashville lives up to its many nicknames, and it's sure to inspire even more as time goes by. It's a great place to make music, learn, work, worship, play, or be yourself. At the risk of sounding like a broken record (which we suppose is appropriate), we'll again state that Nashville is a wonderful place to live or to visit. Whatever your reason for being here (or planning to be here), for however long, enjoy your stay. This city has a lot to offer. Welcome!

GETTING HERE, GETTING AROUND

Question: How do you get to the *Grand Ole Opry?* Answer: Practice, practice, practice! Okay, it's an old joke, slightly paraphrased. But we use it to make the point that, with just a little practice and some practical knowledge, you'll soon find your way without problem to the Opryland area, the downtown/Music Row area, or anywhere else you want to go in metropolitan Nashville.

If you do happen to lose your bearings, don't lose your cool. Stop and ask directions—remember, you're in the land of Southern hospitality! It's reassuring to note that, in Nashville, it seems almost everyone is originally from somewhere else, which means that, like you, they've been lost before and will surely get lost again. Once you understand a few of the ground rules, such as the names and directions of the interstates and primary crosstown routes, you'll discover that getting around in Nashville is a bit like life itself: You're bound to make a few wrong turns along the way, but you'll be wiser for the experience. (Hey, do you think there might be a song in that?)

Of course, if you prefer, you can leave the driving to somebody else. Nashville has a number of transportation alternatives. We'll tell you about them later in this chapter.

GETTING HERE

Airports

NASHVILLE INTERNATIONAL AIRPORT (BNA)
Interstate 40 and Donelson Pike,
8 miles southeast of downtown
One Terminal Drive
(615) 275-1674, (615) 275-1675
(Airport Information Line)
www.flynashville.com

Nashville International Airport has 12 airlines serving more than 72 North American cities and several overseas with nearly 400 daily arrivals and departures. More than eight million passengers fly from or into Nashville International each year. The airport also handles tons upon tons of cargo.

While these figures might still be a far cry from Chicago's O'Hare or Atlanta's Hartsfield, they show significant growth from humble beginnings. When the airfield opened in 1937, it was known as Berry Field and occupied just 337 acres. In the decades since then, Nashville International has undergone numerous expansions, developments, and renovations to become a state-of-the-art facility that now sits on more than 4,500 acres. Additions in recent years include a concourse connector and an international arrivals building. The airport recently welcomed more than a dozen new retail and food and beverage vendors to its terminals. Other renovations in the works include the reconfiguration and consolidation of eight existing security checkpoints to a planned single location with eleven checkpoints. The airport contributes $3.6 billion and more than 56,000 jobs a year to the Nashville-area economy.

The Metropolitan Nashville Airport Authority—an independent, self-financing organization in operation since 1970—owns and operates Nashville International and the John C. Tune general aviation airport (see next airport listing) without the help of local property tax dollars. The Authority has more than 270 full-time employees at Nashville International, where it maintains its own state-certified aircraft rescue, firefighting, and law enforcement division. Numerous U.S. cities and the governments of Bermuda and Canada have studied the Authority as a model airport governance organization.

i *U.S. News & World Report* **in 2007 ranked the country's 100 busiest airports. Based on the most on-time flights and fewest crowded planes, Nashville was reported to be the 7th Least Miserable Airport.**

The airfield itself has four runways with lengths up to 11,000 feet. Parallel runways allow for simultaneous landings and takeoffs. The 820,000-square-foot terminal consists of three levels: ticketing, baggage, and ground level. There are 61 air carrier gates. Covered short-term parking and full-service ground transportation are available.

The airport offers nonstop flights to a total of 49 markets. And you'll be happy to know that this airport, which prides itself on efficiency and customer service, is generally known for on-time performance.

Airlines serving Nashville International Airport include Air Canada, (888) 247-2262; American and American Eagle, (800) 433-7300; Continental, (800) 525-0280; Delta, (800) 221-1212; Frontier Airlines, (800) 432-1359; Northwest, (800) 225-2525; Skyway/Midwest, (800) 452-2022; SkyWest, (800) 221-1212; Southwest, (800) 435-9792; United Express, (800) 241-6522; and US Airways and US Airways Express, (800) 428-4322.

GETTING TO AND LEAVING THE AIRPORT

Nashville International is about 8 miles southeast of downtown Nashville at I-40 and Donelson Pike. It's also near the intersection of two other major interstates: I-65 and I-24.

Once you've driven onto the airport grounds, simply follow the signs to short-term, long-term, or satellite parking; arrivals; or departures. If you're waiting to pick up someone from an arriving flight, look for the blue and white signs leading you to the free "Waiting Area," a parking pulloff where you can watch the arrival boards. There are a number of parking spaces in front of baggage claim on 10-minute timers. You must stay with your vehicle when parking in these spaces. When your 10 minutes are up, you will be immediately asked to leave.

Metropolitan Nashville Airport Authority Police are charged with the responsibility of reducing traffic congestion in front of the terminal. It's a responsibility they take seriously. Unless you're loading a passenger on the arrival ramp or unloading one on the departure ramp, stay out of these areas. Otherwise, the police will politely direct you to one of the parking areas or the waiting area.

The airport facilities include ramps and elevators for travelers with physical handicaps, and complimentary parking is available for vehicles with handicap license plates or decals. Each airline makes its own arrangements for helping disabled travelers get to and from planes. Contact your airline in advance for more information on the services it offers.

PARKING AT THE AIRPORT

Your first 30 minutes of parking are free at all Nashville International lots, including the covered short-term garage. After that, you'll pay up to a maximum of $22.00 a day in the short-term area, $1.50 an hour up to $10.00 a day in the long-term area, or $1.50 an hour up to $8.00 a day in the satellite "economy" lot about a mile from the terminal. If you park in the long-term or satellite lots, you can catch a complimentary shuttle to and from the terminal.

Valet parking is also available, generally between 5:00 a.m. and midnight. Valet rates are $20 per day, with a minimum of $8 for up to four hours.

GROUND TRANSPORTATION FROM THE AIRPORT

Various taxi services are available at the ground

level; just get out by the curb and wait. Please note, however, that the ground transportation area is one level below the baggage claim area, so you'll have to take the escalator or elevator after picking up your luggage.

Taxi meters start at $4.50 and are $2.00 a mile afterward.

Most hotels in the Briley Parkway/airport area offer free shuttle service to their guests. Gray Line Airport Express, (615) 883-5555, which serves hotels downtown and in the Music Row and Vanderbilt areas, offers $12 one-way and $20 round-trip fares.

If you'd prefer to captain your own ship, on-site rental car agencies include Alamo, (615) 361-7467; Avis, (615) 361-1212; Budget, (615) 366-0822; Dollar, (615) 367-0503; Enterprise, (615) 275-0011; Hertz, (615) 361-3131; National, (615) 361-7467; and Thrifty, (615) 361-6050. All of these rental agencies have convenient locations at the airport.

ENJOYING YOUR TIME AT THE AIRPORT

While you probably don't want to spend any more time in the airport than you have to, Nashville International has taken pains to ensure that your stay is as pleasant as possible. You'll find plenty of opportunities to tend to your needs in the areas of food, drink, shopping, and other diversions in an environment appealing to your aesthetic sensibilities.

The modern terminal, designed by New York architect Robert Lamb Hart, features a large central atrium with sloping skylights that contribute to a general atmosphere of openness and accessibility.

The Arts in the Airport program brightens the concourses with visual arts ranging from paintings to sculpture to photography as well as live musical performances. The Airport Sun Project is an ambitious light sculpture created by Dale Eldred and dedicated in 1989. The sculpture illuminates three areas of the terminal, using safety-glass panels, white-painted steel frames, mirrors, and diffraction panels to turn sunlight into a spectrum of colors that is an ever-changing

work of art. Art lovers of all ages will also enjoy the three-dimensional mosaic sculptures by Sherri Warner Hunter—like the Airport Sun Project, a permanent acquisition.

The airport features daily live musical entertainment, ranging from jazz to country. (This is Music City, after all.) Three stages—one at each security checkpoint and one at baggage claim—feature local performers. Performances generally are scheduled for peak travel hours.

Numerous services are available for airport visitors. Business travelers can find computer phone line hookups in specially designated areas throughout the terminal. Internet and e-mail access is available through kiosks on the baggage level and airport concourses. Other consumer services include on-site rental cars, a host of restaurants and a food court, and specialty shops for tourists and golfers. There is a free children's play area on the ticketing level of the concourse connector. You'll also find several bars, news and gift shops, a bank, ATMs, a welcome center, lockers, public telephones, courtesy and hotel phones, tele-services for the hearing impaired, first aid, shoeshines, a massage bar, a nail salon, and a meditation room.

JOHN C. TUNE AIRPORT
110 Tune Airport Drive
(615) 350-5000
www.johntune.com

John C. Tune Airport is a 399-acre general aviation reliever airport in west Nashville, 9 miles northwest of downtown. It opened in July 1986 and has undergone several expansions since, including the completion of a 36,000-square-foot terminal in October 1995. Nearly 100 aircraft, mostly private, are based here. Facilities include rental car delivery by Enterprise, a full-service maintenance facility for piston-powered aircraft, a helicopter service, and a flight school.

GETTING AROUND

Knowing the Laws

A night in jail, or even a ticket from a police officer,

might be fodder for a great country song, but you'd still probably rather avoid these situations if possible. Therefore, it pays to know the following laws pertaining to getting around in the fine state of Tennessee.

Driver's licenses. A valid Tennessee driver's license is required for anyone who lives here and wants to drive. If you've moved here from another state and have a license from there, you'll need to apply for one here within 30 days. Please note that different classes of licenses are issued depending on what type of vehicle you drive. Class D, the most common, is for regular passenger vehicles, pickup trucks, and vans; Class A, B, and C licenses are for various types of commercial vehicles; and Class M licenses are for motorcycles. Tennessee has a graduated license system for teenagers obtaining their first driver's license. The graduated license puts restrictions on those under the age of 18 who have learner's permits or their first license; restrictions include hours a teenager may drive and the number of passengers he or she may have in the car. A detailed explanation of the system is available at the Tennessee Department of Safety's Web site at www.tennessee.gov/safety.

Driving under the influence. Driving under the influence of alcohol or drugs in Tennessee is a serious no-no. The minimum penalty for a first conviction is 24 hours in jail, a $350 fine, court-ordered DUI school, and the loss of your license for a year. In addition, there can also be considerable court costs, increased insurance premiums, and other expenses. So just don't do it.

ℹ️ As you make your way around town, look for the new Wayfinding signs. Placed in strategic locations, the markers will help you to locate attractions and places of interest.

Buckling up. State law requires the driver and all front-seat passengers to wear a seat belt. Under Tennessee's child restraint law, children under one year old or those weighing 20 pounds or less must be placed in a rear-facing child passenger restraint system; children one through three and weighing more than 20 pounds must be placed in a forward-facing child passenger restraint system. Children four through eight and those less than 5 feet tall must use a belt-positioning booster system. Additionally, children through age 12 should be placed in a rear seat if available. Older children and those taller than 5 feet must be sure to buckle up.

Headlights. When it's raining, snowing, or otherwise precipitating enough for you to be using your windshield wipers, the law requires you to have your headlights on as well.

Watching your speed. It's never fun to get caught speeding, but the law provides for even stiffer penalties for those who go too fast in school zones or construction zones. Speeding in a school zone while children are going to or from school or are at recess is considered not just speeding but reckless speeding, which automatically results in six points being added to your driving record. Speeding in a construction zone when workers are present will get you a minimum fine of $250.

Turning right on red. Tennessee law permits right turns at a red light after coming to a complete stop unless otherwise posted.

Interstates, Major Highways, Bypasses, and Crosstown Routes

Nashville's location at the confluence of three major interstates means that getting into or out of town by ground is generally convenient. That's not to say that you won't run into congestion during peak hours—you will, although state and federal highway officials are always working on ways to make area traffic flow more smoothly. (We're giving the Tennessee Department of Transportation, commonly known as TDOT, the benefit of the doubt here; in the interest of full disclosure, however, you'll often hear TDOT described in less-than-flattering terms when road construction projects—like the ongoing work on Interstates 24, 40, and 65—result in major gridlock.)

Interstate 65, which runs north-south, connects Nashville with Bowling Green, Kentucky, and, ultimately, the Chicago area to the north. Going south, it leads to Huntsville before winding up in Mobile, Alabama. Nashville-area exits, from north to south, include Old Hickory Boulevard/Madison (exit 92), Briley Parkway/Dickerson Pike (exit 89), Trinity Lane (exit 87), James Robertson Parkway/State Capitol (exit 85), Shelby Street (exit 84), Wedgewood Avenue (exit 81), Armory Avenue (exit 79), Harding Place (exit 78), and Old Hickory Boulevard/Brentwood (exit 74).

I-40, a major east–west connector, links Nashville with Knoxville and, eventually, Wilmington, North Carolina, to the east; and with Memphis and—if you're in the mood for a *long* drive—Barstow, California, to the west. Nashville-area exits, from east to west, include Old Hickory Boulevard (exit 221), Stewarts Ferry Pike (exit 219), Nashville International Airport/Donelson (exit 216), Briley Parkway (exit 215), Spence Lane (exit 213), Fessler's Lane/Hermitage (exit 212), Second Avenue/Fourth Avenue (exit 210), Demonbreun Street (Music Row)/Broadway/Charlotte Avenue/Church Street (exit 209), 28th Avenue (exit 207), 46th Avenue/West Nashville (exit 205), Briley Parkway/White Bridge Road/Robertson Avenue (exit 204), Charlotte Pike (exit 201), Old Hickory Boulevard (exit 199), and Bellevue/Newsoms Station (exit 196).

Interstate 24 is a diagonal route running northwest–southeast. It will take you from Chattanooga in the southeast to Clarksville or, going farther northwest, to near St. Louis. Nashville-area exits include, from northwest to southeast, Briley Parkway (exit 43), Murfreesboro Road (exit 52), Briley Parkway/Airport (exit 54), Harding Place (exit 56), Antioch/Haywood Lane (exit 57), Bell Road (exit 59), and Hickory Hollow Parkway (exit 60).

Interstate 440 is a major bypass connecting I-40 in west Nashville to I-65 in south Nashville and I-24 in the southeastern part of the city. Its exits are at West End Avenue (exit 1), Hillsboro Pike/21st Avenue (exit 3), and Nolensville Road (exit 6).

Construction is also under way on another bypass—Highway 840—a controversial loop about 30 miles outside Nashville. When com-

i Nashville's famous skyline can help you get oriented if you momentarily lose your way. Or you can always stop and ask someone for directions—remember, you're in the land of Southern hospitality.

pleted, the route will run from an I-40 interchange near Lebanon to an I-40 interchange near Dickson, along the way connecting I-40, I-24, and I-65. As of this writing, on the 78-mile route, 57.1 miles are open to traffic, with 20.9 miles remaining in some phase of construction or development. The entire route is scheduled to be open to traffic by 2011. The last remaining section of Highway 840 was awarded in a separate contract in 2008. It extends from Highway 46 to Highway 246.

The loop is controversial for a number of reasons, including the impact it would have on rural farmland, its contribution to "urban sprawl," and alleged violations of environmental laws.

Other major highways running through Nashville include U.S. Highways 31, 41, and 70.

Briley Parkway, also known as Highway 155, encircles Nashville and bisects all three of its major interstates. Beginning in the east at its juncture with Charlotte Avenue, it runs northeast to meet I-65; heads southeast, briefly following the Cumberland River through the Opryland area and meeting I-40 near Nashville International Airport; then continues south before turning back east, crossing I-24 and becoming one with Thompson Lane. Thompson Lane becomes Woodmont Boulevard, which becomes White Bridge Road northeast of West End Avenue and runs to Charlotte Pike, completing the Highway 155 loop.

i Don't make the mistake of using one of those gigantic broadcast towers you see to get your bearings—Nashville is ringed by several, each identical and prominently placed atop a conspicuous hillside. Plenty of newcomers have gotten lost at night by using a broadcast tower as an orientation point.

Harding Place begins in the southwestern part of the city as Harding Pike (US 70 S.), then branches east from US 70 S. and becomes Harding Place. After crossing Granny White Pike (12th Avenue) in south Nashville, it inexplicably becomes Battery Lane for a brief stretch before resuming the name of Harding Place when it crosses Franklin Road, which is known as both Eighth Avenue and U.S. Highway 31. Harding continues east, then veers northward and becomes Donelson Pike.

Old Hickory Boulevard is even more perplexing. Beginning in the southwest, at Highway 100 on the west side of Percy Warner Park (see our Parks chapter), it runs east until it crosses Nolensville Road (also known as Fourth Avenue or U.S. Highway 31 Alternate) and changes its name to Bell Road. But wait … it's far from through. Back near where we started, Old Hickory also heads north from Highway 100 at Edwin Warner Park (see Parks) before turning into River Road. It also seemingly just materializes just east of Charlotte Avenue's juncture with I-40, then heads north. Up north, way north, Old Hickory masquerades as Highway 45. It passes, from west to east, across Dickerson Pike (known variously as US 31 W., US 41, and Highway 11), I-65, and Gallatin Pike (aka US 31 E. and Highway 6), through the Madison and Old Hickory areas of metropolitan Nashville. It then heads southeast, crossing Lebanon Pike (US 70, Highway 24) in the Hermitage area, and, still acting as Highway 45, crosses I-40 near J. Percy Priest Lake on its way out of town. (Finally!) A word to the wise: Just because you've been on Old Hickory once before and are now on it again doesn't necessarily mean that you're anywhere near where you were the first time. In other words, you probably shouldn't use this boulevard as an orientation point.

TDOT SmartWay

As you whiz down I-65, shaking your fist at the grandma puttering along at 45 mph in front of you, be forewarned: Big Brother is watching.

Since 2002 lovable TDOT has installed 52 video cameras along Nashville's major interstates as part of its SmartWay intelligent transportation system. The idea is to keep tabs on traffic conditions, allow law enforcement to respond quicker to traffic accidents, and help TDOT monitor congested areas so that it can more easily address traffic-flow issues. Cameras are placed on tall poles and can view traffic from as far away as 1 mile. Camera views are refreshed every 15 seconds.

The locations of the traffic cameras are posted on the TDOT Web site (www.cctv.tdot .state.tn.us). In a neat little gimmick, you can click on a camera and get an "I'm right there" view of the interstate that's only two minutes old. That's good to know if you're heading out the door and want to check on traffic conditions—but if you're late for an appointment, don't try using the old "traffic was murder" excuse; checking the veracity of such fibs is just a mouse click away.

Although TDOT has stressed that its cameras will not be used for law enforcement purposes, it bears remembering that if you're tempted to violate the traffic laws, the world will be watching.

HOV Lanes

Nashville's three interstates have so-called HOV lanes, which are intended to reduce both traffic congestion and auto emissions during peak times by encouraging carpooling. HOV stands for "high-occupancy vehicle." Because of federal air-quality standards, the U.S. government requires that the state build these lanes any time it uses federal money to widen an interstate in an urban area. Basically, you're rewarded for being in a vehicle with two or more people by being allowed to drive in the less traveled inner lane, marked with a white diamond painted on the pavement.

If you're driving alone during peak traffic hours—from 7:00 to 9:00 a.m. Monday through Friday for traffic inbound to Nashville, and from 4:00 to 6:00 p.m. Monday through Friday for outbound traffic—stay out of any lanes marked with a diamond. In other words, you must have two or more people in your vehicle (children count) to drive in an HOV lane at these times. Exceptions are granted for buses, motorcycles, and emergency vehicles. Trucks with three or more axles cannot use the HOV lanes during these hours, regardless of how many passengers they have. Failure to abide by these restrictions can earn you a $50 fine.

Local Streets

The Cumberland River, which played such an important role in the founding of Nashville, remains an important orientation point for residents and visitors. If you're trying to figure out how the streets are laid out, start at the river, which runs north–south through the center of town. West of the river, or on the downtown side, numbered avenues run parallel to the river. East of the Cumberland, however, it is streets and not avenues that are numbered, though they still run parallel to the river.

Five bridges cross the Cumberland in the downtown area. From north to south, they are Jefferson Street, Victory Memorial, Woodland Street, Shelby Avenue (for pedestrians and bicyclists only), and the Gateway Boulevard Bridge, which opened in 2004. Additionally, a railroad bridge crosses the river between the Jefferson and Victory Memorial Bridges.

Primary downtown streets running perpendicular to the numbered avenues include James Robertson Parkway, which circles the State Capitol; Union Street; Church Street; and Commerce Street. Broadway serves as the north–south dividing line.

You'll notice that in the downtown area many of the numbered avenues are one-way, so pay attention to make sure you're not turning the wrong way.

The numbered avenues generally change names as they head out of town. For example, First Avenue becomes Hermitage Avenue and then Lebanon Road; Second Avenue actually merges with Fourth Avenue before changing into Nolensville Road; Eighth Avenue becomes Franklin Road. This phenomenon is not limited to numbered avenues downtown, either. It's a simple fact of Nashville that many roads change names, some several times. After a while, you'll get used to it. You'll also notice that many a road is referred to as both a "pike" and a "road" or an "avenue," depending on which sign or map you're looking at. For example, Charlotte Avenue is also Charlotte Pike, Hillsboro Pike is also Hillsboro Road, and Murfreesboro and Nolensville Roads are also known as pikes. There are many other examples of this. In some cases the "pike" designation is more common; in other cases "road" or "avenue" is favored. The "pike" references are holdovers from older days when roads were often known as turnpikes. Don't worry too much about which word you use.

Buses

If your group would like its own bus for travel inside or outside Nashville, you can find dozens of companies listed in the yellow pages under "Buses—Charter & Rental." Many of these offer guided tours of the Nashville area. For more information see our Music City chapter.

GREYHOUND BUS TERMINAL
200 Eighth Avenue S.
(615) 255-3556, (800) 231-2222
From its Nashville terminal, Greyhound offers service to more than 2,000 destinations in the continental United States, including Memphis, site of the closest AMTRAK station.

Public Transportation

METROPOLITAN TRANSIT AUTHORITY
1011 Demonbreun Street
(615) 862-5950
www.nashvillemta.org
Metropolitan Transit Authority, Nashville's public transportation system, serves about 40 bus

routes citywide. About half a dozen of these are "express" routes between two points, and a dozen are "limited-service" routes. The system has five shelters and 16 park-and-ride lots.

i The Nashville Convention & Visitors Bureau partners with several area hotels to offer visitors discounts on hotel rates. You can also get discounted attraction tickets through the CVB. For details check out the CVB's Web site, www.musiccityusa.com, or call (800) 657-6910.

Regular bus fares are $1.45 for adults and 70 cents for seniors. Several package deals, such as 20 fares or unlimited fares for a month, are also available.

MTA's Accessride provides door-to-door van service for disabled people who qualify.

Regional Transportation

REGIONAL TRANSPORTATION AUTHORITY
501 Union Street, Sixth Floor
(615) 862-8833
www.rta-ride.org

The RTA serves Cheatham, Davidson, Dickson, Maury, Robertson, Rutherford, Sumner, Williamson, and Wilson Counties. The RTA organizes carpools and vanpools throughout those counties and operates regional bus routes between downtown Nashville, Hendersonville, and Mount Juliet. Commuters can park for free at one of the many park-and-ride lots located throughout the area, then connect with their carpool, vanpool, or bus. Fares range from 70 cents to $2.25; students, senior citizens, and disabled persons pay reduced rates. Special 20-trip ticket packages are available. For other rates, contact the RTA or visit the Web site.

Taxis

Taxi fares in Nashville are regulated by law. The meter starts at $3 when you get in the cab, and you'll pay $2 a mile to your destination. A $1 charge per additional passenger is added to the total. A fare from the Opryland area or the airport to a downtown location will run about $25.

It's best to reserve your cab at least 30 minutes in advance. You'll often find taxis waiting at the curb near popular downtown restaurants, however, so you might not have to call. By law, taxis are not supposed to "cruise" for customers, but visitors from big cities generally don't know this, and the law is not regularly enforced.

Many companies take credit cards, but others do not; sometimes that decision is left to the discretion of the individual driver, so it's a wise idea to specify that you plan to use a credit card when you call or before climbing into a cab.

Some Nashville cab companies include Allied Cab Company, (615) 244-7433; American Taxi, (615) 865-4100; Checker Cab, (615) 256-7000; and Yellow Cab Metro Inc., (615) 256-0101.

Limousines

Nashville is a town of stars and special occasions, which means it's a limousine kind of town. The yellow pages list dozens of limousine services, most of which are available 24 hours a day, seven days a week. All accept major credit cards. As with any other service, you get what you pay for, and prices cover a wide range. Expect to pay more during peak times such as prom and graduation season, the December holiday season, and during big events—don't even try getting a last-minute limo for the Country Music Association Awards, for example. For such times, reservations have to be made as much as four months in advance.

Standard features in most models include television, stereo (many with CD player and tape deck), privacy partition, moon roof, and cellular telephone. If you're looking to travel in style, you can rent stretch models for up to 10 people with additional luxuries including double bars with crystal champagne glasses. Some companies also offer specials that include dinner. A number of companies rent basic sedans, like Lincoln Town Cars or Cadillacs, as well as limos; these, of course, will be nice but without all the luxuries of a limo.

i The Downtown Trolley Tour, operated by Gray Line Tours, is a one-hour narrated tour of downtown Nashville, Centennial Park, and Music Row. The fare is $12. See our Attractions chapter for details.

Prices range from about $65 an hour for a six-person model to $100 or more an hour for a 10-person stretch with all the amenities. Also plan to add a driver gratuity of 15 to 20 percent; some companies will automatically add this to your bill. Most companies have a three-hour minimum on weekends and a two-hour minimum during the week. Weeknights during nonpeak seasons are generally a little cheaper; if you can, plan your special night during the week to increase your chances of getting what you want.

Here are a few of Nashville's limo companies: Capitol Limousines Inc., (615) 883-6777; Carey Limousine, (615) 360-8700; Celebrity Limousines Inc., (615) 316-9999; Signature Limousine Service, (615) 244-5466; and Super VIP Limousine Service, (615) 889-9680.

HISTORY

The history of Nashville is a tale of drama and adventure as rich as any to be found in a theater or on television. Filled with fascinating characters, the Nashville tale has spellbinding plots with action, battles, victories, defeats, mysteries, political intrigue, and romance. In this chapter we tell you about Nashville's past and highlight some of the people and events that made Nashville the interesting, dynamic city it is today. Pull up an easy chair, sit back, and learn about this fascinating city.

PREHISTORY

The first settlers arrived here in 1779, but they weren't the first to inhabit the area. The land was first a home, hunting ground, and burial ground for prehistoric Indians. Evidence of large Paleo-Indian villages has been found that suggests these people lived here 11,000 to 12,000 years ago. The Mississippi culture of Indians, known as Mound Builders, inhabited the area from about A.D. 1000 to A.D. 1400. By A.D. 1200 their large villages, some occupying hundreds of acres, could be found throughout the area.

Around the middle of the 15th century, the villages mysteriously disappeared, and the area became a hunting ground for various tribes. Cherokee, Chickasaw, Creek, and Shawnee shared the land. The Shawnee, the last of the tribes to have any sort of settlement in the area, were eventually driven out by Cherokee from the east and Chickasaw from the west in the early 1700s.

In the late 1600s and early 1700s, French traders from Canada and what would become Louisiana established a trading post next to a high bluff along the Cumberland River near a salt lick (where animals came for a necessary supply of salt) and a sulphur spring. The spot, later known as French Lick, was just north of where the downtown area is today.

Around 1769, while the area was still being shared by various Indian tribes, another French-Canadian fur trader arrived. Jacques-Timothe De Montbrun, a tall, athletic, dark-skinned man, came to French Lick from Kaskaskia, Illinois. He built a hut at French Lick and spent many winters buying furs from the Indians, which he would then sell in New Orleans. He finally settled in the area in the late 1780s and later operated a store and tavern at the square, where Second Avenue N. is today. De Montbrun, later known as Timothy Demonbreun (pronounced de-MUN-bree-un), is often referred to as the "first citizen" of Nashville.

As Demonbreun and the other traders bartered with the Indians at French Lick, others ventured into the area in search of food and furs. Between 1769 and 1779, "long hunters"—explorers from the colonies of North Carolina and Virginia who lived and hunted in the wilderness for months or even years at a time—could be found here. Some of the long hunters, including Uriah Stone, for whom the Stones River is named, are legendary. Legend has it that Thomas Sharpe Spencer, a large man known as "Big Foot," lived for months in a hollow sycamore tree. Spencer, who planted corn at Bledsoe's Lick, where Sumner County is today, is credited with being the first settler to plant in Middle Tennessee.

THE SETTLEMENT

During the 1770s the colonies along the East Coast in Virginia and North Carolina were becoming crowded. Settlers began hearing the call of the West. In those days, the area we now know as east Tennessee was "the West," and some people settled there in the early 1770s. The leader of the

Watauga settlement in this area—Capt. James Robertson—would soon play a starring role in the history of Nashville.

In the spring of 1775, just weeks before the American Revolution began, Richard Henderson, a North Carolinian who was president of the Transylvania Land Company, met with Cherokee leaders at the Watauga River and convinced them to trade the land between the Ohio and Cumberland Rivers for a few loads of guns, ammunition, rum, and other goods.

In 1779 Henderson sent 45-year-old Robertson to find a suitable spot to build a new settlement. Robertson, a farmer, explorer, surveyor, and negotiator with the Cherokee and Chickasaw, was the right man for the job. He and eight scouts chose the area at French Lick, and Robertson called the spot the Bluffs. Leaving three men behind to tend the corn, Robertson traveled up the Ohio River to obtain "cabin rights" from George Rogers Clark. The rest of his entourage returned to Watauga in August. They told the people of the great river, the streams and creeks, the fertile and uncultivated land, canebrakes of 10 to 20 feet in height, the bountiful supply of fish, and the buffalo and other wild game that came to the salt lick. The salt spring near the bluffs meant a great deal to them as well: Salt was a precious commodity, used in preserving meat.

It was decided that the Wataugans would move to the Bluffs in two groups. The trip through the wilderness was deemed too difficult for women and children, so the first group, led by Robertson, was made up of men and boys. The women and children would come later on boats, led by John Donelson. In October 1779 the first group, a few hundred strong, set out with livestock for the hazardous trek of almost 400 miles through one of the most difficult winters ever seen.

It is generally thought that the group arrived at the north bank of the Cumberland River on Christmas Day 1779. When they reached the river, it was frozen, so they walked across with livestock in tow and settled on the opposite bank. That was the beginning of Nashville.

On December 22, three days before Robertson's party arrived at the Bluffs, Donelson and the second Watauga party began their 1,000-mile river journey. Donelson, in his mid-50s, led a group of more than 200 women, children, elderly men, and slaves in a 33-boat flotilla. Among the passengers was Donelson's 10th child, 13-year-old Rachel, who would eventually marry Andrew Jackson before he was elected seventh president of the United States.

No one in the party had ever traveled the rivers, but they weren't going to let that stop them. The weather, however, was a different story. Only 5 miles into their voyage, severe weather forced them to stop and set up camp for two months. They resumed their journey in late February 1780 but didn't arrive in French Lick until two months later. The severe winter wasn't the only hardship they faced, as Donelson recorded in his journal. Numerous Indian attacks and frostbite claimed lives. One of the more horrifying incidents was the slaughter of a boatload of the travelers by Indians. Twenty-eight members of the Donelson entourage had contracted smallpox and were traveling together on a boat that brought up the rear of the flotilla. Indians captured their vessel, and the other travelers listened in horror as their fellow travelers were killed.

At one point, several groups, faced with dangerous rapids, opted to change course. Some headed down the Mississippi to Natchez, while others turned toward Illinois. Donelson and his party finally arrived at the Bluffs on April 24, 1780.

On May 13, 1780, 256 men from the settlement signed the Cumberland Compact, which spelled out the rights of the settlers. The original document, representing the first civil government in Middle Tennessee, is preserved today in the Tennessee State Library and Archives. High on the bluff on the west bank of the Cumberland, the settlers constructed what would become the capital of the settlement, Fort Nashborough, named in honor of Revolutionary War general Francis Nash of North Carolina.

As the settlers were busy building their new town, hard times were headed their way. The American Revolution continued, and Nashborough settlers were attacked by Indians who had received arms from the British and Spanish. It soon became impossible for settlers to farm or hunt. Indian attacks caused Robertson to move his family to the safety of Fort Nashborough, while the Donelson family moved to Kentucky. In April 1781 Indians attacked Nashborough in the "Battle of the Bluffs." Robertson's wife, Charlotte, was the hero of the day, saving the fort by turning a pack of angry, growling dogs on the attackers. It is said that after this battle, only 70 of the original 400 to 500 settlers remained. Other survivors had moved to safer areas. The Robertsons were among those who stayed. The settlement faced its last severe attack in September 1792.

In 1783 the American Revolution came to an end. The colonies had won their freedom. Also that year the North Carolina Legislature created Davidson County. A year later the legislature established the town of Nashville; the population was 600. In the years that followed, Nashville grew rapidly, evolving from a frontier crossroads into an influential western town.

i **In 1784 Nashborough became Nash-ville. The English "borough" was replaced with the French "ville," most likely as a sign of appreciation for France's assistance during the American Revolution against Great Britain.**

THE JACKSON ERA

In 1796 Tennessee became the 16th state in the Union. Nashville's first church—a Methodist church near the courthouse, jail, and stocks—was built that year, too. Three years later, the town's first newspaper was printed. Between 1796 and 1800 Davidson County's population grew nearly 170 percent, from 3,600 to 9,600. Andrew Jackson is credited for much of the city's growth and influence during the first half of the 19th century. After arriving as a 21-year-old public prosecutor, he achieved success quickly and, in part because he often accepted land grants as payment for his services, became very wealthy. Upon his arrival in town, he boarded at the home of John Donelson's widow (Donelson was mysteriously killed in 1786 while en route

from Kentucky to Nashville), where he met and fell in love with the Donelsons' daughter Rachel, who had separated from her husband, Lewis Robards. Jackson and Rachel Donelson Robards were married in 1791 and repeated their vows in 1794 after discovering—amid something of a social scandal—that Rachel's divorce from her first husband had never been made official. The Jackson marriage remained a topic of gossip for quite some time.

As Jackson was becoming the star of the day, Nashville continued to grow. In 1806 the community was incorporated as a city, and Joseph Coleman was elected the first mayor. By 1810 Nashville's population was approaching 2,000. Residents of the city lived mainly where First, Second, Third, and Fourth Avenues are today.

Meanwhile, Jackson, who had served in the U.S. Senate and as a justice of the state supreme court, was preparing for battle. In 1812 Congress declared war on Great Britain, and the War of 1812 began. Jackson, a colorful figure described as both a "roughneck" and a "gentle-man," became a national hero for his role in the war. He led American troops to victories over the Creek Indians (British allies) and over the British themselves in New Orleans in 1815. News of a peace treaty signed two weeks before the New Orleans battle didn't reach the battlefield in time, so Jackson's last and greatest military victory was actually won after the war had ended.

Jackson had a reputation among his troops as a tough-as-nails military man, and, after one of his soldiers said he was as tough as hickory wood, Jackson's nickname became "Old Hickory." Numerous reminders of the nickname remain throughout Nashville today.

In 1824, despite winning the popular vote, Jackson lost his bid for the presidency of the United States to John Quincy Adams. But he returned victorious in 1828, becoming the first man from west of the Appalachian Mountains to be elected president. More significant, however, was his role in the founding of a new Democratic party characterized by a spirit of reform and interest in the welfare of the common man. The roots of today's Democratic Party date from this

Andrew Jackson is buried at his Nashville home, the Hermitage. JACKIE SHECKLER FINCH

time. Jackson was elected to a second term as president, serving through 1837. His wife, Rachel, died of a heart attack in December 1828, before his first inauguration.

Having a hometown hero in the White House did much to boost Nashville's reputation. While president, Jackson made several trips to his plantation, the Hermitage, 12 miles northeast of Nashville, often entertaining renowned guests there. When his term was up, he returned to

the Hermitage. Jackson died at his home June 8, 1845, and is buried next to his wife in the Hermitage's garden.

Nashville saw much progress during the Jackson era. By 1840 the city had a population of 6,929—a 25 percent increase from the 1830 census. In 1843 Nashville was named the permanent capital of Tennessee. There was much to enjoy about life in Nashville in the mid-1800s. The city was thriving. In 1860, it was the eighth largest city in the South and had two publishing houses, five daily newspapers, five banks, and numerous mills, factories, breweries, and wholesale houses. But the city's growth and prosperity were about to come to a four-year halt.

ℹ️ **William F. Strickland, architect of the Tennessee State Capitol, is buried in a stone vault on the north facade of the first floor, right above the cornerstone.**

THE CIVIL WAR YEARS

Historians say the Civil War had several causes: Political, governmental, and economic forces that continued to separate the North and the South were at work. But the issue of slavery was at the root of the discord. The debate over slavery had been growing for years.

Nashvillians had long discussed the issue, and they watched as the nation became divided over it. Though slavery was allowed in this Southern city, slave owners made up a minority of its total population of 16,988 in 1860. Included in that number were 3,211 slaves (nearly 19 percent of the population) and 719 free African Americans.

Tennessee was the last state to secede from the Union and the first to rejoin after the war ended. Early on, the city had been committed to the Union. Nashville had held pro-Union meetings and at one point even rejected the governor's idea to secede. Nashvillians favored the idea of slavery, but surely not enough to go to war over it.

On April 12, 1861, Confederates attacked Fort Sumter in Charleston, South Carolina, marking the beginning of the Civil War. Three days later, President Lincoln called for Union troops, and the Confederate states took this as a sign to prepare for battle. Virginia, Arkansas, and North Carolina pledged their allegiance to the South, joining South Carolina, Mississippi, Florida, Alabama, Georgia, Louisiana, and Texas. On June 8, when Tennessee voters approved secession, Tennessee became the 11th and final state to join the Con-

federate States of America. The vote in Nashville was 3,029 for secession and 250 for the Union.

As its young men signed up for battle, Nashville mobilized quickly and became a key center for the manufacture and storage of weapons and other supplies to support the Southern army. But Nashville didn't remain a Confederate city for long. When Union troops captured nearby Fort Henry and Fort Donelson, gaining control of the Cumberland River to Nashville, they had a clear shot at the city. The Army of Tennessee could not defend the capital, so the Confederate commander ordered his troops to exit. When the troops abandoned Nashville, the city panicked. Some citizens boarded the first trains out of town; others packed what belongings they could onto wagons and carriages and fled.

They cut the ties on the suspension bridge and set fire to the railroad bridge. Rioting and looting broke out. On February 24, 1862, after Federal troops had closed in, Nashville mayor Richard B. Cheatham surrendered the city.

Nashville's position along the Cumberland River plus its good road and railroad links to other major cities made it a prime target and a highly desirable western base for the Union. The troops girded the city with a string of forts, including Fort Negley, the largest of the fortifications. Trenches and rifle pits surrounded the city.

In March 1862 President Lincoln appointed Tennessee native and former governor Andrew Johnson to serve as military governor to the state. Johnson's goal was to reclaim Tennessee's loyalty to the Union. He required all government officials and other professionals to sign an oath of loyalty to the United States, arresting and imprisoning those who refused. During the occupation, more than 8,000 African Americans sought refuge in Nashville, tripling the African-American population to more than 12,000. They helped fortify the city against attack and served in the Federal army. Two thousand assisted in the construction of Fort Negley. Thousands more served in combat.

Serving as a Union base took a toll on Nashville. Buildings and homes were destroyed to make room for forts. Churches and other buildings were taken over to serve the military's needs.

More than half of the city's trees were cut down. Some of the citizens managed to make a living by providing residents and the military with supplies and services or working for Federal operations.

When Union general William T. Sherman marched through Georgia, leaving Atlanta in flames in November 1864, Confederate general John B. Hood turned his troops north toward Nashville with the plan of recapturing the city. He thought he might then be able to join Robert E. Lee in Virginia and pursue Ulysses S. Grant. Gen. George H. Thomas, who had more than 70,000 soldiers, was prepared to defend Nashville. Hood thought he and his 23,000 soldiers could lure the Federal troops south and then attack Nashville. On November 30, Hood's Confederate soldiers met with a Union force at the Battle of Franklin. Hood attacked, and in less than six hours, the Confederate army suffered about 7,000 casualties (including those killed, wounded, or captured); the Union casualty count was 2,500. The Battle of Franklin was known as one of the bloodiest hours of the Civil War.

i Demonbreun Street is named for French-Canadian fur trader Jacques-Timothe De Montbrun, who is often referred to as the "first citizen" of Nashville. The street is on the area that was once his farm.

The Union force withdrew to Nashville. Hood advanced. By December 2 the Confederates had settled into a position in the hills just south of town. They waited. Thomas waited, too, unwilling to attack until the time was right. On December 8 Nashville was hit by a severe ice storm. Both armies were immobilized but remained ready. On December 15, after the ice thawed, Thomas and his Union soldiers attacked the Confederates. Moving from the river toward the south and the east, the Federal forces pushed Hood's troops back. One day later, Thomas wiped out three Confederate positions, and the rest of the Southern forces retreated to the south. The two-day Battle of Nashville resulted in 6,000 Confederate casualties, many of whom were captured on the battlefield, and about 3,100 Union casualties.

The Battle of Nashville was the last major conflict of the war. On April 9, 1865, Gen. Robert E. Lee, leader of the main Confederate army, surrendered to Gen. Ulysses S. Grant at Appomattox Court House, Virginia.

ATHENS OF THE SOUTH

On April 15, 1865, six days after Appomattox, President Lincoln died after being shot by John Wilkes Booth. Andrew Johnson, military-governor-turned-vice-president, became the 17th president of the United States, the third Tennessean to go to the White House. As Johnson set out to restore the Union, Nashville began its restoration. It had fared better than some other Southern cities had during the war, but there was damage to repair. The next two decades would produce a truly revitalized Nashville, a city that would be a leading commercial center and a growing center of higher education for blacks and whites.

Nashville would soon become known as the Athens of the South for its abundance of colleges and universities. The postwar period marked the opening of such institutions as Fisk University, Vanderbilt University, Meharry Medical College, and Peabody College.

African Americans and Northern missionaries started several colleges. The first was Roger Williams University, founded in 1864 and originally called the Nashville Normal and Theological Institute. In 1866, a free school for African Americans, Fisk School, now known as Fisk University, opened its doors. The school was named for Clinton B. Fish, an official with the Freedmen's Bureau for Tennessee and Kentucky, a federal

i To learn more about Nashville's role in the civil rights movement, visit the Civil Rights Room at the Nashville Public Library. The downtown library, at 615 Church Street, is located at the site of several downtown restaurants where African Americans were once refused service and mistreated before the historic sit-ins of 1960.

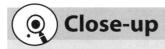

Close-up

The Maxwell House: Much More than Coffee

When John Overton Jr. began construction on his downtown luxury hotel in 1859, many locals derisively referred to the project as "Overton's Folly." After all, Nashville at that time had a population of fewer than 17,000 and little apparent need for such a showplace. Time would prove these naysayers wrong, however, as the Maxwell House Hotel would develop a national reputation—and a name that today lives on, most notably in a popular-brand beverage.

But we're getting ahead of the story. The completion of Overton's hotel, designed by Isaiah Rogers of Cincinnati, was significantly delayed by the outbreak of the Civil War. The first residents of the unfinished building were Confederate troops, who dubbed it Zollicoffer Barracks in honor of Gen. Felix K. Zollicoffer, a former Nashville newspaperman who had joined the rebel army as a volunteer. By 1862 the building, like the rest of Nashville, had fallen into the hands of Union troops, who used it first as a barracks, then a hospital, and, finally, a prison. It was in this last configuration that tragedy struck the building, as several Confederate prisoners

reportedly were killed when a stair collapsed in September 1863.

After the war, construction resumed, and in September 1869 the Maxwell House Hotel officially opened at the corner of Cherry (now Fourth) and Church Streets. It didn't take long for the new hotel to establish itself as a place for the elite to meet. The dining room became famous not only for its menu's quality but also for its quantity, with sumptuous spreads of rich foods, especially during holidays and other special occasions. "Christmas menus might offer a choice of as many as 22 meats, including roast quail, Minnesota venison, Cumberland Mountain black bear and broiled pheasants," according to a history of the hotel prepared by today's hotel (more on that later).

Several U.S. presidents stayed at the Maxwell House, including Tennessee's own Andrew Johnson, Hayes, Cleveland, Benjamin Harrison, McKinley, Theodore Roosevelt, Taft, and Wilson. The wide range of other prominent politicians, civic and business leaders, socialites, and entertainers who sampled the hotel's hospitality includes social reformer

agency that served the needs of newly free blacks. Classes initially were held in a Union military hospital on Church Street. That first year, as many as 1,000 African-American men, women, and children signed up for classes. In the 1870s, the school's chorus, the Jubilee Singers, saved the financially failing university. The group, founded in 1867, toured throughout the United States and later around the world, raising enough money to purchase a 25-acre campus and to fund work on a new school building. On January 1, 1876, Jubilee Hall opened as the country's first permanent building constructed for the purpose of educating African Americans. Today it is a National Historic Landmark.

The year 1892 marked the premiere of one of Nashville's most famous landmarks—the Union Gospel Tabernacle, later renamed Ryman Auditorium. Riverboat captain Thomas G. Ryman built the facility after being inspired by Georgia evangelist Sam Jones, a traveling Southern Methodist minister. Ryman wanted a permanent site for Jones's revivals and other religious gatherings. Jones preached there on a few occasions, but by 1900 the building was gaining a reputation as a premier theater in the South. It hosted theatrical and musical productions and political rallies. After Ryman died in 1904, the venue was renamed for him. It was home to the *Grand Ole Opry* from 1841 to 1874 and, in recent years, has begun serving as

Jane Addams, actress Sarah Bernhardt, orator William Jennings Bryan, Wild West star Buffalo Bill, opera star Enrico Caruso, inventor Thomas Edison, automaker Henry Ford, and the famous midget Tom Thumb.

As you've probably guessed by now, the hotel also became noted for its coffee, provided by local entrepreneur Joel Cheek. That Cheek-Neal brand of coffee was served to President Theodore Roosevelt when he visited Nashville on October 22, 1907. This was a major event to Nashvillians, and crowds lined the streets to watch the popular president arrive. After speaking briefly at the Ryman Auditorium, Roosevelt traveled on to the Hermitage, Andrew Jackson's former home, where he had breakfast. Asked for his opinion of the Cheek-Neal coffee he had been served, the president pronounced it "good to the last drop." Advertising copywriters have been known to kill for phrases like that, of course, and those words have served as a slogan for the Maxwell House brand ever since.

On August 1, 1928, the giant General Foods Corporation bought the Cheek-Neal Company for a price—in cash and General Foods stock—that was reported to be around $45 million, at the time the largest financial transaction in Nashville history. The fortune generated by this sale, incidentally, lives on in Cheekwood Botanical Garden and Museum of Art. Cheekwood is the former estate of entrepreneur Leslie Cheek, who earlier had the foresight to invest in his cousin Joel's coffee company. (For more information about Cheekwood, see our Attractions chapter.)

As for "Overton's Folly," the original Maxwell House Hotel lived on for many more years, being converted into a residential hotel in its later years. The Maxwell House literally went out in a blaze of glory on Christmas night 1961, when it was destroyed by fire. The corner of Fourth and Church Streets is now occupied by a bank and office building commonly referred to as the SunTrust building. But the Maxwell House name lives on, not only in a best-selling coffee brand but also in another Nashville hotel. In 1979 the Clarion Maxwell House Hotel opened at 2025 MetroCenter Boulevard; in 1991, under new ownership, it became the Regal Maxwell House. In 2002 the hotel was renovated and underwent another name change, becoming the Millennium Maxwell House, which advertises "the Southern traditions of gracious hospitality." Enjoy a meal in Praline's, the hotel restaurant, and be sure to try the coffee, which remains "good to the last drop."

host to special engagements of the Opry. Today it is on the National Register of Historic Places, and since reopening in 1993 after a renovation, it is one of Nashville's most popular entertainment venues. (See our Music City and Attractions chapters for details.)

i Native son Andrew Johnson, who never attended school but became president after Abraham Lincoln was shot, held virtually every local, state, and federal office. He was an alderman, mayor, state representative, state senator, governor, congressman, senator, and vice president before becoming president of the United States.

CENTENNIAL EXPOSITION

Tennessee marked its 100th anniversary as a state in 1896 but had to wait until 1897 for the party. From May 1 to October 31, 1897, Nashville hosted the Tennessee Centennial Exposition in West Side Park, now Centennial Park. Officials had begun planning the event in 1893, but a lack of funds forced them to delay the festivities for a year. Support from the railroad companies helped ensure the exposition would be a success.

The six-month celebration, produced at a cost of more than $1.1 million, featured numerous exhibits, amusement rides, dancers, and a dazzling display of lights. The centerpiece of the exposition was a replica of the Parthenon, the temple of Athena, goddess of wisdom, that stands on the Acropolis in Athens, Greece. Nashville's replica, built following plans provided by the king of Greece, was intended to be a temporary structure, like the exposition's exhibit buildings that were constructed of wood and plaster. During the Centennial Exposition, the Parthenon housed works of art.

The Tennessee Centennial Exposition was hailed as a success. It welcomed more than 1.7 million visitors from around the world and was the first such event in America to earn a profit.

After the exposition, the exhibit buildings were torn down, but Nashvillians were fond of their Parthenon, a symbol of the city's reputation as the Athens of the South, and let it stand. The City Parks Board rebuilt the facility out of concrete after it began to deteriorate in the early 1920s. A wide selection of art can be found in the Parthenon's art gallery. In 2001 a $13-million–plus renovation of the Parthenon was completed. (See our Attractions chapter for more information.)

A NEW CENTURY

At the beginning of the 20th century, Nashville was on the verge of major growth, soon to become a leader in finance, insurance, and publishing.

One of the highlights of 1900 was the premiere of Nashville's new Union Station train shed at the corner of Broad and Walnut Streets. The official dedication of the spectacular new Romanesque building took place October 9, 1900. Construction had taken more than two years and involved the razing of more than 200 buildings at the site. Atop the building's tower stood a 19-foot copper figure of Mercury, the Roman god of commerce and travel and messenger to the other gods. The statue was blown down in a windstorm in 1952. A new Mercury was installed in 1997, only to be damaged by the spring 1998 tornado that swept through downtown Nashville. A repaired Mercury graces the tower today. Union Station provided an important link to the country's leading railroad cities.

Banking and insurance were big business for the city, and Nashville became one of the South's

The Parthenon is now an art gallery. JACKIE SHECKLER FINCH

leading financial centers. By 1903 two major insurance companies—National Life and Accident Insurance Company and Life and Casualty Insurance Company of Tennessee—had been formed. Nashville also was growing as a center for distribution for a number of goods.

Two disasters made Nashville headlines in the second decade of the 1900s. One was the flood of 1912. In the early morning hours of November 5, the southeast wall of the round limestone reservoir on Eighth Avenue S. cracked, spilling 25 million gallons of water down the hill into the area's homes. The city repaired the damage, and the reservoir is still in use today. On March 22, 1916, a fire erupted in east Nashville. It reportedly started in a mill on First Street, and winds swept the flames throughout the area. The fire burned for four hours, killing one person, destroying nearly 1,000 buildings, and leaving 3,000 people homeless.

SEGREGATION, WHISKEY, AND WOMEN'S RIGHTS

Racial segregation continued during the early 1900s, as a number of laws were established that restricted the rights of African-American citizens. In 1905 Nashville's African-American community began a boycott of electric streetcars after a law was passed requiring separation of black and white passengers on them. At the time African Americans made up more than 30 percent of the city and county populations. Sadly, segregation continued to become more severe and for some time remained an issue of primary concern only to the population that suffered its unfair consequences. It wasn't until the late 1950s that city schools were desegregated, and following sit-ins at lunch counters in downtown stores and other nonviolent protests beginning in 1960, public facilities were finally open to all citizens by 1963.

A positive change came about as a result of another social issue of the early 1900s: Women in America won the right to vote. Nashville played a key role in the women's suffrage movement. Suffragists had been gathering steam across

America, and in 1914 the National American Woman Suffrage Association held its national meeting at Nashville's Hermitage Hotel.

By March 1920, 35 states had approved passage of the 19th constitutional amendment, which would make it illegal to deny women the right to vote. One more state was needed for the amendment to become law. Suffragettes, led by Carrie Chapman Catt, targeted Tennessee, which had more than 60 chapters of the suffragist organization. In July and August 1920, making the Hermitage Hotel their headquarters, they pushed for the state's legislature to vote in favor of their cause. They won, and on August 18, 1920, Tennessee cast the deciding vote, becoming the 36th state to ratify the 19th Amendment.

The issue of temperance—total abstinence from alcoholic beverages—had been debated for years. The city's first temperance organization had been formed in 1829, 50 years after the first settlers arrived. By the early 1900s Nashville had more than 150 saloons. By 1909, 11 years before Prohibition (1920 to 1933), the Tennessee Legislature declared it illegal to sell alcoholic beverages within 4 miles of a school or to manufacture alcoholic beverages. Only a handful of states had taken this route of total prohibition. The rules were loosely enforced in Nashville until the national Prohibition amendment outlawed the manufacture, sale, and transportation of alcohol. Bootleggers took over after that, however.

GRAND OLE OPRY

During the 1920s a new type of music was beginning to develop: old-time music, later called hillbilly music and eventually known as country music. A Nashville-based radio program would have a lot to do with the development of this emerging music genre.

Nashville's famed *Grand Ole Opry* premiered in 1925. Interested in radio as an advertising medium, the prosperous National Life and Accident Insurance Company launched radio station WSM on October 5, 1925. The station's call letters came from the insurance company's slogan: "We Shield Millions." The station played a mixture of classical, jazz, and other pop music, with a few banjo players, fiddlers, and other performers of the newly popular "old-time tunes" thrown in here and there. Soon after WSM hit the airwaves, popular Chicago radio announcer George D. Hay came to Nashville's fledgling station and started a show similar to the *WLS National Barn Dance* he had hosted in Chicago.

On November 28 the station showcased the talents of 78-year-old fiddler Uncle Jimmy Thompson and his niece/piano accompanist, Eva Thompson Jones. With 1,000 watts, WSM had one of the strongest signals of any station in America, and that night, listeners from around the country called and sent telegrams with their enthusiastic praise of the program. The *Grand Ole Opry* was born.

The *WSM Barn Dance*, as it was called for a time, began airing its old-time music program every Saturday night, mainly featuring local amateur acts. Among the early stars the show produced were Thompson and Uncle Dave Macon. The *Barn Dance* became the *Grand Ole Opry* in December 1927. The name change came about when, one evening, after an NBC classical music program from Chicago had aired, Hay introduced a short program of music from *Barn Dance* regulars by saying, "For the past hour, we have been listening to the music taken largely from Grand Opera, but from now on we will present the *Grand Ole Opry!*" Soon after that the program expanded to a four-hour broadcast, and WSM became a 5,000-watt station reaching 50 percent of America.

After relocating a few times, including a stint at the War Memorial Auditorium, the *Grand Ole Opry* moved to the 3,000-seat Ryman Auditorium in 1941. The Ryman became known as "the Mother Church of Country Music." In 1974, the *Opry* moved to a specially built, state-of-the-art production facility at what was then the Opryland theme park, where it continues to entertain country music fans old and new and remains the longest-running radio program in America. (See our Music City chapter for details.)

DEPRESSION, SUBURBAN GROWTH, AND WORLD WAR II

While the *Opry* was putting the spotlight on Nashville and making stars out of the show's early performers, the nation's economy was spiraling toward disaster. The stock market crash of October 29, 1929, sent the country into the Great Depression. Nashville was by that time an established financial center, and the bank failures, layoffs, and financial failures didn't leave the city untouched.

When Japan bombed Pearl Harbor on December 7, 1941, igniting World War II, Nashville was on its way toward recovery from the Depression. The war gave the city the push it needed to get back on its feet. While thousands of residents headed off to war, area manufacturers went into wartime production. The Middle Tennessee area, with its varied terrain, was chosen as the site of the world's largest military training efforts, which brought in hundreds of thousands of army personnel. Thousands more, stationed at nearby military camps, descended on Nashville on the weekends for entertainment. More than one million came through the city during the first year of war.

Nashville prospered during the war, and by September 2, 1945, when Japan signed its surrender to the Allied forces, the Depression was just a memory. In the following years, Nashville's insurance business boomed. By the early 1960s the city was home to eight insurance companies that had more than $2 billion in assets.

The postwar period also saw Nashville's growth as a religious center. A number of missionary-training colleges were opened, religious publishing houses flourished, and denominational headquarters were established in the city. Nashville had a huge number of churches. The "Protestant Vatican" and "Buckle on the Bible Belt" were added to the city's list of nicknames.

The 1950s brought the interstate highway system, which would greatly influence the lives of Nashvillians as well as Americans everywhere. In 1950 WSM radio announcer David Cobb referred to Nashville as "Music City USA" for the first time. In other music news, country music fans mourned the death of 29-year-old Hank Williams, who was found dead in the backseat of his car January 1, 1953.

HIGHLIGHTS OF THE 1960S

In June 1962 voters approved the merger of Nashville and Davidson County governments. They elected Beverly Briley mayor a few months later and elected a 41-member council. April 1, 1963, marked the beginning of the Metropolitan Government of Nashville-Davidson County. The reorganization made Nashville the first city in America to completely consolidate city and county governments. The move was admired by cities throughout the country.

In the late 1960s hospital management companies were founded here, positioning Nashville as a health-care industry capital.

MUSIC CAPITAL

By the 1960s, Nashville had already become a music city. The *Grand Ole Opry* had been introducing the nation to new country performers for years, and other industry-related businesses had begun operating. Acuff-Rose Publishing, a leader in country-song publishing, was established by Roy Acuff and Fred Rose in 1943. In the late 1940s and early 1950s, RCA Victor, Decca Records, Capital Records, and Mercury Records had set up shop in Nashville.

In 1952 Owen Bradley, a musician and former musical director at WSM, opened a studio in the basement of an old house on 16th Avenue S., a few blocks from Vanderbilt University. That was the beginning of Music Row, the area where the business of country music is carried out every day. In 1955 Bradley began recording in a Quonset hut next door. The building's excellent acoustics, combined with Bradley's production talents, made it a popular recording site. Bradley sold the studio to Columbia Records in 1962 and moved to Williamson County, where he opened

Bradley's Barn, a renowned recording studio that attracted country and rock artists for years.

While Bradley was operating the Quonset hut in the late 1950s, a guitar player by the name of Chet Atkins joined with RCA Victor to establish another studio. In 1957 Atkins, a versatile musician who could play country, jazz, classical, or pop, was producing records and beginning to develop what would become known as the "Nashville Sound," a new style of country music.

Country music legends are honored in downtown Nashville. JACKIE SHECKLER FINCH

Atkins and Bradley used new recording techniques and blended pop elements such as background vocalists and horns into their country recordings to produce a more modern sound that became popular with music fans.

As the recording business grew, other music businesses began operating in Nashville. Song publishers, performing-rights organizations, and booking agencies came to town. The County Music Association was founded in 1958 to promote the growing industry. Country stars also began recording television shows. Jimmie Rodgers, Fred Rose, and Hank Williams were the first inductees into the Country Music Hall of Fame. Pop, rock, and folk music artists could be found in Nashville studios, too. Bob Dylan, for example, recorded an album here in the mid-1960s.

By 1970, when Nashville's population reached 426,029 and Davidson County's registered 447,877, country music was drawing to the city not only performers and music business professionals but also plenty of tourists. In 1971 attendance at the *Grand Ole Opry* topped 400,000 for the first time. National Life opened the 380-acre Opryland USA musical theme park in 1972 and two years later relocated the *Grand Ole Opry* to the new Grand Ole Opry House at the park. Opryland, and the adjacent and enormous Opryland Hotel, an attraction in itself, proved to be huge draws. In the mid-1990s the park was attracting two million or more guests a year, enough to rank it among the country's top 30 amusement parks. Nevertheless, citing poor attendance, officials closed the park for good after the 1997 season. The $200 million Opry Mills mall opened on the property in 2000.

The first Fan Fair, a convention offering country music fans a chance to meet the stars, took place in 1972 at the Municipal Auditorium downtown. The event was held at the larger-capacity Tennessee State Fairgrounds from 1982 to 2000, and marking its 30th anniversary, moved to downtown Nashville in 2001. In 2004 the event was renamed CMA Music Festival/Fan Fair and was expanded to include other styles of music.

Country music reached a new height in popularity in the 1990s. According to the Recording Industry Association of America, in 1993 country music sales accounted for nearly 19 percent of total U.S. record sales. In both 1997 and 1998, country music accounted for nearly $2 billion of the $13.7-billion domestic recording sales.

Music fans can also tune in to country music on TV. For years the Nashville Network took Music City's music straight to televisions around America. Today cable channels such as CMT and GAC provide around-the-clock country music programming. Meanwhile, the CMA's annual Fan Fair brings as many as 40,000 country music fans to Nashville each June for a week of activities. Every Friday and Saturday night, the *Grand Ole Opry*, the show that started it all, still packs 'em in at the Opry House.

While it is undoubtedly the country music capital of the world, Nashville also boasts a strong tradition of gospel and pop music. Today Nashville is the center of the growing contemporary Christian and gospel music industry, and each spring the city hosts the Gospel Music Association's Dove Awards show. You can find every genre of gospel here, from traditional black gospel to Christian rock, pop, country, folk, and rap to Southern gospel.

A number of pop and rock artists come here to record, and some call Music City home. Don't be surprised if you find rockers such as Kid Rock, Bon Jovi, or Metallica sitting beside Amy Grant or Wynonna Judd at a music club or restaurant.

Showcases spotlighting unsigned rock and pop talent from around the country are held regularly in Nashville. The city is also proud of its outstanding songwriting community, which receives national and international acclaim for penning songs in a variety of musical genres. The annual Tin Pan South multiple-day music festival spotlights some of Nashville's excellent writers. Nashville is truly Music City. (See our Music City chapter for an even more detailed perspective.)

A MODERN CITY

Outside the music industry, Nashville has grown tremendously in recent decades. In 1996, the year Tennessee celebrated its bicentennial, Nashville opened its new downtown Bicentennial Capitol Mall State Park and its $145 million, 20,000-seat Nashville Arena, now called the Gaylord Entertainment Center. In 1997 the city lured the National Football League's Houston Oilers—now called the Tennessee Titans—with the promise of a new downtown stadium. The team spent its first year as a Tennessee team in Memphis. In 1999 the Titans moved into downtown Nashville's brand-new, 67,000-seat Coliseum. Music, education, religion, publishing, health care, and now professional sports are the buzzwords of modern-day Nashville.

On April 16, 1998, the city suffered one of the worst disasters in its history when two tornadoes hit the downtown and east Nashville areas, causing more than $175 million in damages. The twisters struck in the middle of the school and workday, damaging hundreds of homes and buildings, including the State Capitol. Windows were blown out of downtown skyscrapers, and hundreds of trees were uprooted. The governor declared Nashville a disaster area. The storms were part of as many as 10 tornadoes that touched down in Middle Tennessee. The Nashville twisters caused only one fatality. The paths of the two twisters were similar to that of a tornado that hit in March 1933, killing 11 people.

Two of Nashville's major attractions opened in 2001. The Frist Center for the Visual Arts premiered in April in the historic building that was formerly Nashville's main post office. With the opening of the Frist Center, Nashville is one of the few U.S. cities that can boast an art gallery of 20,000 square feet of exhibit space. The Country Music Hall of Fame & Museum, another of the city's premier attractions, opened at its new downtown location in May. The massive $37-million facility is a must-visit attraction for any country music fan.

In 2006, Nashville added two more bright stars in its crown as Music City. To honor the people who provide the sounds behind the songs, the Musicians Hall of Fame was unveiled inside the old Tennessee Electric Supply Building at 301 Sixth Avenue S., within sight of the Country Music Hall of Fame and Museum. The museum honors all players—whether stars, session pickers, or sidemen—from all genres of music.

The highly anticipated Schermerhorn Symphony Center opened as the home to the acclaimed Nashville Symphony, which performs more than 100 classical, pops, and special concert events each season. In addition, the Nashville Symphony offers recitals, choral concerts, cabaret, jazz, and world music events in its home. Schermerhorn Symphony Center is located on a full city block in downtown Nashville's rapidly developing SoBro (South of Broadway) neighborhood. The concert hall is the final element of Gateway Plaza, a civic park flanked by the Country Music Hall of Fame & Museum to the south, the Gaylord Entertainment Center to the west, and the Hilton Nashville Downtown to the north. With its ideal acoustics, the center also is one of the few halls nationwide to feature natural interior light through 30 special soundproof windows. A sophisticated and modern building that is neo-classically inspired, the Schermerhorn Symphony Center is a treasure in this artistically rich city.

ACCOMMODATIONS

Accommodations are in demand year-round, but with just a bit of planning, you shouldn't have any trouble finding a place to stay in Music City. Most likely your biggest problem will be choosing from among our numerous and varied lodging options. The Nashville area has about 250 hotels and motels with more than 32,000 rooms combined. We have everything from the spectacular Gaylord Opryland Resort and Convention Center to elegant luxury hotels in historic buildings to budget motels and long-term corporate lodging.

When choosing your accommodations, keep in mind that Nashville covers a wide area. For convenience, you might want a hotel that's closest to your primary interests. Properties are concentrated in three areas: Opryland/Music Valley, near the airport, and downtown. In addition, as you travel away from downtown in any direction, you'll find a number of motels and a few hotels, most of which are near interstate exits. Do you want to stay near the *Grand Ole Opry* and Music Valley? Or would you prefer the Midtown (West End/Vanderbilt) area, close to the heart of Nashville's music industry and Music City's top restaurants and nightspots? Maybe you're here on business and would like to room somewhere near the airport or in the downtown business district. Downtown Nashville is also a good choice if you plan to do lots of sightseeing—you'll be within walking distance of historic Second Avenue, the Country Music Hall of Fame and Museum, the State Capitol, and other attractions.

OVERVIEW

Nashville-area hotels and motels serve more than nine million visitors annually, including tourists and convention delegates. Since it is the country music capital of the world, Nashville welcomes thousands of country music fans each year. June is an especially busy month, when as many as 30,000 country music fans descend on Nashville for the CMA Music Festival/Fan Fair (see our Music City chapter). With convention and meeting facilities, such as the Nashville Convention Center and the Opryland hotel, the city is also a popular choice for conventions and trade shows.

Because Nashville welcomes so many visitors, especially from Memorial Day through Labor Day, it is a very good idea to secure your accommodations in advance. You definitely don't want to arrive in town without a place to stay, only to find out that every room in town is booked for a week! If you're coming for Fan Fair, some hotels suggest you make your reservations a year in advance. December holidays bring many visitors, too, especially to the festive Opryland hotel and surrounding lodgings. During these busy times, you're likely to find that hotel rates are a little more expensive.

In the following listing, we provide a price guide to help you choose a hotel. Our rate information was provided by each property. Most have more than one rate, and in some cases rates span a wide range—from hundreds to even thousands of dollars per night. Our price code is based on the "rack rate," that is, what one night's stay, double occupancy, midweek in peak season would cost you if you walked in off the street. Often you'll pay less than that, however. Many properties offer lower rates on weekends, and most offer a few discounts. AAA and AARP members, for example, get discounts at many hotels. There are a lot of other discount programs, so be sure to inquire about them when you make your reservation. Always ask for the best rate—you can often enjoy significant savings by doing so.

There are so many hotels and motels in Nashville; we have chosen just a small, representative portion of the properties in various areas of town. If you have a favorite trustworthy chain and don't see one of its properties listed here, call the chain's central reservation number to find out if there is a location in Nashville.

Unlike most chapters in this book, this chapter is divided into six geographic categories—Downtown, Midtown (West End/Music Row), East (Opryland/Airport), North, South and Southeast, and West; that's to help you quickly locate a suitable property in your preferred area. We have listed a variety of properties in all price ranges.

All the hotels in this chapter accept major credit cards, and all offer free local telephone calls unless otherwise noted. Amenities vary widely. Some places offer little more than a bed, while others pamper you with every possible luxury. We'll tell you about each property's key amenities. Virtually all properties in town offer nonsmoking and wheelchair-accessible rooms. At some locations, 75 percent or more of the rooms are nonsmoking, and some have a larger number of wheelchair-accessible rooms and more accessible facilities than others. We will tell you if a hotel allows pets, and we'll give details about pet fees or deposits, and whether there is a weight limit. Be sure to state your preferences and needs when making a reservation.

For other accommodations see our Bed-and-Breakfast Inns and Campgrounds chapters.

Price Code

The following price code represents the average cost of a double-occupancy room during peak season. Prices do not include accommodations tax in Nashville-Davidson County. The hotel/motel occupancy tax is 5 percent of the gross room rate, and that's in addition to the state sales tax of 9.25 percent.

$	Less than $75
$$	$76 to $125
$$$	$126 to $175
$$$$	$176 and more

DOWNTOWN

BEST WESTERN DOWNTOWN
CONVENTION CENTER $$$
711 Union Street
(615) 242-4311, (800) 627-3297
www.bestwestern.com

This five-story motel at the corner of Union and Seventh Avenue has been around a while, but its 100 rooms were renovated in mid-1999. Extras include in-room hair dryers, free continental breakfast, and free parking. If you want to stay downtown without spending a bundle, this could be your best bet. It's right across from Legislative Plaza and the capitol, and it's convenient to the Tennessee Performing Arts Center, Nashville Convention Center, Ryman Auditorium, and other downtown attractions. Interstate 24, Interstate 40, and Interstate 65 are less than a mile away.

DOUBLETREE HOTEL—NASHVILLE $$–$$$$
315 Fourth Avenue N.
(615) 244-8200, (800) 222-TREE
www.nashville.doubletree.com

This full-service downtown hotel offers 338 nicely furnished guest rooms, including 10 suites. The Doubletree Hotel, a contemporary-style, nine-story angular building, sits at the corners of Fifth Avenue and Deaderick and Fourth Avenue and Union. It's in the heart of downtown Nashville, a short walk from both the State Capitol and Second Avenue entertainment.

The hotel's spacious corner rooms feature large wraparound windows and have a sitting area with sofa. All rooms have coffeemakers, hair dryers, two dataport phone lines, and TV with free in-room movies. You'll be served complimentary freshly baked chocolate chip cookies on your night of arrival.

Extra amenities for guests on the ninth-floor executive level include terry cloth bathrobes and free breakfast. All guests have access to the indoor pool and exercise room on the second floor. Laundry services are available, and there is a business center with high-speed Internet access in the lobby. Drinks and sandwiches are available in the hotel's lounge. There's also a Starbucks cafe in the lobby. Doubletree Hotel allows pets up to 25 pounds; a $50 refundable deposit is required.

THE HERMITAGE HOTEL $$$$
231 Sixth Avenue N.
(615) 244-3121, (888) 888-9414
www.thehermitagehotel.com

Downtown Nashville's Hermitage Hotel underwent a $17-million renovation in 2002 that was designed to transform the historic property into one of the world's finest small hotels. Less than a year after reopening, the hotel earned AAA's prestigious five-diamond rating. It's the only five-diamond hotel in Tennessee.

First opened in 1910, the hotel is listed on the National Register of Historic Places and is said to be the only remaining commercial Beaux Arts structure in the state.

Over the years it has welcomed such luminaries as Franklin and Eleanor Roosevelt, John F. Kennedy, Richard Nixon, Al Jolson, Greta Garbo, and Bette Davis. Cowboy star Gene Autry once showed up with his horse Champion. Others who have called the hotel home include Jack Dempsey, Minnesota Fats, Al Capone, and Mickey Spillane.

Today, the Hermitage Hotel features 122 spacious and luxurious guest rooms and suites, some of which have a view of the State Capitol. Each room includes a marble bath with double vanities, soaking tub, and separate shower; down-filled duvet; complimentary high-speed Internet connection; three two-line telephones, DVD/CD player; and 27-inch television. The hotel offers concierge service, 24-hour room service, business center, laundry and dry-cleaning service, a fitness room, and many other amenities. Afternoon tea and evening cocktails are served in the grand lobby. Those who are traveling with pets will want to know that the hotel has an excellent pet program that includes custom pet beds, dog-walking service, and a room service pet menu prepared by hotel chefs. There is no weight limit for pets, and no deposit is required.

i The unique men's restroom at the Hermitage Hotel is a landmark that may get as many female visitors as male. The room, decorated in art deco black and green glass, has been the site of photo shoots and music videos.

HILTON SUITES NASHVILLE
DOWNTOWN $$$$
121 Fourth Avenue S.
(615) 620-1000, (800) HILTONS
www.nashvillehilton.com

The Hilton Suites is one of downtown Nashville's most popular hotels. The location can't be beat: It's just off Broadway next to the Gaylord Entertainment Center, between the Country Music Hall of Fame & Museum and the Nashville Convention Center, just a short walk from all sorts of dining, shopping, and entertainment options.

Each of the hotel's 330 suites features a large living room with sofa bed, a separate bedroom with either a king bed or two double beds, and a large bathroom. Each suite has a microwave oven, refrigerator, coffeemaker, iron and ironing board, large work desk, two dataport phones, two TVs with Sony Playstations, and free in-room movies. High-speed Internet access is available. Other amenities include room service, an indoor pool, a workout room, free *USA Today* delivery, a 24-hour business center, and a concierge/transportation desk.

A full, cooked-to-order breakfast, served in the Market Street Cafe on the lobby level, is included in the room rate. Other dining options include the adjacent Palm restaurant, which is frequented by celebrities (actor Robert Redford and singers Tim McGraw and Faith Hill have dined here) as well as plain folks who appreciate a good steak, and Hilton's Sports Grille. (See our Restaurants chapter for more on the Palm.)

HOLIDAY INN EXPRESS NASHVILLE–
DOWNTOWN $$$
920 Broadway
(615) 244-0150, (800) HOLIDAY
www.hiexpress.com

After an $8-million renovation in the fall of 2003, this eight-story hotel at the corner of 10th Avenue and Broadway was rebranded as a Holiday Inn Express. Much larger than the other hotels in that chain, the hotel now has 287 rooms, including 14 two-room suites. In-room amenities include free high-speed Internet access (wireless access is available in public meeting spaces), coffeemakers, hair dryers, large TVs, free movies, two phones, irons, and ironing boards. The hotel has a 1,000-square-foot fitness center, outdoor pool, gift shop, and 5,000 square feet of meeting space. Deluxe continental breakfast is included in the room rate. Two computers are available at the PC station in the lobby. The hotel offers guests free indoor and outdoor parking, as well as use of a complimentary shuttle to travel anywhere within a 5-mile radius of the property.

RENAISSANCE NASHVILLE HOTEL $$$$
611 Commerce Street
(615) 255-8400, (800) 327-6618
www.renaissancenashville.com
Connected to the Nashville Convention Center, this 31-story hotel is a top pick for convention-goers. After a day of meetings and walking the trade-show floor, you can unwind at one of the many nearby restaurants and nightspots.

The Renaissance boasts 673 deluxe rooms, including 24 suites. All rooms feature remote-control TV with in-room movies, computer data-ports, coffeemakers, and direct-dial phones. Extra amenities include laundry and valet service, complimentary shoeshine, covered parking in the adjacent multilevel garage (there is a parking fee), a gift shop/newsstand, concierge service, and free newspapers. Fifty-eight private Renaissance Club–level rooms offer a few extra perks, such as a complimentary continental breakfast and evening hors d'oeuvres in the Club Lounge, comfy bathrobes, express checkout, and a Renaissance Club concierge who is prepared to take care of any special requests.

In-hotel dining options include the Commerce Street Grille, featuring sophisticated Southern cuisine, and Bridge Bagels and Deli, which, along with the adjacent Bridge Lounge, offers a great view of downtown Nashville from the glass-enclosed atrium. Spanning Commerce Street, a new high-energy Bridge Entertainment Bistro on the third floor features eight 60-inch TVs and serves breakfast, lunch, and dinner. You can also order room service 24 hours a day. Combined with the Nashville Convention Center, the Renaissance offers more than 200,000 square feet of space, including nearly 120,000 square feet of exhibit space. The hotel's elegant 18,000-square-foot Grand Ballroom and 11,000-square-foot Convention Center ballroom are perfect for large gatherings, and the exhibit hall can accommodate 615 10-by-10-foot booths. In addition to a complete renovation of all their meeting rooms—which included everything from new carpet to improved furnishings—the Renaissance transformed the hotel's lobby to create a more residential/great-room feel. The lobby also houses a new Starbucks coffee shop.

SHERATON NASHVILLE DOWNTOWN $$$$
623 Union Street
(615) 259-2000, (800) 325-3535
www.sheraton.com/nashvilledowntown
A tasteful choice in downtown Nashville accommodations, this elegant, 28-floor hotel is within walking distance of historic Second Avenue, the capitol, the Gaylord Entertainment Center, the Nashville Convention Center, the football stadium, and numerous restaurants and nightspots. Sheraton Nashville Downtown has 476 rooms and nine suites, which range in size from 300 to 1,500 square feet. Several floors are reserved for nonsmokers. Rooms on the upper floors offer splendid views of the State Capitol and other Nashville sites. Rooms feature voice mail, dataports, coffeemakers, hair dryers, irons, and ironing boards. High-speed Internet access is available. The hotel offers an exercise room, indoor pool, 2,300 square feet of meeting space, and a business center. Valet service is available in the adjacent eight-story garage; there is a fee to park. The hotel's full-service restaurant, Speakers Bistro, offers American cuisine for breakfast, lunch, and dinner. Sessions lounge, on the first floor, is the spot for cocktails and snacks. You'll

often find Capitol Hill legislators gathering here when they're in town. The hotel accepts pets up to 80 pounds at no additional charge; larger pets may be allowed to stay in the room, but you'll need to get approval before making your reservation. The hotel provides pillow beds and water bowls for pets.

i The geographic center of Tennessee is located 1 mile from downtown Murfreesboro. The site is marked by an obelisk.

UNION STATION HOTEL $$$$

1001 Broadway

(615) 726-1001

www.unionstationhotelnashville.com

The Union Station train shed opened in October 1900 and pushed Nashville into the 20th century, linking the city by rail to the country's important railroad cities. The Romanesque Revival–style building took more than two years to complete, and its opening was a grand occasion. When the building reopened as the Union Station Hotel in 1986 after a two-year renovation, it was another

The Union Station Hotel was once a busy railroad hub. JACKIE SHECKLER FINCH

grand affair. What had become something of an eyesore was saved by historic preservationists in the 1970s, and today it is a magnificently restored National Historic Landmark. The Union Station Hotel offers some of the most elegant and luxurious accommodations in town.

Beautiful stained-glass panels adorn the spacious, three-story lobby's 65-foot-high vaulted ceiling, while an abundance of decorative gilded accents lend to the room's classic elegance. Here and there you'll notice reminders of the hotel's past, such as the ornate clock in the lobby, which years ago was used to time incoming trains.

The seven-story hotel has 125 unique guest rooms, including 11 suites, plus 12,000 square feet of meeting space. Some rooms have vaulted ceilings and open toward the lobby. All rooms have exterior views, two dual-line telephones, ergonomically designed desk chairs, irons, ironing boards, plasma TVs, and bathrobes. High-speed Internet access is available. Amenities include concierge service, room service, valet parking, same-day laundry and cleaning service, overnight shoeshine, voice mail, and in-room movies. Copy and fax services are available, too.

Union Station's location near downtown puts you just blocks away from some of Nashville's trendiest restaurants and clubs in the District, West End, and Music Row areas. You might also want to eat at the hotel's Union Station Bar & Grill. The hotel's Broadway Bistro is a casual spot for lunch, dinner, and cocktails. Breakfast is served in the lobby area each morning for about $10 per person. Pets up to 25 pounds are allowed, with a $45 nonrefundable fee.

MIDTOWN: WEST END/MUSIC ROW

BEST WESTERN MUSIC ROW INN $$
1407 Division Street
(615) 242-1631, (800) 780-7234
www.bestwestern.com/musicrow
Popular with tourists, this 102-room hotel sits just off Music Row. It's not fancy, but it does have an outdoor pool, a meeting room, and a laundry room on the fifth floor. There are three large

suites suitable for families. Parking is free, and you can enjoy free HBO movies in your room. A computer with high-speed Internet access is available in the lobby. Just off the lobby is the popular Hall of Fame lounge, which hosts regular songwriter performances. The hotel offers free continental breakfast from 6:30 to 9:30 a.m. Pets weighing up to 20 pounds are permitted for $10 per night.

COURTYARD BY MARRIOTT—
VANDERBILT/WEST END $$
1901 West End Avenue
(615) 327-9900, (800) 321-2211
www.marriott.com
The amenities at this 226-room, eight-story hotel make it popular with business travelers, and it's usually booked solid Monday through Thursday. Each room features a large work desk, separate seating area, coffeemaker, hair dryer, iron, and ironing board. Other amenities include a business center with computers and Internet access, a large outdoor pool, an exercise room with whirlpool, a meeting room, and free parking. A full buffet breakfast ($7.95 a person) is served in the restaurant each morning.

GUESTHOUSE INN & SUITES $$
1909 Hayes Street
(615) 329-1000, (800) 777-4904
www.nashvilleguesthouseinn.com
This comfortable hotel is 1 block off West End, near Baptist Hospital, Vanderbilt, and Centennial Park. It is a good choice for medical guests (relatives of local hospital patients receive special rates), but it is just as popular with tourists, business travelers, and visiting families of Vanderbilt students. The hotel's shuttle provides free transportation to most major area hospitals and nearby attractions. The hotel has 108 rooms, all with a kitchen sink, microwave, refrigerator, coffeemaker, and hair dryer. There are six larger suites that have living rooms with sleeper sofas. A free continental breakfast is served each morning in the lobby's dining area. Other amenities include a small gift shop/convenience store and free parking.

HAMPTON INN—
NASHVILLE/VANDERBILT $$
1919 West End Avenue
(615) 329-1144, (888) 800-5395
www.hamptoninnnashville.com

Located at the corner of West End and 20th Avenue S., this 171-room hotel is convenient to lots of good restaurants, shopping, hospitals, downtown, and Music Row, and it's a popular choice for business travelers. The hotel provides free hot breakfast in the comfortable lobby, where floor-to-ceiling windows offer a view of busy West End. Other amenities include free parking, free Showtime, in-room coffeemakers, free high-speed wireless Internet access, hair dryers, irons and ironing boards, an exercise room, outdoor pool, and a free *USA Today* on weekdays. An extra treat is fresh-baked cookies served 4:00 to 7:00 p.m. Monday through Thursday.

HOLIDAY INN & SUITES VANDERBILT $$$
2613 West End Avenue
(615) 327-4707, (800) 633-4427,
(800) HOLIDAY
www.hiselect.com

This 13-story hotel has a super location on West End, right across the street from Centennial Park and close to Vanderbilt. The hotel is popular with business travelers Monday through Friday. Its proximity to Centennial Sportsplex and Vanderbilt makes it a top choice among sports groups on the weekends. Out-of-towners visiting Nashville for family reunions and weddings often stay here, too.

The hotel has 300 rooms. The Cafe Becca serves breakfast, while the new Commodore Grille offers an expanded menu. Amenities include an outdoor pool, an expanded second-floor fitness center, and satellite TV with free HBO. Every room has a coffeemaker, iron and ironing board, hair dryer, and free high-speed Internet access. The executive-level rooms on the top floor have all that plus comfy bathrobes and a complimentary hot buffet breakfast. A computer, fax, TV, tables, books, and phone and modem hookups are available in the expanded club room/business center, which all guests can access with their room keys. Pets up to 50 pounds are permitted with a $50 nonrefundable fee.

LOEWS VANDERBILT PLAZA HOTEL $$$$
2100 West End Avenue
(615) 320-1700, (800) LOEWS12
(reservations)
www.loewsvanderbilt.com

Tasteful, sophisticated, and luxurious, Loews Vanderbilt Plaza Hotel welcomes many business guests and VIPs. One of the chain's 20 North American properties, this 340-room, 11-story hotel is part of the Loews Vanderbilt Plaza Hotel & Office Complex, which includes an adjacent 13-story office building and a 750-space parking garage. The complex is conveniently located on West End, close to Vanderbilt University, Centennial Park, several good restaurants, downtown Nashville, and Music Row.

Loews will accommodate virtually any request if you give a little notice. Room amenities include a minibar, CD player, safe, coffeemaker, hair dryer, iron and ironing board, fax machine, and dual telephone line with voice mail. High-speed Internet access is available. The Business Class rooms on the Plaza Level feature extra perks, including concierge service, complimentary continental breakfast, and evening hors d'oeuvres served in the Plaza Lounge.

Loews Vanderbilt Plaza has a business center, exercise facility, gift shop, salon and day spa, room service, dry-cleaning service, 24,000 square feet of meeting space, and more. Two restaurants are in the hotel: Ruth's Chris Steak House, a steak lover's dream, and the more casual restaurant, Eat, which serves breakfast, lunch, dinner, and Sunday brunch. For relaxing after a long day of meetings, try the hotel's bar, Drink.

Rates for the hotel's enclosed parking garage are $14 per night maximum. Valet parking is $19. Loews allows pets. If you pay by credit card, there is no pet deposit.

NASHVILLE MARRIOTT AT
VANDERBILT UNIVERSITY $$–$$$$
2555 West End Avenue
(615) 321-1300, (800) 285-0190
www.marriott.com

As you can probably guess from its contemporary brick-and-glass exterior, this is one of the area's newest upscale hotels. Located between Centennial Park and Vanderbilt University, it's convenient to some of Nashville's best restaurants and most popular attractions. The 11-story hotel has more than 300 rooms and five suites, which have a view of either the Parthenon or Vanderbilt University's stadium. Room amenities include a work desk, voice mail, phones with dataports, cable and satellite TV with in-room movies, complimentary in-room coffee, a newspaper delivered on weekdays, iron, and ironing board. Rooms on the concierge level have a few extra amenities. The hotel also has a health club and indoor pool. Parking in the adjacent garage is $14 per day; valet parking is $18. The hotel's upscale restaurant, Latitude, serves breakfast, lunch, and dinner. For more casual meals or snacks, the hotel has a Grab N' Go fast-food restaurant that's open for breakfast and lunch. There is also the Lobby Lounge.

EAST: OPRYLAND/AIRPORT

AMERISUITES AIRPORT $$
721 Royal Parkway
(615) 493-5200, (800) 833-1516
www.amerisuites.com

Located about 2.5 miles from the airport in the Metropolitan Airport Center area off Donelson Pike, this comfortable five-story hotel has 84 suites. Each has a refrigerator, microwave, wet bar, coffeemaker, and free HBO; some suites also have a Jacuzzi. High-speed Internet access is available. There's also an outdoor pool, fitness center, and a large meeting room that can accommodate up to 30 people. A breakfast buffet is included in the room rate. Pets are accepted at a $10 fee.

BEST WESTERN AIRPORT $–$$
701 Stewarts Ferry Pike
(615) 889-9199, (800) 528-1234
www.bestwestern.com

Situated on a quiet hilltop just off I-40 and adjacent to Percy Priest Lake, this 70-room motel is a budget-friendly choice. It's about 8 miles from the Opryland/Music Valley area and about 10 miles from downtown. The three-story property, which opened in the early 1990s, has seven suites with whirlpools, refrigerators, and microwaves. Amenities for all guests include an outdoor pool, free HBO, and free continental breakfast, which is served in the lobby each morning. If your appetite calls for something more substantial, you'll be glad to know that a Waffle House is mere steps away from the front door, and there's a Cracker Barrel across the street. A few other restaurants as well as a grocery store and some convenience shops are close by.

COURTYARD BY MARRIOTT—
ELM HILL PIKE $$$
2508 Elm Hill Pike
(615) 883-9500, (888) 391-8738
www.courtyard.com

This four-story hotel has 145 rooms, including 11 suites. Rooms in the back of the hotel overlook a quiet green space with lots of trees. A free shuttle to and from the airport, which is less than 10 minutes away, is available. Other amenities include free high-speed Internet access in each room, free HBO, an outdoor pool, indoor whirlpool, and exercise room. The 40-seat Courtyard Cafe restaurant offers a full breakfast bar each morning and a soup, salad, and sandwich bar in the evenings. The Market offers a 24/7 selection of freshly made sandwiches, salads, snacks, and beverages. Two 30-capacity meeting rooms provide extra space for business travelers. Local calls are 50 cents each.

EMBASSY SUITES NASHVILLE AIRPORT $$$
10 Century Boulevard
(615) 871-0033, (800) EMBASSY
www.embassy-suites.com

You can't miss it. Visible from I-40, the hotel is in the Century City complex off Elm Hill Pike, 1 mile from Briley Parkway. It's about 3.5 miles from the airport and a short drive from Music Valley attractions. Business travelers and vacationing families will find much to like about this property.

Each of the 296 all-suite accommodations features two TVs, two phones, a wet bar, and refrigerator (a microwave is available upon request). A sleeper sofa in the living room is just right for the kids or an extra person in your party. Free airport shuttles are provided, and complimentary breakfasts and evening beverages are nice perks. For breakfast, choose from the buffet, or order a complete cooked-to-order meal. Evening beverages are served in the hotel's spacious atrium, complete with chirping tropical birds and a babbling brook. Just off the atrium is the Ambassador Grille restaurant, open for lunch and dinner. A lounge area and sports bar are off the atrium. Amenities include a fully equipped fitness center with exercise equipment, sauna, heated pool, and whirlpool. The hotel has 14,000 square feet of meeting space and a 500-capacity ballroom. Meeting planners and a catering staff are available for corporate events. Pets are not allowed.

FAIRFIELD INN BY MARRIOTT AT OPRYLAND $$$
211 Music City Circle
(615) 872-8939, (800) 228-2800
www.marriott.com

This three-story hotel offers 109 rooms and six executive rooms, a heated indoor pool, a fitness center, free deluxe continental breakfast, free wireless high-speed Internet access in each room, and cable TV with Showtime. Located about 1 mile from the Opryland hotel and adjacent to the Music Valley attractions, it's a popular choice with business travelers. Amenities include a free shuttle to nearby Opryland and Nashville International Airport, fax/copy services, and same-day dry cleaning.

FIDDLER'S INN OPRYLAND $$
2410 Music Valley Drive
(615) 885-1440, (877) 223-7621
www.fiddlers-inn.com

This 204-room motel has been in business since 1975. It's one of the more affordable choices in the Music Valley area, appealing to families, bus groups, and budget-minded business travelers. Extras are an outdoor pool, free Showtime, morning coffee and doughnuts, and a gift shop. The Opryland resort is just across the street, offering lots of restaurants, shops, and sightseeing. Music Valley attractions are within walking distance.

GAYLORD OPRYLAND RESORT & CONVENTION CENTER $$$-$$$$
2800 Opryland Drive
(615) 889-1000, (888) 777-6779
www.gaylordhotels.com/gaylordopryland

The Gaylord Opryland Resort is the star of Nashville accommodations. Even if you don't stay at this awe-inspiring property, it's worth stopping by to visit. Thousands of locals, tourists, and business travelers drop by every day to walk through and marvel at the three enormous themed atriums. And it's a tradition for Nashvillians to visit during the holidays when the hotel property turns into a Christmas fantasyland aglow with more than two million lights.

The Opryland resort is one of the largest convention and resort properties in the nation and is the world's largest combined hotel–convention center under one roof. The hotel opened in 1977 with a "mere" 600 rooms. Today it has 2,881 guest rooms (including 200 suites); 600,000 square feet of meeting and exhibit space; 85 meeting rooms; 5 ballrooms; 3 indoor gardens spanning nine acres; dozens of shops, restaurants, and lounges; 3 swimming pools; and a fitness center. You can get a workout just walking from one end to the other. The three indoor gardens are the Conservatory, the Cascades, and the largest, the four-and-a-half-acre Delta, which has a 150-foot-high roof composed of more than 650 tons of glass. The Delta even has its own river—big enough to carry passengers on flatboats on a guided tour of the area. Opryland is undergoing a major expansion which will add more than 400,000 square feet of convention and meeting space and a new 400-room, luxury all-suites hotel adjacent to Gaylord Opryland's current facility.

The hotel was designed for meetings and conventions, and more than 80 percent of its guests are here for such events. It has seemingly endless space and virtually every amenity needed for group functions. The largest of the five ballrooms, the Delta Ballroom, has 55,314 square feet of space. The 289,000-square-foot Ryman Exhibit Hall hosts trade shows and other business gatherings.

There are several types of accommodations here. Each of the garden rooms has a private balcony or patio overlooking one of the themed gardens and costs about 20 percent more than the traditional rooms, which have a window view to the exterior grounds. Guest rooms do not mirror the opulence of the lobbies and gardens, but they are very comfortable and nicely furnished. Room amenities include hair dryers, irons and ironing boards, and voice mail. Dial-up Internet connection is available in the room for a fee. The hotel also has an Internet cafe for those who want high-speed access.

For the ultimate in luxury, the hotel offers four Presidential Suites, which range from 1,500 to 3,000 square feet in size. These fifth-floor suites have one bedroom with a canopy bed (the bedroom connects with two or three other bedrooms outside the suite), living areas, a full wet bar, baby grand piano, whirlpool bath, and at least one fireplace. Some have a full chef's kitchen and a dining room. Presidents George H. W. Bush and Ronald Reagan are among the distinguished guests who have stayed in these suites. Most Presidential Suite guests, however, are business executives; even celebrities and most VIPs opt for the regular rooms. The rate for these spectacular spaces is $3,000 to $3,500 per night. The regular suites range from about $320 to $1,100. Regular room rates aren't nearly as pricey. Opryland offers numerous special deals, such as discounted Internet rates and vacation packages. The savings

can be quite substantial: During the 2008 CMA Awards, for example, the hotel offered a $319 package, which included one night's accommodations, a Silver Club level ticket to the 42nd CMA Awards at Sommet Center, and shuttle transportation to and from the awards.

Gaylord Opryland also offers "drop-in" child care services at its La Petite complex, located just a short walk across the parking lot from the hotel's Cascades Lobby. The La Petite Academy, for infants and toddlers up to age three, is staffed by experienced teachers and other trained child care providers. Children ages 3 through 12 can visit the La Petite Academy Kids Station, a 2,500-square-foot play area where kids can create art, play video games, perform karaoke, or just relax.

Breakfast, lunch, and dinner options at the Opryland hotel are plentiful. Numerous restaurants and lounges offer something for every taste. New outlets in the Delta Atrium are a full-service restaurant called Water's Edge Marketplace; Stax, a build-your-own-burger restaurant; and Paisano's, a casual pizzeria and wine bar.

There are also more than 30 specialty shops selling everything from Jack Daniel's gift baskets to fine bath products.

Of course, the famous Opryland attractions are all nearby: Opry Mills shopping mall, the *General Jackson* showboat and *Music City Queen* riverboats, plus the *Grand Ole Opry* are famous Nashville destinations in their own right. Gaylord's other properties—Ryman Auditorium and Wildhorse Saloon—are located in downtown Nashville.

GUESTHOUSE INN & SUITES $$–$$$
2420 Music Valley Drive
(615) 885-4030, (800) 21-GUEST
www.guesthouseintl.com
This midpriced hotel in the Music Valley area has 185 rooms, including 13 suites. It's right in the middle of all the action of busy Music Valley, convenient to the *Grand Ole Opry* and the airport. Business travelers, tour and travel groups, and individual tourists have kept this well-maintained

ACCOMMODATIONS

property hopping since it first opened in 1987. In fact, if you're planning to stay here in June or any time from September through December, you'll probably need to make your reservations well in advance.

The hotel has 2,500 square feet of meeting space. A complimentary airport shuttle and Opryland hotel shuttle provide convenient transportation. Amenities include free in-room high-speed Internet access, coffeemakers, hair dryers, irons and ironing boards, a guest laundry room, an indoor heated pool, and outdoor whirlpool. Other perks include free Showtime and complimentary deluxe continental breakfast served in the lobby. The lounge, open nightly, serves drinks and snacks and features a variety of live entertainment, including karaoke and local singers and songwriters. Pets can stay here for no additional charge, and there is no weight limit.

HAMPTON INN & SUITES NASHVILLE AIRPORT $$
583 Donelson Pike
(615) 885-4242, (877) 806-8159
www.nashvillehampton.com
This seven-story property is right off I-40 about 1.5 miles from the airport, making it a convenient and moderately priced choice for travel-weary guests who are ready for some downtime. The hotel has 111 rooms, including 31 suites with fully equipped kitchens. Rooms come with coffeemakers, irons and ironing boards, dataport phones, free high-speed wireless Internet service, and complimentary hot breakfast buffet. The hotel has an outdoor pool, exercise room, laundry area, and dry-cleaning services.

HOLIDAY INN EXPRESS AIRPORT $$$
1111 Airport Center Drive
(615) 883-1366, (888) HOLIDAY
www.hiexpress.com/bna-airport
About 2 miles from the Nashville International Airport, this hotel, open since 1987, welcomes lots of business travelers and airline crews. It's located near Donelson Pike. The comfortable and spacious lobby, with its central stone fireplace,

high ceilings, and exposed beams, is an unexpected and welcoming touch. One side of the lobby looks out on a small courtyard area with trees and a park bench. The 206 guest rooms are comfortable and roomy. You can choose a room with two double beds or one king bed. All rooms have coffeemakers, iron and ironing board, free HBO, and dataport phones. A free continental breakfast is served in the atrium. The hotel has an outdoor pool and four banquet rooms.

HOLIDAY INN SELECT NASHVILLE— OPRYLAND/AIRPORT $$–$$$
2200 Elm Hill Pike
(615) 883-9770, (888) HOLIDAY
www.hiselect.com/bna-brileypkwy
Situated right off Briley Parkway, this full-service Holiday Inn is just a couple of miles from both the airport and the Opryland/Music Valley area, and about 7 miles from downtown. The 14-story property has 383 rooms, each with a coffeemaker, hair dryer, iron and ironing board, and two dataports. High-speed wireless Internet service is available (ask about rates). Guests on the top-floor executive level are treated to complimentary coffee and continental breakfast. An indoor pool and sundeck are in the back atrium of the main floor. Nearby are a sauna, fitness center, game room, and gift shop. The Ivories piano bar presents live entertainment Tuesday through Saturday nights. Jackson's Veranda is open for breakfast, lunch, and dinner. Dinner highlights include a pasta bar and weekly prime rib special. You can rent a car at the Enterprise car rental desk. Other services include room service, laundry service, and a free airport shuttle. Pets are permitted with a deposit of $125, $100 of which is refundable.

i March, with an average precipitation of 5.6 inches, is the rainiest month in Nashville.

HOMEWOOD SUITES BY HILTON $$
2640 Elm Hill Pike
(615) 884-8111, (800) CALL-HOME
www.homewoodsuites.com

This attractive, three-story brick hotel opened in 1999 and offers 121 suites, two of which are two-bedroom suites suitable for long-term lodging. The nicely landscaped property is located next to an office park, less than 3 miles from the airport. One-bedroom suites have either a king bed or two double beds and a separate living area with sleeper sofa. All suites have a full refrigerator, microwave, stovetop, tabletop with two chairs, and a coffeemaker. In-room amenities include TVs with cable in the bedrooms and living area, a VCR, two phones, and free high-speed Internet service. The hotel offers a free shuttle within a 5-mile radius, a coin laundry, a fitness center, a business center, an outdoor pool with grills available for guest use, and a 24-hour snack and sundries shop. The room rate includes a full hot breakfast seven days a week as well as a light evening meal with beer, wine, and soft drinks Monday through Thursday. Local phone calls are $1; however, guests can make free local calls at the first-floor courtesy phone. Pets weighing up to 15 pounds are permitted with a $200 deposit, $100 of which is refundable; the refund policy can be flexible, so guests with small or especially clean or well-behaved pets may be able to negotiate a better deal.

HOTEL PRESTON $–$$$
733 Briley Parkway
(615) 361-5900, (877) 361-5500
www.hotelpreston.com
Located 2 miles from the Nashville airport, Hotel Preston has 12 floors with 196 guest rooms and suites. Opening its doors in 2004, Hotel Preston is upscale and personalized. The hotel features a "You Want It—You Got It" program, which offers guests special amenities and comforts such as pet fish companions, lava lamps, CDs, books, rubber duckies, milk and cookies, and more. The exterior of the building reflects its Clarion and Radisson hotel roots, and the interior is sleek and modern. Mustard-colored walls and dark woods warm up the rooms, which display a Southern ambience with their graceful lines. Black-and-white photos add a stylish touch.

Amenities include Starbucks coffee, Tazo tea, pillow-top mattresses, designer toiletries, ergonomic swivel chairs, and high-speed wireless Internet access. Quirky extras include Primp Kits for him, her, and Spot. The hotel includes a 24-hour fitness center, outdoor pool, meeting space for 8 to 800, in-room business work space, same-day dry cleaning and laundry services, and premium channels plus movies on demand. The hotel also offers complimentary 24-hour shuttle service to the airport and service to Opry Mills.

NASHVILLE AIRPORT MARRIOTT $$$–$$$$
600 Marriott Drive
(615) 889-9300, (800) 228-9290
www.nashvillemarriott.com
On 17 acres of rolling wooded hills, the Nashville Airport Marriott offers some of Music City's most comfortable accommodations. It's just off Elm Hill Pike, a few minutes from the airport or Opryland.

Open since 1987, the 18-story hotel has 398 rooms, including six suites. All rooms have high-speed Internet access (an extra fee applies), in-room pay-per-view movies, and free HBO. Guests on the 15th- and 16th-floor concierge levels are treated to a few extras, such as terry-cloth robes, turndown service, complimentary continental breakfast, buffet-style hors d'oeuvres in the afternoon, and a private bar. Rooms feature views of either the airport area, downtown Nashville, or the swimming pool. First-floor rooms have private balconies.

The hotel has excellent recreation facilities, including a sand volleyball court, tennis courts, a basketball court, and a health club with workout equipment and separate saunas in each locker room. With 14,000 square feet of meeting and banquet space, this property is also well equipped to handle business functions. The hotel has an on-site restaurant, a lounge, and a coffee shop. A gift shop, room service, guest laundry area, one-day dry-cleaning service, business center, free airport shuttle, and free parking are among other extras.

RADISSON HOTEL AT OPRYLAND $$$

2401 Music Valley Drive
(615) 889-0800, (800) 333-3333
www.radisson.com

Right across McGavock Pike from the Gaylord Opryland hotel, this comfortable, three-story hotel/motel is in a great location. Each of the 303 rooms has a coffeemaker, hair dryer, voice mail, and free movie channel. High-speed Internet access is available for a fee. Faxing and copying services are available at the front desk for a small charge. The hotel is within walking distance of Music Valley shops, restaurants, and museums. After a long day of fun at nearby attractions, you can come back here for a relaxing soak in the hotel's whirlpool or swim a few laps at the indoor pool. Two saunas and an exercise room offer other opportunities to unwind. The on-site Applebee's Bar and Grill serves a buffet breakfast, buffet lunch, and full-service dinner.

SHERATON MUSIC CITY HOTEL $$$

777 McGavock Pike
(615) 885-2200, (800) 325-3535
www.sheratonmusiccity.com

This recently renovated hotel offers some of Nashville's most comfortable accommodations. The four-story property sits atop a hill on 23 acres in a business park just off McGavock Pike. It's about a five-minute drive from both the airport and the Opryland area. Downtown Nashville is just minutes away, too. The hotel offers 410 spacious rooms, including 56 suites. Room amenities include a sleigh bed with pillow-top mattress, workstation, and 27-inch TV with video games, plus a coffeemaker, hair dryer, iron and ironing board, and a private balcony or patio. High-speed Internet access is available. The 20 second-story Club Level rooms come with extra perks, such as upgraded bath amenities, plush bathrobes, bottled water, turndown service, complimentary breakfast, and evening hors d'oeuvres.

For recreation, you can choose from the indoor pool, outdoor pool, tennis courts, or health club with exercise equipment. The hotel has 32,000 square feet of meeting space and offers business travelers a variety of helpful services, including faxing and wireless Internet access in public areas. Dining choices include the elegant Old Hickory Grill restaurant, offering gourmet Southern specialties, and the Veranda, a piano bar off the lobby, where you can have restaurant items delivered, and room service. Pets are permitted; there is no weight limit or deposit.

NORTH

COMFORT INN MUSIC CITY $-$$

2407 Brick Church Pike
(615) 226-3300, (800) 424-6423
www.nashvillecomfortinn.com

Affordable rates make this 118-room hotel a popular choice with budget-minded families, especially on weekends. Located just off I-65 near Trinity Lane, the hotel is convenient to downtown Nashville and is about a 15-minute drive to Opryland. Some rooms have microwave ovens; other amenities include a fitness room and outdoor pool. A free continental breakfast is served in the lobby each morning. Pets up to 10 pounds are permitted at no additional charge.

DAYS INN AT THE COLISEUM $-$$

211 North First Street
(615) 254-1551, (800) 251-3038,
(800) DAYS-INN
www.daysinn.com

This high-rise hotel is within view of downtown Nashville, less than a mile from I-65, and convenient to the historic Germantown district, where you'll find several good restaurants, the Farmers' Market, and the Bicentennial Capitol Mall state park. The hotel has 180 rooms, some of which offer a great cityscape view. Amenities include free HBO, an indoor heated pool, Henry's Exile Restaurant, a weight room, and a laundry room. High-speed Internet access is available. For business guests there are three meeting rooms—two on the first floor and a larger room on the ninth floor. A daily breakfast buffet is available for an extra charge.

DAYS INN—WEST TRINITY LANE $–$$
1400 Brick Church Pike
(615) 228-5977, (800) DAYS-INN
www.daysinn.com

This 108-room Days Inn is in the Trinity Lane area, just off I–65/24 and minutes from downtown. Other than an outdoor pool, there aren't many amenities here, but the super-affordable rates are a fair trade-off. Rooms have free HBO and hair dryers; some have dataport phones. A free continental breakfast awaits guests in the lobby each morning. Surveillance cameras, extra nighttime security, and card keys offer a little extra peace of mind. There are several restaurants nearby. Pets are allowed for a $10 fee.

MILLENNIUM MAXWELL HOUSE NASHVILLE $$
2025 MetroCenter Boulevard
(615) 259-4343, (800) 457-4460
www.millenniumhotels.com

The Millennium Maxwell House is the namesake of the famous Maxwell House Hotel (see the related Close-up in our History chapter) that opened in downtown Nashville in 1869. The hotel was the site for many important business and social events, and it enjoyed a national reputation. And yes, the hotel is connected to the famous brand of coffee, although the hotel had the Maxwell House name first. President Theodore Roosevelt, on a visit to Nashville in the early 1900s, commented that the coffee was "good to the last drop." The original Maxwell House was destroyed by fire in 1961. The current hotel opened in 1979; it sits just off I–65, 1.5 miles from downtown.

Atop a knoll overlooking downtown Nashville, this 10-story hotel has 287 spacious and well-appointed rooms. Two are bilevel suites with one and a half baths, and two are junior suites with a king bedroom and connecting parlor area. Amenities include an outdoor pool; two lighted tennis courts; a health club with sauna, steam room, and workout equipment; room service and valet/laundry service; in-room movies; two-line dataport phones; and free newspapers daily. Millennium Club Level rooms, on a private,

keyed-access floor, offer free high-speed Internet access, private library, complimentary breakfast buffet, luxury bed linens, turndown service, and other perks, all for about $30 extra. The hotel's free shuttle will take you to any location within a 5-mile radius. On-site Praline's offers breakfast, lunch, and dinner. The sports-bar-themed Maxwell's Lounge is open nightly.

QUALITY INN & SUITES $$
2401 Brick Church Pike
(615) 226-4600, (800) 228-5151
www.qualityinn.com

A nice and affordable choice in the Trinity Lane area off I–65, this five-story hotel was completely renovated in 2004. The hotel has 150 rooms, including 24 two-room suites. Each room has sliding glass doors that open up to a small balcony, but there's not much in the way of a view. A free continental deluxe breakfast is served daily in the lobby. Other amenities include free HBO, free high-speed Internet access, an outdoor pool, fitness room with sauna, and meeting/banquet space for up to 250 people.

RAMADA DOWNTOWN AT THE STADIUM $$
303 Interstate Drive
(615) 244-6690, (800) 2-RAMADA,
(800) 251-1856
www.ramadainnstadium.com

Business travelers and tourists have been relying on this convenient property for about 40 years. Situated on the east bank of the Cumberland River, adjacent to the Titans' stadium, the hotel is popular during football season; if you want a room on a game day, it's a good idea to book it well in advance. The hotel is also a popular choice for youth groups. This Ramada has 120 rooms, including 15 premium rooms and suites. Some rooms have nice views of the downtown skyline. The hotel is close to I-65 and is only about 8 blocks from downtown Nashville. The indoor guitar-shaped swimming pool is a fitting touch for a Music City hotel. Guests can also enjoy a free deluxe breakfast, served daily in the first-floor breakfast room.

SOUTH AND SOUTHEAST

BRENTWOOD STEEPLECHASE INN & SUITES $-$$
5581 Franklin Pike Circle, Brentwood
(615) 373-8585, (866) 770-1274
www.steeplechaseinn.com

One of the Nashville area's few privately owned and operated hotels, the Steeplechase Inn promises nice, comfortable accommodations at an affordable rate. The hotel is popular with business travelers, who account for about 70 percent of bookings on weekdays. The hotel welcomes a lot of guests for weddings and family reunions on weekends.

Steeplechase Inn opened in 1986 and features 48 rooms, including 24 suites, among four separate town house–style buildings. The large rooms have 9-foot ceilings, which add to their spacious feel, floor-to-ceiling draperies, and cherrywood furniture. The 650-square-foot suites have fully furnished kitchens. Some suites have fireplaces; others have whirlpool tubs. Daily deluxe continental breakfast is included in the room rate. Those with heartier appetites might want to walk over to the Waffle House next door. There's also cable TV and free parking.

The inn is off I-65 on the east side of Old Hickory Boulevard. There are plenty of restaurants and shops across the interstate in Brentwood, and the Cool Springs shopping and dining mecca is just a few miles south on I-65.

 In Nashville nearly 55,000 jobs are related to hospitality.

FRANKLIN MARRIOTT COOL SPRINGS $$$
700 Cool Springs Boulevard, Franklin
(615) 261-6100, (888) 403-6772
www.franklinmarriott.com

This 11-story, 300-room hotel is located right across I–65 from Cool Springs's shops and restaurants and offers fast and easy access to Nashville, just a few miles north. The hotel features an indoor pool, sundeck, exercise room, and more than 29,000 square feet of meeting space. There

is an on-site restaurant as well as an equestrian-themed lounge and a coffee shop. Room amenities include wireless high-speed Internet access, hair dryer, coffeemaker, iron and ironing board, a free movie channel, and a free newspaper each weekday. Half of the hotel's rooms are designed specifically for business travelers and include a work desk, executive chair, dataport phones, and voice mail. There are two concierge floors, and three suites are available. Business travelers can take advantage of the full business center, which offers self-service computers, faxing, copying, printing, and other services. There is also an on-site gift shop/newsstand.

HAMPTON INN—BRENTWOOD $$
5630 Franklin Pike Circle, Brentwood
(615) 373-2212, (800) HAMPTON
www.hamptoninnbrentwood.com

Corporate clients doing business in Brentwood's nearby Maryland Farms office park keep the 112-room Hampton Inn—Brentwood busy on weekdays.

Located right off I-65, this four-story property features spacious and nicely decorated rooms plus just enough extras to make sure your stay here is comfortable. In-room amenities include free high-speed Internet access, hair dryer, iron and ironing board, and free movies. An exercise room and outdoor pool are available. A complimentary continental breakfast is served in the lobby each morning.

HILTON SUITES—BRENTWOOD $$-$$$
9000 Overlook Boulevard, Brentwood
(615) 370-0111, (800) HILTONS
www.brentwoodhilton.com

As its name and address suggest, this all-suites property sits atop a hill overlooking Brentwood and I-65. This four-story hotel features 203 two-room suites. The rooms have more than 500 square feet of space and include a bedroom and a living-dining area with a microwave, coffeemaker, refrigerator, and table with four chairs. Each room also has a VCR. King Executive rooms have extra meeting space. High-speed Internet access is available in all suites.

For recreation, there's an indoor pool, whirl-pool, and fitness center. After you work up an appetite, you can enjoy breakfast, lunch, or dinner in the full-service restaurant in the center atrium area. Other amenities include a billiard room, business center, library, gift shop with videos available for checkout, and four meeting rooms. Pets up to 20 pounds are permitted at no charge.

WEST

**BAYMONT INN & SUITES—
NASHVILLE WEST** $$-$$$
5612 Lenox Avenue
(615) 353-0700, (877) BAYMONT
www.baymontinns.com
This property is just off White Bridge Road near Charlotte Pike, 1 block from I-40. If you're not looking for it, you may pass right by, but inside you'll find a courteous and helpful staff and guest rooms with lots of extras. This hotel opened in 1988 and has 105 well-appointed rooms, including six suites. Amenities include a deluxe continental breakfast, hair dryers, irons and ironing boards, and coffeepots in each room. Baymont Inn & Suites is also an affordable and convenient business hotel featuring dataports, working desks with ergonomic chairs, and a business center at the front desk. Free high-speed Internet

access is available in the lobby. The hotel has an outdoor pool.

**HAMPTON INN & SUITES
GREEN HILLS** $$-$$$$
2324 Crestmoor Road
(615) 777-0001, (800) HAMPTON
www.hamptoninn.com
One of Nashville's newer hotels, this Hampton Inn & Suites is distinguished by its lovely redbrick and limestone facade. The classy look mirrors the accommodations; this is definitely one of the company's more upscale properties. The interior is decorated with rich cherry and mahogany woods; bathrooms have cultured marble showers and granite vanities. There are 97 rooms, 27 of them suites. The spacious suites have a bedroom, living room, and fully appointed kitchen. There are also "studies"—rooms with a king bed and sofa sleeper, popular with families with young children. Rooms come with all the amenities, plus complimentary deluxe breakfast and free in-room high-speed Internet access. Complimentary coffee and tea are served in the lobby 24 hours a day; there's also a free shuttle that will take you anywhere within a 3-mile radius of the hotel. Nearby are the Regal Cinema 16 movie theater, shopping at the upscale Mall at Green Hills, and restaurants, so the service comes in handy. The hotel has an outdoor pool, Jacuzzi, exercise room, and guest laundry area.

BED-AND-BREAKFAST INNS

here is something special about spending the night at a bed-and-breakfast inn. Maybe it's the home-away-from-home feeling you get at a B&B—something you just can't get at a hotel. Or maybe it's the hospitality of the hosts, who welcome you into their homes and treat you like a very special friend. It might be the uniquely decorated guest rooms, the fresh flowers, homemade breakfasts, and other attention to detail. Or maybe it's the privacy, the peace and quiet, the relaxing times spent snuggled up in front of a roaring fire or enjoying a soft breeze while you sip a cold drink on a front-porch swing.

More and more people are discovering the delights of bed-and-breakfast hospitality. Many believe the bed-and-breakfast inn is a new concept for America and that our inns are copies of European inns, but American B&Bs, in one form or another, have been around since the earliest colonial days. Today they are becoming increasingly popular among business travelers, vacationing families, and people looking for a close-to-home weekend getaway.

When you stay at a B&B, you get a real Insiders' view of an area. It's a great way to experience an area's color and flavor—a place to become one of the locals for a short time. When you've long forgotten a night in a nondescript hotel, you'll look back with fond memories on your pleasant stay in a special bed-and-breakfast.

Each inn has its own charm, and no two are alike. The innkeepers are just as diverse. Retirees, business executives, artists, secretaries, farmers, teachers, lawyers—friendly people from all walks of life own B&Bs. You'll find some gracious hosts at Nashville-area inns. They are as interesting as their homes, which range from properties on the National Register of Historic Places to modern dwellings with every possible amenity. There are country inns offering spacious, deluxe accommodations as well as cozy, comfortable homes with one or two rooms to rent. Many out-of-towners expect to find large Southern plantation mansions here, but Nashville isn't in the Deep South, and there aren't many properties like that in this area. You will find interesting homes full of character, however.

Business travelers and tourists might enjoy staying at a B&B in or close to the city; there are several of those to choose from. Those who prefer a country setting will find some excellent choices, too—country inns, farmhouses, and cabins on the outskirts of Nashville or in nearby towns.

OVERVIEW

In this chapter you'll find a selection of B&Bs in and around Nashville. We haven't listed all the available properties, but we have chosen a sample that represents several locations, accommodations, and price ranges.

Here are a few Insiders' tips to keep in mind when choosing a bed-and-breakfast.

• The "breakfast" part of your bed-and-breakfast might be a made-to-order country breakfast; an owner's special pancake breakfast; a continental-style breakfast of coffee, juice, and baked goods; or something in between. If you have any special dietary needs, be sure to let your hosts know in advance; they'll usually make a good effort to accommodate your requests.

• Some bed-and-breakfasts accept children; some do so only by special arrangement;

some do not allow kids at all. If you are traveling with children, be sure to find out if your preferred B&B is kid-friendly. Likewise, if you're looking for a quiet adult environment, ask the innkeeper if any children will be staying at your chosen inn during your visit. Policies on children are provided for the B&Bs we list.

- If you're traveling with a pet, you can probably find an inn that accepts them. Be sure to inquire about pet accommodations, especially if your four-legged friend is accustomed to staying indoors; some inns only allow them to stay outside. Also, if you have allergies or just prefer not to be around pets, be sure to ask if the owners have any indoor pets. Pet policies are included in our listings.
- Many inns offer some wheelchair-accessible rooms, but some of the older, historical locations may not be fully accessible. Be sure to inquire about this when you call if accessibility is a concern.
- Virtually all area B&Bs are nonsmoking properties, but most allow smoking on the porch, deck, or other outside areas.
- Credit card policies vary. Check with the inn when making your reservations to see which, if any, credit cards are accepted. We'll tell you if a listed B&B doesn't accept credit cards.
- Advance deposit and refund policies vary. During certain times of year, policies may be more strict due to the demand for accommodations. Be sure you understand the rules before making a reservation.

Price Code

The following key is a general guide to what you can expect to pay for one night's stay. The rates are for double occupancy. If you're traveling alone, you can expect to pay approximately $5 to $15 less. Prices are subject to change.

$	$75 to $100
$$	$101 to $125
$$$	$126 to $150
$$$$	$151 or more

ASSOCIATIONS AND RESERVATION SERVICES

BED & BREAKFAST ASSOCIATION OF TENNESSEE
519 North Highland Avenue
Jackson, TN 38301
(866) 669-5728
www.tennessee-inns.com

This state association is a nonprofit organization established to market Tennessee bed-and-breakfast inns. Its member inns are fully licensed by the state and have passed the association's biennial inspection program. Call the toll-free number for a free brochure that describes each inn, or visit the Web site.

i The Bed and Breakfast Association of Tennessee offers gift certificates in $25 increments. Certificates can be used at its member inns. Order them online at www.tennessee-inns.com or by phone at (800) 820-8144.

NATCHEZ TRACE BED & BREAKFAST RESERVATION SERVICE
P.O. Box 193, Hampshire, TN 38461
(800) 377-2770
www.bbonline.com/natcheztrace

This service has a directory of a few dozen inns in Tennessee, Alabama, and Mississippi. All are along the Natchez Trace, a historic route that runs from Nashville to Natchez, Mississippi. About 10 of the inns are near Nashville. Call or visit the Web site for reservations, details on homes, and a free map of the Trace.

BED-AND-BREAKFASTS IN AND AROUND NASHVILLE

A HOMEPLACE BED & BREAKFAST　　$$$
7286 Nolensville Road, Nolensville
(615) 776-5181

Alfred and Evelyn Hyde Bennett have been operating this B&B since 1990. The couple came across the property one day while taking a drive in the south Nashville countryside to buy a bushel of apples. They ended up buying the one-acre plot of land containing the old Putnam family home and a couple of 1800s-era structures when they realized the property was being auctioned off on the spot, and the lone bidder planned to demolish the house. The Bennetts were newlyweds at the time—Alfred was a retired minister and Evelyn was a retired Metro schoolteacher. They had recently been introduced to bed-and-breakfast hospitality while honeymooning in Scotland, where they had stayed at a variety of inns.

After purchasing the property, they restored the home and buildings and opened up for business. The main building, incidentally, was originally a stagecoach stop; the front of the house was built around 1820 and the back around 1850. Guests from as far away as Switzerland and South Africa have found their way here, and the inn has quite a few repeat visitors.

The main house offers three guest rooms, each with a large full bath, double canopy bed, armoire, dresser with washbasin, fireplace, and sitting area. Downstairs is the Parlor Suite guest room, which has a library. Upstairs is the Doctor's Room, so named because an out-of-town ophthalmologist-veterinarian stayed there when he had appointments scheduled in Nashville. The Honeymoon Suite is also upstairs. It features a Victorian couch, an elegant library table, and several other interesting antiques.

Outside, cheerful and colorful flower gardens brighten each side of the main house. In the backyard is the Victorian Cottage, or "gingerbread house," as Evelyn calls it. The cottage, which served as the cook's cottage in the stagecoach days, is suitable for a lengthy stay and features a small kitchen, an antique bed, and a bath. Water lily and lotus ponds are nearby. The backyard creek house and gazebo offer a view of the creek, stone fences, and meadow. The large gazebo is the setting for barbecues, special receptions, and civic group events.

Guests have access to all other rooms in the main house. A piano, TV, and VCR are in the living room, and the Bennetts have a dulcimer and accordion available, too. Phones are in the living room and dining room. The large front porch has rocking chairs, a porch swing, and a bench and is a nice place to take your morning cup of coffee.

The full breakfast is a special treat. Alfred, of Scottish heritage, dresses for the occasion in his kilt and Prince Charles dinner jacket. Ham quiche and hot biscuits are specialties. Also on the menu are fresh fruit, country ham, Scottish scones, juice, hot tea, and coffee. Waffles and sausage are usually served on Sunday. Evelyn gets many requests for her recipes, and she'll be glad to share them with you. Children are accepted here by prior arrangement, but pets aren't. Guests who stay in any of the rooms for a week or more receive a discount. This B&B does not accept credit cards.

This inn is about 7 miles from the Old Hickory Boulevard–Nolensville Pike intersection, about a 20-minute drive from downtown Nashville.

i Your bed-and-breakfast hosts can recommend good restaurants, attractions, and shopping spots in the area. Be sure to ask about their favorites—there's nothing like a real Insiders' view.

CAROLE'S YELLOW COTTAGE $$
801 Fatherland Street
(615) 226-2952
www.bbonline.com/tn/yellowcottage
Situated on a corner lot in east Nashville's historic Edgefield, 5 blocks from the Tennessee Titans's stadium and within walking distance to other downtown attractions, this spacious 1902 Victorian cottage is a popular spot with business travelers and weekend visitors who want to stay close to the city. The house is listed on the National Register of Historic Places and is surrounded by some beautifully restored 19th-century homes. Each spring the neighborhood has an open house to showcase some of the best. "I feel very elevated, spiritually, to be here," said Carole Vanderwal, who opened Carole's Yellow Cottage in 1995. "Older homes are really a treasure. There are not that many left in the city of Nashville." Vanderwal, who has a degree in Russian language and literature as well as a law degree, plans to become a full-time innkeeper when she retires.

This sunny, one-story cottage has an enclosed backyard with a deck that overlooks perennial gardens. The front yard offers a dramatic view of the downtown Nashville skyline. The Cottage doesn't accept pets.

Inside, the 2,100-square-foot house features 12-foot ceilings, bedrooms with ceiling fans, central heat and air, and original heart-of-pine wood floors. Each of the two guest rooms has its own bath with shower. One room has a large double bed, turn-of-the-20th-century antiques, and a restful buttery yellow and white color scheme. The other room has one double bed, a futon couch that opens into a second double bed, and a taupe color on the walls, with royal blue bedcovers, miniblinds, and coordinating wallpaper trim. The sitting room/library features deep red walls, a love seat, and two chairs. Come here to enjoy a selection of books or watch television before turning in at night. The rooms do not have private phones, but a phone is available. Vanderwal carefully selected original paintings and other artwork for the walls.

Carole serves a full breakfast each morning. She specializes in whole-grain cooking, so you can expect delicious cranberry muffins or eggs with feta and spinach.

1501 LINDEN MANOR $$–$$$
1501 Linden Avenue
(615) 298-2701, (800) 226-0317
www.nashville-bed-breakfast.com

This lovely and comfortable inn, located in the Belmont-Hillsboro Historic District, is a renovated 1893 Victorian home, one of only two Victorians in the area. Owners Tom and Catherine Favreau opened the B&B in the late 1990s after working for 14 years in the Coast Guard and traveling all over the world. They moved to Nashville so that Tom could pursue a songwriting career.

Many of Linden Manor's guests are business travelers or parents of local college students; the inn is especially popular among professors visiting local universities. A few traveling country and pop stars have spent the night here, too. The B&B allows children over age 12 but does not accept pets.

The inn has three large guest rooms, each with a private bathroom. The Vanderbilt Room has a queen-size four-poster bed covered in romantic, floral-print linens. The walls are painted deep red and set off by crisp white trim and stylish area rugs on the wood floors. This room has a fireplace, which makes it especially cozy. The Belmont Room, also with a queen-size bed, has a soothing blue color scheme and a Victorian garden theme. The Linden Room has a king-size bed and a private, outside entrance. The room's private bath has a shower and a Jacuzzi tub. The Vanderbilt and Belmont baths have showers but no tubs.

Guests are welcome in the sitting room, formal dining room, large wraparound porch, and back deck. Catherine serves a full breakfast. A typical menu is French vanilla French toast with strawberries and whipped cream, coffee or tea, and juice. Afternoon refreshments are served on the porch when the weather is nice, and there's always a bottomless cookie jar, popcorn, and plenty of beverages available.

Sometimes guests are even treated to live entertainment. Whenever Tom's songwriter friends from the neighborhood stop by, it's not unusual for an impromptu guitar pull or songswapping session to break out. The atmosphere is relaxed and informal, just like the Favreaus. "Our motto is 'Arrive as a guest and leave as a friend,'" says Catherine.

i Tipping is not expected at local bed-and-breakfasts. If an innkeeper or staff member goes to great lengths to meet a request, however, some gesture of appreciation may be appropriate. For a B&B owner, a bouquet of flowers or bottle of wine might be a suitable thank-you.

HANCOCK HOUSE $$–$$$$
2144 Nashville Pike, Gallatin
(615) 452-8431
www.bbonline.com/hancock

Roberta and Carl Hancock have lived in this historic house since the late 1970s. They opened it as a B&B in 1991 after Roberta, a schoolteacher for 20 years, decided she was ready for a new career. Roberta and Carl, who was formerly in the tobacco business, spent several months renovating the home and the two-story cabin in the side yard.

Hancock House is a 15-room colonial revival log inn. In the late 1800s it was a stagecoach stop and toll gatehouse known as Avondale Station. Over the years two small cabins were attached to the back of the original building. Between the three structures is a courtyard, just off the dining room. The interior features hardwood floors, exposed beams, fireplaces, log walls, area rugs, and period antiques that the Hancocks have collected over more than 30 years.

The main house has five bedrooms, each with a private bath and fireplace. The Chamber room, located on the ground floor, has an antique Murphy bed and a whirlpool tub. The Nannie Dunn room, half a flight of stairs up and off the dining room, has an antique bed. Upstairs are the Bridal Suite, with an antique canopy four-poster bed and a romantic whirlpool for two, and the Felice Ferrell room, named for the home's previous owner, which has an antique elevated bed.

The cabin offers more privacy. It sleeps up to six and has a bedroom, kitchen, and den with sofa bed and fireplace. The bath has a whirlpool tub and shower.

All accommodations include a full country breakfast, served in your room, in the dining room, or outdoors in the courtyard. The Hancocks also serve afternoon tea and other beverages and plenty of fresh fruit. Breakfast, brunch, lunch, and dinner are available by reservation.

Children are welcome at Hancock House, but there are no accommodations for pets. Hancock House hosts weddings, receptions, seminars, and other events.

THE HILLSBORO HOUSE BED & BREAKFAST $$
1933 20th Avenue S.
(615) 292-5501, (800) 228-7851
www.visitnashville.net
Owner Andrea Beaudet describes the Hillsboro House as a cozy Victorian bed-and-breakfast for travelers, featuring private baths, feather beds, morning birds, and homemade breads. This circa 1904 house is in the heart of Nashville's historic Belmont-Hillsboro District, within walking distance of Hillsboro Village shops, Vanderbilt University, Belmont University, and the popular Sunset Grill restaurant. Music Row is just a few blocks away.

Located at the corner of Portland and 20th, just off 21st Avenue, the house was condemned when Andrea, a former music teacher in Maine, purchased it in 1990. She has since carefully restored it and made it a showpiece of the neighborhood. The cheerful yellow two-story house is trimmed in white and bordered by a cream-colored picket fence.

Lots of business travelers have made this charming and casual bed-and-breakfast their home away from home since it opened in 1994. The house is also popular with the neighbors, who send visiting relatives there for the night. "It's comfortable and cozy. Guests get a good night's sleep, a good breakfast, and they're on their way," Andrea says.

Two parlors are on the first floor. Andrea keeps a small refrigerator stocked with refreshments in the main parlor. The living room has a fireplace and makes for a cozy spot to relax during winter. In preparation for the B&B's 10th anniversary in 2004, Andrea redecorated the home. She describes the new decor as "dressed-up vintage yet elegant . . . with whiffs of nostalgia and a sprinkling of whimsy."

Hillsboro House has three minisuites available for guests. Each has a private bath and queen-size feather bed. The second-floor Fairfax suite is a large room with antique 1940s cottage furniture, some of which was hand-painted by a local artist. The bed is dressed in floral and check linens. The bath has a shower only. The spacious Acklen suite, also upstairs, has a verdigris iron bed and wicker furniture. The bath has a deep tub supplied with the B&B's own homemade bath salts. The downstairs Magnolia suite has a traditional cherry four-poster bed and an English country look. The bath has a shower only. All guest rooms have private phones and cable TV.

Upstairs is a cozy library nook, a nice spot for working or reading.

The specialty breakfast is carrot-nut pancakes topped with homemade cinnamon cream syrup. Andrea's peaches-and-cream French toast is another favorite. Breakfasts come with freshly ground coffee, juice, and sausage or bacon; eggs are usually served every other day.

Children and pets are welcome at Hillsboro House. Andrea's Maine Coon cat, Maggie, and her West Highland Terrier, Jock, also live here.

NAMASTE ACRES COUNTRY
RANCH INN $-$$
5436 Leipers Creek Road, Franklin
(615) 791-0333
www.namasteacres.com

This bed-and-breakfast caters to equestrians and their horses but also is popular with casual travelers, hiking enthusiasts, nature lovers, and historians.

Jamie and Joanna Hanson are the innkeepers. The original owners opened the inn with one guest room, and the business grew from there; today they offer a choice of three unique suites and a conference room for business travelers. The property is about 25 miles south of Nashville near the community of Leipers Fork, approximately 1 mile off the Natchez Trace Parkway.

The Trace, a 500-mile wilderness route that connected what was then the northwest United States with the new Mississippi Territory in the early 1800s, is a big part of the appeal here. Guests can ride on portions of the original Trace—the same route traveled by Andrew Jackson and Meriwether Lewis. If you don't have your own horse, the innkeepers can arrange a trail ride for you. Other riding and hiking opportunities are nearby, among them Nashville's Percy Warner Park.

After a day on the trails, you'll enjoy relaxing in your private guest suite. Each of the elaborately themed suites in the Dutch colonial country home has a private entrance, queen-size feather bed, private bath, fireplace, comfortable seating area with reading material, TV/VCR, CD/cassette player, clock-radio, phone, ceiling fan, minifridge, and coffeemaker.

The Cowboy Bunkhouse features rough-sawn lumber walls, log/rope bunk beds, a claw-foot tub, and a private deck. The spacious Indian Lodge has a Southwestern scheme and is filled with an interesting collection of Native American artifacts and paintings. An upper-level deck provides a nice valley view. The Pioneer Cabin features rough-sawn lumber walls, a 12-foot ceiling, and hand-hewn beams. This room's private deck overlooks a pool and rock garden. The inn also has an exercise nook with workout equipment, a seasonal hot tub, gas grills, horseshoe pit, a fire ring for campfires and wienie roasts, and a tree house and swing by the creek. Equestrians will appreciate the stables, six separate pastures, outdoor riding arena, round pen, and horse walker. In the morning, after awakening to the rooster's crow, you can enjoy a delicious and hearty country breakfast—maybe eggs, bacon, ham, sausage, potato casserole, and pancakes.

This inn allows children ages 10 and older, but be sure to inquire about that when you make your reservation. If you have pets other than horses, check with the innkeepers before bringing them.

> **i** If the name of the bed-and-breakfast contains the word *barn*, it usually means the inn has accommodations for guests' horses.

TIMOTHY DEMONBREUN HOUSE $$$$
746 Benton Avenue
(615) 383-0426
timothydhouse.com

The Timothy Demonbreun House may be Nashville's most luxurious bed-and-breakfast. The 22-room mansion is owned by Richard Demonbreun, the great-great-great-great-grandson of Frenchman Timothy Demonbreun, who is considered Nashville's first citizen (see our History chapter). The home is named in Timothy's honor, although he never lived on the property (the home was built long after his death).

The 10,000-square-foot 1906 mansion, located in the Woodland-in-Waverly historic district (see our Relocation chapter), is listed on the

National Register of Historic Places. Richard, an attorney, opened the B&B in 2000 after spending five years and $2 million renovating the home. The meticulous renovation earned the property the Metropolitan Historic Architectural Preservation Award. Since its opening it has become a popular site for wedding receptions, and for video and photo shoots for such stars as Garth Brooks and Kenny Rogers.

The B&B offers four guest rooms, each with a queen-size bed, fireplace, private bath, and access to the heated pool and spa. The home has a wine cellar where guests can select from an assortment of wines, including the B&B's own house wine, which is bottled in California. A full, made-to-order breakfast is served each morning. The B&B has several chefs and a full waitstaff. For those who aren't spending the night here but would enjoy dining at the stately home, private dining is available by reservation.

Children are welcome, but the inn doesn't accept pets.

TOP O'WOODLAND HISTORIC BED AND BREAKFAST $$$–$$$$
1603 Woodland Street
(615) 228-3868, (888) 228-3868
www.topofwoodland.com

Just minutes from downtown, Top O'Woodland exudes Victorian grandeur frozen in time. Authentic Southern hospitality is extended at this Queen Anne Victorian with a neoclassical influence. Original 10-foot chestnut pocket doors, 12 chandeliers, five fireplaces, a turret, and stained-glass windows highlight this historic bed-and-breakfast. The home contains original wallpaper, antique carpet, and period antiques. Play the mahogany Steinway baby grand piano in the Grand Music Entrance Foyer or read by the fire in the parlor. A movie theater on the second floor boasts a 12-foot screen. Relax on the wraparound front porch or in the brick courtyards. A large private courtyard features a lovely koi pond.

Built between 1898 and 1904, Top O'Woodland is known as "the jewel" of the Lockeland Springs Historic Conservation District. Dr. H. B. Hyde built this grand home, and he would meet with his patients here, as well as at his downtown office. Dr. Hyde was the great-grandson of Henry Hyde, one of Nashville's early settlers, for which the Hydes Ferry community was named. The home has had only three previous owners. Belinda Leslie bought it in 2000.

Specializing in weddings, the inn has a wedding chapel parlor and a chaplain on-site. The home has one guest bedroom, the Library, as well as the Locke Room for wedding ceremonies and the Rose Salon as a bridal dressing room.

Walk down the garden path to a separate 600-square-foot cottage, which sleeps five. Mr. Greens Cottage has a king-size four-poster bed, sitting area with daybed, separate bedroom with antique full-size bed, kitchenette, private bath, ceiling fan, and balcony with courtyard view. A flickering fireplace warms the cool evenings.

Enjoy a large gourmet breakfast served in the Tapestry Dining Room. Specialties include tomato pie, fresh fruits, pastries, biscuits, sausage and bacon, and all organic yogurt, milk, cream, and butter. The Art Kitchen is a large, completely renovated kitchen filled with colorful painting and an original gaslight fixture. Children and pets are allowed. (If pets are left unattended in the room, however, it is requested that they be crated.) The inn features wireless high-speed DSL computer access throughout the main house. Special programs include an actor who portrays Edgar Allan Poe on Halloween, and a Mother's Day tea. The owner is with the Nashville Opera Company and will sometimes treat guests with her vocal talent.

CAMPGROUNDS

Nashville and its immediate area offer more than a dozen campgrounds, most of which have sites for both recreational vehicles and tent campers. Some camping opportunities are also available at nearby state parks.

Although most area campgrounds will be happy, when possible, to accommodate campers who just show up looking for a site, you are strongly encouraged to make reservations. Sites tend to fill up, especially during nice weather. You wouldn't want to load up the family and all your camping gear and head for Nashville only to find nowhere to stay.

We list state park camping opportunities under a separate heading. For more information about recreational and other opportunities in Tennessee state parks, see our Parks and Recreation chapters.

All campgrounds are open year-round unless otherwise indicated. Please note that prices are subject to change; off-season rates may be a little cheaper.

PRIVATE CAMPGROUNDS

COUNTRYSIDE RESORT
2100 Safari Camp Road, Lebanon
(615) 449-5527
www.countrysideresort.com
Though adjacent to Interstate 40, Countryside earns its name from the 35 acres of rolling hills that leave all hint of the highway behind. Approximately 100 RV and tent sites are available for overnight use, including RV sites with full hookups, water and electrical sites, and shaded tent sites with water and electricity. Other sites are available on long-term leases.

Countryside has all the basic amenities—showers, fire rings, laundry—plus many extras: a fishing pond, a swimming pool, a tennis court, a playground, volleyball courts, target green golf course, a convenience store, and 30 acres of mowed fields for Rover to stretch his legs. Resort guests also receive a discount for limousine tours of Nashville for hitting the town in style.

Countryside is open year-round. Overnight rates for two persons are $27 for full hookups, $25 for water and electricity, and $22 for tent sites. Discounts are offered for AAA, Good Sam, Coast to Coast, National Campers and Hikers, and seniors. Weekly rates are available.

NASHVILLE COUNTRY RV PARK
1200 Louisville Highway, Goodlettsville
(615) 859-0348
www.nashvillecountryrvpark.com
This year-round campground has 105 sites, ranging from tent camping to full RV hookups to cabins offering full-size beds and bunk beds. Cable TV hookups and high-speed Internet access are available. There is also a swimming pool. Rates, based on double occupancy, are $30 for tent sites and $55 for cabins. Shuttle tours pick up people here for trips to nearby attractions.

NASHVILLE I-24 CAMPGROUND
1130 Rocky Fork Road, Smyrna
(615) 459-5818
http://nashvillei24campground.com
This wooded campground, open since 1971, is affiliated with the Good Sam family of campgrounds. It has 155 sites for tent camping and recreational vehicles plus four cabins. Amenities include a swimming pool, a grocery store, a game room, and two playgrounds. Prices are $15 for tent camping, $21 for full hookups, $25 for single-room cabins, and $40 a night for a cabin with kitchenette and bathroom. Discounts are available for Good Sam members.

NASHVILLE JELLYSTONE PARK

2572 Music Valley Drive
(615) 889-4225, (800) 547-4480
www.nashvillejellystone.com

This campground, formerly known as Holiday Nashville Travel Park, offers a variety of options for travelers. In addition to 233 pull-through sites for recreational vehicles and a tent-camping area, the park has park models, which are trailers with a living room, dining room, kitchen, and bath. Rates range from $22 a night for tent campers to $38 for full hookups and $80–$110 for the park models, all based on two people, with no charge for children 17 and younger. All sites have free cable TV; high-speed Internet hookups are available. Amenities include miniature golf, basketball, planned activities for kids, and summertime concerts.

NASHVILLE KOA

2626 Music Valley Drive
(615) 889-0282, (800) 562-7789
www.nashvillekoa.com

This KOA features 430 sites for various uses, from tent camping through different types of RV hookups. Thirty cabins are also available, and there are four newer lodges that feature bathrooms and kitchenettes. There's a grocery store on-site; recreational opportunities include a swimming pool, miniature golf, a game room, basketball court, bicycle rentals, and two playgrounds.

The campground also contains a 750-seat arena that features live country music seven nights a week. Most shows are free.

OWL'S ROOST CAMPGROUND

7267 Bethel Road, Goodlettsville
(615) 643-1900

Located in a country setting with 60 sites, the Owl's Roost Campground is 20 minutes from downtown Nashville. Open year-round, it features shaded sites at weekly and monthly rates. The daily rate is $19 with $2 for an extra person. Amenities include a dump station; ice; LP gas; laundry; pull-through sites; showers; sites with no hookups; sites with water, electricity, and sewer; and a snack store.

TWO RIVERS CAMPGROUNDS

2616 Music Valley Drive
(615) 883-8559
www.tworiverscampground.com

Two Rivers has 104 RV sites but does not allow tent camping. Full hookups are $25.20 to $35.00 depending on the season, and water and electrical only are $23.40 to $32.50. Discounts are available for senior citizens, members of AAA and other clubs, and groups. A pool, game room, and playground area are also on the campground. There's a full concierge staff on duty at all times, plus showers, laundry, a convenience store, free high-speed Internet access, and free live entertainment in season.

U.S. ARMY CORPS OF ENGINEERS CAMPGROUNDS

Corps of Engineers campgrounds must be reserved through the National Recreation Reservation Service, which bills itself as North America's largest camping reservation service. You can make your reservations by calling the NRRS—which offers more than 45,000 reservable facilities at 1,700 locations managed by the Corps and the USDA Forest Service—toll-free at (877) 444-6777, or by visiting www.reserveusa.com, a Web site with detailed maps, directions, prices, regulations, and about anything else you'd need to know.

Most of these sites offer ample opportunity for fishing, boating, skiing, and swimming, as well as for viewing such wildlife as white-tailed deer, rabbits, raccoons, skunks, wild turkeys, and squirrels.

Please note that most Corps campgrounds require a two-night minimum on weekends and a three-night minimum on holiday weekends. Operating season varies by campground and by year. It's best to check the Web site for current details.

J. Percy Priest Lake Area

ANDERSON ROAD CAMPGROUND

3737 Bell Road
(615) 889-1975
www.lrn.usace.army.mil/op/jpp/rec
(information only)

Anderson Road offers 37 primitive sites, along with hot showers, dump station, picnic shelter, boat launch, laundry, beach, and public telephones. Waterfront sites are $14 a night; wooded sites across the road are $12. The picnic shelter for up to 60 people can be reserved for $120 a day.

POOLE KNOBS CAMPGROUND
Jones Mill Road
(615) 459-6948
www.lrn.usace.army.mil/op/jpp/rec
(information only)
Poole Knobs, near Smyrna, has 88 campsites and a group camping area as well as hot showers, dump station, boat launch, picnic shelter, and public telephones. Prices range from $10 to $22 and depend on whether your site is located on the waterfront or across the road.

SEVEN POINTS CAMPGROUND
1810 Stewarts Ferry Pike, Hermitage
(615) 889-5198
www.lrn.usace.army.mil/op/jpp/rec
(information only)
Seven Points has 60 sites with water and electricity for RV or tent camping. A dump station is available. Prices are $18 to $24. Amenities include hot showers, laundry facilities, a swimming area, and public telephones.

This is one of the Corps's busiest campgrounds in the country; draws include the dayuse area, which offers a beach and group picnic shelter, plus nearby attractions such as the Hermitage and the *Grand Ole Opry*.

i Overnight campers at Tennessee's state parks are charged a $1.00 daily access fee per vehicle in addition to regular campground rates. There is no fee on Wednesday, however. The $1.00 fee covers the first two people in your party; there is an extra 50-cent charge for every additional person over age seven. Revenues collected from the access fee are dedicated to maintenance of park facilities and resources. Montgomery Bell State Park, for example, has used fee revenues to purchase canoes.

Old Hickory Lake Area
CAGES BEND CAMPGROUND
1125 Benders Ferry Road, Hendersonville
(615) 824-4989
www.lrn.usace.army.mil/op/old/rec
(information only)
Cages Bend has 43 sites with electrical and water hookups for $19 to $23 a night. Hot showers, an accessible restroom, a dump station, a boat launch, and laundry facilities are also available. Shopping, grocery stores, gas stations, and a marina are located within about 10 miles. Waterskiing and fishing are popular here; you're also located near religious theme park Trinity City and not too far from Opry Mills shopping mall. The campground generally is open from April through October.

CEDAR CREEK CAMPGROUND
9264 Saundersville Road, Mount Juliet
(615) 754-4947
www.lrn.usace.army.mil/op/old/rec
(information only)
Cedar Creek has 59 sites with electricity and water, as well as hot showers, an accessible restroom, dump station, laundry facilities, picnic shelter (reservable at $35 a day), and boat launch. Area attractions include the Hermitage and the *Grand Ole Opry*. Rates are $19 to $23 a night. The campground generally is open from April through October.

NEARBY STATE PARKS

Tennessee state park campsites are available on a first-come, first-served basis. While the following state parks are open year-round, many of them have reduced capacity during the winter, with portions of the campgrounds closed. In general, this is from early November through early April, but it really depends on the weather.

For more information about state parks, see our Parks chapter. You can also call the individual park or, if you'd especially like to know about other state parks, call the department at (800) 421-6683. A reservation service is available by calling (866) TENN-PKS. Current information can also be found online at www.tnstateparks.com.

State parks have suffered under the state's recent budget mess, and visitors are cautioned to check first before heading out the door. Some parks have had their operations curtailed.

CEDARS OF LEBANON STATE PARK
328 Cedar Forest Road, Lebanon
(615) 443-2769, (800) 713-5180
(cabin reservations)
www.tnstateparks.com

Cedars of Lebanon has 117 campsites, including 30 tent and pop-up sites, as well as an 80-person group lodge and 9 cabins. Campsites with water and electrical hookups are $17.25 a night; tent sites are $14.25. Amenities include hot showers and flush toilets, laundry, dump station, and a camp store that's open in-season. Cabins are $50 to $104 a night, depending on whether you are staying on a weekend or midweek, and the size of the cabin. There is a three-night minimum for holiday weekends; rates are generally cheaper in the off-season. Cabins have a fully equipped kitchen, woodstove, and television; pay phones are nearby. Linens and towels are provided. The group lodge is $165 a night for the first 33 people, and $4.25 for each extra person.

MONTGOMERY BELL STATE PARK
U.S. Highway 70, Burns
(615) 797-9052
www.tnstateparks.com

This almost 4,000-acre park, north of US 70 and 7 miles east of Dickson, offers about 89 RV campsites with electrical and water hookups for $18.50 a night in-season and 27 tent sites (five of them with water) for $12. There are three backcountry campsites. Montgomery Bell State Park also has eight fully equipped two-bedroom cabins (one of which is wheelchair accessible) that sleep five to nine people apiece. The cabins rent by the week only, from June through August, at $350; the rest of the year, they're $60 to $70 a night with a two-night minimum.

Group camping is available in 47 rustic cabins that sleep 120 people in all. Campers are required to bring their own linens, foodstuffs, and campfire supplies such as wood or charcoal. However, on-premise catering is available. A kitchen with two ovens, two stoves, two sinks, and a walk-in refrigerator is provided.

RESTAURANTS

Hungry? If you're not right now, you will be by the time you scan through a few pages of this chapter. We're going to stimulate your appetite by telling you about some of the Southern-style comfort food, hearty pastas, thick and juicy steaks and burgers, freshly baked breads, tasty vegetarian meals, delectable desserts, and spicy international dishes you can find in Nashville. We list ethnic eateries, fine dining spots, barbecue joints, catfish houses, romantic bistros, and much more. Nashville is probably best known, though, for "meat-and-threes." For those of you who aren't familiar with the term, a meat-and-three is a place where you can get a down-home Southern entree—like fried chicken, meat loaf, turkey and gravy, or country-fried steak—accompanied by three vegetables. And when we say vegetables, we mean anything from mashed potatoes, corn, and green beans to deviled eggs, macaroni, and Jell-O. Corn bread, rolls, or biscuits come with the meal, too. We have an abundance of these beloved meat-and-threes, places like Swett's, Sylvan Park, and Elliston Place Soda Shop. They are longtime favorites, and we highly recommend them for their good home cooking and Southern hospitality. Some of our restaurants are nationally known (places like the Loveless Café and the Pancake Pantry), and other establishments that started here have gone on to become national or regional chains—places such as Houston's, O'Charley's, J. Alexander's, and Whitt's Barbecue.

OVERVIEW

In this chapter we're primarily highlighting places that are unique to Nashville. We have lots of fast-food restaurants, fern bars, pizza franchises, and family-style eateries (including the always-popular Cracker Barrel and P.F. Chang's China Bistro), but you already know what to expect from those places. We want to steer you to some of our local favorites. We've arranged this chapter alphabetically by category of cuisine—American, Asian, barbecue, Italian, meat-and-threes, steak, and so on. For information on even more dining options, see our Nightlife chapter. That's where we've listed sports bars, coffeehouses, and the like. Many of those places have great food, and they often serve it late into the night; you'll want to add them to your list of favorites. See our Kidstuff chapter for some especially kid-friendly restaurants.

Most major restaurants take credit cards and debit cards. Some of the smaller establishments, like a few of the meat-and-threes, take cash and personal checks only. We'll alert you to those places that don't accept credit cards. We'll also

suggest whether you should make a reservation. As for smoking, virtually all restaurants offer non-smoking areas. Some restaurants have little or no parking, but those in that situation usually offer free valet parking.

Finally, keep in mind that Nashville's restaurant scene seems to be constantly growing and changing. Operating hours change, businesses change hands, chefs play musical chairs, eateries close and reemerge with new names and menus, and new restaurants open up regularly. If you're planning a special meal out, it's a good idea to call first, at least to make sure of the operating hours.

Price Code

Use the following price code as a general guide for the cost of dinner entrees for two, excluding appetizers, alcoholic beverages, desserts, and tip. Keep in mind that drinks, desserts, and extras for two can significantly add to the bill and will often put you in a new price category. Your tab for breakfast and lunch will most likely be less expensive.

$	$15 or less
$$	$16 to $25
$$$	$26 to $40
$$$$	$41 to $60
$$$$$	$61 and more

AMERICAN/CONTEMPORARY AMERICAN

ANDREW CHADWICK'S ON RUTLEDGE HILL $$$
37 Rutledge Street
(615) 254-8585
www.andrewchadwicks.com

Characterized as "California contemporary cuisine," Andrew Chadwick's focuses on locally grown produce and seafood presented with a sophisticated flair. Located in a historic house on Rutledge Hill, this elegant restaurant features a seldom-seen view of downtown and windows framing the chef's organic gardens. The memorable setting also includes 14-foot ceilings, stained glass, travertine tile floors, and plenty of fireplaces. At Chadwick's all the cooking is done by induction because the historic building wasn't amenable to gas lines. One of only three American institutions that use a professional induction cooktop, Chadwick's has an energy-efficient method of cooking with no flame. Instead, it uses a combination of magnets, electricity, and special pans for rapid heating within the pan itself. The result is delightful, delicious dishes. Begin the meal with hot rolls served with butter sprinkled with house-smoked salt. The lobster bisque is a meal in itself. Poured dramatically at the table over Savoy cabbage and shrimp-and-lobster sausage, the generous serving of bisque is exquisite. Favorite entrees include wild sturgeon with a sauce of smoked tomatoes, and seared lamb served over couscous. Luscious crème brûlée and a glass of dessert wine are a fitting end to a memorable meal.

THE BOUND'RY $$$
911 20th Avenue S.
(615) 321-3043
www.pansouth.net

The Bound'ry, about a block from the Vandy law school, has become a big local favorite. We've found it's a reliable choice for good food and a great atmosphere. There are several cozy dining rooms, all dimly lit and strung with tiny white lights. We like to dine upstairs on the open-air deck. The Bound'ry serves "global cuisine." From the top-selling planked trout to the Tennessee ostrich, there's something for everyone. The filet mignon, wood-oven pizzas, and "wood fish of the day" are among the other favorites. The restaurant is known for its excellent assortment of tapas (a collection of appetizers); you can create a meal from a couple of these choices or order a variety to enjoy family-style. The Bound'ry's bar is a hot spot with singles. For more on that, see our Nightlife chapter. The restaurant is open nightly for dinner. Reservations recommended.

CAPITOL GRILLE $$$–$$$$$
Hermitage Hotel
231 Sixth Avenue N.
(615) 345-7116
www.thehermitagehotel.com

More than a few restaurant critics consider the Capitol Grille to be Nashville's premier dining establishment. The elegant restaurant, located under the lobby of the historic and luxurious Hermitage Hotel, was revamped when the hotel underwent a $17-million renovation in 2002. The Capitol Grille is pure luxury—think truffles, foie gras, caviar, and lobster, all of which are, naturally, on the menu. Creative Southern cuisine is the specialty. While the menu changes from time to time, expect to find such standout dinner entrees as grilled Tennessee Black Angus beef tenderloin with foie gras hollandaise. Fabulous side dishes include fried green tomatoes with spicy pepper relish and white truffle mac and cheese. Desserts don't disappoint. For breakfast there are the traditional eggs and bacon, pancakes, and cereals, as well as Maine lobster and shirred eggs, and eggs Benedict with beef tenderloin medallions. The lunch menu might include Vidalia onion bisque with a miniature Brie cheese sandwich and smoked Virginia bacon; grilled salmon BLT; or Maine lobster raviolis. Capitol Grille is open for breakfast and dinner daily, for lunch Monday through Saturday, and for Sunday brunch. Reservations are recommended.

DEMOS' STEAK & SPAGHETTI HOUSE $–$$
300 Commerce Street
(615) 256-4655

1115 Northwest Broad Street,
Murfreesboro
(615) 895-3701

130 Legends Drive, Lebanon
(615) 443-4600
www.demosrestaurants.com
While its name is frequently mispronounced, Demos' (DE-mo-SEZ) menu never leaves you guessing. This American-Italian-Greek restaurant, owned by Jim and Doris Demos, has lots of pastas with a variety of sauces and four or five steaks that are good for the price. Demos' has a nice, semi-casual/semi-upscale, family-friendly environment. The blackened chicken pasta and Greek-style chicken salad are good choices. Demos' has a weekday lunch special, but be prepared to wait about 20 minutes for a seat, and it's always first come, first served. Demos' is open daily for lunch and dinner.

A recipe for Chicken Florentine Panini sandwiches won a tasty $1 million for Denise Yennie, a Nashville accountant, in a Pillsbury Bake-off Contest.

EASTLAND CAFÉ $$$–$$$$
701 Chapel Avenue
(615) 627-1088
www.eastlandcafe.com
Like its name says, the Eastland Cafe is located in East Nashville and has quickly become a neighborhood favorite. No wonder. The Eastland has a welcoming atmosphere, comfortable surroundings, and ever-changing good food. Casually elegant, the restaurant features dark mahogany wood panels and warmly lit tables. Start with low country shrimp and grits with tasso gravy or goat cheese brulee with chestnut honey, grilled flat-

bread, and balsamic syrup–drizzled oven-roasted tomatoes and peppers. Favorite entrees include grilled Idaho cold water trout cooked with maple balsamic jus, served with sweet potato puree and country green beans sprinkled with spiced pecans; or pan-seared chicken breast with braised collard greens with bacon, cheddar grits and red pepper jelly. For dessert, blueberry beignets with warm white chocolate sauce and powdered sugar are tops. Kids' dinners like pizza, chicken fingers, grilled cheese, and angel hair pasta come with vanilla ice cream with chocolate sauce.

F. SCOTT'S $$$
2210 Crestmoor Road
(615) 269-5861
www.fscotts.com
Casually elegant, warm, and inviting, F. Scott's is considered by many to be one of the best restaurants in Nashville. This is a place where the sophisticated feel comfortable, but it's not necessary to dress to the hilt; you'll fit in whether you're in jeans or a coat and tie. F. Scott's serves American bistro-style food. The menu changes quarterly, but there is always plenty of seafood, pasta, chicken, duck, lamb, pork, and beef. Tempura salmon with ginger sushi rice, coriander-rubbed pork tenderloin with green chile grits and charred tomato vinaigrette, white truffle and Yukon gold potato ravioli, and bourbon pecan and chocolate chip bread pudding with bourbon caramel sauce are just a few tempting examples of the contemporary dishes you might find here. Open nightly for dinner, F. Scott's has three dining rooms and a jazz lounge with live entertainment. In addition to a wonderful dining experience, this is a very pleasant place to stop for a drink. The wine list offers more than 300 different wines.

GREEN HILLS GRILLE $$
2122 Hillsboro Drive
(615) 383-6444
www.greenhillsgrille.com
The always reliable Green Hills Grille serves good food in a comfortable, upscale-casual atmosphere. Whether you're heading out for lunch with the family or planning a relaxed dinner date,

you can't go wrong here. The original location on Hillsboro Drive opened in 1990 and has a devoted following of Green Hills–area residents. The Brentwood restaurant opened in 2002, giving those in the Cool Springs area yet another dining option. (There are also locations in Huntsville, Alabama, and Knoxville, Tennessee.)

Menu favorites include the yummy spinach and artichoke dip, tortilla soup, and Chinese grilled chicken salad. Those with heartier appetites might want to try the baby back ribs, hickory-smoked salmon, or portobello meat loaf. Vegetarians will find a nice selection of entrees, and those who are watching their carbohydrate intake will be glad to know that Green Hills Grille has a good low-carb menu. Be sure to save room for the Heath Bar Crunch Pie, or, if strawberries are in season, go for the yummy strawberry shortcake (it's big enough for two). Green Hills Grille has some good cappuccino drinks and makes a mean martini. Free valet parking is available. The restaurant is open daily for lunch and dinner. Green Hills Grille doesn't accept reservations, but if you're coming for dinner, you can call ahead and put your name on the seating list.

HARD ROCK CAFE   **$$**
100 Broadway
(615) 742-9900
www.hardrock.com

You can't miss the Hard Rock Cafe—right underneath the huge guitar mural facing Broadway. Rock 'n' roll memorabilia is the big draw here. The restaurant features a large collection of guitars once belonging to rock greats. Also adorning the walls are gold and platinum records and a revolving selection of other rock 'n' roll memorabilia. Nashville's Hard Rock also has a wall devoted to country music—look for items from Garth Brooks, Randy Travis, Marty Stuart, and other stars there.

In keeping with the rock 'n' roll mood, the music here is loud, and the atmosphere is lively. As for the food, it's all-American: burgers, sandwiches, salads, daily blue-plate specials, homemade soups, malts and shakes, and yummy desserts. The Pulled Pork Sandwich is the Hard Rock's signature item. The restaurant accepts reservations only for groups of 15 or more. The

Hard Rock's merchandise is sold in the restaurant and in the historic Silver Dollar building a few feet away.

J. ALEXANDER'S   **$$-$$$**
73 White Bridge Road, #130
(615) 352-0981

1721 Galleria Boulevard, Franklin
(615) 771-7779
www.jalexanders.com

J. Alexander's is another local restaurant success story. Since the first J. Alexander's opened on White Bridge Road in 1991, more have popped up all over the country, from Denver to Fort Lauderdale, Florida. The publicly traded company has more than 25 locations. J. Alexander's is known for its casual but nice atmosphere, good service, and contemporary American menu. The restaurant has great prime rib, a variety of salads and homemade dressings, flavorful pasta dishes, homemade soups, and made-from-scratch desserts. One of the first restaurants in the area to open its kitchen to the view of diners, it cooks all the grilled products over a hardwood, open grill. Reservations are not accepted, and there is usually a wait for dinner; come early if you want to avoid the crowd. J. Alexander's is open daily for lunch and dinner. Catering service is also available.

THE MAD PLATTER   **$$$**
1239 Sixth Avenue N.
(615) 242-2563
www.themadplatterrestaurant.com

The Mad Platter is considered one of the best restaurants in Nashville and has been voted Best Romantic Rendezvous in a local readers' poll. In a historic building in Germantown, 2 blocks from the Bicentennial Mall, the restaurant establishes its ambience with white linen tablecloths, fresh flowers, and candlelight. The tiny dining room only accommodates 20 or so tables. *Gourmet world fusion cuisine* is perhaps the best description of the food here. The lunch and dinner menus change daily depending on availability of ingredients, but you can expect expertly prepared and beautifully presented dishes. The Mad Platter's lunch items range from about $5 to $15.

A favorite at lunchtime is the Pasta Mad Platter—linguine with sautéed artichokes, mushrooms, sun-dried tomatoes, spinach, onions, garlic, oregano, chorizo sausage, and Montrachet cheese. Reservations are required for dinner. The Mad Platter serves lunch Tuesday through Friday and dinner Tuesday through Sunday.

MARGOT CAFE & BAR $$$
1017 Woodland Street
(615) 227-4668
www.margotcafe.com
If your epicurean fantasies are set in Provence or Tuscany, you'll enjoy dining at Margot, which specializes in rustic French and Italian cuisine. Chef Margot McCormack opened this restaurant in June 2001. It quickly became a hot spot for east Nashville residents, and the buzz spread around town. It's now one of Nashville's *in* places to dine. Housed in a renovated 1930s gas station building in east Nashville's Five Points area, Margot is cozy and vibrant, with brick walls, antique mirrors, and simple, colorful furnishings setting the tone for either a dress-down or dress-up occasion. Margot also has a nice patio for outdoor dining in the summer. The menu changes daily, and there are usually six entree choices. Recent menu samples include tuna tartar with kalamata vinaigrette appetizer; roast pork chop with Gorgonzola, roasted potatoes, and Swiss chard; and braised lamb shank with soft polenta, escarole, and tomato rosemary broth. Desserts always include sorbet and ice cream, often in exotic flavors, as well as three to five other selections, perhaps a bread pudding, raspberry brown butter tart, tiramisu, or chocolate pot de crème. The restaurant has a nice wine list, with many selections from France and Italy, and about 30 varieties available by the glass. Margot is open for dinner Tuesday through Saturday and Sunday brunch. Reservations are suggested, especially on weekends.

THE MELTING POT $$$$
166 Second Avenue N.
(615) 742-4970
www.meltingpot.com
Voted Best Restaurant in Nashville and Best Place for a Romantic Dinner in a *Nashville Scene* readers' poll, this fondue restaurant is a fun spot when you're in the mood for something a little different for dinner. The atmosphere is relaxed and intimate.

Allow two hours for the complete Melting Pot experience. The menu is based on courses. Your meal starts with a cheese fondue course, prepared by the server; the cheese course is followed by a salad. For the entree course, you cook your choice of meats or vegetables in the melting pot in the center of the table. Lobster tails, center-cut fillet, Cajun-rubbed meats, and sausages are just a few of the choices. The final course is the dessert fondue—a variety of chocolate fondues in which you dip pound cake, cheesecake, bananas, strawberries, pineapple, and nutty marshmallows. If you want only the dessert fondue, come in the late afternoon or after 9:00 p.m. It's a good idea to have reservations, especially on the very busy Friday and Saturday nights. The Melting Pot is open daily for dinner.

THE MERCHANTS $$$-$$$$
401 Broadway
(615) 254-1892
www.merchantsrestaurant.com
Downtown Nashville's Merchants is a casual fine-dining restaurant that serves American food with a Southern flair. The romantic atmosphere and excellent food make this a good choice for a special dinner. The restaurant occupies three floors of a historic building that once housed a pharmacy and hotel. The second floor is the main dining room—it has a more upscale atmosphere and menu than the first floor; the third floor is a banquet space.

If you're dining on the second floor, try the pan-seared salmon fillet with caper dill beurre blanc atop a bed of linguine with shrimp and scallops, all enclosed in a pastry net. Lamb chops are a favorite, too. Your tab will be about 50 percent less in the first-floor Casual Bar & Grill, where a popular entree is the New York strip. For lunch, order the always-in-demand five-pepper chicken. Merchants does a brisk weekday lunch business and opens both floors for the lunchtime crowd. The restaurant has a good wine selection.

Reservations are recommended for second-floor dining, especially on busy Friday and Saturday nights. Merchants is open for lunch and dinner Monday through Saturday and opens at 4:00 p.m. Sunday.

MIDTOWN CAFE $$$
102 19th Avenue S.
(615) 320-7176
www.midtowncafe.com
This small restaurant just off West End has a devoted following of Insiders who like the eclectic American cuisine and casually elegant atmosphere. At lunch it's a prime spot for high-ranking business lunches, while the dinner crowd ranges from business types to romantic couples, mostly 40-somethings and up. Midtown's crab cakes are great as an appetizer, entree, or sandwich. The fresh catch of the day is always in demand, and the Caesar salad is a lunch favorite. Veal, pasta, steaks, and lamb dishes round out the menu. Midtown has a fantastic wine list, too. For dessert, the Key lime pie is good. The restaurant is open for lunch Monday through Friday and for dinner nightly. Reservations are recommended.

PARK CAFE $$$
4403 Murphy Road
(615) 383-4409
www.parkcafenashville.com
Delicious food, low-key sophistication, and a creative environment have made this restaurant in west Nashville's Sylvan Park neighborhood a favorite. Chef Willie Thomas, formerly of acclaimed Nashville restaurants Capitol Grille and the Bound'ry (see separate listings in this chapter), continues to win raves for his "creative American" menu. Colorful art and funky accessories adorn the maze of cozy, dimly lit dining rooms. The frequently Asian-inspired menu is equally interesting. It isn't too lengthy, which simplifies the selection process. Favorites include the pan-seared salmon with coconut jasmine rice, Szechuan green beans, chile plum sauce, and grilled lime, and the grilled tenderloin with

béarnaise sauce, sautéed asparagus, and pommes frites. Park Cafe's desserts are really too good to share with your dining partner, so if you have a sweet tooth, you'll want to order your own. The crème brûlée Napoleon and warm molten chocolate cakes are always popular. Park Cafe is open for dinner Monday through Saturday. Reservations are suggested but are not a must.

PLANTATION HOUSE RESTAURANT $$
2740 Old Lebanon Road
(615) 872-9944
www.plantationhouserestaurant.com
The Donelson area isn't known for its restaurants, but the Plantation House is an exception. In the past decade or so it has become a neighborhood favorite, appealing to nearby families and those who work in the Donelson and Opryland/Music Valley areas. The restaurant's location near the airport and near dozens of hotels means that it's often packed with business travelers as well. The restaurant has an extensive menu with plenty of steak, seafood, and pasta dishes, as well as salads and sandwiches. There is also a small selection of tasty and generously portioned Mexican favorites. Specialties include chicken Alaska, sautéed chicken breast topped with Alaskan snow crab meat, asparagus spears, and béarnaise sauce; and fruity Hawaiian chicken salad. A children's menu has a few selections for less than $4. There are three dining rooms, a banquet room, and an upstairs bar area. The restaurant is open daily for lunch and dinner; it opens Saturday at 3:00 p.m.

PRIME 108 AT UNION STATION HOTEL $$$$
1001 Broadway
(615) 726-1001
www.unionstationhotelnashville.com/dining/
Sounds like a steakhouse, but Prime 108 is named after the Bully 108, the first engine to come through Nashville's Union Station more than a century ago. Located in the lovingly restored Union Station Hotel, Prime 108 serves breakfast, lunch, and dinner—a real boon to guests at the hotel and others who enjoy relaxing in the beautiful landmark. The breakfast menu features the usual, plus an excel-

lent oatmeal souffle that's a great way to start the day. For lunch, choose from soups, salads, sandwiches, and pastas. Prime 108 also specializes in cocktails. Order a 24-Karat Martini—vanilla vodka, amaretto, Chambord, Rose's lime juice, and orange juice—and sip it while it feels as though the clock has been turned back to the station's railroad heyday. A favorite dinner entree is pan-roasted halibut with lobster risotto served with homemade Yukon Gold chips and roasted baby carrots. For dessert, try the poached pear cheesecake or chocolate meringue cake.

SOUTH STREET ORIGINAL SMOKEHOUSE & CRAB SHACK & AUTHENTIC DIVE BAR $$
907 20th Avenue S.
(615) 320-5555
www.pansouth.net
South Street is a superfun place—a great spot to hang out in the spring, summer, and fall because they open up the big garage-door windows and let in the fresh air. If you're lucky, you might get a seat up high in the restaurant's tree house. South Street is within walking distance of Music Row, and music business movers and shakers can be found here daily. Word about this hip place has even spread to the rock 'n' roll world: South Street was selected as caterer for the Rolling Stones when they played Vanderbilt Stadium in 1997 and also for the Eagles when they were in town.

South Street serves "urban Southern" cuisine. The smoked ribs are a favorite, and the Deep South platters—like chicken and roasted pepper enchiladas and crawfish and shrimp enchiladas—are always a hit. The marinated Jack Daniel's strip steak should please the meat eaters. The Crab & Slab, a full slab of ribs with king crab, snow crab, and Dungeness crab, served with corn and potatoes, is a fun way to feed two to four people. The South Street Rita, a frozen margarita, is the proper beverage choice. For dessert, get the New Orleans–style bread pudding with Jack Daniel's sauce. A recent addition is the Tree House Oyster Bar, where patrons can enjoy fresh-shucked oysters. South Street serves lunch and dinner seven days a week. On Saturday the lunch menu is replaced with a brunch menu from 11:00 a.m.

to 3:00 p.m., and the dinner menu is available all day. Seating is first come, first served.

THE STANDARD AT THE SMITH HOUSE $$$
167 Eighth Avenue N.
(615) 259-4114
www.thestandardnashville.com
This three-story 19th-century brick home features a refined Southern-themed menu. Once a boarding house and society club that hosted Nashville's elite, The Standard is a treasure from the past. Magnificently renovated, it offers a cantilevered walnut spiral staircase, chandeliers, Victorian furniture, and a New Orleans-style boardwalk on the side of the house with working gas lamps. The menu offers such treats as crab bisque flavored with Tennessee whiskey, chicken Madeira, and Hot Brown Sandwiches, a Southern favorite of toast points prepared with sliced turkey, mornay sauce, julienne of country ham, and topped with fresh tomatoes and basil. The Standard is well known for its sweet potato fries and its crab cakes served with creole honey mustard and roasted corn salsa. If the Smith House looks familiar, it may be because it starred in a 2004 music video for Allison Krauss and Brad Paisley's "Whiskey Lullaby." The video won the CMA's Music Video of the Year award.

SUNSET GRILL $$$
2001-A Belcourt Avenue
(615) 386-3663, (866) 496-FOOD
www.sunsetgrill.com
Sunset Grill is one of Nashville's favorite restaurants. Since it opened in fall 1990, this Hillsboro Village hot spot has developed a reputation as a good place to see and be seen. It's a music-business hangout and draws lots of other businesspeople and sports personalities, too. On weekdays when the weather is nice, diners don their dark sunglasses and power-lunch on the patio. In winter the patio is enclosed, for those who prefer a more casual setting than the main dining room.

Sunset Grill serves new American cuisine. The Voodoo Pasta is a menu staple. It has grilled chicken, baby shrimp, andouille sausage, and roasted red pepper marinara sauce dusted with Black Magic seasonings and tossed with Cajun fettuccine; a vegetarian version is available, too. There is a good selection of other vegetarian dishes. Other menu favorites include tuna, lamb, and grilled pork tenderloin.

The desserts are beautiful and delicious. Try the chocolate bombe, a brownie crust with double-thick chocolate mousse filling, drenched in chocolate glaze.

Sunset Grill has an excellent wine list—one of the best in town—with about 500 selections, about 70 available by the glass. Sunset Grill also offers wine-tasting classes on Monday (seating is limited, so make a reservation if you don't want to miss out). Sunset Grill is open for lunch Tuesday through Friday and for dinner Monday through Sunday. The restaurant is one of the few places in town that has a late-night menu. You can order till 1:30 a.m. Monday through Saturday.

360 BISTRO $$$
6000 Highway 100
(615) 353-5604
www.360bistro.com

Chef John David Crow has developed a loyal following with his creative flair, unusual ingredients, and glorious creations. An elegant array of entrees ranges from seafood and elk to boar and duck. You can't go wrong with the soup du jour, called the Chef's Whim of the Day. We've never had a bad one, but a favorite is the mussel bisque which shows off Crow's Seattle heritage as chef at The Space Needle. The restaurant's seared duck breast with quince-and-port reduction and creamy polenta is popular, as is the miso-honey tuna featuring seared tuna in a spicy sauce atop lo mein noodles. In addition to an excellent menu, 360 offers over 70 wines by the glass. Or try the interesting wine-tasting flights, weekly selections of wine served in three-ounce tasting portions. The flights are available in light-body reds, full-body reds, light-body whites, and full-body whites. If you can't choose, ask Crow's wife, Sarah, who is a sommelier. She also creates some delightful mojitos.

TIN ANGEL $$-$$$
3201 West End Avenue
(615) 298-3444

Tin Angel is a casual, cozy bistro-style restaurant that serves contemporary American cuisine with an occasional international twist. Favorite dishes include the Mediterranean pasta and the always-popular Mediterranean salad. Tin Angel is one of our reliable standbys—good food, good atmosphere, and rarely a wait. Reservations are not accepted. There is a small parking lot in back of the restaurant, and valet parking is available (except on Monday, Tuesday, and Wednesday evenings). Tin Angel is open Monday through Friday for lunch and dinner, Saturday for dinner, and Sunday for brunch.

THE TIN ROOF $$
1516 Demonbreun Street
(615) 313-7103
www.tinroofcantina.com

The first business to open as part of the redeveloped Demonbreun Street area adjacent to Music Row, Tin Roof wasted no time in becoming the *in* restaurant and bar. With a front patio, back deck, and "Route 66" roadhouse-style decor, it has a fun, easygoing feel that keeps customers returning again and again. Of course, it could be the tasty food that brings them back. Everything here is homemade or prepared fresh, from the grilled chicken to the salsa. The Tin Roof specializes in pressed sandwiches—a French roll loaded with meat, cheese, and other fillings, then pressed and heated until it's all gooey inside—and they serve more than a dozen varieties of them. Another menu favorite is the award-winning white cheese and jalapeño dip, served in a big latte mug and accompanied by homemade tortilla chips. Something you're not likely to find anywhere else is deep-fried hot dogs, served under a mound of slaw. Tin Roof is open Monday through Friday for lunch and Monday through Saturday for dinner. There's live music nightly.

YELLOW PORCH $$$$
734 Thompson Lane
(615) 386-0260
www.theyellowporch.com

More than one potential diner has zoomed past this tiny yellow cottage, which is tucked between a gas station and a row of strip malls on a busy thoroughfare across from 100 Oaks Mall. That's their loss: Yellow Porch offers exquisite continental/fusion cuisine and an excellent wine list, all served in a subdued, dimly lit room that invites friendly conversation and romance. The menu is versatile and creative, often blending disparate elements into a unique signature dish. While the menu often leans toward Asian or Mediterranean inspirations, classic entrees like pork chops are given their due as well. The menu changes often as seasonal ingredients become available—all the more reason to keep coming back. Yellow Porch is open Monday through Saturday for lunch and dinner.

ASIAN

ASAHI JAPANESE SUSHI BAR $$
5215 Harding Road
(615) 352-8877

Asahi serves some of the freshest and most delicious sushi and Japanese dishes in town. If you're not a sushi eater, try one of the teriyaki bento boxes. The tempura is great, too. Beer, wine, and several types of sake are available. This relaxed and friendly restaurant is in the Belle Meade area, at the corner of Harding Road and Harding Place. Asahi is open daily for lunch and dinner.

INTERNATIONAL MARKET & RESTAURANT $
2010 Belmont Boulevard
(615) 297-4453

International Market is one of those real "Insider" places that's really off the beaten path for most tourists. Popular with students at nearby Belmont University, as well as with Music Row workers and residents from the Hillsboro-Belmont-Vandy areas, this cafeteria-style restaurant has been serving Thai and other Asian food since 1975. It's fresh and affordable—you can get a satisfying meal for $6

or less. The buffet features more than two dozen items, including mild to extra-spicy beef, chicken, and pork dishes; rice; egg rolls; and soup. Beverages include bottled beers and juices from the cooler, jasmine tea, and sodas. Next to the seating area are shelves stocked with mostly Asian cooking items—bottles of soy, hoisin, and chile sauces; cans of curry paste and coconut milk; packages of noodles; and boxes of tea—as well as ceramic teapots and bowls and a few gift items. International Market is open daily for lunch and dinner.

KOBE STEAKS $$$
210 25th Avenue N.
(615) 327-9081
www.kobesteaks.net

The family-friendly restaurant serves tasty if somewhat Americanized steak, chicken, and seafood. You'll be seated alongside other diners in one of eight dining rooms, two of which are traditional "Japanese rooms" (which means you'll have to remove your shoes before entering). A dinner at Kobe is as entertaining as it is delicious because the chef cooks up your order right in front of you. It's always fun to watch. Children especially get a kick out of seeing the chef toss shrimp tails into his hat. Kobe's dark, comfortable, and spacious bar area is a nice spot to enjoy a cocktail before dinner. The restaurant is open for dinner only. You can make reservations for Sunday through Thursday. It can get crowded on Friday and Saturday nights, so come early if you don't want to wait.

BAKERY/CAFE

AURORA BAKERY & CAFE PAPILLON $
3725 Nolensville Pike
(615) 837-1933
www.aurorabakery.com

The bright yellow and pink exterior of this busy cafe stands out among the crowded assortment of businesses on Nolensville Pike. Step inside, and you'll be greeted by the heavenly aroma of baked goods that fills the casual space. Owner Patricia Paiva opened the bakery in 1999 and quickly found a devoted following among Nashville's Hispanic population. The native Sri Lankan, whose background is in cross-cultural communications, wants the business to be a welcoming gathering place where people from all cultures can get to know one another. Aurora Bakery specializes in Mexican cakes and pastries and offers a huge assortment of those, including the rich, moist *tres leches* (three milks) cake, a traditional cake in Mexico and Central America. The bakery has gradually added a variety of international specialties, including French croissants, Middle Eastern baklava, Italian pizzelles, and Spanish flan. Patrons fill up their trays with various pastries, cookies, and other treats to take home while others dine on a few basic sandwiches and salads in the adjoining cafe area. The bakery and cafe are open daily during breakfast, lunch, and dinner hours but closed on Sunday.

BREAD & COMPANY $-$$

4105 Hillsboro Pike
(615) 292-7323

2525 West End Avenue
(615) 329-1400

6051 Highway 100
(615) 627-4800

430 Cool Springs Boulevard, Franklin
(615) 771-6600
www.breadandcompany.com

Nashville traditionally has been associated more with biscuits than with baguettes, but when Anne Clay and her son, John Clay III, opened the European-style Bread & Company bakery in November 1992, they were welcomed enthusiastically. The bakery introduced many Nashvillians to hearth-baked, crusty breads. Now we're positively addicted. Bread & Company bakes about 18 different breads, including the always-popular light sourdough farm bread; pane paisano, a round loaf perfect for tearing apart and dipping into olive oil; and the dense and chewy raisin-pecan. The stores also sell outstanding gourmet sandwiches. (We think the Iroquois, a generous portion of almond-tarragon chicken salad, lettuce, and tomatoes between slices of cranberry-pecan bread, is the best sandwich in town.) A rotating

trio of daily soup offerings always includes the popular tomato-basil. The busy cafes also have a daily breakfast bar, where you can get made-to-order omelets, pancakes, waffles, and other morning meals. Bread & Company has gourmet packaged foods and takeout, which can come in very handy for last-minute dinner parties (no one needs to know that you didn't make that Waldorf salad yourself) or for those evenings when you just don't want to cook. Bread & Company is open daily for breakfast, lunch, and dinner.

CITY LIMITS CAFE $

361 Clofton Drive
(615) 646-0062

If you can get past the beautiful, tempting pastries, sweet rolls, cookies, and brownies lined up under the glass case at this cozy, upbeat cafe, you'll find that there are quite a few good sandwiches and salads on the menu. By now that's no secret to Bellevue residents, who have been packing in ever since the restaurant opened in early 2002. Located in a strip shopping center at Old Harding and Clofton, next to the railroad tracks, the colorful and comfortable cafe has about 20 tables indoors and a few outside on the sidewalk. There's also a tiny sitting area with sofas and chairs—just the spot for an afternoon cappuccino.

Sandwiches include tuna and chicken salad as well as heartier choices like roast beef and turkey, all made with a variety of flavorful cheeses, spreads, vegetables, and good breads, which are baked on-site. Place your order at the counter, get a table, and you can pick up your food a few minutes later when your number is called. City Limits Cafe is open daily for breakfast, lunch, and dinner.

> **i** Nashville-based Tomkats Catering has come a long way since it started more than 20 years ago with one truck labeled Ricky Ricardo's Chili Express. The company has catered more than 500 motion pictures and served diet requests from such stars as Sandra Bullock, Nicole Kidman, Gwyneth Paltrow, Matthew McConaughey, and Colin Farrell.

CREMA $
15 Hermitage Avenue
(615) 255-8311
www.crema-coffee.com

The delicious aromas wafting from this new coffeehouse on Rutledge Hill are a great way to wake up or provide a quick pick-me-up at any time of day or night. Crema got its name from the foamy, golden-brown elixir that develops in the filter and encrusts the top of an espresso. Every week Crema features a new coffee along with favorite regulars such as cappuccino, café au lait, tea, mate chai, cider (seasonal), and hot cocoa. Cold drinks include iced coffee, juices, and soft drinks. To go with the drinks, sweet choices include mile-high muffins, croissants, cookies, cakes, cheesecakes, and biscotti. Crema also serves bagels, quiche, and sandwiches.

PROVENCE BREADS & CAFE $–$$
1705 21st Avenue S.
(615) 386-0363

615 Church Street
(615) 664-1150
www.provencebreads.com

Delectable pastries and wonderful artisan breads have made Provence Breads & Cafe one of Nashville's favorite bakeries. Croissants, fruit tarts, biscotti, and chocolate mousse cake are a few of the delicious indulgences available at this trendy and lively bakery/cafe. The extensive list of handmade breads includes sourdough, pistelle, fougasse, New York rye, and organic challah. San Francisco native Terry Carr-Hall opened the Hillsboro Village location in spring 1996 after studying baking in France. The Church Street store, inside the main library downtown, followed in 2003. Provence is a great place to stop for breakfast or lunch. There are two delicious soups du jour, and the choices change daily depending on the produce available at the Farmers' Market. There are about eight sandwich choices, including the vegetarian Montecito, loaded with avocado, Vermont white cheddar, tomatoes, red onion, sprouts, cucumber, and a fig balsamic vinegar on multigrain bread. Provence also has a good selection of cheeses from around the world. The cafes are open daily until early evening. The Church Street location is closed on Sunday.

BARBECUE

BAR-B-CUTIE $
5221 Nolensville Road
(615) 834-6556

501 Donelson Pike
(615) 872-0207

8456 Highway 100
(615) 646-1114

550 Enon Springs Road E., Smyrna
(615) 459-5969
www.bar-b-cutie.com

Hickory pit barbecue is the specialty at Bar-B-Cutie, a Nashville favorite since 1948. Barbecue and ribs are most in demand here, but the restaurant also serves a good mesquite-grilled chicken sandwich as well as turkey and roast beef. Barbecue plates come with two side items and bread. This is a no-alcohol, family-style restaurant. The dining room is busy, and the restaurant does a brisk takeout and drive-through business, too. Bar-B-Cutie is open daily for lunch and dinner.

CARL'S PERFECT PIG BAR-B-QUE & GRILL $
4991 U.S. Highway 70E, White Bluff
(615) 797-4020

We've been tempted to keep Carl's Perfect Pig under our hats, but now that the unassuming little country restaurant has been featured on an Emeril Lagasse–hosted special on cable TV's Food Network, we might as well just come clean. The truth is, we'd be hard-pressed to find any better barbecue or ribs around these parts than the old-fashioned, open-pit kind that's cooked and served up at the Perfect Pig. Located about 30 minutes west of Nashville in the rural community of White Bluff, the restaurant also is a favorite stop for catfish, fried chicken, and "country vegetables" like pinto beans (served with corncakes), yellow squash and cheese, baked beans, turnip greens, potato salad, and coleslaw. Carl's Perfect Pig is open Wednesday through Saturday for lunch and early dinners and for lunch on Sunday.

If you plan to visit on a Sunday, you'll want to get there before the after-church crowd arrives, unless you don't mind waiting in line for a table. The restaurant traditionally closes for a week during the Fourth of July holiday and between Christmas and New Year's.

HOG HEAVEN $
115 27th Avenue N.
(615) 329-1234
www.hogheavenbbq.com

Hog Heaven doesn't look like much—it's a tiny white cinder-block building tucked in a corner of Centennial Park behind McDonald's—but once you taste their barbecue, you'll understand the name of the place. This is some good eatin'. Hog Heaven's hand-pulled pork, chicken, beef, and turkey barbecue is pretty famous among Nashville's barbecue connoisseurs. The menu is posted on a board beside the walk-up window. After you get your order, you might want to hop on over to Centennial Park and dig in, since the only seating at the restaurant is a couple of picnic tables on a slab of concrete right in front of the window. You can order barbecue sandwiches, barbecue plates that come with two side orders, and barbecue by the pound. The white barbecue sauce is just right on top of the chicken, and the regular sauce comes in mild, hot, or extra hot. Quarter-chicken and half-chicken orders are available, and Hog Heaven has spareribs, too. Barbecue beans, potato salad, coleslaw, turnip greens, white beans, green beans, black-eyed peas, and corn on the cob are among the side dishes. The homemade cobbler is a heavenly way to end a meal here. The restaurant is open Monday through Saturday for lunch and dinner.

JACK'S BAR-B-QUE $
416-A Broadway
(615) 254-5715

334 West Trinity Lane
(615) 228-9888
www.jacksbarbque.com

Jack Cawthon opened his first barbecue restaurant in 1976 after studying in the barbecue hot spots of Memphis, Atlanta, Texas, Kentucky, and the Carolinas. Today he satisfies Nashville's appetite for barbecue at two locations and is also known for his catering (some of Music City's biggest stars have called on Jack's for that). The Broadway location backs up to the historic Ryman Auditorium, and diners there can sit on Jack's Backdoor Patio, in view of the Ryman's backstage door. Jack's serves Tennessee pork shoulder, ribs cut St. Louis–style, Texas beef brisket, smoked turkey and chicken, and Texas sausage. Side items include baked beans, potato salad, and coleslaw. For dessert, try the chess pie, chocolate fudge pie, and brownies. Beer is available. Jack's is open daily for lunch and dinner.

NEELY'S BARBECUE $
2292 Metro Center
(615) 251-8895
www.neelysbbq.com

In February 1988 four brothers launched into the barbecue business, opening their first restaurant in downtown Memphis. That was followed by another restaurant in Memphis. In March 2001 the Neelys opened their third location in Nashville, with brother Tony Neely heading to Music City to head up the operation. Since then, Neely's has been voted the No. 1 ribs in Nashville. Open Monday through Saturday, Neely's has lunch and dinner seating capacity for 80 people as well as a drive-through window. Neely's has a long menu with barbecue of all types—chicken, beef ribs, pork ribs, pulled pork, sliced beef, turkey, and chicken wings—and plenty of side choices. The meat is slow-cooked over hickory wood and has a deep-basted flavor that is hard to duplicate without taking time. The Bar-B-Que Spaghetti Dinner (Mother Neely's choice) features a mixture of barbecue and spaghetti sauce poured over pasta and pork, served with coleslaw and fresh bread. Tempting desserts finish off a meal, such as pecan pie, peach cobbler, brownies, cake, and ice cream. If you crave Neely's barbecue at home, try their takeout, catering, or sauce sold in local stores.

WHITT'S BARBECUE $

5211 Alabama Avenue
(615) 385-1553

5310 Harding Road
(615) 356-3435

3621 Nolensville Road
(615) 831-0309

4601 Andrew Jackson Parkway,
Hermitage
(615) 885-4146

2535 Lebanon Pike, Donelson
(615) 883-6907

105 Sulphur Springs Road, Murfreesboro
(615) 890-0235
www.whittsbarbecue.com

Whitt's has been serving barbecue to Nashvillians for about two decades. It has been voted the No. 1 barbecue restaurant time after time in local publications' readers' polls. You can count on speedy service and quality barbecue that's been slow-cooked over hickory coals and topped off with a vinegar-based sauce. Whitt's serves pork, turkey, and beef barbecue in sandwiches or on plates. The plate portions are huge and come with two side items and rolls or corn bread. Whitt's miniature chess, fudge, and pecan pies are the perfect after-meal treat. Whitt's is open Monday through Saturday for lunch and dinner. Whitt's has about a dozen Nashville-area locations, as well as restaurants in Clarksville, Springfield, and other areas of Middle Tennessee. Some locations have dine-in areas; all have drive-through windows. Whitt's does a lot of catering and can accommodate any size group.

BREAKFAST

BEACON LIGHT TEA ROOM $$
Highway 100, Bon Aqua
(931) 670-3880

If you can't get into the often-packed Loveless Café for brunch one Sunday morning, just head down Highway 100 another 15 minutes or so and you'll happen upon the Beacon Light Tea Room. This spot is becoming known among Nashville diners for its fluffy biscuits, country ham, homemade preserves, and other delicious breakfast offerings. While the kitschy Christian-themed decor has grabbed the headlines—there are no velvet Jesuses, but you will find just about everything else—it's the perfect backdrop for this yummy Southern food. For more information see our Meat-and-Three/Southern listings. The restaurant is open Tuesday through Sunday. Breakfast is served on weekends only.

LOVELESS CAFÉ $$
8400 Highway 100
(615) 646-9700
www.lovelesscafe.com

The legendary Loveless Café is the real thing: country cookin' just like Grandma's. Take it from a Southerner who spent half her childhood at her grandparents' farm, where there was always a plate full of fluffy white biscuits sitting atop a dish of greasy bacon and sausage in the kitchen. The meals were Southern and country—always plenty of fried food and bowls of hot gravy. The Loveless always brings back memories of Granny's house. The Loveless is open daily for breakfast, lunch, and dinner. We're partial to the Southern-style breakfasts, which are served all day. Choose from eggs, omelets, sausage, bacon, grits, waffles, and pancakes—all served with plates full of biscuits, bowls of gravy, and homemade blackberry and peach preserves. If you don't know the difference in the types of gravy offered (and we've learned there are many of you in this boat), take note: Cream gravy is the creamy white kind made with milk, flour, and bacon or sausage drippings; redeye gravy is made from ham drippings and black coffee instead of milk. If you prefer, you can order a plate full of fried chicken and vegetables, or country ham and eggs with french fries, or a tossed salad. If you're planning to come here on a Saturday or Sunday, you'll want to call a day or two ahead and make reservations. While you're waiting to be seated, check out some of the photos of celebrities who have dined here. In late 2003, local caterer Tom Morales purchased the Loveless from the McCabe family, who had operated the landmark restaurant for three decades.

Loveless Café was named Best Downhome Dining Spot for 2005.

NOSHVILLE $–$$
1918 Broadway
(615) 329-NOSH

4014 Hillsboro Circle
(615) 269-3535
www.noshville.com

This New York–style deli is famous for its enormous sandwiches, but it also serves a good breakfast. Assorted bagels and cream cheeses, plus eggs, omelets, griddle cakes, assorted toasts, and cereal satisfy just about any morning appetite. Read more about Noshville in the Deli section of this chapter. The deli is open daily but closes early, at 4:00 p.m., on Monday.

PANCAKE PANTRY $
1796 21st Avenue S.
(615) 383-9333

The Pancake Pantry has been a Nashville breakfast tradition for decades. Locals are willing to stand in line as long as it takes to get a table and a stack of pancakes at this Hillsboro Village restaurant. The line usually snakes out the door and down the sidewalk. Urns of complimentary hot coffee are a welcome warmer during wintertime waits. Once inside, the longtime waitresses will make you feel right at home. In addition to a variety of pancakes, you'll find all the familiar breakfast foods on the menu. The busy restaurant is known to draw celebrities regularly, so you'll never know who might occupy the table next to you (try not to stare). The Pancake Pantry is open daily for breakfast and lunch (see our Kidstuff chapter for more).

PFUNKY GRIDDLE $
2800 Bransford Avenue
(615) 298-2088
www.thepfunkygriddle.com

Located in a tiny cottage, the Pfunky Griddle lets you create the pancake of your dreams. Custom-made fireproof tables with built-in griddles are ready and waiting for you to mix and stir up a unique pancake. Be aware that this is a cook-your-own place. When you order pancakes, you get a pitcher of batter and choice of toppings—berries, chocolate chips, nuts, M&Ms, and the like. If you want French toast, you get a bowl of eggs and milk sprinkled with cinnamon and a plate of sliced wheat loaf. If you order eggs, that's what you get—ready for you to cook. If the pancakes seem to taste better here, part of it could be the special batter—hand ground from scratch using whole wheat, cornmeal, buckwheat, rye, and brown-rice flours for the five-grain recipe, and unbalanced, unbromated enriched white flour for the old-time mix. The Pfunky Griddle also serves sandwiches and salads. If the name sounds strange, chalk it up to the owner Penelope Pfuntner. All in all, it's a pfun place.

STAR BAGEL CO. $
4504 Murphy Road
(615) 292-7993
www.starbagelcafe.com

Star Bagel has some of the best bagels in town. There are all sorts of yummy ones to choose from here. Plain bagels and multigrain are two of the most ordered varieties, but there are also cinnamon-raisin swirl, sun-dried tomato, wild blueberry, and egg bagels. Star Bagel's cream cheeses include light plain, wild blueberry, light spicy cucumber, herb and garlic, olive pimiento, and the ever-popular honey walnut raisin. If a heartier breakfast is in order, you can top your bagel with any combination of eggs, bacon, salami, and cheese. For lunch, order from the menu of deli sandwiches such as hot pastrami and Swiss, roast beef and cheddar, and tuna melt—or create your own sandwich. Star Bagel is open Monday through Saturday for breakfast, lunch, and early dinners and on Sunday for breakfast and lunch. No credit cards.

> **i** The Demonbreun Street area adjacent to Music Row, once lined with country music museums and gift shops, is being redeveloped into an upscale live music and dining destination.

BURGERS

BROWN'S DINER $
2102 Blair Boulevard
(615) 269-5509

This weathered building, an expanded dining car, is a genuine tavern—what you might call a dive. But it serves what many people consider the best cheeseburger in town. Plenty of seating is available in the dining room, where there's a big-screen TV. But the real atmosphere is in the dark bar (beer only), a popular hangout for songwriters, businesspeople, and regular working folk, with a TV that's generally tuned to a sports event. Chili dogs, fried fish, and a few sandwiches are among the other menu items, but the burger with fries is really your best bet. This is real Nashville at its most unpretentious. Brown's is open daily for lunch and dinner.

FAT MO'S $
2620 Franklin Road
(615) 298-1111

1216 Murfreesboro Pike
(615) 366-3171

2509 Lebanon Pike
(615) 889-3400

351 White Bridge Pike
(615) 356-4010

2608 Gallatin Road
(615) 226-5012

946 Richards Road, Antioch
(615) 781-1830
www.fatmos.com

Insiders may disagree about who has the best burger in Nashville, but there's no argument about who has the biggest. When your ads and signs proclaim "the biggest burgers in town!" you have to deliver, and this popular establishment offers the Fat Mo's Super Deluxe Burger, more than 27 ounces of fresh beef cooked up in three patties and topped with grilled mushrooms and onions, barbecue sauce, bacon, and jalapeños—enough to feed the whole family. Those with less hearty appetites (or smaller families) can choose from burgers of only 16 or 8 ounces; even the Little Mo's Burger weighs in at 5 ounces, which is bigger than a Quarter Pounder, and it's cooked fresh. And although we've listed only a handful of locations here, there are several more throughout the area where you can indulge. Other sandwiches include fried and grilled chicken, catfish, roast beef, hot dogs, and corn dogs. Fat Mo's also has fries in "plain" and "spicy" varieties, onion rings, cheese sticks, fried mushrooms, and stuffed jalapeños. And be sure to save room for an old-fashioned milk shake, ice cream cone, or sundae. While you'll have to wait several minutes for your order, you'll find the difference between Fat Mo's and fast-food burgers to be well worth the wait. The restaurants are open daily for lunch and dinner.

ROTIER'S RESTAURANT $
2413 Elliston Place
(615) 327-9892
www.rotiers.com

Rotier's—part old-timey diner, part burger joint, part tavern—has Nashville's most legendary burgers. Their cheeseburger has been voted the city's best in local readers' polls for going on a decade. First-timers here might be surprised to see that the burgers are served on French bread instead of buns, so they look more like sandwiches. For the full Rotier's experience, you must have a chocolate shake with your burger. Rotier's is also known for their old-fashioned plate lunches and dinners. Read more about those in the Meat-and-Three/Southern section of this chapter.

CAJUN/CREOLE

BRO'S CAJUN CUISINE $
3214 Charlotte Avenue
(615) 329-2626
www.broscajuncuisine.com

Bro's location has changed a few times in recent years, but the delicious food is still the same. Gumbo, red beans and rice, crawfish étouffée, fried catfish on Friday—all the favorites are still on the menu. (And the rolls of paper towels are still on the tables.) Bro's is one of those Insiders' favorites that has a devoted following. The affable owner, Darrell Breaux of Lafayette, Louisiana, cooks up authentic Cajun foods with just the right amount of spice. During the holidays, the restaurant sells deep-fried turkeys, injected with onions and seasonings (for about $50). Bro's is open for lunch Monday through Saturday until about 3:00 p.m., and on Friday, Bro's is open until about 7:30 p.m.

MOJO GRILL $
1900 Broadway
(615) 321-3363

Tasty New Orleans–style grub with a touch of Tex-Mex and Caribbean makes Mojo Grill an excellent choice when you're in the mood for a hearty meal with a little heat (milder dishes and sandwiches are available for the less adventurous). There are several burritos to choose from; try the Cajun, loaded with jambalaya and topped with crawfish étouffée. Jambalaya is also available as a dish, as are such Big Easy staples as gumbo and red beans and rice. The wings are also great, and you can get them from gringo (mild) to mojo (fiery). Mojo Grill is open daily for lunch and dinner.

CARIBBEAN

CALYPSO CAFE $–$$
5101 Harding Pike
(615) 356-1678
(615) 256-FOOD (catering)

700 Thompson Lane
(615) 297-3888

600 Frasier Drive
(615) 771-5665

1101 Gardiano Avenue
(615) 227-6133

2424 Elliston Place
(615) 321-3878
www.calypsocafe.com

Calypso Cafe puts a fresh, flavorful Caribbean spin on Nashville's traditional meat-and-vegetable plates. At Calypso, the meat is rotisserie chicken with spicy, all-natural Caribbean barbecue or mild Jamaican curry sauce, while the vegetable choices include Cuban black beans, flavorful mustard greens with tomatoes and onions, spiced sweet potatoes topped with coconut, and bean and corn salad. Caribbean sweet corn bread–coconut muffins are a delicious alternative to traditional Southern corn bread. Calypso Cafe also serves a variety of sandwiches, salads with homemade dressings, and desserts. Don't forget to get some refreshing fruit tea, which comes with seemingly endless refills. We love Calypso Cafe, and, judging from the number of new locations popping up around town (see www.calypsocafe.com for locations), we're not the only ones. Calypso Cafe has a small kids' menu and is a great place for takeout. The restaurants are open daily for lunch and dinner.

RUMBA RUM BAR
AND SATAY GRILL $$–$$$
3009 West End Avenue
(615) 321-1350

As you might guess from its name, this restaurant specializes in colorful, exotic drinks and the South Pacific favorite satay, which is skewered grilled meat. Blending Caribbean, Indonesian, Latin American, South American, Spanish, and other global influences, the lively restaurant/bar offers a dining experience that's unique in Nashville. It opened in summer 2003 and quickly found its niche with 30-and-up professionals. The beverage list includes Cuban mojitos, traditional Brazilian caipirinhas, Singapore slings, a variety of martinis, and other cold, tempting selections. The delicious satay—chicken, shrimp, beef, or portobello mushrooms—are attractively served with three dipping sauces (West Indies barbecue, spicy peanut, and Argentinean chimichurri) and make a perfect accompaniment to the fruity drinks. The extensive menu also features tropical salads and a variety of new-to-Nashville beef, pork, and seafood dishes. Especially popular are the coconut shrimp, lobster satay, and tandoori mahimahi. Open nightly and on Sunday for brunch.

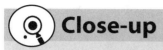 **Close-up**

Hot Chicken Comes Home to Roost

Perhaps one of the oddest food trends to hit an American city in recent years has been the, well, explosion of hot chicken restaurants in Nashville. In fact, this particular variety of Southern food is so, er, sizzling, that a new eatery seems to open up every few months or so. It's fair to say that hot chicken has positively burst upon the scene here.

Okay, enough with the bad puns. What is hot chicken, you may wonder? This is a unique brand of fried chicken that's highly seasoned, some would say to incendiary proportions. When we say this stuff is hot, trust us—it's positively flameworthy. The chicken is served Southern-style, on a slice of white bread; the bread soaks up all the spicy chicken juices and is one of the best parts about eating a hot chicken dinner. The usual accompaniment to all this spicy fried deliciousness is a side of sweet pickles, baked beans, and potato salad. It's all washed down with sweet tea.

Proprietors closely guard their hot chicken recipes, though many seem to have their roots in that granddaddy of Nashville hot chicken outfits, Prince's. Prince's has been a figure on the Nashville scene for more than 50 years, and many folks claim to have that famous Prince's recipe. For their part, the family-owned Prince's maintains their recipe is a closely guarded secret.

Most hot chicken restaurants are little more than shacks, and most operate on a takeout-only basis. It's best to call and order ahead at these places to avoid long waits. Here are two of our favorites.

BOLTON'S SPICY CHICKEN & FISH $
624 Main Street
(615) 254-8015
This east Nashville roadside stand is the only one that offers fish as well as hot chicken. The recipe is reportedly based on Prince's famous concoction—the proprietor's uncle once worked at Prince's and for decades operated a now shuttered famous rival, Columbo's. Since the food is not quite as spicy as the others, you might dare to up the heat level on your food a notch. It's still plenty hot, though. This is a takeout-only place; orders are placed through an iron security window, or you can call your order ahead. Closed Monday.

PRINCE'S HOT CHICKEN SHACK $
123 Ewing Drive
(615) 226-9442
The first of the hot chicken joints, Prince's has been around for 50 years or more. This is the place that started it all; a quintessential dive, the food is legendary, drawing folks from all across the city. The chicken comes in four heat modes, but medium is usually spicy enough for most people. You get your drinks from a Coke machine, and there are just a handful of tables; most business is carry-out. Call your order ahead, or you're likely to wait as much as 45 minutes for your food. Prince's is closed Monday; on weekends, it's open until 4:00 a.m., which makes it popular with the college crowd.

CATFISH

COCK OF THE WALK $$
2624 Music Valley Drive
(615) 889-1930
www.cockofthewalkrestaurant.com

This catfish restaurant in the Opryland/Music Valley area has been a favorite since it opened in the mid-1980s. Many Nashvillians consider the catfish here some of the best around. The large restaurant is themed to the early-19th-century riverboat days, and the staff dresses in period attire. Meals are served on tin plates and in tin cups. The servers, dressed as keel boatmen, flip corn bread in iron skillets. If you're not in the mood for catfish, try the chicken or shrimp. The restaurant is open for dinner Monday through Sunday and also serves lunch on Sunday.

RIVERVIEW RESTAURANT & MARINA $-$$
110 Old River Road, Ashland City
(615) 792-7358

If you have a cravin' for catfish, you may want to head to Ashland City, where this dockside restaurant on the Cumberland River has been serving it up at least since the '70s. They have some of the tastiest catfish around. The restaurant—about a 30-minute drive from Nashville—is nothing fancy, but then you don't need white tablecloths and candlelight to enjoy catfish, do you? You can order hand-breaded catfish fillets for about $8.99, or get all-you-can eat catfish or a whole catfish for $4.00 more. The meals come with coleslaw, hush puppies, and potatoes. White beans and other side items are available, too. A lunch buffet is offered every day except Saturday. Riverview also serves a lot of rib-eye and hamburger steaks and grilled chicken. A salad bar, burgers, other sandwiches, and desserts round out the menu. During the summer, the deck is the hot destination. Patrons will wait for an hour or more for a seat there, especially on busy Friday and Saturday nights. Beer is available. Riverview is open daily for lunch and dinner. The restaurant closes for a couple of weeks during the holiday season and reopens after New Year's Day.

CONTINENTAL/FINE DINING

MIRROR $$-$$$
2317 12th Avenue S.
(615) 383-8330
www.eatdrinkreflect.com

Located in the burgeoning "12 South" district, Mirror wins raves for its excellent food and casual ambience. It's one of the trendiest places to eat in town, but the vibe is warm, friendly, and relaxed. Mirror made a name for itself early on with its tapas menu; the blue cheese polenta fries alone make it worth a visit. The tapas plates are all priced at less than $5.50, and two or three will satisfy a modest hunger, making this restaurant surprisingly affordable. (A regular entree menu is available for those with a bigger appetite.) There's also a creative cocktail menu, and the rose-flavored American Beauty is a favorite. This is a popular late-night hangout; when the weather is nice, take advantage of a few outdoor tables. Mirror is small; reservations are always a good idea. The restaurant is open Monday through Saturday for dinner.

RESTAURANT ZOLA $$$$
3001 West End Avenue
(615) 320-7778
www.restaurantzola.com

Restaurant Zola has won virtually every "Best of" restaurant award Nashville offers, as well as Wine Spectator's "Award of Excellence" several years in a row. Zola has been listed as one of the 101 Top Restaurants in America by *City* magazine. The food is excellent, and the service is flawless. Zola's menu combines flavors from Spain, France, and Italy, with a dash of the South. A sampling from a recent summer menu included Grandma Zola's seafood and chorizo paella, and trout España, which is a boneless trout stuffed with chorizo, Spanish cheeses, and caramelized onion. They've also won awards for their French Laundry Salad, a delightful blend of arugula, radicchio, apples, blue cheese, and fennel with champagne vinaigrette dressing. There are many vegetarian entrees on the menu as well, and some that aren't can be made that way at your request. Many of the ingredients are locally grown and organic; the menu changes frequently, as fresh ingredients become available. Don't be surprised if that promised Santorini Salmon isn't on the menu because a key ingredient didn't pass muster with chef/owner Debra Paquette. The atmosphere is quietly romantic, in a no-pressure kind of way. You don't have to worry about shouting over the table of 20 across the room, but then again, you won't be expected to pop the question over dessert, either—that is, not unless you want to. Zola is open Monday through Saturday for dinner. Reservations are suggested.

DELI

GOLDIE'S DELI $
4520 Harding Road
(615) 292-3589
www.goldiesdeli.net

If you're in the mood for deli food, then head to the Belle Meade Plaza shopping center. Tucked into a long, narrow space there near Starbucks and Office Depot is Goldie's, a great New York–style deli (and you really won't find many of those in these parts). Goldie's has everything you would expect from a good deli, including great Reuben and turkey sandwiches, matzo ball soup, barrels of pickles, and plenty of meats and homemade salads (chicken, tuna, and potato varieties) sold by the pound, plus tasty cheesecake and rugelach for dessert. The busy space seats about 50 at a few tables, which are frequently full, so be prepared to get your order to go. Goldie's is open daily for breakfast, lunch, and dinner, but evening hours vary depending on the day of the week.

NOSHVILLE $–$$
1918 Broadway
(615) 329-NOSH

4014 Hillsboro Circle
(615) 269-3535
www.noshville.com

Nashvillians enthusiastically welcomed the arrival of Noshville, an authentic New York deli that became an instant favorite. Noshville serves tasty, high-quality food in a lively atmosphere. It's a fun place, and the sandwiches are huge. You really don't need to order the "We Dare Ya" size, unless you're feeding two or haven't eaten in a week or so. Trust us on that one. With most regular-size sandwiches priced around $9.95, you'll pay a little more here than at other sandwich places, but you definitely get your money's worth. Meats are piled high. A bowl of kosher pickles on the table makes everything complete. Noshville also serves

a selection of soups, salads, and entrees like homemade meat loaf, corned beef and cabbage, and pot roast served with a vegetable and choice of potato. There are several smoked fish platters available, and plenty of juices, specialty coffees, and desserts (New York cheesecake and rugelach cookies, to name two) on the menu. Noshville is open daily for breakfast, lunch, and dinner and is open until 11:00 p.m. on Friday and Saturday. (For more on the early-morning munchies at Noshville, see this chapter's Breakfast section.)

> **i** The "Martha White" brand of cooking products isn't a fictitious advertising symbol. There was a real Martha, and she was the daughter of Richard Lindsey, who founded Royal Flour Mill in Nashville in 1899. Lindsey named his finest flour after his little girl.

GERMAN

GERST HAUS $$
301 Woodland Street
(615) 244-8886
www.gersthaus.com

This long-running institution has served brats, kielbasa, and Wiener schnitzel to Nashvillians since the turn of the 20th century. Locals were positively aghast when the place was torn down in 1997 to make way for the Titans's football stadium. Fortunately, the owners knew they had a good thing going and built a new version across the street. Today the Gerst Haus is the closest restaurant to the stadium, making it a favorite pregame gathering spot. We like to eat here on Friday or Saturday night, when the restaurant's oompah band performs. In addition to the German specialties, the menu also includes American favorites (steak, fried catfish, barbecued ribs), sandwiches, and salads. You can wash it down with a selection of some 80 beers and ales from around the world—including the house brew, Gerst Amber. The Gerst Haus is open daily for lunch and dinner.

i The Metro Public Health Department of Nashville-Davidson County posts local restaurant inspection scores at its Web site, http://healthweb.nashville.org. You can search for scores by month or by the name of the restaurant.

GREEK

ATHENS FAMILY RESTAURANT $
2526 Franklin Road
(615) 383-2848
www.athensfamilyrestaurant.com

It is fitting that while you are in the "Athens of the South," you should be able to dine at an authentic Greek restaurant. Opened in 2005, Athens Family Restaurant features family recipes from various parts of the Greek islands. The native Greek owners have incorporated the Greek concept into a very broad menu ranging from gyros, souvlaki, moussaka, and spanakopita to the honey-sweet baklava. The food is fresh and tasty, the surroundings reminiscent of Greece, and the cloth-covered tables and comfortable chairs friendly enough to linger over a leisurely meal. Decor includes fishing nets on the walls, Greek paintings, and other island items. The restaurant also serves breakfast, with eggs, omelets, pancakes, French toast, and other early morning treats, as well as heart-healthy choices such as yogurt and fresh fruit, on the menu. The owner is fond of saying that you don't have to spend a fortune to visit Greece. Just stop by his restaurant, and you'll think you are there—if only for a meal.

INDIAN

SHALIMAR $$$
3711 Hillsboro Pike
(615) 269-8577
www.shalimarfinedining.com

One of the first Indian restaurants in Nashville, Shalimar's delicious food and fine service have earned it a very good reputation. Chicken tikka masala and chicken curry are favorite entrees, and the restaurant has a nice assortment of traditional Indian nan breads. For dessert, try the rice pudding or the gulab jamun, sweet dough swimming in a rosewater broth. Shalimar doesn't serve alcohol, but you can bring your own; there's no cork fee. The restaurant is open daily for lunch and dinner and has a popular Saturday lunch buffet. Located in a rather nondescript building in Green Hills, the restaurant has an enclosed patio for outdoor dining.

SITAR $
116 21st Avenue N.
(615) 321-8889
www.sitarnashville.com

This small and casual restaurant is where many folks go when they have a craving for spicy Indian foods. Business execs, the music-business crowd, performers, and students alike frequent Sitar. Many come regularly for the daily lunch buffet, which at $7.99 is a bargain. For dinner, chicken and lamb dishes are favorites, and there are vegetarian meals here, too. Sitar is open for lunch and dinner daily.

ITALIAN

ANTONIO'S OF NASHVILLE $$
7097 Old Harding Road
(615) 646-9166

Bellevue residents often lament the lack of good places to eat on their side of town, but they are blessed with this fine Italian restaurant. Antonio's of Nashville serves gourmet Italian cuisine in a casually elegant atmosphere. It's a perfect place for a romantic date, whether you're wearing blue jeans, a tux, or an evening dress. All foods here are fresh and prepared to order. A favorite is the scaloppini Sorrentino—veal layered with prosciutto, eggplant, and mozzarella and sautéed in a white wine and red sauce. Tiramisu is the ideal end to a meal here, but the fresh berries zabaglione (a sauce of sugar, eggs, cream, and Marsala) is a tempting alternative. Twice a year—on Valentine's Day and New Year's Eve—Antonio's has a four- or five-course special menu; it's a bit more pricey but makes for a memorable special-occasion dinner. Antonio's is open nightly. Reservations are recommended, especially on weekends.

CAESAR'S RISTORANTE ITALIANO $$

72 White Bridge Road
(615) 352-3661
www.caesarsitaliano.com

This casual Italian restaurant has plenty of regulars who return again and again for the authentic and affordable Italian food. With two separate dining areas—one a little more intimate and one a little more family-friendly—it's a good spot for both casual dates and meals with the kids. Owner-chef Caesar Randazzo, a native of Sicily, offers a diverse but pasta-based menu. Especially good are the pastas with Northern Italian white sauces. Try the specialty—ziti alla carbonara, a combination of ziti with fresh cream, asparagus, Italian ham, and Parmesan. Caesar's also has the expected spaghetti and fettuccine with a variety of sauces, as well as lasagna, eggplant, manicotti, and cannelloni. There are several seafood dishes, veal and poultry, pizzas with your choice of about 15 toppings, and sub sandwiches. For lunch, Caesar's has an all-you-can-eat buffet, which is tasty but not quite the same as a nighttime meal.

CITY HOUSE RESTAURANT $$$

122 Fourth Avenue N.
(615) 736-5838
www.cityhousenashville.com

Located in the quaint residential neighborhood of Germantown, City House serves top-notch Italian dishes and memorable desserts. Follow the winding path to a former sculptor's studio that is home to City House with its rustic brick and well-worn wood. House-cured meats, fresh pastas, comforting soups, and simple grated cheese add to the taste and charm. Pan-fried Carolina trout is flavorful with capers, garlic, lemon, anchovies, and parsley. Pizzas are a favorite here, baked in a brick oven behind the counter. Try one with house-cured salami, tomato sauce, and house-made mozzarella. For dessert, it's a hard choice but you can't go wrong with the cream puffs filled with chocolate cream in espresso zabaglione with homemade caramel and candied kumquats.

SOLE MIO $$$

311 Third Avenue S.
(615) 256-4013
www.solemionash.com

The Agnolettis, who moved their restaurant from northern Italy to Music City in 1995, specialize in handmade and hand-rolled pastas, homemade sauces, fresh fish, veal and chicken dishes, and brick-oven pizzas. Lasagna is a signature dish, and the mussels are a favorite as an appetizer. Closed Monday.

MEAT-AND-THREE/SOUTHERN

BEACON LIGHT TEA ROOM $$

Highway 100, Bon Aqua
(931) 670-3880

A few miles past the famous Loveless Café is the Beacon Light, a restaurant that has dished up Southern food along with spiritual succor since 1936. Beacon Light is known for its delicious country ham, biscuits, and homemade preserves, but it's become notorious for the decor, which can only be described as Christian kitsch. Jesus tchotchkes, Jesus paintings, porcelain lions and lambs, and religious knickknacks of all types crowd every nook and cranny of the place. There are even plastic "our daily bread" boxes on each table; toaster shaped, they dispense scripture passages instead of bread. The Southern-fried menu is excellent, by the way. Beacon Light is open for dinner Tuesday through Friday and breakfast, lunch, and dinner Saturday and Sunday. Reservations are accepted.

BRIDGES CAFE AT BELLE MEADE $$

85 White Bridge Road
(615) 353-5705

Located in Belle Meade Drugs, Bridges Cafe serves fresh home-cooked meals like grandma used to put on the table. Using a pencil, diners check boxes for meat and two or three sides. Choices include old standbys like meat loaf, fried chicken, pork loin, grits, beans, squash, potatoes, and green-pea salad. Or choose soup and sandwiches, such as chicken salad and lemon-artichoke soup. End the meal with a filling bread pudding topped with bourbon-ginger sauce or moist coconut cake with walnuts and spices.

ELLISTON PLACE SODA SHOP $
2111 Elliston Place
(615) 327-1090

Plate lunches and milk shakes are the claims to fame of this 1950s-style diner. One of Nashville's oldest restaurants, Elliston Place Soda Shop first opened in 1939, and little has changed here over the years. The restaurant has had only three owners, and it still has some of its original chairs and booths. Old miniature jukeboxes sit on each table; they don't work anymore, but the big jukebox still spins hits from the '50s and '60s.

Monday through Saturday, diners can choose from four entrees, including daily specials like turkey and dressing, fried chicken, and catfish. For the "three" part of your meat-and-three, choose from among 10 vegetables and side dishes, including fresh turnip greens, fried corn, baked squash, and macaroni and cheese. Your meal comes with corn bread or a biscuit. If you want to indulge further, have one of the soda shop's celebrated shakes. If you drive here at lunchtime, you might want to allow extra time to find a parking space. There are metered spaces on both sides of the street, but they're often filled. Plan to circle the block a time or two.

MALLARD'S RESTAURANT $
101 Saunders Ferry Road, Hendersonville
(615) 822-4668

For Southern-style plate lunches and a lake view, eat at Mallard's in Hendersonville. This family-style restaurant has been around more than 20 years; owner Kevin Berry purchased it in 1989. It's at the corner of Saunders Ferry and Gallatin Pike, and nearly every seat has a nice view. Choose from about seven meat entrees, including meat loaf and fried chicken, and about 15 vegetables, including the always-popular squash casserole, spinach casserole, and green beans. If you know what's good, you'll be sure to get some pinto beans because (as any Southerner knows) they

are perfect with the fried corn bread, or any kind of corn bread for that matter. On Friday after 4:00 p.m., Mallard's has all-you-can-eat catfish with fries, coleslaw, and hush puppies for about $8. Mallard's is open daily for breakfast, lunch, and dinner. The restaurant does not accept credit cards.

MARTHA'S AT THE PLANTATION $$$
5025 Harding Road
(615) 353-2828
www.marthasattheplantation.com

Acclaimed chef and cookbook author Martha Stamps focuses on fresh, seasonal ingredients at her cozy restaurant located at the historic Belle Meade Plantation (see our Attractions chapter). The contemporary "new Southern" menu changes four times a year, but for lunch you can usually expect such reliable favorites as chicken croquettes, grilled pork tenderloin, crawfish cakes, and buttermilk-battered fried chicken. The popular Sunday brunch features an a la carte menu that includes country ham and biscuits, Southern-style French toast, shrimp and grits, potato cakes, and eggs. Desserts are a treat and may include fudge pie and orange almond pound cake. The restaurant serves beer and wine. Martha's is open for lunch Monday through Saturday, and for brunch Sunday. Reservations are suggested.

MONELL'S $$
1235 Sixth Avenue N.
(615) 248-4747

CAFE MONELL'S AT THE HERMITAGE
4580 Rachel's Lane, Hermitage
(615) 889-2941
http://monellsdining.ypguides.net/

At Monell's on Sixth Avenue you sit at a big table with other guests and enjoy an all-you-can-eat family-style meal. Guests pass bowls and platters of food around the table and serve themselves. The food is Southern, with entrees like meat loaf, fried chicken, and country-fried steak; plenty of fresh vegetables; home-cooked side dishes; biscuits; and corn muffins. Monell's original location on Sixth Avenue N. is in Germantown in a renovated Victorian house next door to the Mad Platter. Monell's is open for lunch Monday through Friday, for dinner Tuesday through Saturday, and for "Sunday dinner" (also known as lunch) until around 3:30 p.m. Sunday. Breakfast is also served Saturday and Sunday. See the Monell's Express entry for details on Monell's takeout. Monell's doesn't serve alcohol, but you can bring your own wine. Seating is first come, first served. Cafe Monell's at the Hermitage features the same menu, but it's served cafeteria-style. The Hermitage restaurant is open for lunch daily.

MONELL'S EXPRESS $$$
2309 Franklin Road
(615) 292-5336

405 31st Avenue N.
(615) 321-9660

4811 Trousdale Drive
(615) 292-5336
http://monellsdining.ypguides.net/
Monell's Express locations are takeout only and are open for lunch daily. They're conveniently located around Nashville. See the previous entry for details about Monell's menu.

PANCAKE PANTRY $
1796 21st Avenue S.
(615) 383-9333
While famous as a breakfast place, Pancake Pantry packs 'em in at lunch, too. Southern plate lunches and meat-and-three dishes join more traditional fare like patty melts and BLTs.

THE PIE WAGON $
1302 Division Street
(615) 256-5893
This diner has been a favorite among locals for decades. It's been around at least since the early 1920s and was a short-order kitchen when owner Carol Babb purchased it in 1990. It's open for lunch only—hours are 10:30 a.m. to 3:00 p.m. Monday through Friday.

The inexpensive, cafeteria-style cuisine is simple home cookin', or comfort food as some people call it. Lunch entrees might include fried

chicken, meat loaf, or grilled catfish, with vegetables/side dishes like real mashed potatoes, green beans, stewed tomatoes, turnip greens, and macaroni and cheese. There's also corn bread and homemade desserts. The friendly counter workers will treat you like family.

ROTIER'S RESTAURANT $
2413 Elliston Place
(615) 327-9892
www.rotiers.com
Best known for its hamburgers and chocolate milk shakes, Rotier's (row-TEARS) is really an old-fashioned meat-and-three. It's been around since 1945 and is one of Nashville's most beloved restaurants. Walking into Rotier's, you'll find yourself in a building that was once a carriage house for a ritzy West End home. A few solo diners or beer drinkers usually sit at the counter bar, while booths full of Vandy students and white- and blue-collar workers keep the noise level high and the restaurant staff busy.

Rotier's has the meat-and-three (or, in this case, the meat-and-two) down to a science. "Meats of the Day" include hamburger steak, country-fried steak, fried chicken, meat loaf, and salmon croquettes. All are accompanied by two side items plus rolls or corn bread. For breakfast, you can order all the traditional country favorites. The eatery is open Monday through Saturday.

SWETT'S RESTAURANT $
2725 Clifton Avenue
(615) 329-4418

Farmers' Market, 900 Eighth Avenue N.
(615) 742-0699
www.swettsrestaurant.com
Swett's is legendary for its meat-and-three meals. This family-owned restaurant has been serving up Southern food—soul food, if you prefer—since 1954. Diners choose their meat-and-three in a cafeteria line. Entrees, like fried chicken, beef tips, and ham, and a variety of vegetables, including potatoes, corn, and beans, fill the plates. A meat-and-three meal wouldn't be complete without corn bread, and Swett's has some of the

best. Swett's is open daily for lunch and dinner. The Farmers' Market location serves lunch only.

SYLVAN PARK RESTAURANT $
4502 Murphy Road
(615) 292-9275

SYLVAN PARK WEST
2330 Franklin Pike
(615) 269-9716

Sylvan Park on Murphy Road is known as one of the best meat-and-threes in town, which explains why it's always busy. It has been serving Nashvillians for decades; the current owner, Eleanor Clay, purchased it in 2003. Clay added the Sylvan Park West location the following year. Entrees vary daily, but there are usually choices like fried chicken, meat loaf, turkey and dressing, roast beef, and country-fried steak. They're all accompanied by three vegetables or side items like potatoes, macaroni and cheese, white beans, and pinto beans, plus corn bread or biscuits. The star of the dessert menu is the fabulous chocolate pie, but other favorites are the coconut cream, sweet potato, and lemon varieties. Sylvan Park is open for lunch daily and for dinner until 7:30 p.m. Monday through Saturday. Sylvan Park West is open for breakfast and lunch Monday through Saturday.

VARALLO'S RESTAURANT TOO $
239 Fourth Avenue N.
(615) 256-1907

Varallo's Too is run by Todd Varallo, grandson of the legendary Frank Varallo Jr., who for years operated Varallo's on Church Street. Known as Nashville's oldest restaurant, the original location opened in 1907 and was operated by the Varallo family until Frank retired in December 1998. Though Frank and his wife, Eva, are missed, Varallo's Too is still serving up the tasty food that helped make the family famous.

The signature item here is "three-way chili," which is a combination of chili, spaghetti, and a tamale originated by Frank Sr. back in the '20s. The plate lunches feature your choice of meats and vegetables. Favorites like country-fried steak,

meatballs, meat loaf, and turkey and dressing are accompanied by fresh "creamed" potatoes, turnip greens, broccoli casserole, and squash casserole. Homemade peach or blackberry cobbler and banana pudding are among the great ways to end a meal here. If you come for breakfast, you can order what Eva Varallo describes as the best hotcakes in town (made from her own recipe, of course), along with the usual bacon, eggs, and biscuits. Varallo's Too is open weekdays only from 6:00 a.m. to 2:30 p.m. The restaurant does not accept credit cards.

MEXICAN

LA HACIENDA TAQUERIA $
2615 Nolensville Pike
(615) 256-6142
www.lahaciendainc.com

La Hacienda, a Mexican grocery store, tortilla factory, and restaurant, introduced many Music City residents to authentic, freshly prepared Mexican food. La Hacienda is owned by the Yepez family, who sought to create an authentic Mexican restaurant where the area's Hispanic residents could feel at home. They opened the original 60-seat location in 1992 and later expanded it to seat 250. The casual, bustling dining room is packed at lunchtime with workers enjoying a quick Mexican-food fix. The burritos are delicious. They're filled with beans, your choice of meat (chicken, beef, pork, Mexican sausage, tripe, tongue), onions, cilantro, avocado, and salsa. Tacos are just as good. We're partial to the chicken tacos—perfect little soft tortillas topped with flavorful shredded chicken, diced onions, and fresh cilantro and accompanied by an avocado slice, lime wedge, and green and red sauce. There are several combination platters, including the spicy rotisserie chicken served with rice, beans, corn or flour tortillas, and a salad. After your meal, visit the grocery store, where you can pick up a package of tortillas made at La Hacienda Tortilleria. You might even be inspired to take home a Mexican sombrero or piñata. La Hacienda is open daily for lunch and dinner.

LA PAZ RESTAURANTE Y CANTINA $$

3808 Cleghorn Avenue
(615) 383-5200
www.lapaz.com

La Paz combines creative Mexican and Southwestern fare with a more upscale atmosphere than you find at most local Mexican restaurants. Inside it's warm and cozy, even though the rooms are open and spacious and, especially at lunch, somewhat noisy. At night, the lights are dimmed, and it's a little more romantic. There are a handful of these restaurants in the Southeast. We've eaten at the one in Destin, Florida, also and have found the food consistently good. All foods, including the green tomatillo salsa and spicy red salsa that arrive with your chips when you're seated, are made fresh. La Paz serves traditional favorites— burritos, fajitas, tamales, and the like—but often puts a creative spin on them. The restaurant has a full bar, and all imported beers are Mexican. The margaritas are good. Try the Texas variety—all the good stuff in the regular drink, plus orange juice and orange liqueur. La Paz is open daily for lunch and dinner.

i Looking for a late-night meal? A few options include Sunset Grill (open until 1:30 a.m. Monday through Saturday), Prince's Hot Chicken Shack (open until 4:00 a.m. on weekends), and Cafe Coco (open 24 hours a day). The Waffle House, which you can find in virtually every corner of town, is a perennial around-the-clock favorite.

LAS PALETAS $

2907 12th Avenue S.
(615) 386-2101

Paletas are to Mexico what gelato is to Italy. The tasty frozen desserts are similar to our Popsicles, but these aren't like any Popsicle the Good Humor man carried. Las Paletas proprietors Irma and Norma Paz, two daughters of Mexico, have brought their native treats to Nashville, where they operate a "Popsicle factory" in a small shop across the street from Sevier Park. You'll find exotic flavors like hibiscus and tamarind—even jalapeño, if you dare—as well as more traditional fruit flavors (with the fruit frozen inside), chocolate, and vanilla. Las Paletas really is a factory—the sisters provide paletas to Nashville's growing number of Hispanic grocery stores and restaurants. But they do plenty of walk-in business, too; just don't be surprised by the store's rather industrial appearance. La Paletas is closed Sunday and Monday, and is open until 7:00 p.m. the rest of the week during the summer and 6:00 p.m. in winter.

ROSARIO'S MEXICAN RESTAURANT $$

1200 Villa Place, Suite 100
(615) 329-1977
www.rosariosmexicanrestaurant.com

Located in the stylish Edgehill Village, Rosario's features family recipes and a large menu with plenty of choices for everyone. The restaurant's namesake was born and raised in Mexico and became an accomplished cook at age 16. Almost four decades ago, she brought her cooking skills and family recipes to California. Those recipes are now the big draw at Rosario's in Nashville. No one goes away hungry from Rosario's. Take the carnitas main dish, for example—slow-cooked hand-pulled pork served with red chili sauce or green tomatillo sauce, two tortillas, rice, and beans. The tamales are filled with chicken or pork and served on a corn husk with red, green, or poblano mole sauce, rice, and beans. For vegetarians, Rosario's offers several delicious tofu choices, such as Eli's Tofu Burrito with seasoned tofu, corn salsa, cactus salsa, Mexican slaw, and guacamole served with green and yellow squash.

ROSEPEPPER CANTINA
& MEXICAN GRILL $$

1907 Eastland Avenue
(615) 227-4777
www.rosepepper.com

West Nashvillians who typically never think about crossing the Cumberland for dinner are now heading to this lively east Nashville restaurant in droves. Located in a historic neighborhood, Rosepepper Cantina is colorful and fun. It's part bar, part restaurant, with an open, casual, and vibrant feel. When the weather's nice, diners can head to the patio and enjoy a meal alfresco. Inside, the walls are decked out in everything from Mexican and Southwestern art to posters to corrugated metal. Neighborhood regulars with kids in tow dine side by side with couples on dates and friends hooking up for margaritas—and some of the best in town are served here. The flavorful but not too spicy Sonora-style fare includes the usual enchiladas, burritos, fajitas, and tacos, but everything's superfresh (no premade plates under the heat lamps here). House specialties come with beans, rice, lime veggies, and tortillas, and all entrees come with a choice of house salad or soup. Rosepepper Cantina is open daily for lunch and dinner and also has a good happy hour on weekdays. Live music on weekends adds to the festive atmosphere. Reservations accepted.

TAQUERIA EL JALICIENSE $
6341 Charlotte Pike, Cumberland Plaza
(615) 354-5600
A traditional Mexican restaurant that's nowhere near Nolensville Road? El Jaliciense may be a maverick with its location, but this west Nashville taqueria offers tasty, authentic fare at dirt-cheap prices. The decor is standard-issue taco shop—Mexican hats on the walls and Formica-topped tables—but it's frequented by local Hispanics, and many of the waitstaff don't speak English. The menu offers typical Mexican fare (burritos, tacos, enchiladas, chalupas), all of it flavorful, nongreasy, and mildly seasoned; hot sauce is provided for those who prefer their food on the spicy side. Jalisco is a coastal region, and El Jaliciense honors its roots by offering a few shrimp specialties. Try the shrimp in spicy hot sauce or shrimp fajitas for a change of pace. El Jaliciense is open daily for lunch and dinner.

MIDDLE EASTERN

ANATOLIA $$
48 White Bridge Road
(615) 356-1556
http://Anatolia-restaurant.com
Part of Nashville's ever-growing variety of ethnic eateries, the Turkish restaurant Anatolia is an all-around delight. The elegantly uncluttered dining space, adorned with a few Middle Eastern rugs and eye-catching accessories, is comfortable and inviting, and the friendly and professional staff go the extra mile to make you feel welcome. The menu of entrees is divided into two parts: grilled specialties, which include familiar chicken, lamb, and beef kebabs, and "classic Turkish home cooking," a small selection of special recipes. Color photos of the prepared dishes are a thoughtful addition to the menu. If you aren't familiar with Middle Eastern food, you might want to try the Turkish stew, a combination of lamb cubes and 10 vegetables served piping hot with a scoop of rice and a bowl of cool yogurt sauce. Those with more adventurous tastes might consider the homemade Turkish ravioli: ground beef–stuffed pasta in a garlic-yogurt sauce topped with hot butter, red pepper, and mint. Anatolia also has hummus, stuffed grape leaves, soups, and a variety of salads. A small wine list includes a couple of Turkish selections. For dessert, you must try the specialty, kunefe. This heavenly concoction of shredded puff pastry, unsalted cheese, and light syrup, served warm, gets better with every bite. Anatolia is located in the Lion's Head Village shopping center. The restaurant is open for lunch and dinner daily.

KALAMATA'S $-$$
3764 Hillsboro Road
(615) 383-8700
www.eatatkalamatas.com
Freshness and flavor abound at this casual restaurant located in Green Hills's Glendale Center strip mall. Kalamata's specializes in Middle Eastern and Mediterranean foods. Be sure to check out the daily specials on the chalkboard before placing your order. One of the Lebanese-style savory pies topped with spinach, cheese, or meat makes a fine appetizer, as do the traditional tabbouleh and the stuffed grape leaves. The regular menu features about six salads, including fattoush, falafel, tuna salad Nicoise, and chicken salad served atop seasonal fruits. Among the

made-to-order sandwiches are chicken or beef/ lamb gyros, served in a warm pita with lettuce, tomato, and cool, creamy yogurt-cucumber sauce; a falafel pocket; and a Mediterranean grilled vegetable wrap. Those with heartier appetites will be pleased with the beef, chicken, or lamb kebab plates that are served with basmati rice or roasted potatoes, Greek salad, and freshly baked pita. Pistachio baklava, cheesecake, and tiramisu are a few of the tempting ways to end a meal here. Kalamata's sells hummus, tabbouleh, stuffed grape leaves, and a variety of salads by the pound. Open daily for lunch and dinner.

PIZZA

DAVINCI'S GOURMET PIZZA $–$$
1812 Hayes Street
(615) 329-8098
www.davincisgourmetpizza.com
DaVinci's is a great gourmet pizza place located in an old renovated house on Hayes Street. There are many pizzas to choose from here. The "DaVinci" has tomato sauce, mozzarella and provolone cheeses, Italian sausage, roasted red peppers, and onions. There is also a blue cheese and spinach pizza, and shrimp and scallop, barbecue, Southwestern, and oysters Rockefeller varieties, among others. Fresh homemade pesto sauce can be substituted for the red pizza sauce. Select your own favorite toppings to create a custom pizza if you like. The vast selection of toppings includes black olives, red cabbage, capers, roasted chicken, smoked oysters, and artichoke hearts. Domestic and imported beers are available, and for dessert, there's Snickers pie. DaVinci's is open Wednesday through Friday for lunch and nightly for dinner.

HOUSE OF PIZZA $
15 Arcade
(615) 242-7144
House of Pizza has been satisfying downtown workers' pizza cravings for two decades. Located in the historic Arcade mall (see our Shopping chapter), between Fourth and Fifth Avenues and Union and Church Streets downtown, the New York–style pizzeria serves pizza by the slice or by the pie. Don't expect to find any goat cheese, sun-dried tomatoes, or other gourmet ingredients; most of the pizza sold here is of the cheese-and-pepperoni variety, though you do have a choice of crusts. Also on the menu are lasagna, spaghetti, calzones, stromboli, salads, and sub sandwiches. The restaurant seats about 50 to 60. House of Pizza is open Monday through Saturday. They close at 6:00 p.m. Monday through Friday and at 4:30 p.m. on Saturday.

PIZZA PERFECT $
4002 Granny White Pike
(615) 297-0345

1602 21st Avenue S.
(615) 329-2757

3571 Clofton Drive
(615) 646-7877
http://pizzaperfect21st.ypguides.net/
The appropriately named Pizza Perfect has been a favorite for years. Iranian Raouf Mattin opened the Granny White location in 1984 and found a devoted following; it's especially popular with students from Vanderbilt, Belmont, and David Lipscomb. Mattin's former partners, Amir and Ali Arab, own the 21st Avenue store (right in the heart of Vanderbilt) and in 1997 opened the Bellevue location in the small strip shopping center off Old Harding Pike on Clofton. Pizza Perfect makes delicious pizzas with all sorts of yummy toppings. Pizza Perfect also has calzones, sub sandwiches, spaghetti, manicotti, lasagna, and salads. The restaurants are closed Sunday.

PUB FOOD

BIG RIVER GRILLE & BREWING WORKS $$
111 Broadway
(615) 251-4677
www.bigrivergrille.com
This microbrewery and restaurant offers half a dozen ales, along with such pub fare as homemade sausages, California-style pizzas, pulled pork barbecue, grilled chicken, pasta, and sandwiches. There's also a bar and pool room.

BLACKSTONE RESTAURANT & BREWERY $$–$$$
1918 West End Avenue
(615) 327-9969
www.blackstonebrewery.com

The fish-and-chips, artichoke chicken pasta, trout, and filet mignon are favorites at this comfortable West End restaurant/brewery, which is a popular lunch spot for Music Row, West End, and downtown workers. Blackstone brews six ales at its on-site brewery, including the award-winning St. Charles Porter. The restaurant is open daily for lunch and dinner.

BOSCO'S NASHVILLE BREWING CO. $–$$
1805 21st Avenue S.
(615) 385-0050
www.boscosbeer.com

This lively and spacious Hillsboro Village brewpub is a favorite among beer connoisseurs. Appetizers like crawfish cakes and smoked duck spring rolls are nice to munch on with one of Bosco's award-winning handcrafted brews. The individual-size wood-fired oven pizzas are a specialty; there's bound to be one that suits your taste—perhaps the "Germantown Purist," topped with barbecued chicken and red onions, or maybe the "Chesapeake," with pesto, shrimp, and scallops? Bosco's also has a lengthy list of sandwiches, including an oyster po'boy, a Reuben, and a sirloin burger. For heartier appetites, entrees like red snapper étouffée or smoked double cut pork chop, served with appropriate side dishes, fit the bill. Don't miss the $6 weekly lunch specials.

BREWHOUSE WEST $
7108 Charlotte Pike
(615) 356-5005

Located on the west side of Nashville, Brewhouse West carries on the tradition of a roadhouse with cold beer and hot food. The Cajun-themed menu features spicy foods like chipotle chicken wings, Cuban-Jamaican–style mojo-crusted jerk chicken, and molasses-jalapeño dipping sauce. The wooden-sided, tin-roofed building once served as a produce stand and later as a barbecue place. Brewhouse West is a popular watering hole for bikers taking a ride down winding River Road. A lively place, it has seating indoors and out, along with a three-songs-for-a-dollar jukebox boasting classic tunes. An old horseshoe pit was covered to make room for a stage for live music and a circular bar. Brewhouse carries bunches of beer—more than two dozen on tap and about 100 in bottles. It's the kind of place where you visit once as a stranger. When you return, the waiters and servers know your name, as do several of the patrons.

THE CORNER PUB $
4109 Hillsboro Road
(615) 298-9698

This neighborhood bar and restaurant, located across the street from the famed Bluebird Cafe, draws a variety of locals, from college students to old-timers. There's a casual, relaxed feel here that is worlds removed from Green Hills's trendy moneyed vibe. That alone has given this haunt a stable of regulars who like to hang out at the bar and watch sports on one of four TVs. The Corner Pub serves a variety of beers and ales, plus hot and cold sandwiches, burgers, and the like.

MCCABE PUB $
4410 Murphy Road
(615) 269-9406
www.mccabepub.com

The casual and friendly McCabe Pub is a combination neighborhood pub and sports bar. It's known for great hamburgers, lots of good vegetables (mashed potatoes, green beans, squash casserole, broccoli casserole, sweet potato casserole, and steamed veggies, to name a few), and great desserts (Hershey Syrup cake, blackberry crunch, sour cream coconut cake, and more). The home-cooked plate lunches and dinners, with entrees like fried catfish, pork chops, and meat loaf and your choice of vegetables, satisfy nearby Sylvan Park families, couples, and singles and lure out-of-the-neighborhood regulars as well, including the Music Row set. See our Nightlife chapter for more on the sports-bar scene.

SEAFOOD

NEW ORLEANS MANOR $$$$$
1400 Murfreesboro Road
(615) 367-2777
www.neworleansmanor.com

Landlocked Nashville isn't really known for its seafood restaurants, but New Orleans Manor's all-you-can-eat seafood buffet is a longtime favorite of many locals. You'll feel like you're in the Old South when you step up to the big white columned entrance of the Southern colonial–style mansion. Once inside, you'll be seated in one of several spacious rooms and then directed to the buffet. Bring a big appetite because you're sure to want to sample a little of everything. Appetizers include oysters on the half shell, smoked peppered mackerel, salmon pâté, and creamy seafood chowder. The list of a dozen or more entrees includes Alaskan king crab, fried shrimp, shrimp Creole, baked sea scallops, and poached wild Pacific salmon. Maine lobster can be ordered at the beginning of your meal (for an extra charge). Nonseafood choices include prime rib, spinach lasagna, chicken primavera, and, something you won't find too often around town, fried Asian frog legs. Leave room for the desserts; there's something to suit every sweet tooth: pecan pie, chocolate cake, hot apple crisp, and lemon cheesecake are just a few of the choices. Alcoholic beverages and tip are not included in the buffet price. New Orleans Manor is open for dinner Tuesday through Saturday. Reservations are recommended.

STEAK

FLEMING'S PRIME STEAKHOUSE & WINE BAR $$$$
2525 West End Avenue
(615) 342-0131
www.flemingssteakhouse.com

Fleming's is one of many upscale steakhouse chains that seem to have discovered Nashville. Fleming's distinguishes itself from the competition with its easy yet slightly formal atmosphere. There's not the power-broker intensity of the Palm, nor is it nearly as stuffy as Morton's. One thing Fleming's does have in common with its brethren is noise: The decibel level reaches pretty high during the busy dinner hour, so if it's quiet romance you want, you're probably out of luck. Still, with food this good, who wants to talk, right? The steaks are all cooked to perfection. Other entree options include Australian lamb chops, veal and pork chops, salmon, tuna, swordfish, and lobster tails. The wine list includes 100 premium wines by the glass. Fleming's is open for dinner nightly. Valet parking is available.

JIMMY KELLY'S $$$
217 Louise Avenue
(615) 329-4349

Steak lovers have plenty of very good new restaurant choices in Nashville, but generations of Nashvillians continue to return to Jimmy Kelly's, a fixture on Nashville's restaurant scene since 1934. The specialty is aged hand-cut steaks, and the corn cakes are legendary. If you're not in the mood for beef, try the veal chops, lamb chops, or fresh fish. Jimmy Kelly's is comfortable, and the service is top-notch. The restaurant is open for dinner Monday through Saturday. Reservations are recommended.

MORTON'S OF CHICAGO $$$$$
618 Church Street
(615) 259-4558
www.mortons.com

Nashville's Morton's is one of the best in this restaurant chain, which is known for its fine dining, quality service, and elegant atmosphere. Real steak connoisseurs know Morton's as an excellent choice. When you walk into this restaurant, you'll feel as if you've entered an elegant private club. Dark woods, comfortable leather booths, white tablecloths, dim lights, and warm brick set the tone. Morton's is known for its tableside presentation as well as for its huge cuts of prime, aged, grain-fed beef. The waitstaff wheels out carts of uncooked vegetables and entrees for viewing. The food is prepared in an open kitchen, in full view of the patrons. There is also a good selection of fresh seafood and chicken. Morton's has a comfortable bar and a group dining room. It's open nightly for dinner; reservations are recommended.

NICK & RUDY'S $$$$

204 21st Avenue S.

(615) 329-8994

www.nickandrudys.com

Nick & Rudy's entered the Nashville steak house wars in August 2000. One of the few homegrown high-class steak places in town, this one is known for its oysters Rockefeller and oysters on the half shell. This is comfort food for the high-finance set: baked Brie and crab cakes for appetizers; Caesar salads, French onion soup, or lobster bisque for starters. If you have any room after that, go for one of the thick-cut New York strip steaks or a juicy center-cut pork loin. There are a few fish and chicken entrees for those not in the mood for beef. Menu selections change a couple of times per year. The lunch menu offers sandwiches in addition to the New York strip, crab cakes, and lasagna, plus there's a blue-plate special that changes daily. Reservations are recommended. Nick & Rudy's is open for lunch Monday through Friday and for dinner Monday through Saturday.

THE PALM $$$$$

140 Fifth Avenue S.

(615) 742-7256

www.thepalm.com

The Nashville edition of this upscale chain, located across the street from the Gaylord Entertainment Center, opened in 2000 amid much star-studded fanfare. Since then it has hosted such entertainment luminaries as Robert Redford, James Gandolfini, Tim McGraw, and Faith Hill. Top-tier politicos and industry titans—as well as Titans of the NFL variety—are also regulars. The Palm is famous for the cartoons of celebrities that decorate its walls, but it has also quickly earned a reputation as the best restaurant in town. Thick, juicy steaks are the main reason to come; get one with a side of the Palm's signature "half and half," crispy-fried onions and potatoes. A premium wine selection and rich dessert menu ensure that customers walk away satisfied. The Palm is open for lunch and dinner on weekdays and dinner only on weekends. Reservations are recommended for dinner.

i The tabletops and bar at Sperry's in Belle Meade were built on-site from *Liberty* ship hatch covers used in World War II. The bar top is handcarved from this wood. The unique finish was achieved by repeated applications of an epoxy resin, then rubbed to a mirror shine.

RUTH'S CHRIS STEAKHOUSE $$$$$

2100 West End Avenue

(615) 320-0163

www.ruthschris.com

When it comes to steaks, Ruth's Chris Steakhouse, a Louisiana-based chain with about 70 restaurants, is a favorite for special occasions and business dinners. The restaurant is known for excellent beef and live Maine lobsters that are flown in daily. There are chicken and fish choices, too. The ambience is elegant all around—dimly lit, lots of dark wood, dark burgundy chairs, a brass rail bar. The clientele is equally upscale—lots of business owners and business travelers. Ruth's Chris is open nightly for dinner. Reservations are recommended.

SPERRY'S $$$$

5109 Harding Road

(615) 353-0809

www.sperrys.com

This is a neighborhood restaurant, Belle Meade–style. Doctors, lawyers, judges, and well-dressed couples have been dining at Sperry's since 1974. Owned by the Thomas family for more than 25 years, Sperry's is a comfortably upscale restaurant with good food and good service. Deep red carpets and wood tables contribute to the warm and cozy atmosphere. Sperry's is known for its steaks and seafood. Fresh swordfish and tuna, a blue cheese–stuffed fillet, and rack of lamb Dijon are always in demand. There are daily specials. Desserts like bananas Foster and Death by Chocolate cake satisfy tastes beyond the 37205 zip code. Sperry's is open every night for dinner.

NIGHTLIFE

ashville's nightlife, the city has plenty of other options for nighttime fun. In fact, there are probably more after-dark diversions and destinations than you ever imagined. You can dance the night away at a techno or country dance club, catch a game with the gang at the neighborhood sports bar, contemplate a poem during a coffeehouse poetry reading, watch a movie at a unique theater or drive-in, or relax with friends in a cozy pub or bistro. We've compiled a list of some of the places you can go for a night on the town. The nightlife scene is ever-changing, with new venues coming and going regularly, so we recommend that you check out the *Nashville Scene* or *Rage* for an up-to-the-minute rundown of clubs, bars, and restaurants.

Three things to remember:
• If you're going to drink, do it in moderation.
• The drinking age is 21.
• A designated driver is a good thing—if you don't have one, don't drink.

In this chapter you'll find descriptions of some of the best-known nightspots as well as some of the newer locations. If you don't find what you're looking for here, check out our Music City and Restaurants chapters. Unless otherwise noted, the following nightspots do not require a cover charge.

BARS AND PUBS

BAR TWENTY3
503 12th Avenue S.
(615) 963-9998
www.bartwenty3.com
This upscale lounge in "the Gulch District" of 12th Avenue S. is one of Nashville's hottest nightspots. The two-story bar is sleek and minimally furnished with white leather sofas and frosted glass. A DJ spins tunes nightly—there are no live bands—and the bar serves gourmet appetizer-type fare such as mini beef Wellingtons. Bar Twenty3—named for its location at the fork of 11th and 12th Avenues—is open Tuesday through Saturday.

THE BEER SELLAR
107 Church Street
(615) 254-9464
www.beersellar.net/nashville
This casual beer and cigar bar has a huge selection of—you guessed it—beer: 50 draft beers and about 150 bottled brands, including many imports. They pour a lot of flavored brews, too, including cider, vanilla, and cherry. The 175-capacity room is frequented by an eclectic bunch, including college students and the over-60 crowd. The 3:00 to 7:00 p.m. happy hour, featuring pints, brings the after-work crowd. Some come just for the tasty sandwiches or to watch a game on one of the four TVs. Darts, a pool table, and foosball also provide amusement. There's live entertainment every Thursday, and drinks are two-for-one. As for cigars, the Beer Sellar has a variety, and you can buy and smoke them here.

THE BOUND'RY
911 20th Avenue S.
(615) 321-3043
www.pansouth.net
Just a few blocks from Music Row, the Bound'ry's bar is a popular gathering place, usually crowded with the young and single. A cozy yet lively atmosphere, well-made cocktails, and an extensive selection of beer and wine make this a good

place to gather before dinner or for a night on the town. The Bound'ry is also a good place for dinner. Weekends are especially busy. When the weather's nice, you can sit outside.

 Holly Dunn wrote her hit song "Daddy's Hands" as a Father's Day present.

THE CORNER PUB
4109 Hillsboro Road
(615) 298-9698

This sports bar–music club–restaurant, across Hillsboro Road from the Bluebird Cafe, draws everyone from college kids to local suburbanites to old-timers who still lament the loss of the old Joe's Village Tavern that used to sit across the street. Live music is offered Monday, Tuesday, Wednesday, and most Saturdays, with an eclectic array of local bands, from bluegrass to rock. When there's no music on the calendar, this friendly neighborhood hangout is a favorite with the bar crowd. It's a casual, low-key kind of place—the perfect gathering spot for groups of friends. Or belly up to the bar yourself and watch the baseball game—you'll never feel out of place. The food menu features hot and cold sandwiches, burgers, and appetizers like hot wings, all very tasty and satisfying.

FLYING SAUCER DRAUGHT EMPORIUM
111 10th Avenue S.
(615) 259-PINT
www.beerknurd.com

Nashville's Flying Saucer, located behind the Union Station Hotel, is a good choice for beer connoisseurs. If your beer experiences have been limited to the occasional can of Budweiser, or a Corona when you're feeling adventurous, Flying Saucer will wow you with its selection of more than 200 brews from around the globe, dozens of which are on tap. Check the blackboard for the new arrivals. The spacious establishment offers samplers, featuring a selection of five-ounce servings. The black and gold plates on the wall

are tributes to patrons who have tried every beer on the menu at least once. Even if you don't like beer, you can enjoy the casual ambience, tasty bar food, and the covered outdoor patio. Flying Saucer is open daily.

GRAVITY
1530 Demonbreun Street
(615) 252-6670

A late-night lounge with plush red couches and low lighting, Gravity is a chic place on the Demonbreun strip. If you want a crowd, go later than 10:30 p.m. If you like it less crowded, go early or during the week. Live entertainment covers most of the bases—bluegrass, comedy, jazz, rock, Top 40, and variety. The hip crowd at Gravity prefers martinis, but the club also features other cocktails, beer, and wine. Dinner and late-night fare include choices from American, Southern, and Mexican cuisine, with an emphasis on tapas. Parking on Demonbreun Street is tough, particularly on the weekends. Try for a space in the fast-food restaurant lot across the street after normal business hours. Open Wednesday through Saturday from 5:00 p.m. to 3:00 a.m.

MCFADDEN'S
134 Second Avenue N.
(615) 256-9140
www.mcfaddensnashville.com

A sprawling modern Irish pub, McFadden's offers a full-service dining room and bar. Folks actually come here to eat because the food is so good. Try the Dublin fish and chips, featuring beer-battered cod and McFadden's tasty shallot-and-dill tartar sauce. For a filling Irish meal, choose the shepherd's pie, a hearty mix of ground meat and vegetables topped and baked with cheddar mashed potatoes. Along with the customary beer, McFadden's offers some intriguing cosmos—the County Cork cosmo, McFadden's McDreamsicle, and the Dirty Irishman. McFadden's has a 100-foot mahogany bar, a dance floor, and a private party room. The bustling nightlife includes live DJs every Wednesday through Saturday.

THE MERCHANTS
401 Broadway
(615) 254-1892
www.merchantsrestaurant.com

The Merchants offers not only a superb dining experience but also a cozy bar that's a great spot to hook up with friends before a night on the town. The first floor includes a horseshoe-shaped bar, tile and hardwood floors, and lots of exposed brick. It comfortably accommodates about 180 people. Booths with windows are an excellent vantage point from which to watch all the action at Fourth and Broadway. The Merchants, which is housed in a renovated turn-of-the-20th-century hotel, is known for its wine selection and attracts an upscale crowd of people in their late 20s to early 50s.

MERCY LOUNGE
1 Cannery Row
(615) 251-3020
www.mercylounge.com

Located in the historic 1860s Cannery building off Eighth Avenue S., Mercy Lounge opened in 2003 and quickly became one of the nighttime hot spots with one of the coolest vibes in town. Hardwood floors, comfy padded couches and chairs, and funky old lamps and tables create a fun and welcoming feel. The spacious bar is also known for presenting top-notch musical talent, leaning toward rock (artists who've played here include Steve Earle, John Hiatt, Rodney Crowell, and Buddy Miller). There's lots of room to wander about: In addition to a music room and a bar area, Mercy Lounge has pool tables in the back room and an outdoor deck.

MULLIGAN'S IRISH PUB & RESTAURANT
117 Second Avenue N.
(615) 242-8010
www.mulliganspubandrestaurant.com

This cozy Dublin-style pub in the heart of The District features live traditional and contemporary Irish folk music as well as American music from the '60s to the present. We've seen it so packed here that you can barely squeeze in. Starting at 5:00 p.m., Mulligan's has a full menu, featuring such favorites as corned beef and fish-and-chips. Mulligan's serves a variety of whiskeys, ales, and domestic and imported beers.

VIRAGO
1811 Division Street
(615) 320-5149

Virago is a favorite among Nashville's fashionably dressed, young, late-night club-hopping crowd. The swanky, high-tech restaurant/bar—complete with a sunken lounge with a huge flat-screen TV and a DJ booth—is known for its fusion cuisine, large sushi rolls, and exotic drinks. Order a martini and step into Virago's dark, submarine-style lounge to mix and mingle with some of Music City's trendiest scenesters who want to see and be seen. A separate dining room with a nice sushi bar is a plus for those who aren't in the mood for the bar scene.

ℹ️ Music venues aren't the only places to hear great live music in Nashville. Most restaurants, bars, pubs, coffeehouses, and sometimes even bookstores and shopping malls present songwriters and bands on a regular basis.

BREWPUBS

BIG RIVER GRILLE & BREWING WORKS
111 Broadway
(615) 251-HOPS
www.bigrivergrille.com

The beer is good, and so is the food at this huge full-service brewpub across the street from the Hard Rock Cafe. Eight to 10 ales are available at all times. Billiard tables provide a little recreation, while patrons in the dining area feast on a variety of pizzas, pastas, and other tasty entrees.

BLACKSTONE RESTAURANT & BREWERY
1918 West End Avenue
(615) 327-9969
www.blackstonebrewery.com

A comfortable, relaxed place to dine and drink,

Blackstone offers six ales, brewed at the on-site brewery. With a variety of reasonably priced lunch and dinner items, it has a busy lunchtime business. It is a convenient spot for Music Row, West End, and downtown workers to stop after work. Take a tour of the brewery if you like.

BOSCO'S NASHVILLE BREWING CO.
1805 21st Avenue S.
(615) 385-0050
www.boscosbeer.com

Delicious food, great beer, and a fun environment make Bosco's a good pick among Nashville's brewpub selection. The original Bosco's opened in Germantown in 1992 and was the first brewpub licensed in the state and one of the first in the Southeast. Bosco's has been at its 21st Avenue S. address in Hillsboro Village since early 1996. The best-selling beer is Bosco's trademark Famous Flaming Stone Beer. Bosco's also has a variety of special, seasonal, and cask-conditioned beers. Visit the Web site to preview the upcoming weekly selections.

DANCE CLUBS

THE BAR CAR
209 10th Avenue S.
(615) 259-4875

A DJ mixes '70s and '80s tunes with new dance favorites for what has become a legendary disco-soul-funk dance party. Pop star Britney Spears, rapper Snoop Dogg, and former Tennessee Titans star Eddie George are a few of the celebrities who've turned up here. The cover charge ranges from about $3 to $6 and goes up after 10:00 p.m.

GRAHAM CENTRAL STATION
128 Second Avenue N.
(615) 251-9593
www.grahamcentralstationnashville.com

Graham Central Station offers multiple clubs under one roof. Each club has a different theme and atmosphere. Bell Bottoms, for example, has a lighted dance floor, boogie cages, and a DJ playing disco hits from the '70s, '80s, and '90s, and Party on the Roof is an open-air rooftop bar overlooking the Cumberland. There is also a karaoke bar, a lounge area with music videos and exotic drinks, a Top 40 dance club, and a South Beach–themed live music club featuring some of Nashville's local talent. The cover charge ranges from $5 to $12, depending on the day of the week.

Martina McBride sold T-shirts for Garth Brooks one year; the next year she was the opening act on his tour.

THE WILDHORSE SALOON
120 Second Avenue N.
(615) 902-8200
www.wildhorsesaloon.com

Wildhorse Saloon is a combination dance club, restaurant, TV studio, tourist attraction, and concert venue. Its location in the heart of the District makes it a popular place for tourists and locals. The multilevel nightspot has a 3,300-square-foot dance floor and state-of-the art sound, lighting, and video systems. The Wildhorse features live music Tuesday through Saturday, beginning at 7:15 p.m. A rotating schedule of house bands brings in some good regional touring groups, some of which—including Lonestar—have gone on to the big time. Concerts by name country acts are scheduled monthly; tickets usually cost $15 to $20. The cover charge ranges from $5 to $8, depending on the day of the week. The cover usually begins at 7:00 p.m.; on nights when concerts or special events are scheduled, the cover begins at 5:00 p.m. The Wildhorse is open daily 11:00 a.m. to 3:00 a.m. The Wildhorse also serves lunch and dinner. The specialty is barbecue, but they also serve a variety of salads, sandwiches, pastas, and steaks.

DINNER THEATER/COMEDY CLUBS

CHAFFIN'S BARN DINNER THEATRE
8204 Highway 100
(615) 646-9977, (800) 282-BARN
www.dinnertheatre.com
Established in 1967, Chaffin's Barn is Nashville's oldest professional theater. Feast on the all-you-can-eat buffet topped off by the house specialty, Southern-style bread pudding, then enjoy a play. Chaffin's presents a variety of productions, including comedies, musicals, and mysteries (see the Arts chapter). The MainStage Theatre seats about 250; its stage descends from the ceiling. The Back-Stage Theatre seats 60. Shows are presented in the round, so every seat has a good view. Tuesday through Saturday, doors open at 6:00 p.m., and the buffet is open until 7:30. The actors and actresses serve as the waitstaff. The show starts at 8:00. There is one Sunday matinee per production. Reservations are required and weekends usually sell out, so call early if you want to attend on a Friday or Saturday. "Dressy casual" is the dress code. Chaffin's is open year-round except major holidays and the first two weeks of January. Tickets are $55 for adults and $25 for children 12 and under.

ZANIES COMEDY SHOWPLACE
2025 Eighth Avenue S.
(615) 269-0221
www.zanies.com
Zanies presents nationally known comedians as well as up-and-coming talent. Past performers include Jay Leno, Jerry Seinfeld, and Jeff Foxworthy. Photographs of funny people who have appeared at the club line the walls at the entrance. The place is packed when the bigger names appear, so you'll want to get your tickets early and show up early to get a good seat. Tickets usually range from $20 to $40, although special shows cost more. Zanies is open Wednesday through Sunday. Shows begin at 7:00 or 8:00 p.m. Second, and sometimes third, shows are presented Friday and Saturday. Zanies serves snacks and light meals and has a full bar. You must be 18 or older to enter.

First Friday

One of the most popular nighttime events in Nashville is the nationally recognized First Friday, a well-organized dance party/networking event geared for African-American professionals. Held on the first Friday of the month, the parties draw as many as 500 people. The event is held at a different venue each month. Gibson Bluegrass Showcase, Greer Stadium, and the Factory at Franklin shopping mall are just a few of the venues that have hosted the event in the past. First Fridays usually have a theme—Mardi Gras, Leather Night, and Hawaiian Luau, for example—and there is a dress code (no jeans). For more information about First Friday, visit the Web site www.firstfridaynashville.com or call (615) 485-9734.

COFFEEHOUSES

BONGO JAVA
2007 Belmont Boulevard
(615) 385-5282
www.bongojava.com
This was the home of the Nun Bun, the miracle bun with the face of the late Mother Teresa baked right in. In case you don't know the story, in October 1996 hungry Bongo Java worker Ryan Finney picked out a cinnamon bun to munch on. Before he took a bite, he paused. "It looked kind of weird," Finney recalls. "I turned it around and thought, 'Oh my God.'" Staring back at him was a doughy rendition of Mother Teresa's face. A wave of worldwide attention followed. The Nun Bun was featured on TV and in newspapers everywhere. People came to Bongo Java in droves to see the preserved bun, and the coffeehouse sold

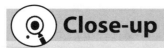 **Close-up**

Nashville and the Bottle: A Continuing Saga

Nashville, a town often associated with cry-in-your-beer songs, has long had a love–hate relationship with "the bottle." Decades before Merle Haggard bemoaned the fact that tonight the bottle let him down, locals had waged battle—literally shedding blood in one infamous landmark case—over alcohol sales.

Travelers during the last quarter of the 19th century knew Nashville as a wild, swinging, "anything-goes" kind of place. Downtown was home to a number of upscale saloons and gambling establishments, including the popular Southern Turf and, at one time, as many as three tracks for horse racing, which is now illegal in Tennessee.

During these years, naturally, many religious leaders and others objected to the drinking, gambling, and carrying on that transpired in the riverfront district. In 1885 steamboat captain Thomas Ryman was persuaded to close the bars and gambling dens on his boats after hearing the exhortations of traveling evangelist Sam Jones. Ryman was so moved by the spirit—and away from the spirits—in fact, that he donated money for a tabernacle. (This building, which now bears the captain's name, later became the home of the *Grand Ole Opry* and is now a popular auditorium for a variety of musical performances. During most shows,

ironically, alcoholic drinks are sold in the lobby.)

Anti-alcohol sentiment picked up during the early 1900s, and one of the most vocal prohibitionists was Edward Ward "Ned" Carmack, editor of the *Tennessean* newspaper. On November 9, 1908, Carmack was shot to death downtown by Duncan B. Cooper and his son, Robin, who objected to the editor's often strident stance. The two were convicted and sentenced to 20 years in prison, but Governor Malcolm Patterson, a friend of the Coopers, pardoned them. The resulting furor helped prompt the passage of a statewide prohibition law that took effect in July 1909. Despite the law, enforcement was often lax, due in part to corruption by local and state officials who disagreed with the ban.

Prohibition remained a controversial political issue throughout the next decade, and one mayor, Hilary E. Howse, was forced to resign from office in 1916 because of his failure to enforce it. He later was reelected.

One side effect of Prohibition was the birth of the downtown area known as Printers Alley. The alley gradually became a hot spot for speakeasies where illegal alcohol was sold. Prohibition in Tennessee, as nationwide, ended with the 1933 passage of the 21st Amendment.

Nun Bun T-shirts and other items before receiving a letter from Mother Teresa asking them to stop the merchandise and promotion. In mid-1997 the bun appeared in a cross-country video produced by Bongo Java friends and was returned. The bun was later stolen in December 2005.

Other than the Nun Bun, coffee and atmosphere are Bongo Java's claims to fame. The coffeehouse opened in a big old house in the early '90s, right in the heart of the Belmont University area. Open until 11:00 p.m. daily, it's a regular hangout for college students and party types and also draws some college professors and regulars

from the neighborhood. When the weather's nice, the front patio is a good spot to hang out; if you want more privacy, the rooms inside the house are comfortable. Upstairs, the Bongo Java After Hours Theatre (615-385-1188) offers a variety of regularly scheduled entertainment, including plays, films, dance, and live music. It's open to all ages. The admission price depends on the show; it's usually $5 to $15. After 7:00 p.m. patrons under 18 must be accompanied by an adult. Bongo Java operates several coffeehouses around town, including Fido (see next entry).

CAFÉ FIDO AND BONGO JAVA ROASTING COMPANY
1812 21st Avenue S.
(615) 777-FIDO
www.bongojava.com

A great place to linger over a latte, Fido, as this coffeehouse is known, opened in October 1996 in the building previously occupied by Jones Pet Store. Located in Hillsboro Village, right next to Vanderbilt University, Fido draws a big college crowd as well as a lot of Green Hills residents, creative artist types, and 40-and-older coffee lovers. Fido's spacious, quiet, and dimly lit room makes for a relaxing environment where everyone seems to feel comfortable. There's plenty of freshly roasted coffee, plus tea, chilled drinks, fresh pastries, and a breakfast, lunch, and dinner menu and brunch on Saturday and Sunday. Fido is open daily until 11:00 p.m. (until midnight on Friday and Saturday).

KIJIJI COFFEEHOUSE & DELI
1207 Jefferson Street
(615) 321-0403
www.kijijicoffee.com

Black-and-white posters of Ella Fitzgerald, Nat King Cole, Billie Holiday, Miles Davis, Louis Armstrong, and other music greats line the walls of this quiet, jazzy coffeehouse, located at the corner of 12th Avenue N. and Jefferson Street, a couple of blocks from Fisk University. Kijiji—the word means "village" in Swahili—is popular with students and university staff, urban professionals, and others in the area. In addition to a variety of domestic and imported coffees as well as teas and smoothies, the menu includes tasty homemade desserts, such as Italian cream cake, red velvet cake, carrot cake, and brownies. Sandwiches, including roast beef and corned beef, are made with freshly baked bread. Kijiji has live jazz music Monday from noon to 2:00 p.m. and on Friday evenings. Friday night is also open-mic poetry night.

> **i** At age 5, *Grand Ole Opry* star Ricky Skaggs hopped on the Opry stage to play Bill Monroe's mandolin.

SPORTS BARS

SAM'S SPORTS BAR & GRILL
1803 21st Avenue S.
(615) 383-3601

Since opening in 2001, Sam's has developed a reputation as one of Nashville's most popular sports bars. Its Hillsboro Village location means it's usually packed with college students as well as young professionals who live or work in the area. Sam's popular two-for-one happy hour runs from 3:00 to 7:00 p.m. weekdays and all day on Tuesday. About two dozen TVs, including a couple of big screens, make it easy to keep up with the game of your choice. Other amusements include video golf games, dartboards, and, on Friday nights, karaoke. The food here is a notch above what you'll find at many sports bars. Everything is freshly made. In addition to a large variety of pizzas, Sam's serves ribs and oven-baked subs, plus the usual wings and chicken fingers. Sam's is open daily for lunch (daily lunch specials are $5.95) and dinner.

SPORTSMAN'S GRILLE
5405 Harding Road
(615) 356-6206

1601 21st Avenue S.
(615) 320-1633

1640 Westgate Circle, Brentwood
(615) 373-1070
http://sportsmangrille.com

Although you can categorize Sportsman's Grille as a sports bar, most people we know go for the food. The original location on Harding Road is a longtime favorite. The dark, comfortable, family-oriented neighborhood hangout is on the edge of Belle Meade, right next to the U.S. Highway 70–Highway 100 split. If you're so inclined, order up a frosty fishbowl glass of Gerst beer before feasting on your choice of catfish, burgers, steak, sandwiches, salads, and pasta. We especially like the red beans and rice and the chicken Parmesan. If you are a sports fan, you can keep up with the action, since sports are always in the background on several TVs positioned around the room. The other two Sportsman's locations offer basically the same menu but have different nightly specials. Sportsman's Grille in the Village, at 21st Avenue S., is near Vandy. The newer Brentwood location, Sportsman's Lodge, is in the Cool Springs area, just off Interstate 65.

MOVIE THEATERS

Nashville isn't lacking in movie theaters. Large multiplexes can be found in every part of town. There are a few theaters, however, that are worth pointing out because of their quality programming, good value, or both.

BELCOURT THEATRE
2102 Belcourt Avenue
(615) 383-9140
www.belcourt.org
The historic Belcourt, located in trendy Hillsboro Village, features movies (focusing on independent, foreign, and reissue films) as well as live music and live theater productions. The nonprofit venue has a full bar and also sells coffee, tea, candy, and popcorn. For more about the theater, see the Arts chapter.

BROADWAY DRIVE-IN THEATRE
3020 US 70 E., Dickson
(615) 446-2786
Those who are old enough to remember going to movies at the local drive-in will get a nostalgic kick from Dickson's Broadway Drive-In, located about 50 miles west of downtown Nashville, near Montgomery Bell State Park. Those who aren't familiar with the drive-in thing can get a blast from the past here. Roll down the windows, tune your radio to the broadcast, and hang your feet out the window if you like. The Broadway—family-owned and -operated since 1950—is

open spring through fall. The theater shows new movies, including many especially kid-friendly flicks. Movies are shown Friday through Sunday and begin at dusk. Get here early enough to make a run to the concession stand (you'll probably have to wait in line) before the movie starts. There's no extra charge for the country air, twinkling stars, and sounds of crickets.

FRANKLIN CINEMA
419 Main Street, Franklin
(615) 790-7122
www.franklincinema.com
At this theater, you can have dinner and a movie at the same time. Kick back in a comfy chair or sofa, and enjoy beer, pizza, and other fun food while you watch a movie. The theater, just 2 blocks off Franklin's historic town square, has two screens. Tickets here can be a bargain. Tickets for movies starting at 6:00 p.m. or earlier are $6; after 6:00 tickets are $8.

REGAL GREEN HILLS 16
3815 Green Hills Village Drive,
at the Mall at Green Hills
(615) 269-5772 (movie information),
(615) 269-5910 (office)
www.regalcinemas.com
Located next to the Green Hills Mall and surrounded by all sorts of restaurants, Regal Green Hills 16 makes doing dinner and a movie (and maybe just a little shopping) supereasy. This theater shows all the latest as well as foreign and independent films. Each spring the Nashville Independent Film Festival (see our Arts chapter) screens its selections here. You can order tickets for Regal theaters in advance by phone, (800) FANDANGO, or at www.fandango.com.

i The AAA Midwest Auto Club listed Nashville second in 2006 in the top 100 destinations in the country, ahead of cities like Las Vegas, Phoenix, New Orleans, and Atlanta.

REGAL IMAX THEATRE
570 Opry Mills Drive, at Opry Mills
(615) 514-IMAX (movie information),
(615) 514-4633 (office)
www.regalcinemas.com
www.imax.com/theatres/usa.html
After oohing and ahhing over IMAX films in
Chattanooga, St. Louis, and Huntsville, Alabama,
we're happy that Nashville now has its own IMAX
theater. You can get completely immersed in
these realistic movies, especially the 3-D variety.
The screen is seven stories tall and 95 feet wide.
The theater screens two different movies on an
alternating schedule several times per day. Ticket
pricing varies depending upon feature. This theater is adjacent to a Regal 20-screen cinema.

SARRATT CINEMA
24th Avenue S. and Vanderbilt Place
(615) 343-6666 (film hot line),
(615) 322-2425
www.vanderbilt.edu/sarratt
Vanderbilt University's Sarratt Cinema may offer
the best movie value in town. It shows mostly a
selection of classics, recent hits, and documenta-
ries for $4, or $3 for Vandy students. The theater
is in the Sarratt Student Center, a couple of blocks
off West End Avenue. The operating hours vary,
so call or visit the Web site for the most up-to-
date schedule. The Sarratt is operated during the
school year only; closed summer months. (Read
more about Sarratt in our Arts chapter.)

MUSIC CITY

They don't call it Music City for nothing. Nashville is truly the place to be if you are a lover of music, whatever the style. Whether you're an aspiring singer or songwriter, an aficionado of live music in intimate settings, a student of country music history, or a starstruck fan eager to discover more about the lifestyle of your favorite artist, you can find plenty in Nashville to meet your desires. By the way, for insight into Nashville's development as a music capital, check out our History chapter. If you're a tourist in Nashville, you've probably been keeping your eyes peeled for a glimpse of a country music star as you stroll down Music Row. You might spot someone ducking into a studio or driving by, but you're probably more likely to bump into your favorite star in an ordinary place like the post office, the mall, or the grocery store. Running into a music star is just about an everyday occurrence here in Music City. We've rubbed elbows with Lorrie Morgan at a Green Hills cosmetics counter, bumped into Steve Earle at the Acklen Station post office, spotted Steven Curtis Chapman at the Nippers Corner movie theater, mingled with visiting rockers R.E.M. on Elliston Place, shopped for greeting cards next to members of Petra at CoolSprings mall, sat next to Emmylou Harris at the Bluebird Cafe … you get the picture. In this chapter you'll find a plethora of attractions, venues, and services related to popular music. If your tastes tend toward more highbrow entertainment like opera and classical music, check out our Arts chapter. Or if you're into dancing to discs spun by DJs, you'll find establishments offering that kind of entertainment in the Nightlife chapter.

OVERVIEW

The main sections of this chapter are as follows:

- **Attractions.** Country music–related museums include general-interest sites, like the Country Music Hall of Fame & Museum and the Grand Ole Opry Museum; a shrine or two tailored to particular artists; and even a wax museum where you can see (almost) lifelike reproductions of the stars. Tour companies offer packages that will take you to various Nashville attractions and, in some cases, past the current or former homes of an assortment of stars.
- **Record stores.** Yes, we still prefer to call them record stores, even though most of them now deal instead in CDs. But there are actually places in Nashville where you can still find vinyl, especially vintage vinyl.
- **Live music.** Here you'll find a world of choices covering practically every musical style you can think of. You'll find venues large and small, including ones specializing in performances by songwriters—and opportunities for you to perform, if that's one of your dreams.
- **Annual events.** It seems that some kind of yearly festival, concert series, jubilee, or other musical event is always going on here, celebrating Nashville's musical heritage, its thriving present, and its promising future.

In addition, this chapter contains a number of Close-ups.

Of course, as we've said elsewhere in this book—and as we'll continue to emphasize—one of the aspects that many newcomers find surprising about Music City is the sheer diversity of its output. While country music remains by far the most visible (or should we say audible?) style, you can find an eclectic selection that includes about any kind of music you might possibly want to hear. This really isn't a new development, as a quick study of the recording industry will attest.

Nashville actually had a thriving rhythm-and-blues scene well before the city became known as the country music capital of the world. From the early days of the city's recording industry on up to today, a stunning array of noncountry artists—including Burl Ives, Ray Charles, Bob Dylan, James Brown, R.E.M., Leontyne Price, Neil Young, REO Speedwagon, Johnny Winter, Carol Channing, Paul McCartney, Elvis Costello, the Allman Brothers, B. B. King, Dave Brubeck, Joe Cocker, Dean Martin, and Yo La Tengo—have recorded albums here. While many of these artists have drawn upon country influences on their Nashville records, others have not, simply recognizing the wealth of talent and facilities available here.

Today Nashville is home to a growing number of veteran rock 'n' rollers, like Steve Cropper of Booker T and the MGs and Blues Brothers fame, Michael McDonald, Steve Winwood, and Steppenwolf's John Kay. John Fogerty and Peter Frampton have also lived here. Elvis Costello, Kid Rock, Mark Knopfler, and Sheryl Crow are frequent visitors. More and more people, perhaps, are realizing that, regardless of category, good music is good music, and music is an international language Nashville speaks fluently.

Price Code

Use the following as a guide to the cost of an adult admission to an attraction. Keep in mind that children's admission prices are generally lower (usually about half the cost of adult admission), and very young children are admitted free to most attractions. Discounts for senior citizens, students, and groups are usually available.

$	$1 to $5
$$	$6 to $10
$$$	$11 to $15
$$$$	$16 and more

ATTRACTIONS

BARBERSHOP HARMONY SOCIETY   **FREE**
110 Seventh Avenue North
(615) 823-3993, (800) 876-SING
www.barbershop.org

In September 2007 the Barbershop Harmony Society moved to Nashville from Kenosha, Wisconsin, into a newly renovated 36,000-square-foot building. Founded in 1938, the Society preserves and promotes barbershop quartet singing. Barbership quartets began in America at the turn of the 20th century, and today the Society has 30,000 members and about 2,000 quartets. It has more than 820 chapters in the United States and Canada, with an increasing number in other countries. The new location houses the Society's headquarters staff, Harmony Marketplace retail gift shop, and merchandising operations. It is also the home of the Old Songs Library, the world's largest privately held collection of sheet music, containing 750,000 sheets and 125,000 titles from the heyday of Tin Pan Alley. The building also houses the Heritage Hall Museum of Barbershop Harmony, which will serve as a repository for barbershop memorabilia, early recordings, costumes, research materials, and historical documents tracing the roots of the barbershop style.

**COUNTRY MUSIC HALL OF FAME &
MUSEUM**   **$$$$**
222 Fifth Avenue S.
(615) 416-2001, (800) 852-6437
www.countrymusichalloffame.com
Located at Fifth Avenue S. and Demonbreun Street, Nashville's $37-million Country Music Hall of Fame & Museum takes up an entire city block and boasts more than 40,000 square feet of exhibit space devoted to the history of country music. The attraction opened the doors at its current facility in May 2001. The four-story museum has more than twice the gallery space of its former home on Music Row, where it had been located since 1967. The Hall of Fame & Museum is made up of three distinct spaces: the conservatory, a large, open space that serves as an introduction to the facility; the museum, which chronicles the history of country music; and the Hall of Fame, which honors the performers.

As you walk through the museum, you'll view music memorabilia, hear clips of country recordings past and present, and learn about the music

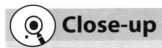

Close-up

Structurally Sound

Look closely at the photo to the right.

Notice anything *musical* about the building?

Of course, you may recognize the eye-catching structure as the new home of the Country Music Hall of Fame & Museum. But there's more to it than that. It's no accident that the dark, narrow windows on the sweeping facade resemble piano keys (some might see them as prison windows). That's just one of many elements that the Hall of Fame's designers incorporated into the modern building as symbols of country music.

Recognizing that country music is an art form whose roots stretch from farms and factories to churches and prisons to country stores and urban bars, the designers, Tuck Hinton Architects, used a variety of materials and included many symbolic representations throughout the attraction. Some symbols, like the windows, are obvious. Others are more subtle. Seen from above, the 130,000-square-foot building's curved facade and drum-shaped segment resemble a bass clef, while the front wall's slanted end is a nod to late-1950s Cadillac tail fins.

A not-so-obvious symbol is the hall's riveted steel structure and Mississippi yellow pine flooring in the conservatory, which allude to early-20th-century bridges and factories. Suggesting an Appalachian stream, or perhaps the flow of artistic inspiration from the Hall of Fame's legendary members, water from a fountain cascades alongside a long staircase; at the bottom, the stream ends in a "wishing well" pool in the spacious conservatory, a space designed to symbolize the "front-porch" origins of country music.

There are several other symbols, but perhaps the most apparent architectural expression of country music is the building's Hall of Fame drum or rotunda, which acknowledges the beloved anthem "Will the Circle Be Unbroken." Around the exterior circumference of the silolike space are slabs of Crab Orchard stone, designed to represent notes from the famous Carter Family song. Atop the drum is a tower/steeple/chandelier modeled after the WSM-AM 650 radio tower, a tribute to the station's role in the creation of the *Grand Ole Opry* and the popularization of country music worldwide. Inside the rotunda, which has an

and its stars. Exhibits are arranged in a chronological fashion, beginning with the roots of country music and continuing to the present. You could spend hours observing the museum's amazing collection of memorabilia, which includes Mother Maybelle Carter's 1928 Gibson guitar, a rhinestone-studded stage suit worn by Hank Williams, matching duds worn by the Dixie Chicks, and even San Quentin Penitentiary parolee Merle Haggard's letter of pardon from California governor Ronald Reagan. A more recent addition to the collection is a set of costumes worn by Reba McEntire in the Broadway production of *Annie Get Your Gun*. Also on view are copies of every gold and platinum country record.

Soundproof booths positioned throughout the museum allow room for one to four visitors to step inside for a more in-depth experience of a variety of historically significant songs and performances. A 1927 recording of DeFord Bailey, the first African-American star of the *Grand Ole Opry*; Ray Price's 1956 chart-topping smash "Crazy Arms"; and an early video of Johnny Cash performing "Folsom Prison Blues" are just a few examples. There are also smaller walk-up listening stations throughout the museum. After the museum, your final stop will be the round, 4,500-square-foot Hall of Fame, where bronze likenesses of the dozens of Hall of Fame members are on display. American painter Thomas Hart

The Country Music Hall of Fame & Museum is a thoroughly musical building. JACKIE SHECKLER FINCH

almost sacred feel, are additional reminders of the unbroken circle, or continuity, of country music, from its earliest days to the present.

For more on the Country Music Hall of Fame & Museum, see the Attractions section in this chapter.

Benton's last work, *The Sources of Country Music,* is exhibited here as well.

Live entertainment at the museum includes songwriter performances and occasional appearances by name country acts. The museum's state-of-the-art Ford Theater is a 214-seat performance venue featuring a digital film presentation on country music around the world. Also on-site are a gift shop and the SoBro Grill, featuring contemporary Southern cuisine. Two-day tickets, group discounts, and package tours that include a stop at historic RCA Studio B and a narrated driving tour of Music Row are available. The museum is open daily except Thanksgiving, Christmas

Day, and New Year's Day. (For more about the museum, see the Close-up "Structurally Sound.")

GRAND OLE OPRY MUSEUM   FREE
2804 Opryland Drive
(615) 871-OPRY
www.opry.com
Located at the Opry Plaza area surrounding the Grand Ole Opry House, this 12,000-square-foot museum tells the story of the *Grand Ole Opry,* the world's longest-running radio show (see our History chapter). There are exhibits on numerous Opry stars, including Roy Acuff, Garth Brooks, Patsy Cline, Little Jimmy Dickens, George Jones,

Marty Robbins, and Tex Ritter. Computer interactive kiosks allow you to learn more about Opry legends and view historical clips. A 10-by-10-foot video wall features highlights from TV's *Grand Ole Opry Live*. The museum is open daily but closes occasionally without notice, so it's a good idea to call before visiting. The museum is closed during January and February.

i *Grand Ole Opry* stars the Whites— daddy Buck and daughters Sharon and Cheryl—had their first recording session in a motel room using bed mattresses to insulate the walls.

GRUHN GUITARS INC.   FREE
400 Broadway
(615) 256-2033
www.gruhn.com
A must-stop for guitarists or serious music fans, world-famous Gruhn's is Nashville's largest guitar dealer. The store specializes in high-quality new, used, and vintage guitars, banjos, and mandolins, with prices ranging from a few hundred dollars to as much as $150,000. Gruhn's has a strong celebrity clientele, but owner George Gruhn is quick to note that his store has "plenty of things that mere mortals can afford." Instruments range from new Martin and Gibson guitars to pre–World War II Martin and Gibson acoustics and 1950s and 1960s electric guitars. Gruhn opened his first store in 1970 at 111 Fourth Avenue N. From 1976 to about 1993, the store was at 410 Broadway. Today Gruhn's occupies 12,000 square feet on four floors at 400 Broadway. In addition to Gruhn, the store has more than a dozen experienced players on staff, plus eight full-time professionals who work in vintage restoration of the store's products. Gruhn's is open Monday through Saturday.

HATCH SHOW PRINT   FREE
316 Broadway
(615) 256-2805
www.hatchshowprint.com
In business since 1879, Hatch Show Print is one of the oldest letterpress poster print shops in America (see our Attractions chapter for more information). The shop is best known for its posters of early *Grand Ole Opry* stars. Today Hatch is owned and operated by the Country Music Foundation, which operates the Country Music Hall of Fame & Museum (see previous listing). The shop still produces its trademark posters and other designs. Its 14-by-22-inch posters advertising local rock bands and would-be country stars can be seen in window displays around town. Hatch sells samples of its posters in the shop. You can drop by Monday through Saturday.

HISTORIC RCA STUDIO B $$$$
Corner of 17th Avenue S.
and Roy Acuff Place
(615) 416-2096, (800) 852-6437
www.countrymusichalloffame.com
Visitors to the Country Music Hall of Fame & Museum can purchase a $16.00 ticket ($8.95 for children ages 6 to 17) that allows them access to RCA Studio B on Music Row. (A ticket to the Hall of Fame is required.) The legendary facility is Nashville's oldest surviving recording studio. More than 1,000 top 10 hits, including tunes by Elvis Presley, Dolly Parton, Willie Nelson, Waylon Jennings, and the Everly Brothers, were recorded at the studio from 1957 to 1977. Tours are offered daily and depart from the Country Music Hall of Fame & Museum (see Hall of Fame listing in this chapter).

LOUVIN BROTHERS MUSEUM &
JOSH SNYDER'S DOG HOUSE   FREE
2416 Music Valley Drive, Suite 104
(615) 889-8834
This museum is dedicated to the influential 1950s and '60s country music duo the Louvin Brothers ("I Don't Believe You've Met My Baby," "Cash on the Barrelhead," "How's the World Treating You"). *Grand Ole Opry* star Charlie Louvin (his brother Ira was killed in a car crash in 1965) opened this museum in 2004 after relocating his collection of awards, photos, and other memorabilia from a small space in Bell Buckle, Tennessee. The museum is open daily from noon to midnight (closed Sunday and Tuesday). A live music show is free on Saturday.

MUSIC CITY WALK OF FAME   FREE
Nashville's Music Mile
walkoffame@visitmusiccity.com
The Music City Walk of Fame on Nashville's Music Mile is a landmark tribute to those from all genres of music who have made significant contributions to preserving the musical heritage of Nashville and have contributed to the world through song or other industry collaboration. Inductees are announced throughout the year and honored at a special ceremony with a permanent platinum-and-granite, star-and-guitar sidewalk marker. Inductions are held twice a year: in April during GMA week and in November to coincide with the CMA Awards. Eighteen stars have already been honored on the sidewalks of Hall of Fame Park between the Country Music Hall of Fame & Museum and the Hilton Nashville Downtown.

RYMAN AUDITORIUM AND MUSEUM $$
116 Fifth Avenue N.
(615) 889-3060
(ticket and schedule information)
www.ryman.com

A statue of Thomas Ryman stands in front of the Ryman Auditorium. JACKIE SHECKLER FINCH

Home of the *Grand Ole Opry* from 1943 to 1974, the Ryman is probably one of Nashville's most famous historic attractions and, today, is one of the city's most popular concert venues. Exhibits and information on the history of the building and country music are displayed on the main floor. Exhibits include memorabilia and photographs of such Opry stars as Kitty Wells, Hank Snow, and Ernest Tubb. Among the other attractions are interactive videos narrated by Johnny Cash, Vince Gill, and Little Jimmy Dickens, life-size bronze statues of Minnie Pearl and Roy Acuff, and a gift shop with a selection of recordings and souvenir merchandise. You can stop by for a self-guided tour any day of the week, but we recommend checking out the exhibits while attending a concert here. (See our History and Attractions chapters, along with the live-music listings in this chapter, for more on the Ryman.)

TRINITY MUSIC CITY U.S.A.   FREE
1 Music Village Boulevard, Hendersonville
(615) 822-8333
www.tbn.org
In mid-1994 California-based Trinity Broadcasting Network purchased the late Conway Twitty's estate, known as Twitty City, and turned it into Trinity Music City U.S.A. Free tours of the Trinity Music Church Auditorium, WPGD Studio, and Twitty mansion are available at designated times throughout the week. The gardens, gift shop, and Solid Rock Bistro are open daily. The state-of-the-art virtual-reality theater features films shot in the Holy Land. Tickets for the film are required and are available at no charge at the theater. Worship services are held in the auditorium Sunday at 2:00 p.m. The *Praise the Lord* program is usually taped here Tuesday at 7:00 p.m.; doors open at 6:00 p.m., and admission to the taping is free. There is also a recording studio on the property.

WILLIE NELSON AND FRIENDS
SHOWCASE MUSEUM $
2613-A McGavock Pike
(615) 885-1515
www.willienelsongeneralstore.com

This museum and gift shop is right beside the Nashville Palace in Music Valley across from the Opryland hotel. There are lots of exhibits on Willie Nelson, including awards, guitars, clothing, and other personal items. Other displays pay tribute to Patsy Cline, Elvis, and other stars. The gift shop has all sorts of souvenir items, including lots of T-shirts and sports merchandise. The museum is open daily, except Thanksgiving and Christmas, with extended hours during the summer.

Tours
Several companies provide guided tours around Nashville. Depending on the type of tour selected, tickets generally range from about $20 for a short, basic tour to upwards of $70 for a tour that includes dinner on the *General Jackson* showboat. The typical tour, however, costs around $30 and lasts about three hours.

GRAND OLE OPRY TOURS $$$$
2810 Opryland Drive
(615) 883-2211, (615) 889-9490
www.gaylordopryland.com
Grand Ole Opry Tours offers about seven different tours. The most popular is the Grand Ole Nashville tour, which includes admission to the Ryman Auditorium, a trip down historic Second Avenue, a visit to Music Row, a drive by the Parthenon and the governor's mansion, and a look at the homes of several music stars, including Martina McBride, the late Minnie Pearl, the late Hank Williams, and others. Tours depart from the Opryland hotel.

GRAY LINE NASHVILLE $$$$
2416 Music Valley Drive
(615) 883-5555
www.graylinenashville.com
This tour company offers 10 to 12 tours. The most popular is the "Discover Nashville" tour, a sightseeing trip that takes you to the State Capitol, Parthenon, Music Row, and other areas and wraps up with a stop at a Broadway-area honky-tonk. The "Homes of the Stars" tour includes a drive past the former or current homes of Alan Jack-

son, Dolly Parton, Ronnie Dunn and Kix Brooks of Brooks & Dunn, Vince Gill and Amy Grant, Trisha Yearwood, the late Tammy Wynette, and others. Gray Line also offers the $10 Downtown Trolley Tour, a one-hour excursion that departs daily from the corner of Second Avenue and Broadway from 10:00 a.m. to 3:00 p.m.

Most tours depart between 9:00 a.m. and 1:30 p.m. The tour bus can pick you up at a hotel if you call at least an hour ahead, or you can board at the Gray Line office.

NASHTRASH TOURS $$$$
P.O. Box 60324, Nashville 37206
(615) 226-7300, (800) 342-2132
www.nashtrash.com

Combining big hair, gossip, a pink bus, and "fancy cheese hors d'oeuvres," NashTrash Tours offers what is definitely the wackiest tour of Nashville you'll find. This 90-minute musical-comedy excursion, hosted by the Jugg Sisters—Sheri Lynn and Brenda Kay—promises "a hilarious, trashy journey through Music City." In addition to dishing out the dirt on country stars, the Juggs make time for makeup and styling tips, casserole recipes, and souvenir shopping. The sisters refer to their tour as *Hard Copy* meets *Hee Haw*.

They take you to lots of local country music "scandal spots," including the Davidson County Jail, the legendary Tootsies Orchid Lounge, the Ryman Auditorium, Printers Alley, Music Row, and the guitar-shaped pool where Elvis was said to have gone skinny-dipping.

Tours are available Wednesday through Saturday. Special tours for private parties can be arranged. The Juggs's Big Pink Bus departs from the north end of the Farmers' Market on Eighth Avenue N. next to the Bicentennial Mall.

SEGWAY OF NASHVILLE TOURS AND TRANSPORTATION $$$$$
119 Third Avenue S.
(615) 244-0555
www.segwayofnashville.com

Segway of Nashville offers customized tours, as well as team building, commercial rentals, special events, and Segway service. See Nashville up

close and personal on this unique two-wheeled personal transportation device. Riders must be at least 14 years old and minors must be accompanied by a parent or guardian. Riders must sign a liability release, must be able to step on and off the platform and maintain normal balance at all times, must have use of left hand, and must wear comfortable walking-type footwear and dress for the weather. Top weight is 250 pounds. Helmets are required and furnished. Cost is $65 per person for a two-hour tour.

RECORD STORES

ERNEST TUBB RECORD SHOPS
417 Broadway
(615) 255-7503

2416 Music Valley Drive
(615) 889-2474

Nashville International Airport
1 Terminal Drive
(615) 275-1155
www.ernesttubb.com

Ernest Tubb founded his downtown store on Commerce Street in 1947. Today the downtown store is at 417 Broadway. It specializes in early and hard-to-find country recordings but also stocks the latest country hits, so you'll find CDs and cassettes by everyone from Hank Snow, Webb Pierce, and Johnny Bush to George Strait and Alan Jackson. The store also has recordings by small-label artists such as Mike Snyder and Johnny Russell. Hours of operation vary. They're open until midnight on Friday and Saturday. The Midnight Jamboree at Ernest Tubb's Record Shop takes place at the Music Valley Drive location. You can find the airport shop near the main entrance, right in front of checkpoints A and B. The airport store features performances by songwriters and up-and-coming artists Monday through Thursday from about 9:00 a.m. to 2:00 p.m.

i Upon her induction into the *Grand Ole Opry* in 1999, Trisha Yearwood was presented with a necklace belonging to her idol, Patsy Cline.

THE GREAT ESCAPE
1925 Broadway
(615) 327-0646

111 North Gallatin Pike, Madison
(615) 865-8052
www.thegreatescape.com

A bargain hunter's paradise for some 20 years, Great Escape offers tens of thousands of used CDs, cassettes, albums, comic books, computer games, and other items. Collectors will find some vintage recordings here. Most CDs cost $6.00 to $9.00, while most tapes and records range from 99 cents to $3.99. The store pays cash for used products. Bring a photo ID if you have products to sell. Both stores are open daily. (See our Shopping chapter for more.)

GRIMEY'S NEW & PRELOVED MUSIC
1604 Eighth Avenue S.
(615) 254-4801
www.grimeys.com

This little Berry Hill shop is well known among local rockers for its great collection of indie rock. If you're a vinyl aficionado, you'll want to check out the store's extensive collection, which includes many new releases on vinyl. The store also sells a lot of soul, funk, electronica, and hip-hop. You'll find just about everything here but mainstream country. Most used CDs are priced at $8.99. If you have music to sell, the store will pay you up to $5 in cash or $6 in trade; be sure to bring a valid ID if you want to sell your stuff. Owned by partners Mike Grimes (a local musician who founded the store in 1999) and Doyle Davis, Grimey's also presents artist in-store appearances, promotes local concerts, and sells tickets to select area shows. The store has a good Web site that provides music news, CD reviews, audio samples of new releases, and more. The store is open daily.

i You can listen to several months' worth of performances of the Ernest Tubb Record Shop's famous *Midnight Jamboree* online at the show's Web site, www.etrecordshop.com/mj.htm.

PHONOLUXE RECORDS
2609 Nolensville Road
(615) 259-3500

Phonoluxe sells used CDs, cassettes, albums, videos, DVDs, and laser discs. For music lovers on a budget, it's a must-stop. CDs are priced from $2 to about $10, and albums start at $1 and go all the way up to $200 for some of the rare, autographed recordings. Phonoluxe sells current and out-of-print recordings. The store pays cash for your used products (up to $5 per CD); just bring a photo ID. In business since 1987, the store is located between Interstate 440 and Thompson Lane. It's open daily.

LIVE MUSIC

Places to Hear Live Music

Music is woven into the very fabric of Nashville; it seems to be everywhere here, as befits a town called "Music City." You're likely to find someone singing out on the street at any time of the day or night. While you may expect buskers to congregate along the Second Avenue entertainment district, they'll also entertain you while you wait in line at the Pancake Pantry. You're even likely to be serenaded at the airport. Live music is such an integral part of this town that you'll find it almost everywhere, from bars, restaurants, and coffeehouses to grocery stores and bookshops, street corners, and churches.

The revitalization of the downtown area—especially in "the District," which is the name given to Second Avenue, Printers Alley, and lower Broadway—has provided a wealth of entertainment opportunities for tourists and locals and given more performers a place to play. In many cases there is no cover charge, which means you can hop around from one establishment to another without spending a fortune. Often these performers are playing for free, so if you like what you hear, drop a bill into the tip jar or in the hat if one is passed around.

When planning this chapter, we had some difficulty deciding how to list the many music clubs that dot Nashville's landscape. We considered breaking it down by genre but ultimately chose not to do that for two primary reasons. First of all, while many of the establishments lean toward a certain genre, like country or blues or rock, many others present a hard-to-categorize variety of musical styles. Second, since we've been harping so much on the fact that Nashville is so much more than just country and has so much cross-pollination of styles, we thought it would be a little hypocritical to arbitrarily segregate these places. Please bear with us. While you may have to skim through a few listings to find that honky-tonk you're looking for, you might also unexpectedly discover a blues bar or classical music venue that really flips your switch. Such is the process of musical discovery, which is one of the things that makes Nashville such a wonderful place.

We list the larger venues, then dive right into the more intimate places. We also provide a separate list of places that hold "open-microphone" songwriters' nights, where any writer with an instrument and a song or two (and a little nerve) can play. Keep in mind that this by no means is a comprehensive listing of Nashville's music venues. We could devote an entire book to that subject. Local publications like the *Rage* and *Nashville Scene* are good sources of information on even more places to hear live music. As far as costs go, in most cases arena shows are going to be priced like … well, arena shows, which generally means tickets will run you $20 and more. Cover charges at the clubs and other smaller venues can vary from "none" to about $10 or even higher for special engagements. Unless otherwise noted, there's no cover at smaller venues.

The Larger Venues

Tickets for shows at these venues are available by calling Ticketmaster at (615) 255-9600, or by calling the venue box office.

ALLEN ARENA, DAVID LIPSCOMB UNIVERSITY
3901 Granny White Pike
(615) 279-7070
http://venues.lipscomb.edu

This 5,000-seat theater opened in October 2001 on the campus of David Lipscomb University. The arena is located on the campus's south end near the tennis courts and softball field on Granny White Pike. While the arena is used primarily for university sporting events, quite a few concerts have been held here. Lipscomb is a Church of Christ–affiliated school, so most of these shows have been of the Christian music variety—bands like dc Talk, Jars of Clay, and Third Day. However, the occasional up-and-coming country artist plays Allen Arena, too.

CHARLES M. MURPHY ATHLETIC CENTER
Tennessee Boulevard, Murfreesboro
(615) 898-2103 (ticket information)
www.goblueraiders.com
Located on the campus of Middle Tennessee State University, the Murphy Center was once the largest arena in the Middle Tennessee area, drawing A-list talent. Elvis played here five times. The Judds' farewell tour in December 1991 made a stop. Major rock acts like Rod Stewart and AC/DC have played the Murphy Athletic Center, as have George Strait, Alan Jackson, Garth Brooks, Pearl Jam, Kenny Rogers, Alabama, and Billy Joel. Things have slowed down a bit, however, since the November 1996 opening of the Gaylord Entertainment Center, and Starwood Amphitheatre also has had an impact. The university, which generally cosponsors concerts with a promoter, hasn't given up on bringing in more big-time performers, but in the meantime it's primarily focusing more on smaller shows.

COLISEUM
1 Titans Way
(615) 565-4300
www.titansonline.com
The 67,000-seat home of the National Football League's Tennessee Titans also plays host to occasional outdoor concerts. The Coliseum is the site of the nightly big-name concerts held during the CMA Music Festival/Fan Fair (see the Annual Events section of this chapter for more on that). In addition, George Strait brought his daylong

Players behind the Music

"Come see what you've heard" is the slogan of the Musicians Hall of Fame & Museum. Opened in 2006, the attraction honors the people who provide the sounds behind the songs. Located on the corner of Clark Place and within sight of the Country Music Hall of Fame & Museum, the attraction honors the players—whether stars, session pickers, or sidemen—from all genres of music.

The multimillion-dollar museum is the brainchild of Joe Chambers, a guitar store owner, who said the idea had been brewing for about a decade. When Chambers found out that Jimi Hendrix's apartment from his seminal years in Nashville had been razed, he decided that Nashville should not lose another piece of music history.

"If people will make a trip to his grave in Seattle, why wouldn't they go to see where he actually lived?" Chambers wondered. "That's what really triggered me to having some kind of museum here."

When another of the Nashville clubs where a young Hendrix performed was being renovated, Chambers tracked down the contractor, and asked to salvage the basement stage. The contractor agreed, and Chambers used his memory of a famous photograph of Hendrix playing on that particular stage to guide the way. Now, the Musicians Hall of Fame will honor the Guitar God with an exhibit featuring the rescued and restored stage.

Chambers's extensive collection includes:

- Lightning Chance's bass, heard on all the early Everly Brothers albums, Conway Twitty's "It's Only Make Believe," and Hank Williams's last recording session, which brought "Your Cheating Heart."

- Pete Drake's steel guitar played on Bob Dylan's "Lay Lady Lay" and George Harrison's album *All Things Must Pass*.

- Scotty Moore's personal items from his long career in Elvis Presley's band.

- Billy Sherrill's cigarette-burned piano on which he composed country classics like "Almost Persuaded," "The Most Beautiful Girl," and "Stand By Your Man."

- The Red Hot Chili Peppers' snare drum heard on their albums *Mother's Milk* and *Blood Sugar Sex Magic*.

- Marshall Grant's basses from Johnny Cash's "Walk the Line" and "Ring of Fire," along with the amp from "Folsom Prison Blues" and "A Boy Named Sue."

- Uriel Jones's drum kit and Eddie Willis's guitars from countless Motown sessions.

"I want to show the diversity of what Nashville has done as a music center. It's hard to put under one umbrella," said Chambers, who also has written such songs as "Somebody Lied" for Ricky Van Shelton, "Old 8x10" for Randy Travis, and "Good Ones and Bad Ones" for George Jones.

Chambers also plans to include an adjoining school of music for young talent, an attached venue for gigs and showcases, and an operational recording studio for museum visitors to witness a real Nashville session.

"I fell in love with Nashville the first time I came here," said Chambers, who arrived in 1978. "It's unexplainable, but I knew this is where I needed to be. The more that I lived here, the more I learned about how many great musicians have been through here and started here. It's really a secret."

With the help of the Musicians Hall of Fame & Museum, it won't be a secret any longer.

For more on the Musicians Hall of Fame & Museum, see the Attractions chapter.

country music festival to the stadium. Tickets to Coliseum concert events are generally sold through Ticketmaster.

CURB EVENT CENTER
2002 Belmont Boulevard
(615) 460-8500 (tickets)
www.belmont.edu/curbeventcenter
Belmont University's 90,000-square-foot state-of-the-art sports and entertainment complex opened in late 2003. The facility includes a 5,000-seat arena, which presents occasional concerts and other entertainment events. Amy Grant and the Chinese Golden Dragon Acrobats were among the first entertainers to perform at the facility. Tickets are available through Ticketmaster. Parking is in the attached garage or along nearby streets.

GAYLORD ENTERTAINMENT CENTER
501 Broadway
(615) 770-2000
www.gaylordentertainmentcenter.com
Although it features ice hockey and other sporting events, the Gaylord was designed primarily for concerts. Extra care has been devoted to the acoustical systems, and the sound is exceptional. The arena, which contains more than a million square feet of total space, seats as many as 20,000 for an in-the-round concert and 18,500 using its 40-by-60-foot proscenium stage. It is also billed as "performer-friendly," with a number of amenities in the form of comfortable dressing rooms, a catering pantry, and bath and shower facilities, so performers are likely to walk onto the stage in a good mood, which is good news for concertgoers. Since its opening in 1996, this venue has hosted the likes of Tim McGraw and Faith Hill, the Rolling Stones, the Dixie Chicks, Jimmy Buffett, Eric Clapton, and Mary J. Blige. Last-minute ticket buyers can take comfort in the fact that 20 box-office windows are available to speed the process.

GRAND OLE OPRY HOUSE
2804 Opryland Drive
(615) 889-6611
www.opry.com

The *Grand Ole Opry* is the show that started it all, and this is where it has happened since the *Grand Ole Opry* moved from the Ryman Auditorium in 1974. Since the Opry is only on Friday and Saturday nights, the Opry House is available for other concerts, awards shows, and special events during the week; concerts by Sheryl Crow, performances of the Moscow Ballet's *Nutcracker,* and self-help guru Dr. Phil McGraw have all graced the famous stage. A typical Opry performance features a mix of country music legends, today's top stars, and up-and-coming new artists. More than just traditional country, the Opry features bluegrass, gospel, Cajun, western swing, country-rock, and comedy. Live broadcast performances (on WSM, 650 on the AM dial) each Friday and Saturday evening feature 20 to 25 performers. The two-hour Tuesday matinees in the summer feature 8 to 10 artists. The lineup is released a couple of days before showtime. It's not unusual, however, for a special guest to drop by for a duet or surprise appearance during these unrehearsed performances. The schedule of showtimes varies and is subject to change, so it's a good idea to call ahead before planning a visit.Tickets range from $30 to $60. Tickets are sometimes still available just before showtime, but since shows often sell out, you might want to order them in advance if you're planning to visit on a specific day. Some ticket buyers cancel their reservations, so you can often get good seats at the last minute. To order tickets and check the schedule, call the listed number. The Great American Country cable network broadcasts an hour of the show every Saturday night.

> **i** Did you know that airmail originated in Nashville? In 1877 John Lillard had the first airmail stamp issued—for balloon service. Although that idea never got off the ground, Lillard was vindicated when the first practical airmail service—on an airplane—departed from Nashville on July 29, 1924.

MARTHA RIVERS INGRAM CENTER FOR THE PERFORMING ARTS
Blair School of Music
2400 Blakemore Avenue
(615) 322-7651
www.vanderbilt.edu/blair
Inaugurated in January 2002, the stunning Martha Rivers Ingram Center for the Performing Arts is a dramatic addition to the Blair School of Music. Its superb acoustics and state-of-the-art stage equipment make it an ideal setting for symphonic, operatic, or chamber orchestra events. The Ingram Center seats around 600; parking is across the street at the Capers Garage.

NASHVILLE MUNICIPAL AUDITORIUM
417 Fourth Avenue N.
(615) 862-6390
www.nashvilleauditorium.com
Once Nashville's premier entertainment venue, 9,600-seat Municipal Auditorium, which opened in 1962, has taken a backseat to some of the newer and larger venues around town. But it still plays host to a wide range of performers. Municipal Auditorium occasionally holds trade shows and family shows such as *Sesame Street Live,* religious crusades, circuses, and truck pulls.

RIVERFRONT PARK
100 First Avenue N.
(615) 862-8400 (Metro Parks office)
www.nashville.gov/parks
Riverfront Park is the site of various seasonal concerts and events, some free and some with an admission charge. The seven-acre park, across the Cumberland River from the stadium, includes a tiered grassy hill that approximates an amphitheater. General capacity for concerts is 10,000.

RYMAN AUDITORIUM
116 Fifth Avenue N.
(615) 889-6611, (615) 889-3060
(reservations and ticketing)
www.ryman.com
If any venue qualifies as Nashville's music mecca, it is the Ryman, former home to the *Grand Ole Opry*. The historic, 2,362-seat former tabernacle is now owned by Gaylord Entertainment, which also owns the Opryland property and the Wildhorse Saloon. Construction on the building began in 1889, with significant financial support from steamboat captain Thomas G. Ryman, who had recently "found" religion and banned drinking and gambling on his boats. It opened in 1892 as the Union Gospel Tabernacle. The auditorium, though built for religious services, soon became well known for hosting lectures and theatrical performances. Through its early history, in addition to legendary preachers such as Dwight L. Moody and Billy Sunday, the stage was graced by speakers ranging from William Jennings Bryan and Helen Keller to Carrie Nation and Booker T. Washington, and by performers including Sarah Bernhardt, Enrico Caruso, Charlie Chaplin, and Isadora Duncan. After Thomas Ryman's death in 1904, the building was renamed in his honor. From 1943 to 1974 it was the home of the *Grand Ole Opry*. After the Opry moved to Opryland in 1974, the Ryman was neglected for years, but it reopened in June 1994 after a full restoration. Now it is noted for its excellent acoustics. Today's Ryman is a fully functioning performing arts center that features concert-quality sound and lighting and has radio and TV broadcast capabilities. The main floor and balcony seat about 1,000 people each. It has been the site of TV specials and is also a popular spot for shooting videos. Original productions—music-themed, of course—have long runs here as well, although the Ryman now focuses only on concerts. In addition, the *Grand Ole Opry* returns to the Ryman for special engagements. Another program is Bluegrass Nights during the summer. The auditorium has featured concerts of a variety of musical genres and artists, including George Jones, Merle Haggard, Coldplay, Neil Young, Bruce Springsteen, Beck, Elvis Costello, and Yo-Yo Ma. See the Attractions section of this chapter for information about Ryman exhibits and tours.

STARWOOD AMPHITHEATRE
3839 Murfreesboro Road, Antioch
(615) 641-5800
www.starwoodamphitheatre.com

The Ryman Auditorium was home to the *Grand Ole Opry* from 1943 to 1974. JACKIE SHECKLER FINCH

Starwood Amphitheatre is the area's only major outdoor venue. It has a capacity of more than 18,000, including 5,200 covered seats in the pavilion and a gently sloping lawn where you can spread a blanket and enjoy the music under the stars. Major concerts in recent years have included Jimmy Buffett, the Dave Matthews Band, Tom Petty and the Heartbreakers, and the Eagles. A word to the wise: Allow plenty of time when going to a Starwood show, as traffic can back up for miles on Interstate 24, as well as on Murfreesboro Road.

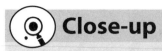 **Close-up**

Vinyl Records Still Going 'Round

Record players may have bit the dust a long time ago in many homes, but vinyl records are still a hot commodity. "There's a whole new generation of consumers that are looking for vinyl," said Cris Ashworth, president of United Record Pressing, one of the largest and last of the business.

"Vinyl has a unique sound, a warmer, richer sound," Ashworth said. "I can play you a CD of a song and a vinyl of a song and nine times out of 10, you'll like the vinyl better."

Many record collectors, DJs, and music lovers still consider vinyl to be the gold standard of recorded music, Ashworth said. "People thought we had disappeared, but we're doing better than ever."

Started in 1962, not far from downtown Nashville, United Record Pressing still looks much as it did back then. With its loud blasts of compressed air and booming presses, the company seems a throwback to a different time.

Vinyl's peak period was when today's baby boomers were listening to rock 'n' roll, blues, and country and buying plenty of albums. Many of the early record-pressing companies have since closed up shop. Vinyl records use analog technology, where a physical groove is etched into the record mimicking the sound wave. CDs, however, transform sound into digital bits of information.

United Record Pressing's 50 or so employees press from 20,000 to 40,000 records a day.

Many of the company's records today are by rap, hip-hop, and R&B artists, such as Christina Aguilera, Black Eyed Peas, Beyond, and Justin Timberlake. A record label will press its latest release to vinyl to get it to the clubs quickly. United Record Pressing can have a record ready to go in 48 hours. Club DJs want the records so they can spin them or "scratch" them. But the company also releases popular reissues, such as those by Elvis Presley, Johnny Cash, Bob Dylan, Bruce Springsteen, and many others.

A whole wall in the facility is dedicated to Elvis, with some of his top album covers and 45 covers. "Those Sun recordings of Elvis were pressed right here," Ashworth said. "It's like a time capsule in here, a real museum."

In fact, '60s furniture decorates the building. The Motown Suite, with its kitschy pink bathroom, is a flashback to when Motown executives would come to town from Detroit with their latest recordings. "If you've heard a Motown record, then you've heard our work," Ashworth said. "We pressed the Motown records."

Visitors are intrigued with the old record players and colorful album covers. "The history of vinyl is here," Ashworh said. "A lot of people don't even realize what we have here."

For more information contact United Record Pressing at (615) 259-9396.

TENNESSEE PERFORMING ARTS CENTER (TPAC)

505 Deaderick Street
(615) 782-4000,
(615) 255-9600 (Ticketmaster)
www.tpac.org

TPAC (pronounced tee-pack) is mainly devoted to productions like its Broadway series and those of its resident groups (for information on such productions and more details about TPAC itself, see our Arts chapter). TPAC is occasionally the site of a pop or rock concert as well as private shows and gatherings for artists' fan clubs during Fan Fair. TPAC consists of four venues: 2,408-seat Jackson Hall, 1,003-seat Polk Theater, 1,668-seat War Memorial Auditorium, and 288-seat Johnson Theater.

Smaller Venues

B. B. KING'S BLUES CLUB
152 Second Avenue N.
(615) 256-2727
www.bbkingbluesclub.com

B. B. King's presents nightly live blues, R&B, jazz, and, occasionally, rock acts. Most of the entertainment is local or regional, but the club features a nationally known performer about twice a month. The cover is $5 Sunday through Thursday, and $10 Friday and Saturday. Expect to pay about $15 to $20 for special ticketed events. B. B. King himself plays here a couple of times per year. B. B. King's serves dinner daily. Barbecue, ribs, catfish, fried chicken, and burgers are on the menu.

THE BELCOURT THEATRE
2102 Belcourt Avenue
(615) 846-3150 (main office),
(615) 383-9140 (box office)
www.belcourt.org

The historic Belcourt Theatre, home to the *Grand Ole Opry* from 1934 to 1936, today is a nonprofit venue that features concerts, films, and events. The 340-seat Hillsboro Village venue features a variety of music, including jazz, blues, and symphony concerts. Past bookings have included Norah Jones, Joan Baez, Kris Kristofferson, the Nashville Chamber Orchestra Quintet, J. J. Cale, and Rickie Lee Jones. The theater sells alcoholic beverages and snacks. Purchase tickets at the theater's Web site, by phone, or at the theater's box office. Shows often sell out quickly. For more on the Belcourt, see our Arts and Nightlife chapters.

THE BLUEBIRD CAFE
4104 Hillsboro Road
(615) 383-1461
www.bluebirdcafe.com

You can't talk about songwriter venues in Nashville without mentioning the Bluebird. And you can't talk at the Bluebird without someone hushing you. That may be an exaggeration, but only a slight one, because here the song is meant to be the focus, not background music for conversations. Insiders know that "Shhh!" has become

a motto of the famous listening room. Owner Amy Kurland opened the Bluebird Cafe in 1982 as a restaurant with live music, and it wasn't long before the music moved to the forefront. A casual look around the 8-by-10-inch photographs covering the walls will tell you why: Practically anybody who's anybody in new country and acoustic music has played here—Vince Gill, Steve Earle, Mary Chapin Carpenter, Guy Clark, Townes Van Zandt, Janis Ian, Maria Muldaur, John Prine, Bonnie Raitt . . . we could go on and on and on. Some, like Garth Brooks, played here as unknowns and went on to become superstar recording artists, while some have made their names as songwriters who pen hits for other people.

The songwriters in-the-round format, in which four songwriters sit in a circle and take turns playing their own songs, was pioneered here by Fred Knobloch and Don Schlitz, and it's a tradition that continues most nights. If you haven't been to an in-the-round, you don't know what you're missing. Reservations for Tuesday through Thursday shows are taken one week in advance; call (615) 383-1461. For Friday and Saturday shows, call Monday of the week of the show. Call early—weekend shows often sell out by noon on Monday. Depending on who's playing, you might get in if you just show up for the evening show, which begins at 9:30 p.m. But if it's a "big" show, don't count on it. The cover is generally $8 (though it can sometimes be $10 or even as much as $15 for special events), and each seat at a table also has a $7 food and drink minimum. You can avoid the minimum by sitting on the benches or sitting or standing at the bar; these positions are filled on a first-come, first-served basis. There's no cover for the early show, which starts at 6:30 p.m. and usually features up-and-coming songwriters. The early show each Monday is open-microphone (for more info on that, see the Open Microphones section later in this chapter). Sunday is Writers Night, during which up to a dozen previously selected writers perform a few of their songs, followed by a performance by a top Nashville tunesmith.

BOURBON STREET BLUES AND BOOGIE BAR
220 Printers Alley
(615) 24-BLUES
www.bourbonstreetblues.com

Bourbon Street features live blues music seven nights a week in an appropriately dark New Orleans–style atmosphere. The club, which was named Blues Club of the Year in 2000 by the Memphis-based Blues Foundation, frequently brings in national acts, including such R&B and soul music stars as Bobby "Blue" Bland, Koko Taylor, and Rufus Thomas. The house band, Stacy Mitchhart & Blues U Can Use, typically plays Wednesday through Sunday. The cover is $5 on weekdays, $10 on Friday and Saturday, with an occasional exception for special engagements. The kitchen serves Cajun American cuisine.

DOUGLAS CORNER CAFE
2106-A Eighth Avenue S.
(615) 298-1688
www.musicdigest.com/douglascorner

A favorite with Nashville's top songwriters, Douglas Corner is a cozy, laid-back little club that features songwriters, artists, and bands six nights a week. Garth Brooks, Trisha Yearwood, Alan Jackson, and Bon Jovi are among the list of better-known names who have performed here. In-the-round performances, featuring a selection of songwriters who take turns performing their tunes, are a highlight. The cover charge varies; on weekends, it's typically around $10. On various nights, there will be a 6:00 p.m. show, when admission is free. Douglas Corner has open microphone on Tuesday nights (see the subsequent Open Microphones section for details).

THE END
2219 Elliston Place
(615) 321-4457

A longtime fixture on Elliston Place, this hole-in-the-wall club is known for booking independent rock acts. We used to visit back in our '80s big-hair days, when the club was known as Elliston Square and the whole area was called the "Rock Block." The vibe hasn't changed much since then. The club is still cramped, the music is still loud, and the sound sometimes isn't so good, but if cutting-edge, indie rock is your scene, this is the place. Owner Bruce Fitzpatrick is a familiar face to Nashville's rock crowd, having worked across the street at the Exit/In for some 16 years and at the long-gone Cantrell's in the early '80s. The End has bands five to seven nights a week. The cover charge is usually $10 to $15. The club sells beer and soft drinks.

EXIT/IN
2208 Elliston Place
(615) 321-3340
www.exit-in.com

After more than three decades, the legendary Exit/In is still alive and kickin'. The club is one of Nashville's oldest music venues, having first opened in 1971. Longtime patrons have fond memories of many fine performances at the Exit/In. R.E.M., Linda Ronstadt, Steve Martin, Jason & the Scorchers, and Bill Monroe are just a few of the performers who have appeared here. Artists who have played here in recent years include Sting, Hootie & the Blowfish, Steve Earle, the Mavericks, Train, Robert Earl Keen, and Social Distortion. The club is essentially just a big room with a capacity of 500 people, a stage in the front, and a bar in the back. Who needs anything more? The show schedule is inclined toward rock and alternative country with a lot of artist-showcase concerts. The cover varies; it's generally $7 to $10 but sometimes can be as much as $30 or more for prime shows.

GIBSON SHOWCASE
161 Opry Mills Drive
(615) 514-2200
www.gibsonshowcase.com/bluegrass

The Gibson Showcase, at Opry Mills mall, has a live bluegrass jam Monday from 7:00 to 10:00 p.m. Ten to 25 pickers usually show up; if you're lucky, a star or two will drop by and jam. There's also a live blues jam on Tuesday from 7:00 to 10:00 p.m. The venue serves a full menu from burgers to steaks and has a full bar. The Gibson Showcase has a glass-enclosed factory room where, during the day, you can watch craftsmen make mandolins, banjos, and guitars. Instruments and accessories are sold here, too.

LEGENDS CORNER
428 Broadway
(615) 248-6334
www.legendscorner.com
Album covers of country greats plaster the walls at Legends, a popular honky-tonk at the corner of Fifth and Broadway, across from the Gaylord Entertainment Center. The bar features a variety of local talent and no cover charge. It's popular with tourists as well as locals who want to kick up their heels on the dance floor or just sit at the bar and drink a beer.

THE NASHVILLE PALACE
2400 Music Valley Drive
(615) 885-1540
www.musicvalleyattractions.com
It's become a part of modern country music lore that Randy Travis had a gig frying fish here and singing on the side when he was "discovered." A popular tourist spot, the Nashville Palace features live country music every night with a $5 cover charge. Name performers such as Vern Gosdin and Ronnie Stoneman (of *Hee Haw* fame) perform here occasionally, and Opry stars often drop by for a bite to eat. Keep an eye out for Porter Wagoner, Marty Stuart, and Gosdin.

RCKTWN
401 Sixth Avenue S.
(615) 843-4001,
(615) 843-4000 (event hot line)
www.rcktwn.com
This youth-oriented nonprofit entertainment venue is the culmination of a longtime dream for Christian music superstar Michael W. Smith, who wanted to create a safe place for teens to congregate and have fun. The original Rocketown operated in the mid-1990s in a Brentwood warehouse before closing. In 2003 Smith provided a big chunk of financing for the club to reopen at its current site in downtown Nashville. Now known as RCKTWN, the expansive two-level entertainment complex includes three music stages; a coffee bar that presents local acoustic music artists, karaoke, and drama; the Sixth Avenue Skatepark, for extreme skateboarding, BMX, and in-line skating; and a small fashion boutique. The largest music area can accommodate 1,200. The club presents a mixture of music styles, including rock, pop, hip-hop, punk, and Top 40. About half of the bands featured are Christian-oriented. Although RCKTWN is accessible to all ages, many activities, including Friday- and Saturday-night shows, are geared for ages 14 to 20; adults make up about 10 percent of the crowd on any given night. The staff keeps an eye on the goings-on, keeping age-appropriateness in mind. Parents or guardians often hang out at the coffee club while the younger set attends a concert or burns off energy in the skate park. The cover charge is $5 to $7. Ticket prices for special concerts may cost about $10 to $18. RCKTWN is open daily from 9:00 a.m. to 9:00 p.m.

ROBERT'S WESTERN WORLD
416 Broadway
(615) 244-9552
www.robertswesternworld.com
You can buy a pair of cowboy boots while you

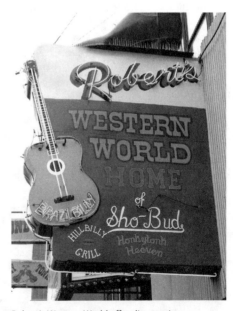

Robert's Western World offers live music on Broadway. JACKIE SHECKLER FINCH

listen to bluegrass and honky-tonk music at Robert's. There's live entertainment day and night—from 11:00 to 2:00 a.m. Stars occasionally show up to hang out and often end up taking the stage for a song or two. Famous faces who've visited Robert's include Merle Haggard, Kid Rock, Brooks & Dunn, Dolly Parton, and Tracy Byrd. The sign out front proudly proclaims the bar as home of BR549, the rowdy traditionalist honky-tonk group that served as house band for a while before signing a major-label record deal. (The band returned for a New Year's Eve concert in 2003.) There's no cover charge.

STATION INN
402 12th Avenue S.
(615) 255-3307
www.stationinn.com

The Station Inn is one of our favorite places to hear live music. A Who's Who of bluegrass, including the Del McCoury Band, Roland White, and Larry Cordle and Lonesome Standard Time, regularly play at the homey (and homely) little club that's almost hidden away down on 12th Avenue S. The club occasionally features country, Americana, and folk performers, including Gillian Welch, Steve Earle, and others. Vince Gill has been known to drop in, too. We like to get there early so we can claim a couple of the old worn-out vinyl seats that line the back wall (they're said to have come straight from Lester Flatt's original tour bus), then settle in for an evening of good music. The Station Inn features live bluegrass nightly. The cover charge generally varies from $10 to $15, depending on the band. There is no cover on Sunday, when an open jam session takes place. Hot shows fill up fast, so come early. The Station Inn doesn't take reservations, and they don't sell tickets in advance. Smoke-free.

i Once a nightclub bouncer, Garth Brooks calls his *Grand Ole Opry* membership the pinnacle of his career.

TEXAS TROUBADOUR THEATRE
2416 Music Valley Drive, #108
(615) 889-2474
www.etrecordshop.com

The 500-capacity Texas Troubadour Theatre takes evident pride in the fact that it is an extension of the Ernest Tubb Record Shop—the legendary Tubb was known as "the Texas Troubadour"—and says that, like its namesake, it endeavors to always treat country music fans right. One example of this generosity is the continuation of the weekly *Midnight Jamboree* radio show, which Tubb started the night of May 3, 1947, the same date he opened his first record shop in downtown Nashville. The *Midnight Jamboree,* which airs on WSM-AM 650 each Saturday after the *Grand Ole Opry,* is the second-longest-running radio show in history, taking a backseat only to the Opry itself. After more than 50 years of the show, it continues its tradition of free admission, even when a star such as Alan Jackson, Travis Tritt, or Marty Stuart is in the lineup. That's the way Ernest Tubb, who started the show as a way for new artists to get on the radio, always wanted it. The other regular program at the Troubadour is *Cowboy Church,* a free, nondenominational, come-as-you-are service every Sunday at 10:00 a.m. That show, broadcast on World Wide Radio, features 45 minutes of music and 10 or 15 minutes of testimony in a laid-back but uplifting atmosphere. (See our Worship chapter for details.) The Troubadour, which is across from Opryland in the Music Valley area, also features theatrical productions such as *A Tribute to the King* (Elvis).

3RD & LINDSLEY BAR AND GRILL
818 Third Avenue S.
(615) 259-9891
www.3rdandlindsley.com

This club, a half mile south of Broadway, boasts live blues, R&B, rock, and alternative music seven nights a week. It's popular with Nashville's session musicians and singers and is a good spot to catch some local favorites, including Jonell Mosser, Mike Henderson, and the Wooten Brothers. The cover charge varies according to the band but is usually about $5 on weeknights and $10 on weekends.

TOOTSIE'S ORCHID LOUNGE
422 Broadway
(615) 726-0463
www.tootsies.net

You can't miss Tootsie's—it's the pale purple club on Broadway. In the old days this was where legendary songwriters like Kris Kristofferson and Willie Nelson gathered to drink and write. Much of the lounge's history is reflected in the photos on the walls. There's a stage downstairs and another upstairs, where you can walk out into an alley to the side door to the Ryman Auditorium (you can't get in that way, but many legendary stars have been known to come out that door and into Tootsie's). Both stages feature live entertainment day and night; there isn't a cover charge. Tootsie's is worth a visit for anyone who wants to soak up a little of Music City's music history.

THE WILDHORSE SALOON
120 Second Avenue N.
(615) 902-8200
www.wildhorsesaloon.com

The Wildhorse, one of the top tourist attractions downtown in The District, is owned by Gaylord Entertainment, which also owns the Ryman Auditorium. This state-of-the-art music club, which opened in June 1994, is host to a continuing parade of country events. Concerts in the huge club have included Merle Haggard, Vince Gill, Billy Joe Shaver, Billy Ray Cyrus, Keith Urban, and many more. The Wildhorse presents house bands, booked from all over the United States, every night except during tapings. New country acts Lonestar and Ricochet have filled the house band slot in the past. Regular admission is $4 weekdays and $6 weekends. Concert tickets range from $6 to about $15. (See our Nightlife chapter for more on the Wildhorse.)

Tootsie's Orchid Lounge is filled with country music history. JACKIE SHECKLER FINCH

Open Microphones

Several area clubs have open-mic nights. Here are some of the more highly regarded open-microphone venues in Nashville.

THE BLUEBIRD CAFE
4104 Hillsboro Road
(615) 383-1461
www.bluebirdcafe.com

Open-mic night at the legendary Bluebird, with host Barbara Cloyd, is Monday at 6:00 p.m. If you're interested in playing, get there at 5:30, sign a slip of paper, and put it in the basket. A drawing determines the order of performers, and unfortunately, not everybody generally gets a chance to play before time runs out at 9:00. If you do get on stage, you can play a maximum of two songs or eight minutes, and your songs should be originals. Now relax and play, keeping in mind that if you do screw up, nobody will boo you. Just about everybody else in the audience is a songwriter, and they know what it's like. And while you should enjoy yourself, forget those dreams of being "discovered" at an open mic. It just doesn't happen that way anymore, but it's a great way to work on your musical- and vocal-presentation skills. By the way, if you're one of the unlucky ones who doesn't get to play, you're guaranteed a spot the next open-mic night you attend. For more information about the Bluebird, see the listing earlier in the Smaller Venues section of this chapter.

DOUGLAS CORNER CAFE
2106-A Eighth Avenue S.
(615) 292-2530 (recording to sign up)
www.musicdigest.com/douglascorner

Douglas Corner's open mic starts at 8:00 p.m. Tuesday. You can reserve your spot in line by calling the listed number between 2:00 and 6:00 p.m. the same day you wish to attend. Calling Douglas Corner's main number won't do you any good. If you forget to call, just show up, and your name will be added to the end of the list. Depending on how many people are waiting to play, you'll get to do two or three songs.

ANNUAL EVENTS

March/April

DOVE AWARDS
Grand Ole Opry House
2804 Opryland Drive
(615) 242-0303
www.doveawards.com

The Gospel Music Association's annual Gospel Music Week traditionally includes the presentation of the Dove Awards, when trophies in more than 35 categories are bestowed upon the industry's best. The show takes place at the Grand Ole Opry House and is televised nationally. Some tickets are available to the public; contact the GMA at the number above, or visit the Web site for more information.

GOSPEL MUSIC WEEK
Renaissance Nashville Hotel, Nashville Convention Center, and various venues
(615) 242-0303
www.gospelmusic.org

If you think gospel music is just something you hear in church, you've obviously never been near the Renaissance Nashville Hotel and Nashville Convention Center when the Gospel Music Association presents its annual Gospel Music Week. As many as 3,000 gospel artists, radio station executives, and music industry types from around the world attend the event. Nashville being the headquarters of the Christian music scene, all the players who don't live in Music City come here for a yearly dose of seminars, showcases, parties, and networking opportunities. All genres of Christian music are represented—from Christian rock to southern gospel to traditional African-American gospel. Seminars covering such topics as artist development, concert promotion, marketing, and getting a record deal take place Monday through Thursday at the convention center. There's also a trade show with dozens of exhibitors. Showcase luncheons and worship services are scheduled throughout the week. These events are for convention registrants, but the nighttime showcases held in various local venues are open to the public. The schedule and ticket prices vary, so check the newspapers or the GMA's Web site for up-to-date information.

ℹ️ Blind since birth, *Grand Ole Opry* star Ronnie Milsap played the violin by age 7, piano by age 8, and guitar by age 12.

TIN PAN SOUTH
Ryman Auditorium and various Nashville venues
(615) 256-3354, (800) 321-6008
www.tinpansouth.com

One of Nashville's treasures is its talented songwriting community. Nashville songwriters pen hits that are heard and loved by millions around the world. In addition to countless country songs, numerous pop hits—such as Eric Clapton's Grammy-winning song "Change the World," written by Music City's Gordon Kennedy, Wayne Kirkpatrick, and Tommy Simms—came from the pens of Nashville tunesmiths. We are fortunate that, on just about any night of the week, we can head out to a club like the Bluebird Cafe or Douglas Corner and hear great songs performed by the talented individuals who wrote them.

For about five days and nights at the end of March and beginning of April, Tin Pan South offers the chance to catch a bunch of top songwriters performing their hits acoustically in an intimate club setting. The Nashville Songwriters Association International sponsors this event, the nation's only festival celebrating the songwriter and the song, and writers from around the country join in. Tin Pan South takes its name from Nashville's songwriting predecessor, the famous Tin Pan Alley in New York. Among the activities are the Songwriters Achievement Awards at the Ryman Auditorium; Tin Pan Jam Night, featuring legendary songwriters; the Tin Pan South Golf Tournament, for members of the corporate community, music executives, and songwriters; and a symposium offering songwriting workshops, song evaluations with writers and publishers, and guest lectures. A highlight of the event is the Tin Pan South Legendary Songwriters' Acoustic Concert at the Ryman Auditorium, which features four or five legendary songwriters. Past performers at this concert have included Steve Winwood ("Higher Love"), Alan and Marylin Bergman ("You Don't Send Me Flowers"), Michael McDonald ("Minute by Minute"), Jimmy Webb ("Up, Up and Away"), Christopher Cross ("Sailing"), Janis Ian ("At Seventeen"), John Phillips ("Do You Believe in Magic"), and Barrett Strong ("I Heard It through the Grapevine"). Tickets are available through Ticketmaster (615-255-9600, www.ticketmaster .com) and at the door if tickets aren't sold out. Ticket prices vary. Shows usually begin at 6:30 and 9:00 p.m.

May

TENNESSEE JAZZ & BLUES SOCIETY SUMMER CONCERT SERIES
Belle Meade Plantation
5025 Harding Road

Cheekwood Botanical Garden & Museum of Art
1200 Forrest Park Drive

The Hermitage: Home of President Andrew Jackson
4580 Rachel's Lane, Hermitage
(615) 301-5121
www.jazzblues.org

The Tennessee Jazz & Blues Society has been sponsoring a summer concert series for more than a dozen years. From late May through early August or September, on various Sunday evenings from 6:00 to 8:00 p.m., the society presents concerts under the stars at either Belle Meade Plantation, Cheekwood, or the Hermitage. Bring a blanket or folding chairs, and pack a cooler with your favorite picnic fare. Everyone is welcome—you can even bring the dog to the Belle Meade Plantation concerts. Admission is $15 to $20 at the gate or through Ticketmaster (615-255-9600, www.ticketmaster.com); children 12 and under are admitted free. Members of the Tennessee Jazz & Blues Society get a $5 discount. Group rates are available by calling the locations in advance.

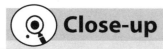

Close-up

It's a Grand Ole Cast

How many of these names do you recognize? Those of you who are die-hard country music fans probably know them all. As of 2008, this was the cast of the *Grand Ole Opry*. The names are followed by the year they joined. The cast changes from time to time, as new members are added and others choose to drop out for a while. New members are invited to join on the basis of their contributions to country music and whether they are available to perform from time to time during the live radio broadcast.

Trace Adkins, 2003; Bill Anderson, 1961; Ernie Ashworth, 1964; Dierks Bentley, 2005; Clint Black, 1991; Garth Brooks, 1990; Jim Ed Brown, 1963; Roy Clark, 1987; Terri Clark, 2004; John Conlee, 1981; Wilma Lee Cooper, 1957; Charlie Daniels, 2008; Diamond Rio, 1998; Little Jimmy Dickens, 1948; Joe Diffie, 1993; the Gatlin Brothers, 1976; Vince Gill, 1991; Billy Grammer, 1959; Jack Greene, 1967; Tom T. Hall, 1980; George Hamilton IV, 1960; Emmylou Harris, 1992; Jan Howard, 1971; Alan Jackson, 1991; Stonewall Jackson, 1956; George Jones, 1969; Hal Ketchum, 1994; Alison Krauss, 1993; Hank Locklin, 1960; Charlie Louvin, 1955; Patty Loveless, 1988; Loretta Lynn, 1962; Barbara Mandrell, 1972; Martina McBride, 1995; Del McCoury, 2003; Mel McDaniel, 1986; Reba McEntire, 1986; Jesse McReynolds, 1964; Ronnie Milsap, 1976; Lorrie Morgan, 1984; Jimmy C. Newman, 1956; the Osborne Brothers, 1964; Brad Paisley, 2001; Dolly Parton, 1969; Stu Phillips, 1967; Ray Pillow, 1966; Charley Pride, 1993; Jeanne Pruett, 1973; Riders in the Sky, 1982; Jeannie Seely, 1967; Jean Shepard, 1955; Ricky Skaggs, 1982; Connie Smith, 1971; Mike Snider, 1990; Ralph Stanley, 2000; Marty Stuart, 1992; Mel Tillis, 2007; Pam Tillis, 2000; Randy Travis, 1986; Travis Tritt, 1992; Josh Turner, 2007, Carrie Underwood, 2008, Ricky Van Shelton, 1988; Billy Walker, 1960; Charlie Walker, 1967; Steve Wariner, 1996; the Whites, 1984; Trisha Yearwood, 1999.

---

i "Nashville Sound" refers to a style of smooth, heavily produced country music in which piano, strings, and backing vocals are more prominent than traditional fiddle and banjo. The style was popularized in the late 1950s and 1960s by producers Chet Atkins and Owen Bradley. Patsy Cline's recordings are among the most popular examples of the famous Nashville Sound.

June

BONNAROO MUSIC FESTIVAL
Manchester
(931) 728-7635
www.bonnaroo.com

Outdoor music festival aficionados may want to know that Bonnaroo—a massive three-day music and camping festival—takes place just down the road at a 700-acre farm in Manchester, about 60 miles southeast of Music City. Since Bonnaroo was first launched in 2002, it has become one of the nation's premier music events, drawing 75,000 or more avid music fans from around the country. The artist lineup is heavy on "jam bands"—artists known for their improvisation in a variety of roots music styles. Performers have included Bob Dylan, the Dead, Widespread Panic, Trey Anastasio of Phish, Dave Matthews, Willie Nelson, and Alison Krauss. There are multiple stages, as well as a central area featuring around-the-clock entertainment activities and food and beverage concessions. Tickets, traditionally available only online at the Bonnaroo Web site, are about $170 to $190 for a three-day pass, which includes camping and parking. Special VIP packages can cost as much as $1,000. An important note: Traffic surrounding the festival can be a nightmare, so do your research and plan a good route—preferably something other than I-24, which has been known to back up for hours during this event.

CMA MUSIC FESTIVAL/FAN FAIR
Various downtown Nashville venues
(800) CMA-FEST
www.cmafest.com

Country music fans have traditionally been a loyal bunch, and country artists bend over backward to show their gratitude during this annual celebration designed to honor music fans. The bond between country fans and their favorite artists is a unique one in the music industry. You wouldn't find many famous rock bands standing in a booth all day to sign autographs for their fans, but country artists do just that. In 1996, for example, Garth Brooks made a surprise visit to the 25th annual Fan Fair and signed autographs for 23 consecutive hours—reportedly without a bathroom break! Since its inception in 1972, Fan Fair, organized and produced by the Country Music Association, has become a tradition for country fans and Nashville's music industry. The first event drew 5,000 to the Municipal Auditorium. In 1982 the event was moved to the Tennessee State Fairgrounds, where it could accommodate more fans. Fan Fair moved from the fairgrounds to downtown Nashville in 2001, and in 2005 the event drew a four-day combined attendance of 145,000. Autograph sessions take place indoors at the Nashville Convention Center, morning and afternoon concerts are staged at Riverfront Park, and headline concerts are presented each night at the Coliseum. Various other activities, including fan club parties and other celebrity events, take place at venues all over town. Typically, more than 200 country music artists participate.

Most major artists participate in the event, although not all stars attend each year. Among the artists who have participated are Tim McGraw, Faith Hill, the Dixie Chicks, Bill Monroe, Billy Ray Cyrus, Kenny Chesney, Brooks & Dunn, Randy Travis, Roy Acuff, Alan Jackson, Toby Keith, Loretta Lynn, Reba McEntire, Ernest Tubb, and Vince Gill. In 1974 Paul McCartney made a surprise visit. In recent years the focus has been primarily on contemporary country acts, and some soap opera stars also take part in a few activities. Net proceeds from the festival are used to advance the growth and popularity of country music. Half the proceeds are donated to charities designated by the participating artists. If you want to attend, plan early. Purchase your tickets well in advance. In recent years Fan Fair has sold out in advance. Wear cool clothing, as it's pretty hot and humid here this time of year; wear comfortable shoes (you'll do a lot of walking); and bring along plenty of patience (you'll do a lot of waiting). Various ticket packages are available. Packages include admission to the autograph sessions, Riverfront Park concerts, and nightly stadium concerts. Ticket prices for Fan Fair 2008 ranged from $300, which included front and center seats at the stadium concerts, to $125 for club-level seats. Those 14 and younger receive a discount on most ticket packages. Single tickets to the nightly concerts are also available. For more information, or to register, call the number listed.

> **Kitty Wells, the first female country singer to become a major star, was also one of the rare country stars actually born in Nashville. She earned the title "Queen of Country Music."**

DANCIN' IN THE DISTRICT
Riverfront Park
(615) 255-3588
www.dancininthedistrict.com

This 12-week concert series is one of Nashville's most popular summertime events. Recent performers have included Blues Traveler, Keb' Mo', They Might Be Giants, and Robert Earl Keen. Held for several years on Thursday at downtown's Riverfront Park, Dancin' in the District switched to Saturday in 2004. The weekly shows happen rain or shine from about mid-June to late August or early September. The fun starts around 4:30 p.m. and lasts until about 10:30 p.m. Food and beverages are available. Admission for everyone over age five is $5 in advance and $8 at the gate. Check the Web site or call for info on advance ticket packages.

JEFFERSON STREET JAZZ & BLUES FESTIVAL
26th Avenue N. and Jefferson Street
(615) 726-5867
www.jumptojefferson.com

In the mid-1900s, Jefferson Street was nationally known for its jazz, blues, and R&B music. As part of an effort to revitalize the historic street's culture, the Jefferson Street United Merchants Partnership began presenting this annual music festival in 2000. The event is usually held the Saturday after Juneteenth, the June 19 celebration of the ending of slavery.

During the festival, the street is blocked off, while nationally known and local jazz and blues acts perform on the stage throughout the day and late into the evening. Performers have included DeFord Bailey Jr., Tyrone Smith, and Marion James. It's a family-oriented event, complete with food and merchandise vendors and activities for children. Admission is free.

OPRY PLAZA PARTIES
Grand Ole Opry House Plaza
2802 Opryland Drive
(615) 871-OPRY
www.opry.com

These free weekend concerts offer a great chance to catch some top alternative country acts without having to stay up until the wee hours. The shows take place from mid-June through mid-August outdoors on the Grand Ole Opry House plaza, located on the street between the Opry House and Opry Mills shopping mall. On Friday the music starts around 6:30 and continues until around 10:45 p.m.; Saturday shows run from about 5:30 to 9:45 p.m. There are usually two bands and two shows each evening. Previous performers have included Asleep at the Wheel, BR549, Jim Lauderdale, and Dale Watson. Come early to get a seat at one of the cafe tables, or bring a lawn chair and make yourself at home. Food and beverages are available.

i Ricky Van Shelton was a pipe fitter, construction worker, car salesman, grocery store clerk, and house painter before becoming a *Grand Ole Opry* member in 1988.

July

DANCIN' IN THE DISTRICT
Riverfront Park
(615) 255-3588
www.dancininthedistrict.com

See the June listing for more information on this summertime concert series.

OPRY PLAZA PARTIES
Grand Ole Opry House Plaza
2802 Opryland Drive
(615) 871-OPRY
www.opry.com

These free Friday and Saturday summer concerts feature mainly alternative country acts. See the June listing for details.

i Nashville's Fourth of July celebration was ranked in the Top 11 celebrations in the United States and granted the title of the Most Musical Boom by *AOL's City Guide* in 2007.

UNCLE DAVE MACON DAYS
Cannonsburgh Village
312 S. Front Street, Murfreesboro
(800) 716-7560
www.uncledavemacondays.com

Grab your banjos and shine your dancin' shoes for the annual Uncle Dave Macon Days in Cannonsburgh Village in historic Murfreesboro. Considered one of America's premier summer festivals, the family-oriented event gathers more than 40,000 people for a hearty helping of fun, Southern style. The festival was established to honor the memory of Uncle Dave Macon, who lived near Murfreesboro and is considered one of the first *Grand Ole Opry* superstars. A master banjo player and performer, he died in 1952 and was inducted into the Country Music Hall of Fame in 1966. Uncle Dave Macon Days is one of the very few old-time music competitions in the country. A purse of more than $6,000 is at stake during Friday and Saturday's highly charged music and dance competitions. Cannonsburgh is an authentic pioneer village with more than 20 restored log structures. Living-history demonstrations take place during the weekend. A Motorless Parade brings horse-drawn buggies and carriages along a route on Saturday morning. Murfreesboro is 30 minutes southeast of Nashville on I-24.

August

BELL WITCH BLUEGRASS FESTIVAL
Old Bell School, Adams
(615) 696-2589
www.adamstennessee.com
Bluegrass musicians and fans alike enjoy this festival, which features competitions in harmonica, bluegrass banjo, mandolin, guitar, clogging, and square dancing. It's organized by a local bluegrass musician and sponsored by the Adams Community Men's Club. Amateur musicians from Tennessee and surrounding states compete for more than $3,000 in prize money. It takes place the second Friday and Saturday in August in Adams, 40 miles north of downtown Nashville. The pickin' starts Friday evening and continues all day Saturday. All final prize money and a trophy for best overall fiddle player are presented Saturday night. Bring your lawn chairs or blankets, and kick back under a shady tree. Concessions and restrooms are available. This is a no-alcohol event. Admission on Friday is $6 for anyone 12 and over, $3 for those ages 8 to 12; admission on Saturday is $8 for everyone. There are no fees for entering the competition. In addition to the music, there is also an arts and crafts show. Rough campsites are available, and parking is free.

DANCIN' IN THE DISTRICT
Riverfront Park
(615) 255-3588
www.dancininthedistrict.com
See the June listing for information on this Saturday-evening summertime street party and concert series.

OPRY PLAZA PARTIES
Grand Ole Opry House Plaza
2802 Opryland Drive
(615) 871-OPRY
www.opry.com

These free Friday and Saturday summer concerts feature mainly alternative country acts. See the June listing for details.

September

DANCIN' IN THE DISTRICT
Riverfront Park
(615) 255-3588
www.dancininthedistrict.com
See the June listing for information on this Saturday-evening summertime street party and concert series.

October

GRAND OLE OPRY BIRTHDAY CELEBRATION
Grand Ole Opry House
2802 Opryland Drive
(615) 871-OPRY
www.opry.com
Grand Ole Opry fans gather each October to celebrate the birthday of America's longest-running radio program. The three-day party is held in mid-October and includes concerts, a Grand Ole Opry performance, and autograph and photo sessions with the stars. Various ticket packages and group rates are available. Call the number listed for more information. For more on the Opry, see our History chapter as well as other entries in this chapter.

November

CMA AWARDS
Gaylord Entertainment Center
501 Broadway
(615) 244-2840 (Country
Music Association)
www.cmaawards.com
The Country Music Association Awards are the industry's most prestigious honors, and the annual star-studded ceremony is the biggest night of the year for Nashville's country music industry. The ceremony is held in early November at the Gaylord Entertainment Center and is televised live on ABC. Awards are presented in more than a dozen categories, including Entertainer of the Year, Album of the Year, and Song of the

Year. Winners are determined by the CMA membership. Some tickets are usually available to the public. For more information call the CMA or visit their Web site.

i Experts say the Ryman Auditorium's acoustics are second only to the Mormon Tabernacle, surpassing even Carnegie Hall.

COUNTRY MUSIC WEEK
Various Nashville locations

For one week each fall, Nashville's music industry participates in a dizzying array of parties and awards presentations. It's schmooze city as industry executives, songwriters, performers, media, and wannabes attend these events at various venues around the city. Most events are invitation-only, but those who are determined will find that it's not too difficult to track down someone with a ticket or invitation to spare. The highlight of the week is the Country Music Association's nationally televised awards show (read more about that in the preceding entry). Performing-rights organizations ASCAP, BMI, and SESAC each host galas, presenting awards to the year's top songwriters.

i Priceline.com in 2007 named Nashville one of the Top 25 destinations in the world to ring in the New Year.

SHOPPING

Shopping. It's a favorite pastime for some, a dreaded inconvenience for others. But whether you view it as a fun activity or a necessary evil, Nashville has the stores that will make your shopping experiences pleasant. From antiques to cowboy boots, and toys to Italian-made suits, Nashville has it all. There are so many shopping districts in and around Nashville that it could take years to discover them all. Major malls are in just about any direction, and you can't go wrong shopping at any of these. Shopping meccas like Rivergate, Cool Springs, and Hickory Hollow are always jam-packed and offer almost any merchandise you want. There are also many neighborhood-type shopping districts, such as Hillsboro Village, Berry Hill, Nolensville Road, and Eighth Avenue S., that make shopping superconvenient. You'll often find some interesting stores and merchandise in these areas. Nashville is a top tourist destination, and naturally we also have tons of country music souvenirs. You'll find most of those in shops and attractions on or near Second Avenue and in the Opryland/Music Valley area. We list some of those shops along with record stores in our Music City chapter. For information on even more shopping opportunities, see our Arts, Attractions, and Annual Events chapters.

We have arranged this chapter by category of goods and have added a section on unique malls. This is definitely not a comprehensive list of stores and shops in Nashville, just a guide to some of the local hot spots and favorites. If we have overlooked your favorite shop, let us know, and we'll try to include it in a future edition. We're always interested in other Insiders' perspectives. Keep this book handy so the next time a gift-giving occasion comes around (or if you just want to treat yourself to something nice), you can glance through our listings. You might find a neat shop, an unusual gift, or a great deal you might have otherwise missed.

NOTABLE MALLS

THE FACTORY AT FRANKLIN
230 Franklin Road, Franklin
(615) 791-1777
www.factoryatfranklin.com
The Factory at Franklin is one of the area's more creative shopping malls. Housed in a renovated 1929 stove factory 6 blocks from historic downtown Franklin, the mall offers an interesting assortment of antiques stores, art galleries, gift shops, and restaurants. You can take a gourmet cooking class or pick up some fancy kitchen goods at the Viking Store, paint your own piece of pottery at Third Coast Clay, or adopt a pet at Happy Tails Humane. The Factory is also the site of special events and concerts.

THE NASHVILLE ARCADE
Between Fourth Avenue N. and Fifth Avenue N., and Union and Church Streets
(615) 255-1034
The Arcade is one of Music City's unique shopping areas. This two-level, glass-covered mall opened in 1903 and was modeled after a mall in Milan, Italy, and others in northern U.S. cities. It is one of only four such structures left in the United States. Today the narrow, block-long mall stays busy with downtown workers and visitors who stop in for a cup of coffee or a quick bite to eat. A fixture at the Arcade is the Peanut Shop, which has been filling the air with the aroma of its freshly roasted nuts since 1927. Other stores include Percy's Shoe Shine, the Arcade Smoke Shop, Arcade Fruit

Stand, It's a Piece of Cake Bakery, Jimbo's ("world class hot dogs and taters"), and other restaurants. The Arcade is open on weekdays.

i Don't go into Robert's Western World on Broadway looking for Western wear. Although they do sell boots, this place is really a bar. It's where the band BR549 got its start.

OPRY MILLS
Opry Mills Drive, exit 11 off Briley Parkway
(615) 514-1100
www.oprymills.com
"Shoppertainment" has arrived in Nashville in the form of this 1.2 million–square–foot shopping mall/entertainment complex. Opry Mills opened in May 2000 at the site of the former Opryland theme park. It's located between Two Rivers Parkway and McGavock Pike, about 7 miles northeast of downtown. Lots of Nashvillians mourned the loss of Opryland and seemed reluctant to embrace the idea that a complex could combine shopping and fun, but Opry Mills has turned out to be a big success. The mall features about 200 stores, including manufacturers' outlets and off-price retailers. The shopping part of the shoppertainment complex includes such stores as Bass Pro Shops Outdoor World, OFF 5th–Saks Fifth Avenue Outlet, Old Navy, Bose, Banana Republic Factory Store, Guess? Factory Store, Ann Taylor Loft, and Mikasa Factory Store. We can't resist stopping in the Blacklion, a huge multidealer store filled with art, antiques, and other furniture; home decor items; garden accessories; and gift items. As for the entertainment, options include the Gibson Showcase, an IMAX theater, Regal Cinemas multiplex, Dave and Buster's, and Checkered Flag. If all that shopping and playing works up an appetite, there are more than a dozen restaurants and specialty food stores where you can relax and refuel, including the Rainforest Cafe, Alabama Grill, and Johnny Rockets.

i Opened in the fall of 2007, Hill Center on Hillsboro Pike is located in the heart of Green Hills. The new outdoor shopping center has 220,000 square feet of retail, dining and office space. Shops include Anthropologie, Posh, Hemline, Francesca's, Whole Foods, California Pizza Kitchen, Pei Wei, Zoe's, West Elm, Swoozie's, Five Guys Burgers, and more.

WESTERN-WEAR STORES

KATY K'S RANCH DRESSING
2407 12th Avenue S.
(615) 297-4242
www.KatyK.com
We love the name of this Western-wear store: Ranch Dressing. Get it? This store is packed with all sorts of interesting clothing, shoes, and accessories. Whether you're looking for a neat $25 shirt or an original Nudies of Hollywood creation for $2,000, you'll have lots to choose from. Ranch Dressing also carries all sorts of kitschy gift items and accessories. Since it opened in 1994, the store has developed a following among music video stylists, recording artists, musicians, and others who want to look like a star.

MANUEL EXCLUSIVE CLOTHIER
1922 Broadway
(615) 321-5444
www.manuelamericandesign.com
Manuel is best known for the flashy rhinestone garb worn by some country music performers, but the store also designs high-quality one-of-a-kind pieces for businesspeople worldwide. Originally founded in Los Angeles in 1972, Manuel today is based in Nashville. Most of the store's business is custom costumes for performers, among them Dwight Yoakam, Brooks & Dunn, Bob Dylan, and Aerosmith's Joe Perry. The prices are steep—a custom coat starts at around $1,250, and shirts start at around $450—but browsing is free. The store welcomes the curious to come in and check out the showroom. Manuel himself is usually there from 9:00 a.m. to 6:00 p.m. Monday through Friday.

TRAIL WEST

1183 West Main Street, Hendersonville
(615) 264-2955

2416 Music Valley Drive
(615) 883-5933

219 Broadway
(615) 255-7030

312 Broadway (Boots 'N' More)
(615) 251-1711

Hendersonville-based Trail West has five Western-wear stores in Middle Tennessee selling clothing and accessories for men, women, and children. The spacious stores are stocked with such brands as Resistol, Stetson, Boulet, Charlie 1 Horse, Corral Boot, and Hat 'n Hand. Although it has a different name, the location at 312 Broadway is essentially the same as the other Trail West stores. In addition to the four Nashville-area stores, there is also a Trail West in Columbia, Tennessee.

CLOTHING AND ACCESSORIES...

...for Women

COCO

4239 Harding Road
(615) 292-0362

A favorite of mostly upscale baby boomers, this women's specialty store in Belle Meade has an extensive collection of designer clothing for all occasions. Styles range from sophisticated chic to career classics and contemporary cutting-edge, and labels include Dana Buchman, Ellen Tracy, Yansi Fugel, Lafayette 148, and Tahari. Coco also sells cosmetics and gift items. Expect to pay full price at this shop. There are only a couple of times a year when you can buy something on sale, usually once after the first of the year and once at the end of summer.

THE FRENCH SHOPPE

2817 West End Avenue
(615) 327-8132

240 East Main Street, Hendersonville
(615) 824-9244
www.frenchshoppe.com

Known for its selection of good-quality career wear, casual weekend clothes at affordable prices, and helpful staff, the French Shoppe has been outfitting fashion-minded Middle Tennessee women since 1968, when the store first opened in Murfreesboro. The family-owned business moved to Nashville in 1978. Merchandise varies somewhat by store. The Hendersonville store sells gift items.

JAMIE INC.

4317 Harding Road, Belle Meade
(615) 292-4188
www.jamie-nashville.com

This Belle Meade boutique carries such top designers as Carolina Herrera, Dolce & Gabanna, Yves Saint Laurent, Ralph Lauren, and Oscar de la Renta. A contemporary department in the back caters to the young and fashionable. Jamie also has Fine Jewelry at Jamie, which offers creations by well-known national and international jewelry artists, and a cosmetics department that specializes in several high-end brands.

OFF BROADWAY SHOE WAREHOUSE

118 16th Avenue S.
(615) 254-6242

Opry Mills, 357 Opry Mills Drive
(615) 514-0290

1648 Westgate Circle, Brentwood
(Cool Springs area)
(615) 309-8939
www.offbroadwayshoes.com

Shoes! With 35,000 to 45,000 pairs of designer shoes in what seems like acres of space, Off Broadway Shoe Warehouse is shoe heaven. This shoe store chain originated in Nashville around 1990. The first location, just off Broadway, near Music Row, was a huge success, which resulted in stores opening nationwide. The Atlanta-based operator now has about 30 stores around the country. Each store has the latest trendy styles as well as the classics—from penny loafers and must-have sandals to hiking boots and towering stiletto heels—at substantial savings. Women's sizes range from 5 to 12; there are lots of narrows and a few wide widths, too. With prices generally 25 to 50 percent less than at most retail stores, it's hard to leave here with only one box.

...for Men

LEVY'S
3900 Hillsboro Pike
(615) 383-2800
www.levysclothes.com
Levy's has been dressing Nashville men since 1855 and is one of the few remaining individually owned clothing stores in the area. This family-owned store is in the Hillsboro Plaza shopping center in Green Hills. Upscale men's business clothing and sportswear are the specialty, although Levy's added women's business and casual clothing recently. Levy's lines include Hart Schaffner & Marx, Hickey Freeman, Brioni, Canali, and Ermenegildo Zegna. The store also carries some of the finest leather in town, including the Bruno Magli label. Many of Levy's knowledgeable sales employees have been with the store for decades, and they'll help you put together all the right pieces, whether you're looking for dressy casual wear for "casual Fridays" or a high-power suit fit for the corner office.

OFF BROADWAY SHOE WAREHOUSE
118 16th Avenue S.
(615) 254-6242

Opry Mills, 357 Opry Mills Drive
(615) 514-0290

1648 Westgate Circle, Brentwood
(Cool Springs area)
(615) 309-8939
www.offbroadwayshoes.com
Although these enormous stores devote most of their space to women's shoes, each has a good selection of men's footwear, too. This is a great place for shoes—you can expect to pay 25 to 50 percent less than you would at department stores.

THE OXFORD SHOP
3830 Bedford Avenue
(615) 383-4442
www.theoxfordshop.com
The Oxford Shop carries high-end suits and casual wear for men, including such lines as Samuelsohn, Southwick, Corbin, Robert Talbott, Bills Khakis, and Barbour. The locally owned store, in business since 1961, also offers expert tailoring and free lifetime alterations on every garment. The Oxford Shop has two sales a year—one after the holidays and another at the end of summer. The store also does two trunk shows every year.

ANTIQUES

There are numerous antiques malls and shops in and around Nashville. Nashville's Eighth Avenue S., Franklin, Goodlettsville, and Lebanon are some of the best-known antiques hot spots, but you can find shops almost anywhere. Take a drive out in the country and you're bound to come across several charming little stores filled with all sorts of furniture and collectibles from years gone by. We've highlighted a few locations, enough to keep weekend treasure seekers busy. Most of the malls are open daily, but hours vary, so it's a good idea to call before visiting. For other information on antiques, see our Annual Events chapter. FYI: An antique, in the strictest sense, is something more than 100 years old, while a collectible is usually at least 20 years old but may be older. But keep in mind that the definition of *antique* can vary around Middle Tennessee. For example, this *Insiders' Guide to Nashville* author usually uses the term to refer to the kinds of relics she finds in her grandparents' attic or chicken coop, but some Nashvillians tend to reserve the term for items like those lovely 250-year-old dressers that fetch upward of $10,000 at some of the area's finer antiques stores.

In *The Treasure Hunter's Guide to Historic Middle Tennessee and South Central Kentucky Antiques, Flea Markets, Junk Stores & More* (Gold-Kiser Co., Nashville, 1995), Maude Gold Kiser offers tips on successful antiquing. Here are some of her ideas:

- If you're a first-timer, go with someone who is experienced and who enjoys it.
- Cash sometimes can improve your negotiating power. Don't expect prices to be dirt cheap in small towns.
- Take along notes about what you're looking for—size, color, and so on. Keep room and specific area measurements with you at all times, as well as a tape measure, a magnet that will not stick to sterling silver or solid brass, and a magnifying glass.
- These goods are bought as-is. Check items carefully for cracks, chips, inadequate repairs, or missing pieces.
- Clean out your car, truck, or van so you'll have maximum room for treasures you find.
- All dealers are on the lookout for merchandise. They will usually be willing to pay you only the wholesale value (but that's still better than what you'll get at a garage sale). And don't expect to get free appraisals.
- Do your gift buying at antiques stores. Antiques or old collectibles will increase in value.
- Don't be afraid to ask questions. Most dealers are in the business because they love antiques and will talk your ear off about their field of expertise.
- Wear comfortable shoes.

A $2.48 yellowed rolled-up document at Music City Thrift Shop turned out to be a rare bargain. The document was an official copy of the Declaration of Independence, one of 200 commissioned by John Quincy Adams and printed in 1823. It sold at a 2007 auction for $477,650.

Nashville's Eighth Avenue S. District

CANE-ERY ANTIQUE MALL
2112 Eighth Avenue S.
(615) 269-4780
Cane-ery Antique Mall specializes in chair caning and wicker repair. The mom-and-pop store, in business since 1976, sells caning and basket supplies and has a good collection of antique repro-

duction furniture hardware as well as salvaged hardware. If you're looking to get a lamp repaired or are searching for lamp parts or shades, you may want to pay a visit. The store also buys and sells all sorts of antique furniture.

DEALER'S CHOICE ANTIQUES AND AUCTION
2109 Eighth Avenue S.
(615) 383-7030
www.dealerschoiceantiqueauction.com
Antiques auctions take place here every other Friday night and draw about 150 dealers and individual antiquers. Dealer's Choice also sells off the floor, but you might want to call before visiting because operating hours vary. You'll find everything from decorator items to fine furnishings here, including Victorian, French, country, and mahogany furniture.

DOWNTOWN ANTIQUE MALL
612 Eighth Avenue S.
(615) 256-6616
Housed in a creaky old historic warehouse beside the railroad tracks, this 13,000-square-foot antiques mall is a fun place to get lost on a rainy afternoon. You never know what you'll find—or should we say excavate—here. The mall's aisles are piled high with all sorts of neat stuff, including furniture from the 1800s to 1950s, collectibles, and textiles. Best of all, most of the antiques here are of the very affordable variety.

In 1950 Aladdin Industries of Nashville fancied up its plain steel lunch boxes and thermos bottles with Hopalong Cassidy decals. Sales jumped from 50,000 to 600,000 lunch kits the first year. The lunch boxes are now collector's items.

TENNESSEE ANTIQUE MALL
654 Wedgewood Avenue
(615) 259-4077
Furniture, glassware, paintings and prints, mirrors, jewelry, and all sorts of treasures in about 150 booths are tucked into this 25,000-square-foot mall.

Also in Nashville

CARISSA'S ARMOIRES & ANTIQUES
1801 21st Avenue S.
(615) 292-6994, (877) CARISSA
www.carissasarmoires.com

Carissa's isn't strictly an antiques store—about 80 percent of their items are reproductions—but if how a piece of furniture looks is more important to you than how old it is, you can't go wrong at this lovely shop. Located in a large building in the trendy Hillsboro Village area, Carissa's is stocked full of one-of-a-kind armoires, handcrafted tables, painted chests and nightstands, creative accessories, and extravagantly upholstered, oversize sofas and chairs. There's a heavy emphasis on Mexican, Indonesian, and French imports. We've never had much luck bargaining on the prices here, but you might be able to get a deal on the antique pieces. Carissa's has a storewide sale each May, when you can select your purchases, then spin a wheel for a discount of up to 35 percent.

GARDEN PARK ANTIQUES BY HERNDON & MERRY
7121 Cockrill Bend Boulevard
(615) 350-6655
www.herndonmerry.com

If you like using architectural elements as furnishings, you'll want to visit this store, which specializes in antique ironwork—fences, gates, window panels, urns, fountains, and statuary from around the world. In addition to individual elements, the store carries one-of-a-kind tables, headboards, and other items of furniture that incorporate salvaged ironwork or other old architectural pieces. If you see a fragment that you like, you can have it transformed into a unique piece of furniture by the store's Herndon & Merry ironworks division next door.

GREEN HILLS ANTIQUE MALL
4108 Hillsboro Pike
(615) 383-9851

Green Hills Antique Mall has 22,000 square feet and more than 20 dealers. Lots of furniture, both antiques and quality reproductions, is beautifully displayed, and you'll also find glassware, books, art, and other items.

PEMBROKE ANTIQUES
6610 Highway 100
(615) 353-0889

The fact that Pembroke Antiques is located near Belle Meade should give you a clue that this isn't your junk-store-variety antiques store. On the other hand, if you're on a budget, don't be put off by the location: Pembroke's prices are actually quite reasonable. The store specializes in quality English and French furniture that has "a sophisticated look but a warm country feel." It's a favorite among local interior designers. This is a good place to find majolica pottery, decorative garden items, and silver. If you're looking for a unique and tasteful item for a wedding or housewarming gift, Pembroke will have it.

POLK PLACE ANTIQUES
6614 Highway 100
(615) 353-1324

Polk Place specializes in items from the American Federal period (1790–1840) and Southern furniture. The store also offers a selection of porcelains, coin silver, copper, pewter, brass, oil paintings, and custom-made lamps.

Franklin

There are two concentrated areas of shops and several others scattered about in Franklin. One concentration is on and near Second Avenue while the other is on Bridge Street, which runs parallel to Main Street.

ANTIQUES OF FRANKLIN
230 Franklin Road, Building 3
(615) 591-4612
www.antiquesatthefactoryfranklin.com

The 15,000-square-foot Antiques of Franklin is the largest retail store at the Factory at Franklin shopping mall (see our Notable Malls section in this chapter for more about the Factory). This store carries practically everything—from roadside castoffs to vintage $20,000 crystal chandeliers.

Furniture styles range from French to Shabby Chic. There is a good collection of antique silver here, as well as old sports memorabilia, rugs, glassware, vintage jewelry, candles, and gift items.

BATTLEGROUND ANTIQUE MALL
232 Franklin Road
(615) 794-9444
Located next to the Factory shopping mall, this 16,000-square-foot mall is filled with French, English, and American furniture, Civil War artifacts, glassware, and linens. The store has especially good prices on furniture.

COUNTRY CHARM ANTIQUE MALL
301 Lewisburg Pike
(615) 790-8908
You'll love browsing through this mall's hodgepodge of antiques and collectibles—lots of furniture, glassware, primitives, and garden items such as benches, obelisks, and other decorative pieces. The mall is about 5 blocks from Main Street in Franklin.

FRANKLIN ANTIQUE MALL
251 Second Avenue S.
(615) 790-8593
If you're planning to go antiquing in Franklin, you'll want to be sure to put the Franklin Antique Mall on your list of stops. In fact, go ahead and put it at the top of your list, and allow plenty of time for browsing here. Housed in the historic handmade brick icehouse building, Franklin Antique Mall has 60 booths. There is a good selection of furniture and glassware, lamp parts, and glass replacement shades, as well as collectible magazines and prints. The furniture selection ranges from rustic to fine quality, and we usually find that the prices are very reasonable.

HARPETH ANTIQUE MALL
529 Alexander Plaza
(615) 790-7965
www.harpethantiquemall.com
Harpeth Antique Mall is in a strip shopping center off Highway 96 near Interstate 65. The 12,000-square-foot mall has merchandise from more than 100 dealers, with lots of art, glass, furniture, prints and maps, books, linens, and other items.

WINCHESTER ANTIQUE MALL
113 Bridge Street
(615) 791-5846
There are about 25 booths in this cozy, two-story cottage located near Franklin's town square. They're filled with reasonably priced American and English furniture, fine porcelain, sterling, linens, and books. This store is a local favorite.

Goodlettsville

Goodlettsville's antiques district stretches along the historic Main Street. To get there, take I-65 North to exit 97 and go west to Dickerson Pike. NOTE: In Goodlettsville, Dickerson Pike, Main Street, and U.S. Highway 41 are the same road.

ANTIQUE CORNER MALL
128 North Main Street
(615) 859-7673
Antique Corner Mall has a little bit of everything, including affordable antique furniture, collectibles, costume jewelry, glassware, lamps, and antique toys.

GOODLETTSVILLE ANTIQUE MALL— ANOTHER ERA
213 North Main Street
(615) 859-7002
www.goodlettsvilleantiquemall.com
You can spend hours treasure hunting in this enormous mall. With 20,000 square feet of space and more than 100 booths, the mall is stocked full of furniture, glassware, collectibles, quilts, clocks, and toys.

RARE BIRD ANTIQUE MALL
212 South Main Street
(615) 851-2635
Scout for furniture, toys, gas station memorabilia, linens, and glassware in more than 50 booths here.

FLEA MARKET

TENNESSEE STATE FAIRGROUNDS FLEA MARKET

Tennessee State Fairgrounds
Wedgewood Avenue at Rains Avenue
(615) 862-5016
www.tennesseestatefair.org

Nashvillians love to shop at the Tennessee State Fairgrounds Flea Market. It's held the fourth weekend of every month from January through November and the third weekend in December. The flea market draws anywhere from 100,000 to 250,000 people from Nashville and neighboring states in a two-day period. Traders, craftspeople, and antiques dealers from about 30 states exhibit antiques, crafts, and new products in more than 2,000 indoor and outdoor booths. There's something to fit every budget—from knickknacks for less than $1 to the priciest antique furniture. The flea market is open from 8:00 a.m. to 5:00 p.m. Friday, 7:00 a.m. to 6:00 p.m. Saturday, and 7:00 a.m. to 4:00 p.m. Sunday. Hint: Come early to avoid traffic jams. Admission is free; it costs $4 to park in the fairgrounds parking lot. A free shuttle will transport you to the top of the hill at the fairgrounds, but it's not too far to walk.

CONSIGNMENT STORES

BARGAIN BOUTIQUE
4004 Hillsboro Pike
(615) 297-7900

Bargain Boutique is in the Green Hills Court shopping center. The store first opened in 1970 and has built a good reputation among consignment shoppers. It sells women's designer clothing, accessories, and shoes, and fashion-savvy bargain hunters will find such names as Ellen Tracy, Dana Buchman, Chanel, and Valentino here. Consignors receive 50 percent of the selling price. Consignment is by appointment only. The store is open Monday through Saturday.

DESIGNER RENAISSANCE
2822 Bransford Avenue
(615) 297-8822
www.designerrenaissance.com

Jodi Miller opened this women's consignment shop in 1988, operating for years in Green Hills. In 2004 she relocated to nearby Berry Hill, setting up shop in a house in the tiny satellite city's hip shopping district. Some of Music City's best-dressed women consign their clothing here. As its name suggests, Designer Renaissance carries designer clothes as well as high-end secondhand clothing. Miller also stocks accessories. Open Monday through Saturday, the store closes on all major (and some minor) holidays. If this store isn't in or near your neighborhood, you might want to call before you come because it sometimes closes on special occasions. If you have items you want to consign, you'll need to make an appointment. Consignors receive 50 percent of the selling price.

FINDERS KEEPERS
778 Rivergate Parkway
(615) 646-0022

8105 Moores Lane, Brentwood
(615) 333-9801
www.f-keepers.com

Finders Keepers is a great place for finding furniture at bargain prices. If you're downsizing or otherwise ready to unload some furniture, you can consign your used stuff here and split the proceeds 50/50 with the store. The stores are large and carry all sorts of furniture, including some brand-new merchandise. Styles range from retro to refined, and the merchandise changes constantly. On any given day you might find a nice antique dresser, an '80s-style black lacquer bedroom suite, a pair of front-porch rocking chairs, or a set of fur-upholstered chairs shaped like cowboy boots. The stores also carry artwork and home decor items. If you have items to sell, the Finders Keepers crew will pick it up free of charge. They'll deliver your purchases for a fee.

SECOND TIME AROUND

121 Indian Lake Road, Hendersonville
(615) 822-6961
www.secondtimearoundbypeggy.com

The friendly staff at this store makes shopping here a pleasure. If you like, the staff will help you put together a whole look. The boutique-type store sells women's clothing, including such lines as Dana Buchman, Anne Klein, and Ellen Tracy. The store is very particular regarding the clothing it accepts, so you can count on good-quality items here. The store has a bridal room, an "after 5" room, and a good selection of well-cared-for shoes and accessories. The store is open Tuesday through Saturday. Second Time Around accepts items by appointment only. Consignors receive 50 percent of the selling price.

TOYS

PHILLIPS TOY MART

5207 Harding Road
(615) 352-5363
www.phillipstoymart.com

In business for more than half a century, Phillips Toy Mart has been in the Belle Meade area for nearly 40 years. An old-timey kind of toy store, Phillips sells all sorts of toys, including games for kids and adults and a large selection of imported educational toys. The store also sells a variety of collector dolls and has one of the largest model selections in the South, including tools and hobby supplies.

i Children's seasonal consignment sales are popular with bargain-hunting Nashville parents. The sales are great for stocking up on good quality, "gently used" children's clothing as well as for selling apparel that your kids have outgrown. The sales are held for a limited time—usually late winter/early spring and late summer/ early fall. Watch the newspapers for details, or visit the Web site www.kidsconsignment-guide.com for a list of upcoming sales.

GIFTS

THE AMERICAN ARTISAN

4231 Harding Road
(615) 298-4691
www.american-artisan.com

Colorful and attention-grabbing glass objects line the large windows of this crafts store in Belle Meade, catching the light and beckoning you to come in to treasure hunt. The American Artisan is a fabulous store filled with crafts handmade by artists all over the United States. This is just the right place to find that special gift or one-of-a-kind item for the person who has everything—or the person who appreciates "designer" crafts. The American Artisan carries many clay and wood crafts, as well as hand-blown glass, metal, and leather items. Beautiful bowls, stemware, wood boxes, jewelry, and quirky objets d'art plus unusual pieces of furniture fill the various rooms in the store. Each year on Father's Day weekend, the American Artisan sponsors the American Artisan Festival in Centennial Park. (See our Annual Events chapter for details.)

CALDWELL COLLECTION

2205 Bandywood Drive
(615) 298-5800
www.caldwellcollection.com

Sisters Ellen Caldwell and Cissy Caldwell Akers stock this gift shop with treasures they find on buying trips to the Tuscany region of Italy as well as to France and other places in Europe. Located behind Davis-Kidd Booksellers in Green Hills, the casual store is best known for its beautiful Italian pottery. The eclectic collection also includes pretty glassware; leather journals; tole; marble fruits; pillows from Florence, Italy; nice Italian artwork; picture frames; linens; collectible memory boxes; and ironware.

CRYSTAL'S

4550 Harding Road
(615) 292-4300, (800) 525-7757
www.crystalgayle.com/crystal%27.htm

Country singer Crystal Gayle ("Don't It Make My Brown Eyes Blue") opened this store in 1987 with the goal of providing top-quality crystal and other gift items in a friendly, relaxed atmosphere. While there are some spectacular high-end items here, the store stocks plenty of affordable merchandise, so whether you want to spend less than $20 or more than $1,000, you'll be able to find something that suits your budget. If it's crystal you want, this is the place. Crystal's carries Waterford, Lalique, Baccarat, and Lladro crystal. The store also carries a nice selection of porcelain, handpainted ceramics, fine jewelry, bookends, and humidors.

MARKET STREET MERCANTILE
111 Second Avenue N.
(615) 228-5336
www.marketmercantile.com
Market Street Mercantile is the general store for collectors—of Jack Daniel's, John Deere, *I Love Lucy,* and Elvis paraphernalia. The shop also carries Nashville souvenirs and a multitude of other items. Open daily 10:00 a.m. to 9:00 p.m.

PANGAEA
1721 21st Avenue S.
(615) 269-9665
www.pangaeanashville.com
This Hillsboro Village boutique has lots of funky and fun clothing and home decor items. Mexican folk art is the main feel, and there is a lot of primitive- or antique-style, natural fiber clothing from Mexico and India, as well as unique and interesting tabletop items. The store has a good selection of candles and candleholders, as well as Mexican mirrors, jewelry, books, and Day of the Dead objects.

TENNESSEE MEMORIES
2182 Bandywood Drive
(615) 298-3253
www.tennesseememories.com
Tennessee Memories is a cozy store brimming with lovely pottery, woodwork, pewter, all sorts of neat collectibles, and other good stuff. The store focuses on high-quality "antiquey," old-fashioned, and Victorian-style items; most of the

merchandise is handmade by Tennessee artisans. The food pantry in the back corner is stocked with an assortment of teas, coffees, cocoas, jams and jellies, spices, and other goodies.

GARDENING STORES

BATES NURSERY & GARDEN CENTER
3810 Whites Creek Pike
(615) 876-1014
www.batesnursery.com
Bates is one of Nashville's favorite garden centers. It has been in business since 1932. It began during the Great Depression, when Bessie Bates, grandmother of the current owner, David Bates, started selling flowers and shrubs from her backyard greenhouse on Charlotte Pike. Today Bates Nursery has a huge selection of flowers, herbs, trees, shrubs, fountains, statuary, and accessories—anything you need for your garden. The store offers free landscaping design services (call for an appointment) and, for a fee, will come to your home and design a more detailed plan for you. Bates has a great Web site. You can log on and search for plants by category, see if they're currently in stock, check the prices, and get detailed instructions on how to care for them.

We like the fact that most of Bates's plants come with a one-year warranty. Combine that with their competitive prices, and it's no wonder that Nashvillians have been shopping here for more than three quarters of a century.

GREEN & HAGSTROM
7767 Fernvale Road, Fairview
(615) 799-0708
www.greenandhagstrom.com
If you're one of the many Nashvillians with garden ponds—or if you're planning to add one to your yard—you'll want to pay a visit to this huge aquatic nursery and garden-supply center just west of Nashville. They sell all sorts of floating and underwater plants, as well as materials for building and maintaining ponds, water-treatment supplies, and more. In addition to plants, they have a variety of decorative fish, including imported Japanese koi and fancy goldfish, which they will

ship anywhere in the United States. The store conducts classes on a variety of pond-related topics.

LITTLE MARROWBONE FARM
1560 Little Marrowbone Road
Ashland City
(615) 792-7255
www.littlemarrowbone.com

Bill and Andrea Henry's little off-the-beaten-path growing nursery has developed a loyal clientele since opening back in the mid-'80s. They specialize in unique varieties of plants, including herbs, hostas, perennials, conifers, hellebores, and—our favorite—adorable tabletop topiaries made from pesticide-free herbs and shrubs. The nursery has a loyal clientele from several surrounding counties and even some from neighboring Kentucky. Their annual herb sale in April is a popular time to visit, but come early for the best selection. The farm—it's nothin' fancy—is about 25 miles northwest of Nashville, off Highway 12 N. You'll have to watch for the plastic-covered growing houses or the address on the mailbox because there isn't a sign marking the nursery. You'll also be hard-pressed to find prices on their merchandise. But not to worry: The prices are always reasonable. In fact, they're so good that we usually feel like we're practically stealing the merchandise. Little Marrowbone Farm is generally open daily, but it's a good idea to call before visiting, as hours vary.

i Nashville's many crafts fairs offer a variety of creative items that make wonderful gifts. See our Annual Events chapter for more information on these events.

MOORE & MOORE WEST GARDEN CENTER
8216 Highway 100
(615) 662-8849
www.mooreandmoore.com

Moore & Moore has been voted Nashville's best garden center by readers of the Nashville Scene on more than one occasion. In business since 1980, this friendly, full-service garden store specializes in native plants from trees and shrubs to woodland wildflowers. If you don't know what to plant or don't know how to plant it, you're in luck because the store offers landscaping and design services. The store also has one of the best selections of bulbs around. Don't miss the garden accessories, especially the designer pottery. The knowledgeable staff is always a good source of free, friendly advice on any gardening topic, from soil science to the latest trends in gardening.

BOOKSTORES

ALKEBU-LAN IMAGES
2721 Jefferson Street
(615) 321-4111

The small, bright yellow building at the corner of 28th Avenue N. and Jefferson Street is home to Alkebu-Lan Images, an independently owned bookstore specializing in African-American books, including fiction, nonfiction, and religious titles. The store also sells some apparel, greeting cards, and gift items such as figurines, notecards, body oils, incense, jewelry, and imported African carvings. Many of the store's products are educationally focused. Alkebu-Lan Images hosts an annual book fair as well as author signings and occasional Saturday-morning storytelling sessions for kids. The store is open daily. Incidentally, translated from Moorish-Arabic, the name *Alkebu-Lan* means "land of the blacks."

DAVIS-KIDD BOOKSELLERS INC.
2121 Green Hills Village Drive
(615) 385-2645, (615) 292-1404
(hours and events hot line)
www.daviskidd.com

Many Nashvillians consider Davis-Kidd to be their favorite bookstore. With more than 100,000 books filling the store's massive two-story space in Green Hills, this is not only a book lover's paradise but a popular and comfortable gathering place, too. Benches are positioned among the rows of books, inviting shoppers to linger and browse as long as they like. The store's cafe, Brontë's (615-385-0043), serves a variety of tasty munchies, coffees, and desserts and is a nice spot to relax any time of day. Davis-Kidd offers

20 percent off Nashville best-sellers. In addition to stocking plenty of current favorites, the store has many backlist titles, including a lot of hard-to-find books. The store's customer service is excellent. Most special orders arrive within a couple of days. Davis-Kidd also has a large magazine and newspaper section, including foreign publications, and a nice selection of greeting cards, stationery, calendars, and gift items. During the holidays the store has a good selection of boxed greeting cards. The children's area has a variety of educational toys as well as books and is a big hit with the little ones. Davis-Kidd also hosts many in-store author signings each month and sponsors three book clubs, which meet several times a month. A few days a week, the store has a program for children (see our Kidstuff chapter for more about that).

LOGOS BOOKSTORE
4012 Hillsboro Pike
(615) 297-5388
www.nashville.logosbookstores.com
This cozy and friendly Christian bookstore in Green Hills, adjacent to the Green Hills Court Shopping Center, is one of about 30 independently owned Logos stores nationwide. The store carries a variety of Bibles and religious books, including an extensive selection of Reformed theology literature. You can also find homeschooling books here. There's a good selection of CDs, greeting cards, and gift items, too. Logos also buys and sells used books and CDs. The knowledgeable staff is always happy to place special orders.

MAGICAL JOURNEY
212 Louise Avenue
(615) 327-0327
www.magicaljourney.com
This New Age bookstore, in a renovated house behind Elliston Place, carries all sorts of metaphysical books and welcomes people of all religious beliefs. Included in the selection of 5,000 books are works on Buddhism, Hinduism, Native American beliefs and practices, and more. The store also carries a large selection of candles as well as incense, crystals, greeting cards, meditation tools, aromatherapy lines, jewelry, music, and other items. The store offers daily psychic readings and massage therapy, as well as monthly Reiki classes and other classes on empowerment and spiritual growth.

ST. MARY'S BOOK STORE & CHURCH SUPPLIES
1909 West End Avenue
(615) 329-1835
www.stmarysbookstore.com
Located at 19th Avenue and West End, St. Mary's Book Store & Church Supplies has been in business for about 80 years. It is a full-line Christian bookstore, with Bibles, hymnals, church supplies, gifts, CDs, and cassettes.

Used Books

BOOKMAN/BOOKWOMAN USED BOOKS
1713 21st Avenue S.
(615) 383-6555
www.bookmanbookwoman.com
This bookstore opened in fall 1995 in Hillsboro Village. Voted Best Used Bookstore several years in a row by readers of the *Nashville Scene*, BookMan has more than 100,000 books, including 10,000 first editions and many signed editions. The store has a large mystery collection as well as a good selection of science fiction, art and photography, history, general fiction/literature, and children's books. Most hardbacks are $10 to $14. The store has thousands of paperbacks, each priced at about $2.95.

i The Public Library of Nashville and Davidson County is online. You can search the card catalog, renew or request books, and view your library record from the convenience of your own computer. You'll find the Web site at www.library.nashville.org. For general library information call (615) 862-5800.

ELDER'S BOOKSTORE
2115 Elliston Place
(615) 327-1867
www.eldersbookstore.com

Elder's Bookstore is one of Nashville's oldest used- and rare-book stores. The store was founded by Charles Elder, but it is now owned and managed by his son Randy. Elder's is known for its tremendous collection of regional, Southern, and Civil War books. Tennessee-history buffs will find plenty to occupy them. Elder's also has a good collection of Native American books, rare and out-of-print books, children's books, cookbooks, art reference books, books on genealogy, late-edition encyclopedias, and more. They have done reissues of important titles through the years. A wonderful place to browse on a rainy afternoon, Elder's is across from Baptist Hospital at 22nd and Church, next to the Elliston Place Soda Shop.

THE GREAT ESCAPE
1925 Broadway
(615) 327-0646

111 North Gallatin Pike, Madison
(615) 865-8052
www.thegreatescape.com

If you're looking for comic books, the Great Escape is the place to go. The Great Escape has more than 100,000 comics in stock, including a huge selection of back issues, and the shop receives weekly shipments of the latest books. Collectors will find collectible comics here that range in price from 50 cents to $500 or more. The Great Escape also has used paperbacks, mostly fiction, with an emphasis on pop culture. The store has a large selection of used CDs, tapes, and records, as well as videos, used video games, gaming cards, and trading cards. The Great Escape Half-Price Store, a few doors down from the Great Escape store on Broadway, offers books, comics, and other items at big discounts; it's open Friday and Saturday.

SPORTING GOODS/OUTDOOR GEAR

ASPHALT BEACH IN-LINE SKATE SHOP
216 Seventh Avenue South
(615) 242-2115
www.asphaltbeach.com

Asphalt Beach is one of the largest, most complete in-line skate shops in the United States. Skater-owned, Asphalt Beach offers sales, repair, parts, accessories, and instruction for fitness, recreation, speed, aggressive, and roller hockey.

BASS PRO SHOPS OUTDOOR WORLD
323 Opry Mills Drive
(615) 514-5200, (800) BASS-PRO
www.basspro.com

This massive store has 154,000 square feet of fishing, boating, hunting, camping, and golf gear and equipment, plus outdoor apparel. From fishing licenses to boats, you should be able to find everything you need here. Even if you're not into the aforementioned activities, you'll want to check out this spectacular store next time you visit Opry Mills. There's a 23,000-gallon aquarium, waterfalls, an adventure travel agency, and a snack bar inside.

THE BIKE PEDDLAR
144 Franklin Road, Brentwood
(615) 373-4700
www.allanti.com

This full-service bike shop specializes in high-end and custom bikes as well as family bikes and equipment, so whether you're looking for a high-end professional frame, a beginner's bike, or a bicycle built for two (or even for four), you should be able to find it here. The knowledgeable staff is more than happy to help. Brands include Trek, Fuji, Waterford, and Seven. In business since 1990, Allanti operates a cycling club and organizes biking tour trips and other events.

BLUE RIDGE MOUNTAIN SPORTS
108 Page Road
(615) 356-2300
www.brms.com

This store carries backpacking, climbing, and camping gear, plus the right clothing to wear while you're engaging in those activities. It also has a good assortment of travel gear. If you're not sure what you need for that upcoming vacation in the Rockies or an afternoon hike at Warner Park, the expert staff will gladly assist you.

BLUEWATER SCUBA
103 White Bridge Road
(615) 356-9340, (800) 356-9640
www.bluewaterscuba.com

Bluewater Scuba offers complete instruction in scuba diving, including S.S.I. (Scuba Schools International) courses. You can learn it all at their indoor pool and then take a diving trip to Florida or a number of more exotic locations with your classmates. The shop is also a full-service travel agency that specializes in trips to the Red Sea (Egypt), Costa Rica, and Thailand. They make one or two trips per month to these and other locations around the world, plus one trip to Florida each month. Bluewater Scuba also sells the top lines of scuba equipment.

CUMBERLAND TRANSIT
2807 West End Avenue
(615) 321-4069
www.cumberlandtransit.com

Adventure-minded outdoor types will find all sorts of clothing and equipment at Cumberland Transit. In business since 1972, the store has gear for backpacking, camping, rock climbing and rappelling, canoeing, fly-fishing, and about every other outdoor activity you can think of. In addition to sporting equipment, the store has men's and women's clothing, travel gear, and luggage. If you need to brush up on your outdoor skills, sign up for one of Cumberland Transit's classes in rock climbing, rappelling, fly-fishing, fly tying, or backpacking. The store's large bike shop spe-cializes in all aspects of biking, including custom frame fitting. The store has a large stock of mountain bikes, road bikes, hybrids, and BMX bikes.

JACK'S GOLF SHOP
4503 Harding Road
(615) 383-8884

Jack's is one of Nashville's favorite golf shops and counts among its customers local country stars as well as several Tennessee Titans players. The shop has a good reputation for its club-fitting service and sells Callaway, Taylor Made, Wilson, Ping, and other top brands. If you just need golf balls or some accessories for your next day on the green, you'll find everything here. Jack's also offers repair services.

PETS AND PET SUPPLIES

AQUATIC CRITTER
5009 Nolensville Road
(615) 832-4541
www.aquaticcritter.com

Freshwater and marine aquarists alike will want to check out this store. It has an excellent selection of fish, plants, corals, and reptiles and a knowledgeable and helpful staff. The fish are guaranteed to be healthy. The store also sells clean, filtered saltwater and provides a variety of services.

THE CAT SHOPPE
2824 Bransford Avenue
(615) 297-7877
http://catshoppedogstore.com/

The Cat Shoppe has been catering to cats and cat people since November 1992. It is stocked full of all sorts of kitty-themed gift items, including picture frames, T-shirts, coffee mugs, and sweaters, as well as food, litter, and grooming tools for your feline friends. The store has lots of cat toys. The helpful staff can recommend pet-sitters, and they'll loan you a trap for catching the neighborhood stray.

Shopping for a pet? The Nashville Humane Association is a great place to find a furry friend who needs a home. It's open daily. Hours are 10:00 a.m. to 5:00 p.m. Monday through Saturday, except Wednesday, when closing time varies. For more information call (615) 352-1010 or visit www.nashvillehumane.org.

THE DOG STORE
2824 Bransford Avenue
(615) 279-9247
http://catshoppedogstore.com/
This store has a huge selection of breed-specific gift items. Whether you're looking for a poodle needlepoint pillow, a Border collie Christmas tree ornament, some Labrador retriever bookends, or a Great Dane coffee mug, you'll probably find it in stock here. The store also sells all-natural gourmet dog food and fancy dog bowls to serve it in, plus dog beds, toys, and ceramic jars for holding puppy treats. Since it opened in spring 1999, the Dog Store has become a favorite of dog lovers and their four-legged friends. The store is owned by Chris Achord, who also owns the Cat Shoppe (see entry above).

NASHVILLE PET PRODUCTS CENTER
2621 Cruzen Street
(615) 242-2223

7078 Old Harding Pike
(615) 662-2525

401 Murfreesboro Road, Franklin
(615) 599-0200

4066 Andrew Jackson Parkway,
Hermitage
(615) 885-4458
www.nashvillepetproducts.com
Nashville Pet Products Center is a locally owned chain of stores that sells pet supplies. The stores stock a variety of premium pet foods, vitamins, shampoos and conditioners, toys, and collars, as well as kennels, carrying cages, doggie sweaters, and books about pets. The stores also have birdcages and supplies and fish supplies, mainly for tropical fish.

FRESH PRODUCE

FARMERS' MARKET
900 Eighth Avenue N.
(615) 880-2001
www.nashvillefarmersmarket.org
The Farmers' Market, at the corner of Eighth and Jefferson across from the Bicentennial Mall, is a favorite spot for buying fresh produce. The indoor-outdoor market is packed with farmers and resellers offering fresh vegetables at very good prices. Indoors, there are a few international markets and specialty shops, including an Asian market, a meat shop, and a fresh seafood shop. The market does a brisk lunchtime business. Swett's, a meat-and-three restaurant (see Restaurants) that has been in business since 1954, has a location here and is always a favorite. You'll also find restaurants serving everything from gyros to barbecue to Jamaican fare. At one end of the market is the seasonally operated Gardens of Babylon, where you can find all sorts of plants and garden supplies. The market has several festivals each year, usually on the second Saturday of the month. Festivals include attractions such as live music, carnival games, and craft making. The Farmers' Market is open every day except Thanksgiving, Christmas Day, and New Year's Day. The Market is moving ahead with the first phase of the renovation of the interior of the Market House. The project includes updated interior space complete with better lighting, a new floor plan, signs, new products, and a larger central seating area. The Market House will remain open throughout construction.

PRODUCE PLACE
4000 Murphy Road
(615) 383-2664
www.produceplace.com
The Produce Place is a natural-foods grocery store that caters to customers who want organic

produce. The store opened in 1988 in the Sylvan Park neighborhood. In addition to fresh fruits and vegetables, the Produce Place carries some gourmet food items, bread by Provence Breads & Café, and sandwiches and other meals-to-go from local caterers. The store also carries health and beauty items and has a reverse-osmosis water-filtering system.

THE TURNIP TRUCK
970 Woodland Street
(615) 650-3600
www.theturniptruck.com

This small, locally owned natural foods market gets much of its produce from six or seven organic farms in the area. In addition to produce, the Turnip Truck sells natural, grass-fed Australian beef; organic meat; and free-range chicken. The store also carries grocery items, including frozen foods, and a full line of supplements. Soups and sandwiches to go are served at the front counter. The Turnip Truck is located in east Nashville's Five Points area at the corner of Woodland Street and South 10th Street. It is open daily.

ATTRACTIONS

There is a lot more to Nashville than music, as you'll see in this chapter. Whether you are a longtime resident, a frequent visitor, or a first-timer, Nashville has a great mix of attractions to entertain and enlighten. In fact, we have so many great places to visit and so many fun things to do, we can't possibly list them all here. For that reason, we're highlighting some of the Nashville area's most popular attractions—the ones residents and tourists alike visit year after year. In this chapter we arrange attractions by the following categories: Historic Sites, Museums, Amusements and the Zoo, and Fun Transportation and Tours. If you're planning an itinerary filled with country music–related locales, you'll find all the information you need in our Music City chapter. We list music attractions there—including country music museums, the hottest live music venues, and annual music festivals. Also, be sure to look in our Parks, Recreation, the Arts, Day Trips and Weekend Getaways, Annual Events, Kidstuff, and Shopping chapters for other fun and interesting places to visit in and around Nashville. Since fees and hours of operation are subject to change, it's a good idea to call before visiting the attractions listed in this chapter.

Price Code

Use the following as a guide to the cost of admission for one adult. Keep in mind that children's admission prices are generally lower (usually about half the cost of adult admission), and very young children are admitted free to most attractions. Discounts for senior citizens, students, and groups are usually available.

$.......................$1 to $5
$$ ....$6 to $10
$$$ .... $11 to $15
$$$$ .... $16 and more

HISTORIC SITES

BELLE MEADE PLANTATION $$$
5025 Harding Road
(615) 356-0501, (800) 270-3991
www.bellemeadeplantation.com

The Greek Revival mansion on this property was once the centerpiece of a 5,400-acre plantation known the world over as a thoroughbred farm and nursery. In 1807 John Harding purchased from the family of Daniel Dunham a log cabin

and 250 acres of land adjacent to the Natchez Trace. Harding and his wife, Susannah, enlarged the cabin as their family grew. In the 1820s they began construction of the present-day Belle Meade (a French term meaning "beautiful meadow") mansion, originally a two-story, Federal-style farmhouse.

Harding, who built a successful business boarding and breeding horses, continued to add to his estate. In 1836 his son, William Giles Harding, established the Belle Meade Thoroughbred Stud. The younger Harding made additions to the mansion in the 1840s. During the Civil War the Federal government took the horses for the army's use and removed the plantation's stone fences. Loyal slaves are said to have hidden the most prized thoroughbreds. The mansion was riddled with bullets during the Battle of Nashville (see our History chapter). After the war William Giles Harding and his son-in-law, Gen. William H. Jackson, expanded the farm. The stables housed many great horses, including Iroquois, winner of the English Derby in 1881. In the early 1900s Belle Meade was the oldest and largest thoroughbred farm in America. It enjoyed international promi-

Guides in period dress lead tours of Belle Meade, once known the world over as a thoroughbred farm.

nence until 1904, when the land and horses were auctioned. The financial crisis of 1893, an excessive lifestyle, and the mishandling of family funds led to the downfall of Belle Meade. The mansion and 24 remaining acres were opened to the public in 1953, under the management of the Association for the Preservation of Tennessee Antiquities. For more information on Belle Meade, take a look at The History of Belle Meade: Mansion, Plantation and Stud by Ridley Wills II (Vanderbilt University Press, 1991). Wills is the great-great-grandson of William Giles Harding and great-grandson of Judge Howell E. Jackson.

The beautifully restored mansion is listed on the National Register of Historic Places. It is furnished with 19th-century antiques and art of the period. The site also includes the 1890s carriage house and stable filled with antique carriages; the 1790s log cabin (one of the oldest log structures in the state); and several other original outbuildings, including the smokehouse and mausoleum. Guides in period dress lead tours of the property. The shaded lawn is a popular site for festivals (see our Annual Events chapter). Acclaimed chef and cookbook author Martha Stamps presides over Belle Meade's restaurant, Martha's at the Plantation (see our Restaurants chapter). Belle Meade Plantation is open daily year-round except Thanksgiving, Christmas, and New Year's Day.

i **The Nashville Visitor Information Center is located in the Gaylord Entertainment Center's glass tower at 501 Broadway. You can find brochures, coupons, and discounted tickets to area attractions there. The center is open daily. For more information call (615) 259-4747 or visit www.nashvillecvb.com.**

BELMONT MANSION $$
1900 Wedgewood Avenue
(615) 460-5459
www.belmontmansion.com
Belmont Mansion was built in 1850 as the summer home of Joseph and Adelicia Acklen. The beautiful and aristocratic Adelicia was said to have been

the wealthiest woman in America during the mid-1800s. She owned more than 50,000 acres of land in Louisiana, Texas, and Tennessee, all of which she inherited after her first husband, wealthy businessman Isaac Franklin, died in 1846. Her wealth placed her in the top half of 1 percent of antebellum society. The Italianate villa is furnished in original and period pieces, including gilded mirrors, marble statues, and art that Adelicia collected as she traveled the world. The Acklens enlarged and remodeled the mansion in 1859. After the expansion, Belmont boasted 36 rooms with nearly 11,000 square feet of living space and another 8,400 square feet of service area in the basement. The property also contained extensive gardens and numerous outbuildings. A 105-foot water tower, which still stands, irrigated the gardens and provided water for the fountains. Also on the property were a greenhouse and conservatory, an art gallery, gazebos, a bowling alley, a bear house, a deer park, and a zoo. Adelicia opened the gardens as a public park.

Today, visitors to Belmont Mansion will hear the fascinating story of Adelicia, an extraordinary woman who led an interesting life. When her second husband died during the Civil War, she was left with 2,800 bales of cotton. She traveled to Louisiana and cunningly "negotiated" the illegal sale of her cotton to England for $960,000 in gold. In 1887 she sold Belmont to a land development company. Two women from Philadelphia purchased the mansion in 1890 and opened a women's school, which later merged with Nashville's Ward School to become Ward–Belmont, an academy and junior college for women. In 1951 the Tennessee Baptist Convention purchased the school, and created a four-year, coeducational college, which became Belmont University (see our Education and Child Care chapter). In 1989, Belmont University separated from the Tennessee Baptist Convention. Today, the mansion is owned by the Belmont Mansion Association and Belmont University. The mansion recently completed a seven-month exterior restoration that returned the home to its former grandeur. In fact, this was the first time since 1859 that stucco work has been done, using a unique scoring that is rarely preserved or restored in Nashville. Open daily. Closed major holidays.

BICENTENNIAL CAPITOL
MALL STATE PARK   FREE
James Robertson Parkway
(615) 741-5280, (888) TNPARKS
www.tnstateparks.com
This 19-acre downtown attraction offers a trip through Tennessee history. It opened in 1996 to commemorate the state's bicentennial. A 200-foot granite map of the state, 31 fountains designating Tennessee's major rivers, and a Pathway of History are among the attractions. The mall also offers a great view of the Tennessee State Capitol. (See our Parks and Kidstuff chapters for more information.)

CANNONSBURGH VILLAGE   FREE
312 South Front Street, Murfreesboro
(615) 890-0355
Get a glimpse of what life was like in the 1800s at this reconstructed pioneer village. The village features restored original buildings such as a church, general store, guest house, and gristmill from Rutherford and other Middle Tennessee counties. There is also an art league exhibit, a historical Murfreesboro exhibit, and displays of antique farm equipment and automobiles. The giant cedar bucket situated near the village entrance is the world's largest—it holds 1,566 gallons. You should allow at least 45 minutes to tour this attraction. Restrooms and a gift shop are on-site. Guided tours cost $2.50 per adult and $1.50 for children ages 7 to 13. The buildings are open Tuesday through Sunday from May 1 through December 1; the grounds are open year-round.

CARNTON PLANTATION $$
1345 Carnton Lane, Franklin
(615) 794-0903
www.carnton.org
This 1826 antebellum plantation was built by Randal McGavock, who was Nashville's mayor in 1824 and 1825. The late-neoclassical plantation house is considered architecturally and historically one of the most important buildings in the area. In its early years the mansion was a social and political center. Among the prominent visitors attending the many social events there were Andrew Jackson, Sam Houston, and James K. Polk.

The home was used as a Confederate hospital after the bloody Battle of Franklin on November 30, 1864. The Confederates lost at least 12 generals during the battle. The bodies of four of the generals were laid out on the mansion's back porch. At that time Carnton was the home of McGavock's son, Col. John McGavock, and his wife, Carrie Winder McGavock. In 1866 the McGavock family donated two acres adjacent to their family cemetery for the burial of some 1,500 Southern solders. The McGavock Confederate Cemetery is the country's largest private Confederate cemetery. Carnton Plantation is open daily.

FORT NASHBOROUGH   FREE
170 First Avenue N.
(615) 862-8400 (Parks Department)
www.nashville.gov/parks
On the banks of the Cumberland River at Riverfront Park stands the reconstruction of the original settlement of Nashville. The original log fort was built slightly north of this location by James Robertson when he and his party first settled in the area in 1779 (see our History chapter). It occupied about two acres of land on a bluff overlooking the river. Named in honor of Gen. Francis Nash, who was killed during the Revolutionary War, the fort is where early Nashvillians met and adopted the Cumberland Compact for government of the new settlement. In 1930 the Daughters of the American Revolution sponsored the construction of a replica of the original structure near the site of Fort Nashborough. The current fort, built in 1962, consists of five reproductions of the early cabins; it is smaller than the original and contains fewer cabins. It was restored and renovated by Metropolitan Nashville–Davidson County government. The reconstruction is authentic in many details. Exhibits of pioneer furniture, tools, and other items are featured, allowing visitors a glimpse at the lifestyle of Nashville's first settlers. The fort is open to the public for self-guided tours daily, weather permitting.

HATCH SHOW PRINT   FREE
316 Broadway
(615) 256-2805
www.hatchshowprint.com

Founded in 1879 in downtown Nashville, Hatch Show Print is the oldest working letterpress print shop in America. For years the shop produced promotional handbills and posters for vaudeville acts, circuses, sporting events, and minstrel shows throughout the Southeast, but it is best known for its posters of *Grand Ole Opry* stars. From 1925 to 1991 it was on Fourth Avenue N., near the Ryman Auditorium; it relocated a few times before settling at its current site, a 100-year-old building between Third and Fourth Avenues. The business is now owned and operated by the Country Music Foundation. Today Hatch finds its letterpress posters and designs in constant demand. The shop continues to create posters and art for such clients as Nike, the Jack Daniel's Distillery, local bands, and national recording artists, including Bob Dylan and Bruce Springsteen. One wall of the tiny space is lined with thousands of wood and metal blocks of type used to produce posters. With its original tin ceilings, wooden floors, metal windows, shelves, and composing tables, the shop appears today much as it did in the early 1900s. Take a peek inside the next time you're downtown. Though formal tours aren't offered, thousands of visitors stop by each year. You can even take home a sample of Hatch's product. Posters are available and range in price from $3 to $300. Hatch is open Monday through Saturday.

THE HERMITAGE: HOME OF PRESIDENT
ANDREW JACKSON $$$
4580 Rachel's Lane, Hermitage
(615) 889-2941
www.thehermitage.com

More than 250,000 people visit this attraction each year, making it the third most visited presidential home in America, behind only Thomas Jefferson's Monticello and George Washington's Mount Vernon. A tour of the Hermitage offers insight into one of America's most interesting presidents, as well as a look at life on a 19th-century plantation. Andrew Jackson, seventh president of the United States and hero of the Battle of New Orleans, lived and died here and is buried next to his wife, Rachel, on the grounds. The Hermitage was first built in 1821 as a Federal-style brick home. It was enlarged in 1831, then rebuilt in Greek Revival style, as it appears today. A National Historic Landmark, managed since 1889 by the Ladies' Hermitage Association, the mansion has been restored to the period of Jackson's retirement in 1837. It contains a large collection of original furnishings and personal belongings, including furniture, porcelain, silver, and rare French wallpaper. Jackson filled the house with elegant and sophisticated pieces from the same dealers who supplied the White House. Among the many notables Jackson welcomed to the Hermitage were Revolutionary War leader the Marquis de Lafayette; Sam Houston, former Tennessee governor, hero of the Alamo, and Texas's first governor; and Jackson's presidential successors, Martin Van Buren and James K. Polk. The Hermitage is surrounded by hundreds of acres of rolling woodlands. On the east side of the house is Rachel's Garden. The flowers and shrubs you see here are typical of the early 19th century.

At the north border is the original "necessary house." The southeast corner of the garden contains the Jacksons' tomb. Rachel died December 22, 1828, weeks before Jackson was inaugurated as president. Jackson is said to have visited the tomb every evening while he lived at the Hermitage. Jackson died in his bedroom on June 8, 1845. Per his directions, he was buried next to his wife. Other members of his family are buried next to the Jackson Tomb. On the other side of the tomb is the grave of Alfred, a slave who lived at the property all his life and was Jackson's devoted servant. Other historic structures on the grounds include the original cabins where the Jacksons lived from 1804 to 1821, the Old Hermitage Church, an original slave cabin, a smokehouse, a springhouse, and a kitchen.

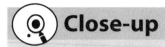 **Close-up**

Carter House ... The Most Battle-Damaged Building from the Civil War

After almost three years serving with Confederate troops in the Civil War, Capt. Tod Carter was going home. The young officer had a furlough and was looking forward to seeing his family again. As with many soldiers, Carter had been through hell. An attorney and a Master Mason, Carter had enlisted and participated in most of the Army of Tennessee battles. He had been captured at Chattanooga on November 25, 1863, but had escaped from a prison train in Pennsylvania in February 1864 and quickly rejoined his troop. Now he had furlough papers in hand and was headed home.

On his way to the family farm in Franklin, Carter stopped and spent the night at a friend's house about 4 miles south of his own home. When Carter awoke the next morning, he realized that the Union army was marching on Columbia Pike to Franklin. "He saw himself cut off from home," said Jamie Gillum, a guide at today's Carter House.

Carter and his friend, who also had a furlough, sat back in the woods and waited for the Union army to pass. When the Confederates came soon after, Carter rejoined his unit and set forth to do battle.

Carter had no idea that the battleground for one of the most horrific fights of the Civil War would take place right at his own home. The Carter House, built in 1830 by Fountain Branch Carter, was caught in the swirling center of one of the bloodiest battles of the War Between the States.

"They said the ground ran red with blood," said Gillum. "It was one of the most fiercely contested battles of the war. It was a complete slaughter.... We are not here to glorify death but to glorify their lives."

The morning of November 30, 1864, dawned a beautiful Indian summer day. At sunrise the Confederate army marched north from Spring Hill in pursuit of fleeing Union forces. General Hood was determined to destroy the Union army before it reached Nashville.

The two forces collided in the Battle of Franklin. Hood sent his Confederates across 2 miles of open fields against the Union front. The Carter House sat directly in the center between the two lines of headlong combat.

Called "The Gettysburg of the West," Franklin was one of the few night battles in the Civil War, beginning about 4:00 p.m. and ending around 9:00 p.m. It was also one of the smallest battlefields of the war—only 2 miles long and a mile and a half wide. "The smoke from the cannons and guns was so thick you could hardly tell friend from foe," Gillum said.

During the battle the Carter family took refuge in their basement. Their home was commandeered by the Union Maj. Gen. John M. Schofield for his headquarters. The head of the family, 67-year-old widower Fountain Branch Carter, and 22 other men, women, and children (many under age 12), barricaded themselves in the basement while the horrible cries of war rang out above them.

The Hermitage has occasional special events. Each summer the Hermitage director of archaeology leads a 10-week excavation of the property. This work has unearthed thousands of artifacts yielding insights into the lives of the slaves who worked here. Your tour of the Hermitage will begin with a short orientation film, followed by a tour of the mansion and grounds. At the visitor center you can get a quick bite at the cafe and browse for gifts at the Hermitage Museum Store. The Hermitage is open daily. It is closed on Thanksgiving, Christmas, and the third week of January. Admission is free on January 8, which is the anniversary of the Battle of New Orleans. On Jackson's birthday, March 15, admission is reduced.

Federal soldiers used the front bedroom and parlor as sniping positions while they fired their muskets at the enemy, who returned fire from the far side of the barn and icehouse. Not one brick in the south wall of the kitchen seems to have escaped a bullet hole.

"Sometime after midnight, they realized that the sounds of war had stopped," Gillum said. Since Tod Carter had not come home, the family feared that he was dead or wounded. His commander told the family where the young man had last been seen. Tod Carter had been heard to cry out, "Follow me, boys, I'm almost home." With a nine-year-old niece carrying the lantern, the four family members found Tod Carter.

He and his horse had been shot down in a small locust grove about 170 yards southwest of his birthplace. "He had probably played in that grove of trees as a child," Gillum said. Carter had sustained eight or nine bullet wounds, and it was a miracle he was still alive. Carter had likely been wounded at about 4:30 p.m. when the battle first started, and he wasn't found until about 4:30 a.m.

"After 12 hours of bleeding, he had probably lost too much blood," Gillum said. "The family carried him back home and his nine-year-old niece held the lantern while a bullet was removed from the back of his eye."

Two days later, Carter was dead. He was 24 years old. "He was buried in the last casket available in Franklin," Gillum said. "There were so many dead that they said you could walk 80 yards across the Carter garden and yard without touching the ground, just stepping on all the dead bodies."

The unofficial count was about 7,500 Confederate and about 2,500 Union casualties. "It's hard to have an exact count of the wounded and casualties because so many of the wounded didn't seek medical attention and marched on to fight in Nashville," Gillum said.

After the battle, the parlor of the Carter House was converted into a Confederate field hospital and witnessed many surgeries and amputations. In fact, soldiers would be dying for decades afterward from wounds they received at the Battle of Franklin. "As late as the 1920s, men were dying of complications from wounds they had received in this battle," Gillum said. "Technically, you could say they were mortally wounded at Franklin but it may have been 60-some years later that they died."

The Army of Tennessee died at Franklin on November 30, 1864, Gillum said. "It was a fight they would never recover from. I think that's why Fountain Branch Carter decided not to repair the bullet holes in his house and buildings. He realized that this was hallowed ground. He wanted people to remember what had happened here and know this was where Americans had shed their blood."

The evidence of over 1,000 bullet holes remains on the site, including the most battle-damaged building from the Civil War. A small 10-by-15-foot building had 167 bullet holes. For more information, contact the Carter House at (615) 791-1861.

---

i The driveway at the Hermitage is shaped like a guitar. Legend has it that Andrew Jackson built the driveway to please his daughter-in-law Emily. The tornadoes that struck Nashville in 1998 destroyed hundreds of trees along the driveway, and more than 1,000 on the property. The trees were more than two centuries old.

**HISTORIC MANSKER'S STATION
FRONTIER LIFE CENTER** $
Moss-Wright Park at Caldwell Road
Goodlettsville
(615) 859-FORT
www.cityofgoodlettsville.com
Bowen Plantation House and Mansker's Station are at this site. The two-story, Federal-style house,

built in 1787, is the oldest brick home in Middle Tennessee. It was built by Revolutionary War veteran and Indian fighter William Bowen, who brought his family to the area in 1785. He received the land as partial compensation for his military service and later expanded the plantation from 640 acres to more than 4,000. In 1807 William Bowen Campbell was born here. He fought in the Seminole War and the Mexican War and served as Tennessee's 15th governor from 1851 to 1853 and a member of Congress in 1855. The restored house was listed on the National Register of Historic Places in 1976. About 200 yards from the house is Mansker's Station, a reconstruction of a 1779 frontier fort where Kasper Mansker lived. Mansker is considered Goodlettsville's first citizen. The fort is near Mansker's Lick, one of the area's salt licks where long hunters came to hunt and trap. John Donelson, one of the founders of Nashville, moved his family here after abandoning his Clover Bottom Station following an Indian attack in 1780. Living-history encampments held here several weekends a year offer demonstrations of frontier skills such as hide tanning, soap making, blacksmithing, butter churning, and fireside cookery. The three largest events are Yulefest, the fall encampment, and the Colonial Fair (see our Annual Events chapter). Historic interpreters in period clothing provide tours daily from March through December. Tours are not available during January and February, but the interpretive center is open year-round.

HISTORIC ROCK CASTLE $-$$
139 Rock Castle Lane, Hendersonville
(615) 824-0502
www.historicrockcastle.com

The late-18th-century house on the shores of Old Hickory Lake was at one time the center of a 3,140-acre plantation, home of senator and Revolutionary War veteran Daniel Smith and his family. Today the property occupies 18 acres and includes the furnished seven-room limestone house, a smokehouse, and the family cemetery. Other buildings were claimed by the creation of Old Hickory Lake in the 1950s. The original

two-room structure was built in the mid-1780s. The multilevel stone house was completed in 1796. The large limestone blocks used in the home's construction were quarried nearby, and the wood for the house came from trees on the property. Smith, a well-known surveyor of the North Carolina (now Tennessee) boundaries and of Davidson County, made the first map of the area. Some say he gave the state its name as well, adopting the Cherokee word *Tanasie*, which may have meant "where the rivers tangle together." (However, accounts of who named the state, and the meaning of the Cherokee word from which the name was taken, vary quite a bit.) Smith and his wife, Sarah, are buried in the family cemetery. You can learn more about the family and the property on a guided tour. Stop first at the visitor center for an orientation. There's a gift shop that sells souvenirs and items representative of the period, such as lye soap, traditional games and toys, and reproductions of Smith's early maps. Rock Castle is 2 miles south of Gallatin Road off Indian Lake Road. This attraction is open daily Tuesday through Sunday.

JACK DANIEL'S DISTILLERY FREE
Highway 55, Lynchburg
(931) 759-6180
www.jackdaniels.com

Founded in 1866, the Jack Daniel's Distillery is the oldest registered distillery in the United States and is on the National Register of Historic Places. This is where the famous Jack Daniel's "smooth sippin' Tennessee whiskey" is made. You can learn all about how this sour-mash Tennessee whiskey is made during a guided tour of the facility, after which you'll be served a complimentary lemonade or coffee. You can't sample the whiskey because the county is dry, but you can purchase a specially designed decanter of it in the distillery's visitor center (except on Sunday). Tours are conducted daily except on major holidays. Plan to spend about 90 minutes on the tour. The distillery is about 80 miles southeast of Nashville, about 26 miles off Interstate 24.

NASHVILLE CITY CEMETERY — FREE
1001 Fourth Avenue S. at Oak Street
www.thenashvillecitycemetery.org

This cemetery was opened January 1, 1822, making it Nashville's oldest remaining public cemetery. It's also one of the few cemeteries in the state listed as an individual property on the National Register of Historic Places. There are some 23,000 graves here, including the graves of many early settlers, whose remains were brought here for permanent burial. Many graves are unmarked. Among the notables buried here are Nashville founder Gen. James Robertson (1742–1814) and Capt. William Driver (1803–1886), who named the American flag "Old Glory." Three Civil War generals are also buried here: Maj. Gen. Bushrod Johnson (1817–1880), hero of the Battle of Chickamauga; Lt. Gen. Richard S. Ewell (1817–1872), a commander at the Battle of Gettysburg; and Gen. Felix Zollicoffer (1812–1862), editor of the city's first daily newspaper, killed at the Battle of Fishing Creek, in Kentucky. In 1878 city officials voted to allow only descendants of owners with unfilled plots to be buried here. This policy is still in place. The property is administered by the Metro Historical Commission (615-862-7970) and maintained by Metro Parks. Many of the grave markers and monuments have been vandalized or have deteriorated and are no longer legible, but an ongoing restoration project has repaired some of the structures. Metal markers containing historical information are located throughout the grounds. The cemetery is open daily. Cemetery records are in the Tennessee State Library and Archives at 403 Seventh Avenue N. (615-741-2764). (See our Annual Events chapter for more about the cemetery.)

OAKLANDS HISTORIC HOUSE MUSEUM — $$
900 North Maney Avenue, Murfreesboro
(615) 893-0022
www.oaklandsmuseum.org

One of the most elegant antebellum homes in Middle Tennessee, this house began around 1815 as a one-story brick home built by the Maney family. The family enlarged the house with a Federal-style addition in the early 1820s and made further changes in the 1830s. The last addition was the ornate Italianate facade, completed in the 1850s. Oaklands was the center of a 1,500-acre plantation. Union and Confederate armies alternately occupied the house during the Civil War. On July 13, 1862, Confederate general Nathan Bedford Forrest led a raid here, surprising the Union commander at Oaklands. The surrender was negotiated here. In December 1862 Confederate president Jefferson Davis boarded at Oaklands while visiting nearby troops. Stop by the visitor center for a video orientation before beginning your tour. There is a gift shop on the property. The house is open Tuesday through Sunday, except on major holidays.

PRINTERS ALLEY — FREE
Between Church and Union and Third and Fourth Avenues

Once the center of Nashville's nightlife, Printers Alley was originally home to Nashville's publishing and printing industry. Speakeasies sprang up here during Prohibition. During the 1940s, nightclubs opened. You could come here to catch performances by such stars as Boots Randolph, Chet Atkins, Dottie West, and Hank Williams. Today you'll find several nightspots here, including the Bourbon Street Blues & Boogie Bar.

RYMAN AUDITORIUM — $$
116 Fifth Avenue N.
(615) 254-1445,
(615) 889-3060 (reservations, tickets)
www.ryman.com

The legendary Ryman Auditorium (see also our History and Music City chapters), home of the *Grand Ole Opry* from 1943 to 1974, has enjoyed a rebirth. After an $8.5-million renovation, the 2,100-seat landmark venue reopened in 1994, restored to its original splendor. Today the Ryman hosts concerts by country, bluegrass, pop, rock, classical, and gospel artists and special engagements of the *Grand Ole Opry*. The Ryman also has hosted several musical productions in recent years. Its excellent acoustics have made it a

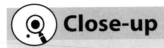 **Close-up**

Schermerhorn Symphony Center

Nashville has a new landmark, comparable to the greatest music halls in the world. Opened in 2006, the $120-million Schermerhorn Symphony Center was designed to be an acoustic masterpiece. Located on a city block between Third and Fourth Avenues S., the center is home to the Nashville Symphony Orchestra. It was named in honor of the late Kenneth Schermerhorn, music director and conductor of the orchestra. The center houses the Laura Turner Concert Hall, named in honor of the mother of Nashville symphony supporters, Cal Jr. and Steve Turner.

Designed by architect David M. Schwarz, the 197,000-square-foot center has 30 soundproof windows above the hall, making it one of the only major concert halls in North America with natural light. The Schermerhorn design was inspired by some of the world's great concert halls, many of which were built in Europe in the late 19th century. The result is a sophisticated and modern building that is neoclassically inspired, with a classic limestone exterior and columns.

The shoebox-shaped hall seats 1,860 patrons. During symphony performances, the seats are ramped in a theater-style layout. During Pops performances and for receptions or banquets, however, the seats can be transported to a storage area by an elevator. In one to two hours, the configuration can change from ramped seating to a flat parquet floor, making it the only building in the world with this ability. Behind the orchestra are 140 seats for choral performances. The seats can be sold to the public when there is no chorus.

The Nashville Symphony will perform more than 100 classical, Pops, and special-events concerts in the Schermerhorn each season. Recitals, choral concerts, cabaret, jazz, and world music events also will be presented. The center also features the Mike Curb Family Music Education Hall, which is home to the symphony's ongoing education initiatives. Another highlight of the new building is a garden and cafe, enclosed by a colonnade. The garden will be open to the public throughout the day and during concerts. For more information contact the Schermerhorn Symphony Center at (615) 687-6400.

---

popular spot among recording artists such as Bruce Springsteen, Merle Haggard, Bob Dylan, and Sheryl Crow.

The building was originally called the Union Gospel Tabernacle. Riverboat captain Thomas Ryman, inspired by the preaching of evangelist Sam Jones, built the facility in 1892 as a site for Jones's revivals and other religious gatherings. It soon became a popular venue for theatrical and musical performances and political rallies. The building was renamed to honor Ryman after his death in 1904. Though it wasn't the first home of the *Grand Ole Opry*, which began in 1925, the Ryman earned the nickname "the Mother Church of Country Music." For 31 years the live *Opry* radio show originated from this building. Country legends such as Hank Williams, Roy Acuff, and Patsy

Cline performed on the stage. While fans packed the wooden pews, others tuned in to their radios to hear the live broadcast. When the *Opry* moved to the new Grand Ole Opry House at Opryland USA, the Ryman became a tourist attraction, and the building was used as a backdrop in such films as *Nashville*, *Coal Miner's Daughter*, and *Sweet Dreams*.

The Ryman remains a top tourist destination. Individuals and groups stop here daily to tour the building. Various exhibits and displays tell about the Ryman and country music history. Audiovisual displays on the main floor feature a variety of memorabilia. An interactive unit downstairs is popular with kids. Self-guided tours are available seven days a week. A concession stand and gift shop are on-site.

The Schermerhorn Symphony Center is home to the Nashville Symphony Orchestra.
COURTESY OF THE NASHVILLE SYMPHONY

SAM DAVIS HOME HISTORIC SITE $$
1399 Sam Davis Road, Smyrna
(615) 459-2341
www.samdavishome.org

This Greek Revival home, built around 1820 and enlarged around 1850, sits on 169 acres of the original 1,000-acre farm that was the home of Sam Davis. Davis, called the "Boy Hero of the Confederacy," enlisted in the Confederate army at the age of 19. He served as a courier, and while transporting secret papers to Gen. Braxton Bragg in Chattanooga, he was captured by Union forces, tried as a spy, and sentenced to hang. The trial officer was so impressed with Davis's honesty and sense of honor that he offered him freedom if he would reveal the source of military information he was caught carrying. Davis is reported to have responded, "If I had a thousand lives I would give them all gladly rather than betray a friend." He was hanged in Pulaski, Tennessee, on November 27, 1863. The home is a typical upper-middle-class farmhouse of the period. A tour of the property also includes outbuildings. Heritage Days takes place here every October (see our Annual Events chapter). The home is open daily.

STONES RIVER NATIONAL BATTLEFIELD FREE
3501 Old Nashville Highway
Murfreesboro
(615) 893-9501
www.nps.gov/stri/

One of the bloodiest Civil War battles took place at this site between December 31, 1862, and

January 2, 1863. More than 83,000 men fought in the battle; nearly 28,000 were killed or wounded. Both the Union army, led by Gen. William S. Rosecrans, and the Confederate army, led by Gen. Braxton Bragg, claimed victory. However, on January 3, 1863, Bragg retreated 40 miles to Tullahoma, Tennessee, and Rosecrans took control of Murfreesboro. The Union constructed a huge supply base within Fortress Rosecrans, the largest enclosed earthen fortification built during the war. The battlefield today appears much as it did during the Battle of Stones River. Most of the points of interest can be reached on the self-guided auto tour. Numbered markers identify the stops, and short trails and exhibits explain the events at each site. Plan to spend at least two hours to get the most out of your visit. Stop first at the visitor center. An audiovisual program and museum will introduce you to the battle. Pick up a brochure or recorded guide to use on the self-guided auto tour. During summer, artillery and infantry demonstrations and talks about the battle take place. The park is administered by the National Park Service and is open daily except Christmas.

TENNESSEE ANTEBELLUM TRAIL   FREE
(800) 381-1865
www.antebellumtrail.com

This 90-mile self-driving tour takes you past more than 50 historical sites as it loops through Davidson, Maury, and Williamson Counties. Several of the antebellum homes along the trail, including Belmont Mansion, Belle Meade Plantation, and Travellers Rest in Nashville, and Columbia's James K. Polk Home, are open to the public (most require an admission fee). You can pick up a free tour map at each of the homes or download one at the Web site above. See the individual listings in this chapter for more about some of the homes featured on the tour.

TENNESSEE STATE CAPITOL   FREE
Charlotte Avenue, between Sixth
and Seventh Avenues
(615) 741-1621
www.tnmuseum.org

Free guided tours of the Tennessee State Capitol are provided throughout the day Monday through Friday at designated times by the staff of the Tennessee State Museum. Tours depart from the information desk on the first floor. If you prefer to take a self-guided tour, pick up a brochure at the information desk. When the legislature is in session, the capitol's hours of operation are extended if either the House of Representatives or the Senate is still in session. On legislative meeting days, visitors can view the Senate and House from their galleries, which are accessed by the second-floor stairwells.

The Greek Revival–style building was begun in 1845 and completed in 1859. Its architect, William Strickland of Philadelphia, began his career as an apprentice to Benjamin Latrobe, architect

A statue of Andrew Jackson stands watch over the Tennessee State Capitol. JACKIE SHECKLER FINCH

of the U.S. Capitol in Washington, D.C. Strickland died before the Tennessee State Capitol was completed and, per his wishes, was buried in the northeast wall of the building near the north entrance. Strickland's son, Francis Strickland, supervised construction until 1857 when Englishman Harvey Akeroyd designed the state library, the final portion of the building.

The capitol stands 170 feet above the highest hill in downtown Nashville. On the eastern slope of the grounds is the tomb of President and Mrs. James K. Polk and a bronze equestrian statue of President Andrew Jackson. During the Civil War, the capitol was used as a Union fortress. In the 1930s the murals in the governor's office were added. Various restoration projects have taken place over the years. In 1996 a bronze statue of Andrew Johnson was erected so that all three U.S. presidents from Tennessee are commemorated on the capitol grounds. The Tennessee State Capitol is open Monday through Friday but is closed on holidays. Parking is available at metered spaces around the capitol complex or in public parking lots downtown.

TRAVELLERS REST PLANTATION HOUSE AND GROUNDS $$
636 Farrell Parkway
(615) 832-8197
www.travellersrestplantation.org
Travellers Rest was built in 1799 by Judge John Overton, a land speculator, lawyer, cofounder of Memphis, and presidential campaign manager for lifelong friend Andrew Jackson. The Federal-style clapboard farmhouse offers a glimpse of how wealthy Nashvillians lived in the early 19th century. The well-maintained grounds feature magnolia trees, gardens, and outbuildings. The house began as a two-story, four-room house, but additions throughout the 1800s increased its size. Changes in architectural styles are evident in the expansions. It has been restored to reflect the period of the original owner and features a large collection of early-19th-century Tennessee furniture. The home served as headquarters for Confederate general John B. Hood just before the 1864 Battle of Nashville. Overton's son John

had financed a Confederate regiment during the war. The Overton family owned the house until 1948. Its last owner, the Nashville Railroad Company, gave the home to the Colonial Dames of America in Tennessee, which manages it as a historic site. Today Travellers Rest is listed on the National Register of Historic Places. Travellers Rest is open daily except Thanksgiving, Christmas Day, and New Year's Day.

MUSEUMS

ADVENTURE SCIENCE CENTER & SUDEKUM PLANETARIUM $$
800 Fort Negley Boulevard
(615) 862-5160
www.adventuresci.com
A fun place to learn and explore, this museum, formerly known as the Cumberland Science Museum, features exhibits on nature, the universe, health, and more. Since the museum opened in 1973, it has been entertaining and educating children and adults with more than 100 hands-on exhibits, live animal shows, science demonstrations, a planetarium, and traveling exhibits. A new Sudekum and Space Chase opened its doors in summer 2008. The first floor for the Space Chase wing includes two primary exhibit galleries—Solar System Survey and Test Bed. Solar System Survey invites visitors to explore the solar system with a 3D walk through the universe. The two-story-high Test Bed features a Space Walker, which allows visitors to feel like they are walking on the moon or other planets, and a Space Climber, which simulates the experience of astronauts working in space. It is open daily except major holidays. (For more information see the listing in our Kidstuff chapter.)

CHEEKWOOD BOTANICAL GARDEN AND MUSEUM OF ART $$
1200 Forrest Park Drive
(615) 356-8000
www.cheekwood.org
This magnificent 1929 mansion, surrounded by 55 acres of botanical gardens, lawns, and fountains, is one of Nashville's favorite attractions. It

was once the private estate of the Leslie Cheek family. Cheek was the cousin and business associate of Joel Cheek, founder of Maxwell House coffee. In 1960 the family gave the estate to the nonprofit Tennessee Botanical Gardens and Fine Arts Center. Today the mansion houses the Museum of Art, a prestigious collection of 19th- and 20th-century American art as well as major traveling art exhibits (see the Arts chapter). The three-story neo-Georgian mansion was built with Tennessee limestone quarried on the property. The house sits atop a hill surrounded by formal gardens designed by Cheekwood architect Bryant Fleming. A walk through these lovely gardens is a must. They feature marble sculptures, water gardens, and bubbling streams. The design includes an award-winning wildflower garden, an herb garden, a perennial garden, a traditional Japanese garden, and a dogwood trail. Along the border of the property is the Woodland Sculpture Trail, a mile-long trail featuring more than a dozen sculptures by artists from around the world.

Cheekwood's Botanic Hall features horticultural exhibits, flower shows, and the annual Season of Celebration holiday show. Inside the main gate are the Pineapple Room Restaurant, offering regional cuisine, and the Cheekwood Museum Gift Shop, where you'll find a selection of books, Tennessee crafts, and nice gift items. The Frist Learning Center offers classes, lectures, workshops, and special events for all ages relating to horticulture and art. Cheekwood is 8 miles southwest of downtown, off Belle Meade Boulevard and Highway 100. Cheekwood is open Tuesday through Sunday. It is closed Monday, except for Memorial Day and Labor Day, and is also closed the second Saturday in June, Thanksgiving Day, Christmas Day, New Year's Day, and on several days in January.

COUNTRY MUSIC HALL OF FAME & MUSEUM $$$$
222 Fifth Avenue S.
(615) 416-2001, (800) 852-6437
www.countrymusichalloffame.com
The Country Music Hall of Fame & Museum is one of Nashville's premier attractions. Originally

located in a barn-shaped building on Music Row, the museum opened in its $37-million home at Fifth Avenue S. and Demonbreun Street in May 2001. The facility takes up an entire city block and boasts more than 40,000 square feet of exhibit space devoted to the history of country music. As you walk through the museum, you'll view music memorabilia, hear clips of country recordings past and present, and learn about the music and its performers. The museum is accredited by the American Association of Museums, certifying that it operates according to the highest standards (fewer than 10 percent of the nation's 8,000 museums are accredited by the association). The museum is open daily except Thanksgiving, Christmas Day, and New Year's Day. (For more about the museum, see our Music City chapter.)

CULTURAL MUSEUM AT SCARRITT-BENNETT CENTER FREE
1104 19th Avenue S.
(615) 340-7481, (615) 340-7500
www.scarrittbennett.org/museum
This museum is on the second floor of the library at the Scarritt-Bennett Center. It features more than 14,000 items from around the world, with an emphasis on pieces from Africa and Asia. Objects relating to religion, social organization, and arts and crafts are on display. Included is a collection of 700 dolls from 21 countries. Three or four temporary exhibits are featured annually. Admission is free, but a $1 donation is suggested. The museum is open daily.

FRIST CENTER FOR THE VISUAL ARTS $$
919 Broadway
(615) 244-3340
www.fristcenter.org
The Frist Center is Nashville's premier art museum. Housed in downtown Nashville's historic former main post office building, the center has approximately 24,000 square feet of gallery space. Its changing lineup of exhibits includes works by renowned artists that are on loan from galleries around the world. The center is dedicated to education, with a goal of making art accessible and interesting to people of all ages and from all back-

grounds. Educational outreach efforts include lectures, concerts, films, gallery talks, and youth and family programs on the center's exhibits and related topics. The Frist Center is open daily except Thanksgiving, Christmas, and New Year's Day. (See our Arts chapter for more details.)

LANE MOTOR MUSEUM $$
702 Murfreesboro Pike
(615) 742-7445
www.lanemotormuseum.org

Opened in 2003, this museum has vehicles that probably wouldn't be seen anywhere else—and most of them are in working condition. Cars that fold in half, drive in the water, lift themselves for a tire change, or open at the top with an airplane-style hatch are just a few of the more than 150 vehicles collected by automobile enthusiast Jeff Lane. The collection is regularly rotated to keep the exhibit fresh for returning guests.

i The area along Demonbreun Street adjacent to Nashville's Music Row that was once home to country music gift shops and country stars' museums is being transformed into an upscale live-entertainment and dining destination.

MUSICIANS HALL OF FAME & MUSEUM $$$
301 6th Avenue S.
(612) 244-3263
www.musicianshalloffame.com

Opened in 2006, the Musicians Hall of Fame & Museum reflects the diversity of what Nashville has accomplished as a music center. With a slogan of "Come see what you've heard," the museum honors the people who provide the sounds behind the music. Located on the corner of Clark Place and within sight of the Country Music Hall of Fame & Museum, the multimillion-dollar museum honors the players—whether stars, session pickers, or sidemen—from all genres of music. The attraction contains such memorabilia as the stage where a young Jimi Hendrix once performed, the famed Studio B door, Scotty Moore's personal items from his long career in

Elvis Presley's band, and Pete Drake's steel guitar played on Bob Dylan's "Lay Lady Lay" and George Harrison's album *All Things Must Pass*.

THE PARTHENON $
Centennial Park, West End
Avenue and 25th Avenue
(615) 862-8431
www.nashville.gov/parthenon

One of Nashville's most dramatic and most recognized attractions, this is the world's only full-size reproduction of the ancient Greek temple. Nashville's magnificent Parthenon, listed on the National Register of Historic Places, mirrors the dimensions of the original to an eighth of an inch. The first Parthenon was built between 1895 and 1897 as the centerpiece for the state's Centennial Exposition. It was a symbol of the city's reputation as the Athens of the South. Like the other exposition buildings, the Parthenon was created of plaster and wood. While the other buildings were demolished after the expo, the Parthenon was so popular that Nashville kept it, and Centennial Park was created around it in the early 1900s. After it had begun to deteriorate, it was rebuilt with concrete from 1920 to 1931. Nashville architect Russell E. Hart and New York architect and archaeologist William B. Dinsmoor worked on the plans. After studying the ruins of the original Parthenon in Greece, Dinsmoor designed the interior, which is accepted by scholars as true to the original. Encircling the Parthenon are 46 Doric columns. Two pairs of bronze doors—the largest in the world, weighing seven and a half tons each—mark entrances on two sides of the building. Inside, the floors are made of Tennessee marble and the ceiling of cypress from the Florida Everglades. Just as it was in ancient Greece, the focus of this Parthenon is a 42-foot statue of the goddess Athena, created by Nashville sculptor Alan LeQuire. It is the tallest indoor sculpture in the Western world. A 6-foot statue of Nike, the Greek goddess of victory, rests in Athena's right hand.

The Parthenon is also the city's art museum and boasts an impressive collection of art, including the Cowan Collection, which features more than 60 works by 19th- and 20th-century American painters. Other gallery spaces showcase temporary art shows and exhibits. Docents provide information about the art collection and about mythology and Nashville history. A gift shop in the main lobby of the gallery-level entrance offers a moderately priced and interesting selection of clothing, games, jewelry, stationery, original art, reproductions of Greek antiquities, and other items. A visit to the Parthenon is a must. It is open Tuesday through Saturday. From June through August it is also open on Sunday.

TENNESSEE AGRICULTURAL MUSEUM FREE
Ellington Agricultural Center
440 Hogan Road
(615) 837-5197

This attraction, a short drive south from downtown Nashville, is at the beautiful 207-acre Ellington Agricultural Center. It operates under the umbrella of the Tennessee Department of Agriculture and is the department's headquarters. The museum, a 14,000-square-foot, two-story horse barn built in 1920, houses an extensive collection of home and farm artifacts from the 1800s and early 1900s, a blacksmith shop, and the Tennessee Agriculture Hall of Fame exhibit. A log cabin area, near the main barn, features five cabins with exhibits relating to early farm life in Tennessee. An interpretive herb garden is next to the cabins, and a nature trail from the cabin area leads to an iris garden, pond, and gazebo. The property is also designated as an arboretum, featuring 80 tree species. Special events held here include the Rural Life Festival in early May and the Music and Molasses Festival the third weekend in October. The museum is open year-round Monday through Friday. On Saturday in the summer, the museum hosts a variety of fun family-oriented events that spotlight farm life. Past summer Saturday themes have included sheep shearing and wool spinning, heirloom gardening, and miniature mules and donkeys.

TENNESSEE SPORTS HALL OF FAME AND MUSEUM $
501 Broadway
(615) 242-4750
www.tshf.net

This attraction, which pays tribute to Tennessee's athletes, is located on the main level of the Gaylord Entertainment Center adjacent to the glass tower. Inductees and honorees include Wilma Rudolph, Peyton Manning, Tracy Caulkins, Pat Head Summitt, and Chandra Cheeseborough. The 7,200-square-foot museum offers interactive games, exhibits on college football and basketball, NASCAR video games, two 30-seat theaters showing sports videos, and more. Don't miss the virtual-reality basketball, where you can go one on one against a virtual version of former University of Tennessee basketball star Chamique Holdsclaw. The attraction is open Monday through Saturday.

TENNESSEE STATE MUSEUM   FREE
505 Deaderick Street (Fifth Avenue, between Union and Deaderick)
(615) 741-2692, (800) 407-4324
www.tnmuseum.org

This museum offers a fascinating look at the history of Tennessee, from prehistoric times through the 20th century. Displays include collections of prehistoric Indian artifacts, firearms, silver, quilts, paintings, and pottery. There is an extensive collection of Civil War uniforms, battle flags, and weapons. You can learn about the long hunters, such as Daniel Boone, who hunted in the area beginning in the 1760s, as well as interesting political figures like Andrew Jackson and Sam Houston.

Other exhibits relate to African Americans, Prohibition, women's suffrage, and important events that shaped the history of the Volunteer State. Replicas of building facades and period rooms are featured, too. A temporary exhibit gallery presents four exhibits each year that relate to art and/or historical subjects of regional and national interest. Allow at least an hour to tour the museum, but be prepared to spend an entire afternoon. The museum is below the Tennessee Performing Arts Center (see the Arts chapter). There are restrooms and a gift shop.

Close-up

Hotel's Indoor Gardens Are a Bona Fide Attraction

A favorite among Nashvillians and visitors, the massive Gaylord Opryland Resort and Convention Center is as much an attraction as it is a hotel. There are nine acres of impressive indoor gardens, 2,881 guest rooms, more than a dozen restaurants and bars, a variety of retail shops, and much more.

The Conservatory, a two-acre bilevel space filled with tropical plants, was the hotel's first indoor garden; it opened in 1983. Wander along the winding path, then walk upstairs and check out the view of the 10,000 tropical plants from above. The 1988 expansion featured the Cascades, another two-acre indoor area. The Cascades's three waterfalls splash down from the top of a 40-foot mountain into a 12,500-square-foot lake. You can linger here at the tropical Cascades Restaurant or enjoy drinks and appetizers at the revolving Cascades Terrace lounge. Each night, visitors crowd around the Cascades's Dancing Waters fountains, which are the focus of a laser show.

The hotel's Delta space opened in 1996. When you step into this four-and-a-half-acre area, you'll be transported to a Mississippi Delta town—complete with a river and flatboats that carry guests through the area. The Delta's glass roof peaks at 150 feet (15 stories). Two- and three-story buildings house a variety of interesting gift shops, meeting rooms, and lounges. The Delta Island Food Court is the place to find drinks and other goodies.

Opened in 2005, Relache Spa features 12 treatment rooms dedicated to pampering, peace, and renewal. The 27,000-square-foot European-inspired spa, fitness center, and full-service salon offers innovative equipment, featuring more than 30 separate stations for cardio, circuit, and weight training. Additionally, Gaylord Opryland's signature restaurants feature spa cuisine for guests seeking the total spa experience.

For more information visit www.gaylordopryland.com. Also, see our Accommodations and Annual Events chapters for more on lodging options and yearly happenings at this Nashville showplace. Admission to the hotel gardens is free; parking at the hotel costs $10.

Indoor gardens are year-round pleasures at the Gaylord Opryland Resort and Convention Center.
JACKIE SHECKLER FINCH

The museum's Military History Branch is in the War Memorial Building 1 block away. There you'll find exhibits on America's involvement in foreign wars, from the Spanish-American War through World War II. Displays feature weapons, uniforms, and battle histories. Admission is free at both museums. The museums are open Tuesday through Sunday and are closed Monday and major holidays.

THE UPPER ROOM CHAPEL AND
MUSEUM   FREE
1908 Grand Avenue
(615) 340-7207
www.upperroom.org/chapel

An interesting attraction here is the chapel's 8-by-17-foot wood carving of *The Last Supper*, based on Leonardo da Vinci's famous painting. It was created by Italian sculptor Ernest Pellegrini in 1953 for the Upper Room, an interdenominational ministry of the United Methodist Church. A short presentation on this piece and the chapel's 8-by-20-foot stained-glass window is given on the hour and half hour inside the chapel. The museum contains religious artifacts, paintings of religious subjects made from 1300 through 1990, manuscripts, books, and seasonal displays of 100 nativity scenes and 73 Ukrainian eggs. Between the wings of the building is the Agape Garden, featuring statues, fountains, and symbols relating to the garden of Gethsemane. Admission is free, but a $2 donation is encouraged. The museum is open Monday through Friday.

AMUSEMENTS AND THE ZOO

NASHVILLE SHORES $$$$
4001 Bell Road, Hermitage
(615) 889-7050
www.nashvilleshores.com

At Nashville Shores, every day is a day at the beach. Located on 385 acres along J. Percy Priest Lake, the water park offers white sandy beaches, swimming pools, seven large water slides, and other water amusements. Pontoon boats and personal watercraft are available for rent at the marina. For landlubbers there's an assortment of amusements, including volleyball and minigolf.

Nashville Shores can get pretty crowded on weekends, so if a jam-packed beach isn't your scene, try visiting during the middle of the week, when it's usually more peaceful. A daily admission price gives you access to all attractions (except the Jet Skis). Admission is cheaper after 3:00 p.m. Check the Web site for other discounts and promotions. If you plan to make four or more visits, you'll save money by purchasing a season pass. Nashville Shores is open daily from mid-May through late August, then weekends only through mid-September. (See our Kidstuff and Recreation chapters for more information.)

NASHVILLE ZOO AT GRASSMERE $$$
3777 Nolensville Road
(615) 833-1534
www.nashvillezoo.org

Nolensville Road between Harding and Thompson Lane is a busy area filled with fast-food restaurants, all types of stores, and lots of traffic. It's an unlikely spot for a wildlife sanctuary, yet just off this road is a 200-acre zoo that is home to more than 300 animals from all around the world. The Nashville Zoo was accredited by the American Zoo and Aquarium Association in 2004; the zoo is among the 10 percent of the nation's more than 2,000 zoos and aquariums that have the accreditation.

Most of the zoo's animals live in naturalistic environments. In some exhibits, moats separate zoo visitors from zoo residents, offering guests unobstructed views of the animals. The Bengal tiger exhibit is one of the zoo's most popular attractions. Other attractions include the two-acre Gibbon Island, home to the zoo's apes; the African Species Yard, where ostrich, zebra, and springbok roam about freely; and the Unseen New World, which houses anacondas, rattlesnakes, bats, scorpions, and other creepy and crawly things. Among the zoo's kid-oriented attractions is an interactive exhibit of playful African meerkats, and the 66,000-square-foot Jungle Gym playground. In 2006 the zoo opened a new giraffe savanna. The one-and-a-half-acre exhibit is the home of the zoo's three rare Masai giraffes— Margarita, Congo, and Savannah.

The land the zoo occupies was donated by the estate of sisters Elise and Margaret Croft for the protection of natural areas and wildlife. The Grassmere name comes from the circa-1815 residence on the property, one of the earliest brick homes in Davidson County. It was built by Michael C. Dunn, an early Nashville sheriff, from whom the Crofts descended. The Grassmere Historic Home, as it is now known, has been restored as an example of a working farm of the 1880s. Farm animals, including Percheron draft horses, Tennessee Walking Horses, chicken, and cattle, live on the property. At the entrance to the park is the Croft Center, a two-story educational facility with lecture rooms, an aviary, an aquarium, reptile and aquatic exhibits, and an amphitheater. Lecture sessions offer up-close visits with animals. In 2007 the zoo opened the African Wild Dog Habitat, featuring four adult female dogs from the Bronx Zoo. Also new are a Louisiana bayou–inspired alligator habitat and a jungle home for ocelots, endangered Central and South American cats who live high in the trees.

Except for New Year's Day, Thanksgiving, and Christmas Day, the zoo is open daily, with extended hours from April through October. (See our Kidstuff chapter for more about the zoo.)

i The Metro Historical Commission's "Nashville FootNotes" brochure will lead you on a walking tour to some of downtown Nashville's historic sites, including Printers Alley, Union Station, the old financial district, and Christ Church Cathedral. You can pick up a tour brochure at the Metro Historical Commission office at 3000 Granny White Pike (615-862-7970), or at the Nashville Visitor Information Center at Gaylord Entertainment Center at 501 Broadway.

WAVE COUNTRY $$
2320 Two Rivers Parkway
(615) 885-1052
www.nashville.gov/parks
The closest seashore is at least a seven-hour drive away, but this water park will do in a pinch. It's a fun place to cool off on one of our hot, humid summer days. Catch a wave, zoom down a slippery slide, or play in the surf. Wave Country has a wave pool, adult slides, a playground, and two sand volleyball courts. Inflatable rafts are available for rent. It's at Two Rivers Park, just off Briley Parkway near Opryland. Wave Country is open daily during the summer beginning on Memorial Day. After the first day of school, the water park is open weekends only. It closes after Labor Day weekend. Admission is half price after 4:00 p.m. All children must be accompanied by an adult 18 or older. (For more on Wave Country, see our Kidstuff chapter.)

i Fort Negley, a Civil War fort in south Nashville that had been closed for nearly 60 years, reopened in 2004. A $2-million renovation at the Union fort added a visitor center and a walking path with interpretive stops. The fort is located just off Eighth Avenue S. on a hill between Greer Stadium and the Adventure Science Center.

FUN TRANSPORTATION AND TOURS

AUTHENTIC TOURS OF HISTORIC BLACK NASHVILLE & MIDDLE TENNESSEE $$$$
P.O. Box 281613
Nashville 37228
(615) 299-5626
www.blacknashvillehistory.com
This three-hour African-American heritage tour is popular with school groups, church groups, and senior citizens organizations. Individuals wanting to take the tour can sign up and join a group outing. The tour includes visits to many historically significant sites, such as Fisk University, Tennessee State University, and Meharry Medical College. Other stops include the north Nashville home of James Weldon Johnson, who wrote the Negro National Anthem, "Lift Every Voice and Sing"; and Fort Negley, the Civil War Union Army fortification that some 2,000 free blacks helped build. Tour guides are authors and historians and

include tour owner Dr. Tommie Morton-Young, a genealogist and author. A three-and-a-half-hour version of the tour includes lunch at one of Nashville's historic black restaurants. The tours are aboard 25- to 55-seat luxury custom buses. Rates vary depending on the size of the group and the length of the tour.

DOWNTOWN TROLLEY TOUR $$
Gray Line Nashville
2416 Music Valley Drive
(615) 883-5555
www.graylinenashville.com
Gray Line Nashville offers a variety of Nashville sightseeing tours. The Downtown Trolley Tour is a $12, one-hour trip that includes a drive by some of Nashville's most famous attractions, including the Ryman Auditorium, State Capitol, Country Music Hall of Fame & Museum, the Parthenon, and Music Row. Trolley tours run regularly from around 10:00 a.m. to 4:00 p.m., departing from the corner of Second Avenue and Broadway, in front of the Hard Rock Cafe. For information on other sightseeing tours, see our Music City chapter.

THE *GENERAL JACKSON* SHOWBOAT $$$$
2812 Opryland Drive
(615) 458-3900, (866) 567-JACK
www.generaljackson.com
March 1819 marked the arrival of the first steamboat in Nashville—the $16,000 *General Jackson*. By the mid-1800s Nashvillians traveled to such cities as New Orleans, Memphis, and St. Louis aboard steamboats outfitted with entertainment. Today you can experience a bit of that bygone era aboard the *General Jackson*. The $12-million, 300-foot-long, four-deck paddlewheel showboat takes guests on sightseeing, dining, and entertainment cruises along the Cumberland River. It carries up to 1,200 passengers. A highlight of the boat is the ornate Victorian Theater, which can accommodate 620 people for banquets and 1,000 for theater presentations. Cruises depart from outside the front-gate area at Opry Mills shopping mall. Except during the winter, an optional lunch buffet is offered on midday cruises Friday through Sunday (Thursday, too, during the summer). Top-notch music and comedy shows are featured during the trip. The evening dinner cruise includes a three-course dinner served in the theater. You can step outside to see the nighttime Nashville skyline and enjoy the sounds of the onboard band. A round-trip cruise to downtown Nashville is 14 miles. The *General Jackson* operates year-round.

i The Francis Craig Orchestra entertained Nashvillians at the Hermitage Hotel from 1929 to 1945, reportedly the longest-running hotel musical act ever.

TENNESSEE CENTRAL RAILWAY MUSEUM $$$$
220 Willow Street
(615) 244-9001
www.tcry.org
The Tennessee Central Railway Museum offers round-trip, one-day excursions aboard comfy, air-conditioned trains to Middle Tennessee locations. The trains depart one to three Saturdays per month and are tied to such events as the mile-long yard sale and flea markets in Watertown, the Wilson County Fair in Lebanon, and fall foliage viewing in Cookeville and surrounding areas. Evening "murder mystery" excursions are sometimes available. You can choose from moderately priced seats in the dining car, first-class seats in a private drawing room, or the priciest seats in the special glass-domed car, which offers panoramic views of the beautiful Tennessee countryside. Refreshments and souvenirs are available for purchase on board. Reservations are required for anyone over age two. Tickets sell out in advance, so plan ahead. Prices range from around $30 to $110, depending on the type of seat purchased. Boarding is 30 minutes prior to departure at the museum's Willow Street location (off Hermitage Avenue), and trains arrive back in Nashville by mid- or late afternoon.

KIDSTUFF

No doubt about it, Nashville is a kid-friendly place. Ask any transplants why they chose to live in Music City, and more often than not, the answer is the same: "We thought this would be a good place to raise children."

That's not idle hyperbole, either. Nashville's diverse arts, sports, education, and religious communities offer a wealth of opportunities for kids of all ages. Nashville's "family-friendly" character manifests in a variety of unusual ways: This is a town where school cafeteria menus are broadcast on the morning news, and kids have access to a teacher-staffed "homework hotline" if they need help with their schoolwork.

Nashville's abundant creative energy has given rise to some unique youth-oriented activities, as well. The city is proud home to the country's oldest children's theater and the world's largest community-built jungle gym.

Here are some of our favorite kid-friendly activities and fun spots. Keep in mind that in a city growing as rapidly as Nashville, some attractions will have closed or moved, and others will have taken their place. Remember to call first to check hours of operation.

Price Code

Admission prices can change, but use our price code as a guide:

$	$1 to $5
$$	$6 to $10
$$$	$11 to $15
$$$$	$16 and up

ARTS AND MUSIC

ALL FIRED UP $$
1807A 21st Avenue S.
(615) 463-8887
www.allfired-up.com

This Hillsboro Village "pottery boutique" frequently draws kids, adults, even singles. But for a fun way to kill a few hours with your budding Picasso, this place can't be beat. It's a growing concept around the country: Choose an unpainted piece of pottery, then let your creativity go wild decorating the piece with a variety of glazes, paints, and other materials provided by the store. Store employees then fire the piece, and you have a beautiful memento of your fun

afternoon to take home. All Fired Up sells snacks and soft drinks, but you're welcome to bring your own food and beverages (even alcohol, for those over age 21). Cost varies depending on the ceramic piece purchased; generally it's $6 per painter, plus an additional $2 to $40 per unfired piece. The store is closed Monday, but it's open days and evenings the rest of the week.

> **i** Tennessee has the largest 4-H club membership in the United States, boasting more than 186,000 members.

ARTQUEST, FRIST CENTER FOR
THE VISUAL ARTS $$ (18 & UNDER, FREE)
919 Broadway
(615) 244-3340
www.fristcenter.org

This museum is a showpiece for everyone, to be sure. But museum officials were particularly concerned about making this a relevant and engaging place for young people, thus education is a key part of the Frist Center's mission. The result is ArtQuest, a hands-on gallery filled with more than 30 activity stations designed to bring the visual arts alive for kids of varying ages. Three- to five-year-olds can take part in simple arts-oriented activities like drawing, painting, and paper sculpture making; older kids can explore multimedia stations that address more advanced topics like the creative process, art and space, printmaking, and more. The Frist Center's various exhibits also come complete with kid-friendly education materials. In addition, a wide variety of programs, workshops, and other education offerings are available throughout the year. As if that weren't enough, the Frist Center demonstrates its commitment to kids at the cash register: Ages 18 and under are admitted free, always. You can't beat that. The Frist Center is open daily except Thanksgiving, Christmas, and New Year's Day. For a more in-depth look at the Frist Center, see our Close-up in our Arts chapter.

CHEEKWOOD BOTANICAL GARDEN
AND MUSEUM OF ART $$–$$$$
1200 Forrest Park Drive
(615) 353-9827
www.cheekwood.org

Education also plays a key role at Cheekwood, Nashville's other art museum. Weekend art classes, workshops, and summer art camps are offered at the Frist Learning Center (yes, it's the same folks who are behind the downtown Frist Center), located adjacent to the Cheekwood mansion. Programs are available for ages as young as four on up to teens. The Frist Learning Center includes art studios and classrooms, and art classes and workshops are held here. Creative types can get instruction in painting, pottery, drawing, jewelry making, and more. Botanical classes and photography/darkroom classes are offered at Botanic Hall, near the Cheekwood entrance. The schedule encompasses classes of just two hours in length to longer extended sessions; Cheekwood's education program also offers adult programs and trips. Cheekwood is closed on Monday. For more on Cheekwood, see our Attractions chapter.

NASHVILLE CHILDREN'S THEATRE
724 Second Avenue S.
(615) 254-9103
www.nashvillechildrenstheatre.org

The acclaimed Nashville Children's Theatre offers a variety of productions and programs for children of all ages—preschool through 12th grade. It puts on about six shows a year. The regular season runs September through May. Nashville Children's Theatre offers creative drama classes on Saturday during fall, winter, and spring, and holds summer camps during June and July. Visit the Web site for showtimes and dates. (See our Arts chapter for more information.)

WEIRD SCIENCE

Nashville offers several attractions for the budding astronomer, scientist, or archaeologist of the family. Fun is the name of the game at these places, and sparking a child's natural curiosity is the rule. No stuffy classrooms here—it's all about imagination and entertainment. If a little education happens along the way, well then, that's just gravy.

ADVENTURE SCIENCE CENTER &
SUDEKUM PLANETARIUM $$
800 Fort Negley Boulevard
(615) 862-5160
www.adventuresci.com

A world of hands-on activities designed to stimulate young minds awaits at the Adventure Science Center, formerly known as Cumberland Science Museum. The first thing visitors notice is the museum's centerpiece, the Adventure Tower. Rising from the ground floor and stretching all the way through the roof, the 75-foot-tall Adventure Tower is packed with hands-on, minds-on experiences that bring science to life. The tower has six concept areas, each an introduction to the rest of the museum. The Heart Crawl, in which you learn about the human heart by crawling through an oversize replica, leads to Health Hall via Vertebrae Ladder. Health Hall contains more interactive health exhibits and also covers such related topics as genetics and nutrition. The Tower's Sound & Light level includes a walk-on piano and a giant walk-in guitar, where kids can pluck the strings and feel the vibrations. Other science concept areas include Creativity & Invention; Energy, Air & Space; and Earth Science. Each can be explored as you climb the Adventure Tower. At the tower's top is a giant model of Earth, from which you get a breathtaking view of the Nashville skyline. Adventure Science Center is open daily except Easter, Thanksgiving, Christmas, and New Year's Day. Be sure to check the museum calendar for special events and kids' festivals, which occur periodically.

> **i** The Nashville Children's Theatre was established in 1931, making it the oldest children's theater company in America.

THE IMAGINARIUM CHILDREN'S ADVENTURE MUSEUM OF MIDDLE TENNESSEE $
7104 Crossroads Boulevard, Brentwood
(615) 373-9596

Open since 1999, this interactive children's museum is located in the Brentwood South Business Center, not far from Cool Springs mall. Kids ages 2 through 10 can explore a variety of hands-on activities, and all of them are wildly creative. The Imaginarium has the largest collection of real dinosaur artifacts on display of any children's museum in the country—everything from bones to teeth to poop, say museum owners. Kids can dig for bones and fossils in the museum's excavation pit. For the career-minded child, there are activity areas such as a working TV studio (WKID), a hospital, and a fire station, all offering a hands-on taste of those worlds. Adventurers can explore a rain forest, "dive" into the Imagiquarium (complete with artifact-laden sunken pirate ship), or tour a space station. The more artsy types can hunker down at an art studio where clay and paints are provided. Thespians can take advantage of the Imaginarium's theater and costume collection or take part in a puppet show. When school is in session, expect to share the Imaginarium with a lot of school groups—kids are bused in from as far away as Kentucky and Alabama. Hours vary depending

on the season, but the museum is generally open Tuesday through Saturday, with Sunday reserved for private parties.

NASHVILLE ZOO AT GRASSMERE $$$
3777 Nolensville Road
(615) 833-1534
www.nashvillezoo.org

Hundreds of species of animals from around the world can be found at the Nashville Zoo, an animal park that is rapidly becoming a world-class facility housing such endangered species as white Bengal tigers. The zoo continues to expand and recently opened its Entry Village, where hyacinth macaws and gibbons greet visitors. Other attractions include zebra, ostrich, cheetah, elephant, and American bison exhibits. Anacondas, rattlesnakes, bats, and scorpions are housed in the Unseen New World. A trip to the zoo is a fun day for the entire family, but the zoo has made itself especially appealing to little ones by offering several unique attractions and programs. The zoo's Jungle Gym is a favorite with local kids (for more information see the Parks and Playgrounds section in this chapter). There's also Critter Encounters, a petting zoo where young ones can get up close and personal with camels, sheep, goats, and other animals. For a more in-depth experience, programs such as Junior Zookeepers allow kids ages 10 through 14 to spend an afternoon with the zoo staff, learning how the animals are cared for. The Nashville Zoo is open daily except Thanksgiving, Christmas, and New Year's Day. (For more about the Nashville Zoo, be sure to see our Attractions chapter.)

VANDERBILT OBSERVATORY FREE
1000 Oman Drive, Brentwood
(615) 373-4897
www.dyer.vanderbilt.edu

Vanderbilt University's observatory is located in the heart of an upscale residential neighborhood, just south of Radnor Lake. Free public observing sessions are held two Fridays per month. The last Friday of the month is usually devoted to kids. The observatory has an impressive 24-inch telescope for viewing the night sky, an extensive astronomy library, a computer center featuring astronomy software, and a mission control center where telescopes around the country are controlled robotically. Vanderbilt professors also lead Q&A sessions. Public observing sessions begin around 7:30 p.m. The observatory is open from March through November. Call for exact program information and times.

PARKS, PLAYGROUNDS, AND ALL-AROUND ACTION AND ADVENTURE

BICENTENNIAL CAPITOL MALL STATE PARK
James Robertson Parkway
(615) 741-5280, (888) TNPARKS
www.tnstateparks.com
There aren't too many places where you can get soaking wet while absorbing some fascinating lessons in state history, geography, and culture. But Bicentennial Capitol Mall is just such a place. This 19-acre park just north of the Tennessee State Capitol opened in 1996, and its fountains—31 of them, designating major state rivers—quickly became a cool place to play during a sultry summer. Nearby on the plaza, a 200-foot granite map of Tennessee lets you walk from Memphis to Knoxville in record time; smaller maps provide details about various facets of the state. There's much more, including clean restrooms and a visitor center. Visit the adjacent Farmers' Market, along with the State Capitol, and you've got one nice (and cheap) afternoon. (For more information on the Bicentennial Capitol Mall State Park, see our Attractions and Parks chapters.)

i The Nashville Zoo's Adopt an Animal program provides an opportunity to sponsor one of the zoo's residents. Adoption levels start at $25 and go up to $250 per year. Fees go toward care and habitat improvement. Depending on the level, adoptive "parents" receive benefits such as adoption certificates, a photo of the animal, and free passes to the zoo. For more information visit www.nashvillezoo.org or call (615) 833-1534.

CENTENNIAL PARK
2500 West End Avenue
(615) 862-8400
www.nashville.gov/parks
The centerpiece of Centennial Park, built to celebrate Tennessee's 100th birthday in 1897, is a full-size replica of the Greek Parthenon that houses an art gallery. Children, however, are more likely to be interested in the abundant outdoor activities at the park. There's a small lake populated with ducks and (in season) pedal boats, and you'll also find a band shell, picnic tables, a steam engine and fighter plane, and lots of green grass. One child close to our hearts is particularly fond of the relaxing two-person swings with footrests. Centennial Park is the site of the Nashville Shakespeare Festival, concerts by the Nashville Symphony, various arts and crafts fairs, and other annual events. For more information on the Parthenon and yearly activities, see our Attractions and Annual Events chapters.

THE DRAGON PARK
2400 Blakemore Avenue
www.nashville.gov/parks
Its official name is Fannie Mae Dees Park, but this highly popular area just off the Vandy campus, at the corner of Blakemore and 24th Avenue S., is usually identified by its dominant feature: a huge sea dragon or serpent covered with brightly colored tile mosaic. The recently refurbished dragon, which seemingly snakes above and below the "surface," is decorated with animals, flowers, rainbows, musical instruments, historical figures, and countless other fanciful scenes. Its tail doubles as a bench where parents can sit while their children play. In addition to the dragon, there's a tunnel through a "mountain" of rocks topped by a sandy "mesa," with a swinging bridge connecting the mountain to a fort with a slide. The park also contains three tennis courts, swings and other playground equipment, wooden benches, picnic tables, a shelter, and two covered tables inlaid with chess and checker boards. A recent addition to Dragon Park is Lily's Garden, a playground for all children designed to accommodate those with special physical or learning disabilities. The

brainchild of a local mom whose own daughter, Lily, was diagnosed with spinal muscular atrophy, the playground has been heralded as a unifying element, connecting the dragon to the rest of Fannie Mae Dees playground and creating a fun atmosphere for all children to enjoy. For more on Lily's Garden, see our Special Needs section at the end of this chapter.

GYMBOREE PLAY & MUSIC
Shoppes at Mallory Lane
Suite 108
Brentwood
(615) 221-9004
www.gymboree.com

This national chain of parent-child play and music centers has one Tennessee location. The concept of an amusement park for the newborn-through-age-five set has taken off nationally, and such Gymboree play standards as "bubble time" and "parachute time" are said to help toddlers build physical coordination and develop social skills. Gymboree facilities have a variety of play equipment and "lesson plans," all age-appropriate and focusing on fun and recreation. A recent addition to Gymboree is Quarter Notes, a music program designed for infants as young as six months. Classes are around 45 minutes long, and children must be accompanied by an adult. Gymboree is closed on Sunday. Class times and costs vary; call for a schedule.

THE JUNGLE GYM NASHVILLE ZOO AT
GRASSMERE $$
3777 Nolensville Road
(615) 833-1534
www.nashvillezoo.org

Lions, tigers, and bears? So what! Nashville kids love the zoo's Jungle Gym so much, some parents bring their children here for this attraction alone. And no wonder: The 66,000-square-foot playground is a massive affair that can accommodate up to 1,000 kids at a time. The Jungle Gym was designed by world-renowned playground architect Robert Leathers and built by volunteers from the community. The playground's centerpiece is the 35-foot-tall Tree of Life tree

house. Kids can also explore the sculpture garden, where they can crawl through a giant snake tunnel, explore a bat cave, climb aboard concrete hippos, bounce through cargo netting, or tear through the Jungle Village. The Jungle Gym is a popular spot for birthday parties, and it's available after hours for such events. Otherwise it's open during regular zoo operating hours. For more information on the Nashville Zoo, see Weird Science in this chapter and our Attractions chapter.

RED CABOOSE PLAYGROUND   FREE
656 Colice Jean Road
(615) 862-8435

Dubbed the "pride of Bellevue," this popular park and playground offers a wide variety of activities for the entire family. The park's community center is home to a comprehensive after-school and summer program for kids, while a summer concert series and other special events frequently fill the eight-acre site on weekends. Built in 1994 in partnership with the community and the Metro Parks Commission, the park has also become home to Bellevue's annual community picnic. The community center has a game room, gym and weight room, and basketball courts, plus a ceramics and pottery studio. The playground is regarded as one of the city's best, with swings for toddlers and other play equipment for older kids, plus a paved walking track for the grown-ups. Three gazebos are ideal for picnics. To read more about Red Caboose Playground and Bellevue Park, see our Parks chapter.

SEVIER PARK   FREE
3000 Granny White Pike
(615) 862-8466
www.nashville.gov/parks

Located on the south end of the up-and-coming 12 South commercial district, Sevier Park is a welcome expanse of green space in an urban-residential area. The park is easily recognized for the pre–Civil War Sunnyside Mansion, which is on the National Register of Historic Places and is the park's dominant feature. Though it looks dilapidated, the historic mansion is undergoing massive renovation. The park's playground and picnic pavilions are frequented by local families. A summer concert series and Friday-night dances have brought music and good times back to Sevier, and the park's rolling hills and meandering creek make it a favorite spot for local dog owners. The park contains tennis courts, basketball courts, and a community center that offers various programs. Community center hours vary depending on the season, so call for availability and a program schedule.

i The Jungle Gym at the Nashville Zoo is the largest community-built playground of its kind in the world. More than 40,000 volunteer hours went into building the rambling play facility, which can accommodate more than 1,000 kids at a time.

WARNER PARKS   FREE
7311 Highway 100
(615) 370-8051 (headquarters),
(615) 352-6299 (nature center)
www.nashville.gov/parks
On a late-afternoon summer drive through Percy Warner Park, we once saw three deer and two rabbits within minutes, and we weren't even looking for them. Percy Warner Park, the largest municipal park in Tennessee, and its neighbor, Edwin Warner Park, span more than 2,700 acres, much of which is rugged, scenic woodland. There's a nature center, picnic areas, playground equipment, hiking trails, bridle trails, and a steeplechase area, as well as two golf courses. The parks are open daily from sunrise until 11:00 p.m., and the nature center is open from 8:30 a.m. to 4:30 p.m. Tuesday through Saturday. (For more information, see our Parks chapter.)

WATER FUN

There's nothing like a good dose of watery fun to bring out the kid in you, as these attractions attest.

METRO AND YMCA POOLS
YMCA corporate office
900 Church Street
(615) 259-9622
www.ymcamidtn.org

Metro Parks aquatics office
222 25th Avenue N.
(615) 862-8480
www.nashville.gov/parks
YMCA of Middle Tennessee operates 37 pools at 23 recreation centers in the area. About half are indoor pools. The Metro Parks department operates more than a dozen pools, including Wave Country (see below). For more information see our Recreation chapter.

NASHVILLE SHORES $$$$
4001 Bell Road, Hermitage
(615) 889-7050
www.nashvilleshores.com
Sandy shores, luscious palms, cool breezes—Nashville's answer to a beach vacation is definitely here. Located on Percy Priest Lake, Nashville Shores offers a wealth of water fun. Seven giant water slides with thrilling names like the "Tennessee Twister" and "Tsunami Raft Ride" beckon the adventuresome; for sunbathing and pool play there are three pools, each targeted to a different age group (so teenagers needn't worry about sunbathing with the kiddies). There's a real beach—white sand is hauled in to the Priest lakeshore—and lake cruises, even cabins on the shore available for rent. Dry fun activities include minigolf, games like Frisbee and horseshoes, volleyball, and live entertainment. Personal watercraft and boats are also available for rent at the marina. With all this to do, it's no wonder Nashville Shores is a popular birthday party and company outing location. Season passes are available. Children two and under are admitted free. Nashville Shores opens in early May and runs through mid-September. For more information see our Attractions and Recreation chapters.

SHELBY PARK
Shelby Avenue and South 20th Street
(615) 862-8467
www.nashville.gov/parks
This park in east Nashville is known for its golf course (see our Golf chapter), but its lake is also a popular fishing spot for kids as well as senior citizens.

WAVE COUNTRY $$

2320 Two Rivers Parkway
(615) 885-1052
www.nashville.gov/parks

Wave Country, just off Briley Parkway, lets you visit the ocean without leaving Nashville. Hold on tight as you ride the wave pool's simulated surf. There are also two water slides and one kiddie slide. Wave Country is open from Memorial Day weekend through Labor Day. (For more on Wave Country, see our Attractions chapter.)

FUN AND GAMES

FAMILY GOLF CENTER AT HICKORY HOLLOW $

5204 Blue Hole Road
(615) 781-0050
www.thefamilygolfcenter.com

Located in Antioch near Hickory Hollow Mall, this miniature-golf attraction may lack the windmills and giant elephants of its counterparts, but it's popular with families who have serious golfers in the mix. There's nothing like sending Junior and Suzie off to test their skills on the challenge-oriented minigolf course while Dad practices his swing on the driving range. In fact, the Family Golf Center has one of the largest driving ranges in the area, including sand traps and putting areas. There are also batting cages and go-karts. A concessions area offers amusement-park foods—hot dogs, ice cream, soft drinks, and the like. Hours vary depending on the season. See our Golf chapter for details on the driving range.

GRAND OLD GOLF & GAMES/VALLEY PARK GO KARTS $$

2444 Music Valley Drive
(615) 871-4701 (recorded information),
(615) 885-8126 (office)
www.grandoldgolf.net

This granddaddy of Nashville minigolf attractions is located near Opry Mills and offers much more than just golf: Go-karts and a video arcade round out the family fun. While Grand Old Golf may be showing its age these days, chances are your little ones won't notice, and the three minigolf courses

can provide an entire afternoon's worth of putting pleasure. Plus, ages 10 and under are half price. Hours vary by season. Group rates are available for birthday parties and corporate outings.

i The Aquatics Center at Centennial Sportsplex is named for Nashville native Tracy Caulkins, who won three gold medals at the 1984 Olympic Summer Games in Los Angeles. Caulkins, a 1981 graduate of Harpeth Hall School, has won an unprecedented 48 swimming titles in her career. She broke five world records and 63 U.S. records—more than any other American athlete in sports history.

LASER QUEST $$$

166 Second Avenue N.
(615) 256-2560
www.laserquest.com

You've seen all the *Star Wars* movies. Now it's your turn to be Luke Skywalker. Laser Quest fits you with a laser gun and sensor pack and turns you loose in a dark maze for a game of high-tech shoot-'em-up. Points are gained or lost depending on number of foes hit and number of times hit by foes. It's kind of like cowboys and Indians in outer space, and it's a harmless way for the kids to release some energy. Be sure to check out Laser Quest's video arcade after your game. Laser Quest's hours vary according to the season and the day of the week.

TIME MACHINE

History is a funny thing. Depending on your outlook, it can make you feel old or make you feel young. Here's hoping these selected historical sites will bring out the inquisitive little kid in you and other members of your family.

FORT NASHBOROUGH FREE

170 First Avenue N.
(615) 862-8400 (Parks Department)
www.nashville.gov/parks

This is where it all got started in 1779, when James Robertson and his fellow settlers established a settlement on the banks of the Cumberland River. This reproduction of the original log fort, which withstood attacks from Natives, is open daily, except Thanksgiving and Christmas, for a free self-guided tour. (See our Attractions chapter for more information.)

THE HERMITAGE: HOME OF PRESIDENT
ANDREW JACKSON $$$
4580 Rachel's Lane, Hermitage
(615) 889-2941
www.thehermitage.com

Andrew Jackson was a brave and adventurous man who was influential in the early expansion of our country. In addition to being seventh president of the United States, he was a military hero, lawyer, planter, statesman, and true romantic (he once shot a man who said bad things about his wife). The Hermitage, 12 miles east of Nashville off Old Hickory Boulevard, is where he made his home. The 1800s mansion, a mixture of Federal and Greek Revival styles, is open daily (closed Thanksgiving, Christmas, and the third week of January). A family admission package is available, and students and senior citizens receive a discount. For more information see our Attractions chapter.

HISTORIC MANSKER'S STATION
FRONTIER LIFE CENTER $
Moss-Wright Park at Caldwell Road
Goodlettsville
(615) 859-FORT
www.cityofgoodlettsville.com

The Frontier Life Center at Historic Mansker's Station offers a look at the lifestyles of the area's early settlers through a reconstructed 1779 forted station. You'll see and hear people in period costumes as they perform activities such as cooking, spinning, and blacksmithing. Special events and festivals are held throughout the operating season. For more information see our Attractions chapter.

TENNESSEE STATE MUSEUM FREE
505 Deaderick Street
(615) 741-2692, (800) 407-4324
www.tnmuseum.org

Tennessee State Museum, at the corner of Fifth and Deaderick Streets, offers exhibits ranging from prehistoric Nashville through the early 1900s, with a large Civil War display. Popular artifacts include a Conestoga wagon and an Egyptian mummy that a Tennessee explorer brought back from overseas several decades ago. The museum is closed on Monday and on New Year's Day, Easter, Thanksgiving, and Christmas. (See our Attractions chapter for more information.)

TRAVELLERS REST PLANTATION &
MUSEUM $$
636 Farrell Parkway
(615) 832-8197
www.travellersrestplantation.org

Nashville's oldest plantation home was built in 1799 by Judge John Overton, a prominent early citizen and friend of President Andrew Jackson. Over the years the plantation has seen many changes; today it's owned by the National Society of Colonial Dames of America. Visitors can tour the plantation, museum, and grounds and get a glimpse of early Nashville life. The plantation's education department has radically expanded its slate of special events and educational programs; everything from plantation holidays to slavery through the eyes of a child to scavenger hunts to an in-depth look at the Mound Builders is now offered. Music events are also on the calendar, and the Celtic Music Festival held each June is a popular evening of traditional music. Travellers Rest is open daily except Thanksgiving, Christmas, and New Year's Day. Kids under six are admitted free; AAA members receive a 10 percent discount. For more information see our Attractions chapter.

Early Nashville life is featured at Travellers Rest Plantation. SANDY BURR

FUN FOOD

DALT'S
38 White Bridge Road
(615) 352-8121
www.daltsgrill.com

Dalt's is a longtime favorite kid-friendly restaurant. A children's meal with beverage is only $2.99. Even finicky eaters will find it hard to resist such kiddie favorites as grilled cheese, hot dogs, mac and cheese, chicken fingers, cheeseburgers, spaghetti, and yummy milk shakes and malts. With its upscale diner atmosphere and tasty grown-up foods like wood-fired pizzas, ribs, steak, chicken, and salads, moms and dads will enjoy dining here, too. Dalt's provides booster seats, high chairs, crayons, and related accessories that make dining out with the kids hassle-free. The restaurant is open daily for lunch and dinner and also serves brunch on Saturday and Sunday.

ELLISTON PLACE SODA SHOP
2111 Elliston Place
(615) 327-1090

Okay, so your kids are now watching reruns of *Happy Days*. But have they ever been in a good old-fashioned diner a la Arnold's? Elliston Place Soda Shop is the real deal, from its tile floor and Formica tabletops to its fare: thick chocolate milk shakes (one is easily enough for two people); root beer floats, banana splits, and sundaes; burgers, fries, and onion rings; and daily "meat-and-three" specials. Elliston Place Soda Shop was established in 1939 by J. Lynn Chandler, and it still packs 'em in. The minijukeboxes in the booths will make you nostalgic, though they don't work; to compensate, there's a Wurlitzer in the back of the room with actual 45 rpm records (remember those?) of pop and country hits.

PANCAKE PANTRY
1796 21st Avenue S.
(615) 383-9333
www.pancakepantry.com
Yes, you'll usually have to wait in line, and yes, the food is worth it. But what puts this Nashville favorite on our kid list is the fact that children really are welcome here. There's a basket of kids' magazines and games at the entrance to occupy the tykes while everyone endures the inevitable wait. Once you do get seated, the waitstaff is accustomed to dealing with kids—a quick look around on any Saturday morning, and it's easy to see why. So if Junior's plate of pancakes ends up on the floor, no fear—no one will bat an eyelash. With a menu of classic comfort-food favorites—pancakes, waffles, grilled cheese, and the like—even picky eaters are bound to find something yummy. Pancake Pantry serves breakfast and lunch daily.

RAINFOREST CAFE
353 Opry Mills Drive
(615) 514-3000 (restaurant),
(615) 871-6848 (reservations only)
www.rainforestcafe.com
Nashville hasn't been friendly to theme restaurants; Planet Hollywood and the NASCAR Cafe are two notable casualties in recent years. But Rainforest Cafe seems to have found its niche, tucked away in the tourist-trafficked Opry Mills shopping megaplex. Entering the Rainforest Cafe can be likened to walking into Disney's *Jungle Book:* Gigantic aquariums, a lush jungle canopy, cascading waterfalls, and a fiber-optic starscape instantly transport visitors into the faux–rain forest theme; there's even a tropical "village" shop offering games, T-shirts, and other retail items. As for the food, it's classic American fare, with a special children's menu offering such tasty kid favorites as mac and cheese, dinosaur-shaped chicken tenders, hot dogs, and the like. (Mom and Dad, meanwhile, will be pleased to find some truly tasty grown-up selections on the menu; this is one theme restaurant that takes its food seriously.) Kids love this place and give cafe operators points for putting an environmental spin on the experience. Groups can take a 45-minute educational tour that addresses such issues as endangered species and rain forest conservation. The restaurant is open for lunch and dinner seven days a week.

STORYTIME

BORDERS BOOKS & MUSIC   FREE
330 Franklin Road, Brentwood
(615) 221-8804

545 Cool Springs Boulevard, Franklin
(615) 771-2870
www.bordersstores.com
The Borders store in Franklin offers regular storytime each Friday at 10:00 a.m. The Brentwood Borders also has various other children's events from time to time. For more details visit the Web site and click on the "My Store" option.

DAVIS–KIDD BOOKSELLERS   FREE
The Mall at Green Hills
2121 Green Hills Village Drive
(615) 385-2645
www.daviskidd.com
Davis–Kidd has an outstanding children's section that includes a toy train. Kidds' Corner storytime is held Monday through Saturday at 10:00 a.m.

NASHVILLE PUBLIC LIBRARY   FREE
Main Library, 615 Church Street
(615) 862-5800
www.library.nashville.org
Former Nashville mayor Phil Bredesen once declared that a "city with a great library is a great city." With that in mind, the city went out to improve its outdated and dilapidated library system. The result: Several glittering new facilities were built, while many existing ones were renovated or expanded. Nashville now has 21 public libraries located throughout the city, and all of them offer free storytimes for children of different ages several times a week. Nashville's main library, called the Downtown library by locals, is one of the city's new facilities, and its marble magnificence has been heralded as the best use of public funds since Nashville's arena opened in 1996. The

⊙ Close-up

Goo Goo

If there were a candy hall of fame, Nashville would have a place in it. Music City is where the first combination candy bar was invented, and it's still made right here at the Standard Candy Company.

The historic candy—the Goo Goo—has been satisfying sweet tooths for more than eight decades. As they say on the *Grand Ole Opry* radio show, which Standard has sponsored since the early 1960s, "Generations of Southerners have grown up on them." Dozens of people—Southerners as well as non-Southerners—from as far away as California and Canada are gaga over Goo Goos. They write the company each week requesting orders of the chewy, gooey candy. But you don't have to write for it; you can find Goo Goos in just about every part of the country, in stores like Walgreens, Wal-Mart, Kroger, and Safeway. They're most plentiful in Music City, however, and tourist attractions and gift stores here usually keep a good supply on hand for visitors who want to take home a taste of Nashville.

Standard, today operated by Jim Spradley and son Jimmy, sells about 25 million Goo Goos (approximately $8.5 million worth) each year. The candy bar has come a long way since its premiere in 1912. The Goo Goo was invented by Howell Campbell, who, in 1901 at the age of 19, founded the Standard Candy Company. The company's first products were hard candies and chocolates, but Howell and original plant superintendent Porter Moore developed a recipe combining fresh roasted peanuts, caramel, marshmallow, and milk chocolate. The recipe became a classic. Today the Goo Goo comes in three varieties—the original Goo Goo Cluster, the Peanut Butter Goo Goo, and the Goo Goo Supreme.

The candy bar didn't have a name at first because no one could decide what to call it. Stories of how the candy got its name vary. Campbell's son, Howell Campbell Jr., says his father took the streetcar to work each morning and would discuss the matter with fellow passengers. One passenger, a schoolteacher, suggested Goo Goo. But some people say the candy was given the name because it's the first thing a baby says.

In its early days the candy bar's circular shape made it difficult to wrap, so it was sold unwrapped from glass containers. Later the Goo Goo was hand-wrapped in foil and advertised as a "Nourishing Lunch for a Nickel." While it wouldn't pass for a nourishing lunch today (the Goo Goo Cluster in the silver package has 240 calories, 11 grams of fat, and just a smidgen of calcium, protein, and iron), Nashville's Goo Goo is still a delicious treat. To learn more about Goo Goos, visit www.googoo.com.

Downtown library offers storytime for preschoolers on Tuesday at 9:30, 10:30, and 11:30 a.m., and for young children on Wednesday at 9:30, 10:30, and 11:30 a.m. Group storytime by reservation is available on Thursday. The Downtown location also offers marionette shows on Friday and Saturday mornings. Other branches offer services such as homework help and after-school reading programs. Library hours vary by location; call the branch nearest you for information or visit the comprehensive Web site.

SPORTING LIFE

CENTENNIAL SPORTSPLEX
222 25th Avenue N.
(615) 862-8480
www.centennialsportsplex.com

Located next to Centennial Park, the 17-acre Sportsplex is operated by the Metro Board of Parks & Recreation. The year-round family sports and recreation complex has facilities for aquatics, fitness, and tennis, plus a two-sheet ice arena where youth hockey and figure-skating clubs practice (as well as Nashville's NHL Predators). Local kids and parents are familiar with the Sportsplex, which has hosted junior National Swim Meets, U.S. Water Polo Olympic Trials, the U.S. Figure Skating Championships, and the Virginia Slims Tennis Championships, to name a few. Sportsplex facilities are open to the public on a pay-as-you-go basis, or you may purchase season passes at a discount. For kids, the Sportsplex offers a full complement of lessons, clinics, and sports camps. A complete list of classes is available on the Web site. Sportsplex facilities are open seven days a week, but hours vary widely because of all the team practices; be sure to call first to ensure the facility you want is open.

JEWISH COMMUNITY CENTER
801 Percy Warner Boulevard
(615) 356-7170
www.nashvillejcc.org
The Jewish Community Center's pool and gym are popular with all ages; for kids, the center has a full slate of programs, including drama and ballet. On the recreation side, there are lessons in swimming and kids' yoga. A variety of sports leagues are also available here, such as soccer, T-ball, summer basketball camps, Little League, and the Tiger Sharks swim team. Membership is open to everyone.

YMCA OF MIDDLE TENNESSEE
900 Church Street (main office)
(615) 259-9622
www.ymcamidtn.org
Part of the Nashville community since 1874, today the YMCA has 23 centers in the Nashville area and surrounding counties. All provide a full complement of programs fulfilling the YMCA's mind-body-spirit credo; youth sports programs such as spring/fall soccer leagues, baseball, and basketball leagues for all ages are a Y mainstay. The majority of Nashville Ys have indoor and outdoor pools, separate gyms for kids, even

nurseries—after all, the Y is the largest child-care provider in Middle Tennessee. Seven Ys have teen centers open to kids ages 10 through 17. Though each is different, they offer such activities as Ping-Pong, foosball, computer labs, skate parks, rock walls, and so forth. A financial assistance program ensures that all youth can take part in the Y's programs, regardless of financial status. The Web site is thorough and offers a good overview of what each facility offers. Or call the YMCA's main office in Nashville.

YOUTH INC. ATHLETICS
Plaza Professional Building
Suite 209, Madison
(corporate office)
(615) 865-0003
www.youthincorporated.org
Youth Inc. has operated in Middle Tennessee since 1945. Programs and activities include sports leagues such as basketball, bowling, rifle, and in-line hockey. YI also operates the Circle YI Ranch, an ACA-accredited summer camp for boys and girls located on 170 acres at Percy Priest Lake. The ranch houses the organization's football training facility, where high school football camps are held. YI also has state-of-the-art football and hockey facilities in La Vergne, Bellevue, and Spring Hill. Boys and girls basketball programs are offered for ages 5 through 14; YI has nonathletic programs as well, including an employment service.

Baseball
LITTLE LEAGUE
www.littleleague.org
The national pastime is alive and well in Music City; there are dozens of Little League teams operating in the city, providing baseball and softball play for kids 5 to 18 years old. City leagues include Charlotte Park, Paul Lawrence Dunbar (ages 10 to 20), McCabe Park (5 to 13), West Park (10 to 20), and North Nashville (10 to 20); these leagues operate dozens of teams—at last count, McCabe had more than 35 teams in its roster. In

addition, the Sounds, Angels, Whitts, Tennessee Patriots, and Nashville Demons operate youth and adult baseball teams. The Triple-A Nashville Sounds, an affiliate of the Pittsburgh Pirates, are also very involved with area youth baseball and softball leagues, offering clinics, sports camps, and other special programs. For information call the Nashville Sounds at (615) 242-4371, or visit the team's official Web site at www.nashville-sounds.com.

Football

BELLEVUE STEELERS
www.bellevuesteelers.com
This football and cheerleading program serves youth ages 5 to 12 in the west Nashville area. The Steelers are a charter member of the Mid-State Youth Football league, which operates in Nashville and the surrounding counties and determines regional championships. The program provides instruction in contact football and cheerleading, plus camps and minicamps. These folks are serious about their football. They were the 2004 and 2005 CCC Mid-State Division II champs. The Steelers field Triple and Double A, B, and C teams, plus Pee Wee and a Varsity team. Organizers are volunteers, so contact information may change; visit the group's Web site for the most current contacts.

TENNESSEE YOUTH FOOTBALL ALLIANCE
6628 Ascot Drive, Antioch
(615) 641-6632
www.tyfa.org
This organization serves boys and girls ages 5 to 14 in football and cheerleading. TYFA has about 15 communities throughout Middle Tennessee, which together sponsor more than 140 teams. Area communities include the South Nashville Sooners. Part of the TYFA's mission is teaching kids the values of fair play, teamwork, and competitiveness. Visit the Web site for more information about TYFA and for information about individual communities and teams, including contact numbers.

WEST NASHVILLE YOUTH SPORTS ASSOCIATION
www.eteamz.com/broncosfb
The West Nashville Youth Sports Association provides tackle football and cheerleading programs for youth 5 to 14 years of age. While the name says West Nashville, kids from all over the Metro area are welcome to participate in the group's programs. Association teams, known as the Broncos, are divided into AAA (11 and 12), BBB (9 and 10), CCC (7 and 8), and Pee Wees. Teams play in the Mid-State Youth Football League and while serious about their play, association staff members pride themselves on putting the emphasis on molding character and being positive role models for kids, not just winning games. Bronco football and cheerleading squads practice and play in Hadley Park in north Nashville. The organization is run by volunteers; the best way to contact the group is via its Web site.

Hockey

NASHVILLE YOUTH HOCKEY LEAGUE
www.nyhl.com

GREATER NASHVILLE AREA SCHOLASTIC HOCKEY (GNASH)
www.gnashhockey.com
While Nashville didn't get its NHL team until 1998, ice hockey has been a presence among the city's youth since 1965, when the nonprofit, all-volunteer NYHL was launched. Today NYHL games are played at the Centennial Sportsplex, with registration beginning in August for the fall/winter season. The NHL Nashville Predators assist the league with fund-raising, organizing youth hockey clinics and camps, and such. NYHL age divisions and teams are Termites (4 through 7), Mites (8 and 9), Squirt (10 and 11), Peewee (11 and 12), Bantam (13 and 14), and Midget (16 and 17). GNASH, Middle Tennessee's high school hockey league, is aptly named for the Predators' lovable saber-toothed mascot, Gnash. Visit the NYHL Web site for current names and phone numbers. Or call the Predators Youth Hockey Department at (615) 770-2372.

STREET PRIDE

(615) 770-2372

www.nashvillepredators.com/play/street-pride.asp

Street hockey is sort of like ice hockey, only the players wear in-line skates and play in parking lots and other large paved areas. Nashville's Street Pride program was launched in 1998 by the Nashville Predators in conjunction with Nike and the National Hockey League. Street Pride is designed for youth ages 6 through 16, and games are played at 29 Metro Parks & Recreation Community Centers and YMCAs around the Nashville area. Nashville also hosts the NHL Breakout, a street and in-line hockey tournament each year.

Soccer

NASHVILLE YOUTH SOCCER ASSOCIATION

www.nysa-soccer.org

Founded in 1972, the nonprofit NYSA has fall and spring soccer programs for boys and girls in six different age groups. The group also hosts soccer camps and special events in conjunction with the Nashville Metros, the city's major-league soccer team. The NYSA is affiliated with the U.S. Soccer Foundation (USSF), the Tennessee State Soccer Association (TSSA), and the Federation International Football Association (FIFA). Games are held at Heartland Soccer Park, located just past Opryland. This is an all-volunteer organization, so check the Web site for current contact and registration information.

TENNESSEE FUTBOL CLUB

P.O. Box 682024, Franklin 37068

www.tnfc.org

Formed in 1999, this league has ballooned to more than 30 teams. Boys and girls teams, soccer camps and academies, and even assistance in college recruiting are available to league members. This group is serious about its play and has some state championships to prove it.

ULTIMATE GOAL

(615) 479-6756

www.ultimategoal.net

Ultimate Goal is an evangelical Christian ministry/soccer club that takes boys' and girls' teams to soccer games overseas and around the United States. Ultimate Goal sends teams to Sweden's Gothia Cup, the world's largest youth soccer tournament; other trips have taken teens and young adults to Mexico, Costa Rica, France, and England. U.S. trips to Florida and Colorado are regularly on the schedule, and there are also soccer programs at home in Nashville. Ultimate Goal is a national organization, and teams generally consist of youth assembled from around the country. But the group has a strong Nashville base and hopes to have its own soccer complex soon. Keep in mind that this is a religious organization geared more toward ministry than toward winning tourneys; scoring points is not, er, the ultimate goal.

SPECIAL NEEDS

LILY'S GARDEN

Fannie Mae Dees Park

Blakemore and 24th Avenues

The brainchild of a local mom, Lily's Garden is Tennessee's first "Boundless Playground," which means it is accessible to children with physical and developmental disabilities. Lily's Garden is located at a corner of Dragon Park and opened in the fall of 2001; play equipment pieces such as ramps, slides, swings, and raised sandboxes are designed to accommodate children with and without wheelchairs. In fact, Lily's Garden has become a gathering spot for all children, and kids without special needs can and do use the equipment.

MERLIN AND THE COURT JESTERS

Metro Parks Centennial Park Office

(615) 883-1730

www.geocities.com/merlin_jesters

For the past several years, Metro Parks has organized this privately funded magic program for youth and adults with mental disabilities. The Court Jesters use magic as a means of changing perceptions of people with disabilities. The troupe has developed quite a reputation for excellence, performing in more than nine states and at such major events as the World Special Olympics Games in Raleigh-Durham, North Carolina. The Court Jesters also offer a program for special ed teachers, showing them how to use magic as a teaching tool.

SPECIAL OLYMPICS TENNESSEE
1900 12th Avenue S.
(615) 329-1375
www.specialolympicstn.org

The Special Olympics offers athletic training and competition for children and adults with mental disabilities. There are more than 10,000 participants in Middle Tennessee. Special Olympics Tennessee hosts eight state games and tournament competitions each year. These events encompass 22 official sports, including softball, aquatics, volleyball, horseshoes, tennis, power lifting, and even bocce (though not all sports are available in all locations). Nashville competitions are held at Vanderbilt and Lipscomb Universities, with aquatic events held at the Centennial Sportsplex.

ANNUAL EVENTS

Want to have some fun? Learn something new? Mingle with a crowd? Maybe just get out of the house? Then check out some of Nashville's annual events. Music City's calendar is full of festivals, celebrations, sporting events, seminars, shows, and other fun and interesting happenings—enough to keep you busy year-round. Just about any weekend—January through December—you can find at least one special event taking place in or around Nashville. What's your pleasure? From art to antiques, gardening to golf, and mules to Moon Pies, there's something for everyone.

Music, of course, is the focus of many of our biggest and best events. Nashville is Music City, and we like to think we have some of the best music events you'll find anywhere. Among them are country and jazz festivals, rock 'n' roll showcases, and special symphony performances in the park. You can find those events in this chapter, but be sure to see our Music City chapter for more information. Even the events that focus on topics other than music usually include musical entertainment in their programming. There's plenty to eat and drink, too. Depending on the event, you can indulge in international fare, country cookin', local restaurants' specialties, or just plain fun food like funnel cakes and cotton candy.

In this chapter we list some of Nashville's favorite events by month, roughly in the order they occur. Schedules are subject to change, so before making plans, it's a good idea to check the local newspapers for up-to-date information on events, dates, and admission prices. Most annual events have a gate charge, but you'll find a few that offer free admission. Children's admission is usually a few dollars less than adult admission. Most events also offer discounts for senior citizens and groups. Some have special rates during designated days or hours, and some offer discounts if you bring a coupon. Keep your *Insiders' Guide to Nashville* handy all year. The next time you're looking for something to do, check our listing of annual events, then go out and have some fun!

JANUARY

"LET FREEDOM SING!"
Schermerhorn Symphony Center
(615) 783-1212
www.nashvillesymphony.org
The Nashville Symphony's annual tribute to civil rights leader Dr. Martin Luther King Jr. traditionally features the local Celebration Chorus and the Celebration Youth Chorus in an uplifting and inspiring program. It is held on the Saturday or Sunday prior to Martin Luther King Jr. Day. In addition to musical performances, the event also includes recognition of winners of the "I, Too, Have a Dream" essay contest, which is open to Middle Tennessee students in grades 5 through 12.

DR. MARTIN LUTHER KING JR. CITYWIDE MARCH AND CONVOCATION
Jefferson Street
(615) 963-5331
www.tnstate.edu/opr
This annual citywide march, organized by the Interdenominational Ministers Fellowship, is Nashville's largest event celebrating Dr. Martin Luther King Jr. Day. Marchers gather at various sites around Nashville and converge on historic Jefferson Street, where they march west to the Tennessee State University campus. After the march, a convocation is held at TSU's Gentry Center basketball arena. The one- to two-hour program includes a keynote speaker, a perfor-

mance by a local church choir, and scholarship presentations. Previous participants have included Nashville mayor Bill Purcell and U.S. senator Lamar Alexander.

i Every January the Department of Public Works' Trees to Trails program recycles thousands of Christmas trees. Trees are chipped and spread along area hiking trails. Be sure to recycle your tree. You can find designated tree drop-offs at parks throughout Nashville. For more information visit www.nashville.gov/recycle or call (615) 880-1000.

FEBRUARY

ANTIQUES & GARDEN SHOW OF NASHVILLE
Nashville Convention Center
601 Commerce Street
(615) 352-1282
www.antiquesandgardenshow.com
Nashville hosts several antiques shows each year. The Antiques & Garden Show, usually held in mid- to late February, happens to be one of our favorites. Named one of the Top 20 Events in the Southeast by the Southeast Tourism Society, the show draws some 30,000 visitors and features more than 80 antiques dealers from the United States, the United Kingdom, and France, as well as about 70 eastern U.S. horticulturists. It benefits the Cheekwood Botanical Garden and Museum of Art (see our Attractions chapter) and the Exchange Club Inc. Charities. The show focuses on high-end items and features a wide range of goods; you'll find furniture, paintings, antique jewelry, rare books, porcelain, and more. Surrounding the antiques are beautifully landscaped gardens as well as booths filled with flowers, herbs, and other garden necessities for sale. High-profile furniture and gardening experts present lectures on a variety of topics, and a Saturday seminar series offers the chance to chat informally with gardeners. The Garden Café, on the trade-show floor, sells reasonably priced lunch items and serves afternoon tea daily. A preview party offers the first chance to view the antiques.

HEART OF COUNTRY ANTIQUES SHOW
Gaylord Opryland Resort & Convention Center, 2800 Opryland Drive
(800) 947-8243
www.heartofcountry.com
Held in mid-February or mid-March, this award-winning event features more than 200 top antiques dealers from around the United States and Canada. Exhibits include unique furniture, paintings, folk art, textiles, and 18th- and 19th-century Americana, and prices run the gamut—from less than $10 to $50,000. There are always special exhibits—Amish quilts, game boards, and American flags, for example—as well as educational seminars and lectures. A Thursday preview party precedes the three-day show. Party tickets are $75 in advance and $80 at the door and include admission throughout the weekend. Daily admission is $10; children 12 and younger are admitted free. Special rates at the Opryland hotel are available for show attendees. Park in the lot designated for the show and take a shuttle to the hotel.

MARCH

COUNTRY RADIO SEMINAR
Nashville Convention Center
601 Commerce Street
www.crb.org
Each February or March more than 2,000 country radio broadcasters from around the country descend on Nashville for the Country Radio Seminar, a week of educational sessions, meetings, artists' showcases, awards presentations, and parties.

SPRING INTO THE ARTS
Downtown Public Library
(615) 862-5800
www.library.nashville.org
This annual-six week celebration of arts and culture in Nashville offers musical and dance performances, puppet shows, craft workshops, story hours, movies, and entertainment by local performers. All events are family friendly, free, and open to the public.

APRIL

CHEEKWOOD SPRING ART HOP

Cheekwood Botanical Garden and Museum of Art

1200 Forrest Park Drive

(615) 356-8000

www.cheekwood.org

Held the Saturday before Easter, this event features egg hunts for kids, music, storytelling, art activities, a scavenger hunt, and, of course, the Easter Bunny. Admission for nonmembers is $10 for adults and children; admission for members is $5 for adults and children.

MULE DAY

Maury County Park, 1018 Maury County Park Drive, Columbia

(931) 381-9557

www.muleday.com

Even if you're not particularly interested in mules, you're bound to enjoy this old-time festival, held the first or second weekend (Thursday through Sunday) at Maury County Park in Columbia, about 43 miles south of downtown Nashville. The Mule Day tradition began in 1934. Farmers used to bring their mules to town for a livestock show and market once a year, and the festival grew around this annual happening. Today the festival features a mule parade downtown, mule shows, mule pulling, arts and crafts, a flea market, square dancing, a clogging contest, a liars' contest, and more. You can enjoy "pioneer foods" such as roasted corn, fried pies, and apple fritters as well as traditional festival fare like hamburgers, hot dogs, and soft drinks. This event generates interest from across the country and has drawn as many as 265,000 people (plus about 500 mules) in one year. While attending Mule Day, impress your friends by informing them that a mule, as defined by the *Random House Webster's Dictionary*, is "the sterile offspring of a female horse and a male donkey." To get to Maury County Park from Nashville, take Interstate 65 south to the first Columbia exit and turn right. Follow the signs about 10 miles to the park. Traffic at the park usually moves at a snail's

pace, so allow plenty of time for parking and exiting. Admission is $7 for adults and teens; $5 for children 12 and younger.

i The Nashville Convention Center at 601 Commerce Street is the site of several popular consumer shows each year. A few local favorites are the Nashville Boat and Sports Show, held in January (314-567-0020, www.boatshows.com); the Southern Women's Show in April (800-849-0248, www.southernshows.com); and the Home Decorating and Remodeling Show in September (800-343-8344, www.showprosintl.com).

TIN PAN SOUTH

Various Nashville venues

(615) 256-3354, (800) 321-6008

www.tinpansouth.com

The Nashville Songwriters Association International (NSAI) sponsors this annual music festival that celebrates songwriters and songwriting. Concerts, awards, and a golf tournament are held during the week. See our Music City chapter for information.

CMT FLAME WORTHY VIDEO MUSIC AWARDS

Gaylord Entertainment Center

501 Broadway

www.cmt.com

Billed as country music's only fan-voted awards, CMT's Flame Worthy Video Music Awards celebrate country music videos.

GOSPEL MUSIC WEEK

Renaissance Nashville Hotel, Nashville Convention Center, and other venues

(615) 242-0303

www.gospelmusic.org

This industry event attracts artists, record company personnel, radio representatives, concert promoters, and others who work in the gospel music industry. Read more about it in our Music City chapter.

DOVE AWARDS
Grand Ole Opry House
2804 Opryland Drive
(615) 242-0303
www.doveawards.com

The Gospel Music Association presents its annual Dove Awards each spring. Read more about it in our Music City chapter.

> **i** If you enjoy gardening, you may be interested in Cheekwood's many plant shows held throughout the year. The botanical garden and museum hosts shows devoted to daffodils, wildflowers, bonsais, roses, hostas, daylilies, and more. See our listings in this chapter, or call Cheekwood at (615) 353-2148 for more information.

NASHVILLE EARTH DAY FESTIVAL
Centennial Park
2500 West End Avenue
(615) 242-5600
www.nashville.gov/earthday
www.teamgreenonline.com

Nashville celebrates Earth Day with a free, family-oriented festival on the weekend closest to the April 22 holiday. The event is usually held at Centennial Park and features live alternative-country, folk, blues, and bluegrass music; food and drink booths; and speakers from the mayor's office and Tennessee Environmental Council.

MAIN STREET FESTIVAL
Downtown Franklin
(615) 591-8500
www.historicfranklin.com

This two-day, free-admission event held during the last full weekend in April averages an attendance of about 140,000. The Southeast Tourism Society has listed it as one of the top 20 events in the Southeast. It's a fun time and definitely worth the short drive to Franklin. The festival takes place on 5 city blocks in the historic downtown area, from First Avenue to Fifth Avenue, and encompasses the town square. Crafts and food booths line the streets. More than 200 artists and craftspeople from across the United States exhibit their works. Food vendors offer such items as barbecue, burgers, hot dogs, roasted corn, and Greek, Italian, Mexican, and Asian fare. A children's area on Third Avenue off Main Street caters to kids eight and younger. Bring the youngsters here for face painting, pony rides, games, a jump on the Moon Bounce, and a ride on the Ferris wheel. Four stages offer continuous entertainment, including music, dance, and storytelling. At 7:00 p.m. Saturday a locally popular musical act performs. Park along nearby streets and in downtown lots.

> **i** In 1897 Nashville candymakers Williams Morrison and John Wharton invented a machine to spin the sugary treat called fairy floss or cotton candy. The confection became a big hit at fairs and festivals.

NASHVILLE RIVER STAGES
Downtown, Riverfront Park
(615) 346-9000
www.nashvilleriverstages.com

River Stages is a three-day music festival featuring dozens of nationally known bands on six stages. See the Music City chapter for more information.

MAY

COLONIAL FAIR
Historic Mansker's Station, Moss–Wright Park at Caldwell Road, Goodlettsville
(615) 859-FORT
www.cityofgoodlettsville.com

This re-creation of an 18th-century market draws some 5,000 to 6,000 attendees during the first weekend in May. Crafters and merchants sell reproductions of 18th-century clothing, baskets, copperware, flint-rock firearms, knives, and other goods. Native Americans display and sell skins and other items typical of the period. The juried crafts show requires that every artist, merchant, and costumed participant adhere to the 1750–1790 time period. Re-enactors take on such characters as beggars, trollops, and other people you might find at an 18th-century fair. Musical entertainment, jugglers, sword swallowers, and other entertainment from the period are scheduled. Admission is $8 for adults, $5 for children ages 6 through 12.

i Fans of *The Blair Witch Project* may be interested to know that Middle Tennessee has its own legend, the Bell Witch. It started in 1818 when John Bell and his family were reportedly tormented by strange noises in and near their house in Adams, Tennessee, about 40 miles north of Nashville. These days some people claim they still see ghostly images and hear eerie noises. For $10 you can tour a supposedly haunted cave in the area. Call (615) 696-3055 or visit www.bellwitchcave.com for details.

TENNESSEE CRAFTS FAIR
Centennial Park
West End Avenue and 25th Avenue N.
(615) 385-1904
www.tennesseecrafts.org
The crafts fairs at Centennial Park are among Nashville's most popular events. This one, a juried crafts festival produced by the Tennessee Association of Craft Artists, is the largest market of Tennessee crafts you'll find anywhere. Some 175 contemporary and traditional artisans, all from the Volunteer State, set up on the lawn of Centennial Park, and as many as 50,000 visitors stop by during the three-day show, held the first weekend in May. You can find affordable gifts for around $25 as well as collectible items costing thousands of dollars. Children's crafts activities, live music, demonstrations, and food will keep you in the park for hours. Admission is free. TACA also hosts the Fall Crafts Fair here on the last weekend of September (see that month's section for details).

TENNESSEE RENAISSANCE FESTIVAL
Near Castle Gwynn, Triune
(615) 395-9950
Weekends in May, ending on Memorial Day, the wooded grounds across from Triune's Castle Gwynn turn into a medieval village where you'll find jousting knights, fair maidens, fortune-tellers, gypsy jugglers, and entertainers plus medieval-themed arts and crafts and food. Twice daily, knights in full armor mount large Percherons and engage in combat. In addition to jousting exhibitions, you can enjoy drama and comedy (presented in Olde English) at two stages on the grounds as well as Renaissance music. All vendors, entertainers, and some 150 volunteer greeters wear period costumes. Dozens of crafts vendors and artisans offer such items as clothing, glass, candles, wood crafts, pewter jewelry, silver crafts, and weaponry. Free children's activities include storytelling, games, and coloring. For an extra charge, adults can try their luck at such games of skill as archery and ax throwing. Triune is about 20 miles south of downtown Nashville between Franklin and Murfreesboro. The castle is 8 miles from Interstate 24, off the Highway 96 exit, or 6 miles from I-65. Admission is $18 for adults, $6 for children ages 5 through 12. A season pass is $65. Parking is free.

IROQUOIS STEEPLECHASE
Percy Warner Park
(615) 343-4231
www.iroquoissteeplechase.org
The Iroquois Steeplechase, one of Nashville's most popular sporting and social events, takes place the second Saturday in May. First held in 1941, this is the nation's oldest continually run weight-for-age steeplechase. Some 30,000 attend every year. Various parties and gala events precede the running of the Iroquois Steeplechase. If you come, plan to make a day of it. You can picnic or have a tailgate party. Thousands take blankets, lawn chairs, and their favorite food and drink to a spot on the grassy hillside overlooking the course. Gates open at 10:00 a.m. The seven-race card culminates with the featured Iroquois Memorial at 4:00 p.m. Admission is $15; admission for children 6 to 12 is $5. Children ages five and under are admitted free. Special ticket and party packages are available, too. The event benefits Vanderbilt Children's Hospital.

JUNE

OPRY PLAZA PARTIES

Grand Ole Opry House Plaza
2802 Opryland Drive
(615) 871-OPRY
www.opry.com

These free outdoor concerts take place on Friday and Saturday evenings during the summer and feature mainly alternative country and roots music performers. See our Music City chapter for details.

PERFORMING ARTS SERIES

Centennial Park, Riverfront Park,
and other area parks
(615) 862-8424
www.nashville.gov/parks

Looking for some inexpensive entertainment? You can't find anything more affordable than Metropolitan Nashville Parks and Recreation's free summer schedule of concerts, dance, and theater performances. Events are held at parks throughout the city. Contact the parks department or check the entertainment listings in local daily and weekly publications for more information.

AMERICAN ARTISAN FESTIVAL

Centennial Park
West End Avenue and 25th Avenue N.
(615) 298-4691
www.american-artisan.com

This invitational festival, held mid-June during Father's Day weekend, features 160 craftspeople from around the country. It's sponsored by the American Artisan, the upscale crafts gallery on Harding Road in west Nashville (see our Shopping chapter). You'll find pottery, wood, blown glass, leather, photography, metal, furniture, quilts, and more. It's a great place to find unique jewelry—there are usually about 24 jewelry booths at this festival. There's good food, too, with an emphasis on healthy items. You can choose from Thai specialties, fajitas, gyros, and more. A children's art booth and musical entertainment round out the offerings. If you're not in the market for crafts, it's still a fun event. This is a great place to people-watch. Adults of all ages, children, babies in strollers, and dogs (on leashes, of course) wander through the rows of crafts booths and relax in the picnic area. If you're planning to come here, be sure to wear comfortable clothing; it can be pretty hot and humid in Nashville this time of year. And the park grounds can be muddy in places, so choose appropriate footwear. Admission is free.

> **i** Looking for a unique gift for that special someone? Check out one of Nashville's crafts fairs. Centennial Park and the state fairgrounds host several such events each year. You'll find everything from modern art to old-fashioned country crafts.

CMA MUSIC FESTIVAL/FAN FAIR

Various downtown Nashville venues
(800) CMA-FEST
www.cmafest.com

Tens of thousands of hard-core country-music fans, more than 70 hours of concerts, and long lines of autograph seekers: That's this event in a nutshell. This mid-June festival attracts fans from around the world. (Read more about it in the Music City chapter.)

NASHVILLE INDEPENDENT FILM FESTIVAL

Regal Green Hills 16
(615) 742-2500
www.nashvillefilmfestival.org

This early- to mid-June event features several days of film and video screenings from renowned and up-and-coming filmmakers from around the world, including Tennessee. As many as 200 films are featured, along with 15 to 20 workshops, film analyses, forums, and other events, some of which are led by well-known entertainment industry figures. Admission ranges from $5 to $8 for a single film; an all-festival pass is available for $250 to $350. Other ticket packages are available. Call for a schedule of daily and evening shows, or watch for a listing in local publications. NIFF members receive discount tickets as well as special benefits throughout the year, such as free admission to monthly screenings and discounts on tickets at Regal Green Hills 16.

RC COLA AND MOON PIE FESTIVAL
Bell Buckle town square
www.bellbuckletn.org

An RC Cola and a Moon Pie—if you have to ask, you're probably not a Southerner. The RC–Moon Pie combo is a classic. The tiny, charming town of Bell Buckle celebrates the big round chocolate-and-graham-cracker-covered marshmallow treat the third Saturday in June. It all started in 1995, when the town wanted to celebrate the 75th birthday of the Moon Pie, which is made in nearby Chattanooga. As you might guess, this event doesn't take anything too seriously. It's purely for fun. Festival activities might include a Moon Pie toss, Moon Pie hockey, synchronized wading, a Moon Pie dessert recipe contest, a Moon Pie song contest, and a "womanless beauty pageant," featuring high school football players in drag. You wouldn't want to miss the crowning of the Moon Pie King and RC Cola Queen. A 10K run, country and bluegrass music, and clogging demonstrations add to the fun. The event is held in conjunction with a crafts fair. Bell Buckle is about an hour's drive from Nashville, off I-24 between Murfreesboro and Shelbyville. The historic town has been a magnet for the arts community, attracting sculptors, potters, and other artisans. While you're here, you might want to check out the Bell Buckle Café (www.bellbucklecafe.com), a popular spot with musicians. Admission is free. Parking is $3 to $5.

JEFFERSON STREET JAZZ & BLUES FESTIVAL
26th Avenue N. and Jefferson Street
(615) 726-5867

Historic Jefferson Street, once known for its jazz, blues, and R&B music, is the location of this family-oriented music festival, which usually takes place on the third Saturday in June. (Read more about it in our Music City chapter.)

THE VINNY
The Golf Club of Tennessee
1 Golf Club Lane
Kingston Springs
(615) 794-9399
www.golfhousetennessee.com

Since its inception in 1993, the Vinny, country star Vince Gill's annual pro-celebrity golf tournament, has raised more than $3 million for Tennessee Junior golf and youth programs. The two-day event includes PGA Tour players plus sports and entertainment celebrities. The Pro–Celebrity Am takes place on Monday, while amateurs play with the celebrities on Tuesday. Pros who have participated in the event include John Daly, Fuzzy Zoeller, and Lanny Wadkins. In addition to Vince Gill and his wife, Amy Grant, celebrity participants have included Alice Cooper, NFL quarterback Brett Favre, Charley Pride, and Kix Brooks of Brooks & Dunn. The event is not open to the public, although many junior golfers are able to participate as volunteers, and the state's top junior golfers have a chance to play in the tournament.

JULY

INDEPENDENCE DAY CELEBRATION
Riverfront Park
First Avenue N.
(615) 862-8400

This is Nashville's largest one-day event, drawing up to 80,000 to the riverfront to celebrate the Fourth of July. It's a free afternoon and evening of music and fireworks, sponsored by the mayor's office and Metro Parks and Recreation. You'll find food and alcohol-free drinks, too, but you'll have to pay for that. The family-oriented celebration usually kicks off around 4:00 p.m.; a variety of locally popular bands and the Nashville Symphony perform at the riverfront stage. If you come early, you can find a spot to sit and relax on the tiered hillside facing the Cumberland River; it's a great place to listen to the bands while watching boats travel up and down the river. If you prefer, you can walk along First Avenue while sampling festival food and people-watching. The fireworks display begins around 9:00 p.m.

CELEBRATION OF CULTURES
Scarritt-Bennett Center
1008 19th Avenue S.
(615) 340-7500
www.scarrittbennett.org

This two-day international festival began in 1996 as a way to celebrate the cultural diversity of Nashville and Middle Tennessee. Japanese, Korean, African-American, Chinese, Greek, Kurdish, and rural Appalachian are among the more than 40 cultures represented. Dancers, musicians, storytellers, and exhibits provide the entertainment. Bring your appetite, and sample a variety of ethnic food offerings, including Ethiopian, Indian, Mediterranean, and soul food. A family activity area features storytelling and international games and crafts such as origami, Guatemalan worry dolls, and Muslim handpainting.

UNCLE DAVE MACON DAYS
Cannonsburgh Village
312 South Front Street, Murfreesboro
(800) 716-7560
www.uncledavemacondays.com
This nationally recognized old-time music and dance festival is named for Uncle Dave Macon, a pioneer of the *Grand Ole Opry*. The four-day event, which begins the Thursday following July 4, offers national championship competitions in old-time clogging, old-time buck dancing, and old-time banjo. There's plenty of fiddling, too. Musicians of all ages bring their instruments and get together for impromptu concerts throughout the event. The motorless parade on Saturday features mules, horses, and wagons. A gospel celebration is held on Sunday. The festival also features a juried crafts show, a variety of food vendors, and historical photo displays, all set against the backdrop of Murfreesboro's Cannonsburgh Village, a re-creation of a pioneer village. The village is off Broad Street on Front Street. Admission is free.

i Nashville's record high temperature of 107 degrees Fahrenheit was set in July 1952. The record low—17 degrees below zero—was set in January 1985.

AUGUST
BELL WITCH BLUEGRASS FESTIVAL
Old Bell School
U.S. Highway 41, Adams
(615) 696-2589
www.adamstennessee.com
This event is popular with bluegrass musicians and fans. Held the second Friday and Saturday in August, it features mainly amateur musicians from Tennessee and surrounding states.

TENNESSEE WALKING HORSE NATIONAL CELEBRATION
Celebration Grounds, Shelbyville
(931) 684-5915
www.twhnc.com
This event, the World Grand Championships for the high-stepping Tennessee Walking Horse, has been called "the world's greatest horse show." The 10-day celebration begins in late August. When you're not watching the action in the show ring, you can enjoy the trade fairs, dog shows, and elaborately decorated barn area. Shows run three to four hours, so you'll want to allow plenty of time here. Ticket prices (adults and children) are $7 to $20 for reserved seats, $5 to $10 general admission. A 10-day package is $105 per person. Groups of 30 or more receive discounts of approximately 30 percent on certain nights. Shows begin at 7:00 p.m., but the grounds are open all day. Shelbyville is southeast of downtown Nashville, about a 50-minute drive. The show site is a mile off U.S. Highway 231 S., or 25 miles from I-24.

MISS MARTHA'S OLD FASHIONED ICE CREAM CRANKIN'
First Presbyterian Church
4815 Franklin Road
(615) 254-1791
Who can pass up an opportunity to dig into some delicious homemade ice cream on a hot August day? Every year on the first Sunday in August, 250 to 300 ice cream makers crank out dozens of their favorite frozen concoctions for you to sample.

Categories are vanilla/vanilla base, chocolate, specialties (sorbets, yogurts, sherberts), and fruit. Bring a blanket or lawn chairs, find a comfortable spot on the lawn, kick back, and enjoy every rich and creamy spoonful. Adults can enjoy the live music while kids play games. A stacking contest features area ministers in a two-minute race to see who can stack the most scoops of ice cream on a cone. While you're enjoying the tasty treats, volunteer judges are choosing the best in each category. Tickets are $5 in advance and $8 on the day of the event. Children under age three are admitted free. Proceeds benefit the Martha O'Bryan Center, a family-services center serving the James A. Cayce Homes and surrounding east Nashville communities.

SEPTEMBER

TENNESSEE STATE FAIR

Tennessee State Fairgrounds
Wedgewood Avenue at Rains Avenue
(615) 862-8980
www.tennesseestatefair.org

Focusing on livestock and agriculture, the Tennessee State Fair features 4-H Club and Future Farmers and their projects in the Agriculture Hall. Although this isn't one of the better-known state fairs, there's plenty to see and do here. The carnival midway, open until midnight, features all your favorite adult and kiddie rides and games. There are usually crafts, antiques, a petting zoo, and concerts, too, as well as plenty of fair food. The fairgrounds is 4 blocks off I-65. Admission is $8.00 for adults and teens, $4.00 for children ages 3 through 12, and 25 cents for those ages 2 and under. Parking is $2.

AFRICAN STREET FESTIVAL

Tennessee State University main campus
28th Avenue N.
(615) 963-5561
www.africanamericanculturalalliance.com

This three-day family-oriented ethnic celebration is held the second or third weekend of September. It is a major event, drawing tens of thousands to the historic Jefferson Street area. The festival features more than 100 merchants from 25 states, exotic food concessions, and eight hours of daily entertainment. There is something for everyone. The stage show features art, lots of music—blues, gospel, African drums, jazz, rap, and reggae—as well as poetry and drama. Other attractions are African dance lessons, children's storytelling, a teen tent, art show, fashion show, and lectures. Day-care assistance is provided on-site. It's held on the west side of the TSU campus, a mile from downtown, near 28th Avenue N. and Interstate 40. Admission and parking are free. An MTA trolley provides free transportation around the campus.

BELLE MEADE FALL FEST

Belle Meade Plantation
5025 Harding Road
(615) 356-0501, (800) 270-3991
www.bellemeadeplantation.com

Around this time of year, leaves have begun changing from green to red, orange, and gold, and the unmistakable feeling of fall is in the air—a perfect time to celebrate the changing of the seasons at a fun outdoor event. This mid-September festival features antiques, crafts by noted artisans, local retail merchandise, food by local restaurants, a children's festival, and music. Admission is $6 for adults, $2 for children 6 to 12. The price includes a tour of the Greek Revival mansion. (See our Attractions chapter for more information on Belle Meade Plantation.)

i During the summer, Full Moon Pickin' Parties take place at Percy Warner Park's steeplechase barn, roughly at the time of each full moon. The parties feature a variety of small jam sessions. Musicians who bring their instruments get in free. For everyone else, admission is about $15 in advance or $20 at the gate. For reservations or more information, contact Friends of Warner Park at (615) 370-8053.

TACA FALL CRAFTS FAIR
Centennial Park
West End Avenue and 25th Avenue N.
(615) 385-1904
www.tennesseecrafts.org
Nearly 200 crafters from around the country, selected for the quality of their work, exhibit at this juried market of fine crafts, held the last weekend in September. The fair is loaded with pottery, art jewelry, blown glass, photography, sculpture, and more. Crafts demonstrations and live music round out the activities. A food court with picnic tables is the perfect place to recharge or do some people-watching. Admission is free. The fair is presented by the Tennessee Association of Craft Artists, which also presents the Tennessee Crafts Fair here the first weekend in May (see that section's related entry).

LIVING HISTORY TOUR
Nashville City Cemetery
1001 Fourth Avenue S. at Oak Street
(615) 862-7970
www.thenashvillecitycemetery.org/
For one afternoon only in late September, the Nashville City Cemetery is transformed into a theater of sorts, with actors portraying notable Nashvillians who were laid to rest at the historic cemetery. Visitors walk along the paths, taking in miniskits throughout the graveyard. At dusk a candlelight tour begins. The whole thing lasts about 90 minutes and is suitable for children. The event, which began in 1999, raises money to support the cemetery. Admission is about $7 and includes refreshments. (See our Attractions chapter for more on Nashville City Cemetery.)

OCTOBER

HERITAGE DAYS
Sam Davis Home Historic Site
1399 Sam Davis Road, Smyrna
(615) 459-2341, (888) 750-9524
www.samdavishome.org
This event is a living-history celebration featuring such activities as lye soap making, blacksmithing, quilting, and food preserving. It's held on the Thursday and Friday closest to October 6 at the Sam Davis Home. (See our Attractions chapter for more information on the Sam Davis Home Historic Site.) Admission is $5 for everyone ages three and up. Smyrna is 20 miles southeast of Nashville. The Sam Davis Home is off I-24 E.

SOUTHERN FESTIVAL OF BOOKS
War Memorial Plaza, downtown
between Charlotte and Union,
and Sixth and Seventh Avenues
(615) 770-0006
www.tn-humanities.org
More than 30,000 book lovers attend this annual three-day event sponsored by the Tennessee Humanities Council. Some 200 authors from around the country, with an emphasis on those from the Southeast, gather for readings, panel discussions, and book signings. A children's area features children's authors and activities. Admission is free. Tickets to the Friday-night dinner and awards presentation are approximately $40 a person. The festival is usually held the second weekend of October.

OKTOBERFEST
Historic Germantown
Eighth Avenue N. and Monroe Street
(615) 256-2729
Live German music, German food and drink, plus dozens of booths full of German and American arts and crafts are featured at this annual event. It's held on the second Saturday in October in historic Germantown. The festival opens with worship services at the Church of the Assumption Catholic Church and the Monroe Street United Methodist Church, which cosponsor the event. Admission is free. To get there, take I-65 to the MetroCenter exit and proceed to Eighth Avenue. The festival site is 2 blocks north of the Bicentennial Mall.

FALL MUSIC FESTIVAL
Moss–Wright Park
745 Caldwell Road, Goodlettsville
(615) 859-7979
www.goodlettsvillechamber.com

All kinds of music, plus dancing, food, and a barbecue cook-off, are featured at this event, which takes place in mid-October.

GRAND OLE OPRY BIRTHDAY CELEBRATION
Grand Ole Opry House
2804 Opryland Drive
(615) 889-3060
www.opry.com

Grand Ole Opry fans gather each October to celebrate the birthday of America's longest-running radio program. The three-day party is held in mid-October and includes concerts, a *Grand Ole Opry* performance, and autograph and photo sessions with the stars. (See our Music City chapter for more information about the event, and our History chapter for more on the Opry.)

HEART OF COUNTRY ANTIQUES SHOW
Gaylord Opryland Resort &
Convention Center
2800 Opryland Drive
(800) 862-1090
www.heartofcountry.com

This popular antiques show is one of two Heart of Country shows held in Nashville each year. The other event takes place in February. See our February listing for more details.

NAIA POW WOW
Long Hunter State Park
2910 Hobson Pike
Nashville
(615) 232-9179
www.naiatn.org

The Native American Indian Association sponsors this annual event that brings together Native Americans from throughout North America. As many as 25 tribes are represented, and the general public is invited. It's held on the third weekend of October. Competitive dancing, arts and crafts, storytelling, demonstrations, and fine-art displays are among the festivities. Food booths feature traditional foods from various tribes. Admission is $6 for ages 12 and older and $3 for those under 12.

HANDS ON NASHVILLE DAY
Throughout Nashville
(615) 298-1108
www.hon.org

One day a year, usually on a Saturday in October, Nashville's volunteer-services organizations plus thousands of volunteers get together to provide community service at nonprofit agencies and schools. While some paint and clean schools, clean up parks, landscape school grounds, and build small play areas at schools and community centers, others organize intergenerational parties for senior citizens and walk dogs at the humane society. In addition to providing needed services, the event raises the community's awareness of Nashville's nonprofit organizations.

NOVEMBER

CMA AWARDS
Gaylord Entertainment Center
501 Broadway
(615) 244-2840 (Country Music
Association)
www.cmaawards.com

Each fall the Country Music Association presents its annual awards, the industry's most prestigious honors. The star-studded ceremony, held at the Gaylord Entertainment Center, is televised live on ABC. Some tickets are usually available to the public. Read more about it in our Music City chapter.

COMMUNITY OF MANY FACES
Downtown Public Library
615 Church Street
(615) 862-5800
www.library.nashville.org

The annual celebration of the diverse cultures and communities of Nashville features multicultural, music, and dance performances; puppet shows; craft workshops; book talks and story hours; movies; and entertainment by local performers. All events are family friendly, free, and open to the public.

CHRISTMAS VILLAGE
Tennessee State Fairgrounds
Wedgewood Avenue at Rains Avenue
(615) 256-2726
www.christmasvillage.org
This annual event at the fairgrounds features more than 250 merchants with seasonal and gift items. You'll find Christmas ornaments, hand-painted and personalized items, clothing, pottery, jewelry, toys, and food items. Kids can also visit with Santa. The three-day mid-November event benefits the Vanderbilt Bill Wilkerson Hearing & Speech Center and Pi Beta Phi philanthropies. Admission is $7 for anyone 10 and older; children 9 and younger get in free. Advance tickets are available for $6 (call or visit the Web site for details).

CHRISTMAS PASTIMES
Belle Meade Plantation
5025 Harding Road
(615) 356-0501, (800) 270-3991
www.bellemeadeplantation.com
Belle Meade Plantation decks the halls the way they did it in the late 1890s, offering a look at how Nashvillians—at least some of them—celebrated Christmas more than a century ago. Admission is $7 per person. Wassail tours are available by reservation. The exhibit runs from mid-November through early January.

COUNTRY CHRISTMAS
Gaylord Opryland Resort &
Convention Center
2800 Opryland Drive
(615) 889-1000
www.gaylordhotels.com/gaylordopryland
An outing to the Opryland Hotel during the holidays is a tradition for many Nashvillians, and the hotel is a popular place to take visiting friends and relatives this time of year. Wide-eyed visitors marvel at the hotel's outdoor lights display of more than two million bulbs. The decorations indoors are spectacular as well. About a million visitors show up for the festivities each year. If you wait until late in the season to visit, you'll probably end up in a major traffic jam (often extending for miles down Briley Parkway), and once inside the hotel, you'll find it jam-packed as well. To avoid the crowds, get in the spirit early and come in November—the earlier the better. If you plan to visit only the hotel, you'll have to pay only for parking (about $10 during this event). Of course, once inside, you're bound to want to stop in one of the many food and drink spots for a holiday treat. Country Christmas includes a breakfast with Santa for the kids, a room full of life-size ice sculptures, and an art, antiques, and crafts fair. Several events, such as the Yule Log lighting ceremony and nightly Dancing Waters fountain shows, are free.

CHRISTMAS AT BELMONT
Belmont Mansion
1900 Wedgewood Avenue
(615) 460-5459
www.belmontmansion.com
Belmont Mansion, on the campus of Belmont University near Music Row, is decorated in Victorian style during the holidays, trimmed with hundreds of yards of garland, fruit, and dried flowers. Christmas at Belmont begins around the Friday after Thanksgiving and continues through December 31. Tours of the 1853 mansion are available Tuesday through Saturday. A free classical and folk music concert is held once during the event (usually on the second Monday in December). Admission is $10 for adults, $3 for kids ages 6 through 12. (For more information on Belmont Mansion, see our Attractions chapter.)

GOODLETTSVILLE ANTIQUE FESTIVAL
Goodlettsville Antique Community
Main Street, Goodlettsville
(615) 859-7979
www.goodlettsvillechamber.com
Goodlettsville's numerous antiques malls and shops have a Christmas Open House with special decorations, refreshments, and sales. It takes place usually the last weekend in November. From downtown, take I-65 N to exit 97, then go west to Dickerson Pike. The malls are on Main Street. (For more information on these shops, see the Antiques section of our Shopping chapter.)

DECEMBER

YULEFEST
Historic Mansker's Station
Moss–Wright Park at Caldwell Road
Goodlettsville
(615) 859-FORT, (615) 859-7979
www.goodlettsvillechamber.com

"A 1780s Candlelight Christmas" is the theme of Yulefest, held the first weekend in December. Guides in period dress re-enact colonial Christmas customs at this historic site, which features a reconstruction of a 1779 frontier fort, Mansker's Station. There are refreshments, music, decorations, and horse-drawn wagon rides, too. The historic brick structure on the site is Bowen Plantation House; built in 1787, it was the first brick home in Middle Tennessee and is listed on the National Register of Historic Places. Admission is free. Mansker's Station and Bowen Plantation House are at Moss–Wright Park at Caldwell Road, between Longhollow Pike and Gallatin Road. (For more info about Mansker's Station and Bowen Plantation House, see our Attractions chapter.)

TRIBUTE TO AFRICAN AMERICANS IN THE BATTLE OF NASHVILLE
National Cemetery and area sites
(615) 963-5561
www.africanamericanculturalalliance.com

A lecture, tour, and wreath laying are highlights of this event, which takes place over three days in mid-December. The tour includes stops at locally significant sites such as Fort Negley and Shy's Hill. National Cemetery is at 1420 Gallatin Road. Admission is free.

NASHVILLE GAS CHRISTMAS PARADE
Downtown Nashville
(615) 734-1754, (615) 734-1702
www.nashvillegas.com

As many as 100,000 spectators turn out for the annual Christmas parade, which features more than 100 floats, bands, clowns, and other attractions—Santa, too. The parade starts at Gaylord Entertainment Center and marches along Broadway, Second Avenue N., and the Woodland Street Bridge, wrapping up at the Titans's stadium. Before the parade are a 5K race and 1-mile fun run. Participants vie for prizes for best costumes and best time. It all takes place the first Sunday in December. The fun starts around 10:00 a.m. Admission is free.

DICKENS OF A CHRISTMAS
Downtown Franklin
(615) 591-8500
www.historicfranklin.com

You'll feel like you've stepped back in time to a Charles Dickens Christmas during this event, held the second full weekend in December in historic downtown Franklin. For those two days, 2 blocks of Main Street are themed to the 1800s. You'll see carolers in Victorian costumes as well as characters such as Scrooge and the ghosts of Christmases past, present, and future. In the store windows, artisans dressed in period clothing demonstrate crafts of the 1800s. Shopkeepers dress in period clothing, too. Take a free ride in a horse-drawn carriage, then visit a street vendor for a bag of kettle corn, some sugarplums, plum pudding, tea, or hot cider. Admission is free.

NASHVILLE BALLET'S *NUTCRACKER*
3630 Redmon Street
(615) 297-2966
www.nashvilleballet.com

The Nashville Ballet's version of *The Nutcracker* was an immediate hit when it opened in the late 1980s, and it has become a holiday tradition for many Nashvillians. In addition to the Nashville Ballet, the production features local children and the Nashville Symphony. Tickets range from about $21.50 to $72.50 and are available through Ticketmaster and at the TPAC box office.

THE ARTS

Ballet. Symphony. Museums. Broadway musicals. Opera. Independent film. Nashville has it all … and more. These are essential elements of a thriving arts scene befitting a city with the nickname "Athens of the South." Recent years have seen a steady growth in the number of arts groups busily creating new works or new interpretations of old favorites. That's not surprising because Nashville has long been a magnet for creative, energetic people. If there's a downside to all the activity, it may well be that the abundance of artistic and cultural opportunities can lead to difficulty in making a decision. The area's arts scene is rapidly changing, too. The opening of the Frist Center for Visual Arts in 2001 provided the city with its first art museum equipped with enough gallery space to land some prestigious touring exhibitions. Construction began in December 2003 for the Schermerhorn Symphony Center. Located downtown across from the Country Music Hall of Fame & Museum, the $120-million facility opened in fall 2006.

While it's not technically the arts, Nashville's recently renovated public library system has become a focal point for a variety of arts-oriented activities. Works by local artists and photographers are on exhibit at a variety of library locations, including the beautiful Main Library downtown.

Nashville's burgeoning arts scene has sparked interest in the surrounding counties, too. In 2001 Williamson County launched its first professional theater company, the Boiler Room Theatre, named for its location in the old boiler room of the Factory in Franklin. A little farther afield in Dickson, about 30 minutes from Nashville, is the Renaissance Center, a state-of-the-art facility focusing on all areas of the arts, including music, multimedia, visual arts, and drama. The Renaissance Center's emphasis is on education; a variety of classes and workshops are held here, as well as concerts, exhibitions, and theatrical productions.

With all this activity, you might expect Nashvillians to be a surprisingly cultured lot, hopping from art opening to avant-garde theatrical work to ballet performance to independent film screening. Well . . . with all due respect to the locals, Nashville's arts often appear to function in a void. "Nashville doesn't support the arts" is a frequent complaint among local artsy types, and it's not uncommon for local productions to be greeted with a sea of empty seats. But on the upside, those who do enjoy this abundance of cultural activity have become spoiled by readily available tickets and shows that rarely sell out. That is changing, however. Galvanized by such highly publicized events as the Frist Center's opening and the community effort to save the Belcourt Theatre, Nashvillians are showing renewed interest in community arts. The Metro Nashville Arts Commission's *Arts and the Economy* report has shown large attendance increases at arts events in recent years.

Art lovers can rejoice: The cultural arts are alive and well in Nashville and getting stronger every year. Serious art aficionados are urged to look into season tickets, subscription packages, and memberships that make participating in many activities much more affordable than purchasing tickets by the event. The following information looks at performing and visual arts opportunities around the Nashville area; listings for specific theaters where concerts may take place can be found in our Music City chapter.

TICKETS

TICKETMASTER
(615) 255-ARTS, (615) 255-9600 (charge by phone)
www.ticketmaster.com
Ticketmaster, a nationwide service, handles ticket sales for a number of local concerts, plays, and other productions at a variety of venues. If you're going to order tickets by phone, have your credit card ready—and be aware that Ticketmaster always adds a surcharge (generally $3 or more) to the price of each ticket. Ticketmaster outlets are located in area Kroger stores and Hecht's department stores.

ARTS CENTERS

THE RENAISSANCE CENTER
855 Highway 46 S., Dickson
(615) 740-5600, (888) 700-2300
www.rcenter.org
Located 30 minutes from Nashville off I-40, this unique nonprofit center offers a broad spectrum of visual arts and performing arts programming, education, and community outreach for the entire Middle Tennessee area. Opened in 1999 by the Jackson Foundation, a local organization, the Renaissance Center is an impressive arts facility, drawing visitors from Nashville and beyond. Officials with TRC like to say they have something for everybody, and it's certainly true. The visual-arts department includes gallery exhibitions, artist-in-residence programs, and community classes in a variety of disciplines. The music department offers concerts and recitals, group and individual classes, workshops, and even specialty classes such as songwriting and classes for toddlers. Concerts run the gamut—country great Vince Gill, '60s rockers Three Dog Night, and the Indiana State University Wind Ensemble have all been on the calendar. The center also presents four Southern gospel concerts each year and schedules songwriter showcases as well. The second Monday of each month, during regular semesters, Recitals in the Rotunda, featuring area

university faculty and accomplished students, are presented at 7:00 p.m.

TRC's theatrical arts department is home to the Gaslight Dinner Theatre, Renaissance Center Community Theatre, and the in-house Renaissance Repertory Company. The Community Theatre, which features local amateur thespians, has staged such productions as *Driving Miss Daisy* and *Anything Goes*. Shows are held in TRC's Performance Hall; tickets usually cost around $15 for adults, with discounts for seniors and children. The Renaissance Rep is a professional company that stages its own productions and also serves as cast and directors for TRC's Gaslight Dinner Theatre. Gaslight is open to the public Friday nights; tickets are $30. The dinner is buffet-style, and the menu changes with each new production. Call for reservations. Performances typically sell out weeks in advance, so call early if you want a seat. A special Senior Lunch Matinee is presented at noon on Friday for senior citizens 55 and older. In addition, TRC is involved in an expansive arts outreach program, television production, and offers one-of-a-kind training in 3-D animation at its 3D University.

SARRATT PERFORMING ARTS
Great Performances at Vanderbilt series
207 Sarratt Student Center
Vanderbilt University
(615) 322-2471
www.vanderbilt.edu/sarratt
The Great Performances series is one of eight student program committees of Vanderbilt's Sarratt Student Center. The series brings a variety of theatrical and musical programs, literary readings, and dance of all types to the Nashville community. Launched in 1978, it has evolved into a season of 10 to 15 events, most held at Vanderbilt's 1,200-seat Langford Auditorium. Since students are involved in all programming decisions, Great Performances has earned a reputation for discovering fresh, emerging talent. Tickets are available at Ticketmaster locations or the Sarratt box office. Great Performances at Vanderbilt also offers residency programs that bring artists together

with students, teachers, and interested patrons. Artists-in-residence typically provide master classes, lectures, demonstrations, and school day performances to Vanderbilt and the community. The Sarratt Student Center is located off 24th Avenue S. on Vanderbilt Place, near West End Avenue. It houses the Sarratt Cinema, Sarratt Gallery, university art studios, a Ticketmaster outlet, radio station WRVU, and student newspaper offices.

i To keep track of concerts, theater, exhibits, and other arts events in Nashville, be sure to pick up a copy of the *Nashville Scene* each week. The *Scene,* available free at locations all over town, comes out Wednesday afternoon; listings cover an eight-day period, from Thursday to Thursday.

TENNESSEE PERFORMING ARTS CENTER
505 Deaderick Street
(615) 782-4000,
(615) 255-ARTS (tickets),
(615) 782-6560 (season ticket info)
www.tpac.org
The Tennessee Performing Arts Center, commonly known as TPAC (pronounced tee-pack), is a private, nonprofit corporation located in a huge downtown complex. It has four stages: 2,472-seat Jackson Hall, 1,075-seat Polk Theater, 288-seat Johnson Theater, and the 1,668-seat War Memorial Auditorium, the historic landmark located at the corner of Charlotte and Seventh Avenue, across the plaza from TPAC. These stages are home to three local resident groups: the Tennessee Repertory Theatre, Nashville Opera, and the Nashville Ballet. In July 2002 the "Rep" officially became a division of TPAC, merging administrative staffs. As Nashville's primary performing arts facility, TPAC underwent a much-needed $7.9-million renovation in 2003. The project transformed the Jackson Hall lobby into a stunning gathering space. TPAC serves area schools through a variety of programs. They include live performances at TPAC, arts workshops, in-school visits, and more. TPAC also

sponsors various teacher-training workshops and professional development seminars to help bring arts into Nashville's schools.

DANCE

NASHVILLE BALLET
3630 Redmon Street
(615) 297-2966,
(615) 782-6560 (subscriptions)
www.nashvilleballet.com
Nashville Ballet, founded in 1981 as a nonprofit civic dance company, became a professional company in 1986. Each year it presents a four-program series, accompanied at the majority of series by the Nashville Symphony, at the Tennessee Performing Arts Center's Polk Theater and Jackson Hall. Every other year the ballet features a fifth series. The company's classically based repertoire is balanced with modern, neoclassical, and contemporary works. Of course, what makes this company unique is its Music City location, and the Nashville Ballet has cleverly incorporated this into one of the company's most original concepts: combining dance with live performances by renowned singer-songwriters—folkie Nanci Griffith and country artist Hal Ketchum are two notable names. Most ballet performances are at TPAC, though special performances such as the children's ballet have been held on various stages around the city, including Belmont University and the Downtown public library. Children's ballet performances are all originals and based on folktales; they are free. Single ticket sales to regular performances range from around $25 to $50, though hot tickets like *The Nutcracker* tend to be more expensive. The popular *Nutcracker* is also a sellout each year, so get your tickets early. Season ticket subscribers receive a 20 percent discount on all shows.

Nashville Ballet, which has an affiliated School of Nashville Ballet, serves the community with varied educational and outreach programs. Children's ballet performances entertain and educate youth through artistic presentations in an interactive setting; Nashville Ballet also presents a free Ballet Story Hour during the season at each of the public library branches. The Nashville School of Ballet offers youth and adult classes to the community in ballet and modern dance as well as Pilates. Beginner to advanced levels are available.

CLASSICAL MUSIC AND OPERA

BELMONT UNIVERSITY SCHOOL OF MUSIC
1900 Belmont Boulevard
(615) 460-6408
www.belmont.edu/music
Belmont's comprehensive music program offers studies in diverse music styles, and its free solo and group concerts cover a wide range as well, from classical and jazz to bluegrass and rock. Camerata Musicale, a chamber music ensemble created in 1987, performs several times a year in the Belmont Mansion. Other groups, including the Belmont Concert Band and the University Orchestra, perform at various locations on campus. The Faculty Concert Series features a variety of music performed by the school faculty. Student showcases are often an opportunity to catch the stars of tomorrow before they're famous—Trisha Yearwood, Brad Paisley, and Lee Ann Womack are just a few graduates of the Belmont's music business program (see our Education and Child Care chapter). Most performances are held in the Massey Performing Arts Center, which includes the 999-seat Massey Concert Hall and 100-seat Harton Recital Hall.

BLAIR SCHOOL OF MUSIC
2400 Blakemore Avenue
(615) 322-7651
www.vanderbilt.edu/blair
The Blair School of Music at Vanderbilt University presents about 140 free concerts each year by groups including the Vanderbilt Orchestra, Chamber Choir, Symphonic Wind Ensemble, Opera Theatre, and Jazz Band as well as the Nashville Youth Symphony, a precollege orchestra of community youth. Performances are held

at Steve and Judy Turner Recital Hall, Ingram Hall, and Langford Auditorium campus. In addition, the highly respected Blair Concert Series features about 20 concerts and recitals a year, including shows by special guests such as fiddler/multi-instrumentalist extraordinaire Mark O'Connor. Tickets are $12 for adults, $10 for Vanderbilt faculty and staff, and $5 for students and seniors; season tickets are available.

DAVID LIPSCOMB UNIVERSITY DEPARTMENT OF MUSIC
3901 Granny White Pike
(615) 279-5932, (800) 333-4358
http://music.lipscomb.edu
Lipscomb's Department of Music presents concerts by soloists and groups, including the A Cappella Singers, who perform sacred music; the Jazz Band, which performs four concerts a year; the Lipscomb University String Ensemble; and the Early Music Consort, which combines medieval and Renaissance music with ethnic styles from around the world. Admission is free to student performances. For performances by touring artists or name performers—there are about three of those each year—a ticket is required.

Cultural Arts

The following organizations provide assistance, information, funding, and other support to the Nashville arts community.

Metro Parks and Recreation— (615) 862-8424, www.nashville .gov/parks

Tennessee Arts Commission— (615) 741-1701, www.arts.state .tn.us

Tennessee Films, Entertainment & Music Commission—(615) 532-2770, www.filmtennessee.com

---

NASHVILLE CHAMBER ORCHESTRA
2002 Blair Boulevard
(615) 256-6546
www.nco.org

The Nashville Chamber Orchestra presents a broad mix of new music and traditional classics within a chamber music format. Though primarily a string orchestra, the flexible group, led by music director and conductor Paul Gambill, adds brass, winds, and percussion when at its full size of about 35 members. Many NCO musicians also double as studio session players, prompting influential local critics to dub the NCO a group of "super-pros." The NCO presents a six-concert season with additional performances offered at various locations around the region. The season begins in early October; concerts are held at such venues as TPAC's Polk Theater, War Memorial Auditorium, and the Belcourt Theatre. Tickets are available by calling (615) 256-6546, or visiting the venue box office. Ticket prices vary but are around $25, with discounts for students and seniors.

NASHVILLE OPERA ASSOCIATION
3628-D Trousdale Drive
(615) 832-5242
www.nashvilleopera.org

Artistic director John Hoomes, who joined the Nashville Opera in February 1995, and executive director Carol Penterman have been credited with not only significantly improving the quality of the company's productions but also expanding its audience through innovative marketing and education programs. Nashville Opera, founded in 1980, merged with Tennessee Opera Theatre in September 1997 to form the Nashville Opera Association. That umbrella group now consists of the Nashville Opera, which produces professional, full-scale operas; Tennessee Opera Theatre, an education division that trains young singers and promotes local talent; and the Nashville Opera Guild, a group of 400 fund-raising and promotional volunteers. The opera season runs October through April, during which four productions are staged. Past productions have included *Tosca*, *The Barber of Seville*, *La Bohème*, and *Porgy and Bess*. Foreign-language performances have English supertitles. Performances are held at TPAC's Polk Theater and Jackson Hall; individual tickets range from $17 to $75, but season subscribers receive a substantial discount. Tickets can be purchased by calling (615) 255-ARTS, or at any Ticketmaster location.

THE NASHVILLE SYMPHONY
Schermerhorn Symphony Center
Fourth Avenue S.
(615) 783-1200
www.nashvillesymphony.org

The Nashville Symphony, the largest performing arts organization in Tennessee, puts on more than 200 concerts—ranging from classical and Pops series to children's concerts and special events—during its 37-week season. It also performs with the Nashville Ballet and the Nashville Opera (see previous entries). The resurgence of the symphony after filing for bankruptcy in February 1988 is a testimony to the Nashville community's support. A reorganization plan developed by the chamber of commerce, local government, volunteers, and business leaders had the symphony back on track by fall 1988. The Schermerhorn Symphony Center opened in September 2006 at Fourth Avenue S., across from the Country Music Hall of Fame & Museum. The number of performances has increased substantially now that the symphony has moved into its new home. Attendance at symphony performances has almost quadrupled. The Nashville Symphony has garnered acclaim, attracting such prominent guest artists as Van Cliburn, Isaac Stern, Jean-Pierre Rampal, and Rosemary Clooney. You can catch the Nashville Symphony, which has been under the direction of Maestro Kenneth Schermerhorn since 1983, at Ryman Auditorium, the Grand Ole Opry House, outdoor venues like Centennial Park and Cheekwood, and other sites throughout Middle Tennessee and in adjacent states. Many of these performances are free. The Nashville Symphony offers various ticket subscription packages. Single tickets range from about $23 to $70. Tickets are required for all ages; however, those ages 17 and under receive a 50 percent discount.

THEATER

You'll find an abundance of theatrical opportunities in Nashville, ranging from professional companies to amateur and dinner theater to children's shows. We've included some of the more visible groups, but independents are always popping up, so keep your eyes open.

ACT I
1411 Eastland Avenue
(615) 726-2281
www.act1online.com

ACT I, a group of local artists—the acronym stands for "Artists Cooperative Theater"—performs a varied selection of classic and contemporary plays at the Darkhorse Theater at 4610 Charlotte Avenue. ACT I presents three to five productions each year, from September to May. Past productions have included *Hair*, *Bus Stop*, *Elephant Man*, *Pygmalion*, and *Julius Caesar*. Tickets may be reserved by phone or on the Web site beginning one month before each production. Prices are $15 for adults and $12 for students and seniors. Season tickets are available. Students through high school with a valid ID are admitted free to Thursday evening and Saturday matinee performances.

ACTORS BRIDGE ENSEMBLE
1312 Adams Street
(615) 341-0300
www.actorsbridge.org

What started in 1995 as a theatrical training program has evolved into a progressive professional theater company. Actors Bridge stages original and contemporary theatrical productions on various stages around town, including the Darkhorse Theater, and the ensemble's home base, the Neuhoff Site, off Monroe Street in Germantown. Under the guidance of artistic director Bill Feehely, Actors Bridge Ensemble has produced numerous original works to critical acclaim, including the musical *Francis of Guernica* by hit songwriter Marcus Hummon; *American Duet*, by Feehely and Hummon; and *The Vampire Monologues* by local actor Jeremy Childs. As part of its mission, the nonprofit theater company aims to raise social consciousness and serve the community. A good example is the 2008 season presentation of *Marisol* by Jose Rivera. In the play, a band of guerrilla angels has decided that God is senile and must be assassinated for the greater good of the universe. In 1999 Actors Bridge launched its New Works Lab, which allows playwrights to see their work in staged readings. Lab readings are open to the public; several full-fledged productions began as Lab readings, including Feehely's play *Working with Glass*. Actors Bridge also offers classes using the Meisner Technique, an acting technique developed by Sanford Meisner and taught by Feehely. Many Actors Bridge actors have also gone on to work on Broadway (*The Civil War*) and in film (*My Dog Skip*, *The Castle*). Season tickets are around $50. Ticket prices to Actors Bridge events are generally $12 to $15.

THE BOILER ROOM THEATRE
230 Franklin Road, Building 6
The Factory at Franklin
(615) 794-7744
www.boilerroomtheatre.com

Williamson County's first resident professional theater company is located in a converted boiler room of the Depression-era Allen Manufacturing Co. factory. Now a dining and retail complex, the Boiler Room Theatre adds a nice mix of live entertainment to this piece of suburban renewal. Under the guidance of president and artistic director Jamey Green, the Boiler Room presents a season of four theatrical and musical productions, plus special events. It's a varied slate. Past productions have included *A Dickens Christmas Carol*, the Nashville original *Macbeth: The Musical*, *Six Degrees of Separation*, and *Man of La Mancha*. The BRT Harlequins children's theater program has two six-week workshops each year. Held on Saturday in the spring and fall, the workshops culminate in a performance. There's also a kid's summer camp focusing on all aspects of the theatrical arts, with programs for children and teens. Shows are staged in the 120-seat theater. Ticket prices range from $15 for children under 12 to $20 for adults; matinees are a few dollars cheaper.

CHAFFIN'S BARN DINNER THEATRE
8204 Highway 100
(615) 646-9977, (800) 282-BARN
www.dinnertheatre.com

Having opened in 1967, Chaffin's Barn is Nashville's oldest professional theater. For one price, you can enjoy an all-you-can-eat country buffet followed by a stage production. It could be Shakespeare, a musical, a mystery, or a comedy. Chaffin's has two theaters running simultaneously: the 300-seat MainStage theater, with its stage that "magically" descends from the ceiling at showtime, and the more intimate 60-seat BackStage theater. The two theaters share the buffet line and starting times. Chaffin's, which uses local and out-of-town actors and holds open auditions, presents 16 productions each year. You'll generally find a musical or comedy on MainStage. BackStage usually has a mystery or comedy. Past productions have included the Tony Award–winning *Cabaret,* the original work *Murder in Music City,* and Rodgers and Hammerstein's *Sound of Music.* Chaffin's also offers a special children's Christmas matinee through each December. MainStage performances are held Tuesday through Saturday year-round, with dinner served from 6:30 to 7:30 p.m. and showtime at 8:00 p.m. One Sunday matinee is presented sometime during each production's run. Two reduced-rate senior matinees are also held for each show; call for details. Reservations are required. Season memberships offer a great bargain: Members and a guest are entitled to attend each production at a two-for-one rate. A membership sampler offers the same deal on just five shows. Group discounts are also available. (See also our Nightlife chapter.)

CIRCLE PLAYERS
505 Deaderick Street
(615) 322-PLAY
(615) 255-ARTS (Ticketmaster)
www.circleplayers.net

Circle Players, founded in 1949, is Nashville's oldest volunteer nonprofit arts organization. The troupe has been one of the Tennessee Performing Arts Center's resident groups since 1980. They stage about nine productions a season, which typically runs from early September through mid-May. The Players present a wide range of theater—musicals, comedies, and drama—in TPAC's 288-seat Johnson Theater. Past performances have included *Joseph and the Amazing Technicolor Dreamcoat, To Kill a Mockingbird,* and *Smokey Joe's Cafe.* Performances are generally at 8:00 p.m. Friday and Saturday and 2:30 p.m. Sunday. Tickets are $15 for adults, $12 for seniors, and $10 for folks 17 and younger. Season ticket holders get to take advantage of ticket exchange privileges, allowing Circle tickets to be exchanged when they cannot be used for the performance day normally attended.

DAVID LIPSCOMB UNIVERSITY THEATER
3901 Granny White Pike
(615) 966-5715
www.theater.lipscomb.edu

Lipscomb University Theater, under the direction of Dr. Larry Brown, stages three or four productions a year. They can vary from Shakespeare or other classics to musicals and new works. Productions are presented in the university's intimate 128-seat University Theater. Past shows have included the world premiere of *The Queen's Two Bodies,* named best play at the 2000 Christians in Theater Arts Conference, and *Macbeth.* The group, which includes theater majors as well as other interested students, also presents an occasional dinner theater, usually an original murder mystery, in the home of David Lipscomb on campus. Most of the group's shows are free admission. Admission to the dinner theater/murder mystery productions is $10.

i The seasons of many concert and theater groups in Nashville run from September to April or May—roughly in line with school schedules.

LAKEWOOD THEATRE COMPANY INC.
2211 Old Hickory Boulevard, Old Hickory
(615) 847-0934
www.lakewoodtheatre.com

Lakewood Theatre Company is a community theater group that maintains its own venue in a historic former bakery just down the street from Andrew Jackson's home, the Hermitage (see our Attractions chapter). The building is one of Davidson County's oldest and was renovated by the company in 1983. The company, begun for children in the community, continues to offer a summer children's workshop. It also continues to offer a variety of productions. Past shows include Cole Porter's *Anything Goes*, Neil Simon's *The Star Spangled Girl*, and the timeless kids' classic, *The Boxcar Children*. Most productions run for three weekends, except for musicals, which run for four. Plays are at 7:30 p.m. Friday and Saturday nights and 2:30 p.m. Sunday. Tickets are $10 for adults, $8 for students and seniors. Season tickets are available at $45 for adults, $35 for students and senior citizens. Reservations are strongly suggested.

NASHVILLE CHILDREN'S THEATRE
724 Second Avenue S.
(615) 254-9103
www.nashvillechildrenstheatre.org
Established in 1931, NCT is the country's longest-running children's theater group. The not-for-profit group has been recognized internationally as a model for excellence in the field of theater for young audiences and has received numerous awards. The theater holds after-school and in-school workshops and a summer drama day camp. Nashville Children's Theatre produces at least five shows from May through September. Shows run for four to five weeks. During production, school performances are usually presented at 10:00 and 11:30 a.m. each weekday. A weekend family series features shows on Saturday and Sunday. Check the Web site for the season performance schedule. Past productions have included *The House at Pooh Corner* and *Charlotte's Web*. The theater is currently undergoing a $5.7-million renovation and expansion project that will more than double its existing space. Improvements include a larger lobby and box office, additional restrooms, a soundproof cry room for infants and small children, and an outdoor courtyard. The theater has been ranked one of the top five in the United States by *Time* magazine. Tickets are $5 a person during the week for school groups, $7 a person for weekend groups, and on the weekends, $10 for adults and $8 for children. The NCT stages productions in two theaters: the 690-seat Hill Theatre and the more intimate Cooney Playhouse, where kids and adults sit on the floor and join in the action and excitement of the play. (See our Kidstuff chapter for more on NCT.)

Darkhorse Theater

One of Nashville's most popular venues for live theater is the Darkhorse Theater, located at 4610 Charlotte Avenue, across from Richland Park. The 136-seat alternative theater presents new works, classical theater, dance, film, live music, and multimedia shows. The venue is home to several performing arts groups, including ACT I and Actors Bridge Ensemble, and also hosts productions from groups such as Nashville Shakespeare Festival and People's Branch Theatre. For more information on the theater, its resident groups, and season schedule, visit the Web site www.darkhorsetheater.com or call the theater at (615) 297-7113.

THE NASHVILLE SHAKESPEARE FESTIVAL
1604 Eighth Avenue S.
(615) 255-2273
www.nashvilleshakes.org
The Nashville Shakespeare Festival is dedicated to producing the plays of the Bard as well as works by other classical, modern, and emerging playwrights. It is best known for its free "Shakespeare in the Park" productions, which since 1988 have drawn thousands of Nashvillians to Centennial Park. Past performances have included *As*

You Like It, A Midsummer Night's Dream, Macbeth, and *Julius Caesar.* In addition to the popular summer Centennial Park productions—which are free—NSF stages winter shows at the Belcourt Theatre and Darkhorse Theater. The festival also takes its "Shakespeare sampler," a combination of 50-minute condensed versions of the Bard's classics with a workshop, on tour to high school students throughout Tennessee.

PEOPLE'S BRANCH THEATRE
(615) 254-0008
www.peoplesbranch.org
People's Branch Theatre, established in 2000, has developed a reputation as the city's leading alternative theater, presenting inventive and experimental productions. The nonprofit Actors' Equity–affiliated company's productions have included Samuel Beckett's *Waiting for Godot* and C. S. Lewis's *Till We Have Faces.* All performances take place at Belcourt Theatre in Hillsboro Village. Tickets are $15 ($10 for students, seniors, and Equity members) and can be reserved by phone or purchased at the door. Various season memberships are available.

TENNESSEE REPERTORY THEATRE
505 Deaderick Street
(615) 782-4000
www.tnrep.org
Called "the Rep," Tennessee Repertory Theatre, the state's largest professional theater company, was established in 1985. In July 2002 it became a division of TPAC. Its programs, staged in TPAC's Polk Theater, have ranged from blockbuster musicals to Pulitzer Prize–winning plays to original productions. Past productions have included 2002 Tony winner *Proof,* Harold Pinter's acclaimed *Betrayal,* Edward Albee's *Who's Afraid of Virginia Woolf?,* David Mamet's *A Life in Theatre,* and musicals such as *Evita.* The Rep also offers post-show discussions and other programs for the audience. The Rep uses professional actors—most of them based in Nashville—for all its productions. It creates all costumes and set designs and conducts all rehearsals at its offices and studios at 427

Chestnut Street. Individual tickets range from $10 to $45. Subscriptions are available. Tickets can be ordered through www.tnrep.org, via any Ticketmaster outlet, or by phone through Ticketmaster at (615) 255-ARTS.

VANDERBILT UNIVERSITY DEPARTMENT OF THEATRE
Neely Theatre, West End at 21st Avenue S.
(615) 322-2404
http://sitemason.vanderbilt.edu/theatre
Vandy's theater department stages four major productions a year representing a range of time periods and genres. Recent productions have included Shakespeare's *As You Like It* and *Romeo and Juliet,* Thornton Wilder's *Our Town,* and Tony Kushner's *A Dybbuk.* Shows are held at Neely Auditorium, a flexible black-box theater that seats about 300. Ticket prices are $7 general admission and $4 for graduate students and those in groups of 10 or more. Undergraduates are admitted free with student ID.

ART GALLERIES AND MUSEUMS

Art is practically everywhere you look in Nashville—from the architecture of the famed skyline to the public parks. But the city's art landscape changed dramatically in April 2001 with the opening of the Frist Center for the Visual Arts, Nashville's first major art exhibition center. More on that later, however. Nashville is home to several public art collections as well as many privately owned galleries that display works from local, regional, national, and international artists. Admission is free to many public museums, though a few charge a fee while others accept donations. There's no charge to visit the private galleries, which display and sell artwork on consignment and are probably hoping you'll buy something. You'll also find changing displays at a variety of alternative exhibit spaces, including banks, restaurants, bookstores, coffeehouses, schools, and, periodically, places like the Country Music Hall of Fame and the Ryman Auditorium. See the "Listings" section each week in the *Nashville Scene* for details.

THE AMERICAN ARTISAN
4231 Harding Pike
(615) 298-4691
www.american-artisan.com

This crafts gallery has been a Nashville fixture for more than 30 years. Gallery owner Nancy Saturn, a prominent figure on the local arts scene, has brought together an eclectic array of one-of-a-kind American craft pieces, ranging from woodcrafts, handblown glass, and ceramic works to jewelry and furniture. The gallery is also famous for its annual American Artisan Festival, held at Centennial Park each Father's Day weekend. The gallery is open Monday through Saturday.

i Belmont University's Singing Tower was built around 1850 as a water tower; it was transformed into a carillon in 1928 and is now a historic landmark. The carillon is still played for special events and concerts.

ARTS AT THE AIRPORT FOUNDATION
1 Terminal Drive, Suite 501
(615) 275-2040
www.flynashville.com

The Arts at the Airport program brings a variety of changing visual arts exhibits as well as musical performances to all three levels at Metro Nashville International Airport. Arts in the Airport also has a permanent collection, which includes Tennessee artist Jack Hastings's two 15-foot mobiles, *Dancing on Air.*

THE ARTS COMPANY
215 Fifth Avenue N.
(615) 254-2040, (877) 694-2040
www.theartscompany.com

This company is primarily known for the services it offers the arts community: curatorial services, project development, and such. But the Arts Company/Nashville's gallery represents regional, national, and international artists in photography, painting, sculpture, and contemporary outsider art. The gallery's Salon Saturday, on the third Saturday of each month, is a chance for artists to showcase new works. The company also presents new exhibits on a quarterly basis at a variety of "satellite" locations, including Provence Breads & Cafe in Hillsboro Village and Pinnacle National Bank on Commerce Street downtown. The gallery is open Monday through Saturday.

BENNETT GALLERIES
2104 Crestmoor Road
(615) 297-3201
www.bennettgalleriesnashville.com

A fixture on the local art scene since 1976, Bennett Galleries specializes in a variety of works from notable local artists as well as regional, national, and international names. Artist wine-and-cheese receptions are a popular cheap date. The gallery is open Monday through Saturday.

CENTENNIAL ARTS CENTER
25th Avenue N.
(615) 862-8442
www.nashville.gov/parks/cac.htm

Centennial Arts Center, run by Metro Parks and Recreation, is located in a corner of Centennial Park. The center hosts a variety of shows and exhibits featuring local artists and also offers classes in painting, drawing, sculpture, and pottery through the Metro Parks Cultural Arts Program. It is open Monday through Friday; admission is free.

CHEEKWOOD BOTANICAL GARDEN AND MUSEUM OF ART
1200 Forrest Park Drive
(615) 356-8000
www.cheekwood.org

The Cheekwood estate, formerly owned by the Leslie Cheek family, which made a fortune with Maxwell House coffee, is a feast for lovers of architecture, gardens, and art. The 55-acre estate includes a three-story neo-Georgian mansion and 12 lush garden areas filled with streams, water gardens, and sculptures. Opened to the public in 1960, the mansion itself has been turned into the prestigious Cheekwood Museum of Art, which has a permanent collection of more than 8,000 pieces, including American paintings of the Ashcan School, Worcester porcelain, silver, and sculpture by Tennessee artist William Edmondson. The museum also hosts a variety of innovative traveling exhibits, such as a one-of-a-kind show of works by world-class photographers Diane Arbus, Irving Penn, Mary Ellen Mark, Ansel Adams, and more. The show's only appearance was at Cheekwood.

The grounds are equally impressive. The Monroe Carell Woodland Sculpture Trail is a mile-long forest path featuring contemporary pieces by modern sculptors. The Japanese garden, called Shomuen, is a tranquil place where bamboo, ginkgo, waterfalls, and granite lanterns invite meditation. Herb, wildflower, dogwood, and water gardens are just a few of the other botanic "collections" you can explore as you wander the beautifully landscaped grounds. Cheekwood is open Tuesday through Sunday. The museum is closed Monday except for federal holidays. The Pineapple Room restaurant (615-352-4859) is open Tuesday through Sunday for lunch. Cheekwood is closed Thanksgiving, Christmas Day, New Year's Day, the second Saturday in June, and part of January. Admission is $10 for adults, $8 for seniors, $5 for college students and youth ages 3 through 13, and free for children younger than 3. For more information about Cheekwood, see our Attractions chapter.

CHROMATICS SECOND FLOOR GALLERY
625 Fogg Street
(615) 254-0063, (888) 254-0063
www.chromatics.com

Known locally for its photoimaging and film lab services, in 1993 Chromatics began developing its second floor into what is today a rather impressive photography gallery and has brought some prestigious names to the space—Mary Ellen Mark and David Doubilet to name two. The gallery also features works by local Chromatics clients. The gallery is open Monday through Friday when there is an exhibit, and by appointment after hours and weekends.

THE COLLECTOR'S GALLERY
6602 Highway 100
(615) 356-0699

The Collector's Gallery, founded more than 25 years ago, emphasizes well-known 20th-century Southeastern artists. It is the only gallery that shows the works of Tennessean Carl Sublett. The gallery is open Tuesday through Saturday and by appointment.

CUMBERLAND GALLERY
4107 Hillsboro Circle
(615) 297-0296
www.cumberlandgallery.com

Carol Stein's Cumberland Gallery, founded in 1980, focuses on paintings, photography, and sculpture by established and up-and-coming state and regional artists. The gallery is open Tuesday through Saturday and by appointment Sunday and evenings.

FINER THINGS
1898 Nolensville Road
(615) 244-3003
www.finerthingsgallery.com

Finer Things specializes in two- and three-dimensional contemporary art. Shows in the exhibition gallery change every six weeks. The Outdoor Sculpture Gallery features more than 50 sculpture works by artists from all across the country; Finer Things also hosts an annual sculpture competition here. The gallery's boutique features fine handcrafted jewelry, crafts, and art. Finer Things is open Tuesday through Saturday.

FRIST CENTER FOR THE VISUAL ARTS
919 Broadway
(615) 244-3340
www.fristcenter.org

Nashville's first major art museum opened in April 2001 with all the fanfare and hoopla you'd expect. Located in the former downtown post office, an art deco historic landmark, the Frist Center features 24,000 square feet of gallery space. Local, state, regional, and significant national and international exhibitions are all showcased here. The Center's ArtQuest Gallery is a unique, interactive gallery allowing kids of various ages to get hands-on with art. There's also a gift shop, and the Frist Center Cafe has become a popular downtown eatery in its own right. The gallery is open daily except Thanksgiving, Christmas Day, and New

Year's Day. The Frist stays open until 8:00 p.m. on Thursday and 9:00 p.m. on Friday. Admission is $8.50 for adults, $7.50 for ages 65 and over, and $6.50 for college students with ID. Ages 18 and under are always free, as are Frist Center members. For more on the Frist Center, see our Close-up in this chapter.

HANGING AROUND
113 17th Avenue S.
(615) 254-4850
www.hagallery.com
This Music Row–area gallery features mainly contemporary works by local artists. It is open Monday through Saturday.

HIRAM VAN GORDON MEMORIAL GALLERY
Tennessee State University
3500 John Merritt Boulevard
(615) 963-7509
www.tnstate.edu
TSU's Hiram Van Gordon Memorial Gallery features permanent, changing, and traveling exhibits of both individual artists and groups, including faculty and student art. The gallery is open Monday through Friday; weekend tours are available by appointment.

LEU ART GALLERY
Belmont University
1900 Belmont Boulevard
(615) 460-6770
www.belmont.edu
Leu Gallery features changing individual and group exhibits by faculty members and students and some regional and national artists as well as traveling exhibits. It is open daily.

LOCAL COLOR GALLERY
1912 Broadway
(615) 321-3141
www.localcolornashville.com
Local Color, one of Nashville's most popular galleries since 1990, features works from more than 60 local artists in a variety of media and styles. The gallery is open Tuesday through Saturday.

MIDTOWN GALLERY
1912 Broadway
(615) 322-9966
www.midtowngallery.com
Midtown Gallery represents more than 60 regional, national, and international artists. While the emphasis is on contemporary oil, acrylic, and watercolor painting, you'll also find pastels, mixed media, photography, and wood, metal, and stone sculpture. Exhibits change every six weeks. The gallery is open Tuesday through Saturday.

PARTHENON MUSEUM
Centennial Park
West End Avenue
(615) 862-8431
www.nashville.org/parks
Many visitors don't know that Nashville's signature landmark, the Parthenon, actually houses an art museum. Inside you'll find two galleries where exhibits by local, regional, national, and international artists are staged. The Parthenon also has a permanent collection bequeathed to the museum by insurance executive John M. Cowan, who died in 1930. The Cowan Collection features some of the finest American paintings from 1765 to 1923. Of course, no visit to the Parthenon is complete without visiting *Athena*. It took Nashville sculptor Alan LeQuire eight years to re-create the lost *Athena Parthenos* statue by fifth-century Greek sculptor Pheidias. The original was said to be Pheidias's greatest achievement, but Nashville's is the largest indoor statue in the Western world. It was made even more striking in the summer of 2002 when the entire statue was covered in gold leaf. The purpose of the gilding was to make Nashville's *Athena* more closely resemble Pheidias's original. Expect to spend a little less than an hour in the Parthenon; admission is $5 for ages 18 through 61, $2.50 for seniors and kids, and free for children ages four and under. Some special exhibits may require an additional fee. The Parthenon is open Tuesday through Saturday; from June through August it is also open on Sunday.

i The Parthenon Museum's *Athena* stands 41 feet, 10 inches tall, making it the largest piece of indoor sculpture in the Western world. The statue of Nike in Athena's right hand stands 6 feet, 4 inches tall.

SARRATT GALLERY
Sarratt Student Center
Vanderbilt University
24th Avenue S. near Vanderbilt Place
(615) 322-2471
www.vanderbilt.edu/sarratt/gallery
Sarratt Gallery, in the main lobby of the Sarratt Student Center, has about 10 major exhibits and a student show each year featuring national and regional contemporary artists. The gallery is open, subject to the school calendar, from 9:00 a.m. to 9:00 p.m. Monday through Friday and 10:00 a.m. to 10:00 p.m. Saturday and Sunday. During the summer and holiday and semester breaks, it closes at 4:30 p.m. weekdays and is closed weekends. Admission is free. For more on the Sarratt Center, see our Arts Centers section at the beginning of this chapter.

STANFORD FINE ART
6608-A Highway 100
(615) 352-5050
www.stanfordfineart.com
Stanford Fine Art displays changing exhibits of American and European painting from the 19th and early 20th centuries. The gallery is open Monday through Saturday.

TENNESSEE ARTS COMMISSION GALLERY
401 Charlotte Avenue
(615) 741-1701
www.arts.state.tn.us
The Tennessee Arts Commission Gallery displays only work by Tennessee residents, with six to eight exhibits a year. A professional panel juries the competition, which takes place every two years. The commission offers annual fellowships in crafts, photography, and visual arts to the state's top artists. The gallery is open Monday through Friday. Admission is free.

TENNESSEE STATE MUSEUM
505 Deaderick Street
(615) 741-2692, (800) 407-4324
www.tnmuseum.org
This museum, which is dedicated to exhibits related to various aspects of Tennessee history, sometimes features art displays that are complementary to its mission. Tennessee State Museum is open Tuesday through Sunday. Admission is free, but donations are accepted. (See also the Attractions chapter.)

THE UPPER ROOM CHAPEL & MUSEUM
1908 Grand Avenue
(615) 340-7207
www.upperroom.org
The Upper Room is a ministry of the Methodist Church; it started as a daily devotional that has mushroomed into a global ministry headquartered in Nashville. The chapel and museum near Music Row has a collection of religious art and artifacts that is open to the public. The Old Masters gallery features paintings from 1300 to 1900, including copies of Raphael paintings. Rare books and antique English porcelains are also on display. Seasonal events include a collection of 100 Nativity scenes in December and January and a Lenten Easter display of more than 70 Ukrainian eggs. The focal point of the chapel is a nearly life-size wood carving of Da Vinci's painting *The Last Supper*. The museum is open Monday through Friday. A $2 contribution is recommended.

VANDERBILT UNIVERSITY FINE ARTS GALLERY
23rd and West End Avenues
(615) 343-1704, (615) 322-0605
(current exhibit information)
www.vanderbilt.edu
Vandy's art gallery features six exhibitions a year representing a diverse range of Eastern and Western art. The Samuel H. Kress collection of Renaissance paintings is a highlight. In January 2008 Vanderbilt University received about 150 original Andy Warhol photographs and prints to be added to the university's permanent col-

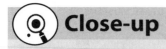

Close-up

Frist Center for the Visual Arts

Nashville's newest fine art museum opened its doors in April 2001, launching a new era in the city's history and forever changing its cultural landscape.

The Frist Center was born from that perfect marriage of necessity and opportunity. The story begins with a building, Nashville's landmark downtown post office, which was built in 1933–1934. On the National Register of Historic Places since 1984, it once served the city as its main post office. But when a new mail-handling facility opened near the airport in 1986, the downtown building was turned into a branch office that required just a small portion of the 125,000-square-foot structure.

Around the same time a group of Nashville's citizens began a long-range community visioning process. Among the needs they identified was for a major art museum, centrally located and large enough to land significant touring shows, something that Nashville's existing museums were not equipped to do. The unused downtown post office was deemed ideal.

Enter the charitable Frist Foundation. The Frist family and Dr. Thomas Frist Jr., chairman of HCA, have long supported Nashville's arts community (Cheekwood's Frist Learning Center is one example). They rallied behind the arts center project, and in 1998 the Frist Foundation, Metropolitan Nashville, and the U.S. Postal Service formed a unique public–private partnership. The U.S. Postal Service agreed to sell the building for the purpose of an arts center, provided they could still maintain a customer service window there

(today Nashville probably has the only art museum with a working post office on its lower level).

Renovations began in November 1999. In addition to retrofitting the building for its new use, careful attention was paid to repairing the building's unique historic features. The original hardwood floors and art deco ornamental details such as lighting fixtures and decorative metal grillework were painstakingly preserved. The hard work paid off, however, and today the building is regarded as a work of art in itself.

While work went on inside the building, an advisory council hammered out the nuts and bolts of the museum's mission. From the beginning it was envisioned as a place where the entire community, regardless of age or economic background, could "connect with art." With that in mind, an extensive education and community outreach program was planned, including the decision to allow visitors under age 18 free admission, always.

It was also determined that the Frist Center would have no permanent collection but would accommodate changing exhibitions exclusively, giving visitors a reason to return again and again. The center's Main Level Gallery features short-term exhibitions of two to three months' duration. The main level also includes an Orientation Gallery, providing information about present and future exhibits as well as exhibits at Nashville's other art institutions. There's also a 250-seat auditorium, a gift shop, and the Frist Center Cafe.

Exhibitions of up to three years' duration are

lection. The inclusion of these invaluable pieces serves as a resource to students, but is open and free to the public. The gallery is open daily; hours vary. It is closed Sunday and Monday during the summer break.

WATKINS GALLERY
Watkins College of Art and Design
2298 MetroCenter Boulevard
(615) 383-4848
www.watkins.edu

staged in the Upper Level Gallery; adjacent to that is Frist's unique ArtQuest Gallery, which fulfills its educational mission by providing various hands-on activities explaining basic art principles. The Media and Technology Resource Center offers library resources for those wishing to learn more about the works on exhibit. There are also three studio-classrooms and a computer lab used for the educational programs.

The Frist Center opened with an exclusive exhibit, European Masterworks: Paintings from the Collection of the Art Gallery of Ontario. The collection of masterpieces by the likes of Rembrandt, Monet, Degas, and Van Gogh made its only stop at the Frist Center. Exhibits of pieces from Nashville's own private and public collections, a massive sculpture by Nashville artist Michael Aurbach, and an exhibit looking at the building's unique history filled out the center's four galleries.

Since then, the Frist Center has brought world-class exhibits to the city, quickly becoming the focal point of a vibrant arts scene. The 2008 schedule included successful exhibitions of Auguste Rodin's sculptures and Tiffany lamps from the Neustadt Collection. The exhibition of more than 50 paintings and sculptures from the Phillips Collection in Washington, D.C., featured the works of such artists as Picasso, Monet, Renoir, and Degas, and it drew nearly 200,000 visitors during its four-and-a-half-month run.

The fine arts in Nashville received a significant boost when the Frist Center opened in April 2001.
TIMOTHY HURSLEY, COURTESY OF THE FRIST CENTER FOR THE VISUAL ARTS

The Watkins College gallery holds student, faculty, and outside exhibits throughout the year. In addition, lectures and seminars are held at Watkins College, located north of downtown at the Metro-Center Complex. The gallery is open Monday through Friday.

ZEITGEIST GALLERY

1819 21st Avenue S.
(615) 256-4805
www.zeitgeist-art.com

Zeitgeist exhibits works by contemporary regional mixed-media artists, emphasizing conceptual and design-oriented works in formats such as three-dimensional art, furniture, and lighting. The gallery is open Tuesday through Saturday.

FILM

THE BELCOURT THEATRE

2102 Belcourt Avenue
(615) 383-9140, (615) 846-3150
www.belcourt.org

The historic Belcourt, built in 1925, was barely saved from the wrecking ball by a massive grass-roots effort; today it's Nashville's only art-house theater. With a diverse programming of independent, foreign, and art cinema, Belcourt's offerings are always daring, to say the least. Music and performing arts events flesh out the calendar. The theater serves food, wine, and beer along with the traditional popcorn and soft drinks. For a current schedule visit the Belcourt Web site or check the film listings in the *Nashville Scene*.

NASHVILLE INDEPENDENT FILM FESTIVAL

(615) 742-2500
www.nashvillefilmfestival.org

NIFF is best known for the annual June film festival that has brought the likes of maverick director John Waters to town and draws 10,000 or more attendees. The film festival continues to grow in influence and scope; its recently expanded slate of offerings has included a Kid's Film Fest, animation workshop, gay/lesbian and Latino festivals, and documentary subjects, plus the usual indie fare. Year-round, NIFF sponsors screenings of notable independent films for its members. The festival, and most screenings, are held at the Regal Green Hills 16 Cinema (see our Nightlife chapter).

SARRATT CINEMA

Sarratt Student Center
Vanderbilt University
(615) 343-6666 (cinema hot line),
(615) 322-2471
www.vanderbilt.edu/sarratt

Sarratt Cinema is located on the ground floor of the Sarratt Student Center. During the school year about a dozen cutting-edge independent and studio releases are shown here each weekend; in April a student film festival is held. Films are selected by the student-run Sarratt Film Committee, so expect some cutting-edge cinema. That said, the schedule also includes escapist fare like *American Pie II* and *Planet of the Apes*. Ticket sales begin 30 minutes prior to screening time, and prices are notoriously low.

WATKINS FILM SCHOOL

Watkins College of Art and Design
2298 MetroCenter Boulevard
(615) 383-4848
www.watkins.edu

This highly selective film school program is gaining national recognition for the quality of its diverse programs. Watkins offers a four-year bachelor of fine arts degree in film, with five areas of specialization: screenwriting, cinematography, producing, directing, and editing. The school also offers a post-graduate certificate in film. The Community Education Program offers noncredit screenwriting courses as well as other classes in filmmaking for those in the community. The free Friday Night at the Movies series features classic, foreign, and art-house films in Room 500 of the Watkins complex at MetroCenter, all open to the public.

i For First Art Saturday, art galleries throughout downtown host receptions and art openings on the first Saturday of every month. A free shuttle provides transportation among the participating galleries from 6:00 to 10:00 p.m.

GENERAL INSTRUCTION AND AWARENESS

METRO PARKS AND RECREATION ARTS PROGRAM

Centennial Park Office
511 Oman Street
(615) 862-8424
www.nashville.gov/parks

Metro Parks and Recreation provides a variety of activities in music, dance, visual arts, crafts, and theater for all ages from children through seniors. Offerings include instruction, concerts, festivals, and other performances (such as Shakespeare in the Park), and resources and services. Activities take place at various venues, including the Centennial Arts Center Courtyard, the Parthenon, the Centennial Park band shell, Z. Alexander Looby Theater, and Shelby Park.

METROPOLITAN NASHVILLE ARTS COMMISSION

Cummins Station
209 10th Avenue S., Suite 416
(615) 862-6720
www.artsnashville.org

The Metropolitan Nashville Arts Commission works hard to connect various arts organizations with the community, providing leadership and resources to all forms of the arts. The commission assembles an annual *Arts Directory* and other information to help make the arts more accessible to all. The commission's Web site contains the *Artist Registry,* an illustrated catalog of Nashville-area artists; the *Arts Directory,* a guide to Nashville-area arts organizations; the commission's mission statement; a billboard with announcements and links to other arts-related sites; and a grant application for not-for-profit arts organizations.

PARKS

Nashville is known worldwide as "Music City," and no doubt you've heard the nicknames "Athens of the South," "Twangtown," and "Third Coast." But did you know Nashville is also called the "City of Parks"? Nashville owes that nickname to the abundance of parks and greenways here. You never have to travel far in Nashville to find green spaces. As of 2008, the Metropolitan Board of Parks and Recreation operated 113 parks and greenways totaling more than 10,570 acres. The 2,058-acre Percy Warner Park is the largest; it's about three times larger than New York City's Central Park. The smallest is the nearly quarter-acre Bass Park, a playground in east Nashville. Metro Parks maintains 21 community and recreation centers, the 145,000-square-foot Centennial Sportsplex, 87 ball fields, 7 golf courses, more than 45 picnic shelters, 80 playgrounds, and 14 swimming pools. Add to that the attractions at the numerous state parks and natural areas in and around Nashville, and you can see that Nashvillians rarely have an excuse for staying indoors. Not that we do stay in. Nashvillians love their parks and can be found enjoying the great outdoors seven days a week year-round. Nashville-area parks offer a variety of opportunities for recreation and relaxation. Whether you're looking for a quiet spot to commune with nature, a curvy paved in-line-skating route, a lake for waterskiing or fishing, a wide-open field for flying a kite or playing Frisbee, a cozy picnicking spot, or trails for hiking and biking, there is a place for you. (Check out the Recreation chapter for a more in-depth look at recreation options at parks.)

OVERVIEW

Nashville's first public park was the eight-and-a-half-acre Watkins Park, at Jo Johnston Avenue and 17th Avenue N. Watkins Park was given to the city by brick manufacturer and construction contractor Samuel Watkins in 1870. The property had served as an unofficial park known as Watkins Grove in the 1850s but was ravaged in the early 1860s by the Civil War. Around the turn of the 20th century, area residents were using the then-treeless and barren lot as a pasture and unofficial dump. With donated materials and some city funds, the park board stepped in and built an entrance and walkways, planted flowers, installed water and lighting systems, and placed benches on the property. In 1906 the Centennial Club took over and added the city's first playground, including swings, a skating area, and a merry-go-round. It was such a success that in 1909 the board opened children's playgrounds on vacant lots throughout Nashville. Watkins Park, by the way,

is still there at 616 17th Avenue N. Today it has a community center, tennis courts, a basketball court, and a picnic shelter.

In November 2002 Metro Parks produced its first parks and greenways master plan, which is designed to guide the maintenance of existing green spaces and plan for the development of parks and recreational programs for the next two decades. The plan recommended $262 million in improvements and investment for the first 10 years. The funding of $35 million in 2004 to improve parks and greenways was the largest single appropriation in the history of the parks department. The establishment of greenways has been a major focus of the parks system in recent years. Often located along scenic roads, river floodplains, waterways, old railroad tracks, and wildlife areas, greenways provide space for conservation, recreation, and alternative transportation. The Metro Greenways Commission envisions Nashville and Davidson County linked together by a system of linear parks, bike paths, and hiking trails that connect neighborhoods to schools, shopping areas, downtown, and other points of activity. As of 2008, three new nature centers have been completed, and Fort Negley has a new interpretive center. The first phase of a new youth soccer complex was built near the airport and a complete renovation of the Warner Sports Fields is currently underway. The department also has developed 36.5 miles of trails with about 14 more miles under development.

In this chapter we've chosen to list only a portion of Nashville's many parks and green spaces—just enough to get you in the mood for getting out and about. To ensure that your park excursions are safe and enjoyable, take note of the rules and hours of operation. Many parks are open from sunrise to sunset, and unless otherwise noted, you can assume those are the operating hours. Be aware that even in a friendly city like Nashville, unless there is a park event taking place, it isn't a good idea to be in most parks after dark. Similarly, cars parked in an area where the activities nearby—fishing, golfing, and so on—would keep their owners absent for a prolonged time may be especially vulnerable. Most parks offer wheelchair-accessible attractions and barrier-free access. Some are more accessible than others, so if accessibility is a concern, it's a good idea to contact Metro Parks, Tennessee State Parks, or the individual park for more information. Metro Parks's Special Recreation Program serves children and adults with disabilities. The programs are held in community centers, schools, and various spots around town. Admission is free at most area parks, but special activities or programs might require a fee.

STATE PARKS AND NATURAL AREAS

There are more than 50 parks in the Tennessee State Parks system. Beginning in July 2006, all Tennessee state parks have been free to all visitors (many of the state parks previously charged an access fee). For more on Tennessee's state parks and natural areas, visit the Web site www .tnstateparks.com or call (615) 532-0001 or (888) TN-PARKS.

BICENTENNIAL CAPITOL MALL STATE PARK
600 James Robertson Parkway
Jefferson Street between Seventh
and Sixth Avenues
(615) 741-5280, (888) TN-PARKS
www.tnstateparks.com
Don't let the word *mall* throw you off: This is not a shopping mall, but rather a mall similar to the National Mall in Washington, D.C. This 19-acre downtown attraction, Tennessee's 51st state park, is part park and part outdoor history lesson. It opened in 1996 on the north side of the Tennessee State Capitol to commemorate the state's 200th birthday celebration and preserve the last unobstructed view of the capitol. The park is at the site of the French Lick, a salt lick and sulfur spring that drew wildlife, Indians, trappers, and, eventually, settlers. French-Canadian traders and hunters set up trading posts here beginning in the late 1600s. The spring still flows underground. (See our History chapter for more information.)

For an overview of the entire mall, head to the State Capitol grounds (the capitol is at Charlotte Avenue between Sixth and Seventh Avenues). Across James Robertson Parkway, in the mall's concrete plaza entrance, a 200-foot granite map will take you on a walking trip through Tennessee. The map highlights major roads, rivers, and other details of the state's 95 counties. At night the county seats light up. A variety of other granite maps detail topics such as the state's geography, musical diversity, and topography. Just past the railroad trestle is the Rivers of Tennessee Fountains, with 31 fountains of varying heights, each representing one of the state's major rivers. The Walkway of the Counties on the east side represents the topographic features and diverse vegetation of east, middle, and west Tennessee. This is also where time capsules from the 95 counties are buried; they will be opened during Tennessee's tercentennial celebration in 2096.

At the northern end near Jefferson Street is the focal point of the mall: the Court of Three

Stars, a red, white, and blue granite map representing the three divisions of the state. For an excellent view of the capitol, head here. Surrounding the Court of Three Stars is the 95-bell carillon, which has one bell for each county in the state. The Pathway of History, starting at the west side of the mall, features marble columns that divide state history into 10-year increments. A World War II memorial, paid for by veterans of the war, takes the shape of an 18,000-pound granite globe supported by a constant stream of water; visitors can rotate the globe to view areas of the world as it was from 1939 to 1945 and see Tennessee's ties to the war's major battlefields. Other features of the mall include the McNairy Spring Fountain—atop the sulfur spring that created the French Lick. Placards in the mall recount the history of French Lick and of Sulphur Dell,

The history of Nashville is recounted at the Bicentennial Capitol Mall State Park. JACKIE SHECKLER FINCH

the historic ballpark where professional baseball was played from 1885 to 1963. The mall also has a visitor center and 2,000-seat amphitheater. Guided group tours are available. Restrooms are near Seventh Avenue, and a gift shop is near Sixth, at opposite ends of the railroad trestle. Mall-designated parking is available along Sixth and Seventh Avenues. On weekends, holidays, and Monday through Friday after 4:30 p.m., parking is available at state employee parking areas. Handicapped parking is at the corner of Sixth and Harrison. Buses and RVs can park at Eighth and Jefferson. The park closes at dark. The visitor center is open 9:00 a.m. to 5:00 p.m. daily. The park is patrolled 24 hours a day.

BLEDSOE CREEK STATE PARK
400 Zieglers Fort Road, Gallatin
(615) 452-3706
www.tnstateparks.com
One of more than a dozen state parks that were closed in 2001 due to budget cuts, Bledsoe Creek State Park had reopened by 2004 with new features, including a new bathhouse facility and several other planned improvements, including a new office, two boat docks, boat launching ramps, and 26 campsites. Most, if not all, sites have electrical and water hookups as well as picnic tables and grills. Reservations are not taken for campsites. The park also has 6 miles of hiking trails (including a 1-mile paved, wheelchair-accessible trail), three playgrounds, fishing areas, two picnic shelters, and wildlife-viewing opportunities. An environmental education area, this 164-acre park is 6 miles east of Gallatin off Highway 25, on the Bledsoe Creek embayment of Old Hickory Lake in Sumner County. Bledsoe Creek State Park, named for long hunter and Revolutionary War veteran Isaac Bledsoe, who came to the area in the 1770s, is in an area rich in history. The settlement of Cairo in Sumner County occupied an area near here in the 1780s. Also nearby are the historic sites of Wynnewood, Cragfont, Rock Castle, and Bledsoe's Fort. The latter, on Highway 25, 5 miles east of Gallatin, was built by Bledsoe in 1783 to protect settlers from Indian attacks. Isaac and his brother Anthony were killed not far from there by

Indians and are buried at the Bledsoe Monument. Cragfont is the rock house that sits on a bluff about 3.5 miles north of the park entrance. It was the home of Gen. James Winchester, veteran of the American Revolution and the War of 1812. The park is open daily from 7:00 a.m. to sunset.

CEDARS OF LEBANON STATE PARK
328 Cedar Forest Road, Lebanon
(615) 443-2769
www.tnstateparks.com
This park, which is connected to the largest red cedar forest in the United States, is about 31 miles east of Nashville in Wilson County, 6 miles south of Interstate 40 on U.S. Highway 231. Only about 900 of the total acres are used for recreation. The remaining 8,100 acres are operated as a natural area by the Parks Division and as a state forest by the Forestry Division. Numerous wildflowers and other native plants can be found in the open limestone glades, including 19 rare and endangered plants, such as the Tennessee coneflower, which is said to exist only in Middle Tennessee. Approximately 600,000 people visit this state park every year. It is named for the cedar forests in the biblical lands of Lebanon. The cedar trees here, however, are actually eastern juniper, a coniferous cousin of the fragrant-wooded cedar. By 1900 the junipers had been cut down, used for making pencils, cross-ties, and cedar oil. In the 1930s the area was replanted by the Civilian Conservation Corps.

Accommodations include 117 campsites, nine modern two-bedroom cabins, two small two-person cabins, and an 80-person-capacity group lodge with separate sleeping facilities. Among the other attractions are 11 picnic pavilions, an "Olympic-plus-size" swimming pool, 8 miles of hiking trails through the cedar forests and glades, and 6 miles of horseback-riding trails. The park offers horse rental and guided trail rides from March through November. The Merritt Nature Center (open Tuesday through Saturday during the main season) is a popular spot, offering exhibits, plus a recreation director and a naturalist who conduct programs during the summer. Visitors can participate in such activities as guided tours, arts and crafts, and hayrides during the warm-weather months. The cabins, lodge, campground, and assembly hall are available by reservation year-round. If you're interested in reserving the group lodge, make your plans well in advance. The park is open 8:00 a.m. to 10:00 p.m. year-round.

HARPETH RIVER STATE PARK
Off U.S. Highway 70 at Cedar Hill
Road, Kingston Springs
(615) 797-6096
www.tnstateparks.com

This park, considered a satellite area of Montgomery Bell State Park about 11 miles west, offers recreation on the river, hiking, and a bit of education, too. The state acquired the property in July 1979, and in winter 1996–1997 acquired another 30 acres for a total of 133 acres. The Harpeth Scenic River Complex offers canoe-access points at the Highway 100 bridge just past the Warner Parks, at the 1862 Newsom's Mill ruins, and at the McCrory Lane Bridge at Hidden Lake. Downstream the Narrows of the Harpeth provide upstream and downstream access. One nice thing about canoeing the Harpeth is that the Bell's Bend 5-mile loop allows you to put in and take out at the same area. Be sure to see the Recreation chapter for more information on canoeing the Harpeth—it's one of our favorite summer activities. While you're at the Narrows site, be sure to check out the historic 290-foot-long tunnel hand-cut through solid rock; it is an industrial landmark listed on the National Register of Historic Places and is one of the oldest existing human-made tunnels in the nation. Montgomery Bell, an early iron industrialist, built the tunnel to supply waterpower to his iron forge on the river. Bell is buried on a hillside across the river. The wooden walkway leading from the parking area will take you to the front of the tunnel. If hiking is on your itinerary, the trails begin about 150 yards from the parking lot. The trail to the top of the bluff over the tunnel (it's steep, but short—the three trails combined total only about 1.5 miles) offers a fantastic view of the Harpeth River valley. If you have a fear of heights, stay close to the

trail—the drop-offs are steep! A historical marker at Scott Cemetery on Cedar Hill Road tells about Mound Bottom, an ancient Indian ceremonial site along the river. Indians of the Mississippian period were believed to have lived here around 800 years ago. Archaeologists say the town was an important political and ceremonial center. If you're interested in visiting Mound Bottom, a park ranger can take you, but be sure to call the park office ahead of time to schedule the trip. This park doesn't have restroom facilities.

i For $1,400 to $1,500, you can sponsor a historical marker and post to erect at a historically significant site in Tennessee. The Tennessee Historical Commission can purchase only a few of the signs each year, so most of the new markers must be paid for by sponsors. If you or your group are interested in sponsoring a new marker, contact the Tennessee Historical Commission, 2941 Lebanon Road, Nashville, (615) 532-1550.

LONG HUNTER STATE PARK
2910 Hobson Pike, off I-40 and Interstate 24
on Highway 171, Hermitage
(615) 885-2422
www.tnstateparks.com

The 2,600-acre Long Hunter State Park, situated on the east shore of J. Percy Priest Lake (see our Recreation chapter), is a popular site for boating, swimming, waterskiing, and fishing. If you prefer to stay dry, there are plenty of activities on terra firma too, such as hiking, bird-watching, picnicking, and backcountry camping. The park offers boat rentals, playgrounds, a gift shop, and more. Spanning more than 14,000 acres, the U.S. Army Corps of Engineers's Percy Priest Reservoir is one of the largest lakes in the state. The 110-acre, landlocked Couchville Lake is part of Priest and is surrounded by a 2-mile paved trail. That barrier-free area also has a fishing pier. Nonsupervised swimming is permitted at Bryant Grove but not at Couchville Lake or in the two boat ramp areas on Priest Lake. Stop by the visitor center for more information on the park or to check in if you plan to camp. If you want to camp, come prepared.

You'll hike 6 miles and spend the night at a backcountry camping area. Long Hunter State Park was named for the hunters and explorers of the 1700s who stayed in the area for months or years at a time. Among them were Uriah Stone, for whom nearby Stones River is named. (See our History chapter for related information.) The park is open daily 7:00 a.m. to sunset year-round.

i When visiting area parks, keep your eyes open for the official Tennessee state creatures. The official state insects are the firefly (often referred to as a lightning bug), which glows at night, and the ladybug, a small reddish-orange bug with black spots on its wings. You might also see or hear the state bird, the mockingbird, which not only has its own melodious song but also is skilled at mimicking the songs of other birds. The state animal is the raccoon, which you'll recognize by its bushy ringed tail and banditlike mask of dark fur around its eyes.

MONTGOMERY BELL STATE PARK
1020 Jackson Hill Road, Burns
(615) 797-9052
www.tnstateparks.com

This approximately 3,800-acre park is located along US 70, about 2 miles west of White Bluff and 7 miles east of Dickson. The park is named for the state's first capitalist and industrialist, Montgomery Bell, who operated an iron forge on the Harpeth River. Bell came to Tennessee from Pennsylvania in the early 1800s and for a few years operated the Cumberland Iron Works, which had been established by James Robertson, a founder of Nashville. Bell purchased the business and turned the area into an industrial capital. He built the 290-foot tunnel at the Narrows of the Harpeth (see the Harpeth River State Park listing) to supply water for the business. The tunnel is now on the National Register of Historic Places and is said to be the nation's oldest remaining human-made tunnel. Other remains of Bell's iron empire include Laurel Furnace, built in 1810, and ore pits. Another interesting historical note about the park: It was the birthplace of the Cumberland Presbyterian Church, first organized in 1810. Every Sunday during June, July, and August, services are held at the park's replica of Rev. Samuel McAdow's chapel. Everyone is welcome.

Montgomery Bell's accommodations and recreational opportunities make it a popular choice for family reunions, church groups, and company outings. There are 118 tree-covered campsites, most of which have water and electrical hookups. All sites have a picnic table and grill. A 120-person-capacity group camp—open April through October—contains individual cabins, a dining hall, bathhouses, and a fishing dock. Montgomery Bell State Park's inn, conference center, and restaurant overlook the park's Lake Acorn. The inn has 120 rooms and five suites. The conference facility accommodates up to 500 people. The restaurant seats 190 and serves three meals a day. Other accommodations include eight two-bedroom, fully equipped cabins that are available year-round. Cabins are available Monday through Saturday; a minimum two-night reservation is required. Privately owned boats are allowed at 17-acre Lake Acorn, 26-acre Creech Hollow Lake, and 50-acre Lake Woodhaven (check with the park for regulations). Lake Woodhaven has a year-round boat launch. Lake Acorn has canoes, paddleboats, and johnboats available for rent. Hikers will find about 20 miles of trails. An 11.7-mile overnight trail has three primitive overnight shelters. The park also offers a challenging 18-hole golf course (see our Golf chapter for more about that), two tennis courts, playground, ball field, basketball courts, and more. See our Recreation chapter for information on nearby mountain biking trails. Hours are 6:00 a.m. to 10:00 p.m.

RADNOR LAKE STATE NATURAL AREA
1160 Otter Creek Road
(615) 373-3467
www.tnstateparks.com,
www.radnorlake.org

In the late photographer John Netherton's book *Radnor Lake: Nashville's Walden* (Rutledge Hill Press, 1984), Nashville author John Egerton writes, "Words will never suffice to describe it. Radnor must be experienced through the senses. It must be seen, smelled, heard." It's true. Radnor Lake, a natural area spanning more than 1,100 acres just 6 miles south of downtown Nashville, must be experienced—in every season. But beware—Radnor Lake can become addictive. The lake is just 0.5 mile east of Granny White Pike and 1.5 miles west of Franklin Pike (U.S. Highway 31). Otter Creek Road winds its way around the 85-acre lake, offering wonderful views of the lake and surrounding hills. You'll find people of all ages and all walks of life taking in the natural beauty along the route. Walkers, joggers, bird-watchers, bicyclists, babies in strollers, photographers, and pets (on leashes) share the road, which is closed to motor vehicles. The park is open during daylight hours.

Radnor is a state natural area and therefore not a recreation-oriented park. Primary activities are hiking, nature observation, photography, and research. Some activities, such as jogging on the wooded trails, boating, swimming, and picnicking, are not permitted. All plants, animals, rocks, minerals, and artifacts are protected by state law—so observe and enjoy, but don't disturb! Many of the lake's one million annual visitors come for the hiking trails. Radnor offers six connecting trails, ranging in length from 0.25 mile to 1.5 miles. The Spillway Trail and Lake Trail, both wheelchair accessible, are the easiest. Ganier Ridge Trail and South Cove Trail are the most strenuous. The trails are especially nice and fragrant to walk in January, after they have been paved with the mulch of recycled Christmas trees. Before or after your hike or walk, be sure to spend at least a few relaxing moments at the lake near the nature center, just off the Spillway Trail. You can get up close looks at one or more of the 26 species of ducks and Canada geese as well as frogs and turtles—including large snappers. Radnor is also home to some 240 bird species, plus deer, coyotes, and other creatures. Radnor naturalists conduct a variety of environmental activities, such as birds of prey programs, wildflower hikes, canoe floats, and nighttime "owl prowls." You can make reservations for these programs by phone or at the visitor center.

Radnor Lake was created in 1914 by the Louisville & Nashville Railroad Company to provide water for steam engines and livestock at the Radnor Railroad Yards. L&N officials and their guests also used the site as a private hunting and fishing ground. At the request of the Tennessee Ornithological Society, L&N in 1923 declared Radnor a wildlife sanctuary and banned all hunting. In 1962, when the area was purchased by a construction firm that had plans for a housing development, Nashvillians protested and were able to preserve the area. With the financial support of the federal government and thousands of Nashvillians, the Tennessee Department of Conservation purchased the land in 1973, and it became the state's first natural area. When residential development threatened the park again in 2004, the nonprofit Friends of Radnor Lake group and other Nashvillians rallied in an effort to help raise some $850,000 to purchase additional nearby acreage from a developer to protect the scenic natural area.

ℹ️ *The Parks of Nashville, A History of the Board of Parks and Recreation,* by Leland R. Johnson, was published in 1986 by the Metropolitan Nashville and Davidson County Board of Parks and Recreation. The book is an excellent source of information about Nashville parks. It can be found at libraries, some park offices, and, occasionally, at stores where used books are sold.

METRO PARKS AND GREENWAYS

The Metro Parks system consists of regional parks, community parks, neighborhood parks, and mini-parks. The regional parks are 50 to 500-plus acres in size and include large, undisturbed tracts of land important for the protection of wildlife habitats. Hiking and picnicking are popular activities at these parks. The four largest regional parks are Shelby Bottoms Greenway in the downtown area; Hamilton Creek Park in the eastern part of Davidson County; the Warner Parks, which serve the south and southwestern parts of the county; and Beaman Park in north Nashville. There are at least nine additional regional parks of 50 to 200 acres, including Centennial Park, one of the parks system's showpieces. Community parks are 20 to 50 acres in size, serve several neighborhoods, and offer numerous recreational facilities, including community centers; there are more than a dozen community parks in Nashville. There are more than three dozen neighborhood parks, which are 5 to 20 acres in size and are designed to serve the immediate surrounding neighborhood; these parks may have playgrounds, tennis or basketball courts, ball fields, and picnic areas. Miniparks, which are smaller than five acres, include urban plazas, playgrounds, and other small spaces; there are more than 20 of these parks in Nashville. For more on the Metro Parks system, visit the Web site www.nashville.gov/parks or contact Metro Parks at (615) 862-8400. The Greenways Commission's Web site, www.nashville.gov/greenways, is a good resource as well.

ALVIN G. BEAMAN PARK
4111 Little Marrowbone Road
(615) 862-8400
www.beamanpark.org
Work on this 1,500-acre woodland greenway in northwest Davidson County, between Joelton and Ashland City, began in 1996, and the park opened in 2005. The first phase of the park was completed in 2004 and includes a short entry road, two parking access areas for the hiking trails, and a few picnic areas. Beaman Park is Metro's second largest park, second only to the Warner Parks. The park is named for the late Sally and Alvin G. Beaman. Sally originally donated the funds to purchase the property as a tribute to her late husband, who was a parks board member and founder of the Beaman Automotive Group. Nature education and hiking are the focus of Beaman Park. The master plan calls for 2 miles of paved trails and 12 miles of unpaved hiking trails. A nature center has been completed there. The greenway is a protected natural resource that's home to a variety of rare plants not found in other area parks. For additional information call Friends of Beaman Park at (615) 299-9586 or visit www.beamanpark.org.

CEDAR HILL PARK
860 Old Hickory Boulevard
(615) 865-1853
www.nashville.gov/parks
This 225-acre, hilly park is near Goodlettsville on Dickerson Road at Old Hickory Boulevard. With a four-diamond baseball and softball complex, it's a top pick for the area's teams; the complex is used by leagues five days a week and is the site of tournaments on weekends. Cedar Hill Park was originally known as Old Center Park, taking its name from a nearby school. Metro purchased the property in 1964, and in 1965 it was renamed Cedar Hill Park because it was covered with cedar trees. It reopened to the public in 1977 and that year hosted the National Men's Fast-Pitch Softball Tournament. In addition to its baseball and softball diamonds, Cedar Hill Park has seven tennis courts, a playground, a walking and jogging track, seven picnic shelters that stay very busy, and restrooms. Many visitors come here just to walk the path around Cedar Hill Lake. The lake is also the site for regional fishing rodeos for the disabled. The park is open from sunrise to 11:00 p.m.

CENTENNIAL PARK
2500 West End Avenue
(615) 862-8400
www.nashville.gov/parks
Home of Nashville's famous replica of the Greek Parthenon, Centennial Park sits on 132.3 acres at West End Avenue and 25th Avenue N., 2 miles west of downtown. The land was once a farm, purchased in 1783 by John Cockrill, brother-in-law of Nashville founder James Robertson. After the Civil War, the land served as the state fairgrounds, and from 1884 to 1895 it was West Side Park racetrack. In 1897 it was the site of the Tennessee Centennial Exposition, which celebrated (one year late) Tennessee's 100th anniversary of statehood. Construction on the exposition buildings began in October 1895, when the

cornerstone for a Parthenon replica was laid. Several elaborate, temporary white stucco buildings were constructed for use during the event, which attracted more than 1.7 million people from around the world. When the celebration was over, the other buildings were removed, but Nashvillians chose to keep the magnificent Parthenon (see our History and Attractions chapters), the only full-size replica of the Athenian structure. The Parthenon and Centennial grounds were preserved as a public park. The city's new park system, which was begun in 1901, built a pool, driveways, and walkways; stocked the lake with fish; and planted flowers and shrubs. Centennial Park opened to the public in 1903 as Nashville's second city park. The Parthenon was rebuilt of concrete from 1921 to 1931, and the structure received renovations in 1962. A $13-million renovation began in the 1980s and was completed in 2001. A highlight of the Parthenon is the 42-foot *Athena Parthenos,* the largest piece of indoor sculpture in the Western world.

Various other changes and additions have been made to the park over the years. Today Centennial Park offers playgrounds, paddleboating on Lake Watauga (a large pond), picnic facilities, swings, a band shell, a sand volleyball court, and plenty of grassy areas just perfect for spreading out a blanket. Various monuments around the park are reminders of Nashville's history. Monuments of James Robertson and leaders of the Centennial Exposition were erected in 1903. The steam locomotive was put in place in 1953, and the F-86 jet aircraft landed in Centennial in 1961. Despite the park's many attractions, one of the most popular activities for kids (and grown-ups) is observing and feeding the ducks and pigeons at the pond. The park is the site of various arts and crafts exhibits, concerts, and other popular events throughout the year. The Art Center, in the northernmost corner of the park, features works by local artists and offers arts classes. Across 25th Avenue, the Centennial Sportsplex has ice rinks, tennis courts, and an Olympic-size pool. For more on Centennial Park, see our Kidstuff chapter. For more on the Parthenon, see our Attractions and Arts chapters.

i More than 1,000 trees have been planted at Centennial Park since the 1998 tornadoes. (See our History chapter for information on the destructive storms that hit Nashville that year.)

ELMINGTON PARK
3531 West End Avenue
(615) 862-8400
www.nashville.gov/parks
This popular neighborhood park, on 13.3 acres at West End and Bowling Avenues, was developed by the Works Progress Administration during the 1930s. The property the park encompasses was once part of Edwin Warner's "Elmington Estate." The park board purchased the property in 1927 with assistance from area citizens. Today Elmington is a multipurpose park, offering two tennis courts, a baseball diamond, various playground pieces, and picnic tables. A community group helped raise funds for a playground and trees for the property. The grassy front field is the site of a nearby college's cricket games as well as an annual Swing for Sight hole-in-one golf benefit, dog shows, and various community events. It is also used by students of West End High School, which sits at the top of the hill in back of the park.

i The year 1933 saw one of the state's toughest elections. In a race to determine the state bird, the mockingbird beat the robin by a mere 450 votes.

FANNIE MAE DEES PARK
2400 Blakemore Avenue
(615) 862-8400
www.nashville.gov/parks
Fannie Mae Dees Park is known by many as Dragon Park because of the mosaic sea-serpent centerpiece sculpture that winds its way through the playground area. But it's the park's recent addition—Lily's Garden, featuring playground equipment that is accessible to children with disabilities—that has given this urban green space a new lease on life. Children of all ages and abilities enjoy playing on the colorful structures. (See the

Kidstuff chapter for more about Lily's Garden.) As for the dragon, a grant from the Tennessee Arts Commission brought artist Pedro Silva from New York to Nashville to design the sea creature. The work itself was funded by grants from Vanderbilt University and local businesses. Individual artists created the graphics in the mosaic design of the serpent's coils. Nashville children were involved in the work, piecing the tiles together at various community centers and then bringing them to the park. The piece was dedicated April 25, 1981.

If you've never visited this park, it's worth stopping by just to marvel at the sea serpent. Look closely—you'll see many interesting and fanciful designs, including sailboats, scuba divers, mermaids, and flowers. A portrait of local civic leader Fannie Mae Dees, the park's namesake, can be found on the loop near the serpent's tail. The sculpture is more than art, however; its tail serves as a bench—a great spot to relax while the kids enjoy the playground. (See Kidstuff for related details.) In addition to playground equipment, the seven-and-a-half-acre park features tennis courts and picnic shelters. The park is on Blakemore Avenue at 24th Avenue S. a couple of blocks from Hillsboro Village.

HADLEY PARK
1037 28th Avenue N.
(615) 862-8400
www.nashville.gov/parks
This 34-acre urban community park is the site of a new $5-million regional community center, completed in 2005, the first of five such centers targeted under Metro's Parks and Greenways Master Plan. The Hadley Regional Community Center serves as a model for others in Nashville. It includes an indoor walking track, pool, community meeting rooms, and a fitness room. The new regional centers will be twice as large as existing centers and will offer a broader array of programs and services. Hadley, located at 28th Avenue N. and Centennial (John Merritt Boulevard), was also pegged for other much-needed upgrades in the master plan report, so visitors can expect to see more improvements here. In addition to

a community center, the park has playground equipment, a dozen or more tennis courts, softball and baseball diamonds, a band shell, and picnic shelters. The park board purchased the property in 1912 at the request of Fisk University's president and leaders of the north Nashville community. That year Nashville mayor Hilary Howse proclaimed Hadley Park the first public park for African-American citizens that had been established by any government in the nation.

A park board member named the park Hadley Park but did not specify which Hadley he had in mind. The city's African-American newspaper assumed it to be John L. Hadley, whose family had a house on the property. Around the time the park was purchased, the family's plantation became the site of Tennessee State University. Some say the park might have been named for Dr. W. A. Hadley, a pioneering African-American physician who worked with the park board on the 1897 Centennial Exposition. The entrance gates were built in the late 1930s by the Works Progress Administration. On each side of the main entrance, next to the library, the stone columns contain a listing of the 11 African-American soldiers from Davidson County who were killed during World War I.

HAMILTON CREEK PARK
2901 Bell Road
(615) 862-8400
www.nashville.gov/parks
Biking and boating are popular activities at Hamilton Creek Park, a 790-acre park on Bell Road along J. Percy Priest Lake. The U.S. Army Corps of Engineers leases the property to Metro Parks. In 1975 the parks board participated in the construction of a sailboat marina at the Hamilton Creek embayment; it opened in 1980, and today it stays busy. Boat slips and boats are available for rent. The park also has a boat-launching ramp, concession stands, restrooms, and hiking and nature trails. The BMX track is the site of national races that attract anywhere from 2,000 to 3,000 people. The park boasts about 9 miles of mountain biking trails that range in difficulty from challenging

beginner to advanced. The beach area along the lake is used as a remote-control motorboat area. Some visitors come here to swim, but there are no lifeguards. See our Recreation chapter for more on Hamilton Creek Park.

Parks Information

For additional information on state parks, natural areas, and Metro parks and greenways, contact:

Tennessee State Parks (Tennessee Department of Environment & Conservation), 401 Church Street, L&C Tower, seventh floor; (615) 532-0001 or (888) TN-PARKS; www.tnstateparks.com

Metropolitan Board of Parks and Recreation, 511 Oman Street in Centennial Park (administrative office), (615) 862-8400, www.nashville.gov/parks; 2565 Park Plaza in Centennial Park (sports and recreation office, park rangers), (615) 862-8424

The Metro Greenways Commission and Greenways for Nashville, Metropolitan Board of Parks and Recreation, 511 Oman Street in Centennial Park; (615) 862-8400; www.nashville.gov/greenways

---

HARPETH RIVER GREENWAY
Morton Mill Road
(615) 862-8400
www.nashville.gov/parks
This greenway is along the Harpeth River on Morton Mill Road near Old Harding Pike in Bellevue. Along the boardwalk following Morton Mill Road, you'll find an overlook with benches. A long-range plan calls for the greenway to extend from Morton Mill to the Bellevue Center mall area on US 70 S. It currently consists of a 1-mile trail with more than 800 feet of boardwalk along Morton Mill Road.

MILL CREEK/EZELL PARK GREENWAY
Harding Place at Mill Creek
(615) 862-8400
www.nashville.gov/parks
When completed, this greenway will include about 4.5 miles of trails in three segments. A 1-mile paved trail along a scenic stretch of Ezell Park was the first segment to be completed. This trail connects to a 1-mile loop near the Antioch Community Center at Blue Hole Road that links Antioch Middle School and neighborhood recreation facilities.

RED CABOOSE (BELLEVUE PARK)
656 Colice Jean Road
(615) 862-8435
www.nashville.gov/parks
This is one of Metro's most popular parks. It's in the west Nashville community of Bellevue along US 70 S. Formerly the site of Bellevue Junior High School, the land was transferred from the Metro Board of Education to the park system in 1982. A community center and park were completed in 1984. In the mid-1990s the community raised the funds and volunteered time and labor to renovate the playground; with matching funds from Metro Parks, the nearly eight-acre park now boasts some of the most expensive structures in the park system. The natural wood play structure is the focus of the park. Its connecting slides, bridges, tunnels, and other features entertain children for hours. Tire swings, toddler swings, a sand area, and the much-loved old red caboose provide other options for fun. While the youngsters are playing, grown-ups might enjoy getting some exercise on the 0.25-mile paved walking track that surrounds the playground. Three gazebos provide shade and spots for picnicking, and a restroom facility has been built on the park grounds. The on-site Bellevue Community Center is open Monday through Friday; hours of operation vary according to season. The community center features a bas-

ketball gym, weight room with free weights and machine weights, two club rooms, a game room with pool tables and Ping-Pong tables, and restrooms. These activities are free. In the winter adult volleyball leagues and church basketball leagues play here. The center also has a pottery and ceramics room, where classes are conducted by the arts department. The community center staff can provide information on class fees and instructions on how to sign up. Bellevue's park is also the traditional location for the Bellevue Community Picnic, an annual spring event featuring arts and crafts, exhibits, music, food, and a fireworks display. (See Kidstuff for more information.)

RIVERFRONT PARK
100 First Avenue N.
(615) 862-8400
www.nashville.gov/parks
Riverfront Park in downtown Nashville is the site of lots of summertime revelry. It's the site of the big Fourth of July celebration and fireworks display, as well as the free Dancin' in the District concert series, Fan Fair concerts and activities, and other events. Prime viewing spots on the tiered, grass-covered hill fill up fast, so arrive early if you want to sit there. The seven-and-a-half-acre park overlooks the Cumberland River. It's just a short walk from bustling Second Avenue and Broadway. Commercial and private boats dock at Riverfront Park. You can also find a replica of Fort Nashborough here that is open to the public. The replica is near where the original Fort Nashborough of the late 1700s stood (see our Attractions chapter). The park was created to commemorate Nashville's bicentennial and pay tribute to the city's river heritage. The first phase opened July 10, 1983.

SHELBY BOTTOMS GREENWAY AND NATURE PARK
East end of Davidson Street,
adjacent to Shelby Park
(615) 862-8400
www.nashville.gov/greenways
Considered one of the jewels of the Metro parks system, this 810-acre park on the Cumberland River has 5 miles of primitive hiking trails and 5 miles of paved multiuse trails. Along the trails there are boardwalks, interpretive stations, and several rustic bridges. The area also includes an observation deck for birders, lots of bluebird boxes, and a wetlands waterfowl refuge.

One of Metro Nashville's newest parks is Bell's Bend Park, which opened at the end of 2004. The park, located along the Cumberland River at 4107 Old Hickory Boulevard in west Nashville, was pegged as a possible site for a landfill in the early 1990s. In fall 2001 Nashville Mayor Bill Purcell chose to preserve the undeveloped property. Amenities at Bell's Bend include trails, parking lots, and entry roads.

SHELBY PARK
Shelby Avenue and South 20th Street
(615) 862-8467
www.nashville.gov/parks
Shelby Park, a historic and scenic park covering 361.5 acres, recently received a boost to its reputation with renovations as well as improvements to the adjacent Shelby Bottoms (see previous entry). When the park board opened Shelby as a public park in 1912, it was a showpiece park, but it deteriorated along with the east Nashville neighborhoods in later years. It's enjoying a renewed popularity today. A true community-use park, Shelby Park is bordered on various sides by a renovated historical neighborhood, middle-class contemporary homes, and lower-income homes, bringing a diverse mix of visitors to the park. Some come to fish in the lake, walk the paved winding roads, or play golf at the 27-hole golf course or the 9-hole course. With a four-diamond adult softball complex and additional ball fields for kids, Shelby Park is one of the five large ballparks operated by Metro Parks. Four tennis courts, a playground, hiking/nature trails, eight picnic shelters, restrooms, and a boat ramp are among the other attractions here. Shelby is also home to Nashville's first dog park, which opened in 2004. At the turn of the 20th century,

a real estate development company named the park for John Shelby, an army surgeon who owned much of the original property and built the Fatherland and Boscobel mansions in east Nashville during the 1800s. The company operated an amusement park on the Shelby Park site. The city's first municipal golf course opened here in 1924, and the park was home to Nashville's first city park baseball league, organized in 1915 by the YMCA.

i Nashville's oldest model-airplane-flying field is located at Edwin Warner Park, at Old Hickory Boulevard and Vaughn Road, across from the steeplechase grounds. The field dates from the 1940s. Members of Edwin Warner Model Aviators show up regularly to fly model planes. The field is also a popular spot for watching meteor showers.

TWO RIVERS PARK
3150 McGavock Pike
(615) 862-8400
www.nashville.gov/parks

This park is a great place to cool off on a hot summer day. This is where you'll find a skate park (see our Recreation chapter) as well as Wave Country water park. Wave Country has a wave pool, water slides, a children's playground, and volleyball pits, and it gets packed on summer days. (See our Attractions and Kidstuff chapters for more information.) Other attractions at the 384.5-acre Two Rivers Park include 18 holes of golf, baseball and softball diamonds, six tennis courts, and a playground. The park also has concession stands, picnic shelters, restrooms, Two Rivers Lake, and more. The property is the site of Two Rivers Mansion, a restored 1859 Italianate home available for event rentals. The mansion and an adjacent 1802 house are listed on the National Register of Historic Places. (Call 615-885-1112 for information on the mansion.)

WARNER PARKS
Edwin Warner Park, 50 Vaughn Road
(615) 370-8051

Percy Warner Park
2500 Old Hickory Boulevard
(615) 370-8051

Warner Parks Nature Center
7311 Highway 100
(615) 352-6299
www.nashville.gov/parks

The jewel in Metro Parks's crown, Warner Parks encompass at least 2,681 acres in southwest Nashville, making the collective pair one of the largest city parks in the country. Acres of wooded hills, open fields, and miles of scenic paved roads and nature trails provide Nashvillians with excellent recreation and environmental-education opportunities. (See Kidstuff for related information.) The parks are named for brothers Edwin and Percy Warner and were acquired between 1927 and 1930. Col. Luke Lea donated the first 868 acres of the land to the city in 1927, with the encouragement of his father-in-law, Percy Warner, a prominent local businessman, park board chairman, and lifelong outdoorsman and nature lover. Following Percy's death, Edwin Warner joined the park board and became the driving force behind the development of the parks and the acquisition of additional acreage. In 1937 the park board designated all the property west and south of Old Hickory Boulevard as Edwin Warner Park. The stone structures in the park, including the miles of dry-stacked stone retainer walls, were constructed from 1935 to 1941 by the Works Progress Administration, which provided jobs during the Great Depression. The WPA built seven limestone entrances, two stone bridges, a steeplechase course, picnic shelters, stone pillars, scenic drives, overlooks, and trails.

The main entrance to 2,058-acre Percy Warner Park is at the intersection of Belle Meade Boulevard and Page Road. Other entrances are off Chickering Road, Highway 100, and Old Hickory Boulevard. Percy Warner offers miles of hiking and equestrian trails as well as paved roads that wind along forest-shaded hillsides and through open fields. Bicyclists will find the roads make for a challenging workout. In addition to its recreation opportunities, Percy Warner Park is a nice place for a Sunday-afternoon drive or picnic. Percy Warner Park also has a steeplechase course—the site of the annual Iroquois Steeplechase (see Annual Events)—as well as two golf courses, picnic shelters, restrooms, and equestrian facilities.

Edwin Warner Park, divided from Percy Warner by Old Hickory Boulevard, offers paved and nature trails, playgrounds, ball fields, a polo field, model-airplane field, restrooms, and picnic shelters, including several reservable shelters. It's a popular spot for dog walking as well as for company picnics, family reunions, and other group events. The main entrance to Edwin Warner is at Highway 100 near the Warner Parks Nature Center, but you can also enter the park at Vaughn Road off Old Hickory Boulevard. The Warner Parks Nature Center serves both parks and includes the Susanne Warner Bass Learning Center, a natural-history museum, office and reference library, organic vegetable and herb garden, pond, bird-feeding area, and wildflower gardens. The park offers environmental programs year-round for adults and children. Programs include wildflower, insect, and tree hikes; bird-watching hikes and bird banding; exotic-plant removal; and sunrise celebrations. The programs are free, but reservations are required. The parks' 5,000-square-foot learning center features a gathering area where you can review park maps, an exhibit hall, classroom, collections room, offices, and a large porch and patio. Warner Parks is a strictly protected sanctuary. The parks are open from 6:00 a.m. until 11:00 p.m.

Walkin' the Dog

Shelby Dog Park, Nashville's first dog park, opened in 2004 at Shelby Park (Shelby Avenue at South 20th Street). The dog park allows owner-supervised dogs to play and socialize off-leash in a fenced area. There are several rules that owners must follow. Contact Metro Parks for details (615-862-8400), or visit the Web site www.nashville.gov/parks. Dogs are welcome at all other Metro parks, but must be leashed at all times. "Unofficial" spots where Nashvillians have been known to let their dogs off-leash include Percy Warner Park's steeplechase racetrack, and the area behind Eakin Elementary School on Fairfax Avenue, where a group of dog owners meets in the late afternoon on weekdays.

RECREATION

The typical Nashvillian isn't one to sit around idly and let the world go by. No, there's just way too much to do here for that. Whatever your preferred method of recreation, you'll probably find it in this city. We've mentioned elsewhere in this book how Nashville has earned the nickname "City of Parks," among many others. That's appropriate to bring up again here because many of the recreational opportunities available in Middle Tennessee are at parks. We're talking about activities as varied as bicycling, hiking, swimming, tennis, and skating, to name just a few. And many parks have fields for team sports like baseball, softball, and soccer. But parks don't have a monopoly on the action in Nashville. Tens of thousands of acres of water in area lakes just beg to be swum, fished, boated, and skied. You can put on your boots and cowboy hat and, instead of boot scootin', go for a horseback ride through the country. You can enjoy nature's beauty on an easy-paced walk or a strenuous hike.

Bad weather? That's okay. It doesn't have to ruin your day. As you'll discover in this chapter, we have plenty of indoor recreational opportunities as well, like indoor swimming and tennis, bowling, billiards, and pumping iron. So you don't need to climb the walls—although, if you really want to, that's an option as well (see the Climbing section in this chapter for details). You'll also find recreational opportunities in our Campgrounds, Golf, Kidstuff, and Parks chapters as well as in Day Trips and Weekend Getaways.

PUBLIC PARKS, PLAYGROUNDS, AND PROGRAMS

METROPOLITAN BOARD OF PARKS AND RECREATION
Administration Office
511 Oman Street
(615) 862-8400 (general information)

Centennial Sportsplex
222 25th Avenue N.
(615) 862-8480

Sports and Recreation Office
2565 Park Plaza
(615) 862-8424
www.nashville.gov/parks

The Metropolitan Board of Parks and Recreation, informally known as Metro Parks, not only maintains more than 100 parks and greenways throughout Davidson County but also provides ample opportunities for people of all ages to enjoy themselves. Facilities include more than 85 ball fields; 21 community centers; 14 swimming pools, some of which are open year-round; more than 45 picnic shelters; 80 playgrounds; and 7 golf courses. Metro Parks programs range from sports leagues for youth and adults to arts classes and workshops for all ages. Community centers offer activities including arts and crafts, exercise classes, sports, games, tutorial help, nature, anti-drug programs, Boy Scouts, and Girl Scouts. Centennial Sportsplex, at the edge of Centennial Park (see our Parks chapter), contains two ice rinks offering lessons for all ages and skill levels, as well as open skating sessions; an aquatic center offering lessons and open swim times; a tennis center with indoor and outdoor courts, including a stadium court; and a full fitness center. More information about activities available at Metro Parks is in this chapter under the specific activity, such as swimming or tennis. You can also find more detailed descriptions of some parks in our Parks and Kidstuff chapters. In addition to the playgrounds maintained by Metro Parks, most area elementary schools also have playgrounds, so there's bound to be one near you.

i *National Geographic Adventure* magazine chose Nashville as one of the Top 50 Adventure Towns in the United States for 2007. The top adventure towns are selected by meeting above-average standards in five categories: wilderness, small town, mountain, waterfront, and city.

BICYCLING

Nashville's many parks make it an ideal city for bikers of varying experience. If you're a beginner, you can find relatively flat paths that require little exertion; if you're eager for a challenge, there are plenty of hills that will test your stamina. One excellent guide to biking throughout Nashville and surrounding areas is *Bicycling Middle Tennessee: A Guide to Scenic Bicycle Rides in Nashville's Countryside,* by Ann Richards and Glen Wanner (Pennywell Press, Nashville). You can also request "Cycling Tennessee's Highways," a free collection of bicycling touring maps covering various sections of the state, from the Tennessee Department of Transportation by writing to Bicycle & Pedestrian Coordinator, Department of Transportation Planning, 5050 Deaderick Street, Suite 900, James K. Polk Building, Nashville 37243. Here are some highly recommended areas to bike in the Nashville area.

BOWIE NATURE PARK
7211 Bowie Lake Road, Fairview
(615) 799-5544
www.fairview-tn.org/park.htm
This 722-acre park west of Nashville is a popular spot for mountain biking, hiking, and horseback riding. The 15 miles of multiuse woodland trails are in good shape and can be fairly challenging, especially for beginners, though the park has smoother areas through sections of woods and fields. Bowie is also known for its scenic beauty and vistas of lakes, rivers, forest, and native grassland. There is a $2 trail access fee for biking and horseback riding. Hikers can use the trails free.

HAMILTON CREEK PARK
2901 Bell Road
www.nashville.gov/parks,
www.harpethbikeclub.com
Hamilton Creek Park, located on the west side of Percy Priest Lake, has 9.2 miles of mountain biking trails. Novices will want to start with the east trail, which traverses cedar glens and wooded hills and has few obstacles. More skilled bikers will want to head out on the west trail, which features longer climbs, rock gardens, and log crossings. Trailheads are at the beach, just off Ned Shelton Road. Hamilton Creek also has a BMX track used for national, state, and local races. For more information on Hamilton Creek trails and other area trails, call the Harpeth Bike Club at (615) 316-9417 or visit the club online at the Web site listed above.

MONTGOMERY BELL STATE PARK
1020 Jackson Hill Road, Burns
(615) 797-9052, (800) 250-8613
www.tnstateparks.com
Some of the area's most elaborate mountain biking trails can be found at scenic Montgomery Bell State Park, west of Nashville. Miles of trails, including beginner- and expert-level trails, recently have been developed at property on the opposite side of U.S. Highway 70 from the main park. By 2008 about 30 miles of trails were completed. The trails are off Jones Road, about 3 miles east of the park entrance. Tommy Hatcher, of the Harpeth Bike Club (www.harpethbikeclub .com), considers these trails as among the best the Nashville area has to offer.

NATCHEZ TRACE PARKWAY
(800) 305-7417
www.nps.gov/natr/
The Natchez Trace Parkway is very popular with bicyclists, even though there's no shoulder. Begin at the northern terminus at Highway 100, just across from Loveless Café, and—if you are so motivated—you can bike the road, which is part of the National Park system, as far as Natchez, Mississippi. For more information see *Bicycling the*

Natchez Trace, A Guide to the Natchez Trace Parkway by Glen Wanner (Pennywell Press, Nashville).

RADNOR LAKE STATE NATURAL AREA
1160 Otter Creek Road
(615) 373-3467
www.tnstateparks.com,
www.radnorlake.org
Otter Creek Road, which encircles the lake, is a great route for biking, and it's closed to motor vehicles. It's packed with walkers and joggers, however. For more information see our Parks chapter.

SHELBY BOTTOMS GREENWAY AND NATURE PARK
East end of Davidson Street,
adjacent to Shelby Park
(615) 880-2280
www.nashville.gov/greenways
Some of the trails at this 810-acre greenway and nature park are paved and others are mulched. For more information see our Parks chapter.

WARNER PARKS
Highway 100
(615) 370-8051 (headquarters),
(615) 352-6299 (nature center)
www.nashville.gov/parks
An 11-mile loop begins at the main drive near the Belle Meade Boulevard entrance to Percy Warner Park. The one-way road, which winds through fields and wooded areas, is suited for all skill levels, though the steep hills make it challenging in spots. Biking is permitted in paved areas only. For more information see our Parks chapter.

> **i** The Natchez Trace Parkway Bridge is the nation's first segmentally constructed concrete arch bridge. Spanning 1,648 feet above Highway 96, the double-arch structure offers motorists a majestic view from 155 feet above the valley floor.

BOATING

Registration, Rules, and Regulations

It is legal to travel on any navigable stream in Tennessee. But before you do, you should know the rules so you can avoid hurting someone or ending up in trouble with the law. If you have bought a new boat, your dealer generally will register it for you. If you've bought the boat from an individual or are new to the area, you'll need to go to the county court clerk's office in your county—in Davidson County, the clerk is at 700 Second Avenue S. (615-862-6050). Bring a bill of sale and other appropriate information on the boat; you'll pay sales tax on the amount paid plus $2. While there, you should apply for registration in your name. The office will notarize the card and give you a 30-day temporary registration; then you mail the card to the Tennessee Wildlife Resources Agency (TWRA). You can register for a one-, two-, or three-year period. Registration fees are based on the length of the boat.

TWRA enforces and administers the provisions of the Tennessee Boating Safety Act. Enforcement officers are on the water to assist boaters, enforce laws, and provide control. Every TWRA officer has the authority to stop and board any vessel, issue citations, and make arrests. Most TWRA boats are identified by orange and green stripes near the bow and the words *wildlife resources* on the sides; some, however, are unmarked. Boaters who are signaled to stop must do so immediately. It is unlawful to operate any sail or powered vessel while under the influence of alcohol or drugs. A person with a blood-alcohol content of 0.08 is presumed to be under the influence and can be fined up to $2,500 on the first or second offense and $5,000 on the third offense, jailed for 11 months and 29 days, be placed on mandatory probation, and be prohibited from operating a vessel for 1 to 10 years. As with motor vehicles, anyone operating a sail or powered vessel has given implied consent to a sobriety test. Failure to consent to testing is a separate offense that may result in suspension of operating privileges for six months.

Reckless operation of a vessel, including water skis, is an offense punishable by a $2,500 fine and six months in jail. The Coast Guard can also impose civil penalties up to $5,000 and one year in jail. Examples of reckless operation include operating a vessel in swimming areas; riding on seat backs, gunwales, transoms, or pedestal seats in a boat traveling faster than an idle speed; excessive speed in crowded, dangerous, or low-visibility areas; operating an overloaded vessel; towing a skier in a crowded area where he or she is likely to be hit by other vessels or to strike an obstacle; and using a personal watercraft to jump the immediate wake of another vessel.

People younger than 12 are prohibited from operating any vessel of eight and a half horsepower or larger unless they are under the direct supervision of an adult who can take immediate control of the vessel. An exception for unaccompanied operators is made if the person is 10 to 12 years old and has successfully completed a TWRA-approved boating education course, and the boat is more than 14 feet long and powered by an outboard motor of less than 15 horsepower.

A life jacket or other approved personal flotation device must be worn by each person onboard a vessel being operated within specifically marked areas below any dam. In fact, it's a good idea to wear one anytime you're in a vessel, wherever you are; the law requires that an approved personal flotation device be onboard and readily accessible for every person in the vessel.

Boating safety classes are available through TWRA. For more information about these classes or about other rules of the waterways, call TWRA's boating division at (615) 781-6522, or visit the Web site at www.tnwildlife.org.

Popular Waterways

Nashville's two big lakes, J. Percy Priest and Old Hickory, are both managed by the U.S. Army Corps of Engineers, which also manages some launching ramps on Cheatham Lake (Cumberland River). You'll see a variety of watercraft on these lakes, from fishing and skiing boats to houseboats, sailboats, and Jet Skis. Signs to boat ramps are marked at various locations around the lakes.

The Corps of Engineers operates nearly a dozen launching ramps on Old Hickory Lake in such areas as Hendersonville, Old Hickory, Hermitage, and Gallatin. The Corps has about 14 ramps at various sites on Priest Lake.

A number of private marina operators lease land from the Corps, and their offerings vary. Most, but not all, have a launching ramp, for example, and while most sell fishing and marine supplies, only a few sell fishing licenses.

i J. Percy Priest Lake was named in honor of Representative James Percy Priest, who was a high school teacher and coach and a reporter and editor for the *Tennessean* before being elected to Congress in 1940. He represented Nashville and Davidson County until his death in 1956. Old Hickory Lake was named for President Andrew Jackson, whose nickname was "Old Hickory."

J. Percy Priest Lake

3737 Bell Road (visitor center)
(615) 889-1975
www.lrn.usace.army.mil/op/jpp/rec
Percy Priest, about 10 miles east of downtown Nashville, covers 14,400 acres and has 265 miles of shoreline. Launching ramps are available at the following Corps recreation areas: Cook, (615) 889-9551; Seven Points, (615) 889-9552; Anderson Road, (615) 361-9805; Poole Knobs, (615) 459-6948 (campground); Vivrett Creek; Smith Springs; Hurricane Creek; Fate Sanders; Lamar Hill; Stewart Creek; Fall Creek; Jefferson Springs; West Fork; and East Fork. For those launch areas that don't have phones, call the Priest Lake visitor center at the number above for information. The visitor center is located near the west side of the dam and is open on weekdays. To make campsite and picnic shelter reservations at the above areas, call (877) 444-6777 or visit www.reserveusa.com.

Other marinas on Priest Lake include the following:

ELM HILL MARINA
3361 Bell Road
(615) 889-5363
www.elmhillmarina.com
Elm Hill, the largest marina on Priest Lake, has a launching ramp and sells cold sandwiches, along with gasoline and fishing and marine equipment. The marina has a restaurant that's open seasonally and also has private docking and restrooms, water hookups, and a pumping station. Fishing boats and pontoon boats are available to rent.

FATE SANDERS MARINA
3157 Weakley Lane, Smyrna
(615) 459-6219
In addition to a launching ramp and fishing supplies, Fate Sanders also offers a restaurant that serves catfish daily.

FOUR CORNERS MARINA
4027 Lavergne Couchville Pike, Antioch
(615) 641-9523
In addition to a boat launch and slips, Four Corners has boat rentals and sells gas and bait-and-tackle supplies. The marina's restaurant serves burgers, catfish, and fried chicken. You can even buy your fishing license here. A long-standing institution, Four Corners is a favorite with locals who remember visiting the marina when they were kids.

HAMILTON CREEK SAILBOAT MARINA
2901 Bell Road
(615) 862-8472
This marina is operated by Metro Parks and Recreation. It has its own trailer parking and launch ramp, and Insiders like it because there's little boat traffic and the scenery is beautiful. Facilities include a bathhouse and restrooms, nearby grocery store, a beach area, and picnic areas with tables and grills.

LONG HUNTER STATE PARK
2910 Hobson Pike, Hermitage
(615) 885-2422
www.tnstateparks.com
At Couchville Lake, a 110-acre lake off Percy Priest, you can rent 14-foot johnboats as well as canoes.

NASHVILLE SHORES YACHT CLUB AND MARINA
4001 Bell Road, Hermitage
(615) 883-0413
www.nashvilleshores.com
The Nashville Shores marina is one of several attractions offered by this popular water park. Facilities include boat and Jet Ski rentals, lake cabin rentals, picnic areas, restrooms, water hookups, restaurants, and minigolf and arcade. An added attraction is the water park's water slides and swimming pools, open under separate admission. (See our Attractions and Kidstuff chapters for more.)

Old Hickory Lake

No. 5 Power Plant Road, Hendersonville (resource manager's office)
(615) 822-4846, (615) 847-2395
www.lrn.usace.army.mil/op/old/rec
Old Hickory Lake, located northeast of Nashville on the Cumberland River, has more than 22,000 acres of water and 440 miles of shoreline. The visitor center/resource manager's office is located in Rockland Recreation Area in Hendersonville. Launching ramps are available at the following Corps recreation areas (not all have phones): Rockland, (615) 822-4846; Avondale; Cages Bend, (615) 824-4989; Cedar Creek, (615) 754-4947; Lone Branch, (615) 758-5299; Old Hickory Beach, (615) 847-8091; Martha Gallatin, (615) 444-4452; Nat Caldwell; and Laguardo, (615) 449-6544. Please note that listed numbers are not for making campsite reservations; for that, call the toll-free National Recreation Reservation Service line at (877) 444-6777. Launching ramps at Rockland are open year-round; the others are open seasonally. (See also our Campgrounds chapter.) Commercial marinas, all of which are open year-round, include:

ANCHOR HIGH MARINA
128 River Road, Hendersonville
(615) 824-2175
www.anchorhighmarina.com
Anchor High, located at mile marker 216.3, has a "ship store" with fishing and marine supplies,

sandwiches, and drinks, plus the Anchor High Bar and Grill. You'll also find a picnic area with tables, drinking water, and restrooms. Private and transit docking are available.

CEDAR CREEK MARINA
9120 Saundersville Road, Mount Juliet
(615) 758-5174
Cedar Creek has a launching ramp and a small store that sells fishing licenses, bait, oil, and other supplies as well as sandwiches during the warmer months. There's also a picnic area and shelter with tables and grills, private boat docking, and a vessel pump-out station. Cedar Creek is wheelchair accessible.

CHEROKEE RESORT
450 Cherokee Dock Road, Lebanon
(615) 444-2783
Cherokee Resort offers a marina with private and transit docking as well as a swimming pool and a 150-seat steak house restaurant with an additional 175-seat banquet room. Fuel and oil are available.

CREEKWOOD MARINA
259 Sanders Ferry Road, Hendersonville
(615) 824-7963
Creekwood Marina offers slip rental only. There is no launching ramp. The marina has gas and pump-out service, restrooms with showers, and electric meters (except for the pontoon slips), and it is prewired for cable and phone service.

DRAKES CREEK MARINA
441 Sanders Ferry Road, Hendersonville
(615) 822-3886
www.drakescreekmarine.com
This full-service marina sells Regal yachts and Nautiques ski boats, as well as used boats. The marina has a complete service department and offers private and transit docking as well as dry storage. It also offers electrical hookups and marine supplies, plus there's a restroom and picnic areas.

i For information on lake elevation, water temperature, and fishing conditions at J. Percy Priest Lake or Old Hickory Lake, call the U.S. Army Corps of Engineers's fishing information lines Monday through Friday. The number to call for Priest Lake is (615) 883-2351; the number for Old Hickory is (615) 824-7766. The information is updated on weekdays. On weekends, call TVA's Lake Information Line at (800) 238-2264 for information on either lake.

GALLATIN MARINA
727 Marina Road, Gallatin
(615) 452-9876
Gallatin Marina has a restaurant, a store that sells limited marine supplies, a private launching ramp (there's a $5 fee for nonmembers), a picnic area for boaters, private and transit docking, a gas dock, and, for members, a swimming pool.

OLD HICKORY YACHT CLUB & MARINA
2001 Riverside Road, Old Hickory
(615) 847-4022
Old Hickory Marina has a public access boat ramp, private and transit docking, an eating area with concessions (they're known for their chili dogs), gas, bait, and restrooms.

SHADY COVE RESORT AND MARINA
1115 Shady Cove Road, Castalian Springs
(615) 452-8010
Shady Cove has a launching ramp, private and transit docking, a snack bar serving sandwiches and other deli-type foods during warmer months, gas, fishing and marine supplies, bait, a campground with camper dumping station (propane and a grill are available), electrical hookups, a swimming pool with bathhouse, boat and motor rentals (fishing boats, canoes, and paddleboats), a laundry facility, picnic area, and playground.

Cheatham Lake (Cumberland River)

1798 Cheatham Dam Road, Ashland City
(resource manager's office)
(615) 792-5697, (615) 254-3734
www.lrn.usace.army.mil/op/che/rec

Cheatham Lake, an impoundment of the Cumberland River, is 67.5 miles long, extending through Nashville to Old Hickory Dam. The lake has 320 miles of shoreline. Cheatham Lake is 42.3 miles to downtown Nashville's Riverfront Park and 45 miles to the public boat launching ramp at Shelby Park. The Corps maintains launching areas (phone numbers are seasonal) at Cheatham Dam Right Bank, (615) 792-1371; Lock A, (615) 792-3715; Sycamore Creek; Johnson Creek; Pardue; Harpeth River Bridge, (615) 792-4195; Bluff Creek; Brush Creek; Cleese's Ferry Right Bank; and Cleese's Ferry Left Bank. At this writing, the Corps's Bull Run and Sam's Creek launching areas had been closed, but the two areas may reopen—Bull Run under Ashland City management and Sam's Creek under Cheatham County management. Ashland City operates River Bluff Park. In addition, Metro Parks maintains ramps at Shelby Park in Nashville, Peeler Park in Madison, and Lock 2 at Old Hickory Dam. As for commercial marinas, there are two on Cheatham Lake close to Nashville. The Commodore Yacht Club is private, but we're told they will occasionally accept transits, with reservations. Boaters are advised to call ahead to make sure, at (615) 352-9981.

THE NEW ROCK HARBOR

525 Basswood Avenue
(615) 356-1111, (800) 542-ROCK
www.rockharbormarine.com

This popular marina is just a 10-minute drive from downtown Nashville and 15 water miles from Riverfront Park, making it a natural for day excursions. Rock Harbor has both wet slips and dry stack storage, gas and diesel fuel, restrooms and showers, cable TV and phone hookups, and electrical hookups. Transient slips are available with reservations.

RIVERVIEW MARINA

110 Old River Road, Ashland City
(615) 792-7358

Riverview Marina, just off the Highway 49 bridge in Ashland City, has a launching ramp and dock and provides dockside diesel and gas sales and transient moorage spaces. The marina also has a popular restaurant that's known for its catfish (see our Restaurants chapter for the Riverview Restaurant & Marina listing under "Catfish").

BOWLING

Bowling in greater Nashville generally will cost you around $3.00 a game. You may pay as little as 50 cents or as much as $3.50 plus an extra $1.00 to $2.75 for shoes if you need them. Most facilities, however, have reduced-price hours (generally in the morning or afternoon), and some offer all-you-can-bowl specials at certain times. Be aware that during league play (hours vary from location to location), some bowling centers will have limited or no lanes open, so as with many businesses, it's always a good idea to call first. Many local bowling alleys offer regularly scheduled "cosmic bowling" nights, which include music, disco, laser and black lights, and a general party atmosphere. There are at least two dozen bowling centers in Nashville and surrounding areas. We'll list a few local favorites.

CUMBERLAND LANES

3930 Apache Trail, Antioch
(615) 834-4693
www.jaymarFEC.com

Cumberland Lanes offers 32 lanes, automatic scoring, a game room, snack bar, and lounge. Friday and Saturday night it stays open until 2:00 a.m. Cumberland Lanes also has birthday party packages available for kids and has launched a youth bowling league. Call the information line for a list of specials, such as lunch-and-bowl specials and cosmic bowling.

DONELSON BOWL

117 Donelson Pike
(615) 883-3313

Donelson Bowl has 24 lanes with automatic scoring, a games arcade, and a snack bar serving beer and food. Special prices are available throughout the week, and this center also offers reasonably priced 10-game cards, which can be used at any time.

HERMITAGE LANES
3436 Lebanon Pike, Hermitage
(615) 883-8900
www.hermitagelanes.com
Hermitage Lanes has 32 lanes with automatic scoring, six pool tables, and about 120 video games. The bowling alley also has a full-service restaurant and bar, where you can watch sports on TV, listen to live music, or play darts. Hermitage Lanes is known for its great birthday parties and also has daily specials, including cosmic bowling on Saturday.

MADISON BOWL
517 Gallatin Road N., Madison
(615) 868-1496
There are 32 lanes with automatic scoring, a game room and video arcade, and a snack bar here. A discounted 10-game card can be used at any time.

TUSCULUM LANES
5315 Nolensville Road
(615) 833-2881
www.jaymarFEC.com
Tusculum Lanes, in south Nashville, offers 24 lanes with automatic scoring, snack bar, pro shop, and video games. Tusculum frequently offers "Cyber Bowl." It also has a summer youth club that offers significant savings.

CANOEING

The Harpeth River is a blessing to canoeists who don't want to drive far. Three businesses on the river in nearby Kingston Springs rent canoes for trips of varying lengths and times on the Harpeth, which is designated a State Scenic River and nature sanctuary. Because of the Harpeth's 5-mile "hairpin" loop in this area, you can put in and take out at nearly the same spot. Along the quiet, relaxing route—there are no major rapids to negotiate—you'll pass peaceful farmland and green, rolling hills. It's a great way to get away from it all for a few hours. The following renters of canoes are generally open from March or April through October, weather permitting. Each canoe will carry three adults, or two adults and two small children. Canoeing has grown in popularity, and it's recommended that you call ahead to reserve your canoes, especially on busy holiday weekends like Memorial Day and July 4.

FOGGY BOTTOM CANOE RENTAL
1270 US 70, Kingston Springs
(615) 952-4062
www.foggybottomcanoe.com
Foggy Bottom rents canoes for $29.95 per boat for a one-and-a-half to two-hour trip; you can keep your canoe all day for $40. Prices include paddles and life jackets. Primitive campsites nearby come free with canoe trips.

PIZZA SHACK RESTAURANT AND MARKETPLACE
1203 US 70, Kingston Springs
(615) 952-4211
"We feed 'em and we float 'em," says the operator of the Pizza Shack, which is, yes, a pizza restaurant that rents canoes. Canoes rent for $30 all day. Pizza, along with picnic tables near the river, makes this a popular site. Group rates (five or more canoes) are 10 percent off during weekends and 20 percent off during weekdays.

TIP-A-CANOE STORES INC.
Harpeth River Outpost,
1279 US 70, Kingston Springs
(615) 254-0836, (800) 550-5810
www.tip-a-canoe.com
Tip-A-Canoe is the area's oldest outfitter and one of the oldest canoe outfitters in the nation. Canoes rent for $50 for anywhere from two to four and a half hours. Six- and eight-hour trips are an additional $10. Two-, three-, four-, and five-day

tours are also available. Group rates (20 percent off) are available if renting six or more canoes. Visit the Web site for other discount offers.

i **The Harpeth River, a popular spot for canoeing, is normally rated Class I, which means it's suitable for beginners and children. About 20 percent of the time, the Harpeth is Class II, and suitable only for experienced canoeists. Beginners and children under age 12 are advised not to canoe the river during those times.**

CLIMBING

CLIMB NASHVILLE
3630 Redmon Street
(615) 463-ROCK
121 Seaboard Lane, Suite 10, Franklin
(615) 661-9444
www.climbnashville.com
Climb Nashville's 13,000-square-foot climbing facility on Redmon Street is one of the largest indoor climbing gyms in the Southeast. Located in Sylvan Park, near the intersection of West End Avenue and Interstate 440, the gym offers 11,000 square feet of 40-foot-tall climbing wall space. The facility also has weight training and cardiovascular equipment and offers yoga classes. The Franklin facility, located near the Cool Springs Galleria mall, has more than 6,000 square feet of climbing space and a great bouldering cave. Each location offers something for all skill levels, but the Franklin location specializes in parties and groups, while the West End–area facility draws the most hard-core climbers. First-time climbers should go for the introductory package, which includes a lesson, equipment, and climbing fee. Various admission packages and memberships are available, and walk-ins are accepted. The facilities are closed on Monday.

FOSTER FALLS SMALL WILD AREA
U.S. Highway 41, Jasper
(423) 942-5759
www.tva.gov, www.friendsofscsra.org

Scenic Foster Falls is probably the top destination for Nashville-area rock climbers. In fact, it is known for having some of the best climbing ledges in the entire Southeast. Permits are not required for climbing or rappelling. The area centers on a 60-foot waterfall, which is visible from the surrounding sandstone overlooks. The climbing area, which is on land owned and managed by the Tennessee Valley Authority and the South Cumberland State Recreation Area, is about 11 miles south of the South Cumberland State Park Visitor Center. You can stop at the visitor center for information on climbing at Foster Falls as well as at the nearby Great Stone Door. The visitor center is located about 3 miles off Interstate 24 E., on U.S. Highway 41, between Monteagle and Tracy City. Monteagle is about 90 miles southeast of Nashville. TVA provides picnic facilities, restrooms, and a seasonally operated campground at Foster Falls.

FISHING

Middle Tennessee has 10 lakes and more than a dozen rivers and streams within a two-hour drive of Nashville, which is good news for anglers. The three closest lakes to Nashville are Cheatham, J. Percy Priest, and Old Hickory.

Vernon Summerlin, author of *Two Dozen Fishin' Holes: A Guide to Middle Tennessee* (Rutledge Hill Press, 1992) and former copublisher of the now-defunct *Tennessee Angler* magazine, was gracious enough to answer some of our questions and share his thoughts on Nashville-area fishing with us. You'll find Vern's insights throughout this section of the chapter.

Gamefish species caught in Middle Tennessee include rainbow and brown trout, walleye, sauger, rockfish (also known as stripers), stripe (also known as white bass), bream, black bass (largemouth, smallmouth, and spotted), catfish, and crappie. Not all species will be found in all waters—their presence is often dependent upon habitat and Tennessee Wildlife Resources Agency (TWRA) stocking programs.

Anyone 13 or older who fishes in Tennessee must have a license. You are exempted if you are: (1) a landowner fishing on your own farmland; (2) on military leave and carrying a copy of your leave orders; or (3) a resident born before March 1, 1926. Disabled resident veterans and blind residents are eligible for free licenses. Licenses go on sale March 1 of each year. An annual resident fishing and hunting combination license costs $21. A stamp permitting you to fish for trout costs an additional $12. Nonresident licenses start at $10.50 for a three-day (no trout) fishing license and $20.50 for a three-day all-fish license. In addition, special permits are available for TWRA-managed lakes and Reelfoot Preservation (Reelfoot Lake). Fishing licenses are available at sporting goods stores, marinas, hardware stores, and bait-and-tackle shops. You can also order them online or by phone from the TWRA (see subsequent entry).

Tennessee has a Free Fishing Day each June, when everyone can fish without a license, and a Free Fishing Week in June for children ages 13 through 15. Contact TWRA for dates (see the subsequent entry for information).

Here are some resources for additional information on fishing in Middle Tennessee.

TENNESSEE WILDLIFE RESOURCES AGENCY
Ellington Agricultural Center
440 Hogan Road
(615) 781-6622
www.state.tn.us/twra

The latest laws governing fishing in Tennessee are available in the booklet *Tennessee Fishing Regulations*. The booklet, as well as other information about fishing, hunting, and other outdoor activities, is available from this office, which is responsible for Middle Tennessee, or Region 2.

You can purchase an instant fishing license from the TWRA online or by phone, using a credit card (there is an extra fee of $3.95 for either service). To order online, visit the TWRA's Web site. From there, you will be able to print a temporary license, which you can use until a permanent license arrives by mail.

Lake Fishing

Cheatham Lake

Cheatham Lake is 67.5 miles long, with 320 miles of shoreline, and looks like a river until you get to the lower section. It is an impoundment of the Cumberland River downstream from Old Hickory Dam to Cheatham Dam, and it runs right through downtown Nashville, which is 42 miles upstream from Cheatham Dam. (Most people simply refer to this lake as the "Cumberland River.")

Largemouth bass are taken on quarter-ounce jigs and plastic worms at creek mouths where the current is quiet—next to downed trees or other completely or partially submerged structures. Spinnerbaits and crankbaits also can be effective. Topwater baits work best early and late in the day. Similar tactics work for smallmouth and Kentucky bass.

Crappie take small jigs and minnows. Bream, including bluegill, like worms and crickets. Catfish prefer minnows, chicken livers, and nightcrawlers. Walleye and sauger like minnows and jigs fished near the bottom in the cold-weather months (November through March). Fish for rockfish below the dams year-round.

The public launch access points are fairly limited, but the easiest access is from Shelby Park in Nashville, Cleese's Ferry west of Nashville off Highway 12, and at Cheatham Dam in Ashland City. Several of the ramps are within 6 miles of the dam, which is also where the best fishing is found.

Summerlin thinks the best fishing is at Lock A, Brush Creek, and Sycamore Creek. Bank-fishing opportunities are available at the ramps and the recreation areas at Lock A, Harpeth River, and Sycamore Creek. Camping is available at Lock A and Harpeth River Bridge.

i For a quick check of when and where to fish in Middle Tennessee, visit the Tennessee Wildlife Resource Agency's Web site, www.state.tn.us/twra. There you will find a listing of area lakes and rivers that includes the type of fish caught there and when you can expect to catch them.

J. Percy Priest Lake

J. Percy Priest Lake, an impoundment of the Stones River, is the most popular lake in Middle Tennessee. It is 42 miles long with 265 miles of shoreline. About 20 recreation areas, some with camping and most with boat ramps, make the lake very accessible; parts of it are only a five-minute drive from Nashville. Many people consider Priest Lake's midsection—from Fate Sanders Marina to Hobson Pike Bridge—to be the most productive. The many islands in this section are usually home to bass on the deep side in summer and winter and on the shallow side in spring and fall.

Priest Lake offers excellent fishing for crappie, largemouth and smallmouth bass, rockfish, white bass, and hybrids, thanks to an abundance of cover and a strong forage base. Smallmouth tend to dwell near Cook, Elm Hill, Seven Points, and Vivrett Recreation Areas as well as Long Hunter State Park and Hamilton Creek Park. They are generally receptive to jigs dressed with pork, crawfish, and tubes. In spring you're likely to catch smallmouth using artificial deep-diving crankbaits, including Deep Wee-R, Hellbender, and Rapala, along with spinnerbaits, 4-inch worms, and jigs. Largemouth bass prefer worms, spinnerbaits, and crankbaits offered near cover like stumps, trees, and humps in the upper section of the lake above Fate Sanders Marina, but they are found throughout the lake in all seasons. Rockfish congregate during summer nights on Suggs Creek and between Seven Points and Long Hunter State Park. They are receptive to live shad or shiners drifted, or surface lures like Red Fin or a jointed Thunderstick retrieved through what is known as "the jumps" (rockfish feeding on schools of shad). Crappie are taken year-round but are easiest to find in the spring when they're spawning in the shallows and are receptive to a minnow dropped among the limbs of downed trees and bushes along the bank. Worms and crickets are reliable for catching bream close to the banks and rocky bluffs. There are lots of good spots for bank fishing around the recreation areas like Elm Hill and Cooks.

Old Hickory Lake

Old Hickory Lake is another impoundment of the Cumberland River, and its flow is regulated by Old Hickory Dam. There are 97.3 river miles from Old Hickory Dam upstream to Cordell Hull Dam and 440 miles of shoreline. There are about 12 Army Corps of Engineers ramps on the lake between Old Hickory Dam and Highway 109 south of Gallatin, and you'll also find nine marinas on the lake. The presence of coontail milfoil, an aquatic plant, from Shutes Branch to Bull Creek makes for a prime largemouth habitat. Spinnerbaits, crankbaits, and artificial worms are the favored offerings. Catfish are plentiful throughout Old Hickory, with heavy concentrations around the Gallatin steam plant and Cedar Creek. You'll also find plenty of bream, stripe, and crappie. Sauger are taken below the dam in winter. Occasional rainbow trout are taken from Old Hickory—escapees from the Caney Fork River, which is Middle Tennessee's trout hot spot. Old Hickory also offers good fishing from its bank.

River and Stream Fishing

Several Middle Tennessee rivers and streams are popular with creek anglers seeking smallmouth bass. Preferred waters for stream fishing include the Buffalo, Duck, Elk, and Harpeth Rivers in addition to the Caney Fork below Center Hill Dam. The information we include for these areas is general rather than specific; experienced stream anglers realize that streams are fragile ecosystems that are more susceptible than reservoirs to heavy fishing pressures.

Author and angler extraordinaire Vernon Summerlin was a great source of information, with much of the following coming from his book *Two Dozen Fishin' Holes: A Guide to Middle Tennessee* (Rutledge Hill Press, 1992). While it is legal to travel on any navigable stream in Tennessee, please keep in mind that the banks are often privately owned land. Look to public lands for bank fishing, and get permission before traipsing onto private property.

As a general rule, the area's larger streams contain more species, as you might expect. The smaller streams are good places to find large-mouth and smallmouth bass, rock bass, bream, and rough fish, such as carp, suckers, and baitfish. On smaller streams, Summerlin suggests fishing deep holes and structure, then moving on. "Go prepared to catch about a two-pound fish on about four-pound-test line on an ultralight rod-and-reel outfit," he says. "You can retrieve most of your lures, so keep it light with a small tacklebox that will fit in your pocket. The heaviest thing you want to carry is your fish."

Buffalo River

The Buffalo River, a scenic Class I and II water-way, provides good fishing for largemouth and smallmouth bass, rock bass, and bream. You'll also find trout in some sections. Good canoe access is available off the Natchez Trace Parkway at Metal Ford.

Caney Fork

Caney Fork offers fishing on 27 miles from Center Hill Dam to Carthage. Trout fishing is popular below the dam, but be prepared to catch rock-fish, walleye, stripe, bream, and smallmouth and largemouth bass. Use light to medium equipment unless you're going for the big (up to 40 pounds) rockfish.

i Winter anglers crowd the waters around the Gallatin steam plant to fish for rockfish, which are drawn to the abundant bait attracted to the warm waters near the plant. Many rockfish caught here tip the scales at about 20 pounds, and some weigh as much as 40 pounds.

Duck River

Rainbow and brown trout are in abundance on the Duck River below Normandy Dam. You'll also find saugeye, muskellunge, bass, bream, crappie, and stripe.

Elk River

The Elk River below Tim's Ford Dam is clear and cold. For the first 12 miles below the dam, trout are plentiful. Anglers like to fish large gravel areas near deep pools here.

Harpeth River

The four branches of the Harpeth River—Little, Big, South, and West—converge near the Pasquo-Bellevue area. The Harpeth, a State Scenic River, offers more than 100 miles of largely Class I water that is easily navigable by canoe. Game-fish include bass, bream, catfish, crappie, stripe, rockfish, and sauger. There's limited access to the South Harpeth, but you can find bank access and a good place to put your canoe in on the Big Harpeth at Pinkerton Park in Franklin. The section known as the Narrows of the Harpeth has an easy 5-mile loop at Harpeth River State Park off US 70. Canoe rentals are available at various canoe liveries in the area (see the Canoeing section of this chapter for more information).

FITNESS CENTERS

Nashville's fitness scene has grown tremendously. Whereas once there were only a handful of "health clubs"—many of them catering to image-conscious Belle Meade ladies—today Nashvillians have available to them a variety of options. Yoga studios, Pilates, boxercise, and tai chi centers have joined the more typical fitness clubs offering weights and treadmills. While we can't offer a comprehensive listing of fitness centers, here are a few of our favorites. As with everything else, studios close and new ones open with regularity; it's always wise to call ahead.

BAPTIST WELLNESS CENTER
2011 Church Street
(615) 284-5066
www.baptisthospital.com
Baptist Wellness Center, on the campus of Baptist Hospital (see our Health Care and Wellness chapter), provides fitness testing and individualized programs supervised by exercise professionals. The cardiovascular center features treadmills, exercise bikes, and rowing, ski, and stair machines. Other features include a complete weight room with free weights and a variety of machines,

steam room, saunas, whirlpool, aerobics classes, a cushioned indoor track, and a heated lap pool. Membership is available, but guest passes can be purchased as well. A one-time pass costs $10; for 5 to 10 visits, you'll pay $7 a day; 11 to 19 visits, $6 a day; and 20 or more visits, $5 a day.

CENTENNIAL SPORTSPLEX
222 25th Avenue N.
(615) 862-8480
www.nashville.gov/sportsplex
Machine weights, a separate free-weight room, stationary bikes, treadmills, step machines, aerobics, steam room, and sauna are available at Centennial Sportsplex, the complex run by the Metropolitan Board of Parks and Recreation. Sportsplex also has 2 pools, 1 Olympic and 1 recreational, 2 ice-skating rinks, 15 outdoor tennis courts, and 4 indoor courts. Annual memberships are available; you can also pay $6 a day ($5 for children to use the pools only) or buy 10-pass packages for $54.

THE CLUB AT WESTSIDE
11 Vaughns Gap Road
(615) 352-8500

THE CLUB AT GREEN HILLS
3820 Cleghorn Drive
(615) 383-3456
www.wactn.com
These clubs have fully equipped gyms complete with cardio equipment, free weights and weight machines, basketball courts, and classes in yoga and the like. The Westside club has tennis courts. All locations have sauna and steam rooms. Massage therapists add to these facilities' spalike atmosphere. Annual memberships are available, but visitors can buy a $10 to $15 daily guest pass. If you're coming with a member, however, it's free.

GORDON JEWISH COMMUNITY CENTER
801 Percy Warner Boulevard
(615) 356-7170
www.nashvillejcc.org
The Jewish Community Center has a pool and gym and offers fitness and recreation programs for all ages. Personal trainers, classes in everything

from aerobics to yoga to swimming, and sports leagues are available. Membership is required, and various plans are available.

HIKING

BOWIE NATURE PARK
766 Fairview Boulevard W., Fairview
(615) 799-5544
www.fairview-tn.org/park.htm
This park, named for local naturalist Dr. Evangeline Bowie, is located about 30 minutes west of Nashville. It offers 15 miles of trails that are popular for hiking, mountain biking, and horseback riding. The park's 722 acres offer a variety of native habitat to explore, from oak-hickory and white pine forests to streams, rivers, and five lakes. Park naturalists offer a variety of programs throughout the year, and Bowie is home to the annual Fairview Nature Fest each August.

LONG HUNTER STATE PARK
2910 Hobson Pike, Hermitage
(615) 885-2422
www.tnstateparks.com
Located along the shores of J. Percy Priest Lake, east of Nashville, this 2,315-acre park has 28 miles of trails for day hiking and overnight backpacking. Trails include the Lake Trail around Couchville Lake, a self-guided barrier-free nature trail; the mile-long Deer Trail, which takes you through old fields and new forests; and, for shorter walks, the Nature Loop Trail and Inland Trail. The more strenuous Day Loop Trail and Volunteer Trail wind along the lake, climb overlook bluffs, and travel through hardwood forests and cedar glades.

MONTGOMERY BELL STATE PARK
US 70, Burns
(615) 797-9052, (800) 250-8613
www.tnstateparks.com
This 3,850-acre park offers at least 19 miles of trails, including a 0.75-mile walk in the woods to an 11.7-mile overnight trail. The backcountry trail has three overnight shelters. Montgomery Bell is located west of Nashville and about 7 miles east of Dickson.

RADNOR LAKE STATE NATURAL AREA
1160 Otter Creek Road
(615) 373-3467
www.tnstateparks.com
Radnor Lake State Natural Area is a point of pride for many Nashvillians, whose protests in the '60s saved it from being turned into a housing development. Located just 7 miles from downtown Nashville, the beautiful and peaceful area is surrounded by both level walking paths and steep climbs—six in all—offering something for everyone. No fishing, boating, or hunting is allowed, but there are plenty of opportunities for bird-watching and photography. Pets and joggers are allowed only on the paved road.

SHELBY BOTTOMS GREENWAY AND NATURE PARK
East end of Davidson Street,
adjacent to Shelby Park
(615) 880-2280
www.nashville.gov/parks,
www.nashville.gov/greenways
This 810-acre greenway includes 5 miles of paved trails and 5 miles of primitive hiking trails. The park—popular with hikers, bikers, skaters, and bird-watchers—also features a river-look observation deck and a shorebird pond.

WARNER PARKS
Highway 100
(615) 370-8051 (headquarters),
(615) 352-6299 (nature center)
www.nashville.gov/parks
Percy Warner Park and Edwin Warner Park, more than 2,680 acres combined, are ideal for hiking, jogging, or biking, with miles of nature trails and scenic paved roads. Maps and literature are at the nature center trailhead (7311 Highway 100).

HORSEBACK RIDING

JURO STABLES
735 Carver Lane, Mount Juliet
(615) 773-7433
www.jurostables.com

At JuRo Stables anyone from beginner to seasoned riders can take a trip—paced to suit the rider—through wooded trails along Percy Priest Lake or gallop along the "back 40," an open field. Rates are $22 for one hour for adults and $17 for children. JuRo, which also has primitive camping and cookout facilities, gives English and western riding lessons. Reservations are preferred. JuRo is open daily.

RAMBLIN' BREEZE RANCH
3665 Knight Road, Whites Creek
(615) 876-1029
www.acowboytown.com
Ramblin' Breeze Ranch, located about 8 miles north of downtown Nashville, offers a one-hour, 3-mile trail ride through 116 acres of woods and pastures and around a lake. One-hour rides are $25.63 plus tax for adults and $21.05 plus tax for children 7 to 12. Lead-around rides for children 3 to 6 are $21.05 plus tax. Call to inquire about lengthier rides. The ranch is open daily, but in the winter operation depends on the weather. Reservations are suggested. The ranch also offers riding lessons, fishing, canoeing, primitive camping, hiking, and hayrides. Some activities might require a few days' notice. Check out the Saturday night Wild West Dinner Show for gunfights, cowboy singing, and cowboy grub.

POOL AND BILLIARDS

BUFFALO BILLIARDS & HAVANA LOUNGE
154 Second Avenue N.
(615) 313-7665
www.buffalobilliards.com
The Second Avenue location of this hangout makes it a popular stop on the honky-tonk crawl circuit. The atmosphere is fun and lively, but on weekends it can get unbearably crowded—and smoky, since Buffalo Billiards is also known as a cigar and martini bar. There are 12 pool tables, 5 dartboards, 4 foosball tables, plus a DJ spinning music. The menu features sandwiches with

chips and hot peppers, and the kitchen stays open late. Buffalo Billiards is open until 3:00 a.m. on Friday and Saturday and 2:00 a.m. the rest of the week.

GEORGE'S ELLISTON PLACE POOL HALL
2200 Elliston Place
(615) 320-9441
This pool hall is popular with college students and 20-somethings out for a night on the town. In addition to billiards, there's beer and a relaxed, easy atmosphere.

H CUE'S UPSTAIRS POOLROOM
1602 21st Avenue S.
(615) 329-0690
This Hillsboro Village mainstay usually doesn't get hopping until late at night, but if you want to be sure to get a table without having to wait, show up before 7:00 p.m. H Cue's has only four tables, so if it's packed, you're in for a wait. In addition to pool, there's pinball and video games. The bar serves beer and light snacks.

HERMITAGE LANES
3436 Lebanon Pike
(615) 883-8900
www.hermitagelanes.com
Hermitage Lanes has six pool tables and 120 video games in addition to its 32 bowling lanes.

J.O.B. BILLIARDS CLUB
960 South Gallatin Road, Madison
(615) 868-4270
www.jobbilliards.com
Thirty-two tables are available in this clean 18,000-square-foot playing area that stays open until 3:00 a.m. on Friday and Saturday, until 2:00 a.m. Monday through Thursday, and until midnight on Sunday. The club also has a pro shop and a sports lounge. Frequented by serious players, J.O.B. hosts league play Monday through Wednesday.

MELROSE BILLIARDS
2600 Franklin Pike
(615) 383-9201
Locals have been frequenting Melrose Billiards (sometimes referred to as Chandler's) since 1942. Known as the "real deal," the neighborhood pool hall is a favorite with serious players. There are 11 regulation tables and one snooker table, as well as table tennis and shuffleboard.

SNOOKER'S OF HICKORY HOLLOW
1015 Bell Road
(615) 731-5573
Favored by locals and serious pool sharks, Snooker's has 20 pool tables plus go-karts and video games. A bar serves beer and wine coolers, and the restaurant offers such sports bar fare as burgers, barbecue, french fries, and the like. Snooker's is open until 2:00 a.m. Sunday and weekdays and until 3:00 a.m. weekends. Go-karts close an hour earlier

SKATING

Many skating rinks, while offering limited hours during the week, are available for private party rentals during the "closed" hours. Call the specific rink for details.

CENTENNIAL SPORTSPLEX
222 25th Avenue N.
(615) 862-8480
www.nashville.org/sportsplex
Public ice-skating sessions are held for two to five hours a day at Sportsplex, which has two rinks open to the public (one doubles as the Nashville Predators's hockey practice facility). Visit the Sportsplex for a schedule. Admission is $6 for adults, $5 for seniors and ages 12 and younger, plus $2 for skate rental. Hours for public skating vary, so call ahead.

HENDERSONVILLE SKATING RINK
750 West Main Street, Hendersonville
(615) 824-0630
Hendersonville Skating Rink specializes in private parties during the week. In-line skaters and roller

skates are allowed on the wooden floor, though only roller skates are available for rent. The cost to skate varies according to the day and time. You'll pay about $4.50 max, including skates, on weekends.

NASHVILLE SKATE PARK
3150 McGavock Pike
(615) 862-8400
www.nashville.gov/parks

Metro Parks opened this state-of-the-art skate park in 2004. Located at Two Rivers Park across from the Wave Country water park in the Donelson area, the 20,000-square-foot, $500,000 facility offers smooth, concrete surfaces for freestyle in-line skating, skateboarding, and BMX bike riding. The park provides ramps, pipes, bowls, and other components designed to allow skaters to perform all sorts of tricks. The park is free to the public.

SIXTHAVENUE SKATEPARK
401 Sixth Avenue S.
(615) 843-4001,
(615) 843-4000 (event hotline)
www.sixthavenueskatepark.com

SixthAvenue SkatePark is part of the nonprofit RCKTWN entertainment complex for youth. The 11,000-square-foot indoor wood park is for extreme skateboarding, in-line skating, and BMX freestyling. Admission is $7 per session. The park welcomes skateboarders, bikers, and in-liners at any time. On weekends, the skate park stays open until midnight. A $39 monthly membership is a good deal for avid skaters.

SKATE CENTER
402 Wilson Pike Circle, Brentwood
(615) 373-8611,
(615) 373-1827 (information line)

119 Gleaves Street (Rivergate area)
(615) 868-7655,
(615) 868-3692 (information line)

1505 Plaza Drive, Smyrna
(615) 459-7655
www.skatecenter.com

These centers, each with wooden floors, charge $5.00 to $8.00 admission (prices can vary for special events). Roller-skate rental is $1.50. In-line skates are also allowed. Skate Centers have a variety of special events, including after-school fun skates, family night, Christian night, and ladies' night. The rinks are also available for parties.

SPORTS LEAGUES

METROPOLITAN BOARD OF PARKS AND RECREATION
Sports and Recreation Office
2565 Park Plaza
(615) 862-8424
www.nashville.gov/parks

Metro Parks offers adult sport leagues in softball (men's, women's, and coed), basketball (men's and women's), and volleyball (women's and coed). Youth leagues are available in basketball, flag football, soccer, kickball, tennis, volleyball, and track and field; other youth competition includes a Punt, Pass & Kick contest. There is a $20 fee to participate in T-ball and youth basketball; other youth sports leagues are free. Metro Parks can provide information on other youth leagues, such as Little League and Babe Ruth baseball.

HOCKEY

NASHVILLE MEN'S HOCKEY LEAGUE
Centennial Sportsplex
222 25th Avenue N.
(615) 862-8480
www.nashville.org/sportsplex

There are three adult divisions: a beginners' C league, intermediate B league, and A league for advanced players. Since games are structured in multigame segments year-round, registration times are frequent. Call the Sportsplex for the next registration period.

NASHVILLE WOMEN'S ICE HOCKEY
(615) 883-1858

Launched in 2000, the NWIH was formed to promote women's ice hockey and help women develop their skating and playing skills regardless of age or skill level. NWIH has a house league with two to three teams (depending on the number of participants) and a travel team—the Nashville Athenas—that has been to Cincinnati, St. Louis, Indianapolis, and Atlanta. The travel team is chosen about once per quarter. NWIH practices/plays once per weekend at Centennial Sportsplex with the exception of August, during which they take a break. New players get their first two ice times free, including loaner equipment if needed.

RUNNING

NASHVILLE STRIDERS
(615) 870-3330
www.nashvillestriders.com
This is the largest running club in Middle Tennessee. The Striders sponsor a variety of events, from weekly fun runs and fitness walks to the arduous Kroger-to-Kroger run, a 22-miler used as a training run for the Country Music Marathon. The organization counts more than 1,000 members.

i Wilma Rudolph, who grew up in Clarksville, overcame polio to become an Olympic track champion. In the 1960 Olympics, at age 20, she won gold medals for the 100-meter race, the 200-meter race, and the 400-meter relay.

SWIMMING

With the abundance of water in and around Nashville, many people enjoy taking dips at J. Percy Priest and Old Hickory Lakes. Those who prefer pools have plenty of options as well.

Lakes

J. PERCY PRIEST LAKE
Anderson Road Day Use Area
4060 Anderson Road
(615) 361-9805

COOK DAY USE AREA
12231 Old Hickory Boulevard, Hermitage
(615) 889-9551
www.lrn.usace.army.mil/op/jpp/rec

The U.S. Army Corps of Engineers maintains two swimming areas on J. Percy Priest Lake: at Anderson Road and Cook. Both charge a day-use fee of $1 per person or $4 per vehicle. Children 12 and under are admitted free. Annual passes are $25.

NASHVILLE SHORES
4001 Bell Road, Hermitage
(615) 889-7050
www.nashvilleshores.com
Nashville Shores, a water park, features a private white-sand beach on Priest Lake. There's also a lot more for your wet and dry amusement. For one price you can spend a day swimming in the lake or pool, cavorting on various water slides, getting soaked by the Bucket of Fun Waterfall, or cruising the lake in paddleboats or the 100-passenger *Nashville Shoreliner*, and more. Nashville Shores is open from late spring through summer. Admission is $18.95 for adults and $15.95 for children 3 to 12 and for seniors. Season passes are available. For more on Nashville Shores, see our Kidstuff and Attractions chapters.

OLD HICKORY LAKE
No. 5 Power Plant Road, Hendersonville
(resource manager's office)
(615) 822-4846, (615) 847-2395
www.lrn.usace.army.mil/op/old/rec
The U.S. Army Corps of Engineers maintains swimming areas at four beaches on Old Hickory Lake: Lock 3 in Hendersonville, Cedar Creek in Mount Juliet, one in Old Hickory, and one in Laguardo. There is no charge to swim at Lock 3. For the other beaches it costs $1 per person or $4 per carload. Children 12 and under are admitted free. Annual passes, good at similar day-use facilities at any Corps project, are $25.

Pools

The Metro Parks department operates more than a dozen pools, including two pools at Centennial Sportsplex. The outdoor pools are open seasonally—in general, from early June to mid-August—while the indoor pools are open year-round, with the exception of Napier, which is open only during the summer. Hours vary. Wave Country, which is outdoors, and Centennial Sportsplex, which is indoors, have admission fees, but there is no charge for open swimming at any of the other pools. The only charge is for classes, which are generally $40 for 10 sessions, $50 at Sportsplex.

Although lifeguards are on duty at all pools, children younger than 12 should be accompanied by an adult, especially if they are shorter than 4 feet. Most Metro pools offer competitive swim teams during the summer, with competitions culminating in a big meet at Centennial Sportsplex at the end of summer. For specific hours and other information, call the individual pool or the aquatics office, (615) 862-8480, or visit Metro Parks online at www.nashville.gov/parks.

Nashville YMCAs operate a total of 21 pools: 11 outdoor and 10 indoor. See the subsequent YMCAs section of this chapter for more information, or call or drop by the organization's corporate office at 900 Church Street (615-259-9622).

CENTENNIAL SPORTSPLEX
222 25th Avenue N.
(615) 862-8480
www.nashville.org/sportsplex
The Sportsplex's Aquatic/Fitness Center features two pools: one for recreational swimming and the other, which is Olympic size, for lap swimming. The daily rate is $6 for adults and teens and $5 for children 12 and younger and seniors 62 and older (children younger than 12 must be accompanied by an adult guardian). Lessons are available.

CLEVELAND
North Sixth Street and Bayard Street
(615) 880-2253

COLEMAN
Thompson Lane at Nolensville Road
(615) 833-7210

EAST
Woodland Street at South Sixth Street
(615) 254-5903

GLENCLIFF
160 Old Antioch Pike
(615) 862-8470

HADLEY
28th Avenue N. at Albion Street
(615) 321-5623

HARTMAN
2801 Tucker Road
(615) 880-1718

LOOBY
2301 Metro Center Boulevard
(615) 259-1560

NAPIER
73 Fairfield Avenue
(615) 242-9212

PEARL–COHN
904 26th Avenue N.
(615) 862-8471

RICHLAND
46th Avenue N. at Charlotte Pike
(615) 292-4363

ROSE
1000 Edgehill Avenue
(615) 742-3155

WHITES CREEK
7277 Old Hickory Boulevard
(615) 876-4300
Glencliff, Hartman, Napier, Pearl-Cohn, and Whites Creek are indoor pools and offer classes for $40. The big outdoor pools (Cleveland, Hadley, Looby, and Rose) are in parks or by community centers. They are about three times larger, in general, than the smaller playground pools (Coleman, East, and Richland). The larger pools feature locker rooms and have five or six lifeguards on duty, and most have diving areas. Although there are no concession stands, and no food is permitted inside the pool gates, most have picnic tables nearby.

WAVE COUNTRY
2320 Two Rivers Parkway
(615) 885-1052
www.nashville.gov/parks
Wave Country features simulated surf, along with two water slides and one kiddie slide. The water park is open from Memorial Day weekend through Labor Day. Admission is $6 for adults and teens, $5 for youth ages 5 through 12, and free for kids 4 and younger. See our Attractions and Kidstuff chapters for more.

TENNIS

CENTENNIAL SPORTSPLEX
222 25th Avenue N.
(615) 862-8490
www.sportsplextennis.com
The Metro Board of Parks and Recreation has more than 160 tennis courts available free at parks around town. Call for information on courts near you. In addition, Metro Parks's Centennial Sportsplex has 15 outdoor courts and four indoor courts. Outdoor courts are $5 per hour. The indoor court fee is $12 per hour from noon to 4:00 p.m. Monday through Friday, and $15 per hour for all other times. Indoor contract time is available from October through March; you may reserve one court for up to two hours weekly. Call or visit the Web site for details on how and when to sign up for contract time.

YMCA INDOOR TENNIS CENTER
207 Shady Grove Road
(615) 889-8668
Membership in the YMCA makes you a member here, or you can belong to the Tennis Center only. Four indoor courts are available at $12 an hour during the summer, and $15 in winter; three outdoor courts are free to members.

YMCAS

YMCA OF MIDDLE TENNESSEE
900 Church Street
(615) 259-9622 (main office)
www.ymcamidtn.org
The YMCA of Middle Tennessee is a not-for-profit health and human-services organization committed to helping persons grow in spirit, mind, and body. The organization operates 23 facilities in 11 counties. The Y offers its members a wide variety of programs and services, including indoor and outdoor pools, aerobics classes, wellness equipment, athletic fields, and gymnasiums. In addition, the YMCA has programs like youth sports, year-round child care, summer camp, personal fitness, family nights, volunteer opportunities, outreach, and activities for teens and older adults. A comprehensive list of local Ys and the facilities each has to offer is available at the Web site.

YMCA centers are community-based, and each center is designed to meet the needs of its community. For information on how to become a member of the YMCA, call your local Y or the main office. Membership requires a joining fee, which is onetime as long as you keep your membership current, plus a monthly charge. "Citywide" joining fees range from $50 for ages 8 to 18 to $100 for a family and entitle you to use the facilities at any of the Ys. "Center-only" joining fees, which allow admission to one particular facility, are less expensive. Monthly membership dues range from $33 for youth and teens to $83 for a family for the "citywide" option; if you want access to only one center, dues are cheaper. Financial assistance is available through the Y's Open Door program at all centers, in accordance with the Y's philosophy that its programs and services should be available to everyone, regardless of ability to pay. If your annual income is $65,000 or less, you qualify for reduced rates based on your income. The program is very popular.

Following is a listing of the main YMCA centers that are convenient to Nashville-area residents.

BRENTWOOD FAMILY YMCA
8207 Concord Road, Brentwood
(615) 373-9622

CLARKSVILLE AREA YMCA (PROGRAM FACILITY)
260 Hillcrest Drive, Clarksville
(931) 647-2376

COOL SPRINGS YMCA
121 Seaboard Lane, Franklin
(615) 661-4200

DONELSON–HERMITAGE FAMILY YMCA
3001 Lebanon Road
(615) 889-2632

DOWNTOWN YMCA
1000 Church Street
(615) 254-0631

FRANKLIN FAMILY YMCA
501 South Royal Oaks Boulevard, Franklin
(615) 591-0322

GREEN HILLS FAMILY YMCA
4041 Hillsboro Circle
(615) 297-6529

HARDING PLACE FAMILY YMCA
411 Metroplex Drive
(615) 834-1300

INDOOR TENNIS CENTER
207 Shady Grove Road
(615) 889-8668

JOE C. DAVIS YMCA OUTDOOR CENTER
3088 Smith Springs Road, Antioch
(615) 360-2267

MARGARET MADDOX FAMILY YMCA EAST CENTER
2624 Gallatin Road
(615) 228-5525

MARYLAND FARMS FAMILY YMCA
5101 Maryland Way, Brentwood
(615) 373-2900

MAURY COUNTY FAMILY YMCA
1446 Oak Springs Drive, Columbia
(931) 540-8320

NORTHWEST FAMILY YMCA
3700 Ashland City Highway
(615) 242-6559

OAKWOOD COMMONS YMCA
4656 Lebanon Pike, Hermitage
(615) 871-0002

ROBERTSON COUNTY FAMILY YMCA
3332 Tom Austin Highway, Springfield
(615) 382-9622

RUTHERFORD COUNTY FAMILY YMCA
205 North Thompson Lane
Murfreesboro
(615) 895-5995

SUMNER COUNTY FAMILY YMCA
102 Bluegrass Commons Boulevard
Hendersonville
(615) 826-9622

UPTOWN YMCA
424 Church Street, 30th floor
(615) 251-5454

YOUTH DEVELOPMENT CENTER
(outreach programs)
213 McLemore Street
(615) 259-3418

GOLF

It should come as no surprise that Nashville is full of golf courses. First of all, there's the terrain, which varies from flat to gently rolling to downright hilly. That means whatever your playing style, you can find a course with a layout to your liking. Second, consider that this is, after all, a city of business. What better way to clinch a plum contract than with a putter in your hand? Add in the fact that a lot of us around here like sports of any kind. And don't forget the music. Country music and golf go together like country ham and biscuits. Just ask Vince Gill, well-known golf tournament host. Gill is renowned for his vocal and guitar skills, but he's equally passionate about his golf. His annual pro-celebrity tournament, the Vinny, attracts country stars, PGA pros, and other celebrities. Since it began in 1993, the Vinny has raised almost $4 million to benefit the state's high-quality junior golfers' program, becoming one of the nation's top pro-celebrity events in the process.

Gill has also lent his considerable drawing power to other local golf events, including the Ladies Professional Golf Association tournament, which he hosts with his wife, Amy Grant. The popularity of these events serves notice that Nashville is a prime location to watch and play competitive golf. The area's public courses have been ranked among the best in the nation, and most of them are reasonably priced. The seven courses operated by Metro Parks in particular are bargains. Golfers with more discriminating standards can pay more to play on tournament-quality courses like Gaylord Springs and Hermitage.

This chapter covers a selection of area courses that are open to the general public. We'll also look at practice ranges and opportunities for instruction. Distances are measured from the white (men's) tees. Greens fees include riding cart unless otherwise indicated but do not include tax; please note that these prices were in effect in 2006 and are subject to change. Walkers are allowed, generally for a lower fee, unless otherwise indicated. Fore!

METRO PARKS COURSES

Metro Parks maintains seven public golf courses in five parks. They are open year-round, weather permitting, with the exception of the Vinny Links youth course, which is open May through October. From December through February, each course is closed one day a week. During these months, it's a good idea to call first to ensure your course is open. The six year-round courses each have a putting green, snack bar, and pro shop; lessons are available at all but Shelby and Vinny Links. Metro Parks's courses, which range from 9 to 27 holes, charge $6.00 to $12.50 per 9 holes, depending on the course and the day of the week. Riding cart rental is an additional $10 per nine holes. Club rental is $6.50 to $10.00. Those with their own carts pay a trail fee of $7.00 per day.

Annual memberships entitle members to play at any Metro course. Members pay a surcharge of $1.50 to $3.00, depending on the course. Memberships for Davidson County residents are $570, $380 for seniors (62 and retired or 65 and older), and $240 for those 18 and younger. Out-of-county residents pay $765, $570, and $270, respectively.

> **i** It's not unusual to see deer, wild turkeys, and other wildlife at Harpeth Hills Golf Course at Percy Warner Park.

Bear Trace Golf Trail

Serious golfers may want to check out Tennessee's Bear Trace Golf Trail, which features five spectacular and affordable 18-hole courses throughout the state. Each course was designed by the "Golden Bear" himself, golf great Jack Nicklaus. The course closest to Nashville is Tim's Ford, near Winchester, about 90 miles south. Other courses are Cumberland Mountain near Crossville, Harrison Bay near Chattanooga, Chickasaw near Henderson, and Ross Creek Landing near Clifton. For details, call (866) 770-BEAR or visit www.tngolftrail.net.

HARPETH HILLS GOLF COURSE
2424 Old Hickory Boulevard
(615) 862-8493
www.nashvillefairways.com

Harpeth Hills, one of two Metro courses in Percy Warner Park, is a busy course, and you'll generally need to reserve your tee times a week in advance. This scenic, slightly hilly 18-hole course is 6,481 yards and par 72, with bent grass greens and no water. Harpeth Hills is Metro's most expensive course. Greens fees for 18 holes and a cart are $40 on weekends and $38 on weekdays. From December through February, Harpeth Hills closes on Wednesday.

MCCABE GOLF COURSE
46th Street and Murphy Road
(615) 862-8491

McCabe is a fairly level, easy-to-walk course with 27 holes—par 70 and par 36. The par 70 covers 5,847 yards. There's no water, but there are some challenges, notably the 162-yard 15th hole, a par 3 with a trap on each side. This is one of Metro's most popular courses. Greens fees at McCabe are $22 on weekends and $20 on weekdays. Cart rental is $20. McCabe is closed Thursday from December through February.

i Of the seven Metro Parks golf courses, the easiest to walk are McCabe, Percy Warner, and Vinny Links. The most challenging are Harpeth Hills, Ted Rhodes, Shelby, and Two Rivers. Additional details about Metro golf courses are available at www.nashville.gov/parks/golf.htm.

PERCY WARNER GOLF COURSE
Forrest Park Drive
(615) 352-9958

This scenic nine-hole, 2,474-yard course at the Belle Meade Boulevard entrance to Percy Warner Park features traditional, tree-lined fairways and is par 34. There's no water. It costs $11.00 to play nine holes at Percy Warner on weekends and $10.00 on weekdays. If you want to play 18 holes, the prices are double. The course is closed Tuesday from December through February. Percy Warner has no riding carts, but pull carts are available for $2.50.

SHELBY GOLF COURSE
2021 Fatherland Street
(615) 862-8474

Shelby is very hilly—fit for a mountain goat, as one golfer put it. The 18-hole, 5,789-yard, par 72 course has a pond on the 11th hole and creeks running throughout. Greens fees at Shelby are $20 throughout the week and $28 on the weekends. Cart rental is $6 for each nine holes. From December through February, Shelby is closed Wednesday.

TED RHODES GOLF COURSE
1901 Ed Temple Boulevard
(615) 862-8463

There's water everywhere at Rhodes, coming into play on about 14 of the 18 holes. The scenic par 72 course is 6,207 yards. Greens fees for 18 holes at Ted Rhodes are $24 on weekends and $22 on weekdays. Cart rental is $12. This course is closed Monday from December through February.

GOLF

TWO RIVERS GOLF COURSE
3140 McGavock Pike
(615) 889-2675

Two Rivers is marked by rolling hills, with one water hole on both the front and the back nines. It's 18 holes, 6,230 yards, and par 72. Two Rivers's greens fees for 18 holes are $24 on weekends and $22 on weekdays. Cart rental is $12 per person. The course is closed on Monday from December through February.

VINNY LINKS
2009 Sevier Street
(615) 880-1720

This nine-hole, 1,314-yard, par 29 course along the Cumberland River opened in May 2001 at the site of the former Riverview Golf Course. It is part of the First Tee program, which aims to promote golf and make the sport affordable for young people. The course was based on a Donald Ross design. There is one par 4 hole; the rest are par 3s. While this walking-only course is geared toward youth, adults can play, too. Fees are $6 for adults and $3 for those age 18 and younger. It's open from April through October.

OTHER PUBLIC COURSES

COUNTRY HILLS GOLF COURSE
1501 Saundersville Road, Hendersonville
(615) 824-1100
www.countryhillsgolfcourse.com

Country Hills is a short course, at 5,862 yards, but it's a hilly, wooded, and tough par 70, so it plays long. The biggest challenge is the number 3 hole, a 363-yard par 4 dogleg left with water. Holes 4 and 5 feature water. Greens fees are $32 weekdays and $40 weekends, with varying morning and afternoon specials offered. The nine-hole rate is $20 all day. Country Hills has a pro shop, driving range, putting green, and snack bar. Lessons are available from pro James Pashel and assistant pro Rusty Pence.

FORREST CROSSING GOLF CLUB
750 Riverview Drive, Franklin
(615) 794-9400
www.americangolf.com

During the Civil War, Confederate general Nathan Bedford Forrest and his men crossed the picturesque Harpeth River at a spot between where holes number 3 and number 4 are today. The name of this rolling course commemorates the event. Water comes into play on 15 of the 18 holes on this 6,968-yard, par 72 course. Forrest Crossing, which offers corporate events and tournament packages, also has a putting facility, driving range, and full-service snack bar. Greens fees are $47 weekdays and $57 Friday, Saturday, and Sunday. Walking is allowed after 2:00 p.m.

GAYLORD SPRINGS GOLF LINKS
18 Springhouse Lane
(615) 458-1730
www.gaylordsprings.com

Gaylord Springs, a links-style course designed by Larry Nelson, lines the Cumberland River. The course, highlighted by large mounds and a bunch of water, has five sets of tees. The "everyday" tees at this course are blue instead of white, with a total distance of 6,165 yards. A 19th-century springhouse sits at the back of the green on the signature hole, the 338-yard number 4. Greens fees range from $70 to $110 for 18 holes. Walking is not permitted. The 43,000-square-foot clubhouse is a complete facility with rooms for meetings and banquets, a grill room, and complete locker-room facilities for men and women. The pro shop offers high-quality rental clubs and golf shoes as well as brand-name balls for the double-sided driving range. PGA pros on staff are available for lessons.

GREYSTONE GOLF CLUB
2555 U.S. Highway 70 E., Dickson
(615) 446-0044
www.greystonegc.com

Since opening in 1998, this scenic, par 72, 6,002-yard course has become a favorite. It was voted among the 100 best values in the United States by Maximum Golf and has hosted several high-profile events, including the Men's and Women's Tennessee State Opens and the 2000 and 2002 PGA Tour's first-round qualifiers. Designed by Mark McCumber, the course is marked by rolling hills and offers several challenging holes. The par 3 16th hole is especially scenic. The kidney-shaped green is guarded by a creek in front and a stone wall. Water comes into play at seven holes. In addition to the snack bar, pro shop, and driving range, the course has the King's Court restaurant, which on Sunday is open to the public as well as to golfers. Fees are $36 Monday through Friday and $50 on weekends.

i Gaylord Springs is noted for its golf, especially during the Senior Classic. Not as many people seem to realize it also has a great practice putting green.

HERMITAGE GOLF COURSE
3939 Old Hickory Boulevard,
Old Hickory
(615) 847-4001
www.hermitagegolf.com

The Hermitage Golf Course has two 18-hole courses—the General's Retreat and the newer President's Reserve. The General's Retreat is an 18-hole, par 72 course. It measures 6,011 yards. It's mostly a flat, open course with some elevated greens. The bent grass greens are large and undulating. Fairways are Bermuda grass in summer and rye the rest of the year. Six lakes come into play on the course, which lies along the Cumberland River. Hermitage, which is noted for its driving range and putting green, also has a snack bar, pro shop, and PGA instructors. It specializes in golf outings. Fees are $49 Monday through Thursday, $59 Friday through Sunday and holidays. You can reserve your tee time up to five days in advance by phone or up to 90 days in advance at the Web site.

The President's Reserve, opened in the spring of 2000, shares the same pro shop and other facilities. President's Reserve, also a par 72, features six sets of tees, with a distance of about 6,000 yards from the white ones. The course is built around a huge natural-wetland area with a slough running down its middle. Six holes are on the Cumberland River. Fees for President's Reserve are $69 Monday through Thursday and $71 Friday through Sunday. If you play a lot, you may want to ask about the frequent player program.

i The Hermitage Golf Course has received *Golf Digest* magazine's four-star rating and was named one of the "100 Best Bargain Golf Courses in the United States" by *Maximum Golf* and "One of America's 100 Best Golf Courses for $100 or Less" by *Travel + Leisure Golf.*

HUNTER'S POINT GOLF COURSE
1500 Hunters Point Pike, Lebanon
(615) 444-7521
www.hunterspointgolf.com

Hunter's Point, a 6,212-yard, par 72 course, is flat, with water coming into play on about one-third of the 18 holes. Number 15, a 446-yard par 4, challenges you with water to the left and right of the green and trees to the left of the fairway. Greens fees are $13.50 on weekdays and $20.50 on weekends. Carts are $12 per person. Hunter's Point has a pro shop, putting green, driving range, and a snack bar.

THE LEGACY GOLF COURSE
100 Raymond Floyd Drive, Springfield
(615) 384-4653
www.golfthelegacy.com

This par 72 course, designed by PGA veteran Raymond Floyd, opened on Memorial Day 1996. But it looks a lot older. That's because Floyd designed the 6,755-yard Legacy—which is marked by undulating greens and water on four of the 18 holes—around a collection of mature trees. Fees are $32 weekdays, $43 weekends. The Legacy has a driving range, a snack bar, and a pro shop, and lessons are available.

LONG HOLLOW GOLF COURSE
1080 Long Hollow Pike, Gallatin
(615) 451-3120
Long Hollow, a 5,622-yard, par 70 course, is on rolling land, with water a factor on seven of its 18 holes. Watch out for number 10, a 420-yard par 4—there's water out of bounds to the right on the second shot and trees to the left. Greens fees are $17 weekdays without cart, $34 with cart; and $19 on weekends without cart, $38 with cart. Long Hollow has a snack bar, pro shop, and driving range and offers lessons.

MONTGOMERY BELL STATE PARK GOLF COURSE
1020 Jackson Hill Road, Burns
(615) 797-2578
www.tnstateparks.com
This course, part of Montgomery Bell State Park, is 5,927 yards and par 71. It's hilly and features water on three holes. Reserve your tee times up to six days in advance. Fees for 18 holes are $36 with cart weekdays, $39 with cart weekends. The course has a pro shop, practice green, driving range, and snack bar.

NASHBORO GOLF CLUB
1101 Nashboro Boulevard
(615) 367-2311
www.nashborogolf.com
Nashboro Golf Club, five minutes south of the airport off Murfreesboro Road, is set on rolling hills and beautifully lined with trees. Half of the 18-hole course runs through the Nashboro Village housing development, and water comes into play on six holes. The course covers 6,384 yards and is par 72.

Nashboro has PGA golf pros on staff and offers a driving range, practice putting green, pro shop, and large snack bar with satellite television. Tournament and league packages are available. Fees are $37.00 Monday through Thursday and $43.50 on weekends. Area residents with a Tennessee driver's license can join the Links Club

and save $3.00 on the greens fees for an 18-hole round. Walkers are permitted Monday through Thursday only.

PINE CREEK GOLF COURSE
1835 Logue Road, Mount Juliet
(615) 449-7272
www.pinecreek.net
Smaller, undulating greens that can be hard to reach are characteristic of this 6,249-yard, par 72 course, which was built on a farm and has remained largely unaltered. Pine Creek's rolling layout is marked with water and pine trees, both of which come into play on many of the 18 holes. A lake marks the 136-yard, par 3 number 6 hole. Fees are $40 Monday through Friday and $50 Saturday and Sunday. You can schedule tee times up to seven days in advance.

RIVERSIDE GOLF COURSE
640 Old Hickory Boulevard, Old Hickory
(615) 847-5074
www.riversidegolfcourse.net/
Riverside Golf Course on the Cumberland River features a 9-hole and an 18-hole course. The 1,558-yard, nine-hole executive course is mostly par 3s, with a couple of par 4s. It's a good choice for beginners and good practice for your irons. The 18-hole par 70 course is 5,465 yards. It's flat, and water comes into play on about half the holes. Riverside has a lighted driving range, a 150-yard grass tee, PGA instructors, a snack bar, and pro shop. Fees for the 18-hole course are $32 weekdays and $38 weekends and holidays. Walking fees for the nine-hole course are $11; a cart is $16.

i Metro's busiest golf courses are Harpeth Hills and McCabe. About 85,000 9-hole rounds are played at Harpeth Hills per year, while McCabe, which has 27 holes, registers about 110,000 9-hole rounds annually.

SMYRNA MUNICIPAL GOLF COURSE
101 Sam Ridley Parkway, Smyrna
(615) 459-2666
www.townofsmyrna.org/golf

This 6,028-yard, par 72 course is fairly flat with just a few water hazards. Fees are $34, $37 weekends. Smyrna Municipal has a snack bar and pro shop. Smyrna Municipal Golf Course also has a nine-hole executive course. The 1,507-yard, par 29 course is part of the nationwide First Tee junior golf program. Fees on the nine-hole executive course are $15 with cart; $13 with a cart for seniors 55 and older and juniors 17 and under.

WINDTREE GOLF COURSE
810 Nonaville Road, Mount Juliet
(615) 754-4653
www.windtreegolf.com
The front nine is relatively flat, but the back nine is hilly at Windtree, which features Bermuda grass fairways, bent grass greens, and water on several holes along the 6,069-yard, par 72 course. The signature hole is the scenic number 16, a 420-yard, par 4 downhill shot from the highest point on the course; don't let the view distract you. Fees are $46 Monday through Friday and $50 weekends; regular players will find it worthwhile to join the free Links Club, which reduces fees by $3. Seniors with a Links Club card can play for $22 from Monday through Friday. Walkers are allowed during the week and after 2:00 p.m. on weekends. Windtree has a pro shop, driving range, and practice putting green. A pro is available for lessons.

GOLF INSTRUCTION

ART QUICK GOLF ACADEMY
501 Metroplex Drive
(615) 834-8121
Art Quick, a PGA professional who still plays the Senior Tour, has been teaching since 1950. But there's nothing old-fashioned about his approach, which uses computerized TV simulators much like those used in baseball and football training. He says it's "one of the best setups in the nation." Rates are $35 for half an hour or $180 for six lessons. The academy is closed Friday and Sunday.

THROUGH THE GREEN
1725 New Hope Road, Joelton
(615) 746-0400
www.ttggolf.com
Through the Green, an indoor-outdoor golf teaching center that's geared especially toward women and children, offers complete video analysis of your golf game. Women can benefit from accelerated programs taught by PGA and LPGA professionals. The course has an 18-hole championship layout. A short-game practice area simulates course situations. Prices are $70 for a 45-minute session.

PRACTICE RANGES

FAMILY GOLF CENTER AT HICKORY HOLLOW DRIVING RANGE
5204 Blue Hole Road
(615) 781-8388
This year-round driving range, located at the corner of Bell and Blue Hole Roads, offers both grass tees and mats, as well as a covered area, so you can stay dry while you practice your swing in the rain. There are about 60 hitting stations. The adjacent family fun center, which is open March through November, has minigolf, go-karts, and batting cages. (See our Kidstuff chapter for more on that.)

HARPETH VALLEY GOLF CENTER
7629 Old Harding Pike
(615) 646-8858
Harpeth Valley's large, lighted grass range features grass tees and sand. There's also a two-acre short-game practice area with bunkers, a practice putting green, and a nine-hole par 3 course. Five resident teaching pros can give you tips.

HERMITAGE GOLF LEARNING CENTER
4000 Andrew Jackson Parkway
(615) 883-5200
Hermitage is noted for its driving range and its 10,000-square-foot putting green. Lessons are available.

SPECTATOR SPORTS

Music City? Bah, humbug—as anyone who lives here can tell you, sports rule this town. When the Tennessee Titans made it all the way to Super Bowl XXXIV in January 2000, only to lose in the final seconds 23–16, it was a thrilling, albeit heartbreaking, moment for the entire city. The Tennessee Titans have been enthusiastically embraced by Nashville since moving here from Houston in 1997; although the post-2000 seasons haven't displayed quite the same winning performance, Titans fans have maintained their reputation as the best (and *loudest*) in the league. Win or lose, we love our team.

It's not just football that we love. The NHL's Nashville Predators took several years to make it to the Stanley Cup playoffs, but their fans are as loud and devoted as they come. One particularly avid group, called the Rafter Rats of Cell Block 303 because they sit together in Section 303 at the top of the Gaylord Entertainment Center, has been known to get the entire arena chanting "you suck!" at the opposition's goalie. National sports media have dubbed Nashville hockey fans the league's loudest and most loyal. Coincidence? We think not.

There's something for everyone here. During the summer you'll find devoted followers of the city's AAA baseball team, the Nashville Sounds, as well as our soccer team, the Metros. The opening of the Nashville Superspeedway in Wilson County has delighted the legion of NASCAR fans, who travel by the thousands to the Busch Series Grand Nationals in April. And college sports? Don't get us started—you haven't seen Nashville until you've been here when Alabama's Crimson Tide rolls into town—and usually rolls over rival the Vanderbilt Commodores. Vanderbilt's men's and women's basketball programs are leaders in the SEC, however, which provides an opportunity for a little payback.

Nashville is home to numerous colleges and universities that offer plenty of sports action. We'll highlight some of the most popular programs in this chapter. The two schools with the biggest fan followings here are the UT-Knoxville Volunteers and the University of Kentucky Wildcats. Both universities are three hours away, but they have thousands of alumni living in Nashville. Banners and flags decked in the Vols' orange and white and Kentucky's blue and white decorate the entire town when either team is playing—whether the game is in Nashville or not.

Since 1998 Nashville has had its own collegiate football bowl, the Gaylord Hotels Music City Bowl. The first game, in December 1998, drew a sold-out crowd of 41,600 to Vanderbilt stadium, where Virginia Tech defeated Alabama. The next year the bowl moved to the new 67,000-seat stadium. Nashville is also home to the first National Women's Football Association team—the Nashville Dream.

While we're still on the subject of football, we'll also mention the Nashville Kats, our entry in the Arena Football League. This is an altogether different breed of the sport—a high-scoring, crowd-pleasing, rock 'n' roll indoor hybrid. The Kats, who played their home games at Gaylord Entertainment Center, moved to Atlanta in 2001. That same year, Bud Adams, the Titans's controversial owner, was approved for an AFL expansion franchise. Adams resurrected the Kats. A new version of the Kats took the field at Gaylord Entertainment Center in 2005.

Tickets for many sporting events are available through Ticketmaster (615-255-9600). Be sure to see our Golf and Recreation chapters for information on other sporting activities.

AUTO RACING

HIGHLAND RIM SPEEDWAY
6801 Kelly Willis Road, Ridgetop
(615) 643-8725
www.highlandrim.com

Highland Rim Speedway, a 0.25-mile, high-banked asphalt oval, features stock car racing every Saturday night from March through October as well as special events throughout the year. Weekly races are held in nine divisions: Late Models, Sportsman, Super Stocks, Pro Trucks, Pro 4 Modifieds, Pure Stocks, Challengers (four-cylinder front-wheel-drive cars), Mini Modifieds, and Rim Runners (a beginners division). Every other week, there's an Open Wheels division.

Before achieving their current NASCAR stardom, drivers such as Darrell Waltrip, Bobby Hamilton, Donnie and Bobby Allison, and Red Farmer raced at Highland Rim. Seating is about 5,000, including VIP skyboxes, and the atmosphere is family-friendly, with no alcohol. The small track makes for some truly exciting races. Races are on Saturday night; admission is $10 for general admission and $5 for children 6 to 12. Tickets for special events are generally $12 and sometimes $15.

Highland Rim Speedway is 20 miles north of Nashville; just take Interstate 65 north to exit 104, then take Highway 257 west for 2 miles. Parking is free.

i In 1990 Darrell Waltrip, a resident of Franklin, became the first NASCAR driver to top the $10-million career-winnings mark.

MUSIC CITY MOTORPLEX
Tennessee State Fairgrounds
25 Smith Avenue
(615) 726-1818
www.musiccitymotorplex.com

The fairgrounds' speedway has gotten a new lease on life, thanks to new management that came on board in October 2003 and made a number of changes, including the return of the NASCAR Dodge Weekly Series on Saturday and

significantly increasing the number of scheduled events. Admission price for Friday Night Thunder is $10 for adults and $3 for children 6 to 11. Children 5 and under are admitted free. The cost for Sunday Family Fun is $5 per adult and $2 for children 6 to 11. Preferred seating, VIP seating, and season passes are available. The grandstand seats just over 15,000—about 8,000 in the covered upper area and the rest in the uncovered lower area. Nashville racing fans fondly recall the Nashville Speedway's glory days, when such legends and legends-to-be as Dale Earnhardt, Darrell Waltrip, Jim Weatherly, Lee and Richard Petty, Fireball Roberts, Curtis Turner, Junior Johnson, Cale Yarborough, and Bobby Allison could be found speeding around the track. But as other tracks around the country expanded, Nashville gradually became too small to compete for the big events. Meanwhile, in 2001 the $125-million Nashville Superspeedway in Wilson County (see subsequent listing) opened, taking this track's major events with it.

MUSIC CITY RACEWAY
3302 Ivey Point Road, Goodlettsville
(615) 876-0981 (information)
www.musiccityraceway.com

Music City Raceway offers National Hot Rod Association drag racing on Tuesday, Friday, and Saturday nights from February to November. Admission is generally $5 Tuesday night, $10 Friday and Saturday nights. Children 12 and under are admitted free. For directions to the track, call (615) 264-0375 or visit the Web site.

NASHVILLE SUPERSPEEDWAY
4847-F McCrary Road, Lebanon
(866) RACE-TIX
www.nashvillesuperspeedway.com

Located amid rolling hills and farmland, Nashville Superspeedway has certainly earned its moniker. Built by Dover Motorsports for a hefty $125 million, the Superspeedway opened in 2001. The speedway is enormous, with a main grandstand seating 25,000 and additional seating boosting capacity to 150,000. The infield alone covers more than 80 acres. The track is 1.3 miles and features

14-degree banking in the turns. One of only three concrete tracks on the NASCAR circuit, this track required a special concrete paving machine to be custom-built for its laying. The schedule features two NASCAR Nextel Cup Series races: the Pepsi 300 in April and the Federated Auto Parts 300 in June. Indy Racing League Series events occur in July, and NASCAR Craftsmen Trucks series races are run in August. Races are an all-day event here, with a slate of prerace activities such as an "Expo Row," featuring vendors hawking racing-themed items, and a Kids Zone, where the little ones can enjoy games and refreshments. Some races open or close with concerts; country artists John Michael Montgomery and Darryl Worley have both performed at the speedway.

Parking lots usually open at 9:30 in the morning, and the gates open at noon. Prerace activities begin around 2:00 p.m. Parking is available on-site. If you're bringing an RV, be sure to call ahead to reserve a spot in the RV lot. A one-day ticket runs around $45 to $125. Season tickets are available for $199 to $429.

BASEBALL

NASHVILLE SOUNDS
Herschel Greer Stadium
534 Chestnut Street
(615) 242-4371
www.nashvillesounds.com

The Nashville Sounds, a AAA affiliate of the Pittsburgh Pirates, enjoyed a resurgence in popularity in 2003—their 26th season. The team got off to a 14–1 start, an amazing accomplishment in minor league baseball. The Sounds went on to enjoy their best record in 10 years and advanced to the Pacific Coast League championship series. Talk about building a new baseball stadium helped generate interest in the team.

The team, originally a AA affiliate of the Cincinnati Reds when it came to town in 1978, had a memorable second season, setting a minor-league season attendance record and winning the Southern League championship. Nashville was a AA affiliate of the New York Yankees from 1980 to 1984, then moved to AAA and affiliated with the Detroit Tigers in 1985. From 1987 to 1992 the Sounds were the Cincinnati Reds's AAA farm team, and they joined the White Sox organization in 1993 before affiliating with the Pirates in 1998. The Sounds have won two league championships—in 1979 and 1982—and were runners-up in 1981, 1993, and 1994. In 1999 they finished with an 80–60 record, fourth best in the league.

Promotional events and giveaways include regular visits by the Famous Chicken and other crowd-pleasers. Unique promotional days include "Bark in the Park," in which fans can bring the family dog and take part in a puppy parade and other fun and games. The team offers promotions and programs for about any type of group imaginable. One of the most popular is Faith Nights, geared toward church groups. Launched in 2002, these events include a contemporary Christian concert performance and have proven to be a big hit. Another success story is the Sounds Kids Club, which for $10 entitles members to free admission to 10 Kids Club Games, an autograph session with team mascot Ozzie, discounts on Sounds merchandise, and other perks.

The nature of a "farm team" can make being a fan both rewarding and frustrating. It's rewarding because you have the opportunity to watch the stars of tomorrow; frustrating because, when they start becoming stars, they are generally shipped up to the major leagues. Nashville Sounds fans have had the opportunity to enjoy the early careers of such stars as Steve Balboni, Don Mattingly, Willie McGee, Otis Nixon, Buck Showalter, Hal Morris, Chris Sabo, and Doug Drabek, who as a Pittsburgh Pirate was the National League's 1990 recipient of the Cy Young Award.

The Sounds play about 72 home games from April through Labor Day. Game times vary; gates open two hours before starting time. Lower-level seats are $12, upper-level seats are $10, and general admission is $8. Prices for children 12 and younger and senior citizens are $1 less. Various ticket plans offer a substantial savings if you want to attend more than one game. The Sounds also have a Family Fun Pack, which combines admission, hot dogs, soft drinks, and a coupon, all for $56 for a family of four. You can usually park in the stadium lot or at the nearby Cumberland Science Museum.

> **i** Sportswriter Grantland Rice, who penned the phrase "The One Great Scorer . . . writes not that you won or lost, but how you played the game," was born in Murfreesboro in 1880.

BASKETBALL

MIDDLE TENNESSEE STATE UNIVERSITY
MURPHY ATHLETIC CENTER
Monte Hale Arena
Tennessee Boulevard, Murfreesboro
(615) 898-2103,
(888) YES-MTSU (tickets)
www.goblueraiders.com

MTSU's Blue Raiders men's and women's teams are members of the Sun Belt Conference. The 1999–2000 season was their last in the Ohio Valley Conference. Men's basketball coach Kermit Davis was named the Sun Belt Coach of the Year in 2008 by collegeinsider.com after leading the Blue Raiders to a school record for conference wins and taking his team to a league tournament title. The Blue Raiders won 11 of their last 14 games in 2008 and captured 14 wins against Sun Belt Conference teams—the most league wins ever for a Middle Tennessee team in a single season. In 2007 the Lady Raiders and head coach Rick Insell won their fourth straight Sun Belt Tournament title. In 2007, for the first time in school history, the Lady Raiders ranked in the Associated Press and ESPN/USA Today polls.

> **i** In 1957 Tennessee A&I State (now Tennessee State) University in Nashville became the first historically black college to win a national basketball title. In that year the Tigers won the National Association of Intercollegiate Athletics championship.

TENNESSEE STATE UNIVERSITY HOWARD
GENTRY COMPLEX
3500 John Merritt Boulevard
(615) 963-5841 (tickets)
www.tsutigers.com

Tennessee State University has a rich athletics history. The Tiger men's basketball team won three NAIA national championships (1956–57, 1957–58, 1958–59), won the College Division National Championship in 1958, and won four Black College National Championships (1948–49, 1949–50, 1952–53, and 1953–54). The TSU Tigers have played in the Ohio Valley Conference since 1988. In 2008, the Tigers advanced to the Ohio Valley Conference semifinals for the first time in 10 years. Tennessee State's 15 wins in 2008 were the most for the Tigers since the 1995–96 season when TSU finished with a 15–13 record. The women's basketball team began play in 1977–78. At this writing, the Lady Tigers had won two OVC championships and made two appearances in the NCAA tournament. The Tigers and Lady Tigers play their home games in the 10,500-seat Howard Gentry Center, the largest facility in the OVC. Single-game tickets are $10 for men's and women's. Season tickets are about $65. Parking passes are $30.

VANDERBILT UNIVERSITY
2601 Jess Neely Drive
(615) 322-GOLD,
(877) 44-VANDY (tickets)
www.vucommodores.com,
www.commodoregameday.com (tickets)

Vanderbilt University's basketball program is the showcase of the school's athletic department. For the men's team, the 2007–2008 season was the ninth under Coach Kevin Stallings, who came from Illinois State University. The men finished their 2008 season 26–8. The Commodores are always a formidable opponent at Memorial Gym, the SEC's oldest arena. The newly renovated gym has an unusual design—benches are behind the goals instead of on the sidelines, and the bleachers start below the level of the floor—which seems to have a disconcerting effect on many visiting teams. The women's team has blossomed under sixth-year coach Melanie Balcomb, formerly with Xavier University. The Commodore women finished in 2008 with a 25–9 record. Generally, for men's and women's games, single-game tickets are available in mid-September. Various season ticket packages are available in the three-tier gymnasium. Parking is available in two garages within walking distance of Memorial Gym and at lots on campus (be sure not to park in the lots that are permit only). Many people park on the street in the residential neighborhood surrounding Vanderbilt.

i Memorial Gym at Vanderbilt University was dedicated in 1952 as a memorial to all Vanderbilt men and women who served in World War II. It was built by late master architect Edwin Keeble.

FOOTBALL

MIDDLE TENNESSEE STATE UNIVERSITY
Floyd Stadium/Jones Field
Greenland Drive, Murfreesboro
(615) 898-2103 (season tickets)
www.goblueraiders.com
Coach Rick Stockstill has settled into his post. In 1999 the Blue Raiders moved from the NCAA Division I-AA to the top Division I-A. The school's other athletic programs have been in Division I-A since 1952. The MTSU football team also left the Ohio Valley Conference and entered the Sun Belt Conference with the 2001 season. In its first season MTSU went on to an 8–3 overall record and the Sun Belt Conference co-championship. In 2007, Middle Tennessee ended the season 5–7 overall and 4–3 in Sun Belt Conference play. Season football tickets range from $60 to $95 for five home games. Individual game tickets are $10.

TENNESSEE STATE UNIVERSITY
Home games at the Coliseum
1 Titans Way
(615) 963-5907 (tickets)
www.tsutigers.com

Tennessee State University's football team competes as an NCAA Division I-AA team and as a member of the Ohio Valley Conference. TSU football has a proud legacy as one of the nation's great historically African-American football programs, compiling an overall 232–65–11 record in their heyday under coach "Big" John Merritt. But a few years after Merritt's death in 1983, things got tough for the program. Under head coach James Webster, the Tigers finished their 2007 season with a 5–6 overall record and 4–3 in the Ohio Valley Conference. The Tigers are co-champions of the OVC's Sgt. Alvin York Challenge for 2007, finishing tied with Austin Peay with a 2–1 record among Tennessee's OVC football schools. TSU will hold the cup since they beat Austin Peay in head-to-head competition. About 100 TSU football players have been drafted by the NFL, including Ed "Too Tall" Jones, Richard Dent, Joe Gilliam Jr., Eldridge Dickey, Larry Kinnebrew, Claude Humphrey, and Jim Marsalis. Season tickets were $70 for five home games in 2008. Individual game tickets are $20. Parking passes are an additional $30.

TENNESSEE TITANS
The Coliseum
1 Titans Way
(615) 565-4300,
(615) 565-4200 (ticket office)

Baptist Sports Park
460 Great Circle Road
(615) 565-4000
www.titansonline.com
Titans quarterback Steve McNair had a career year in 2003–2004. McNair was named the NFL's Most Valuable Player, an honor he shared with Indianapolis Colts QB Peyton Manning. It marked only the third tie since the Associated Press started the MVP award in 1957. Additionally, McNair was the first black quarterback to be named MVP. He led the Titans to a 10–4 season and the team's fourth playoff appearance in five years. The Titans ended the 2003–2004 season with a divisional playoff loss to the New England Patriots (who went on to win the Super Bowl that year). Nashville is still buzzing about the phenomenal 1999–2000

season in which the Titans won 16 of 20 games, concluding with a thrilling 23–16 Super Bowl loss to the St. Louis Rams. While the Titans's next few seasons weren't quite as winning, Nashville has wholeheartedly embraced its team and coach Jeff Fisher.

The team, which relocated to Tennessee from Houston in 1997, spent its first season in a temporary home at Memphis's Liberty Bowl. For the 1998–1999 season, the team, still known as the Oilers, played its home games at Vanderbilt Stadium in Nashville; while repeating the previous year's overall record of 8–8, there was improvement with a club-record 7–1 mark against AFL season division opponents. But everything really clicked in fall 1999 with the new name, new look, and $292-million, 67,000-seat, open-air stadium. Then a spate of injuries and other calamities befell the Titans in the subsequent 2001 and 2002 seasons, and dreams of a Super Bowl rematch quickly faded. Tennessee ended its 2007–2008 season with an overall record of 10–7. Quarterback Vince Young entered the game as the youngest quarterback to ever start a playoff game in franchise history at 24 years and 233 days.

Still, Titans fans are loyal, and game tickets remain some of the hardest to come by in Nashville.

For the 2008–2009 season, one-day tickets cost $35 to $70, but be advised: Individual tickets typically sell out for the season the same day they are put on sale, which is usually a Saturday in July. The team makes available about 3,000 tickets per game for individual purchase. Individual tickets are sold through Ticketmaster or at the Titans ticket office, located on the east side of the Coliseum. All season tickets have been sold out for years, and there is already a waiting list of more

i Catherine Masters, a Nashville entrepreneur, founded the National Women's Football Association, the world's largest league for full-contact women's football. From two teams the first season in 2002, the Nashville Dreams and the Alabama Renegades, the league has grown to 30 teams.

i Tennessee Titans fans who want to attend away games should contact the Titans' official fan travel company at (800) 363-TRIP for information about packages that include game tickets, or contact the opposing team for ticket availability. Only a limited number of seats are available for away games, and tickets for those games are not available through the team's ticket office.

than 7,500. You can obtain a form to get on the waiting list by visiting the Web site or calling the ticket office. Parking at the stadium is by permit only. If you don't have a permit, don't even try to park near the stadium—traffic gridlock is a hallmark of Titans games. Shuttles operate from remote lots located around the city; MTA also operates shuttles to and from the stadium on game day.

VANDERBILT UNIVERSITY
2601 Jess Neely Drive
(615) 322-GOLD (tickets)
www.vucommodores.com

Vanderbilt University's reputation for academic excellence unfortunately hasn't translated recently to winning performance by its football team. The Commodores football team dates from 1890. The early years of VU football featured some of the most powerful teams in the country under College Hall of Fame coach Dan McGugin. McGugin's teams at Vanderbilt dominated Southern football until the 1930s. Vanderbilt has been to three bowl games in its history, defeating Auburn 25–13 in the 1955 Gator Bowl, losing to Texas Tech in the 1974 Peach Bowl, and falling to Air Force in the 1982 Hall of Fame Bowl. Although the team hasn't had a lot of success in recent years, the university does have 34 all-Americans in football and several alumni who went on to play in the NFL.

Head coach Bobby Johnson came on board in 2002. Johnson joined Vandy from Furman University, where in 2001–2002 he guided that team to the NCAA I-AA championships. He replaced

Woody Widenhofer, who resigned as head coach at the end of the 2001–2002 football season. In five years at Vandy, Widenhofer had an overall record of 15–37. The 2007–2008 season had a 5–7 record. In 2007 Vanderbilt upset #6-ranked South Carolina 17–6, beating a top-10 team for the first time in 33 years. It was the highest-ranked team Vanderbilt had beaten since defeating #6 LSU in 1937.

Most home games are held at 41,448-seat Dudley Field, located on Natchez Trace near West End Avenue, where the team has played since 1922. Occasionally, though, a really hot match—such as Commodores–UT Vols games—will be waged at the Titans's stadium downtown. Tickets can be purchased online or at the Vandy ticket office on Jess Neely Drive, off Natchez Trace. Single-game tickets are usually around $25. A "Family Zone" package offers season tickets for two adults and two youth (ages 17 and under) for $200, but the tickets are good only in the south end zone.

HOCKEY

Nashville's relationship with professional hockey dates from the Dixie Flyers, a minor-league team that was here from 1962 to 1971. The Nashville Knights of the East Coast Hockey League were here from 1989 to 1996, and the Nashville Night-hawks of the Central Hockey League lasted just one season, disappearing in 1996. A second Central Hockey League team was also short-lived. But now Nashville is truly in the big leagues with the 1998 arrival of the Predators, who play in the National Hockey League.

NASHVILLE PREDATORS
Gaylord Entertainment Center
501 Broadway
(615) 770-PUCK (ticket information)
www.nashvillepredators.com
The Predators began play in the 1998–1999 season after a two-year pursuit of an NHL expansion franchise by Nashville officials and private investors bore fruit in June 1997. Nashville, the NHL's 27th franchise, is part of the Central Division of

the Western Conference, with the Chicago Black Hawks, Detroit Red Wings, St. Louis Blues, and Columbus Blue Jackets. The Predators play their home games at Gaylord Entertainment Center. Barry Trotz, the head coach, came to Nashville after several years with the Portland (Maine) Pirates of the American Hockey League. Craig Leipold is majority owner of the Predators.

The Predators really came into their own in 2003–2004—the team's sixth season and its most exciting up to that point. They made it to the first round of playoffs for the first time. By 2008, the Predators had compiled one of the best records in the NHL over the past four seasons, averaging 99.5 points per season. Trotz has coached all 738 regular season games in the Predators' 10 years. He has made the club one of just seven teams to make the NHL Stanley Cup Playoffs each season from 2003 through 2007, guiding Nashville to franchise records in wins (51), road wins (23), points (110), and goals (272) in 2007. Trotz earned a spot as an assistant coach with the Western Conference at the 2007 NHL All-Star Game. The Predators's season runs from early October to early April. Single-game tickets range from $15 to $100; season tickets are offered in various packages; a full 43-game season ranges from $520 to $4,100.

RUNNING

COUNTRY MUSIC MARATHON AND 1/2 MARATHON
Elite Racing
220 Great Circle Road, Suite 134
(615) 742-1660, (800) 311-1255
www.cmmarathon.com
Inaugurated in 2000, the Country Music Marathon is a certified course and qualifying race for the Boston Marathon. The marathon starts at Centennial Park and ends at the Titans's stadium; along the course, roads are shut down, and thousands of Nashvillians line the streets to cheer the runners on, hand out water and fruit, and generally watch the spectacle. Concert stages also line the course, and bands perform rock and country music for the duration of the race. While

the event draws elite international runners, it's open to anyone, and we get some rather offbeat entries: A group known as "the Dollys" have run in blond bouffant wigs, sequined minidresses stuffed with balloons, and cardboard cowboy boot cutouts above their running shoes. Another racer strummed a guitar the entire 26.2 miles. The race also draws its share of local notables: Tennessee's U.S. Senator Bill Frist and Titans coach Jeff Fisher ran in recent years. The course is rather rigorous, though, with plenty of hills. Held in April, the race is subject to unpredictable weather, seasonably cool one year and broiling hot the next. Prize money is available to Davidson County runners. At the Ninth Annual Country Music Marathon in April 2008, 22,500 runners and walkers participated. Steve Cropper and Friends performed for the group that evening.

NASHVILLE STRIDERS
P.O. Box 917, Madison 37116
(615) 870-3330
www.nashvillestriders.com
Middle Tennessee's largest running club—with some 1,000 members—sponsors such events as weekly fun runs and fitness walks, road races, and track events. Striders track events are held at local university tracks, such as David Lipscomb University and MTSU. Through the Striders you can also volunteer to work race events such as the Country Music Marathon. The nonprofit group's Web site is a great resource, providing a calendar of upcoming race events and online registration forms. When the race is over, they'll post the results there, too.

SOCCER

NASHVILLE METROS
Ezell Park, 5135 Harding Place
(615) 832-5678
www.nashvillemetrossoccer.com
Begun in 1991, the Nashville Metros is the longest continuously owned and operated franchise in the United Soccer League. This is the little club that could: By sheer determination, the club has rebounded from a transitional 1999 season, when a major sponsor pulled out and the club nearly folded. Two of the team's minority owners took the club over and reorganized, briefly renaming it the Tennessee Rhythm Futbol Club and moving it to Franklin. Responding to fans, in 2001 the team returned to Nashville's Ezell Park as the Metros but also moved from the A-League to the more development-oriented PDL. That change happened largely because the Metros's temporary home at Ezell Park does not meet such A-League standards as a capacity of 5,000 or have such amenities as showers and a press box. The Metros season runs April through July. Tickets can be purchased as a $40 "Flex Pass," meaning they can be used for any regular-season match. Single-game tickets are $5.

DAY TRIPS AND WEEKEND GETAWAYS

There is plenty do in Nashville. If you don't believe that, just take a look through some of the other chapters in this book. But every now and then, we get the urge to hit the road, to get away from it all and explore new territory. Lucky for us, Nashville is centrally located. Three interstates travel through Music City, offering easy access to a number of great destinations in any direction. Highways and back roads can provide an altogether different experience, taking us on a slower pace through charming towns, historic locations, beautiful farmland, rolling hills, and mountain villages. In this chapter we feature some of our favorite day trips and weekend getaways. Most of these are within an easy three-hour drive from Nashville. It's a good idea to call ahead for the latest information on operating hours and rates. The next time you're feeling a little restless, stressed out, or bored, or if you're just in search of a fun way to spend a day or weekend, consider one of these trips, or pick up a map and plot your own getaway. Think of it as a minivacation.

Attractions Price Code Key

Use the following as a guide to the cost of an adult's admission to an attraction. Keep in mind that children's admission prices are generally lower (usually about half the cost of adult admission), and very young children are admitted free to most attractions. Discounts for senior citizens, students, and groups are usually available.

$	$1 to $5
$$	$6 to $10
$$$	$11 to $15
$$$$	$16 and more

Restaurants Price Code Key

We use dollar signs to indicate the cost of dinner for two, excluding appetizers, alcoholic beverages, desserts, and tip.

$	$15 or less
$$	$16 to $25
$$$	$26 to $40
$$$$	$41 to $60
$$$$$	$61 and more

HUNTSVILLE, ALABAMA

For a quick but fun getaway, check out Huntsville, Alabama. Huntsville's location and attractions make it an easy, educational, and enjoyable trip for adults and kids alike. It's about 110 miles south of Nashville. Head down Interstate 65 south, and take either exit 351, for U.S. Highway 72, or exit 340B, for Interstate 565, if you want to go straight to the U.S. Space & Rocket Center.

If you've chosen Huntsville as your getaway destination, it's most likely because of the U.S. Space & Rocket Center, Alabama's top tourist attraction. We'll tell you more about that in just a minute. But first, a little background info on the Rocket City.

Huntsville is named for the area's first settler, Tennessee pioneer John Hunt, who settled in a log cabin 10 miles north of the Tennessee River in 1805. The city was designated as the county seat in 1810. In 1940 Huntsville, then a cotton mill town, was selected as the site of a U.S. Army chemical weapons manufacturing plant. The army turned nearly 40,000 acres of cotton fields into the Redstone Arsenal, which produced chemical weapons and other ammunition. After the war, the arsenal switched its focus to missiles and rockets. In 1950 the army brought Dr. Werner Von Braun and 117 German rocket scientists to this small mill town, where they produced the United States's first rocket. That rocket, the *Redstone,* launched an artificial satellite in 1959, followed a couple of years later by the launch of astronaut Alan B. Shepard Jr. on a 15-minute suborbital tour. When the National Aeronautics & Space Administration (NASA) was established, Von Braun's team led the organization's new Marshall Space Flight Center.

During the 1960s Huntsville welcomed the world's greatest rocket scientists to work toward the goal of putting a man on the moon. The town's population grew by 50,000 in four years. The Huntsville scientists developed the Saturn rockets for the Apollo moon program. On July 15, 1969, the world's most powerful rocket, the 363-foot *Saturn V,* was launched, propelling three astronauts to the moon. Neil Armstrong walked on the moon July 20.

Today Huntsville's population is about 160,000. The area has one of the highest per-capita incomes in the Southeast, and Huntsville has been listed by *Kiplinger's Personal Finance* magazine as among America's best 15 small- to medium-size cities in which to live.

For more information on Huntsville, call (800) SPACE–4U or visit www.huntsville .org.

Attractions

ALABAMA CONSTITUTION VILLAGE $$
109 Gates Avenue, Huntsville, AL
(256) 564-8100, (800) 678-1819
www.earlyworks.com
Alabama Constitution Village is a living-history museum that offers a trip through Alabama history. This attraction is just off the Courthouse Square, on the same block where, in 1819, delegates wrote the constitution that made Alabama the 22nd state. Costumed "villagers" will take you on a guided tour through reconstructed Federal-style buildings, including a cabinetmaker's shop, print shop, confectionery shop, library, and post office. Alabama Constitution Village is open from March through October on Tuesday through Saturday. Santa's Village is open in November and December.

BURRITT MUSEUM & PARK $
3101 Burritt Drive, Huntsville, AL
(256) 536-2882
www.burrittonthemountain.com
Sitting atop Monte Sano Mountain is the Burritt Museum & Park, a museum of regional history housed in the 14-room mansion of prominent physician Dr. William Henry Burritt. You might find it interesting to know that this 1930s home is built in the shape of an *X* and is insulated with 2,200 bales of wheat straw. This attraction includes the mansion, which serves as a museum; Historic Park, which features 19th-century restored farm structures; and nature trails that wind through the dense forest surrounding the buildings. Living-history demonstrations are presented at Historic Park. The attraction is closed on Monday and major holidays.

EARLYWORKS CHILDREN'S MUSEUM $$
404 Madison Street, Huntsville, AL
(256) 564-8100, (800) 678-1819
www.earlyworks.com
This hands-on museum makes learning about history fun for everyone. There's a 16-foot story-telling tree, a musical bandstand where you can hear tunes made popular by Alabama performers, a "floating" keelboat, an interactive architecture exhibit, and more. The museum is open Tuesday through Saturday except on major holidays.

1819 WEEDEN HOUSE MUSEUM $
300 Gates Avenue, Huntsville, AL
(256) 536-7718
www.weedenhousemuseum.com
The 1819 Weeden House Museum is the state's oldest building open to the public. It's a block from Alabama Constitution Village (see earlier entry). Inside the Federal-style brick structure, you can get a glimpse of the life of prominent families

of the 1800s. The works of artist and poet Maria Howard Weeden, who lived in the house all her life, are on display. This attraction is open Monday through Friday.

HISTORIC HUNTSVILLE DEPOT $$
320 Church Street, Huntsville, AL
(256) 564-8100, (800) 678-1819
www.earlyworks.com
The Historic Huntsville Depot is the site of one of the oldest railroad buildings in America. During your self-guided tour of the two-story brick circa-1860 depot, look for Civil War graffiti—actual messages left by imprisoned soldiers. There are also a number of Civil War artifacts along the way. A robotic ticket agent at the restored 1912 ticket office tells about what life was like as a Southern Railway worker in the early 1900s. Outside, you can explore historic locomotives and railcars. The depot is open to the public Tuesday through Saturday March through December.

HUNTSVILLE BOTANICAL GARDEN $$
4747 Bob Wallace Avenue
Huntsville, AL
(256) 830-4447, (877) 930-4447
www.hsvbg.org
Just 0.5 mile from the Space & Rocket Center is the Huntsville Botanical Garden. This 112-acre garden features wooded paths, grassy meadows, and a beautiful collection of tended gardens filled with the colorful blooms of annuals and perennials from early spring through late fall. Enjoy the beautiful roses, daylilies, and irises, and visit the fern glade and demonstration vegetable garden to learn about the benefits of these plants. An aquatic garden features a large gazebo where you can rest and enjoy the view. More than 300 species of butterflies flutter about in the Butterfly House, which is open May through September. If you like, bring your lunch and have a picnic in the shade. The garden shop offers a selection of books and gifts. The garden is open daily except on major holidays, with extended hours April through October.

U.S. SPACE & ROCKET CENTER $$$$
1 Tranquility Base, Huntsville, AL
(256) 837-3400, (800) 63-SPACE
www.spacecamp.com
The U.S. Space & Rocket Center, about a two-hour drive south on I-65, welcomes as many as 400,000 visitors each year. This attraction features dozens of interactive exhibits, displays of NASA artifacts, and actual Apollo, Mercury, and space shuttle spacecraft. You can see the *Apollo 16* command module that returned from the moon and check out the moon buggy that was developed here.

If you ever wanted to fly in the space shuttle, here's your chance, sort of. You can command an "orbiting" craft in the Land the Shuttle simulator, or experience a shuttle launch and a few seconds of weightlessness aboard the Space Shot simulator, which speeds you to the top of a 180-foot tower at 45 mph with 4 Gs of force. Take a virtual trip into deep space on the Mission to Mars simulator or strap on a harness for a climb up the Mars Climbing Wall. The IMAX movies on the Spacedome Theater's 67-foot domed screen are a thrill, too.

Museum guests also can check out the U.S. Space Camp (800-63-SPACE), where as many as 18,000 children and adults participate each year in intensive astronaut-training activities. You can watch some of the activities, but if you want to participate, you'll need to make reservations about two weeks in advance. Activities include training simulators, rocket building and launches, scientific experiments, and lectures about space exploration. The five-day Space Camp program for children ages 9 through 11 costs $899. Other camp programs include Space Academy, for children 12 through 14; Advanced Space Academy, for ages 15 through 18; and Adult Space Academy. Prices and the duration of the camps vary but generally max out at $999 for a six-day program for teens. One of the most popular camps is the Parent-Child Space Camp, three days of training and activities for $399 or six days for $999.

There are a variety of admission prices to the U.S. Space & Rocket Center. A combination ticket that includes all attractions at the facility is available, or you can choose a ticket for admission to the museum only or to the IMAX theater only. The U.S. Space & Rocket Center is open daily except on major holidays.

CHATTANOOGA, TENNESSEE

Chattanooga is a great family getaway destination. You can make it a day trip if you're really determined, but this city is best enjoyed as a weekend getaway. You'll need at least that much time to visit a selection of the city's many attractions.

Chattanooga is an easy 133-mile drive from Nashville via Interstate 24 E. You'll enjoy some nice scenery along the way. In the eastern part of the state, near the Tennessee-Georgia line, Chattanooga is in the Eastern Time Zone, so set your watch ahead an hour to keep up with local time.

The Chattanooga Visitor Center, next to the Tennessee Aquarium downtown, is a good first stop. You can pick up brochures on attractions, accommodations, shops, and restaurants as well as tickets to attractions. The visitor center is open 8:30 a.m. to 5:30 p.m. daily except Thanksgiving and Christmas days.

Chattanooga has changed enormously in recent years. A few decades ago this river city was declared the "dirtiest city in America" by the Environmental Protection Agency, but after an $850-million riverfront and revitalization plan, Chattanooga is now often called the "best mid-sized city in America." The revitalized downtown area includes the $45-million Tennessee Aquarium (see subsequent entry), which opened in 1992 and continues to spur new development in the area, and the Tennessee Riverpark greenway. Numerous other attractions, including museums, restaurants, festivals, and excellent retail shopping, have done much for the city's image.

Chattanooga is known worldwide thanks to "King of Swing" Glenn Miller's No. 1 hit single "Chattanooga Choo Choo," released in 1941. The song sold more than one million copies. But before that, the city was known as a major center of trade and, later, as one of the key strategic locations during the Civil War.

As far back as 10,000 years ago, Chattanooga was a center of trade and migration among Native Americans. In 1815 Cherokee descendant John Ross established a trading post and ferry across the Tennessee River. His post was at Ross's Landing, where the Tennessee Aquarium is today. A small town of Cherokee and white settlers grew up around the trading post.

Chattanooga became a railroad hub before the Civil War, linking producers in the South with northern manufacturers. In fall 1863 a series of Civil War battles took place on Lookout Mountain, Missionary Ridge, and at Chickamauga, which is considered the bloodiest battle of the Civil War. The city was a key to the Union's control of the South. Many local attractions tell the stories of the Civil War battles that took place in the area.

We list some of Chattanooga's best-known attractions as well as a few off-the-beaten-path locations. We also provide a few choices for dining and overnight accommodations. Call the Chattanooga Area Convention and Visitors Bureau, (423) 756-8687 or (800) 322-3344, or visit www.chattanoogafun.com for more information on the city's attractions, accommodations, and dining choices.

> Tennessee has more than 3,800 caves. One, in southeast Tennessee's Lookout Mountain, contains Ruby Falls—the country's highest underground waterfall (145 feet). Ruby Falls is 1,120 feet underground.

Attractions

THE BATTLES FOR CHATTANOOGA ELECTRIC MAP & MUSEUM $$
Lookout Mountain, 1110 East Brow Road
Lookout Mountain, TN
(423) 821-2812
www.battlesforchattanooga.com
This is an electronic battle map of Chattanooga's Civil War history, with more than 5,000 miniature

soldiers and hundreds of lights. Located on Lookout Mountain, at the entrance to Point Park, the museum features a weapons collection and other relics. A gift shop specializes in Civil War books and souvenirs. After learning about the battles, walk to Point Park (see subsequent entry), the site of Chattanooga's famous "Battle Above the Clouds." The museum is open daily, with extended summer hours.

BLUFF VIEW ART DISTRICT
Corner of High and East Second Streets (next to the Hunter Museum)
Chattanooga, TN
(423) 265-5033, (800) 725-8338
www.bluffviewartdistrict.com

The Bluff View Art District is in a quiet area of downtown Chattanooga, along the Tennessee Riverwalk and just a 0.25-mile walk from the Tennessee Aquarium. The district includes the Hunter Museum of American Art and the Bluff View Inn as well as a handful of restaurants. From this area you can climb the steps to the century-old steel-truss Walnut Street Bridge, a 0.75-mile linear park and pedestrian bridge, the longest pedestrian-walkway bridge in the world.

CHATTANOOGA AFRICAN AMERICAN MUSEUM $
200 East Martin Luther King Boulevard
Chattanooga, TN
(423) 266-8658
www.caamhistory.com

The Chattanooga African American Museum is dedicated to preserving the history of African Americans in the Chattanooga area. Exhibits include a wall dedicated to African Americans who have achieved "firsts" in their professions, an authentic African dwelling, and exhibits on the lives of blacks in Chattanooga, including Civil War displays and displays highlighting achievements in performing arts and sports. The museum is open Monday through Saturday. At the other end of the building is Bessie Smith Hall, a 264-seat performance hall/cabaret named for the legendary "Empress of the Blues" Bessie Smith, a Chat-

tanooga native. The venue presents prominent blues acts as well as other music and arts programs. The African American Museum features a Bessie Smith exhibit.

CHICKAMAUGA/CHATTANOOGA NATIONAL MILITARY PARK FREE
Fort Oglethorpe, GA
(706) 866-9241
www.nps.gov/chch

History and Civil War buffs will want to be sure to visit this attraction, America's first and largest national military park. Just across the state line from Chattanooga, Chickamauga/Chattanooga National Military Park is dedicated to the memory of Union and Confederate soldiers who died in the 1863 battle here. An audiovisual presentation explaining the battle and its significance in the war is offered at the Chickamauga Battlefield Park Headquarters and Visitor Center. A collection of Fuller guns is also on display. Point Park (see subsequent entry), atop Lookout Mountain, is an extension of the park and serves as a memorial to the soldiers.

CREATIVE DISCOVERY MUSEUM $$
321 Chestnut Street, Chattanooga, TN
(423) 756-2738
www.cdmfun.org

Creative Discovery Museum is a neat place for kids. It's 2 blocks from the Tennessee Aquarium in downtown Chattanooga. The 42,000-square-foot museum is loaded with interactive, hands-on attractions that make learning fun. Main exhibit areas include the Artist's Studio, where kiddies can learn about printmaking, sculpting, and painting; the Inventor's Clubhouse, which allows visitors to manipulate various pulleys, motors, magnets, and other devices to create their own inventions; a Musician's Studio, with instruments from around the world and a recording studio where the little ones can play instruments, compose songs, and experiment with studio recording; and an Excavation Station, where kids can dig for "bones," study paleontology, or dress up like a dinosaur. You'll also find a two-and-a-half-story climbing structure, the Little Yellow House for preschoolers, a cafe, and a gift shop. The museum is open daily March through Labor Day but is closed Wednesday from September through February.

HUNTER MUSEUM OF AMERICAN ART $$
10 Bluff View, Chattanooga, TN
(423) 267-0968
www.huntermuseum.org
The Hunter Museum of American Art has more than 1,500 pieces in its permanent collection. Among them are works by Mary Cassatt, Childe Hassam, Thomas Hart Benton, Ansel Adams, Helen Frankenthaler, Louise Nevelson, George Segal, and Thomas Cole. Its collection of contemporary glass sculpture includes works by Harvey K. Littleton, William Morris, Dale Chihuly, and Toots Zinsky. Because space is limited, only about 20 percent of the museum's collection is on view. Pieces are rotated every two to four years. The museum sits on an 80-foot limestone bluff overlooking the Tennessee River on one side and downtown Chattanooga on the other. The museum is located in two different buildings, one a 1904 Greek Revival mansion and the other a contemporary structure built in 1975. The two buildings are connected by an elliptical stairwell and outdoor sculpture garden. The museum is open daily.

INTERNATIONAL TOWING & RECOVERY HALL OF FAME & MUSEUM $$
3315 Broad Street, Chattanooga, TN
(423) 267-3132
www.internationaltowingmuseum.org
One of Chattanooga's more offbeat attractions, the International Towing & Recovery Hall of Fame & Museum is all about the history of wreckers and tow trucks. Exhibits include wreckers and towing equipment dating from 1916. The museum is open daily.

LOOKOUT MOUNTAIN INCLINE RAILWAY $$
At St. Elmo Avenue, at the foot of Lookout Mountain, Chattanooga, TN
(423) 629-1411
www.lookoutmtnattractions.com

Put the Incline Railway on your must-do list. A ride on the Incline Railway, the world's steepest passenger railway, is a memorable and breathtaking experience. The Incline's trolley-style railcars take you to the top of scenic Lookout Mountain and back; near the top of the track, the grade reaches 72.7 percent. As you ride toward the clouds, you'll get a panoramic view of Chattanooga. The observation deck at the top is the highest overlook on Lookout Mountain. On a clear day, you can see as far as 100 miles. At the upper station, you can visit the Incline's machine room and see how the giant gears and cables make the whole thing work. After checking out the views at the top, visit Point Park (see next entry), just a short, 3-block walk from the upper station, for other spectacular views.

The Incline is both a National Historic Site and a National Historic Mechanical Engineering Landmark. It was built in 1895 as a fast and inexpensive way to transport residents and visitors to and from the St. Elmo neighborhood and the top of Lookout Mountain. The mountain soon developed as a popular summer vacation resort of the late 1800s and early 1900s. To get to the Incline from I-24, take any Lookout Mountain exit and follow the signs. Free parking is available at the lower station. Incline Railway daily, round-trip, and one-way tickets are available. The Incline is open daily except Christmas Day.

POINT PARK $
Atop Lookout Mountain
Lookout Mountain, TN
(423) 821-7786
www.lookoutmtnattractions.com
A unit of the Chickamauga/Chattanooga National Military Park (see previous listing), Point Park was built in 1905 to commemorate the November 1863 "Battle Above the Clouds," one of the most dramatic battles of the Civil War. Panoramic views of Chattanooga and the Tennessee River and a history of the Battle of Lookout Mountain await visitors. Monuments, markers, and a museum pay tribute to the soldiers who fought and died in the area. The park is on the northern crest of Lookout Mountain. Point Park is open daily.

ROCK CITY GARDENS $$$
1400 Patten Road, Lookout Mountain, GA
(706) 820-2531
www.seerockcity.com

SEE ROCK CITY. You've seen the barns and bird-houses painted with that slogan, and if you've ever been to Chattanooga, chances are that you have seen Rock City. If you haven't been to Rock City, one of Chattanooga's best-known attractions, be sure to stop by on your next visit. Rock City Gardens began more than 60 years ago, when Frieda Carter and her husband, Garnet, developed a 10-acre garden among huge boulders and natural rock formations on this mountaintop. It opened to the public in 1932. The ingenious advertising campaign followed in 1937, when Garnet Carter hired a young man named Clark Byers to paint barn roofs with messages. Over the next 32 years, Byers painted the SEE ROCK CITY slogan on more than 900 barns in nearly 20 states. In the '50s Rock City added bird-houses to its campaign. But it all came to an end after the Beautification Act of 1965. Barns and birdhouses were painted over. Today, fewer than 100 of the painted barns remain, but the legend lives on. The SEE ROCK CITY slogan can be seen on subways, gardens, birdhouses, and other spots around the world.

Now that you know the history, what can you expect at Rock City Gardens? Lovely gardens and great scenery mostly. Take a self-guided tour along the Enchanted Trail, where you'll observe unique rock formations and various gardens with more than 400 species of wildflowers, shrubs, and other plants. The trail takes you through a couple of tight squeezes—the Needle's Eye and Fat Man's Squeeze—between massive boulders. At the top, at famous Lover's Leap, you can supposedly see seven states—Tennessee, Kentucky, Virginia, North Carolina, South Carolina, Georgia, and Alabama. The walk through the charming Fairyland Caverns and Mother Goose Village is especially fun for the kids. The whole trip takes about 60 to 90 minutes. Rock City Gardens is open daily except Christmas.

RUBY FALLS $$$
Lookout Mountain, 1720 South Scenic Highway, Chattanooga, TN
(423) 821-2544
www.rubyfalls.com

Ruby Falls, America's highest underground waterfall open to the public, is one of Chattanooga's oldest and most popular tourist attractions. This 145-foot natural waterfall is more than 1,100 feet inside Lookout Mountain. Your guided tour begins with a 260-foot elevator ride into the caverns. Then you make the trek to the falls. Along the way, your guide will tell you all about the history of the falls and point out interesting calcite formations. This tour takes about two hours. Lookout Mountain Caverns is a National Landmark and is on the National Register of Historic Places. Lookout Mountain Tower provides a spectacular panoramic view of Chattanooga. Ruby Falls also has a Fun Forest play area for kids. A gift shop and concession stand are nearby. Ruby Falls is open daily except Christmas.

Each fall, from September 15 to November 15, the Tennessee Department of Tourist Development opens its Fall Color Forecast Line, (800) 697-4200, which provides weekly recorded updates about the changing leaf colors across the state and about upcoming outdoor events.

TENNESSEE AQUARIUM $$$$
1 Broad Street, Chattanooga, TN
(423) 265-0698, (800) 262-0695
www.tennesseeaquarium.com

The Tennessee Aquarium, the world's first and largest freshwater aquarium, is an attraction you don't want to miss. In fact, it's the reason many people visit Chattanooga. The aquarium opened in 1992 as the centerpiece of Chattanooga's downtown revitalization effort and has drawn up to a million visitors each year. The aquarium is in the center of Ross's Landing Park and Plaza on the banks of the Tennessee River, next to the Chattanooga Visitor Center. A self-guided tour through the aquarium takes about two hours.

The Tennessee Aquarium in Chattanooga is the world's first and largest freshwater aquarium. JACKIE SHECKLER FINCH

During your visit you'll travel through a number of natural freshwater habitats, including a 60-foot canyon and two living forests. The aquarium provides habitat for more than 9,000 animals, including an 80-pound blue catfish, river otters, alligators, piranhas, a boa constrictor, stingrays, sharks, and colorful fish that can be found in the Gulf of Mexico. The aquarium also hosts special exhibits. Tickets are sold daily except Thanksgiving and Christmas. Various discounted combination tickets good for admission to the aquarium, the IMAX 3-D theater next door, and Creative Discovery Museum are available.

i Earl Mitchell, a salesman for Chattanooga Bakery, created the Moon Pie after coal miners said they wanted a snack that was filling and as big as the moon. His chocolate-covered marshmallow treat has filled the order since 1917.

TENNESSEE VALLEY RAILROAD MUSEUM $$
4119 Cromwell Road, Chattanooga, TN
(423) 894-8028, (800) 397-5544
www.tvrail.com

This is the largest operating historic railroad in the South. The museum was founded by a group of Chattanoogans who wanted to preserve operating steam passenger trains. It features a number of classic pieces from railroad's golden age, among them a 1911 steam locomotive, 1926 dining car, and 1929 wooden caboose. Passenger trains depart regularly for various Chattanooga destinations. The schedule varies according to season, and prices vary.

Accommodations

Chattanooga has all types of hotel, motel, and bed-and-breakfast accommodations. We're listing a couple of favorites. For other options, check out the many brochures available at the Chattanooga Visitor Center downtown, or contact the Chattanooga Area Convention and Visitors Bureau (423-756-8687; 800-322-3344; or www.chattanoogafun.com).

BLUFF VIEW INN
411 East Second Street,
Chattanooga, TN
(423) 265-5033, (800) 725-8330
www.bluffviewinn.com

A bed-and-breakfast overlooking the Tennessee River, Bluff View Inn offers accommodations in three early-1900s restored homes. Your room comes complete with a complimentary gourmet breakfast. Expect a room here to run approximately $120 to $300 a night. Smoking, red wine, and the burning of candles are strictly prohibited.

CHATTANOOGA CHOO CHOO HOLIDAY INN
1400 Market Street, Chattanooga, TN
(423) 266-5000, (800) TRACK-29
www.choochoo.com

A fun place for the whole family, the Chattanooga Choo Choo Holiday Inn downtown is the city's most famous place to spend the night. For some 60 years this was the site of Chattanooga's Terminal Station. During the height of the railroad era, it saw dozens of arriving and departing trains each day. Today visitors here can sleep and eat in authentic railcars. The Chattanooga Choo Choo Holiday Inn is a 30-acre complex with 315 guest rooms, 48 sleeping parlors aboard railcars, meeting space, restaurants, indoor and outdoor pools, a Model Railroad Museum, formal rose gardens, and more. Rates range from approximately $105 to $160 a night for a standard room to about $240 for a suite. Train cars are $175.

Restaurants

BACK INN CAFE $$$$
412 East Second Street
Chattanooga, TN
(423) 265-5033, (800) 715-8338
www.bluffviewartdistrict.com

Casual fine dining is the specialty at this restaurant, which is located in historic Bluff View Inn's Martin House, an early-1900s mansion that offers a spectacular river view. Dine indoors or out. Wine and a selection of imported and domestic beers are available. The cafe is open daily for breakfast, lunch, and dinner.

BIG RIVER GRILLE & BREWING WORKS $$
222 Broad Street, Chattanooga, TN
(423) 267-BREW
www.bigrivergrille.com

Just a few steps from the Tennessee Aquarium, this eatery is a fun and casual spot to grab a bite or sample a handcrafted ale. The brewing apparatus overlooks the bar area. In addition to fresh-brewed beers and homemade sodas, the menu features such tempting entrees as smoked chicken enchiladas, fresh-grilled seafood, and salads. There's a kid's menu, too. Next door is Big

River Billiards, where you can order a wood-fired pizza to munch on while you enjoy a game.

CHATTANOOGA CHOO CHOO $–$$$$
1400 Market Street, Chattanooga, TN
(423) 266-5000
www.choochoo.com
The Chattanooga Choo Choo's Dinner in the Diner offers gourmet meals aboard an authentic dining car. At the Choo Choo's Station House (more affordable and suitable for families), singing waiters and waitresses will deliver your meals. Southern favorites are served for breakfast, lunch, and dinner at the Gardens, while Café Espresso offers gourmet coffee and desserts. The Choo Choo also has two lounges, an ice cream shop, and the Silver Diner pizza and snack eatery.

REMBRANDT'S COFFEE HOUSE $
204 East High Street, Chattanooga, TN
(423) 265-5033
www.bluffviewartdistrict.com
Rembrandt's is a good spot to stop for a cup of gourmet java and indulge in handmade chocolates and fresh-baked pastries. Seating is available indoors or on the garden terrace outdoors. Rembrandt's is open daily for breakfast, lunch, and dinner.

MAMMOTH CAVE, KENTUCKY

This area of central Kentucky, an hour and a half north of Nashville, is known for its unique karst topography: limestone formations, sinkholes, and caves. There are hundreds of caves in the area, many of them privately owned; quite a few are open to the public. While it's close enough to be a day trip, avid spelunkers and outdoorsy types may want to spend a weekend here, exploring the massive Mammoth Cave system and the area's scenic hiking trails and waterways.

MAMMOTH CAVE NATIONAL PARK
Cave City, KY
(270) 758-2180 (information),
(800) 967-2283 (reservations)
www.nps.gov/maca

Mammoth Cave National Park, the granddaddy of all caves, is about one and a half hours north of Nashville. To reach it, just take I-65 north from Nashville to Park City, Kentucky. Follow the signs to the park visitor center, about 10 minutes away. This is an excellent place to start your trip.

Mammoth Cave is a fascinating place to visit, especially for families with kids. The national park is 52,700 acres; Mammoth Cave itself is the longest recorded cave system in the world, with more than 360 miles explored and mapped. During the War of 1812, a commercial saltpeter-mining operation provided gunpowder for American troops. In 1842 the cave was used as a tuberculosis hospital.

The cave system is home to an enormous diversity of plants and animals, a complex geology, and a rich cultural heritage tracing back 4,000 years. There are more than 130 species of wildlife that use the cave regularly, and some 42 of them have been identified as troglobites: animals adapted exclusively to life in the darkness. Eyeless cave shrimp and eyeless fish, bats, cave crickets, and more all call Mammoth Cave home. As befits this unique natural treasure, it has been declared a World Heritage Site as well as an International Biosphere Reserve. It became a national park on July 1, 1941.

Park service interpreters lead a variety of hikes through this fascinating cave system. Tours range from the easy to the highly difficult. The one-and-a-half-hour Travertine Tour, which passes by such unique geologic features as stalagmites and stalactites, is ideal for families with toddlers and young children, or those who have difficulty walking.

For those interested in history, a three-hour, 3-mile Violet City Lantern Tour is offered on a seasonal basis. Visitors trace the path of the cave's famous explorers by the light of a coal lantern; highlights include views of a saltpeter mining operation, evidence of prehistoric exploration, ruins of the tuberculosis hospital, as well as some of the cave's largest rooms and passageways. A shorter History Tour hits many of the same highlights, as well as artifacts left by Native Americans.

Both tours involve climbing stairs and tolerance of heights and enclosed spaces.

Athletic types and amateur spelunkers may want to try an extremely strenuous, six-hour, 5-mile Wild Cave Tour. Here you will crawl, climb, and squeeze through small passages to see hidden treasures and hot spots off the usual tour route. Helmets, lights, and knee pads are available, or you can bring your own. It's also advised that you wear long pants, hiking boots, and bring gloves. This is a rigorous tour: You must be over age 16 and have a chest size of less than 42 inches to participate.

Tours range in price from $4 to $45, depending on length. A caution: Mammoth Cave is one of the country's most popular national parks. One of our *Insiders' Guide* authors made the mistake of "just showing up"—only to find a four-hour wait for the next tour! Tours can and do sell out, but you can reserve your tickets in advance either online at www.nps .gov/maca or by calling the park reservation line at (800) 967-2283.

Aboveground there's plenty to do and see, as well. The Mammoth Cave area is home to the Green and Nolin River valleys and Nolin Lake; canoeing, camping, fishing, hiking, and other recreational activities are plentiful. Accommodations in the park include a hotel and several cottages. Call (270) 758-2225 for details or reservations.

i Kentucky's Mammoth Cave, the world's longest recorded cave system, is inhabited by 12 species of bats, including two endangered species.

Camping

There are three campgrounds inside Mammoth Cave Park. The Headquarters Campground has 111 sites at $16 per night. You'll find an RV dump station, flush toilets and hot showers, water, grills, and picnic tables. A camp store nearby has a coin laundry and camping supplies; ranger-led talks, hikes, and other programs are available seasonally. Reservations are accepted through the National Park Service Reservation Line, (800) 967-2283, or online at http://reservations.nps.gov.

Houchins Ferry camping area has 12 riverside primitive campsites and is open year-round at $12 per night. Amenities include grills and tables, chemical toilets, and drinking water. Houchins Ferry operates on a first-come, first-served basis.

Maple Springs Group Campground accommodates people with horses and large groups at $30 per night (there is a limit of 24 people per campsite). There are three sites for groups with horses and four sites for groups without horses. Amenities include water, chemical toilets, potable water, picnic tables, and grills.

You can also camp on riverbanks and islands along the Green and Nolin Rivers with a free backcountry-use permit available at the visitor center.

i Temperatures inside Mammoth Cave range from the mid-50s to the low 60s, year-round. No matter when you visit, it's a good idea to bring a sweater along.

Trails

Hiking and horseback trails wind through the forests above Mammoth Cave. Many of the trails are shared; if you don't want to meet a horse on your walk, better stick to the Ganter Cave Trail, which is closed to horses. If you like to ride but didn't bring your horse, Double-J Stables offers guided trail rides through the park. Call (800) 730-4773 for information.

Hikers can take advantage of more than 70 miles of trails at Mammoth Cave. Trailheads are at the North Side, South Side, and the visitor center; maps and guides are available at the visitor center.

The Heritage Trail near the visitor center accommodates those with disabilities; the trail features wheelchair turnouts, rest areas with benches, and lights for evening use. Other easily accessible trails are the Pond Walk, a 2,200-foot trail around Sloan's Crossing Pond; and the trail at Sand Cave on the east boundary of the park. An audio guide is available at the visitor center.

Boating and Canoeing

Both the Green and Nolin Rivers flow through Mammoth Cave National Park. The Green River is dotted with sandbars, islands, and subsurface springs; the Nolin River has a narrower channel. Both rivers flow at a gentle pace—5 mph or slower—making them perfect for canoeing or kayaking.

Boat launches for the Green River are at Dennison Ferry, Green River Ferry, or Houchins Ferry. Dennison Ferry access is steep and suitable for kayaks, johnboats, and canoes only. The best take-out points are at Green River Ferry or Houchins Ferry.

There are no canoe rentals within the park, but several livery services outside the park boundaries rent canoes and lead canoe excursions.

MEMPHIS, TENNESSEE

Just about three hours west of Nashville via Interstate 40 is Memphis, Tennessee's largest city, the adopted home of the King—and much more.

Memphis, named for the ancient Egyptian capital (you were wondering about that pyramid?), has a rich history filled with proud events as well as shameful ones. It's a jumpin', swingin' Mississippi River town that, essentially, is to blues, R&B, and rockabilly what Nashville is to country music. It's a city with a past inextricably linked to the civil rights movement. It's one of fewer than a handful of cities that legitimately can claim the title "Barbecue Capital of the World." And it's a city that, perhaps not surprisingly, shares a sometimes intense sibling rivalry with Music City. Nowhere is this more evident than in the world of professional sports: In the '90s the two cities bitterly vied for an NFL franchise. Nashville won that battle, but Memphis quickly rebounded by landing an NBA team. The NBA Memphis Grizzlies played their inaugural season at the Pyramid Arena in 2002.

Memphis is a city built on cotton and river trade that has grown into a major commercial hub. The river remains a major transportation route, and the sky is another. Northwest Airlines has one of its three U.S. hubs here at Memphis International Airport, and FedEx is headquartered here.

Memphis's past includes a role as one of the South's largest slave markets in the early and mid-1800s. Because of its location, it was a strategic city during the Civil War. At the start of the war, it was a Confederate center, but Union forces captured it in 1862. Racial problems continued to plague the city; they came to a climax in 1968, when escaped convict James Earl Ray assassinated Rev. Martin Luther King Jr. at the city's Lorraine Motel. (One positive outcome in the aftermath of King's assassination was an effort by local, state, and federal officials to improve relationships with, and conditions within, the African-American community.)

Today there are many reasons to visit Memphis. Many people immediately think of Elvis Presley when they think of Memphis, but he isn't the only King enshrined here. You also can celebrate the legacies of Martin Luther King Jr. and the still-vibrant bluesman B. B. King while contemplating the mysterious power of the mighty Mississippi, that natural force often referred to as Old Man River.

For more information on Memphis, visit www.memphistravel.com (the Memphis Convention and Visitor's Bureau's Web site) or call (800) 873-6282.

Attractions

BEALE STREET

This historic downtown street packs a lot of action, most of it music-related, into 4 blocks. W. C. Handy, the musician and composer who became known as "Father of the Blues" for his efforts to popularize the genre, made the street famous with his song "Beale Street Blues." A statue of Handy stands on Beale Street today. Other attractions on this street include B. B. King's Blues Club, Rum Boogie Cafe, A. Schwab Dry Goods Store, and the W. C. Handy House Museum.

BROOKS MUSEUM OF ART $$
1934 Poplar Avenue, Memphis, TN
(901) 544-6200
www.brooksmuseum.org

Opened in May 1916, the Brooks Museum of Art is Tennessee's oldest and largest fine-art museum, with more than 40,000 square feet of gallery space. Located in Memphis's lovely Overton Park, the museum is housed partially in its original Beaux Arts–style building, which is a registered U.S. National Landmark. The Brooks is known for an outstanding and varied permanent collection, especially its Italian Renaissance and Baroque paintings and sculpture, English portraits, and European and American paintings. Many of these fine works were donated to the Brooks in 1952 by the Kress Foundation; the bequest included paintings and sculptures by French masters Alfred Sisley, Auguste Rodin, and Camille Pisarro, as well as American artists Georgia O'Keeffe, Thomas Hart Benton, and Winslow Homer. In addition, the Brooks hosts traveling and special exhibits throughout the year. The museum also has a full-service restaurant, the Brushmark, which offers excellent food. The museum is closed Monday and on Thanksgiving, Christmas, New Year's Day, and July 4.

i Memphis's famous Peabody ducks started as a prank in the 1930s when friends of hotel general manager Frank Schutt slipped three live ducks in the Peabody fountain. Since then ducks have been in the fountain every day. They were trained to perform their famous "march" in 1940.

GRACELAND, HOME OF
ELVIS PRESLEY $$$–$$$$
3734 Elvis Presley Boulevard
Memphis, TN
(901) 332-3322, (800) 238-2000
www.elvis.com

We've heard many people use the word "tacky" to describe the 15,000-square-foot Memphis mansion of Elvis Presley—and it is true that the home does have its garish highlights. But it was, honestly, nowhere near as bad as we'd expected (maybe that just means we're tacky, too). Remember, much of the decor was from the '70s, a period not generally associated with subtlety. Keep in mind, too, that Elvis was a rock 'n' roll star. Beyond that, he was just a poor country boy who got way too rich and way too famous, way too soon.

Visiting Graceland, for us at least, actually served to make the King seem more human. By the time we reached the backyard memorial gardens, where Elvis and family members are buried, we felt a genuine sadness.

The Graceland mansion tour, which takes about one and a half hours to complete, takes visitors through selected portions of the mansion. You won't see the King's bedroom or the infamous bathroom where he died, but you will see the pool room, where he hung out with his Memphis Mafia friends, and the kitchen, where so many of those famed peanut-butter-and-banana sandwiches were made. You'll see the TV room, the music room, the all-white formal living room, his baby grand piano, his dining rooms, and the den. You'll visit his racquetball building and his trophy room, which features gold records, stage costumes, and other mementos.

Tours start every three to five minutes. The mansion is open daily, except Tuesday, from December through February. Graceland is closed on Thanksgiving, Christmas, and New Year's Day. Parking is available across the street from the mansion.

Anytime is a good time to visit Graceland, but for a real dose of local color, try to plan your trip in August during Elvis Week. Elvis Week commemorates the music and legacy of the King, and it's always held the week of the anniversary of his death, which was August 16, 1977. Fans and fan clubs from all around the world descend on Memphis by the thousands for a full week of activities; on August 15 of every year, there's a candlelight vigil. Elvis impersonators are literally on every street corner in mid-August, making this a unique—if somewhat surreal—experience. A caution: Elvis Week is a monumental event. If you do plan to participate, it's wise to make your travel arrangements early.

LICHTERMAN NATURE CENTER $$
5992 Quince Road, Memphis, TN
(901) 767-7322
www.memphismuseums.org
Once the suburban estate of a wealthy Memphis family, this 65-acre property was donated to the city for the purposes of a nature center, becoming the first accredited nature center in the United States. Lichterman has been dubbed "Memphis's Central Park." Nature trails wind through the grounds, and a boardwalk surrounds a 10-acre lake, making this a scenic and peaceful retreat in the midst of urban sprawl. A $7.5-million renovation and expansion included a bright and airy 16,000-square-foot visitor center, a special-events pavilion, and a greenhouse. There's also a small amphitheater where special events and nature talks are held. Plant sales, guided nature walks, and kids' events are among the activities you can take part in. Lichterman is open Tuesday through Saturday.

MEMPHIS ROCK 'N' ROLL
SOUL MUSEUM $$
191 Beale Street, Suite 100
Memphis, TN
(901) 205-2533
www.memphisrocknsoul.org
This attraction is located 1/2 block south of Beale Street, on the second floor of the Gibson Beale Street Showcase. The main highlight is the Smithsonian's Rock 'n' Soul: Social Crossroads exhibit, which features artifacts and music from such Memphis notables as Elvis Presley, Otis Redding, B. B. King, and Jerry Lee Lewis. More than just a music museum, these galleries examine the history of Memphis music and its impact on popular culture. Tours take about an hour. Downstairs in the Gibson facility, you can watch as a Gibson guitar is made. The museum is open daily.

THE MEMPHIS ZOO $$
2000 Galloway Street, Memphis, TN
(901) 725-3400, (800) 288-8763
www.memphiszoo.org
The Memphis Zoo, considered by many one of the best in the country, is in Overton Park. Favorite exhibits include the China Exhibit (home to giant pandas Ya Ya and Le Le), Cat Country, Primate Canyon, an aquarium, and a tropical birdhouse. The zoo is open every day except Thanksgiving, Christmas Eve, and Christmas Day.

i Volney was the lion seen roaring at the beginning of MGM movies. He lived at the Memphis Zoo until his death in 1944.

MUD ISLAND RIVER PARK $$
125 North Front Street, Memphis, TN
(901) 576-7241, (800) 507-6507
www.mudisland.com
How'd you like to walk along—or in, if you prefer—the Mississippi River from Cairo, Illinois, to the Gulf of Mexico? You can do just that—and all in a matter of minutes—at Mud Island. The River Walk, a 5-block-long scale model of the lower Mississippi River, is just one highlight of this fascinating attraction devoted to the river, its history, and its culture.

Mud Island, a 52-acre island just offshore, is connected to downtown Memphis by an automobile bridge (the Auction Street Bridge, north of the island), a pedestrian bridge, and a monorail. Other highlights here include the Mississippi River Museum, with exhibits that include a reproduction of an 1870s steamboat, a Union gunboat, and other river vessels; American Indian artifacts; and a Hall of River Music, which offers insights into the development of jazz, blues, and rock 'n' roll. Back outside on the pavilion, you'll find the *Memphis Belle*, a B-17 bomber from World War II. The River Walk ends in the "Gulf of Mexico"—a 1.3-million-gallon pool where you can enjoy a leisurely pedal-boat ride. Canoe and kayak rentals are available for exploring the harbor. Those who prefer to stay on dry land can rent a bicycle and cruise around the park or downtown Memphis. Mud Island is open April through October. It is closed Monday in the spring and fall.

NATIONAL CIVIL RIGHTS MUSEUM $$$
Lorraine Motel, 450 Mulberry Street
Memphis, TN
(901) 521-9699
www.civilrightsmuseum.org
The Lorraine Motel is where, on April 4, 1968, Rev. Martin Luther King Jr. was assassinated. So it is fitting that the building today be devoted to the ideals of King and other leaders of the civil rights movement. An introductory film provides an overview, and interactive audiovisual exhibits evoke the emotions and tensions of the times. The "Brown v. Board of Education of Topeka"

exhibit explores the 1954 Supreme Court decision that ruled segregation in public schools unconstitutional. In another dramatic exhibit, visitors can sit on a bus and put themselves in the place of Rosa Parks, whose refusal to surrender her bus seat in Montgomery, Alabama, in 1955 was a catalytic event in the struggle for civil rights. The National Civil Rights Museum is closed Tuesday.

THE PEABODY MEMPHIS DUCKS FREE
149 Union Avenue, Memphis, TN
(901) 529-4000, (800) PEABODY
www.peabodymemphis.com
The Peabody, a luxury hotel, is famous for its ducks, a pampered quintet who twice a day march through the lobby amid great ceremony. At 11:00 a.m. the ducks leave their hotel room,

The Lorraine Motel is where the Rev. Martin Luther King, Jr., was killed in 1968. JACKIE SHECKLER FINCH

take an elevator ride to the main floor, then march across the red carpet, rolled out just for them, to the lobby fountain. There they frolic until 5:00 p.m., when they reverse the process. It's a great photo opportunity, especially for the little ones, and it's free. For more about the Peabody, see our listing of Memphis accommodations.

SUN STUDIO $$
706 Union Avenue, Memphis, TN
(901) 521-0664, (800) 441-6249
www.sunstudio.com

Graceland may attract most of the attention, but Sun Studio has the ghosts. Here, at Memphis Recording Service, part of the Sun Records company, is where 18-year-old Elvis Presley cut his first tracks in 1953. By the next year, Sun owner Sam Phillips had signed Presley to his label and released his first single, "That's All Right, Mama," with "Blue Moon of Kentucky" on the flip side. Despite two top-five hits, including a No. 1, in the next year, Phillips soon sold Elvis's contract to the larger RCA Victor label for $35,000—a huge sum then, but nothing when you consider what was to come. Yet Phillips says he never regretted his decision. Sun also recorded such legends as Johnny Cash, Roy Orbison, B. B. King, Muddy Waters, Carl Perkins, Jerry Lee Lewis, and Charlie Rich—pioneers whose music has shaped the face of popular music with an influence that continues to be felt today.

Sun, which reopened in the 1980s after being closed for years, has recently been the studio for recordings by acts including U2, Bonnie Raitt, and Def Leppard. There's still magic between these walls, as you'll discover when you take the 40-minute tour. Actually, "tour" can be something of a misnomer because most of the presentation takes place in a single room. But what a room it is! The outtakes you'll hear from those early recording sessions serve as a brief audio history of rock 'n' roll's formative years. And you can hold the microphone once used by the poor teenager from Tupelo, Mississippi, who became the King of Rock 'n' Roll. Sun Studio is open daily. Tours begin every hour on the half hour from 10:30 a.m. to 5:30 p.m.

Accommodations

Memphis has thousands of hotel rooms and other accommodations. You shouldn't have any problem finding a suitable property, although it's a good idea to make reservations in advance, especially if you want to stay at a particular location. We're listing just a few favorites. For other options, visit the Memphis Convention & Visitors Bureau Web site, www.memphistravel .com, where you can search for hotels and book a room online. If you're on the road to Memphis, you can pick up information on accommodations at the Memphis/Shelby County Visitors Center (901)-543-5333), located at 12036 Arlington Trail, in Arlington, Tennessee, about 15 minutes east of Memphis off I-40.

HOLIDAY INN—MT. MORIAH
2490 Mt. Moriah Road, Memphis, TN
(901) 362-8010, (800) 477-5519
www.himemphis.com

This moderately priced hotel in east Memphis is convenient to Graceland, museums, and several shopping malls. The property was built in 1974 but was completely renovated in 1999 and upgraded again in 2003. Each of the 195 comfortably furnished guest rooms includes a large work desk, coffeemaker, hair dryer, iron, and ironing board. About half the rooms have microwave-refrigerators. The hotel has a full-service restaurant and lounge, room service, an exercise room, an outdoor pool, a coin-operated laundry, a complimentary airport shuttle. The rate is about $100 per night, but specials and discounts may reduce the price.

THE PEABODY MEMPHIS
149 Union Avenue, Memphis, TN
(901) 529-4000, (800) PEABODY
www.peabodymemphis.com

The elegant Peabody hotel is Memphis's only historic hotel. First opened in 1869 (and rebuilt and renovated since then), the Peabody has a well-earned reputation as one of the South's finest hotels. In fact, *Travel + Leisure* magazine listed the Peabody among its "Top 100 Hotels in the

Continental U.S. & Canada." If you're looking for luxury and can afford the best, this is the place. The hotel has 464 rooms, including 15 suites. Basic guest rooms range from $200 to $260 per night. Peabody Club Floor rooms, which include complimentary hors d'oeuvres, continental breakfast, and use of the Peabody Athletic Club, among other perks, are $300 to $325. Suites range from $350 to $1,500. Amenities include 24-hour room service, a concierge, valet/laundry service, a workout room, and a shopping area. The hotel has several restaurants, including its highly rated gourmet restaurant Chez Philippe. Even if you don't spend the night at the Peabody, you can visit the hotel's magnificent Italianate Renaissance Revival–style lobby and have a drink in the bar. Visiting the lobby to see the famous Peabody ducks waddle along a red carpet and into a marble fountain is a Memphis tradition. For more on the ducks, see the "Attractions" part of this section.

TALBOT HEIRS GUESTHOUSE

99 South Second Street, Memphis, TN
(901) 527-9772, (800) 955-3956
www.talbothouse.com

Talbot Heirs Guesthouse offers some of Memphis's most unique accommodations. The inn's eight spacious suites are on the second floor of a downtown Memphis building, right across the street from the famous Peabody Memphis and about 2 blocks from Beale Street. Each uniquely furnished suite has a queen-size bed, private bath, full kitchen, and separate living area. Suite One, with its bright purple walls, black-and-white floor, and black leather sofa, is the hippest room. Those with tamer tastes might enjoy staying in Suite Two, which has a more subdued color scheme and traditional furnishings. Extras in each suite include high-speed Internet connection, dual phone lines, CD player, satellite TV, iron, and ironing board. Guests also have access to a laundry room and exercise equipment. A complimentary continental breakfast is delivered to your room daily. If you provide a grocery list, Talbot Heirs will have your kitchen stocked upon your arrival. Talbot Heirs Guesthouse is best suited for couples or single travelers, although children are welcome here. Rooms range from $130 to $275 per night.

i Memphis's famous Peabody Memphis is named for George Peabody, an international financier and philanthropist who was good friends with Robert Brinkley, who built the hotel. The hotel originally was to be named the Brinkley House, but in 1869, just before the facility opened, Peabody died, and Brinkley named the grand hotel in his honor.

Restaurants and Nightclubs

ALFRED'S ON BEALE $$

197 Beale Street, Memphis, TN
(901) 525-3711, (888) 433-3711
www.alfredsonbeale.com

Alfred's is located in one of Beale Street's few historic buildings to survive the 1970s' "urban renewal" push that demolished so many of the street's architectural treasures. Alfred's is a restaurant, bar, and club; there's a rooftop patio and a covered patio area downstairs that are perfect for enjoying those sultry Southern nights. Inside, the main restaurant seats around 125. Food is classic Southern fare, and the homemade cobbler is delicious. Live entertainment is offered nightly and includes karaoke and various live music. Alfred's is home of the Memphis Jazz Orchestra, a 17-piece big band that is featured every Sunday night. Alfred's also houses the largest collection of gold records in the United States, along with a wide-ranging collection of Elvis photos.

i For a free copy of the Tennessee Department of Tourist Development's *Tennessee Vacation Guide,* call (800) GO2-TENN or visit www.tnvacation.com.

B. B. KING'S BLUES CLUB $$$

143 Beale Street, Memphis, TN
(901) 524-KING
www.bbkingsclub.com

Listen to live blues while savoring some down-home Southern cooking, like barbecue and catfish, at B. B. King's. For an unusual twist, tried the fried green tomatoes—six graham-cracker-and-cornmeal-crusted fried green tomatoes drizzled with basil oil and served with carmelized onion marmalade, herb cream cheese, and strawberry preserves. We highly recommend the catfish, fried in cornmeal batter. Here's a tip: Skip the tartar sauce and eat your catfish with hot sauce, the way they do in Mississippi, where B. B. King grew up. B. B. King's is open seven days a week, with live entertainment nightly.

FRANK GRISANTI'S ITALIAN RESTAURANT $$$$
1022 Shady Grove Road, Memphis, TN
(901) 761-9462, (888) 761-3309
www.frankgrisanti.com
This award-winning family restaurant has been a Memphis tradition for nearly a century and is currently operated by a third-generation Grisanti. Grisanti's specializes in Northern Italian cuisine such as pastas, pizzas, fresh seafood, and steaks. We favor a famous recipe of Elfo Grisanti, featured in many cookbooks—gulf shrimp and fresh mushrooms sautéed in garlic butter sauce and served on spaghetti pasta. Once located on Main Street in downtown Memphis, today Grisanti's can be found in east Memphis's Embassy Suites hotel off Poplar Avenue.

THE RENDEZVOUS $$–$$$
52 South Second Street, Memphis, TN
(901) 523-2746, (800) 464-7359
www.hogsfly.com
The entrance to this world-famous barbecue restaurant is actually in the alley across from the Peabody Memphis's main entrance. The Rendezvous is noted for its ribs and pork. Many consider a slab of ribs at the Rendezvous the holy grail of barbecue; others wonder what all the fuss is about. We will tell you that the Rendezvous specializes in dry ribs—that is, seasoned with dry-rub spices, not everyone's cup of tea. You can slather on the sauce yourself when your plate arrives, however. Give them 24 hours' notice and the Rendezvous

will prepare a real treat—five mouth-watering pounds of barbecued shrimp served at your table in a big, old iron skillet.

THE GREAT SMOKY MOUNTAINS

The Great Smoky Mountains National Park, encompassing more than 521,000 acres and spanning 800 square miles in Tennessee and North Carolina, is America's most visited national park. Nearly 10 million visitors come to the Smokies each year, drawn by the beauty of the mountains, the Appalachian mountain culture, recreational opportunities, and abundance of animal and plant life.

The Great Smoky Mountains are a range of the Blue Ridge Mountains, which are part of the Appalachian Mountains. The Smokies, which earned their name from the bluish, smokelike haze that rises from the dense tree growth and other vegetation, are truly a natural wonder. You can see more than 100 native species of trees; more than 1,000 types of flowering shrubs and plants; several hundred miles of clear, sparkling streams fed by mountain springs; and all kinds of mammals, birds, fish, reptiles, and other animals. As a result, the park has been designated an International Biosphere Reserve. Sadly, though, the park is being threatened by air pollution and lack of funds. Its famous smoky haze is now mixed with vehicle exhaust and emissions from coal-fired power plants.

The Smokies's most famous animal resident is *Ursus (Euarctos) americanus,* more commonly known as the black bear. Park officials say the bear population, which has risen sharply in recent years thanks to plentiful food supplies, is about 1,800 (about two bears per square mile). If you spend much time in these mountains, chances are very good that you will see one or more black bears.

You will also find plenty of activities. Nature lovers will relish the opportunities for hiking, swimming, fishing, camping, white-water rafting, horseback riding, and nature-watching. In the towns of Gatlinburg and Pigeon Forge, you can get married in one of many wedding chapels, play golf, shop, browse for arts and crafts, be entertained by top-notch singers and musicians, bungee jump, and ride go-karts. You can visit Cherokee, North Carolina, an Indian reservation, and gamble in a casino. There's something for almost everybody.

The Smokies are in the Eastern Time Zone, so set your watch ahead one hour. To get there, take I-40 E. from Nashville to Knoxville—about a three-hour drive. Then continue east on the Interstate 640 bypass toward Asheville, North Carolina (you can bypass downtown Knoxville via I-640 if you wish). Exit onto U.S. Highway 441 S. and follow the signs. You'll pass through Sevierville and the resort towns of Pigeon Forge and Gatlinburg before arriving at the entrance to the park. (The part of US 441 that passes through Sevierville, Pigeon Forge, and Gatlinburg is known as Parkway; as it enters the park and leads on to North Carolina, it becomes known as Newfound Gap Road.) An alternative route for those who would like to bypass the busy and often traffic-snarled Pigeon Forge area is to enter the park from the Townsend, Tennessee, side (often referred to as the "peaceful side of the Smokies"). From I-40 in Knoxville, take U.S. Highway 129 S. to Alcoa/ Maryville. In Maryville proceed on U.S. Highway 321 N. through Townsend. Continue straight on Highway 73 into the park.

In addition to the towns we just mentioned, this section covers attractions in Townsend, as well as Cherokee, North Carolina. In this area, literally hundreds of possibilities await you. To describe them all would require a thick book. We've chosen to cover some of our favorite activities, which, with a few exceptions, lean toward the "natural." If you prefer to bungee jump or ride go-karts or helicopters, don't worry if you don't find those activities described in this section. We guarantee that, once you get here, you won't have any trouble finding them. They are everywhere, especially in "action-packed Pigeon Forge," to quote the advertisements.

For more information on opportunities in the Smoky Mountains, these numbers may be of help:

Visitor's Tip

If you're visiting east Tennessee's Great Smoky Mountains National Park, consider spending some time in the peaceful mountain town of Townsend, Tennessee, just 30 minutes from Pigeon Forge and Gatlinburg. Townsend has beautiful scenery, recreation, attractions, entertainment, shopping, dining, and accommodations. For more information, call the Townsend Visitors Center, (800) 525-6834. For a free vacation guide, call the Smoky Mountain Visitors Bureau, (800) 525-6834, or visit www.smokymountains.org.

- Cherokee Welcome Center, (800) 438-1601, www.cherokee-nc.com
- Gatlinburg Chamber of Commerce, (865) 436-4178 or (800) 588-1817, www.gatlinburg.com
- Great Smoky Mountains National Park, (865) 436-1200, www.nps.gov/grsm
- Pigeon Forge Department of Tourism, (865) 453-8574 or (800) 251-9100, www.mypigeon forge.com
- Sevierville Chamber of Commerce, (865) 453-6411 or (800) 255-6411, www.sevierville chamber.com
- Sugarlands Visitor Center, (865) 436-5615
- Townsend Visitor Center, (865) 448-6134 or (800) 525-6834, www.smokymountains.org

Natural Attractions

CADES COVE

Take scenic, winding Little River Road (U.S. Highway 73), off US 441 near the Sugarlands Visitor Center, to reach Cades Cove, about 25 miles away. This 6,800-acre valley, the park's most popular destination, was once home to a thriving frontier community that lasted from the mid-1700s to the mid-1800s. As you pass through the valley on a one-way, 11-mile loop road, you'll see old log homesteads and barns, smokehouses, a working corn mill, three historic churches with cemeteries, and, most likely, an abundance of wildlife. Cades Cove offers several hiking trails, ranging from 2 to 11 miles round-trip. From May through September the 11-mile loop is closed to motor vehicles until 10:00 a.m. on Wednesday and Saturday to allow bicyclists to enjoy the park. On Saturday in December the road is closed until noon to allow for hayrides, biking, and walking.

On the way to Cades Cove, stop at the Townsend Y, where the middle and west prongs of the Little Pigeon River come together. This peaceful and popular spot is ideal for picnicking, swimming, or floating on inner tubes. A large, grassy bank looks down on the curve of the river. The Cades Cove Visitor Center is located about 6 miles around the loop at the Cable Mill area.

NEWFOUND GAP ROAD

Newfound Gap Road, or US 441, leads through the center of the Great Smoky Mountains National Park, winding southeast on its way over the mountains and into North Carolina. This route will take you to or near a number of scenic overlooks, hiking trails, and other points of interest, including Chimney Tops, Mount LeConte, Clingmans Dome, Newfound Gap, and Cherokee (descriptions follow).

CHIMNEY TOPS

The gap between these dual peaks, about 2,000 feet high, has the appearance, to some, of a flue; hence the name. You can see the peaks from the Chimney Tops overlook on Newfound Gap Road. Just 5 miles up the road from the Sugarlands Visitor Center is the Chimneys picnic area. This highly popular spot, in a ravine, contains plenty of picnic tables and a mountain stream filled with big boulders that are perfect for resting, sunning, or walking across the stream.

MOUNT LECONTE

Mount LeConte, which at 6,593 feet is the Smokies's third highest peak, is visible throughout the park. But you must hike or ride on horseback to

reach it, as it is accessible only by five trails ranging from 11 to 16 miles round-trip. Two overlooks provide magnificent views from the top of Mount LeConte, and you can make reservations for rustic (that is, no showers) mountaintop lodging by calling Wilderness Lodging at (865) 429-5704. A maximum of about 50 guests per night can stay at Mount LeConte. You'll need to make your reservations as much as a year in advance. The lodges begin taking reservations for the following season on the first business day of October, and all the Saturdays in the coming year are usually booked on the first day of reservations; bookings for the remainder of the year are usually filled by the end of October. You may call at other times of the year to inquire about cancellations.

i Elevations in the Great Smoky Mountains National Park range from 800 feet to 6,643 feet. If you're planning to hike in the park, keep in mind that temperatures are 10 to 20 degrees cooler on the mountaintops.

Guests at the lodge are served two meals a day: a dinner of beef stew, applesauce, and biscuits, and a hearty hiker's breakfast the next morning. If you stay more than one night, the lodge will pack a lunch for you.

NEWFOUND GAP

At this site, 15 miles up Newfound Gap Road from Sugarlands Visitor Center, President Franklin Delano Roosevelt officially dedicated the Great Smoky Mountains National Park in 1940. A parking area includes restrooms and provides some great photo opportunities of Smoky Mountain ranges. Here you can also get on the Appalachian Trail, a 2,000-mile trail that stretches south to Georgia and north to Maine. Charlie's Bunion, a 1,000-foot sheer drop-off, is a 4-mile eastward hike from here.

CLINGMANS DOME

Clingmans Dome, at 6,643 feet, is the highest point in all of Tennessee and the third tallest peak east of the Mississippi River. A 7-mile road from Newfound Gap Road takes you to a parking area from which you can take a steep 0.5-mile hike to the peak's observation tower. Here you'll discover a spectacular 360-degree panorama of the Smokies—one of the most incredible vistas you'll encounter. Sometimes Clingmans Dome is above the level of the clouds; while this can limit visibility, it also offers an eerily dreamlike view. Clingmans Dome is closed from December through March.

ROARING FORK MOTOR NATURE TRAIL

The Roaring Fork Motor Nature Trail, off US 321 E., is a one-way, 6-mile loop that contains a number of homesteads from the early 19th century as well as an abundance of natural beauty. Several hiking trails are accessible from the Roaring Fork road; these range from the easy Grotto Falls (3 miles round-trip) to the strenuous Trillium Gap (9 miles round-trip). This area contains three waterfalls, one of which—Meigs Falls—is visible from the road.

GREENBRIER

The entrance to this wooded area, which lies along the middle prong of the Little Pigeon River, is a few miles outside downtown Gatlinburg off US 321 E. It's a popular place to float in inner tubes—various stores and gas stations on US 321 rent them—over the river's rapids, which range from mild to moderate in this area. Other people prefer simply to relax on rocks, enjoy a picnic lunch, or hike on one of several trails, which range from about 3 to 8 miles round-trip. The narrow 4-mile road that winds through the Greenbrier area is secluded and filled with beautiful scenery, including plants and wildlife.

Other Attractions
CHEROKEE, NORTH CAROLINA

Cherokee, an Indian reservation 35 miles from Sugarlands Visitor Center, contains the Cherokee Museum and Gallery as well as numerous shops that sell Native American arts and crafts. The reservation is also home to Harrah's Cherokee

Casino, featuring video poker, craps, blackjack, and pull tabs, along with live entertainment and dining; call (800) HARRAHS for details.

DOLLYWOOD $$$$
1020 Dollywood Lane
Pigeon Forge, TN
(865) 428-9488, (800) 365-5996
www.dollywood.com

Dollywood, owned by Dolly Parton, is a theme park devoted to music, arts and crafts, and rides for the entire family. Many of the park's attractions reflect Dolly's down-home mountain heritage. Rides include the Tennessee Tornado spiral loop roller coaster, Smoky Mountain River Rampage white-water rafting ride, Mountain Slidewinder water toboggan, Dollywood Express steam train, an old-fashioned carousel, and a few kiddie rides. A water park, Dolly's Splash Country (www.dollyssplashcountry.com), features numerous water slides and pools for all ages.

Dollywood is also home to the Southern Gospel Music Hall of Fame and Museum and Eagle Mountain Sanctuary, featuring the largest presentation of nonreleasable bald eagles in the country. The Smoky Mountain Home is a replica of Dolly's childhood home. The interactive Chasing Rainbows attraction lets you "share the stage" with Dolly, see what you look like in one of her wigs, and listen to some of her songs. The Dreamland Forest is a large children's play area.

Dozens of daily shows range from contemporary country and '50s rock 'n' roll to Southern gospel and the music of Dolly and other songwriters of the Smokies. During certain weekends, the park features, for an additional charge, concerts by many of today's country superstars. Dollywood is also home to five of the South's largest festivals—Festival of Nations, KidsFest, Bluegrass & BBQ, National Harvest, and Smoky Mountain Christmas. Dollywood, 1 mile off the Parkway in Pigeon Forge, is open April through December, although the days and hours of operation vary. Call or check the Web site for the schedule.

GREAT SMOKY ARTS AND CRAFTS COMMUNITY   FREE

US 321 N., Glades and Buckhorn Roads,
Gatlinburg, TN
(800) 565-7330
www.artsandcraftscommunity.com

Glassblowers, candle makers, potters, basket weavers, visual artists, doll makers, wood-carvers, and many other types of artists and craftspeople have their wares on display and for sale on this 8-mile loop of shops, studios, and galleries. Many offer free demonstrations of their work. The loop begins 3 miles from traffic light No. 3 in downtown Gatlinburg. The community holds special shows during Thanksgiving week, early December (Christmas), and early April (Easter).

OBER GATLINBURG   FREE

Ski Mountain Road, Gatlinburg, TN
(865) 436-5423, (800) 251-9202
www.obergatlinburg.com

Ober Gatlinburg is a ski resort and amusement park atop 3,500-foot Mount Harrison. You can drive to it by way of the winding and often steep Ski Mountain Road or ride the aerial tramway at 1001 Parkway (traffic light No. 9) in downtown Gatlinburg. Skiing is seasonal, with primarily human-made snow, but the rest of the park is open year-round. Amusements include an alpine slide, bungee jumping, an ice-skating rink, arcade games, shopping, and a black bear habitat. Admission is free, with prices varying per attraction. The Ober Gatlinburg Restaurant, which overlooks the ski slopes, is a great place to refuel or unwind.

RIPLEY'S AQUARIUM OF THE SMOKIES $$$$

88 River Road, Gatlinburg, TN
(865) 430-8808, (888) 240-1358
www.ripleysaquariumofthesmokies.com

The highlight of Gatlinburg's spectacular $70-million aquarium is the world's longest aquarium tunnel. Submerged in a million gallons of water, the clear acrylic tunnel allows guests an up-close look at most of the aquarium's residents, including 10-foot tiger sharks. A 340-foot moving walkway transports you along under the water; if you want a closer look, you can step off the path, then step back on when you're ready to move along. The aquarium is home to 10,000 exotic fish from around the world and has more than 30 tanks and exhibits. In addition to many species of sharks, residents include moray eels, jellyfish, giant red-bellied piranhas, the giant Pacific octopus, and the Japanese spider crab, the world's largest crustacean. Fascinating dive shows occur regularly in the Coral Reef exhibit. There are lots of interactive areas, including Sting Ray Bay, where you can pet a stingray (which, by the way, can range in size from 5 inches to 10 feet across), and the Discovery Center, which allows kids to examine horseshoe crabs. The 115,000-square-foot, 1.3-million-gallon aquarium opened in December 2000 and has become one of the area's most popular attractions. The aquarium is open 365 days a year.

Be[ar] Aware

The Great Smoky Mountains National Park is home to about 1,800 black bears. Here are a few bear facts: The bears are most active in early morning and late evening during spring and summer. They usually mate in July. Females and their newborn cubs emerge from their winter dens in late March or early April. In addition to being good tree climbers, black bears are good swimmers and can run 30 miles per hour. If you see a bear, do not approach it; although rare, black bear attacks on humans have occurred!

Recreation

DEER FARM RIDING STABLES $$$$
Happy Hollow Lane, Sevierville, TN
(865) 429-BARN
www.deerfarmzoo.com

Half-hour- and hour-long rides in the foothills of the Smokies are available year-round, weather permitting, at Deer Farm, which is also the site of an exotic petting zoo with zebras, donkeys, camels, reindeer, kangaroos, wallabies, prairie dogs, miniature goats, exotic cattle, miniature horses, and much more.

i The Tennessee Department of Tourist Development operates 13 welcome centers along Tennessee's interstates. Each welcome center has a toll-free telephone system that allows travelers to make hotel, motel, and campground reservations anywhere within the state.

SMOKY MOUNTAIN OUTDOORS UNLIMITED $$$$
3229 Hartford Road, Hartford, TN
(800) 771-RAFT
www.smokymountainrafting.com

Smoky Mountain Outdoors Unlimited takes rafters onto the Big Pigeon River. You and your rafting colleagues, with a guide, will take a bus to your entry point near the North Carolina state line. (First you'll receive a thorough briefing on proper use of oars and general rafting safety.) Then you'll put your raft into the water for a 6.5-mile trip back to headquarters. Along the way you'll pass through more than 40 Class I and II rapids, more than a dozen Class IIIs, and four Class IVs (the roughest of the trip). If this sounds too adventurous for you, inquire about the 5.5-mile trip on the lower section of the river—it has less speed and is suitable for kids. No experience is necessary, but whitewater rafting can be a risky activity, and you'll have to sign a waiver releasing the company from liability. We came through our trip unscathed, exhilarated, and determined to try it again someday. The business operates May through September and is closed on Friday, Sunday, and Monday.

Accommodations

We'd like to caution you from the start that, while you certainly can take a day trip to the Smokies, you'll more than likely want to make the trip last more than one day. There are many hotels and motels in the area, but our preferred lodging would be a mountain cabin, cottage, or chalet. You can rent anything from a cozy one-room cabin to a luxury chalet with five or more bedrooms accommodating 15 or more people. Features, which vary according to property, include fireplaces, gorgeous mountain or forest views, mountain streams, decks, barbecue grills, outdoor hot tubs, indoor whirlpools, pool tables, TVs and VCRs, and much more, including all the amenities of home. Prices also vary significantly, with such a wide range of properties available. You can pay less than $100 a night or as much as $500 or more. The average price for a fully equipped two-bedroom chalet is generally around $125 to $150 a night.

Some rental companies:

- Alpine Chalet Rentals, 103 Silverbell Lane, Gatlinburg, Tennessee; (865) 436-4370 or (800) 235-2661; www.alpinechaletrentals.com
- Baskins Creek Vacation Rentals, 215 Circle Drive, Gatlinburg, Tennessee; (865) 436-7811 or (800) 436-7811; www.baskinscreek.com
- Jackson Mountain Homes, 1662 East Parkway, Gatlinburg, Tennessee; (865) 436-8876 or (800) 473-3163; www.jacksonmountainhomes.com

Just be sure to make your reservations in advance, especially during peak times like the start of autumn, when thousands of visitors come to see the beautiful fall colors.

Shopping

Many people travel to the area simply to shop. Pigeon Forge has several major outlet malls offering discounted prices on brand-name merchandise. Here are some of our favorites:

BELZ FACTORY OUTLET WORLD
2655 Teaster Lane, Pigeon Forge, TN
(865) 453-3503
www.belz.com

PIGEON FORGE FACTORY OUTLET MALL
2850 Parkway, Pigeon Forge, TN
(865) 428-2828
www.mypigeonforge.com

RIVERVIEW FACTORY STORES
2668 Teaster Lane, Pigeon Forge, TN

RIVERVISTA FACTORY STORES
2732 Teaster Lane, Pigeon Forge, TN
www.mypigeonforge.com

TANGER OUTLET CENTER AT FIVE OAKS
1645 Parkway, Sevierville, TN
(865) 453-1053, (800) 408-8377
www.tangeroutlet.com

TANGER OUTLET CENTER
161 E. Wears Valley Road
Pigeon Forge, TN
(865) 428-7002, (800) 408-5775
www.tangeroutlet.com

Restaurants

APPLEWOOD FARMHOUSE
RESTAURANT $$–$$$
250 Apple Valley Road, Sevierville, TN
(865) 428-1222

APPLEWOOD FARMHOUSE GRILL $$
250 Apple Valley Road, Sevierville, TN
(865) 429-8644
www.applebarncidermill.com

In our opinion, a visit to the Smokies isn't complete without a meal at one of these quaint restaurants, situated in the midst of an apple orchard. The Southern-fried chicken, turkey and dressing, and chicken and dumplings are delicious, and all meals start with complimentary homemade apple fritters and apple juleps. The Farmhouse Restaurant, the original eatery here, serves five-course dinners; vegetables are family-style. The Farmhouse Grill offers basically the same menu, but dinners are three-course, and there are more a la carte options. While you wait for your table— and you'll probably have to wait—you can relax in a rocking chair on the porch or visit the Apple Barn Cider Mill & General Store on the property (we always take home a jar or two of the tasty apple butter from the store).

i Before 1819, Cades Cove, in the Great Smoky Mountains National Park, was part of the Cherokee Nation. The Cherokee name for the cove was Tsiyahi, which translates to "place of the river otter."

HOFBRAUHAUS RESTAURANT $
634 Parkway, Suite 14, the Village
Gatlinburg, TN
(865) 436-9511
www.thevillageshops.com/hofbrauhaus

Reubens made with steamed, lean corned beef on pumpernickel rolls are the specialty at this cozy little restaurant, upstairs from the Cheese Cupboard in the Village collection of shops. The restaurant, established in 1969, also serves roast beef, turkey, pastrami, and other deli sandwiches; bratwurst; and beer.

THE OLD MILL RESTAURANT $$$
2934 Middle Creek Road
Pigeon Forge, TN
(865) 429-3463
www.old-mill.com

This restaurant serves Southern specialties like catfish and fried chicken in a scenic location next to a working mill on the Little Pigeon River. Before or after your meal, you can visit the mill and even buy some cornmeal.

i If you're traveling from Nashville to East Tennessee on I-40, you'll enter the Eastern Time Zone (one hour ahead of Central Time Zone) before you get to the Rockwood and Harriman areas. If you're traveling east on I-24, you'll enter the Eastern Time Zone a few miles before you reach Chattanooga.

i Have you ever wondered where East Tennessee's Frozen Head State Natural Area got its name? The 11,869-acre wilderness area in Wartburg is named for a 3,324-foot peak that often is capped in ice or snow. For more information, call the park at (423) 346–3318.

PANCAKE PANTRY $–$$

628 Parkway, Gatlinburg, TN
(865) 436-4724
www.pancakepantry.com

Nashvillians who enjoy dining at their hometown Pancake Pantry (see our Restaurants chapter) will want to try out Gatlinburg's version. This warm and cozy restaurant opened in 1960 and has the distinction of being Tennessee's first pancake house. In addition to pancakes, waffles, eggs, and other breakfast items—which are served all day—the menu includes gourmet sandwiches, soups, and salads, which are available for lunch. It's located near traffic light No. 6.

THE PARK GRILL $$$$

1110 Parkway, Gatlinburg, TN
(865) 436-2300
www.parkgrillgatlinburg.com

THE PEDDLER RESTAURANT $$$$

820 River Road, Gatlinburg, TN
(865) 436-5794
www.peddlergatlinburg.com

Both these restaurants, which share ownership, are in big log buildings. The Peddler, a long-time favorite, is noted for its steaks, marinated chicken, grilled seafood, and salad bar. The newer Park Grill is a little more family-oriented, with a wide children's menu. Specialties include ribs and trout. Homemade desserts like Jack Daniel's Crème Brûlée, with real Jack Daniel's whiskey, and creamy custard, with freshly caramelized sugar, are prepared daily.

RELOCATION

If you're relocating to Nashville, have recently moved here, or are in the market for a new home in the area, this chapter is for you. In the following pages we'll tell you about Nashville-area neighborhoods, give you the scoop on the real estate scene, and provide a list of resources that will come in handy. Nashville has come a long way since the pioneering folks of 1779 established a settlement on the banks of the Cumberland River. The city has continued to grow and expand its boundaries in every direction, and the population has boomed. Today more than 1.3 million people live in the 13-county Nashville–Davidson–Murfreesboro Metropolitan Statistical Area. (MSA counties are Davidson, Cannon, Cheatham, Dickson, Hickman, Macon, Robertson, Rutherford, Smith, Sumner, Trousdale, Wilson, and Williamson.)

Newcomers arrive daily, lured by Middle Tennessee's low cost of living, affordable housing, opportunities for higher education, and overall quality of life. Nashville is one of the most affordable cities of its size. Its cost of living consistently ranks below the national average. According to the American Chamber of Commerce Researchers Association, Nashville's cost of living in the second quarter of 2008 was rated 91.8 of the national average.

Housing in Nashville is among the most affordable in the country. According to the aforementioned ACCRA report, the average cost of a new, 2,400-square-foot home in Nashville is $245,097. (For comparison, the same home would cost $264,989 in Richmond, Virginia, and $258,989 in Atlanta.) Renters will find plenty of available properties. The average rent for a 950-square-foot, unfurnished, two-bedroom, two-bath apartment in Nashville is $995, according to ACCRA. While that figure is a bit higher than some other Southern cities, renters can find a variety of properties and rates by exploring the different areas of Nashville. Many apartment communities have offered competitive new-resident discounts and other move-in incentives in recent years.

Nashvillians live in the city, in the suburbs, and out in the country. We make our homes in modern houses, high-rise condos, renovated historic houses, downtown lofts, apartments, farmhouses, mansions, cottages, and town houses in communities and neighborhoods that are as diverse as the people who live in them.

OVERVIEW

If you're a newcomer, you will soon find out that the Nashville area is made up of many different "neighborhoods"—suburbs, urban and rural areas, and historic districts—each with its own personality and appeal. Belle Meade is as different from Madison as Hillsboro Village is from Antioch.

The top restaurants, clubs, and shops are, for the most part, on the west side of the Cumberland River. However, east Nashville is experiencing a renaissance, with quite a few good restaurants and trendy nightspots, as well as rising property values. If you never cross the river and explore the east side, you're missing a treat—lots of good neighborhoods, historic homes, plenty of shopping, good food, and numerous recreation opportunities.

Within Metro Nashville are seven satellite cities that were incorporated before Nashville and Davidson County merged in 1963 to form Metro. These cities—Belle Meade, Berry Hill, Forest Hills, half of Goodlettsville, Lakewood, Oak Hill, and Ridgetop—have their own planning and zoning boards, city officials, and various city services.

They are somewhat indistinguishable from surrounding Nashville areas and generally have a suburban feel.

While people relocating to the Nashville area often head straight to Davidson County, existing residents are moving to surrounding counties, including Cheatham, Dickson, Robertson, Rutherford, Sumner, Williamson, and Wilson. In fact, according to U.S. census figures, between 1990 and 2000 Williamson and Rutherford Counties had Tennessee's highest population growth rates: 56.3 percent and 53.5 percent, respectively. The population of the aforementioned surrounding counties increased from about 23 percent to about 31 percent, while Davidson County's population increased 11.6 percent, to 569,891. The Nashville economic market includes Maury County to the southwest and Montgomery County to the north, adding 204,000 or so to the population.

Many cite taxes, schools, housing prices, and quality of life as their reasons for moving to outlying areas. According to a study by the UT Center for Business and Economic Research, between the years 2000 and 2020, Davidson County's population is expected to increase 11 percent—to 605,030—while surrounding counties will experience growth rates ranging from 34 percent to 81 percent.

Not surprisingly, major development is occurring along the interstate system and major secondary arteries into Davidson County. Easy access to Interstate 40, Interstate 24, and Interstate 65 makes living in a surrounding county an appealing option for many Nashville workers. According to the U.S. Census Bureau and Metro Planning Commission, nearly 75,000 passenger vehicles from Sumner, Williamson, Rutherford, Wilson, and Cheatham Counties travel to Nashville each day. The Federal Highway Administration reports that Nashvillians travel an average of about 32 miles per person per day. A good portion of that is the commute to and from work. The construction of Interstate 840, a route extending from Lebanon in the east to Dickson, west of Nashville, will make it even easier to zip around the area.

Regardless of the region in which you choose to live, it's a good idea to learn about the school districts, tax rates, level of services, restrictions, and zoning laws. For example, if you want to live on a lake, you should know that most lake areas allow for very limited shoreline access, but there are some areas designated for shoreline development that might allow for a dock if you obtain a permit. If you plan to build on acreage that requires a well or septic tank, consult local officials to make sure the land will percolate—a necessary component in obtaining a permit to install a septic system. Some areas in Middle Tennessee are rocky, making it difficult to support septic systems.

Of course, you also have price to consider. Fortunately, Nashville has something for every budget. With a little patience, you will find what you're looking for, whether it's an efficiency apartment or a custom-designed new home.

GETTING ESTABLISHED

This section offers information on resources related to Metro government, schools, utility connections, vehicle registration and driver's licenses, libraries, hospitals, and more. See our Education and Child Care, Retirement, Health Care and Wellness, Media, and Worship chapters for other useful newcomer information. Most of the listings in this section apply to the Metropolitan Nashville–Davidson County area only.

METRO GOVERNMENT
(615) 862-5000 (information)

Metro Nashville's Web site—www.nashville .gov—is an excellent source of information on all things related to Metro government. You'll find information on business, education, employment, health care services, residential resources, transportation, and much more.

Chambers of Commerce and Visitor Bureaus

The Nashville Chamber of Commerce can provide general information about the area as well as information on businesses. For information on other local chambers of commerce and visitor bureaus in the Nashville area, see the individual writeups on counties, cities, and neighborhoods in this chapter.

NASHVILLE CHAMBER OF COMMERCE
(615) 743-3000
www.nashvillechamber.com

NASHVILLE CONVENTION & VISITORS BUREAU
(615) 259-4700, (800) 657-6910
www.nashvillecvb.com

GREATER NASHVILLE BLACK CHAMBER OF COMMERCE
(615) 876-9634
www.nashvilleblackchamber.org

Utility Connections

For a list of utility service providers outside the Metro Nashville–Davidson County area, contact the Nashville Chamber of Commerce or visit the Web site www.nashvillechamber.com.

NASHVILLE ELECTRIC SERVICE
(615) 736-6900
www.nespower.com

NASHVILLE GAS CO.
(615) 734-0665
www.nashvillegas.com

METRO WATER SERVICES
(615) 862-4600
www.nashville.gov/water

TRASH REMOVAL AND RECYCLING
Metropolitan Nashville Department of Public Works' Waste Management Division
(615) 880-1000
www.nashville.gov/pw

Phone Service

BellSouth is the dominant local phone service provider. Several other companies provide local service as well. For a more comprehensive list of providers, see the "Customer Guides" section on establishing phone service in the front of the local phone book or visit the Nashville Chamber of Commerce's Web site, www.nashvillechamber.com.

BELLSOUTH
(888) 757-6500
www.bellsouth.com

MCI TELECOMMUNICATIONS
(800) 539-2000
www.mci.com

SPRINT COMMUNICATIONS
(800) 877-2000
www.sprint.com

Cable Television

COMCAST
(615) 244-5900
www.comcast.com
For counties outside Davidson, contact the Tennessee Cable Telecommunications Association at (615) 256-7037, or visit www.tcta.net.

Vehicle Information

Driver's License

TENNESSEE DEPARTMENT OF SAFETY
(615) 741-3954
www.tennessee.gov/safety
A driver's license must be obtained within 30 days of establishing residency in Tennessee. A regular operator license costs $19.50. Written, vision, and road tests are required. Road and written tests aren't necessary for those with a valid out-of-state license. New driver's license laws took effect in mid-2004. First-time applicants and new and returning residents of Tennessee now must provide proof of U.S. citizenship or lawful permanent residency, two proofs of identity, two proofs of Tennessee residency, and proof of a Social Security number (or a sworn affidavit stating that you have never been issued

a Social Security number). Additionally, anyone issued a Tennessee license since January 1, 2001, is required to provide documentation of U.S. citizenship or lawful permanent residency at the time of their first renewal.

Effective July 1, 2004, those who are not eligible for a Tennessee driver's license because they are not U.S. citizens or lawful permanent residents may apply for a Certificate for Driving (the certificate is not a valid form of identification, although this is currently being challenged in the courts). Call or visit the Web site for a list of local examining stations, a list of accepted forms of documentation, and other information.

i In 1978 Tennessee became the first state in the nation to require the use of safety seats for children who are passengers in motor vehicles. Within a decade all 50 states passed laws mandating some form of child restraint in automobiles.

Vehicle Titling and Registration

DAVIDSON COUNTY CLERK
(615) 862-6251
www.nashville.gov/cclerk

To title a vehicle in Tennessee, you will need either the clear title from the previous state or the lien holder's name and address, as well as your registration and a valid emissions test certificate (see subsequent entry). In Davidson County, to obtain or renew your vehicle registration, you must present current registration (if renewing), a valid emissions test certificate, or car title or the lien holder's name and address, and the required fees. The Tennessee Department of Safety mails vehicle registration renewal notices. However, if you do not receive a renewal form, last year's copy or other proof of vehicle ownership is adequate. For other counties, contact the county clerk's office for renewal information.

Vehicle Emissions Testing

(615) 399-8995
www.tennessee.gov/safety

Residents of Davidson, Rutherford, Sumner, Hamilton, Williamson, and Wilson Counties must have their vehicles tested before registering or renewing their vehicle registration, unless their vehicle is a 1974 or earlier model. The cost for emissions testing is $10 (cash only). Call the listed number or visit the Web site for the testing station nearest you.

Voter Registration

DAVIDSON COUNTY ELECTION COMMISSION
(615) 862-8800
www.nashville.gov/vote

You may register to vote if you are a citizen of the United States, if you are or will be at least 18 years of age before the next election day, and if you are a Tennessee resident. You may vote if you have registered at least 30 days prior to an election. For more information or to download a voter registration application, visit the Web site listed above.

Metropolitan Nashville Public Schools

- **General Information**, (615) 259-8400, www.mnps.org
- **Student Assignment** (to find out what school child will attend), (615) 259-4636
- **Adult Basic Education** (GED preparation and Adult English Language Learners classes), (615) 259-8551
- **Adult/Community Education**, (615) 259-8549
- **Community Relations**, (615) 259-8485
- **Director of Schools Office**, (615) 259-8419
- **English Language Learners**, (615) 298-8467
- **Homework Hotline** (Monday through Thursday 5:00 p.m. to 8:00 p.m.), (615) 298-6636
- **Magnet School Information**, (615) 259-4636
- **Special Education**, (615) 259-8699
- **Transportation**, (615) 782-3870

Hospitals

Nashville, known as the "Silicon Valley of Health Care," has several excellent hospitals. There are more than 30 hospitals, medical centers, clinics, and specialty centers in the region, as well as thousands of health care professionals. Following is a listing of area hospitals. See our Health Care and Wellness chapter for details on each, as well as for other health care information.

ALVIN C. YORK VETERANS AFFAIRS MEDICAL CENTER
3400 Lebanon Pike, Murfreesboro
(615) 867-6000

BAPTIST HOSPITAL
2000 Church Street
(615) 284-5555
www.baptisthospital.com

CENTENNIAL MEDICAL CENTER
2300 Patterson Street
(615) 342-1000
www.centennialmedctr.com

CENTENNIAL MEDICAL CENTER AT ASH-LAND CITY
313 North Main Street, Ashland City
(615) 792-3030
www.centennialashlandcity.com

HENDERSONVILLE MEDICAL CENTER
355 New Shackle Island Road, Hendersonville
(615) 338-1000
www.hendersonvillemedicalcenter.com

HORIZON MEDICAL CENTER
111 U.S. Highway 70 E., Dickson
(615) 446-0446
www.horizonmedicalcenter.com

MIDDLE TENNESSEE MEDICAL CENTER
400 North Highland Avenue, Murfreesboro
(615) 849-4100
www.mtmc.org

NASHVILLE GENERAL HOSPITAL AT MEHARRY
1818 Albion Street
(615) 341-4000
www.nashville.gov/generalhospital

NASHVILLE VETERANS AFFAIRS MEDICAL CENTER
1310 24th Avenue S.
(615) 327-4751

NORTHCREST MEDICAL CENTER
100 NorthCrest Drive, Springfield
(615) 384-2411
www.northcrest.com

PORTLAND MEDICAL CENTER
105 Redbud Drive, Portland
(615) 325-7301
www.portlandmedcenter.com

SAINT THOMAS HOSPITAL
4220 Harding Road
(615) 222-2111
www.saintthomas.org

SKYLINE MEDICAL CENTER
3441 Dickerson Pike
(615) 769-2000
www.skylinemedicalcenter.com

SOUTHERN HILLS MEDICAL CENTER
391 Wallace Road
(615) 781-4000
www.southernhills.com

STONECREST MEDICAL CENTER
200 StoneCrest Boulevard, Smyrna
(615) 768-2000
www.stonecrestmedical.com

SUMMIT MEDICAL CENTER
5655 Frist Boulevard, Hermitage
(615) 316-3000
www.summitmedicalcenter.com

TENNESSEE CHRISTIAN MEDICAL CENTER
500 Hospital Drive, Madison
(615) 865-0300
www.tennesseechristian.com

UNIVERSITY MEDICAL CENTER
1411 Baddour Parkway, Lebanon
(615) 444-8262
www.universitymedicalctr.com

VANDERBILT CHILDREN'S HOSPITAL (MONROE CARELL JR. CHILDREN'S HOSPITAL)
2200 Children's Way
(615) 936-1000
www.vanderbiltchildrens.com

VANDERBILT UNIVERSITY MEDICAL CENTER
1211 22nd Avenue S.
(615) 322-5000
www.mc.vanderbilt.edu

WILLIAMSON MEDICAL CENTER
2021 Carothers Road, Franklin
(615) 435-5000
www.williamsonmedicalcenter.org

Libraries

The Nashville Public Library has 20 branches throughout Davidson County in addition to the main location downtown. The library also operates the Nashville Talking Library, an audio reading service that broadcasts around-the-clock readings to those who cannot read normally printed matter because of a visual or physical impairment or because of a reading disability. Visit the library online at www.library.nashville.org for more information about the library system or to search the card catalog and check for availability of materials.

MAIN LIBRARY
615 Church Street
(615) 862-5800
www.library.nashville.org

NASHVILLE TALKING LIBRARY
505 Heritage Drive, Madison
(615) 862-5874

BELLEVUE BRANCH
650 Colice Jeanne Road
(615) 862-5854

BORDEAUX BRANCH
4000 Clarksville Pike
(615) 862-5856

DONELSON BRANCH
2315 Lebanon Road
(615) 862-5859

EAST BRANCH
206 Gallatin Avenue
(615) 862-5860

EDGEHILL BRANCH
1409 12th Avenue S.
(615) 862-5861

EDMONDSON PIKE BRANCH
5501 Edmondson Pike
(615) 880-3957

GOODLETTSVILLE BRANCH
106 Old Brick Church Pike, Goodlettsville
(615) 862-5862

GREEN HILLS BRANCH
3701 Benham Avenue
(615) 862-5863

HADLEY PARK BRANCH
1039 28th Avenue N.
(615) 862-5865

HERMITAGE BRANCH
3700 James Kay Lane, Hermitage
(615) 880-3951

INGLEWOOD BRANCH
4312 Gallatin Road
(615) 862-5866

Close-up

Nashville-Area Property Tax Rates

The following are the 2007 property tax rates per $100 of assessed value. Rates for cities are in addition to county rates, unless otherwise noted.

Cheatham County—$2.78

Ashland City—$0.46

Kingston Springs—$0.78

Davidson County

(General Services District)—$4.04

(Urban Services District)—$4.69

Belle Meade—$0.26

Goodlettsville—$0.66

Ridgetop—$0.85

Dickson County—$2.63

Burns—$0.33

Charlotte—$0.17

Dickson—$0.90

White Bluff—$0.44

Rutherford County—$2.44

Eagleville—$0.92

LaVergne—$0.50

Murfreesboro—$1.41

Smyrna—$0.86

Sumner County—$2.28

Gallatin—$1.12

Goodlettsville—$0.66

Hendersonville—$0.63

Millersville—$0.86

Mitchellville—$0.64

Portland—$1.03

Westmoreland—$1.40

White House—$1.02

Williamson County—$2.31 (county only)

Brentwood—$2.79 county + $0.49

Fairview—$2.26 county + $0.70

Franklin—$2.20 county + $0.43

Franklin Special School District—$220 + $0.43

Nolensville—$2.26 county + $0.06

Spring Hill—$2.26 (county only)

Thompson Station—$2.26 county + $0.10

Wilson County—$2.48

Watertown—$0.75

Lebanon—$0.37

Lebanon Special School District—$0.39

Source: State of Tennessee, Comptroller of the Treasury

MADISON BRANCH
610 Gallatin Pike S., Madison
(615) 862-5868

NORTH BRANCH
1001 Monroe Street
(615) 862-5858

OLD HICKORY BRANCH
1010 Jones Street, Old Hickory
(615) 862-5869

PRUITT BRANCH
117 Charles E. Davis Boulevard
(615) 862-5985

RICHLAND PARK BRANCH
4711 Charlotte Avenue
(615) 862-5870

SOUTHEAST BRANCH
2325 Hickory Highlands Drive, Antioch
(615) 862-5871

THOMPSON LANE BRANCH
380 Thompson Lane
(615) 862-5873

WATKINS PARK BRANCH
612 17th Avenue N.
(615) 862-5872

Z. ALEXANDER LOOBY BRANCH
2301 Metro Center Boulevard
(615) 862-5867

NEIGHBORHOODS

With so many great neighborhoods, choosing one in which to live can be tough. You can use the neighborhood descriptions in this section to aid you in your search or just to learn more about the different communities in and around Nashville. We use the term *neighborhood* pretty loosely. While Green Hills could be considered a neighborhood, the area also has several smaller neighborhoods that have their own character and style. The same is true for most other areas we call "neighborhoods." If you are relocating or are considering moving to another part of town, we highly recommend making several exploratory visits to different parts of town so you can get a good feel for what these areas are like.

In what follows, we describe some of the major neighborhoods, starting with those in Metro; these are grouped by area. A listing of counties follows. In local real estate and apartment guides, most listings are categorized into numbered areas that correspond to areas on the Nashville-area neighborhoods map in the front of the book. Area 2, for example, includes Green Hills, Bellevue, and Belle Meade; Area 13 is Cheatham County; and so on. We'll refer to these well-known numbered areas to help orient you to a particular neighborhood or county.

Following this Neighborhoods section is a listing of real estate agencies, services, and publications that can assist you in relocating or finding a new home.

Metropolitan Nashville–Davidson County

This very urbanized county includes those satellite cities mentioned previously as well as other extensive residential areas. Following is an overview, including some history of Metro neighborhoods.

Downtown Area

SECOND AVENUE

Among downtown Nashville's numerous historic neighborhoods, the oldest—Second Avenue, or "the District" as we sometimes call it—offers city living in the truest sense. Serious urbanites who want to feel the pulse of the city—day and night—can live here in the heart of downtown, among the neon lights and hustle and bustle of Music City.

Development of residential properties in downtown Nashville is booming. In 2004 several hundred lofts, townhomes, condos, and apartments were built in the area, making this one of the hottest real estate markets in town. One of the newest developments is the 31-story Viridian luxury condominium tower (615-254-3325, www.viridiannashville.com), which was completed at the end of 2006. The $70-million building, at 415 Church Street, behind the L&C Tower, includes 305 units ranging from 690-square-foot studio spaces to 2,747-square-foot penthouses. Prices range from $130,000 to $1.25 million. The Viridian has a grocery store on the ground level—the first grocery store in downtown Nashville since 1967—as well as a parking area, fitness center, and rooftop swimming pool.

Other residential spaces include the Kress Lofts at 237 Fifth Avenue N. (www.marksvillage.com), which consists of 21 condominiums in the revamped historic Kress department store building; loft prices here listed for about $120,000 to $145,000.

The Second Avenue area is rich in history. Second Avenue Historic District is listed on the National Register of Historic Places. Until 1903 Second Avenue was called Market Street. The center of commercial activity in the last half of the 1800s, the street was lined with two- to five-story brick Victorian warehouses that were 1 block deep. Their back entrances on Front Street (now First Avenue) received goods unloaded from vessels that had traveled down the Cumberland River. Groceries, hardware, dry goods, and other items were sold out of the buildings' Market Street entrances. Most of the buildings were built between 1870 and 1890. Later, as the railroads became the preferred method of transporting goods, and as shipping on the Cumberland declined, many of the buildings closed their doors; others served as warehouses. In the 1960s, when Nashvillians moved to the suburbs in droves, these historically significant buildings were largely unoccupied.

Burgeoning interest in historic preservation during the 1970s was a boon to this district. Businesses such as restaurants and retail shops opened in the old warehouses, and development boomed during the late 1980s. Today Second Avenue's restored 100-year-old warehouses contain unique shops, galleries, restaurants, nightclubs, and offices. For information about residential options in the downtown Nashville area, call the nonprofit Nashville Downtown Partnership at (615) 743-3090 or visit the Web site at www.nashvilledowntown.com.

i If you are experiencing a non-life-threatening emergency in Davidson County, the number to call is (615) 862-8600. See the first page of the phone book for other emergency numbers.

GERMANTOWN

Bordered by Eighth and Third Avenues N. between Jefferson and Hume Streets and spanning about 18 city blocks, historic Germantown is Nashville's oldest residential neighborhood. In the past few years, investment and redevelopment in the area have boomed.

German immigrants established the community in the late 1840s, and it grew into a truly diverse neighborhood, home to both wealthy and working-class families. The diversity is reflected in many of the area's homes. Architectural styles here include Italianate, Eastlake, and Queen Anne Victorian homes as well as modest worker cottages. After World War II, many German residents moved out. That exodus, the rezoning of the area to industrial in the 1950s, and the city's urban renewal projects in the 1960s led to the demolition of many of Germantown's historic homes. Preservationists arrived in following decades, however, and have renovated many of the buildings. Much of the new development, such as the row of frame town houses along Fifth Avenue N., is modeled after the area's older buildings.

Today Germantown boasts an interesting mixture of residential, commercial, office, and retail, as well as a diverse community of professionals, blue-collar workers, and others who enjoy living in the inner city. The area attracts lots of single professionals and older professionals who work from their homes. Some of the new properties in Germantown recently have been priced in the $225,000 to $325,000 range, with some going as high as $525,000.

i Nashville's historic Germantown area was designated as an Inner City Arboretum by the Nashville Tree Foundation in 1993. Germantown contains more than 135 varieties of trees and major shrubs. For more information about the Nashville Tree Foundation and its Arboretum designations, visit www.nashvilletreefoundation.org or call the tree hotline at (615) 292-5175.

Germantown has its own neighborhood association, Historic Germantown. Visit the association online at www.historicgermantown.org, or write to it at P.O. Box 281074, Nashville 37228. Germantown is within walking distance of the Farmers' Market on Eighth Avenue N. and the Bicentennial Capitol Mall. Other neighborhood hot spots include the Mad Platter and Monell's restaurants on Sixth Avenue N. On the second Saturday in October, Germantown invites all of Nashville to Oktoberfest, its celebration of German and American food, music, arts, and crafts.

Fisk-Meharry

Between Charlotte Avenue and Jefferson Street and 12th Avenue N. and 28th Avenue S., Fisk-Meharry is a large historic neighborhood full of renovation potential. It is named for nearby Fisk University and Meharry Medical College. Fisk opened in 1866 as a free school for newly freed slaves and is the home of the world-famous Jubilee Singers. Meharry, founded in 1876, was the first medical college for African Americans and today educates 6 out of every 10 of the country's African-American physicians and surgeons.

Architectural styles here include late-1890s and early-1900s two-story post-Victorian brick homes and American foursquares and stone-and-brick Tudors and clapboard cottages built from 1910 to 1940. According to Metro Planning Department figures, the average home sale price in Fisk-Meharry between 1995 and 2000 was $51,120; the median price was $56,500.

Edgefield

There are several historic districts on the east side of the Cumberland River. The closest to the downtown business district is historic Edgefield, which extends from South Fifth Street eastward to South 10th Street, between Woodland and Shelby Streets. It includes most blocks on Shelby, Boscobel, Fatherland, Russell, and Woodland Streets. Edgefield is one of Nashville's oldest suburbs and was the city's first residential National Trust Historic District (1977) and first locally zoned Historic District (1978, only the second in the state at the time). Edgefield was also Nashville's first urban neighborhood to begin revitalization. Because of Edgefield's designation as one of only two locally zoned historic preservation districts, all new construction, additions, demolition, alterations, and fences must be approved by the Metro Historical Commission.

Though it has changed over the years, Edgefield retains much of the charm of an early Nashville suburb. Tree-lined streets, HISTORIC EDGEFIELD signs marking neighborhood boundaries, an active neighborhood association, and a mix of professionals, young families, and longtime residents combine to create a definite neighborhood feel.

With the addition of the Tennessee Titans's stadium nearby, interest in east Nashville is increasing. Property values have risen considerably, but this is still an affordable neighborhood for first-time home buyers.

The first major residential development east of the Cumberland, this community dates from the mid-1800s, when landowner Dr. John Shelby subdivided much of his property into residential lots. At that time, a suspension bridge over the Cumberland River connected downtown Nashville with this east-bank area. A railroad bridge connected the areas by 1857.

This area was dubbed "Edgefield" by another resident, Neil S. Brown (Tennessee's governor from 1846 to 1850), who was inspired by his view of the distant fields enclosed by forests. By 1869 Edgefield, which had incorporated as a city, had more than 3,400 residents, 675 homes, and 7 churches. Italianate and Eastlake homes, including middle-class frame cottages and large brick mansions, could be found throughout the area. In 1880 Edgefield was incorporated into Nashville's city limits.

The devastating east Nashville fire of 1916 destroyed nearly 650 homes in the area and claimed one life. The Queen Anne and Italianate homes that burned were replaced by modern bungalows. In the 1950s and 1960s, as Nashvillians moved to more distant suburbs, Edgefield lost some of its prestige, becoming a largely working-class neighborhood. Many homes were turned into apartments, while urban renewal projects further chipped away at the neighborhood's character.

Thanks to the arrival of preservationists in the 1970s, Edgefield today boasts a wonderful assortment of lovingly restored old homes, including two- and three-story Victorians, post-Victorian Princess Anne cottages, American foursquares, and bungalows. In addition to restoration of historic properties, Edgefield has seen the construction of new single-family homes, apartments, and condominiums. Residents formed the nonprofit neighborhood association Historic Edgefield Inc. in 1976. The organization sponsors a tour of homes each spring, proudly showcasing some of the neighborhood's best restoration projects as well as homes in the process of being restored. Historic churches and a museum of neighborhood history have been featured also. For more information visit Historic Edgefield's Web site at www.historicedgefield.org, or write to the association at P.O. Box 60586, Nashville 37206.

East End

This small, middle-class, urban neighborhood east of downtown Nashville is home to professionals, blue-collar workers, and artists, many of whom were drawn to its historic appeal, quietness, and convenience to downtown. East End is between the neighborhoods of Edgefield and Lockeland Springs, extending from Woodland Street to Shelby Avenue between 10th and 14th Streets. The 360-plus-acre Shelby Park is nearby, as is the hip Five Points commercial district, home to several good restaurants and an organic foods market.

The neighborhood was named East End because at one time it was at the eastern city limits of Edgefield, which was incorporated in 1868. Electric streetcar lines linking east Nashville to the downtown business district were installed by 1890 and contributed to the influx of residents. Development took place here from about 1875 to the early part of the 20th century, when East End was considered a working-class neighborhood. East End boasts nice examples of a variety of architectural styles, including Victorian, Italianate, Eastlake, and Queen Anne. For more about East End, visit the Web site www.eastendnashville.org.

Lockeland Springs

The third historic neighborhood in the urban area of downtown/east Nashville is Lockeland Springs, just past East End between Gallatin Road and Shelby Avenue, 2 miles northeast of downtown. It's bordered by 14th Street, Eastland Avenue, and Shelby Park. The area was named for Lockeland Mansion, built in the early 19th century by Col. Robert Weakley, whose wife, Jane Locke, was the daughter of Gen. Matthew Locke of North Carolina. Water from the property's Lockeland spring, which some believed to have curative powers, won a grand prize for its mineral composition and "salubrious quality" at the St. Louis Exposition in 1904. The city of Nashville purchased the mansion in 1939, demolished it, and built Lockeland School on the site.

Like East End, Lockeland Springs benefited from the electric streetcar lines installed in the late 1800s. Streetcars allowed residents to travel easily to Nashville's business district across the Cumberland River and made it practical for the middle class to move away from the crowded city.

The well-preserved and architecturally diverse homes in this neighborhood were built from about 1880 to 1940. In the past two decades, the neighborhood has seen quite a bit of renovation. This large area is popular with professional renovators as well as first-timers eager to try their hand at restoring a home. Middle-class workers, professionals, and artists enjoy the community feel of this neighborhood.

Lockeland Springs has been called the next Hillsboro Village. Several trendy restaurants and nightspots have popped up in the area, including Rosepepper Cantina and Chapel Bistro.

For more on Lockeland Springs, visit the Lockeland Springs Neighborhood Association online at www.lockelandsprings.org.

North and Northeast Nashville

Inglewood

Inglewood is a friendly and pleasant community that, according to some local Realtors, is one of the best investment values in Nashville, appealing to first-time buyers as well as investors looking for good rental properties. The neighborhood is just east of Lockeland Springs, off Gallatin Pike. It is bordered roughly by the railroad track at Gallatin Pike, north of Trinity Lane, and extends to Briley Parkway.

Lovers of historic houses will feel right at home here. Inglewood boasts lots of 1920s and 1930s homes with brick and stone exteriors, marble fireplaces, ceramic tile, and good structural quality. There are some newer ranch-style homes, too. You'll find small lots as well as large, well-shaded lots with houses set back off the road. Tidy, well-maintained yards, colorful window boxes, perennial gardens, and lots of green areas add to Inglewood's cheerful personality. Many 30- to 45-year-old residents, as well as younger professionals, make their home in this settled community.

i **If you're in the market for a new home and planning to visit open houses, keep in mind that they are usually held on Sunday. When the Tennessee Titans have a Sunday home game, however, some open houses are held on Saturday instead. *The Tennessean*'s weekend editions list the date, location, and other details about open houses.**

MADISON

Until recently, it was sort of hard to pinpoint the location of the Madison community—one of Nashville's earliest suburbs. If you weren't familiar with the north and east Nashville areas, you could drive right through Madison without even knowing it. Even some longtime Nashvillians are not quite sure where Madison begins and ends. To help identify itself, the community installed signs at several entry points to the area in 1999. Madison doesn't have an identifiable town square or center, just lots of retail areas lining Gallatin Road and established neighborhoods tucked along the side streets.

This neighborhood sits on the northeast edge of Metro Nashville–Davidson County, 8 miles from downtown Nashville. It's south of Goodlettsville and southwest of Old Hickory. The busiest part of town extends along Gallatin Road between Neeley's Bend Road and Old Hickory Boulevard. The community was established in 1840, although a church known as the Spring

Hill Meeting House existed in what is now south Madison in the late 1700s.

Between 1859 and 1865, Madison Stratton was hired as a contractor for the L&N Railroad, which passed through the area. The depot he constructed was named for him, putting Madison on the map. The Nashville-Gallatin interurban streetcar track also ran through this community. The old depot was in an area known as Amqui. As the story goes, trains came to such a quick stop in Madison that if you wanted to load something on the train, you'd better do it "damn quick." Madison residents dropped the *d, n,* and the *ck* and came up with the more polite *Amqui* to name their section of town.

Today Madison is home to more than 32,000, including many longtime residents, and has one of the oldest commercial districts in the state. Here you'll find the more-than-200-year-old Spring Hill Cemetery (not to be confused with the community of Spring Hill between Franklin and Columbia). Madison Park and Cedar Hill Park offer recreation opportunities. There are also facilities for bowling, golfing, horseback riding, and skating.

This area is especially appealing for first-time buyers who are attracted to the affordable 1950s-era homes. In some sections you'll find tree-lined streets and large lots with ranch-style houses; others feature older cottages on small lots. For more on Madison call (615) 865-0448 or see www.madisonchamber.net.

GOODLETTSVILLE

Goodlettsville is one of those cities that offers the best of both worlds: a quiet, small-town feel with all the conveniences of city life close by. An incorporated city within Metropolitan Nashville–Davidson County, Goodlettsville is north of Nashville and Madison and east of Hendersonville.

It encompasses areas around Dickerson Pike, Long Hollow Pike, and I-65. Goodlettsville incorporated in 1857 and again in 1958, but like Nashville's other satellite cities, it remains part of Metro government. Goodlettsville straddles the

Davidson and Sumner County lines, so the property taxes vary depending on the county.

Goodlettsville residents receive Goodlettsville city services, not Metro services. The city has a separate police department, including 30 uniformed officers; a separate fire department with 15 full-time firefighters plus volunteers; and separate public works departments, a planning commission, and city manager/city commission government structure. Goodlettsville's easy access to I-65 and the excellent security provided by its police and fire departments make the area appealing to industries. Many businesses have relocated or moved their distribution operations here.

Goodlettsville was originally known as Manskers Station, established by pioneer Kasper Mansker around 1780. The road connecting the area to "Nashborough" was built in 1781. Today Goodlettsville is home to about 14,000 people, including several country music stars. The area has a real mix of residential properties—everything from large homes surrounded by acres of lawns to historic houses to mobile-home parks. Lots of fields and green spaces give this area a rural feel, but the bustling Rivergate area is just minutes away.

For more on Goodlettsville call the chamber of commerce at (615) 859-7979 or visit www.goodlettsvillechamber.com.

East Nashville

DONELSON

Affordable homes draw lots of young families to this southeast Nashville community, which was developed in the 1950s and '60s. The dominant architectural style here is the one-story ranch. According to a market value report by local real estate appraisers Manier & Exton, homes in the Donelson area have maintained strong appreciation rates since 1993.

In addition to affordability, good location is another plus here. Situated between the Stones and Cumberland Rivers, Donelson offers easy access to the airport and downtown (via I-40) as well as J. Percy Priest Lake. The Tennessee School for the Blind also is located here.

Donelson, named for John Donelson, one of Nashville's founders, is a conservative community with many longtime residents. It boasts a strong chamber of commerce and lots of civic-minded residents. Residents joined to raise money for improvements to the neighborhood playground at Two Rivers Park. The hot spot is Lebanon Road, which is lined with lots of shops, churches, and fast-food restaurants. Upscale stores and restaurants, however, are scarce here, so folks in search of other shopping and dining choices need to go into town, or perhaps head to the Rivergate area. For more information about this area, contact the Donelson-Hermitage Chamber of Commerce at (615) 883-7896 or visit www.d-hchamber.com.

i **Rediscover East! is a nonprofit organization dedicated to preserving the character of east Nashville and enhancing the quality of life for those living, working, or visiting in the area. For more information on the organization, visit the Web site www.rediscovereast.org or call (615) 226-8118.**

HERMITAGE

This east Davidson County community lies between the Stones and Cumberland Rivers. Hermitage Station, a stop along the Tennessee & Pacific Railroad line, once was here. The Hermitage, home of President Andrew Jackson, is nearby (see our Attractions and History chapters).

Affordable land and fairly easy interstate highway access encouraged a lot of speculative building in the Hermitage–Priest Lake area in the 1980s, and the community experienced one of the largest population gains in the area. Today lots of affordable single- and multifamily residences lure home buyers to this neighborhood. For more information about this area, contact the Donelson–Hermitage Chamber of Commerce at (615) 883-7896 or visit www.d-hchamber.com.

OLD HICKORY

Located in eastern Davidson County between the Cumberland River and Old Hickory Lake,

Old Hickory is an unincorporated community of about 9,800 residents. The village was built in 1918 by the DuPont Co. of Philadelphia. The company constructed hundreds of homes for workers at its gunpowder plant, which produced smokeless gunpowder for use in World War I. Today, the area appears much as it did in 1918. Some of the historic homes are being renovated by new owners. The community, which includes the small, incorporated town of Lakewood, is well established and offers affordable housing.

West End/Vanderbilt/Hillsboro Village

BELMONT-HILLSBORO

Recently, Belmont-Hillsboro has become the hot residential district. Property values have skyrocketed as the academic crowd, artists, musicians, and young professionals clamor for a home in the historic, middle-class neighborhood. In 2001 the average sales price for a Belmont property was $216,556; homes for sale in the area were snapped up within 53 days (the average number of days on the market for the county overall was 77). Prices have increased since then. More recently, many of the finer homes have been selling from $450,000 and up to $650,000 or more.

Situated between 21st Avenue S./Hillsboro Road and Belmont Boulevard, the area extends north toward Wedgewood and south toward Interstate 440. It's convenient to downtown, Music Row, Vanderbilt University, Belmont University, Green Hills, West End, hospitals, and bus lines. The neighborhood hot spot is Hillsboro Village, a shopping district of eclectic stores, restaurants, and pubs that scores high on the "hip" meter. This is where you'll find Sunset Grill, the Fido/Bongo Java coffeehouse, Pancake Pantry (a Nashville landmark), Provence bakery and restaurant, and the historic Belcourt Theatre. Nearby, on Belmont Boulevard, you'll find Bongo Java coffeehouse, the International Market & Restaurant, and other hangouts popular with the college crowd.

In the 19th century the area was part of the estate of Adelicia Acklen (see the Belmont Mansion entry in our Attractions chapter). In the early 1900s an electric streetcar line along Belmont Boulevard accelerated the neighborhood's transition to a streetcar suburb. Most homes here were built between 1910 and 1940 and range from 1,200-square-foot cottages to 3,500-square-foot bungalows and foursquares on sidewalked streets. Renovators will find some good opportunities here. Belmont-Hillsboro Neighbors, a neighborhood association that formed in 1970, sends out a newsletter every other month. Visit the association online at www.belmont-hillsboro.org, or call the hot line at (615) 386-3711 for neighborhood information.

HILLSBORO–WEST END

One of Nashville's oldest neighborhoods, Hillsboro–West End is a large middle- and upper-middle-class neighborhood extending from around Blakemore Avenue to just past I-440, and from Hillsboro Road to West End.

Many Nashvillians refer to this neighborhood as the "Vanderbilt area." The location is great: It's close to Vanderbilt University, Hillsboro Village, Belmont University, Green Hills, and West End, which means there are plenty of places to shop and dine. In fact, many of Nashville's best restaurants are just minutes away. On West End, Zola and Houston's restaurants are longtime favorites. The area is also home to Eakin Elementary School, which is regarded as one of the city's best.

Residents of Hillsboro–West End include young professionals, music business types, physicians, and university professors, many of whom can be found daily walking their dogs or jogging on wide tree-lined sidewalks. Homes are situated on small, shaded lots, and there are lots of winding, shaded streets leading to little pocket neighborhoods that have their own unique personalities. As for architectural styles here, you'll find mostly classic Tudors, Cape Cods, and bungalows built between 1920 and 1940. There also are some newer properties, including condos.

Prices start at about $175,000 and can go as high as $525,000 or more.

Homes here often offer a substantial value for their price and are generally considered good investments. Renters will find some good older homes and some apartments, too. For more information on this neighborhood, visit the Hillsboro–West End Neighborhood Association online at www.hwen.org, or contact the association by mail at P.O. Box 120521, Nashville 37212.

Waverly-Belmont to Melrose

WAVERLY-BELMONT/SUNNYSIDE (12TH SOUTH)

Since the late 1990s, this urban neighborhood has become one of the hottest areas for renovation. In the past few years, the "12th South Neighborhood Commercial District" (or 12th South, as it's commonly known), which borders Waverly-Belmont and Belmont-Hillsboro, received several hundred thousand dollars in improvements from the Metropolitan Development & Housing Agency and Public Works, including new lights, sidewalks, and banners designed to encourage pedestrian-friendly retail and office spaces and to create a more friendly neighborhood feel. The 12th South area has transformed into a hip, eclectic neighborhood with an interesting assortment of businesses, including trendy restaurants, a popular pizzeria, clothing boutiques, and the Las Paletas Mexican Popsicle shop (see our Restaurants chapter).

Renovators are also doing their part, restoring many of the area's old homes, most of which were built from the 1890s to 1930s. These homes provide the first impression of the area's personality, but the neighborhood also gets some of its character from its racially and socioeconomically diverse residents.

Waverly-Belmont is a large neighborhood extending from Belmont Boulevard to Ninth Avenue S. and from Gale Lane north to Bradford Avenue, near Wedgewood. The area includes Waverly Place, adjacent to Woodland-in-Waverly, which is also sometimes considered part of the Waverly-Belmont district. It is convenient to I-440, Music Row, Green Hills, universities, downtown, and the Melrose shopping district. In the center of the neighborhood is Sevier Park and its antebellum Sunnyside Mansion.

The area's great assortment of historic homes makes it appealing to those with an eye to the future. The neighborhood is filled with large Queen Anne, American foursquare, and 1900–1915 Princess Anne homes as well as smaller 1900s shotgun homes and 1920s and 1930s Tudors and bungalows awaiting a renovator's touch.

Neighborhood groups include Montrose Avenue Alliance, Sunnyside Community Citizens Inc. (www.sunnyside.org), and Waldkirch Avenue Neighbors.

i Several neighborhood associations sponsor annual home tours in Nashville's historic neighborhoods. Richland–West End, Edgefield, East End, and Hillsboro–West End are among the areas that have tours. You can find information about the tours in local newspapers or at the associations' Web sites. See the individual write-ups in this chapter for details and contact information for the various neighborhood associations.

WAVERLY PLACE

When you turn off Eighth Avenue S. onto Douglas Avenue (at Zanies), you'll be greeted by a WELCOME TO WAVERLY PLACE sign. Waverly Place is a small, historic district tucked between Woodland-in-Waverly and Waverly-Belmont, from Eighth to 10th Avenues S. and Wedgewood to Bradford Avenues. It is often considered part of the larger Waverly-Belmont, also referred to as Sunnyside (see separate listings in this section), a larger district that is ripe for renovation.

Sidewalks line both sides of the street, and the small lots are accented with numerous tall trees, ivy, and colorful flowers. Waverly Place features a wide mix of architectural styles, including frame-and-brick cottages, American foursquares, Tudors, and one- and one-and-a-half-story bungalows from the 1890s and 1930s. The area's population is as diverse as its properties, and people of various races and income levels find this pleasant little neighborhood to their liking. First-time home buyers and renovators have shown increasing interest in this area.

Neighborhood hot spots include Zanies comedy club, Douglas Corner songwriters' club, and the Eighth Avenue S. antiques district.

WOODLAND-IN-WAVERLY

One of Nashville's first streetcar suburbs, Woodland-in-Waverly is south of Wedgewood Avenue, between I-65 and Eighth Avenue, convenient to downtown, Music Row, colleges, the Melrose area, and Eighth Avenue antiques shops. This is one of Nashville's three "historic preservation zoning districts" (the others being Edgefield and Second Avenue). This zoning means that all exterior additions, alterations, demolitions, new construction, and fences must meet the approval of the Metro Historical Commission.

According to the Historical Commission, Woodland-in-Waverly could serve as a model for neighborhood design now being emulated by progressive new subdivision developments. Part of Woodland-in-Waverly was listed on the National Register of Historic Places in 1980. The neighborhood features many well-preserved homes built mainly from the 1890s through the 1930s. Queen Anne, English Tudor, and American foursquares and bungalows are among the architectural styles found in this small neighborhood, which offers plenty of choices for renovators.

In the 1830s the area was farmland owned by historian and author A. W. Putnam, who named his house Waverly and his farm Waverly Place for the novel by Sir Walter Scott. The farm was sold in 1858. Development increased in the late 1880s following the installation of an electric streetcar line on Eighth Avenue S. that provided easy access to downtown Nashville. This streetcar suburb was a fashionable address and remained so until around 1940, when automobiles became the preferred method of transportation. The neighborhood eventually evolved into an urban middle-class neighborhood. A few houses built during this period still remain.

In the mid-1960s many of the historic homes were demolished to make room for I-65, which divided and reduced the size of the neighborhood. At the same time, many buildings had fallen into disrepair, and many Nashvillians were moving to outlying suburbs. Today a few duplexes and ranch-style homes dot the areas around I-65.

Woodland-in-Waverly is a good area for first-time buyers who want to live in an urban neighborhood. For more information on the area, visit the Woodland-in-Waverly Neighborhood Association online at www.nashvilleneighborhood.com, or write to P.O. Box 4006, Nashville 37204.

MELROSE

This neighborhood was named for the Melrose Estate, which was granted to its first owner, John Topp, in 1788. Named for the Scottish ancestry of the then-reigning mistress, the mansion was the site of many notable events in Nashville society. The original two-story brick building burned in 1950 and was rebuilt as a one-story structure. The rebuilt home was gutted by fire in 1975.

Melrose is bounded by Wedgewood Avenue and I-440 between Franklin Pike and Granny White Pike. It's convenient to downtown, I-440, and Nolensville Road. You'll find a variety of home styles here, ranging from late Victorian to contemporary.

Neighborhood hot spots include the Sutler live music venue and Melrose Lanes bowling alley. The Eighth Avenue S. antiques district is also nearby.

i Apartment rents in the West End–downtown areas are typically the highest in Nashville, averaging around $1,215 per month during the second quarter of 2008. Rents in North Nashville are the lowest, averaging about $675 per month.

BERRY HILL

This tiny satellite city, developed in the 1940s and early '50s, covers approximately 1 square mile, between Thompson Lane near 100 Oaks Mall and Craighead Avenue, and between Franklin Road and into Woodlawn Cemetery.

The city was incorporated in 1950 and today has its own mayor, city manager, and city commissioners. The city provides police protection and other services for its citizens. In 2008 there were approximately 700 residents and about 500 businesses.

Berry Hill's residential area is transitioning into a quaint commercial district. Businesses have opened in some of the small 1950s cottages that were once homes. Bohemian types are discovering the Berry Hill District, where you can shop for garden supplies, vintage clothing, used records, and quirky gifts in a tree-lined 3-block area. Music Row has also discovered Berry Hill; more than 40 recording studios, including one owned by Martina McBride, have moved into the area. Restaurants include the upscale Yellow Porch and the casual Calypso Cafe (see our Restaurants chapter). Berry Hill's city offices are at 698 Thompson Lane (615-292-5531; http://tn-berryhill.civicplus.com).

i **The satellite city of Berry Hill has been dubbed a "little Music Row" thanks to the growing number of recording studios that have discovered the area. Albums by Shania Twain and Barenaked Ladies, to name two, were recorded or mixed in Berry Hill.**

West and Southwest Nashville

RICHLAND–WEST END

Historic Richland–West End encompasses a triangular area between Murphy Road, I-440, and West End. Developed in the early 1900s on the outskirts of the city, this was an upscale suburb popular with professionals who wanted to escape the noise, smoke, and crime of the city. After World War II some homes were converted to apartments, but young professionals and upper- and middle-income families have been restoring them since the 1970s.

The neighborhood has lots of longtime residents, and many take an active part in the community. The Richland–West End Neighborhood Association, formed in 1974, keeps watch over the area's residential quality and sponsors an annual tour of homes. Richland–West End features lots of well-preserved early-1900s homes, including spacious bungalows, built from 1910 to 1930, and American foursquares.

Sidewalks, lots of old trees, and a definite community feel are strong selling points for this neighborhood. Location is another plus: it's a straight shot down West End/Broadway to downtown, I-440 access is right off West End, and it's close to Music Row, Green Hills, Belle Meade, and Hillsboro Village. For more information visit the Richland–West End Neighborhood Association's Web site at www.rwena.org.

SYLVAN PARK

This historic west Nashville neighborhood has enjoyed a wave of popularity in recent years. Young professionals, families, creative types, and retirees in search of affordable homes moved to this former blue-collar area and have carefully restored many of the homes. Interest has now expanded to the adjacent Sylvan Heights area near 37th and Charlotte Avenues.

Sylvan Park also has a trendy commercial district that's home to several popular restaurants, including Park Cafe, Sylvan Park, and McCabe Pub, as well as the Produce Place market (see our Restaurants and Shopping chapters). Also in the neighborhood is McCabe Park and Community Center, which has one of Metro's most popular golf courses and offers other recreational opportunities (see our Golf chapter).

If you're new to the area, note that you can usually recognize Sylvan Park by its street names. When the area was planned back in the 1880s, the streets were named after states in hopes that people from across the country would want to relocate to the neighborhood.

Lots of trees, sidewalks, nice landscaping, cheerful window boxes, and a business district contribute to the personality and close-knit feel of this charming neighborhood. There are a lot of 800- to 1,000-square-foot houses here, but they can be pricey, typically starting at about $110 per square foot. You'll find mostly 1910 to 1940s frame-and-brick bungalows, and these can range from 800 to 2,500 square feet. A tour of the neighborhood also will reveal some 1900 to 1915 Princess Annes, 1930s brick cottages, and spacious Queen Anne homes. This neighborhood definitely represents a good investment: Houses recently have appreciated as much as 20 percent a year.

Sylvan Park is between West End Avenue and Charlotte Pike and is convenient to West End, I-40, I-440, and downtown. To learn more about Sylvan Park, visit the Sylvan Park Neighborhood Association online at www.sylvanpark.org, or write to P.O. Box 92324, Nashville 37209.

GREEN HILLS

Green Hills is considered one of Nashville's most desirable addresses. This Area 2 community is bounded by I-440, Belle Meade, Oak Hill at Harding Road, and Forest Hills. It's minutes from Vanderbilt, West End, Music Row, Hillsboro Village, and downtown. If you're looking for an upscale neighborhood; large, well-landscaped lots; and tree-lined streets, you can't miss with Green Hills. Families will find the good schools a bonus.

The area was developed in the 1930s and '40s, and building continues today, so you'll find everything here from modern and spacious homes loaded with amenities to pockets of cluster housing and smaller older properties. There are also some nice condominiums/town houses. According to a market value report by local real estate appraisers Manier & Exton, the average 2005 sale price in Green Hills was $583,113. Those who want the privacy and square footage of a house but aren't in a buying mode might find a suitable private rental here. There is a smattering of apartments and condos, too—old and new.

The upscale Mall at Green Hills is the centerpiece of a large retail sector that extends for several blocks along Hillsboro Road. Green Hills also boasts the world-famous Bluebird Cafe songwriters' club, Davis-Kidd Booksellers, and several good restaurants, including F. Scott's, Shalimar, and Green Hills Grille (see our Restaurants chapter). One drawback here is traffic, which can get pretty congested along Hillsboro Road.

Neighborhood groups include the Green Hills Neighborhood Association (P.O. Box 159339, Nashville 37215, or 615-726-3735).

FOREST HILLS

This desirable west Nashville satellite city extends from Harding Road to Old Hickory Boulevard and from Belle Meade toward Oak Hill and Franklin Road. Forest Hills is home to about 4,700 residents. There is no commercial area.

First developed in the 1950s and '60s, Forest Hills boasts spacious ranch-style homes as well as some architect-designed custom homes. Newer housing developments can be found along Old Hickory Boulevard and Granny White Pike. Houses sit on large, well-tended lots that offer a good amount of privacy. Some have great views. Homes here have sold from $200,000 to more than $1 million in recent years. Renters will find an occasional upscale rental. Good schools and a convenient Area 2 location add to the appeal of this neighborhood.

Nearby Radnor Lake offers a wonderful, if sometimes crowded, nature retreat (see the Parks chapter). Also worth a look: the Bison Meadows park at Hillsboro Road and Tyne Boulevard, which features "evergreen buffalo" sculptures by artist Alan LeQuire.

If you want to learn more about Forest Hills, you may be interested in reading the book *Historic Homes of Forest Hills,* which is available at the Forest Hills city office at 4012 Hillsboro Road (615-383-8447).

OAK HILL

A popular choice for music business executives and "move-up" families, Oak Hill is where you'll find the Governor's Mansion and other stately homes, including former homes of the late Tammy Wynette and Minnie Pearl. Covering an area of 8 square miles, Oak Hill extends from Forest Hills to I-65 and from Woodmont Boulevard to Old Hickory Boulevard. You'll find Oak Hill divided between Area 1 and Area 2 on the Nashville real estate maps.

As its name suggests, this residential community of 5,000 boasts lots of rolling tree-covered hills. It is characterized by low-density development, with most homes situated on at least one- to two-acre lots. Many of the ranch-style and two-story colonial homes here were built during the past 30 to 40 years. There are also some beautiful contemporary homes. Incorporated in 1952, this is a well-established, stable neighborhood, and residents often prefer to renovate rather than move out. You'll occasionally come across a newly built home. In recent years, home sales have averaged more than $350,000, with at least one property selling for more than $2.5 million.

Oak Hill is home to Radnor Lake (see our Parks chapter) and is close to the Melrose shopping area, Harding Mall, 100 Oaks Mall, and Nipper's Corner. Oak Hill's city office is at 5548 Franklin Road (615-371-8291).

BELLE MEADE

If living in one of the area's most prestigious neighborhoods is a must, look no farther than Belle Meade. This traditionally old-money west Nashville community is the address of choice for many of Nashville's most prominent citizens, including former vice president Al Gore. A city of about 1,120 homes and about 3,200 residents, Belle Meade is the fifth richest city in America and the richest in the state. According to the 2000 U.S. Census, its annual per-capita income was $104,908. The median household income was $144,720.

It is one of Nashville's oldest communities—actually a city in itself, having incorporated in 1938. Today it has its own police force, street signs, and building codes, and the powers-that-be keep a pretty tight rein on the neighborhood. It was originally part of the Belle Meade Plantation, a world-renowned thoroughbred farm. The plantation's Belle Meade mansion is now a tourist attraction (see our Attractions chapter).

Belle Meade's unique and architecturally interesting homes are surrounded by large, professionally landscaped lawns. Many homes here were built during the 1920s, but Nashville's elite find this address so de rigueur that many are willing to pay top dollar for an older home, demolish it, and build an enormous, new traditional-style home in its place.

According to a market value report by local real estate appraisers Manier & Exton, the average sale price of a sampling of existing Belle Meade homes in 2008 was $1,325,696. In recent years some homes have sold for more than $2.5 million, and some have sold for $200,000.

Belle Meade is bounded roughly by US 70 (Harding Road), Lynnwood Boulevard, Chickering Lane, and Page Road, and it is bisected by Harding Place. Belle Meade is a residential-only city. Nearby hot spots include Belle Meade Plantation, Cheekwood, the members-only Belle Meade Country Club, and Belle Meade Boulevard, popular with residents and other Nashvillians who come to jog, play Frisbee, and hang out at the entrance to Percy Warner Park. Belle Meade also is home to three houses of worship: the Temple, St. George's Episcopal Church, and Emmanuel Baptist Church.

Belle Meade's city offices are at 4705 Harding Road (615-297-6041).

WEST MEADE/HILLWOOD

Another Area 2 community, West Meade/Hillwood is just west of Belle Meade, across the railroad tracks that parallel Harding Road/US 70. The area is bounded by White Bridge Road, Davidson Drive, and I-40 and encompasses the Vaughns Gap Road area to the south.

This well-established neighborhood is one of Nashville's oldest planned communities. Most homes were built in the 1950s and '60s, so there are lots of ranch-style dwellings. Houses sit on large, shady lots, and the neighborhood's winding streets take you over hills and along forested areas. The Hillwood area, which developed around the Hillwood Country Club, has some of the largest and most expensive homes, with prices ranging from $175,000 to more than $525,000. According to a market value report by Manier & Exton, in 2005 the average sale price of a sampling of existing homes in West Meade was $366,021.

There is a definite neighborhood feel here, and residents are active in the community. This is a convenient location with lots of good shopping and restaurants nearby on White Bridge Road and in the Harding Road area. The Green Hills mall is just minutes away. Hot spots include Percy Warner and Edwin Warner Parks, and Cheekwood.

BELLEVUE

For those who want a fashionable Area 2 address but find such areas as Belle Meade, Hillwood/West Meade, and Green Hills a little pricey, Bellevue is a good choice, offering lots of newer, upscale homes that are affordable for many first-time buyers. This west Nashville community is about 2.5 miles west of the US 70–Highway 100 split, about 7 miles from Green Hills, and about 13 miles from downtown. Most areas are easily accessible to I-40. Bellevue is bordered on one side by the Warner Parks along Tennessee Highway 100 and on the other by Charlotte Pike.

As the WELCOME TO BELLEVUE sign on US 70 S. informs you, this community was established in 1795. The rolling green hills and wooded valleys inspired the name (French for "beautiful view"). Bellevue remained a largely rural area until the mid-1900s. Development moved in this direction in the 1940s, but it hasn't completely taken over yet. Despite rapid growth since the 1970s, the area still offers a pleasing mix of urban and rural life. Bellevue has maintained a sort of small-community feel that some Nashville suburbs lack. A few farm areas remain around the perimeter, but the conveniences of "city life" are close by for those in the more rural areas.

The local chamber of commerce and civic-minded residents keep watch on the area's growth. Though there has been a lot of development on US 70, Bellevue's proximity to the Warner Parks on Highway 100 (see our Parks chapter) keeps residents from feeling crowded.

Lots of young professionals and families have joined the longtime residents here. Those looking for a house will find many single-family homes, some in pocket neighborhoods and new subdivisions. There are also condominiums to fit every budget as well as an assortment of apartment complexes. Prices have been increasing steadily since the early 1990s. According to the aforementioned market value report, the average listing price for a home in Bellevue in 2008 was $245,979. Renters will discover that the newer apartments here carry some of the highest rents in Nashville, although some of the older complexes offer significantly lower rates.

Recreational opportunities abound here. In addition to Warner Parks, the northern terminus of the Natchez Trace Parkway is just a few miles down Highway 100, offering a scenic retreat for Sunday drivers or biking enthusiasts, and the nearby Harpeth River, with several access points, is a great spot for canoeing. Other hot spots include Regal Cinemas's Bellevue 12 movie theater near the mall, Red Caboose Park on US 70, and Loveless Café on Highway 100. Neighborhood groups include the Bellevue Area Citizens for Planned Growth. The Bellevue Chamber of Commerce is located at 177 Belle Forest Circle (615-662-2737).

South and Southeast Nashville

CRIEVE HALL

Development of this Area 1 neighborhood centered on Trousdale Drive and Blackmon Road in the 1950s, so you'll find lots of ranch-style homes here. Unlike many of Nashville's new developments, Crieve Hall boasts large lots accented with big shade trees. Homes are well maintained and nicely landscaped. It's a nice, quiet area convenient to downtown, Harding Mall, the 100 Oaks/Berry Hill area, and the Nashville Zoo at Grassmere.

Crieve Hall is a stable neighborhood, with many longtime residents. Good schools are nearby. Properties here are in demand. In 2005, for example, homes stayed on the market about 58 days.

ANTIOCH

Affordable housing and location lure many Nashvillians to this diverse southeast Nashville community, which has experienced an enormous boom in new home construction in the past few years. Antioch is convenient to I-24, the airport, and Starwood Amphitheatre and is a short drive from downtown via I-24. The area is bordered to the north by Harding Place and extends west from Percy Priest Lake to just past the I-24/Bell Road intersection.

Development boomed here with the opening of the Hickory Hollow Mall and Smyrna's Nissan plant. In the past two decades, Antioch has undergone tremendous growth, including lots of commercial development along Bell Road, Nolensville Pike, and Harding Place. Large numbers of new housing developments and apartment complexes have joined the ranch-style homes built here in the 1960s. The arrival of new residents and increase in commercial development have resulted in major traffic snarls in the Hickory Hollow area and along Nolensville Pike. Road construction here seems to be never-ending. Antioch has been praised for its ethnic diversity and integration of its schools. Antioch has many homes that are affordable for first-time buyers. Renters can choose from many affordable apartment complexes.

Nearby recreational areas include Long Hunter State Park and J. Percy Priest Lake.

Neighboring Counties

Cheatham County

The area's best-kept neighborhood secret may be just west of Davidson County: Cheatham County (Area 13). Some real estate agents expect this 305-square-mile county to be the next boom area, but houses are still affordable here, and most of the new developments feature one-acre lots, large by Middle Tennessee standards. In recent years it has been one of the state's fastest-growing counties. Between 1990 and 2000 the population increased 32.3 percent to nearly 36,000. In an effort to keep the growth at a manageable level, the county has a development tax of $3,750 per each new house, which will deter some development. There's also a county adequate-facilities tax of $1 per square foot of heated living space, among other fees.

Cheatham County is convenient to Bellevue in west Nashville, easily accessible to I-24 and I-40, and is a 25- to 40-minute drive to downtown Nashville, depending on which side of the county you're on. In addition to location, strong drawing points of this rural area include quality of life and lots of outdoor-recreation opportunities. The 20,000-acre Cheatham Wildlife Management Area is popular for hunting, horseback riding, and hiking, and Harpeth River State Park is a good spot for canoeing, fishing, and hiking. Cheatham Lake is popular with boaters.

Those interested in lake property should determine eligibility for private-use privileges before beginning any construction. A shoreline-management plan classifies the lake into limited development areas, which are the only areas where private-use privileges such as mowing, moorage, electrical lines, and construction of steps are permitted. Contact the Resource Manager's Office, 1798 Cheatham Dam Road, for more information.

The four largest cities in Cheatham County are Ashland City, Kingston Springs, Pegram, and Pleasant View. For more information contact the Cheatham County Chamber of Commerce (615-792-6722, www.cheathamchamber.org), or visit www.cheathamcounty.net.

Ashland City

In central Cheatham County, Ashland City developed around a shallow area along the Cumberland River where riverboats ran aground and had to unload their cargo. Locks have since solved that problem, and today Ashland City is a rapidly growing area.

In 2000 Ashland City's population was 3,641. Ashland City is home to one of the area's largest employers, A. O. Smith Water Products Co. (formerly State Industries), with a workforce of about 2,000, as well as other growing industries. With the widening of Highway 12 to Nashville to four lanes, the city has paved the way for more growth. Ashland City is about a 40-minute drive from downtown Nashville; from courthouse to courthouse, it's about 20 miles. Ashland City's courthouse, with its croquet lawn, is still the focus of downtown. The city is also known for its antiques shops and catfish restaurants. The 3.7-mile Cumberland River Bicentennial Trail, a former railroad right-of-way, is popular for walking, horseback riding, and bicycling along river bluffs, past waterfalls, and through wetlands.

Ashland City has some of Cheatham County's most affordable homes. A sample listing in February 2008 was a new three-bedroom, two bath, 1,725-square-foot home on 1 acre for $175,600. Finding a rental property here isn't easy. Those that are available often are snapped up by newcomers awaiting construction of new homes.

KINGSTON SPRINGS

Kingston Springs, on the south side of Cheatham County, appears to be one of the next neighborhood hot spots. Between 1990 and 2000 its population increased more than 81 percent, to about 2,773, supporting data from a 1999 report by the UT Center for Business and Economic Research predicting that through 2020, Kingston Springs is expected to experience an 81 percent growth in population—the highest rate in the area.

The area is a nature lover's paradise. All sorts of songbirds, as well as deer, wild turkey, and other wildlife, make their homes here. Affordable homes, easy access to Nashville via I-40, and a quiet rural setting are also part of the scenic bedroom community's appeal. Those who want to live in a country-style home with a big wraparound porch or in a log cabin or hillside chalet will feel right at home in Kingston Springs. Some of the rolling wooded hills and farmland are being developed into subdivisions, but in an effort to control the growth, Kingston Springs has implemented a 75-cent-per-square-foot adequate-facilities tax (impact fee)—in addition to the county's $1-per-square-foot tax—on new residential development; there's also a 25-cent-per-square-foot building permit fee inside the city limits.

Kingston Springs has some of the county's most expensive homes and lots. A one-acre or smaller lot might cost $45,000. A few of the newer homes list for $275,000 or more. Kingston Springs hot spots include the Harpeth River State Park (see our Parks chapter); the private Golf Club of Tennessee, where country star Vince Gill hosts his annual Vinny charity golf tournament; Cliff View Golf Course, a nine-hole public course; and two city parks near the quaint downtown area.

PEGRAM

At 3,440 acres, this is the smallest of Cheatham County's four cities. This quaint little rural town (population 2,146) is on the south side of the county, next to Bellevue and about a 25-minute drive from downtown Nashville. Like Kingston Springs, Pegram's population is expected to grow by 81 percent by the year 2020, the highest rate in the area.

If you'd like to get a feel for what Pegram is like, visit on July 4, when the town puts on the big Pegram Fish Fry; you can get all the catfish you can eat.

PLEASANT VIEW

Incorporated in 1996, Pleasant View, a growing community of about 3,000 residents, is located in northern Cheatham County. There is no property tax; the city operates on state and local sales taxes. Pleasant View is the kind of community where the volunteer fire department hosts an annual parade and barbecue for residents. The city also has its own three-member police department. There is a lot of new home construction under way. New developments include Pleasant View Village, a multiphased "new urban"–style community with a village square, sidewalks, and commercial spaces. A typical new home in Pleasant View sells for about $175,000 to $200,000.

Dickson County

Dickson County (Area 15), just west of Nashville past Cheatham County, is a largely rural area with the lowest population density of any county surrounding Metro Nashville. Officials with the Dickson County Chamber of Commerce (615-446-2349, www.dicksoncountychamber

.com) say that is changing fast. Like most counties surrounding Metro, Dickson County is growing. In 2000 its population was 43,156, a 23 percent increase over 1990's figure.

The 600-acre Dickson County Industrial Park, established in 1976, is attracting a steady stream of industry. The county's chamber of commerce actively recruits new businesses. At the same time, many city dwellers and suburbanites are deciding they want to live in the country and are heading to Dickson County areas such as Dickson, White Bluff, Burns, and Charlotte. Lower home and land prices are a big draw.

DICKSON

Affordable homes and a quiet, small-town setting are luring more people to Dickson these days. New subdivisions are being developed in this city of 12,200-plus. Land sales are strong, too, especially small farm properties of 20 acres or less. According to the aforementioned market value report, in 2005 the average sale price of a sampling of existing homes in Dickson was $130,010. Dickson is about 40 minutes from downtown Nashville and easily accessible to I-40, so it's a feasible choice for Nashville workers who don't mind the commute; it's a shorter drive for those who work in west Nashville.

Dickson County was established in 1803, and the city of Dickson dates from 1899. There are a few historic homes here, but most of the area is still rural. Most of the longtime family-owned businesses in the Main Street downtown district have been replaced with antiques stores and specialty shops. Dickson voters approved liquor-by-the-drink a few years ago, so there are a few modern restaurants, grills, and pubs around the city. Shopping is sparse, but new retail is coming in. Among the offerings are a Wal-Mart Supercenter and a Goody's clothing store. For recreation there are nearby Montgomery Bell State Park, the Great Caves Park, and a few golf courses, including GreyStone Golf Club on US 70 E.

Dickson's annual Old Timers festival, honoring senior citizens, is held the first weekend in May and attracts as many as 20,000 to the downtown area for a parade, entertainment, and arts and crafts.

A sign of Dickson's progressive growth is the Renaissance Center, an educational technology center on Highway 46. This unique public facility offers traditional art, music, and drama education; instruction in high-performance computing; a 450-seat performing arts theater; computer classrooms; a 136-seat domed interactive theater with graphic- and laser-projection systems; a science theater; and more (see our Arts chapter).

For more information call the Dickson County Chamber of Commerce at (615) 446-2349.

Robertson County

With a strong agricultural base and diverse manufacturing industries, Robertson County (Area 14), about a 35-minute drive north of Nashville, is growing fast. By 1997 the county's population had already exceeded projections for the year 2000. According to the 2000 U.S. Census, Robertson County's population is 54,433. County officials attribute the growth to improved quality of life. Recent developments in the county include a boom in retail growth (Lowe's, Wal-Mart, and a few restaurants), the addition of an 18-hole public golf course, a $4-million-plus YMCA, a new greenway in Springfield, and improvements to schools. The county is also home to NorthCrest Medical Center. A portion of US 41 was widened to four lanes, improving access to Springfield, the county seat and largest community.

The majority of this 476-square-mile county is farmland. Principal crops include tobacco, corn, wheat, and soybeans. There are also dairy and beef cattle farms here. Historic family farms and beautiful country scenery surround Robertson County's incorporated cities and towns, which include Adams, Cedar Hill, Coopertown, Cross Plains, Greenbrier, Orlinda, Ridgetop, Springfield, and White House.

Robertson County has 17 public schools and two private schools. To contact the Robertson County Chamber of Commerce, call (615) 384-3800 or visit www.springfieldtennchamber.org.

SPRINGFIELD

Renovations and new construction are increasing in busy Springfield, population 14,329. Buyers have snapped up and begun renovating several historic homes. The highest concentration of older residences, including Victorian homes, is in the district north and west of the historic town square. New-home prices are keeping pace with the increase in new construction. Springfield has three golf courses, a bowling alley, and a movie theater. The largest city park, J. Travis Price Park, has soccer fields, a baseball complex, trails, a playground, picnic shelters, and a lake. Retail and dining choices are limited but increasing. Residents who want a night on the town can drive to Nashville in about 45 minutes. In February 2008 two sample real estate listings in Springfield were a new three-bedroom, two-bath, single-story home on .75 acres for $175,000; and a home built in 1995 on a .75-acre lot with three bedrooms and two baths for $147,000.

Rutherford County

In the geographic center of Tennessee, Rutherford County (Areas 21–34), southeast of Nashville, is one of the fastest-growing areas in the nation. Most statistics put it neck-and-neck with adjacent Williamson County in population growth. From 1990 to 2000 Rutherford County's population grew 53.5 percent, reaching an estimated 182,023. With Murfreesboro's Middle Tennessee State University, Smyrna's Nissan Motor Manufacturing Corporation USA plant (the county's largest employer), three hospitals, and other industries, the county has a diverse economic base and is enjoying a booming economy.

Despite the growth, Rutherford County maintains a small-town charm. Its 615 square miles still include nearly 234,000 acres of farmland. The area is also rich in history. The Battle of Stones River, one of the major battles of the Civil War, was fought near Murfreesboro. You can take a self-guided tour of the battlefield today (see our Attractions chapter).

Affordable homes and easy access to Nashville via I-24 are among the county's other pluses.

When it comes to buying a home or property, you'll get more for your money here than in Williamson County. Rutherford County encompasses Murfreesboro, LaVergne, Smyrna, and tiny Eagleville (population 501).

For more information call the Rutherford County Chamber of Commerce at (615) 893-6565 or visit www.rutherfordchamber.org.

MURFREESBORO

Rutherford County's largest city, Murfreesboro was home to 68,816 (plus some 18,000 students at MTSU) as of 2000. And the population is growing every day. This city, established in 1812, still has the feel of a small town. Its charming and historic downtown area received a boost in 1985 with the initiation of the Main Street program, which included new sidewalks, underground wiring, landscaping, and more than $6 million in interior and exterior renovations. The courthouse, built in 1859, is the focal point of the historic and still-lively town square. (The first courthouse, built in 1813, burned before the Civil War. It served as the state capitol from 1819 until 1826, when Nashville became the capital.) A variety of shops and businesses line the square. The landmark City Cafe on East Main Street continues to be the hot spot with Murfreesboro seniors and the downtown business crowd.

On the tree-lined streets surrounding the square, you'll find some wonderfully restored old homes, the grandest of which are on West Main between the courthouse and MTSU's campus. East Main Street has some especially lovely Victorian architecture. There are several neighborhoods of 1950s and 1960s ranch-style brick homes as well as newer developments around the city's perimeter.

In 2005 the average sale price of a sampling of existing homes in Murfreesboro was about $175,784, according to the aforementioned market value report.

Recreation opportunities in Murfreesboro abound. Hot spots and activities include Stones River; Old Fort Park, a 20,000-square-foot playground; historic Cannonsburgh, a reconstructed pioneer village; Uncle Dave Macon Days, an old-time festival held in July; several golf courses; Stones River Greenway, a walking and biking trail; outlet mall shopping; and concerts and sporting events on the MTSU campus.

i Every now and then, when one of Nashville's country stars sells their home, they hold a moving sale and invite the public. Trisha Yearwood, Wynonna Judd, Barbara Mandrell, and Tanya Tucker all have held sales. You can't count on the stars showing up in person at these events, but you never know...

SMYRNA

This former farming community between La Vergne and Murfreesboro enjoyed a boost when the Nissan plant came to town, bringing 6,000 jobs and hastening the development of farmland into subdivisions. In 2000 Smyrna's population was 25,569, the second highest in the county. While you won't find many tree-lined streets here, you will find plenty of new construction and affordable housing. The average selling price in 2008 was $169,873, according to the aforementioned report. Nearby I-24 provides easy access for Nashville commuters.

Aviators will want to take note of this city. The Smyrna Airport, formerly Sewart Air Force Base, is still active. Area hot spots include Stones River, Smyrna Town Centre (fitness center), Smyrna National Golf Course, a bowling alley, and several parks.

LA VERGNE

Just across the Davidson County line in northeast Rutherford County, La Vergne has experienced dramatic growth. Between 1990 and 2000 the city's population grew an astounding 149.2 percent, to a total of 18,687. The city is a top pick for incoming industries. The largest employer is book distributor Ingram Book. It's about a 30-minute drive from downtown Nashville and is close to the Nashville International Airport. Relatively inexpensive homes make this area a viable choice for

first-time home buyers. The average selling price here was about $145,595 in 2008, according to a sampling by real estate appraisers.

Neighborhood hot spots include Percy Priest Lake and La Vergne Park.

Sumner County

Sumner County (Area 9), Nashville's northeastern neighbor, has several diverse communities and recreational opportunities that make it a popular choice for everyone from young families to country music stars. This county's communities have distinct personalities. Some remain largely rural, while others have a definite urban feel. Country general stores, pastures, rolling creeks, and antebellum homes are common sights in the more rural areas, while Old Hickory Lake, with its hundreds of miles of shoreline on the county's southern border, boasts some luxurious, upscale properties. Sumner County is also a historic area, the site of two settlements established by long hunters in the late 1700s (see our History chapter for details).

Like many other Middle Tennessee counties, Sumner County is growing. It is the third most populous county in the MSA, behind Davidson and Rutherford. In 2000 the population was 130,449. Lots of major business developments in Gallatin, numerous recreational and upscale residential areas in Hendersonville, abundant retail stores in Goodlettsville, and an extensive industrial base in Portland have contributed to the growth.

In recent years the average home sale prices have been between $165,000 and $225,000. You'll pay a premium for anything along Old Hickory Lake, however, where Nashville-area residents flock for boating, fishing, and recreation. If you're interested in lake property, be sure you understand the regulations that govern the property and where the property lines lie. Docks are allowed along certain areas. For more information on Sumner County, contact the chambers of commerce in the county's cities or visit www.sumnercountytourism.com.

HENDERSONVILLE

Hendersonville, Tennessee's 10th largest city, offers small-town appeal, resident country music stars, Old Hickory Lake, good schools, and plenty of shopping in nearby Rivergate. It's about a 30-minute drive from downtown Nashville, with easy access from I-65 and Gallatin Pike/U.S. Highway 31E. Some of the biggest country music stars, including Garth Brooks and Johnny Cash, have lived here, along with lots of retirees, families, and professionals. In 2000 the city's population was 40,620.

Hendersonville's 534 square miles offer plenty of residential choices. There is a rural side, a lake side, and lots of apartments, condominiums, and high-density developments. Houses on Old Hickory Lake are in big demand and generally range from $275,000 to $2 million. You can find homes in older neighborhoods for less than $100,000; new homes will start a little higher. In 2008 the average sale price of a sampling of existing homes in Hendersonville was about $245,998. In addition to recreation on Old Hickory Lake, residents can go out and play at the 135-acre Drakes Creek Park, which has a lighted jogging and fitness trail, soccer fields, softball and baseball fields, a youth football field, picnic areas, and playgrounds.

For more information call the Hendersonville Chamber of Commerce at (615) 824-2818 or visit www.hendersonvillechamber.com.

GALLATIN

About 45 minutes from downtown Nashville, 10 to 15 miles northeast of Hendersonville on US 31E, is Gallatin, the Sumner County seat. Gallatin is one of Tennessee's original five "Main Street Communities." Its quaint downtown district features more than 25 historic buildings, some of which were built before the Civil War. There are also several historic attractions nearby, including Cragfont and Wynnewood.

In 2000 Gallatin's population was 23,230. The economic base here is 50 percent industrial and 50 percent agricultural.

Old Hickory Lake, Bledsoe Creek State Park, and numerous city parks offer lots of recreation

opportunities. The Gallatin Civic Center has an indoor swimming pool, volleyball and racquetball courts, two basketball courts, a track for walking and running, a fitness room, an aerobic room, a weight room, meeting rooms, and a video arcade.

Call the Gallatin Chamber of Commerce at (615) 452-4000 for additional information or visit www.gallatintn.org.

GOODLETTSVILLE

Half of this historic area, 20 minutes from downtown Nashville, is in Davidson County and half is in Sumner County. See the listing under Metro Nashville–Davidson County Neighborhoods for more information.

Wilson County

As the Nashville area continues to expand on all sides, Wilson County (Area 11), about 20 minutes east, is experiencing a boom in residential, commercial, and industrial development. From 1980 to the mid-1990s, the population increased nearly 44 percent. As of 2000 the population was 88,809.

An abundance of affordable land is luring families in search of a more peaceful lifestyle. With its wide-open spaces, small historic towns, and easy access to Nashville via I-40, Wilson County offers what many are finding to be the right mix of country and city life. Businesses also have chosen to make Wilson County home, and Cracker Barrel Old Country Stores, Bay's Bread, and Texas Boots are among those with corporate headquarters or offices here. Dell Computer set up shop here in 1999.

For more information call the Lebanon/Wilson County Chamber of Commerce at (615) 444-5503 or visit www.lebanonwilsontnchamber.org.

MOUNT JULIET

How this small town got its name is something of a mystery. Some say it was named for Aunt Julie Gleaves, a sort of guardian angel of the area, someone who was always helping others. The problem with that story is that she was only

18 years old in 1835, the year Mount Juliet was formed. Most believe the city was named for a castle in County Kilkenny, Ireland. Whatever its beginnings, Mount Juliet, incorporated in 1972, is reputed to be the only town in the world with that name.

If you like rolling green hills, spacious lots, and a relaxed lifestyle, Mount Juliet may be for you. Just about 25 minutes from downtown Nashville and a short drive from the Nashville International Airport, Mount Juliet is an increasingly popular choice for families. As of 2000, 12,366 people called Mount Juliet home. Affordable housing is a big draw, although Mount Juliet's prices are generally the highest in Wilson County. According to data published in February 2008, the average estimated housing value in Mount Juliet is about $189,900. Development is increasing in the area. As many as 500 new homes were expected to be built in Mount Juliet in 2008.

LEBANON

Lebanon, named for the biblical land of cedars, may be the largest city in Wilson County, but it's also big on small-town appeal. About a 30-minute drive from Nashville, Lebanon (population 20,235) offers a slower pace.

The city was laid out in 1802 and chartered in 1819. A Civil War battle was fought on the town square in 1862, and after the Confederates' defeat, many homes and businesses were burned. The town was rebuilt, and today the Public Square boasts lots of historic buildings. This area, once the site of mule sales, is known mainly for its great collection of antiques shops. In fact, Lebanon has earned the nickname "Antique City of the South"—for antiques lovers, a visit to this town is a must—and has been featured in *Southern Living* magazine.

Homes in Lebanon range from around $75,000 to $400,000—less than in Mount Juliet but higher than in some other areas in the county. Some historic properties can be found near Cumberland University as well as on West Main and West Spring Streets.

Nearby hot spots include Cedars of Lebanon State Park, south of Lebanon on U.S. Highway 321; Fiddlers Grove at James E. Ward Agricultural Center; Lebanon Golf and Country Club; Cumberland River, north of town; Don Fox Park; and Lebanon Community Playground.

Williamson County

Wealthy Williamson County (Area 10), south and southwest of Nashville, is the fastest-growing county in the state. Between 1990 and 2000 the county's population skyrocketed 56.3 percent, to 126,638. The estimated population for 2006 was 165,804. According to the county chamber, per-capita income in 2008 was $39,150. The median household income in 2008 was $90,087.

Williamson County includes the rapidly expanding Cool Springs business community, one of the hottest retail and corporate office locations in the country. Cool Springs straddles Brentwood and Franklin along I-65. The area offers the 1.3-million-square-foot Cool Springs Galleria shopping mall, tons of additional upscale shops, dozens of restaurants, new executive-level homes, and new office complexes. Williamson County is a definite relocation hot spot in Middle Tennessee, luring more and more Nashvillians and newcomers with its high quality of life, excellent schools, beautiful rural settings, and upscale shops and restaurants. It's about a 20- to 25-minute commute to Nashville via I-65 (if there are no traffic snarls, that is), so neighborhoods here are popular with Music City workers who prefer the Williamson County lifestyle. Lots of music business executives, country stars, professionals, and families live in Brentwood, Franklin, Leiper's Fork, and other areas of the country.

Given the high per-capita income, it's no surprise that you'll find some spectacular homes here. Of course, if you're shopping for real estate in this area, be prepared to spend big. Property and homes here can be pricey.

Williamson County has two public school districts, four private schools, and one hospital. Recreation-wise, there are plenty of options, including several public and private golf courses, more than 20 parks, Natchez Trace Parkway, and several historic attractions. And there are plenty of good country roads—just perfect for a Sunday-afternoon drive.

For more information about the county, call the Williamson County–Franklin Chamber of Commerce, (615) 794-1225, or visit the Williamson County Convention and Visitors Bureau's Web site at www.williamsoncvb.org.

BRENTWOOD

Nestled among green rolling hills, about 8 miles south of downtown Nashville, is the popular middle-class suburb of Brentwood. A mix of suburban and rural areas covering 35.4 square miles, Brentwood has seen its population grow dramatically since the city incorporated in 1969. Since 1980, the population has more than doubled to 32,456. Brentwood's location along I-65 and Franklin Road just across Old Hickory Boulevard offers easy commuter access to Nashville.

The city's well-planned new residential and commercial developments lend a brand-new, fresh look. Planned growth includes green spaces around office buildings and commercial complexes and one-acre lots in subdivisions.

Home buyers can choose from established neighborhoods of two-story or ranch-style homes and newer developments in upscale "McMansion" subdivisions offering superspacious floor plans, modern amenities, and security. In 2008 the average sale price of a sampling of existing homes in Brentwood was about $575,900. Current development is pushing toward the Cool Springs Galleria mall area, and you'll find some condominiums and apartments here. Several city parks offer tennis courts, ball fields, playgrounds, trails, and picnic pavilions. For more on Brentwood visit the Brentwood Chamber of Commerce Web site at www.brentwood.org or call (615) 373-1595.

FRANKLIN

Although it's only about a 30-minute drive from downtown Nashville, Franklin seems worlds away. Its old-fashioned but revitalized town square remains the hub of this town. The 15-block original downtown area is listed on the National Register of Historic Places. Restored 19th-century buildings downtown that house trendy boutiques, antiques stores, restaurants, art galleries, and other unique shops line the square. Franklin's participation in the National Main Street Program brought brick sidewalks, period lighting, underground wiring, and trees to the downtown area.

Many fine old homes on the streets near the square have been restored. The 2-block Lewisburg Avenue Historic District features numerous late-19th- and early-20th-century homes. Sound appealing? Tens of thousands of new Franklin residents would agree. Between 1990 and 2000, Franklin's population grew more than 108 percent, to a total of 41,842.

If you're shopping for a historic home, take note: These properties get snapped up quickly, and they've been selling for higher than market value. Homes in Franklin generally are on smaller lots and have less square footage than Brentwood properties, but they're also less expensive. In 2008 the average sale price in Franklin was $390,900. Folks looking more for a lifestyle than a house feel that's a fair trade.

Franklin's farmland also is in great demand for development. For more on Franklin visit the city's Web site at www.franklin-gov.com.

FAIRVIEW

This quiet, rural community about 25 miles southwest of downtown Nashville has little in common with its Williamson County neighbors Brentwood and Franklin. Fairview is about 10 miles from Bellevue on Highway 100; it's also accessible via I-40. As of 2000, Fairview's population was 5,800. Many of its residents work in nearby Franklin, Brentwood, and Dickson. Fairview's industrial park, developed in the early 1990s, has attracted new industries to the area.

Fairview incorporated in 1959, so many of the homes here are brick ranches, although a few subdivisions and condos have been built recently. Properties are much more affordable than in other parts of Williamson County, with prices starting below $100,000. Lots in some subdivisions are two acres or more, while others feature the tiny parcels commonly found in Middle Tennessee's new developments. There are also some small-acreage listings for "gentleman farmers" whose budgets make trendy Franklin and Leiper's Fork areas off-limits.

The hot spot in Fairview is the Bowie Nature Park. Bicycling and horseback-riding trails, picnicking, and a small lake are among the attractions at this lovely and rarely crowded park (also see our Recreation chapter). For more on Fairview visit www.fairview-tn.org.

REAL ESTATE

There's a lot of buying, selling, and building going on in and around Nashville. In some areas new subdivisions and apartment complexes seem to pop up almost overnight.

Local Realtors report a robust real estate market—in-town and suburban homes as well as condos—in and around Nashville, continuing a trend that's lasted several years. In 2005 the average number of days on the market in Middle Tennessee was 65.

New jobs, a diversified economy, and incoming business have contributed to the housing boom. Relatively low interest rates have made it easier for first-time buyers to purchase a home and for families moving up to buy a more upscale property.

As a result of recent accelerated construction, there are many new homes on the market. Counties surrounding Metro Nashville are growing rapidly. Williamson and Rutherford Counties have been growing fastest, Rutherford being particularly popular among first-time buyers. Some local Realtors expect to see more buyers looking to other counties—Cheatham and Dickson, in particular—in search of more value for their dollar.

REAL ESTATE AGENCIES

If you are considering buying or selling a home, you may want to consider working with a Realtor, who can help ensure your home search, purchase, or sale goes more smoothly. A Realtor's knowledge of the market and the ins and outs of real estate transactions can save buyers and sellers time, headaches, and hassles.

We've compiled a list of several of the area's best-known and a few otherwise notable real estate companies as a place to start. Certainly, there are many other good firms in and around Nashville, so don't limit your options. For information on other companies, call the Greater Nashville Association of Realtors at (615) 254-7516 (www.gnar.org) or the Tennessee Association of Realtors at (615) 321-1477. In addition, the Tennessee Real Estate Commission (615-741-2273), which issues real estate licenses and time-share licenses to brokers, affiliate brokers, and firms, also offers information to the public on how to proceed with complaints against firms. For those interested in building a home, a helpful resource might be the Tennessee Board for Licensing Contractors (615-741-8307 or 800-544-7693, www.state.tn.us/commerce).

The Sunday edition of the *Tennessean* is also a great source of information on properties for sale or rent. Each week you'll find hundreds of properties, a list of interest rates from area lenders, information on Realtors, plus news on the housing market. Searchable databases of thousands of Middle Tennessee Regional Multiple Listing Service properties are available online at the MTRMLS's site, www.realtracs.com, as well as at the *Tennessean*'s Web site, www.tennessean.com, and at other sites. In addition, many real estate companies have their own Web sites; some even include "virtual" tours of selected homes. Other helpful home-hunting resources include several free real estate and apartment guides (see our list at the end of this chapter), which you can find at grocery stores and other locations around town.

Metro Nashville–Davidson County Area

CRYE-LEIKE OF NASHVILLE INC.
5111 Maryland Way, Brentwood
(regional headquarters)
(615) 373-2044,
(800) 373-8893 (relocation)
www.crye-leike.com

Crye-Leike, one of the largest real estate companies in the nation, has had a presence in Nashville since 1992. Crye–Leike of Nashville has more than 900 sales associates at its 18 branch and franchise offices in the Middle Tennessee area.

Crye-Leike's relocation division offers complete relocation services to assist transferring employees and their companies in every state and in more than 20 countries. Crye-Leike's Web site is a popular resource for searching for residential or commercial properties. The site displays more than 71,000 listings and offers 360-degree panoramic movie tours of some properties. Users can sign up to receive an e-mail notification whenever a new property that meets their criteria becomes available. The company publishes two four-color homes magazines each month: the *Crye-Leike Homebuyer's Guide*, available free at area grocery stores, convenience stores, and other locations, and the *Crye-Leike Premier Homes Buyer's Guide*, which features homes in the $300,000-and-up price range.

In addition to residential and relocation services, the full-service real estate company offers commercial business and investment real estate services, property leasing and management services, REO foreclosure services, mortgage lending facilities, insurance services, title services, home services, auction services, apartment locator services, franchise sales, and builder resource services.

i If you're thinking about buying a new home and would like to do a little market research, visit the Web site www.tnrealestate.com. There, you can find out the selling prices and other details of specific properties throughout the state. The data are compiled from county property tax assessors' files. The office of the Davidson County Property Assessor has all county properties listed at its Web site, www.padctn.com; the site includes photos of properties and information on recent sales.

HAURY & SMITH
2033 Richard Jones Road
(615) 383-3838
www.haurysmith.com
This locally owned and operated company has been in business since 1960. About 24 agents and brokers handle residential, commercial, farmland, and resort properties. The company also offers relocation services.

REALTY EXECUTIVES FINE HOMES
3902 Hillsboro Pike
(615) 463-7900

1600 Westgate Circle, Suite 106
Brentwood
(615) 376-4500,
(800) 291-1966 (relocation)
www.realtyexecutives.net
Realty Executives' international network has hundreds of offices. The company has been in business nationally since 1965, making it the second oldest real estate company in the United States. The local Realty Executives office opened in 1997. The Nashville-area office has about 80 Realtors. The company serves all needs, including residential, land, relocation, new homes, and commercial properties. Offices are open daily and offer both buyer and seller representation.

RE/MAX PREMIER PROPERTIES
3354 Perimeter Hill Drive, Suite 140
(615) 777-5550

105 Northcreek Boulevard, Goodlettsville
(615) 855-0880, (877) 225-9739
www.metronashvillehomes.com
This full-service real estate and auction company has been in business for about three decades. The offices have about 55 sales associates who cover all areas of Nashville and surrounding counties. The company handles residential and commercial properties as well as farms and vacant land.

SHIRLEY ZEITLIN & CO.
4301 Hillsboro Pike
(615) 383-0183

278 Franklin Road
(615) 371-0185

341 Cool Springs Boulevard, Suite 100
Franklin
(615) 794-0833
www.shirleyzeitlin.com

Founded in 1979, Shirley Zeitlin & Co. is one of the most recognizable names in Nashville real estate. Specializing in relocation and upper-end properties, the full-service company has more than 100 full-time Realtors. It landed the exclusive agreement to relocate the Houston Oilers (now Tennessee Titans) football team to Nashville—a real coup for Zeitlin, who has served as president of the Greater Nashville Association of Realtors and the State of Tennessee Association of Realtors during her 30-plus years in the business. The company was a finalist in a competition conducted by the United States Chamber of Commerce and Dun and Bradstreet to determine the best businesses in the Southeast. The company's Web site links to all listed properties in the area and also provides virtual tours of selected properties. Senior citizens may be interested in Zeitlin & Co.'s program that takes care of assisted living arrangements, estate sales, and other details that accompany a change in lifestyle.

VILLAGE REAL ESTATE SERVICES

2206 21st Avenue S., Suite 200
(615) 383-6964, (888) 383-6964

615 Woodland Street
(615) 369-3278

707 Monroe Street
(615) 248-1884

1717B Church Street, Suite 101
(615) 321-0577

301 Church Street
(615) 279-7200

202 Church Street, Franklin
(615) 790-4881
www.villagerealestate.com

This agency specializes in unique, eclectic, and historic urban homes in areas such as downtown

Nashville, Belmont/Hillsboro, Hillsboro/West End, Richland, Sylvan Park, historic Edgefield, Forest Hills, Oak Hills, Green Hills, and Belle Meade. In business since October 1996, the agency donates 10 percent of its proceeds to children's clubs and other community organizations citywide through its Village Fund. In 2008 Village opened its first office in Williamson County in historic downtown Franklin. This is the company's sixth location in the greater Nashville area.

Surrounding Area

AGEE AND JOHNSON REALTY AND AUCTION

728 West Main Street, Lebanon
(615) 444-0909
www.ageeandjohnson.com

This company handles residential properties, farm auctions, and commercial properties and offers relocation services in Wilson, Rutherford, DeKalb, Trousdale, Smith, and Summer Counties. In business since 1977, it has 27 agents and brokers.

BOB PARKS REALTY

201 South Church Street, Murfreesboro
(615) 896-4045, (800) 365-RELO
www.bobparks.com

Founded in 1975, Bob Parks Realty is one of the state's largest real estate companies. The independently owned company has 10 Middle Tennessee offices and more than 550 agents and brokers who handle commercial and residential properties. The company has a real estate auction division, a relocation division, and provides moving services, such as hiring a moving company and arranging for utility cut-on. Call the main headquarters at the number above for the location of the office nearest you.

CLARK MAPLES REALTY AND AUCTION CO.

2245 Keeneland Commercial Boulevard, Murfreesboro
(615) 896-4740
www.clarkmaplesrealty.com

Lots of referrals and repeat customers have helped keep this locally owned company in busi-

Looking for a Good Home

If you're looking for a home in the Nashville area, or even if you're already settled in, you might want to consider sharing your home with a companion. A furry, four-legged companion. Local animal shelters are filled with dogs and cats in need of good, loving homes. If you would like to add a pet to your household, consider adopting from one of the local shelters. There are several shelters in Middle Tennessee. The two largest such facilities in Nashville are the Metro Animal Services Facility, which is operated by the Metro Public Health Department of Nashville/Davidson County, and the privately funded Nashville Humane Association.

The Metro Animal Control Facility
5125 Harding Place
(615) 862-7928
www.metronashvilleanimalcontrol.com
The Metro Animal Control Facility is on Harding Place, near Nolensville Road. The state-of-the-art facility can house about 400 animals per month; in any given month, about 100 to 200 pets are adopted. You can adopt a pet there Monday through Saturday during designated hours. Fees, including rabies vaccination fees and spay/neuter fees, range from $79 to $104 for dogs and from $54 to $69 for cats. If the animal was already spayed or neutered when it arrived at the Metro facility, the total cost for adoption is only $29 and includes rabies vaccination.

The Nashville Humane Association
213 Oceola Avenue
(615) 352-1010
www.nashvillehumane.org
The Nashville Humane Association adopts out as many as 2,000 pets each year. The facility, located just off White Bridge Road in west Nashville, has space to house about 145 animals. Adoptions take place daily except Wednesday, when the shelter is closed. Adoption fees are $79 for dogs and $69 for cats and include spaying/neutering and vaccinations. Newly adopted pets also receive two months of free pet health care insurance. Visit the Humane Association's Web site to view some of the pets available for adoption or to obtain more information.

i Woodmont Boulevard was Nashville's first street paved with concrete. It was originally called Concrete Boulevard.

ness for more than 30 years. The company offers a full range of properties, including residential, commercial, and acreage, and handles as many as 80 auctions in Tennessee each year. There are approximately 25 brokers and agents.

COLDWELL BANKER LAKESIDE REALTORS
530 West Main Street, Hendersonville
(615) 824-5920, (800) 933-5920
www.coldwellbankerlakeside.com
Established in the early 1970s, this is one of the oldest real estate companies in Hendersonville. The office specializes in residential properties, including lakefront, and has about 65 agents.

COLDWELL BANKER/SNOW AND WALL REALTORS

1980 Old Fort Parkway, Murfreesboro
(615) 893-1130
www.snowandwall.com
In business since 1982, this Coldwell Banker franchise specializes in residential properties in and around Murfreesboro. There are about 50 agents and brokers.

GOLDSTAR REALTY

303 South Main Street, Ashland City
(615) 792-1910
www.goldstarrealty.net
This company specializes in new construction, residential, and agricultural properties in Cheatham and surrounding counties. It has been in business since 1989 and has about 13 brokers and agents.

RE/MAX ELITE CARRIAGE HOUSE

2500 North Mount Juliet Road
Mount Juliet
(615) 754-4766, (800) 548-0131

4473 Lebanon Pike, Hermitage
(615) 872-0766, (800) 807-9099
www.mynashvillehome.com
This locally owned company has been in business since the late 1980s. It handles residential, commercial, and farm properties. With about 70 agents, the company prides itself on its emphasis on personal service.

REAL ESTATE RESOURCES

Services

APARTMENT SELECTOR

2720 Old Lebanon Road, Suite 115
(615) 833-3151, (800) 394-2736
www.aptselector.com
Call either of the listed numbers for free assistance in locating an apartment in Nashville or surrounding cities. Fees are paid by the landlords. Listings also include condominiums, houses, and duplexes. The database contains information on current availabilities, size, amenities, and policies.

In business since 1959, the company providing this service has several offices nationwide. You can move into an apartment in as little as one to three days after contacting the office, or look two to three weeks in advance of your move and have your new apartment reserved.

MORRIS PROPERTY MANAGEMENT INC.

413 Welshwood Drive
(615) 833-5117
www.morrisproperty.com
Founded in 1969, this company manages and maintains hundreds of units, serving the needs of both the property owner and the resident renter. Morris Property Management also has a Realtor division to assist buyers and sellers with real estate transactions. The company also handles commercial leasing.

Publications

The following publications are distributed free at participating grocery stores, convenience stores, hotel lobbies, area chambers of commerce, colleges, and other locations.

APARTMENT FINDER

(800) 222-3651
www.apartmentfinder.com
This handy guide has loads of color photos and information, including rental rates. Complexes are arranged geographically.

CRYE-LEIKE HOMEBUYERS GUIDE

(615) 373-2044, (800) 373-8893
www.crye-leike.com
This guide features color photos and a brief description of Crye-Leike properties arranged by area. It is published every four weeks.

FOR SALE BY OWNER

5331 East Bend Drive, Old Hickory
(615) 804-3177
www.FSBOmonthly.com
This monthly publication features color photos and descriptions of properties that are for sale by owner (and therefore, typically wouldn't be listed

by the MTRMLS). The Web site has a searchable database of homes.

HOMES OF MIDDLE TENNESSEE
1854 Air Lane Drive
(615) 884-5470, (800) 874-1490
Published every four weeks, this guide has color photos, descriptions, and prices of homes listed by various agencies.

i Nashville was tapped No. 2 on the list of Best Places for Relocating Families by Worldwide ERC and Primacy Relocation. The 2007 report focused on "the ease with which a family can move to a city and the ease of settling into a new life there."

NASHVILLE HOMES MAGAZINE
1854 Air Lane Drive
(615) 884-5470, (800) 874-1490
This is a big, thick book filled with more than 200 pages of properties for sale. It's published every two weeks. Listings are arranged by area.

REAL ESTATE THIS WEEK
1854 Air Lane Drive
(615) 884-5470, (800) 874-1490
This biweekly guide features Nashville and Middle Tennessee homes and property for sale, listed by area and price.

HEALTH CARE AND WELLNESS

Everyone knows that Nashville is Music City, but it's also a leading center for the health care industry. In fact, Nashville is rapidly carving out a name for itself as the "Silicon Valley of Health Care." Currently it's home to nearly 300 health care companies, including HCA, the largest for-profit provider of health care services in the nation. HCA manages about 182 hospitals and 94 outpatient surgery centers in 22 states, England, and Switzerland, and employs thousands of people at its headquarters near Centennial Park.

The health care industry has been in a state of flux, however. In Nashville, a spate of mergers, acquisitions, and a headline-grabbing Medicare fraud case have brought new corporate identities for some major local players. Among the big changes are the reorganization of HCA's regional hospitals into the 14-hospital TriStar Health Systems network and the 2001 purchase of Baptist Hospital by Saint Thomas Health Services, creating a five-hospital organization that is the area's largest nonprofit health care provider.

But while the landscape has changed, Nashville has emerged on the winning side of the corporate shuffle. Today residents of Middle Tennessee can choose from several nationally recognized hospitals for their health care needs. In addition, Nashville remains a center for health care education. Vanderbilt University and Meharry Medical College are both nationally recognized medical schools. Vanderbilt, Belmont University, David Lipscomb University, Tennessee Tech, and Aquinas Junior College all offer degrees in nursing. Meharry's School of Dentistry has one of only four Regional Research Centers for Minority Oral Health in the United States. All of which assures Nashville's place as a health care leader for years to come.

OVERVIEW

Saint Thomas Hospital's Heart Institute is one of the top five cardiac programs in the nation. Among the "firsts" to its credit are the first heart transplant in Tennessee (in 1985) and the first Regent aortic valve installation in the United States (in 1999). In the 2006 HealthGrades hospital quality ratings, Saint Thomas Hospital ranked among the top 5 percent of all hospitals in the nation, and No. 1 in Tennessee for overall cardiac services and heart surgery. Saint Thomas received five-star ratings for cardiac services, cardiac interventions, heart surgery, and treatment of atrial fibrillation. Baptist Hospital is the largest non-profit medical center in Middle Tennessee and also the region's busiest emergency room, receiving about 50,000 visits per year. Baptist has been at the national forefront in health care treatment, building the nation's first facility dedicated solely to laser and laparoscopic surgery and the region's first outpatient surgery center.

TriStar Health Systems can claim recognition in several departments as well. In 2000 the Solucient Leadership Institute, a leading source of health care information, bestowed honors on three TriStar hospitals: Centennial Medical Center and Hendersonville Medical Center were named among the country's top 100 hospitals for stroke, cardiovascular, and orthopedic medicine, while Summit Medical Center, in Hermitage, was recognized for its breast cancer clinical research program.

Centennial's Sarah Cannon Cancer Center is also widely regarded as the leading program of its kind in the Southeast. Meanwhile, TriStar's Hendersonville hospital recently pioneered a groundbreaking procedure for Parkinson's disease patients.

Vanderbilt University Medical Center is another major player in the health care field. In 2008, 10 Vanderbilt programs ranked among the country's best in the *U.S. News & World Report* annual survey of America's best hospitals. Among the departments receiving top honors were Vanderbilt's kidney disease treatment center, ranked 10th; gynecology, ranked 10th; the urology departments, ranked 13th; and its ear, nose, and throat facilities, ranked 16th.

In early 2004 Vanderbilt Medical Center's state-of-the-art $172 million Monroe Carell Jr. Children's Hospital opened its doors. The only free-standing children's hospital in the area, the new facility serves children of Middle Tennessee, southern Kentucky, and northern Alabama. In December 2003 StoneCrest Medical Center, a new TriStar Health Systems hospital in northern Rutherford County, opened, replacing Smyrna Medical Center, an emergency and outpatient facility. In time for fall 2008 enrollment, Vanderbilt University School of Nursing unveiled its new Doctor in Nursing Practice (D.N.P.) degree.

HEALTH DEPARTMENT

METROPOLITAN HEALTH DEPARTMENT FOR NASHVILLE AND DAVIDSON COUNTY
311 23rd Avenue N.
(615) 340-5616 (recorded general information)
www.healthweb.nashville.org
Since the introduction of TennCare, the state's experimental replacement for Medicaid, the Metro Health Department largely has moved out of primary service and assumed more of a preventive function. Still, the department takes an active role in such areas as HIV testing and the treatment of sexually transmitted and other communicable diseases, as well as food inspection, air-pollution control, animal control, and other environmental issues.

In addition to the Health Department's main clinic, the Lentz Public Health Center at 311 23rd Avenue N. (615-862-5900), the Health Department also operates the Downtown Clinic for the Homeless, 526 Eighth Avenue S. (615-862-7900);

East Public Health Center, 1015 East Trinity Lane (615-862-7916); and Woodbine Public Health Center, 224 Oriel Avenue (615-862-7940).

The Sexually Transmitted Disease Clinic (615-340-5647) and Communicable Disease Program (615-340-5632) are housed at the 23rd Avenue center, which also runs special programs such as the Adolescent Pregnancy Initiative (615-340-0411) and Car Seat Loaner Program (615-340-5648).

Clinic hours are 8:00 a.m. to 4:30 p.m. Monday through Friday except holidays. For direct-dial numbers of the department's programs, check the blue pages of your telephone directory under Nashville government.

ℹ **The Tennessee Disability Information and Referral office provides free information about community services throughout Tennessee for persons with disabilities as well as their family members and service providers. For information visit the comprehensive Web site at www.kc.vanderbilt.edu/kennedy/tdir or call (615) 322-8529 or (800) 273-9595 (hearing impaired).**

HOSPITALS

BAPTIST HOSPITAL
2000 Church Street
(615) 284-5555
www.baptisthospital.com
Baptist Hospital, Middle Tennessee's largest non-profit community hospital, has 2,500 employees and more than 700 physicians serving locations in Davidson and surrounding counties. Baptist, which is licensed for 683 acute care beds, 66 bassinets, and 27 neonatal intensive care unit beds, offers a wide variety of services. Specialty areas include cardiac services, neuroscience services, oncology, and women's services. The hospital also has a large bariatrics (weight reduction) program. Baptist has served the Nashville area since 1919; today it is part of Saint Thomas Health Services. Locals remember Baptist for its mid-'90s rhinestone-studded advertising campaign, which brought stars like Garth Brooks and Naomi Judd to television sets explaining why their families

chose Baptist. Baptist remains the hospital of choice for many of Nashville's rich and famous—including the NFL Titans and NHL Predators, for which Baptist is the official sports medicine provider.

Baptist's expansive main campus spans 6 city blocks. Here patients will find such specialty clinics as the Mandrell Heart Center—yes, it's named for that Mandrell—the Institute for Aesthetic and Reconstructive Surgery, the Diabetes Center, Baptist Sleep Center, 55 Plus (for adults 55 and older), a comprehensive inpatient and outpatient Rehabilitation Unit, and the 10,000-square-foot Sports Medicine Center. In addition to traditional medical care, Baptist offers a variety of free health screening services. Screenings for prostate and skin cancer, glucose, ovarian cancer, colorectal cancer, heart disease, blood pressure, and cholesterol are offered at various health events Baptist hosts around the community each year. Baptist's CareFinders Physician Referral service provides free referrals to the community. Call (615) 284-MD4U (6348) or visit the hospital's Web site.

The Baptist Wellness Center provides such services as smoking cessation, stress management, weight management, and more than 40 different health education programs for adults and children. It also has an indoor track, pool, fully equipped weight room, multipurpose gym, steam and sauna rooms, and a variety of aerobic exercise programs. (See also our Recreation chapter.) Baptist has a sports rehabilitation clinic at Club K, a state-of-the-art sports medicine/athletic training facility in Antioch. Baptist's Certified Athletic Trainers help with sports medicine rehabilitation and teach injury prevention.

CENTENNIAL MEDICAL CENTER
2300 Patterson Street
(615) 342-1000
www.centennialmedctr.com
Part of the TriStar Health System facilities, Centennial has 615 beds and a medical staff of 1,200. TriStar is the name used by the family of hospitals in Middle Tennessee and southern Kentucky owned by Nashville-based HCA, the world's largest private provider of health care. Fourteen

TriStar hospitals are located in the area. Centennial Medical Center is the largest in the TriStar system; its main campus covers some 40 acres in the heart of Nashville, stretching roughly from Centennial Park all the way to the city's other mega health complex, Baptist Hospital. It offers a full array of primary-care as well as emergency, cardiac, neurologic, orthopedic, obstetric, psychiatric, and other specialty services. Centennial has been recognized as one of the top hospitals in America in the areas of cardiology, stroke, and orthopedics. The hospital's physicians have been nationally recognized for their contributions in the field of stroke intervention. Centennial is also known for its Spine Surgery Program, which has been ranked No. 1 in the state and No. 3 in the nation for the number of spine surgeries performed.

Centennial Medical Center is composed of five main facilities: the Sarah Cannon Cancer Center; the Women's Hospital, a freestanding facility dedicated to women's health; Parthenon Pavilion, a psychiatric facility; Centennial Heart Center; and Centennial Tower, a tertiary-care facility.

Parthenon Pavilion is Middle Tennessee's oldest and largest full-service psychiatric facility. The 158-bed hospital, located at 2401 Parman Place (615-342-1400, www.parthenonpavilion.com), provides inpatient and outpatient mental health services, plus specialized programs and treatment for adolescents, adults, and geriatric patients. Parthenon also provides 24-hour emergency assistance and crisis intervention, referral, and educational programs. Workshops about mental health issues are offered free to community groups and organizations through the Community Education Team.

The Sarah Cannon Cancer Center is named for the late *Grand Ole Opry* star better known as Minnie Pearl. The center is actually a network of 16 affiliated medical facilities in the Middle Tennessee–southern Kentucky area; devoted solely to cancer diagnosis and treatment, the center has become the largest community-based, privately funded clinical research program in the country. Since 1992 more than 5,000 cancer patients have participated in clinical trials through SCCC. The center's main office is located at Centennial

Medical Center, 250 25th Avenue North, (888-323-7398, www.sarahcannon.com).

The Women's Hospital at Centennial, located at 2221 Murphy Avenue (615-342-1919), offers a comprehensive array of women's health care services above and beyond the general OB/GYN care. Among the specialty services available are family birth services, lactation support, a Sleep Disorders Center, neonatal intensive care unit, various education classes, a Women's Surgical Unit, and menopause care and services.

TriStar's MedLine offers a physician referral service at (615) 342-1919 or (800) 242-5662. An online service is also available at Centennial's Web site.

i In 1928 a German shepherd named Buddy became the nation's first guide dog for the blind, trained in Switzerland for Morris Frank of Nashvillle.

CENTENNIAL MEDICAL CENTER AT ASHLAND CITY
313 North Main Street, Ashland City
(615) 792-3030
www.centennialmedicalcenter.com
Centennial Medical Center at Ashland City, part of HCA's TriStar Health Systems, has served Cheatham County since 1987. It provides a number of on-site outpatient services—including surgery, radiology, respiratory therapy, ultrasound, CT scans, and mammograms—for pediatric through geriatrics as well as transfers to other TriStar hospitals.

HENDERSONVILLE MEDICAL CENTER
355 New Shackle Island Road,
Hendersonville
(615) 338-1000
www.hendersonvillemedicalcenter.com
This facility, part of TriStar Health Systems, has 110 beds offering medical and surgical care, obstetrics, gynecology, critical care, 24-hour emergency services, MRI (magnetic resonance imaging), a cardiac catheterization lab, and outpatient services.

The hospital has completed several major expansion projects, to the tune of some $30 million. An emergency department and intensive care unit, a community classroom, a surgical wing, and a medical professional building have been constructed.

HORIZON MEDICAL CENTER
111 U.S. Highway 70 E., Dickson
(615) 446-0446
www.horizonmedicalcenter.com
TriStar's Horizon Medical Center services the needs of Middle Tennesseans in Dickson, Hickman, Houston, Humphreys, and Perry Counties. The hospital, located 45 miles west of Nashville, has been open since 1958. The 176-bed regional referral facility is recognized for primary-care, long-term-care, and geriatric psychiatric-care services.

MIDDLE TENNESSEE MEDICAL CENTER
400 North Highland Avenue
Murfreesboro
(615) 849-4100
www.mtmc.org
Middle Tennessee Medical Center is a private, not-for-profit hospital. Established in 1927, MTMC has a long tradition of providing health care for residents of Rutherford, Cannon, Coffee, Warren, and DeKalb Counties. It became affiliated with Saint Thomas Health Services in 1986. One of the fruits of that affiliation was the opening of the Baptist Women's Pavilion at MTMC, which provides such women's services as labor and delivery rooms, a neonatal intensive care unit, obstetrics, and education programs. The Women's Imaging Center offers mammography services and osteoporosis screening. MTMC provides a full range of medical and surgical care, including women's care, pediatrics, cardiac care including catheterization and stents, home health services, wellness programs, and sleep disorders treatment. More than 200 physicians representing more than 30 different specialties are on staff. MTMC also provides a variety of medical/surgical care, including orthopedics, neurosurgery, ophthalmology, neurology, plastic surgery, oncology, nephrology, gastroenterology,

and internal medicine. MTMC also operates a busy 24-hour emergency room facility.

The Regional Cancer Center, located at 509 East Bell Street, is connected to the ambulatory surgery center and outpatient diagnostic center via an atrium. Radiation treatment, a resource center, and meeting rooms are available. MTMC unveiled its expanded Diagnostic Labs facility in 2000. In addition to conventional X-ray equipment, it performs advanced diagnostic services such as nuclear medicine, CT scans, and MRIs. In 2002 the Emergency Department was greatly expanded, and it treats more than 50,000 patients per year.

NASHVILLE GENERAL HOSPITAL AT MEHARRY
1818 Albion Street
(615) 341-4000
www.nashville.gov/generalhospital
When Metro General Hospital opened as City Hospital on April 23, 1890, one physician and seven nurses staffed the 60 beds that served Nashville residents. The hospital's mission was to provide health care services for those unable to care for themselves. Today city-owned NGH serves as the clinical teaching hospital for Meharry Medical College. The hospital, which moved to the Meharry campus in 1999, is licensed for 150 beds and provides a full complement of primary- and acute-care services. A shared clinical affiliation among Metro General, Meharry Medical College, and Vanderbilt University Medical Center came full circle in 1999 with the formation of a formal alliance between the academic partners and the hospital. Today Vanderbilt provides executive management of the hospital, while Meharry manages its clinical and educational programs.

Medical/surgical, obstetrical/pediatric, emergency, ancillary, and ambulatory care are provided throughout the facility. Meanwhile, the Primary Care Center, Maternal and Infant Care Clinic, and OUR KIDS Center provide ancillary services to the community. The Maternal and Infant Care Clinic offers comprehensive family planning and prenatal and pediatric care in a family-centered environment. The clinic's professional clinic staff includes certified nurse-midwives, social workers, nurse practitioners, and a nutritionist who manage the care of children from birth through age 18. The OUR KIDS Center, jointly supported by the hospital, Vanderbilt University Medical Center, and the Junior League of Nashville, is the only center in Middle Tennessee providing both medical and psychological services for children who are suspected victims of sexual abuse. The center is at 1804 Hayes Street.

i The Nashville City Hospital, now called Nashville General Hospital at Meharry, opened its School of Nursing in 1892—the first training school of its kind located between the Ohio River and New Orleans.

NORTHCREST MEDICAL CENTER
100 NorthCrest Drive, Springfield
(615) 384-2411
www.northcrest.com
Located 30 miles north of Nashville, the former Jesse Holman Jones Hospital is now a member of the TriStar family. Since 1995 the hospital has been located in a 43-acre, 109-bed medical complex. NorthCrest provides a full array of inpatient and outpatient services to residents of Robertson County and the surrounding area. Among the hospital's specialties are its in-house cardiovascular lab, 24-hour emergency services, obstetrics and women's services, sleep disorder care, pulmonary rehabilitation, and medical/surgical services. NorthCrest has an accredited chest pain center and an accredited CT scan (one of only a few in the state) and also performs angioplasty. The center sponsors a variety of free educational classes, support groups, and seminars promoting good health.

SAINT THOMAS HOSPITAL
4220 Harding Road
(615) 222-2111
www.saintthomas.org
Saint Thomas Hospital, founded in 1898, is one of the nation's top five cardiac-care centers and a member of Ascension Health, the nation's largest

not-for-profit Catholic health system. The 541-bed facility provides specialty health care services for more than two million residents of Middle Tennessee, southwestern Kentucky, and northern Alabama. The hospital is located in west Nashville. Saint Thomas has consistently ranked high in independent industry surveys of top hospitals (see the beginning of this chapter). In 2008 Saint Thomas Hospital was named one of the nation's 100 Top Cardiovascular Hospitals. This marked the sixth time the hospital received the recognition, based on excellence in care, efficiency in operations, and sustainability of cardiovascular performance. Saint Thomas is the only hospital in Nashville and one of only four in Tennessee receiving this honor.

Saint Thomas is best known nationally for its Heart Institute. As of April 2008, the Institute had performed more than 276 heart transplants, 157,000 cardiac catheterizations, 31,000 coronary angioplasties and stents, 56,000 open heart operations, including valve replacement surgery, and had treated 81,000 cardiac rehabilitation patients. While the Heart Institute gets most of the limelight, Saint Thomas's Dan Rudy Cancer Center is also renowned and has been recognized by the Commission on Cancer of the American College of Surgeons. The Rudy Center offers comprehensive, multidisciplinary care for cancer patients, as well as support services for patients and their families. Saint Thomas also provides 24-hour emergency room services and a full array of inpatient and outpatient services. Among the specialty clinics available at Saint Thomas are the Center for Breast Health, Joint Replacement Center, Neurosciences Institute, Center for Diabetes, Pulmonary Care, and the Vascular Institute. Saint Thomas is also the only hospital in Nashville with an attached hotel and overnight accommodations, Seton Lodge and the Inn at Saint Thomas.

In 2001 a new era began for Saint Thomas when Ascension Health acquired the assets of Nashville's Baptist Hospital (see listing, this chapter). This created a family of hospitals known as Saint Thomas Health Services (STHS), which consists of Baptist, Saint Thomas, Middle Tennessee Medical Center in Murfreesboro, Baptist Hickman Community Hospital in Centerville, and Baptist DeKalb Hospital in Smithville. STHS is the largest nonprofit hospital system in Middle Tennessee.

SKYLINE MEDICAL CENTER
3441 Dickerson Pike
(615) 769-2000
www.skylinemedicalcenter.com
This TriStar-affiliated medical center opened in 2000 as a replacement for Nashville Memorial in Madison. Skyline is a 203-bed facility covering 59 acres; in addition to the hospital and 24-hour emergency room, it includes a 200,000-square-foot medical office plaza. Skyline offers specialized care in neurosurgery, oncology, surgical services, orthopedics, and cardiology. Skyline also provides a wide array of community education and health and wellness programs.

SOUTHERN HILLS MEDICAL CENTER
391 Wallace Road
(615) 781-4000
www.southernhills.com
Southern Hills, part of HCA's TriStar system, opened in 1979 and serves the communities of southern Davidson, northern Rutherford, and Williamson Counties. The center has 300 physicians on staff, covering more than 20 specialties. The facility has 120 acute-care beds and 20 skilled nursing beds. The emergency room, one of the busiest in Nashville, averages more than 3,000 cases per month. Southern Hills is recognized for neurosurgery, neurology, orthopedics, cardiology, obstetrics, and oncology. The center established a stroke program in 2003 that includes a whole-body, eight-slice-per-second CT scanner. Additions in 2005 include an Advanced Wound Care Center, an all-digital Cardiac Catherization Laboratory, and a new Radiation Therapy Center. The Joint and Spine Centers of Excellence were established in 2001; since then, Southern Hills has been rated by independent firm HealthGrades as among the best in the nation for total knee replacement and hip fracture repair.

Emergency, Information, and Referral Numbers

Emergencies requiring ambulance, police, or fire departments—911

Baptist Care Finders (physician referrals)—(615) 284-MD4U, (800) 625-4298

Crisis Center (crises ranging from people who can't pay their heating bill in winter to suicide attempts)—(615) 244-7444

HealthLink (Saint Thomas's free physician referral service)—(615) 298-3200 or (800) 298-3200

MedSource Physician Referral (Middle Tennessee Medical Center's referral service)—(615) 893-4357 or (800) 427-8497

Mental Health Cooperative (24-hour mobile crisis support)—(615) 726-3340

Tennessee Poison Center—911 or (615) 936-2034, (800) 222-1222

TriStar Med Line—(615) 860-6600

Vanderbilt Physician Referral—(615) 322-3000

Vanderbilt Psychiatric Hospital (for psychiatric referral and assessment)—(615) 327-7000, (800) 365-2270

STONECREST MEDICAL CENTER
200 StoneCrest Boulevard, Smyrna
(615) 768-2000
www.stonecrestmedical.com
StoneCrest Medical Center opened in November 2003 as a replacement for the 60-bed Southern Hills Medical Center at Smyrna emergency department. Part of the HCA-owned TriStar

Health System, the $75-million facility, located at the intersection of Interstate 24 and Sam Ridley Parkway in the heart of Smyrna and La Vergne, has 75 beds, with room for 150. There are more than 130 physicians on staff. Among the full array of acute-care services offered are emergency care, general surgery, cardiology, obstetrics and other women's services, cancer care, and intensive care. A 160,000-square-foot physicians' building is adjacent to the hospital.

SUMMIT MEDICAL CENTER
5655 Frist Boulevard, Hermitage
(615) 316-3000
www.summitmedicalcenter.com
This community hospital, in operation since 1970, moved in 1994 to its current 188-bed medical and surgical facility. With more than 300 physicians on staff, it provides emergency care, diabetes management, and obstetric services, as well as laparoscopic and other same-day surgeries, psychiatric care, neurosurgery, and pediatric services. Summit, a part of HCA's TriStar system, also has a women's health center and orthopedic care.

TENNESSEE CHRISTIAN MEDICAL CENTER
500 Hospital Drive, Madison
(615) 865-0300
www.tennesseechristian.com

PORTLAND MEDICAL CENTER
105 Redbud Drive, Portland
(615) 325-7301
In March 2006 HCA acquired the two Tennessee Christian Medical Centers from Adventist Health Systems. With this acquisition, the Madison center has become part of Skyline Medical Center. The Tennessee Christian Medical Center in Portland was renamed Portland Medical Center. As of September 1, 2006, Portland was managed by Hendersonville Medical Center. Tennessee Christian Medical Center, which admitted its first patient in 1908, now has 273 acute-care beds. Portland Medical Center has 38 beds, more than a dozen physicians, and more than 130 employees and provides intensive and coronary care, medical

and surgical care, and comprehensive OB/GYN care, including a newborn nursery. Tennessee Christian has a 400-member medical staff serving 35,000 patients a year and providing outpatient and inpatient acute care as well as behavioral and rehabilitation programs. In addition to the services provided at Portland Medical Center, the Madison hospital offers cardiac catheterization; cardiopulmonary services; day surgery; 24-hour emergency services, staffed by MDs and nurses specially trained in emergency medicine; an endoscopy lab; home health services; occupational medicine; radiology; inpatient rehabilitation and behavioral services, including adolescent treatment with partial hospitalization, aftercare, and outpatient services as treatment options; adult acute treatment; an adult stress-disorders unit; and a center for addictions (based on 12-step programs pioneered by Alcoholics Anonymous).

UNIVERSITY MEDICAL CENTER
1411 Baddour Parkway, Lebanon
(615) 444-8262
www.universitymedicalcenter.com
The 257-bed University Medical Center is part of the Naples, Florida–based Health Management Associates system. Facilities include an Outpatient Center with a full range of diagnostic and treatment procedures, from CAT scans to MRI and cataract surgery to tonsillectomies. The Heart Center is a full-service diagnostic facility with capabilities ranging from nuclear cardiology to cardiac catheterization. The Orthopaedic Center performs procedures including total joint replacement as well as back, knee, and hip surgeries. The Emergency and Chest Pain Center features the latest in emergency-treatment technology and chest pain testing.

UMC also has a Cancer Care Center, a full-service center offering both chemotherapy and radiation therapy; an Aesthetic Image Center, for plastic and reconstructive surgery; progressive and pediatrics care units; and its own home health agency. McFarland Specialty Center offers rehabilitation (including physical, occupational, speech, and recreational therapies), psychiatric care for adult and geriatric patients, and skilled nursing for total care of those with physical or cognitive disabilities. The Women's Pavilion offers all-in-one labor/delivery/recovery rooms, plus programs that meet the additional needs of women in all stages of life. The hospital also has a Health Works Program to help business and industry obtain high-quality health care in a cost-effective manner.

VANDERBILT CHILDREN'S HOSPITAL (MONROE CARELL JR. CHILDREN'S HOSPITAL)
2200 Children's Way
(615) 936-1000
www.vanderbiltchildrens.com
The Children's Hospital moved into its new eight-story, $172-million, curved-glass-and-granite facility in early 2004. The freestanding Children's Hospital has 17 specialty units, including neonatal and pediatric intensive care, pediatric surgery, kidney center, lung center, and long-term-care unit. The 206-bed hospital has 38 beds in its pediatric emergency department, 12 operating rooms with room for four more, a 36-bed pediatric critical care unit, a 60-bed neonatal intensive care unit, and a 12-bed myelo-suppression unit. The hospital boasts such child-friendly features as a 45,000-gallon fish pond at the main entrance, colorful wall murals and floor designs, a toy train that encircles the pharmacy, a movie theater, and a performance stage. The facility was built to be family-friendly. Each of the patient rooms is private; the rooms are large and contain furniture that converts to sleeping space for parents. Additional small, hotel-like rooms are available for family members to use as well. Parents and family members will appreciate the comfortable quiet spaces on each floor, kitchen and laundry areas, computer hookups, desk space, and garden areas.

VANDERBILT UNIVERSITY MEDICAL CENTER
1211 22nd Avenue S.
(615) 322-5000
www.mc.vanderbilt.edu
Vanderbilt University Medical Center and the Vanderbilt Clinic have a world-class reputation

for excellence that is unsurpassed in the region. Physicians refer patients to Vanderbilt from not only throughout Middle Tennessee but also east and west Tennessee, Kentucky, and Alabama. Vanderbilt treats more than 300,000 people a year. Both the medical center and the clinic consistently rank among the premier health care facilities in the nation. *U.S. News and World Report* recently listed nine of Vandy's specialties among the top in the nation.

The Vanderbilt-Ingram Cancer Center, a National Cancer Institute Clinical Cancer Center, provides comprehensive care and state-of-the-art research. The Vanderbilt program provides leading-edge treatments, some of which may not be available anywhere else in the world. In 2002 the Vanderbilt-Ingram Cancer Center at Franklin opened; the 8,000-square-foot facility is Williamson County's first radio-oncology center.

Vandy has several programs that are one-of-a-kind in Middle Tennessee. These include a Level I Trauma Center and a Level I Burn Center, both of which provide the highest level of immediate, 24-hour service available; a Lifeflight air emergency transport system; and a Level IV Neonatal Intensive Care Unit, which provides the highest level of that type of care available.

Vandy also has the only Middle Tennessee transplant program that provides all major solid organ transplants: heart, kidneys, lungs, liver, and pancreas. The Vanderbilt Stallworth Rehabilitation Hospital, which has 80 beds, provides complete inpatient and outpatient services for pediatric and adult patients with orthopedic and neurologic injuries or disabilities. It includes the Vanderbilt Center for Multiple Sclerosis.

The Children's Hospital (see previous entry) moved into its new $172-million facility in early 2004. It is the only children's hospital in the area. The Psychiatric Hospital at Vanderbilt, located at 1601 23rd Avenue S., provides inpatient, partial hospitalization, and intensive outpatient services to children, adolescents, and adults with psychiatric and substance-abuse problems.

Other special centers include the Adult Primary Care Center, the Arthritis Center, the Balance and Hearing Center, the Bill Wilkerson Center for Otolaryngology, the Breast Center, the Child Development Center, the Geriatric Evaluation Program, the Vanderbilt Brain Institute, and the Voice Center. At the Breast Center, women can obtain comprehensive breast health care, including mammography, breast ultrasound, examination, biopsy, and surgical evaluation; the center also offers a breast cancer support group. The Child Development Center evaluates children who have, or are suspected of having, developmental problems. The Voice Center is a one-of-a-kind facility for treating vocal disorders and counts many notable recording artists among its clients.

The Vanderbilt Dayani Center offers a wide range of health assessments and screenings, aerobics and exercise programs, rehab programs, nutrition consultation, therapeutic massage, and classes in smoking cessation and weight management. Facilities include an indoor track, indoor pool, and fully equipped weight room.

WILLIAMSON MEDICAL CENTER
2021 Carothers Road, Franklin
(615) 435-5000
www.williamsonmedicalcenter.org
Williamson Medical Center is a not-for-profit community hospital dedicated to "making health care services cost effective, convenient, and accessible to area residents and employers." The 185-bed facility offers comprehensive inpatient and outpatient services, 24-hour emergency care, and preventive health screenings and wellness activities. The medical center is staffed with nearly 350 physicians representing 39 medical specialties from oncology to sports medicine, allergies to reproductive health. The center is known for its orthopedic surgery. Recent additions to Williamson Medical Center are a neonatal intensive care unit, a Breast Health Center, the Heartburn Treatment Center of Middle Tennessee, and the Surgical Weight Loss Center. Williamson Medical Center partners with the community to provide outreach programs to businesses, schools, government, and citizens of Williamson County. Among these activities are community and corporate health fairs, classes in CPR, seminars, and

health screenings. In addition, the center provides a full-time physician for Williamson County Health Department patients.

i We love Nashville, but the climate here can be the kiss of death for allergy sufferers. If you've never suffered from allergies before, chances are you will after one spring in Middle Tennessee. The Baptist Hospital Allergy Center Report offers daily pollen and mold spore counts online at www.baptisthospital.com, or call the Baptist Allergy Center at (615) 340-4620.

VETERANS HOSPITALS

ALVIN C. YORK VETERANS AFFAIRS MEDICAL CENTER
3400 Lebanon Pike, Murfreesboro
(615) 867-6000
This 213-bed veterans hospital, part of the VA Tennessee Valley Healthcare System, provides primary care and subspecialty medical, surgical, and psychiatric services. Affiliated with Vanderbilt University School of Medicine and Meharry Medical College, the hospital provides long-term rehabilitation and nursing home care and long-term inpatient psychiatric care. It has a primary care program and provides subspecialty care in dermatology, gastroenterology, hematology/oncology, infectious diseases, neurology, pulmonology, nephrology, rheumatology, and sleep evaluation.

NASHVILLE VETERANS AFFAIRS MEDICAL CENTER
1310 24th Avenue S.
(615) 327-4751
The Nashville VA Medical Center is one of two main campuses in the VA Tennessee Valley Healthcare System. The other is in Murfreesboro. The 238-bed Nashville campus offers primary, secondary, and tertiary care to veterans living in Middle Tennessee and Kentucky. The hospital is affiliated with Vanderbilt University School of Medicine and Meharry Medical College and has active residency programs in all major medical and surgical specialties and subspecialties. The Nashville campus

is a Veterans Health Administration resource for solid organ and bone marrow transplants. In order to meet the increasing need for outpatient services, the center completed a $43-million renovation project to expand its facilities.

WALK-IN CLINICS

The following clinics, which do not require appointments and which see patients of all ages, prefer that patients come in no later than an hour or so before closing so there is still time to be seen.

BRENTWOOD FAMILY CARE CENTER
5046 Thoroughbred Lane, Brentwood
(615) 370-8080
Brentwood Family Care Center is open 8:00 a.m. to 6:00 p.m. Monday through Friday and 9:00 a.m. to 2:00 p.m. Saturday.

CHRISTIAN FAMILY MEDICAL CLINIC
385 Wallace Road, Suite 307
(615) 837-9080

2531 Elm Hill Pike
(615) 884-0215

1719 Gallatin Road
(615) 612-6330
www.christianfamilymedical.com
These family practice and urgent care centers treat adults and children older than age two. Labs and X-ray facilities are located on-site. Hours at the Wallace Road and Elm Hill Pike locations are 8:30 a.m. to 7:00 p.m. Monday through Thursday, 8:30 a.m. to 5:00 p.m. Friday, and 9:00 a.m. to 1:00 p.m. Saturday. Hours at the Gallatin Road clinic are 9:00 a.m. to 5:00 p.m. Monday through Friday and 9:00 a.m. to 2:00 p.m. Saturday.

GREEN HILLS MEDICAL CENTER
2001 Glen Echo Road
(615) 292-0012
Nonurgent medical services are provided at this walk-in clinic. Hours are 8:30 a.m. to 4:30 p.m. Monday through Friday (the center closes for lunch from 12:30 to 1:30) and 9:00 a.m. to 2:00 p.m. Saturday.

HARDING MEDICAL CENTER
4126 Nolensville Road
(615) 834-2170

Harding Medical Center is open 8:00 a.m. to 6:00 p.m. Monday, 8:00 a.m. to 5:00 p.m. Tuesday through Thursday, and 8:00 a.m. to 4:30 p.m. Friday. The clinic is sometimes open Saturday from 9:00 a.m. to 2:00 p.m.

MADISON MINOR MEDICAL CENTER
1114 North Gallatin Road, Madison
(615) 868-9959

Madison Minor Medical Center is open 9:00 a.m. to 7:00 p.m. Monday through Friday and 9:00 a.m. to 6:00 p.m. Saturday.

NASHVILLE FAMILY MEDICAL CLINIC
476 Harding Place
(615) 315-8717

This walk-in clinic treats adults and children older than age two. A lab and X-ray facility are located on-site. Hours are 8:00 a.m. to 8:00 p.m. Monday through Thursday, 8:00 a.m. to 5:00 p.m. Friday, and 9:00 a.m. to 5:00 p.m. Saturday.

VANDERBILT WALK-IN CLINIC
919 Murfreesboro Road, Franklin
(615) 791-7373

The Vanderbilt Walk-In Clinic is open 7:30 a.m. to 7:30 p.m. Monday through Friday, until 8:00 p.m. Saturday and Sunday. Recently added to this facility is the Vanderbilt Orthopedic Clinic, which provides orthopedic care in hand, spine, shoulder, and sports medicine, as well as physical therapy and occupational therapy.

i BlueCross BlueShield of Tennessee, one of the area's largest health insurance providers, has added an alternative medicine discount called BluePerks to its regular insurance plans. The program features discounts of up to 30 percent on massages, spa services, vitamins, holistic medicine, and more. For details visit www .bcbst.com or call (800) 227-5911.

VINE HILL COMMUNITY CLINIC
601 Benton Avenue
(615) 292-9770

Immunizations, nonurgent care, physical exams, and mental health services are offered here. The Vine Hill clinic is operated and staffed by the Vanderbilt School of Nursing. Hours are 8:00 a.m. to 8:00 p.m. Monday through Friday.

i Dr. David Satcher, former president of Nashville's Meharry Medical College, served as U.S. Surgeon General from 1998 to 2002. Satcher also has led the national Centers for Disease Control, based in Atlanta.

SPECIAL SERVICES

AGAPE
4555 Trousdale Drive
(615) 781-3000
www.agapenashville.org

Agape (pronounced uh-GAH-pay), meaning "Christian love," is a licensed child-placement agency offering temporary foster-home care and adoptive services in Middle Tennessee since 1966. Maternity services include counseling and foster care for unwed mothers. Also, professional counseling, available on a sliding scale, includes marriage and family counseling as well as individual counseling for everyone. A major objective of the agency is strengthening family life through workshops and seminars. Hours are 8:00 a.m. to 4:30 p.m. Wednesday and Friday and 8:00 a.m. to 7:00 p.m. Monday, Tuesday, and Thursday.

HOPE CLINIC FOR WOMEN
1810 Hayes Street
(615) 321-0005
www.hopeclinicforwomen.org

Hope Clinic offers free pregnancy tests, crisis intervention counseling, post-abortion counseling (individual and support groups), abortion education, maternity clothes, and baby items. STD testing (excluding HIV) is $10. The center also provides referrals for medical care, social services, adoption, and housing. All services are confidential. Hours are 9:00 a.m. to 5:00 p.m. Monday, Wednesday, and Friday; 9:00 a.m. to 8:00 p.m. Tuesday and Thursday; and 9:00 a.m. to noon Saturday.

HOUSECALLS USA
(877) 244-7362
www.hoteldocs.com

When you're on vacation, you generally travel without many of the conveniences of home—such as your family physician. With HouseCalls USA (formerly HotelDocs), however, if you find yourself in need of medical assistance, you can simply call the listed toll-free number, and a board-certified local physician will be dispatched to your hotel, home, or worksite within the hour.

HouseCalls visit fees range from $200 to $250—much less than the cost of a typical emergency room visit. A phone consultation with a physician is $50; if a house call is required, the $50 will be credited toward the cost of the visit. Medication, which most doctors bring with them, costs extra unless the doctor provides a free sample. Payment is required at the time of the visit, but most insurance plans will reimburse you for the cost of services. Major credit cards, travelers checks, personal checks, and cash are accepted.

Various types of doctors and specialists are available, including physicians, dentists, chiropractors, optometrists, podiatrists, audiologists, acupuncturists, nurses, pediatricians, ophthalmologists, obstetricians, gynecologists, allergists, dermatologists, nutritionists, and internal specialists. Many doctors speak a variety of languages, as well.

HouseCalls USA is based in Miami and serves dozens of cities in the United States, Canada, and the Caribbean. The service is available 24 hours a day, 365 days a year.

PLANNED PARENTHOOD OF MIDDLE AND EAST TENNESSEE
Midtown Health Center
412 D. B. Todd Boulevard
(615) 321-7216
www.ppmet.org

Planned Parenthood provides family planning and crisis pregnancy services. Hours are 9:15 a.m. to 6:30 p.m. Monday, 9:15 a.m. to 4:30 p.m. Tuesday and Thursday, 8:15 a.m. to 3:30 p.m. Wednesday, and 9:15 a.m. to 3:30 p.m. Friday. Saturday hours vary, so call ahead. Appointments are available for gynecological exams and Pap smears, all birth-control methods, counseling, abortions from 7 to 14 weeks, testing for sexually transmitted diseases including HIV, and hormone replacement and gynecological care for menopausal women.

The clinic accepts walk-ins for pregnancy testing without an appointment during Family Planning Clinic hours. Emergency contraceptive pills are available, but appointments are requested.

HOSPICE CARE

Hospices work to improve the quality of life for the terminally ill and provide supportive care for both the patient and family members. Hospices typically help patients who have a life expectancy that is measured in months and who are no longer receiving treatment toward a cure. Request for hospice services typically can be made by the patient, physician or other health care personnel, and family and friends. Care is provided by an interdisciplinary team that typically includes physicians, nurses, home health care workers, clergy, social workers, and trained volunteers. Hospice staff members will visit a patient to assess his or her needs. Pain management, spiritual support, counseling, respite care, and bereavement counseling are among the services provided. Hospice workers are typically available 24 hours a day. All or part of the hospice care may be covered by Medicare, Medicaid, or private insurance companies. There are several hospices in the Nashville area, including the following.

ALIVE HOSPICE INC.
1718 Patterson Street
(615) 327-1085, (800) 327-1085
www.alivehospice.org

One of the area's best-known and largest hospices is Alive Hospice, which began providing hospice care in 1976. In 2008 its team of nurses and other professionals cared for about 450 people each day.

The not-for-profit agency provides end-of-life care for patients in Davidson, Cheatham, Dickson, Robertson, Rutherford, Sumner, Williamson, and Wilson Counties, regardless of ability to pay. Alive Hospice provides in-patient/residential care at its 30-bed residence facility as well as in-home hospice services. Nursing services include the complete spectrum of skilled-nursing care and pain management, with 24-hour on-call availability. Arrangements can be made for physical, speech, and occupational therapies related to symptom control. Individual counseling for patients and families is available through the Grief Center at Alive Hospice. Social workers, chaplain services, and volunteer help are also available.

HOSPICE OF MURFREESBORO
726 South Church Street, Murfreesboro
(615) 896-4663
www.mtmc.org

Hospice of Murfreesboro, which serves primarily Rutherford County, is a department of Middle Tennessee Medical Center. Its services, however, are not limited to patients at that hospital.

Most services are provided in patients' homes. The hospice has an active volunteer component that helps out in such ways as occasionally delivering dinner and staying with a patient, so family members can run errands or tend to other needs.

Other benefits include grief support groups, which are free and open to the community, and Camp Forget-Me-Not, a summer camp for children who have experienced the loss of a loved one.

i **Family members and friends of patients in local hospitals often receive discounts on lodging at designated hotels and motels. Some hospitals have information about nearby accommodations on their Web sites.**

TRINITY HOSPICE OF TENNESSEE
2625 Perimeter Place, Suite 124
(615) 365-0343, (800) 889-HOPE
719 East College Street, Suite 401
Dickson
(615) 740-9905
www.trinityhospice.com

Trinity Hospice's Nashville and Dickson locations serve terminally ill patients residing within 50 miles of the nearest office. Services for all patients include nursing care, social work, counseling and education, home health aides, and bereavement follow-up for family members and caregivers for a year after a patient's death. In addition to traditional hospice services, Trinity offers a special program of care for terminally ill patients in nursing homes.

WILLOWBROOK HOSPICE
1164 Columbia Avenue, Franklin
(615) 791-8499, (800) 790-8499
www.willowbrookhealth.com

Willowbrook works with patients who have been diagnosed as having six months or less to live if their disease runs its normal course. The hospice's main focus is on comfort and pain management, working to help patients spend their final days at home rather than in an institution, and teaching family members how to care for their dying loved one. The patient's personal physician works with Willowbrook's hospice team to develop an individual plan of care.

ALTERNATIVE HEALTH CARE

We've already established that Nashville is a national leader in the field of health care. The area has also come a long way when it comes to "alternative" health care. A growing number of holistic medicine practitioners can be found here, but remember: This isn't California. This is the Bible Belt, where people tend to be a little more conservative on the average, and apparently that philosophy largely extends to folks' attitudes toward medicine.

Still, attitudes are changing. One of Nashville's largest hospitals has opened a holistic health center: Saint Thomas's Total Health Institute (see separate listing in this section). Formerly known as the Institute for the Healing Arts, the center offers such therapies as acupuncture and massage.

The Nashville area also has several schools training holistic medical practitioners. The Natural Health Institute of Nashville (615-242-6811, www.natural-health-inst.com), located at 209 10th Avenue S. in historic Cummins Station, offers a 600-hour program of professional massage and bodywork therapy; graduates are eligible for licensure and national certification.

The Cumberland Institute for Wellness Education (615-370-9794, www.cumberlandinstitute.com), at 500 Wilson Pike Circle in Brentwood, is Tennessee's oldest training program for massage therapy. Students receive massage therapist certification upon completing the 500-hour program.

Nashville has also wholeheartedly embraced chiropractic practitioners, once viewed as being on the fringe of the medical profession. Today there are more than 100 chiropractors practicing in Nashville. Dozens of other alternative practitioners—herbalists, energy healers, iridologists, color therapists—have set up shop in Nashville as well. Natural food stores and any of the many free alternative newspapers are good sources of information on such practitioners.

Keep in mind that not all of these practitioners are licensed medical doctors. Be sure to ask plenty of questions if you have doubts about anyone's credentials.

INTEGRATED HEALTH CARE CENTER
602 West Iris
(615) 383-1995
This clinic is headed by an M.D. and specializes in using an integrated approach for a variety of disorders. Among the disciplines practiced here are acupuncture and herbal medicine for treatment of allergies, PMS, headaches, addictions, and depression.

INTEGRATIVE HEALTHCARE CENTER
1711 19th Avenue S.
(615) 467-6462
www.integrativehealthcarecenter.com
This nonprofit agency located in Hillsboro Village assists those seeking relief from the side effects of illness, cancer treatment, surgery, stress, and pain. The center offers a variety of mind/body/spirit therapies, including psychotherapy, psychiatry, and energy therapy and other types of body work. The approach is intended to complement traditional medicine, so the therapists work collaboratively with physicians and other therapeutic practitioners. The center's therapists receive seven years of intensive training.

i The free, bimonthly publication *Health & Wellness* contains listings of alternative medicine practitioners in the Middle Tennessee area. Pick up a copy at health food stores, bookstores, cafes, and wellness centers, or contact the magazine at (615) 356-8404 or at www.healthandwellnessmag.com.

MIND–BODY MEDICAL CENTER
1201 Villa Place Suite 202
(615) 320-1175
www.mindbodymedicalcenter.com
This general, natural medicine, and prevention-based medical practice provides a variety of natural approaches to healing. The center is led by Stephen Reisman, M.D., who created the center in 1991. There are also two M.D.s on staff who are trained in traditional Chinese medicine. Some of the services offered are chelation therapy, acupuncture, intravenous vitamin therapies, nutritional counseling, energy balancing, weight loss programs, and stress reduction and relaxation.

EDUCATION AND CHILD CARE

Education has come a long way since the 1855 founding of Hume School, a notable institution because it made Nashville the first city in the South to establish a public school system. On that site today stands Hume-Fogg High, a "magnet" for academically talented students in grades 9 through 12. The newer school, one of a growing number of public magnet programs in Metropolitan Nashville–Davidson County, represents an ever-expanding number of educational opportunities in the area for young and old alike. Perhaps it's no surprise to find a large quantity of high-quality learning institutions in a city that has been called the "Athens of the South." But it's reassuring to discover that Nashville schools—technical as well as academic, from pre-kindergarten through doctoral programs—are continuing to explore, innovate, and improve, helping create new generations of leaders in a stunning range of fields. Today's students, even in the early grades, are as likely to be utilizing high-tech tools like CD-ROMs and the Internet as they are to be using books or calculators.

According to a study by the Center for Regional Economic Issues at Ohio's Case Western University, Nashville is one of the 10 most educated metropolitan areas in the United States. *U.S. News & World Report* and academic journals have recognized the Nashville region's diverse and outstanding educational institutions. This diversity includes not only the area's public schools but also literally scores of private elementary and secondary schools, both secular and with church or religious affiliations. Nashville also has highly respected single-sex institutions, including the all-girls Harpeth Hall School and the all-boys Montgomery Bell Academy. Some 20,000 Davidson County students attend private schools—that's about 23 percent of the total number of school-age children in the county. Tuition in area private schools ranges from about $1,000 to more than $19,000 per year.

Higher education, of course, has long been one of Nashville's bragging points. The most prominent institutions are Vanderbilt University, with its highly ranked schools of education, medicine, business, and law; Meharry Medical College, a leading educator of African-American doctors and dentists, which has an alliance with Vanderbilt; and Fisk University, which is highly acclaimed not only among historically African-American colleges and universities but also among all postsecondary schools. And these are far from the only options you'll find in this area. In fact, the region has some 19 colleges and universities offering baccalaureate, graduate, or professional degrees to more than 85,000 students annually.

OVERVIEW

This chapter looks at the Nashville metropolitan area's public school systems; the "best and brightest" private schools, colleges, and universities; and arts and special-needs schools. We also address the child-care issue—which, in some areas, is becoming more and more inseparable from the school issue, as some schools allow children to enter pre-kindergarten as early as age three.

EDUCATION

Public Schools

Nashville/Davidson County

i Metro's Board of Public Education meets on the second and fourth Tuesday of each month. Meetings are open to the public and take place at the Administration Building of Metropolitan Public Schools, 2601 Bransford Avenue, beginning at 5:00 p.m. The meetings are televised live on Metro's Government Access Channel 3 (Comcast Cable TV in Davidson County).

METROPOLITAN NASHVILLE PUBLIC SCHOOL SYSTEM
Central Office, 2601 Bransford Avenue
(615) 259-8400, (615) 259-INFO
www.mnps.org

In the 2007–2008 school year, Metro had 137 schools: 74 elementary schools, 35 middle schools, 16 high schools, 4 special education schools, 1 gifted and talented center, 4 alternative learning schools, and 3 charter schools. All public schools in Nashville–Davidson County are under the direction of the consolidated city-county government. The school board consists of nine elected members and a director, who is appointed. The average teacher salary is $61,567. Approximately two-thirds of Metro teachers have a master's degree or higher.

There were 74,155 enrolled in Metro schools in the 2007–2008 school year and 4,915 teachers. The ethnic makeup of the student population reflects the area's diversity: 35.3 percent of students that year were Caucasian, 48.3 percent were African American, 13 percent were Hispanic, 3.1 percent were Asian, and about 0.2 percent were Native American. The number of Kurdish students is growing, as well. More than 40 Metro schools offer English Language Learners programs; this growing program serves more than 5,000 students. About 64 percent of ELL students are Hispanic; the predominant languages spoken by ELL students are Spanish, Kurdish, Arabic, Somali, and Vietnamese.

Each Metro student is assigned to a school depending on where the student lives. This is called their "zone" school. School bus transportation is provided. However, there are different options for each child, including magnet schools, which we will cover later in this chapter. A five-year, $206.8 million capital plan that began in the 1998–1999 school year has built new schools and improved old ones countywide. Rezoning is also keeping many students closer to home; much of this is the result of a U.S. District Court's 1998 ruling that ended voluntary desegregation after parents sued over the long bus trips their children endured.

KINDERGARTEN

One year of state-approved kindergarten is required for enrollment in first grade in the Metropolitan Nashville Public School System. Kindergarten programs are available at all elementary schools. Kindergarten enrollment for children who will be five years old on or before September 30 requires the child's birth certificate, a record of a recent physical examination, an up-to-date Tennessee state immunization form, and proof of residence (a rent receipt or utility bill will work). The child's Social Security number or card is optional.

ENRICHMENT PROGRAMS AND OPTIONS

Metro Schools offer a variety of unique enrichment programs. Gifted students in pre-K through grade six, for example, can take part in the Encore program, which supplements regular classes with an extended enrichment curriculum. Students in grades seven and eight can take high school classes such as Algebra I and first-year foreign language, often for high school credit. High school students can take part in PA classes and the Scholars Program, which recognizes its graduates with a Distinguished Scholars Diploma.

SPECIAL EDUCATION

Special education programs consist of individual education plans created by committees of parents, teachers, principals, and school psychologists. One committee meets to assess the student's needs; another creates the plan for meeting those needs, which is devised according to the student's disabilities. Students in special education programs may continue in the Metro system until they are 22 years old, if they desire. Whenever possible, they are mainstreamed.

CHARTER SCHOOLS

In Tennessee charter schools are an option for academically at-risk students and children with special needs. The state's first charter schools began operation in 2003–2004. At this writing, Nashville has three charter schools: the K-4 Smithson-Craighead Academy at 3307 Brick Church Pike (615-228-9886, www.smithsoncraig head.org); Lead Academy at 1704 Heiman Street (615-498-2916, www.leadacademy.org); and KIPP Academy at 123 Douglas Avenue (615-406-8239, www.kippacademynashville.org). The schools were created to offer an alternative to students who are zoned to attend a low-performing school. Charter schools are paid for by tax dollars, as are other public schools, but are operated by independent nonprofit organizations. The schools have the freedom to control their own curriculum, staffing, organization, and budget but are held accountable for their results. For more on the state's charter schools, visit the Tennessee Department of Education's Web site, www.state.tn.us/education.

i Student performance ratings and other data for all of Tennessee's public schools are available on the state Department of Education's Web site, www.state .tn.us/education. The School System Report Card is updated annually.

METRO MAGNET AND OTHER OPTIONAL SCHOOLS

Magnets offer alternatives to assigned or zoned schools and help offer voluntary desegregation for some students. They also allow students to study a theme related to their areas of interest or expertise. No transportation to magnet schools is provided by Metro schools, but bus routes from Metro Transit Authority are available. For information call the transit authority at (615) 862-5950.

A random lottery is held to select students for Metro's magnet schools. All students who meet the academic requirements may apply for admission to Metro's three academic magnets (Meigs Middle, Hume-Fogg High, and Martin Luther King High). Any student may apply through the lottery for admission to the various thematic magnet schools.

Applications for admission must be submitted by deadline (dates vary). Applicants will be assigned random magnet lottery numbers, which they will receive in the mail. If your child is selected for admission, you will receive a letter in the mail; you must sign and return the letter in order for your child to enroll. Students who are not selected will be placed on a waiting list. (Nashville School of the Arts does not have a lottery; the school selects 70 percent of its students by audition and 30 percent by essay or interview.)

For more information on magnets, visit the Metro Schools Web site or call (615) 259-8676 or Metro Schools' information line listed at the beginning of this entry.

In addition to magnets, the system has nine Enhanced Option Schools and 10 Design Centers. The Enhanced Option Schools are kindergarten and pre-K programs that encourage learning through smaller class size and a longer school year. Enrichment and Encore programs are available to gifted students. Enhanced Option programs are offered at Bordeaux, Buena Vista, Caldwell, Fall-Hamilton, Glenn, Kirkpatrick, Napier, Park Avenue, and Warner zones.

Design centers have specialized programs developed to meet the needs of students in a particular area or "cluster." Most programs are K–4, but as of 2006, there are also two preschools and three 5–8 programs. Each program has a particular theme, such as advanced academics or language/literature. For the majority of the centers, students living within the school zone have first choice to enroll in a design center and do not need to apply. Students living in the "high school cluster" have second priority and must apply through the lottery. Students living outside the cluster are required to apply through the lottery and go on a waiting list until space becomes available.

Private Schools

Nashville
AKIVA SCHOOL
809 Percy Warner Boulevard
(615) 356-1880
www.akivanashville.net
Akiva is a coed Jewish day school serving around 100 students in kindergarten through sixth grade. The school, founded in 1954 by Rabbi Zalman Posner, is open to all children who have at least one Jewish parent, without regard to synagogue affiliation. It combines "excellent secular education with intense Jewish education." The student-teacher ratio is 8 to 1. Jewish studies include classical and conversational Hebrew; the Hebrew Bible in its original text; Jewish prayer, laws, traditions, holidays, and history; along with Mishnah, Talmud, and Jewish thought. The school is SACS-accredited. Some athletics programs use the Gordon Jewish Community Center facilities. Annual tuition for the 2008–2009 year was $11,775.

i Helpful resources for homeschooling in the Nashville area include the Middle Tennessee Home Education Association (615-477-6917, www.mthea.org), the Tennessee Home Education Association (858-623-7899, www.tnhea.org), and the Tennessee Department of Education (888-854-3407, www.state.tn.us/education).

CHRIST PRESBYTERIAN ACADEMY
2323A Old Hickory Boulevard
(615) 373-9550
www.christpres.org
Christ Presbyterian Academy, or Christ Prez as it's called by the locals, opened in 1985 as a ministry of Christ Presbyterian Church, PCA. In 2008 its enrollment was 886 students in grades K–12, with a faculty/ staff of 150. The education is Christian-based, so Bible study is required each year of attendance. Students do not have to be members of Christ Presbyterian Church to enroll, but they must be professing Christians, and at least one parent must be a professing Christian. Several notable figures in Christian music—Michael W. Smith among them—have sent their children here.

Christ Prez is known for its Bridges curriculum, which is based on the work of University of Southern California psychology professor Dr. J. P. Guilford. Guilford's research in the '40s, '50s, and '60s pioneered the idea that intelligence is not fixed at birth but can be developed with proper techniques. Today the Bridges Learning System is a nationwide program for middle and high school students who don't learn at their full potential under traditional educational methods. Not all students are enrolled in Bridges at Christ Prez, but those who need the assistance have it available to them. Christ Prez is accredited by the Association of Christian Schools International and by SACS. In 2007–2008 tuition rates at Christ Presbyterian were $8,810 for K–5 and $10,530 for grades 6–12.

DAVID LIPSCOMB CAMPUS
Elementary School
4714 Granny White Pike
(615) 269-1783
www.dles.lipscomb.edu

Middle School, 3901 Granny White Pike
(615) 269-1785
www.dlms.lipscomb.edu

High School, 3901 Granny White Pike
(615) 269-1784
www.dlhs.lipscomb.edu

David Lipscomb Campus, part of Church of Christ–affiliated David Lipscomb University, serves children in pre-kindergarten through high school. Enrollment totals more than 1,500. The private school's mission is "to serve students so that they may master knowledge and skills appropriate to them and become Christ-like in attitude and behavior."

The school began in 1891 when Lipscomb and James A. Harding founded the Nashville Bible School, which later became David Lipscomb College and is now Lipscomb University. The original objective of the Nashville Bible School was to provide a well-rounded general education, offering instruction in a full range of academic subjects as well as the Bible. Students of all ages—many of the younger ones children of the college's professors—attended, helping establish a close relationship between the college and the campus school. The school, which moved in 1903 to its present location, was renamed in 1918. Four years later, the Campus School was separated in identity from David Lipscomb College, but the Campus School and Lipscomb University continue to share a common organization and commitment to education founded on biblical principles.

David Lipscomb Campus School offers a comprehensive and challenging academic curriculum designed to prepare students for college. Primary emphasis in all grades is on language skills, math, science, social studies, and Bible, with supplemental instruction in art, music, foreign languages, computer skills, and physical education. A full range of athletic and extracurricular activities begins with elementary class plays and continues in the middle school and high school with interscholastic and intramural athletics, drama, music, forensics, student publications, academic competitions, and various civic and social clubs.

All members of the faculty and administration are Christians, and the curriculum for all grades includes daily Bible instruction and participation in regular chapel services. About 98 percent of all graduates from the Campus School enter colleges and universities. Each year's senior class has included at least one, and as many as five, National Merit Semi-Finalists. David Lipscomb Campus School is accredited by the Southern Association of Colleges and Schools.

i "Rockin' Around the Christmas Tree" singer Brenda Lee, the only female inducted into both the Rock and Roll and the Country Music Halls of Fame, attended Maplewood High School in Nashville.

DAVIDSON ACADEMY
1414 Old Hickory Boulevard
(615) 860-5300
www.davidsonacademy.com

Davidson Academy, an interdenominational Christian school, is a private, coed, college preparatory day school for students in grades K3 through 12. The school took its name from the first school west of the Cumberland Mountains. The original Davidson Academy was founded in 1785 in Madison; its namesake, which opened in the fall of 1980, has more than 800 students. The student-teacher ratio is 20 to 1. The average class size is 19 in pre-K and kindergarten, 21 in grades one through six, and about 17 in grades seven through 12. Honors and Advanced Placement courses are offered in grades nine through 12. Students take educational and cultural field trips to historical landmarks in the state and as far away as New York and Europe. Student achievement scores are above average in all subjects. The average composite score on the ACT college entrance exam for Davidson Academy students is 22; 99 percent of the school's graduates go on to college. Annual tuition in the 2008–2009 school year was $7,200 for grades PK4 through 12. The cost for the K3 program was $135 per week. The school's mission statement reads: "Davidson Academy is dedicated to providing boys and girls opportunities for intellectual, spiritual, social, and physical growth; to instilling and strengthening Christian values in an interdenominational setting; to preparing students for higher education, leadership, and service; and to offering programs and services to meet the ever-changing needs of students and their families."

ENSWORTH SCHOOL
211 Ensworth Avenue (K–8)
(615) 383-0661

Highway 100 (grades 9–12)
(615) 301-5400
www.ensworth.com

Ensworth, founded in 1958, traditionally served boys and girls K–8, but the school added grades 9–12 when its stunning new 15-acre campus opened on Highway 100 in west Nashville. The school is located on the site of the historic Devon Farm, adjacent to Edwin Warner Park.

The school's 2007–2008 enrollment was about 1,000. The average class size is 21, with a student-faculty ratio of 8 to 1. Ninety-eight percent of Ensworth students continue on to college. The curriculum includes English (personal journals are kept at many grade levels), social studies (a thematic, not chronological, approach), foreign language (French and Spanish studies begin in pre-first grade, while seventh and eighth graders can elect to study Latin), computers (three computer labs), science (four lab facilities), music (regular instrumental and choral instruction), math (emphasis on problem solving and logical thinking), art (biweekly art classes), physical education, and outdoor education and life skills (personal responsibility, decision making, health, and communication skills). Students also have scheduled classes in and free time to use the 20,000-volume library. The school offers competitive sports for boys and girls and is a member of the Harpeth Valley Athletic Conference. Applicants should demonstrate average or above-average abilities on developmental and achievement tests. Priority is given to youngsters who are children or siblings of graduates or children of faculty members. Ensworth is SACS-accredited.

i The nonprofit Tennessee Association of Independent Schools has helpful information about how to select a private school, as well as information on its member schools. Visit the association online at www.taistn.org or call (615) 321-2800 for more information.

EZELL-HARDING CHRISTIAN SCHOOL
574 Bell Road, Antioch
(615) 367-0532
www.ezellharding.com

Ezell-Harding, an independent school established in 1973, has an enrollment of about 900 students from pre-K through 12th grade. It is accredited by SACS. A quest for excellence is apparent in the accomplishments of the 2007 senior class with three National Merit Semi-Finalists, two National Merit Commended Scholars, and one National Merit Achievement Participant Scholar. EHCS, a member of the Tennessee Secondary School Athletic Association, fields boys' teams in baseball, basketball, football, golf, soccer, tennis, track, and cross-country, and girls' teams in basketball, golf, soccer, softball, tennis, volleyball, track, and cross-country.

FATHER RYAN HIGH SCHOOL
700 Norwood Drive
(615) 383-4200
www.fatherryan.org

Father Ryan, a Catholic coed high school, is operated by the Catholic Diocese of Nashville and accredited by the Southern Association of Colleges and Schools. For more than 60 years, its mission has been "to develop within each student a sense of purpose, a love of God and one's fellow man, and a strong respect for life."

The school has a 76-member faculty, with 58 percent holding a master's degree or higher. The student-faculty ratio is 11 to 1. Enrollment is 907 students from seven Middle Tennessee counties. Ninth-grade students are admitted from the parochial schools and other area schools. Placement is based on the results of placement tests in December, plus academic records and eighth-grade teacher recommendations. The school requires 24 credits for graduation, including one credit in religion for each year attended. Honors and advanced courses are offered at all grade levels in every major subject.

Extracurricular activities include drama, newspaper and yearbook journalism, band, and student government. The National Honor Society and Mu Alpha Theta encourage academic achievement. The athletic program includes football, basketball, soccer, baseball, track, volleyball, golf, swimming, tennis, softball, cross-country, wrestling, lacrosse, ice hockey, bowling, and competitive cheerleading.

FRANKLIN ROAD ACADEMY
4700 Franklin Road
(615) 832-8845
www.frapanthers.com

"A well-rounded education in a caring Christian environment" is the objective at Franklin Road Academy, founded in 1971. The school, which serves 935 coed students in pre-kindergarten through 12th grade, is divided into a Lower School, Middle School, and Upper School. Its mission is "to prepare students intellectually for higher levels of education while also providing programs and facilities for the physical, social, spiritual, cultural, and emotional development of the 'whole child.'"

Pre-kindergarten, for four- and five-year-olds, stresses social and academic growth with programs "geared to the cultivation of thinking abilities, language development, reading and math readiness, and refinement of gross and fine motor skills." These youngsters receive an early introduction to computers, and computer science instruction starts in first grade. Enrichment classes at Franklin Road Academy include computer science, library skills, physical education, music/band, and art. To graduate, students must accumulate 24 units, including Old and New Testament Survey, foreign language, fine or performing arts, and physical education, in addition to math, English, science, and social studies. Many teachers hold master's degrees, and some have doctorates. The student-teacher ratio at Franklin Academy is 10 to 1. The school is accredited by the Southern Association of Colleges and Schools. The class of 2007 earned over $3.7 million in scholarship offers, with 80 seniors receiving 340 acceptances to 112 different colleges and universities throughout the country. One student was named a National Merit Finalist, two were named National Merit Commended Scholars,

and one student received an appointment to the United States Military Academy.

FRA has 22 sports teams, including basketball, softball, football, baseball, soccer, tennis, cross-country, indoor track, track and field, riflery, cheerleading, golf, volleyball, and wrestling. There's also an extended-hours program and a summer program. The school's arts program includes a 655-seat theater featuring state-of-the-art sound and lighting technology, a 300-seat auditorium, and an amphitheater. Separate rooms are devoted to art, band, dance, drama, and voice, and there are soundproof private practice rooms.

HARDING ACADEMY
170 Windsor Drive
(615) 356-5510
www.hardingacademy.org

Harding Academy, organized in 1971 as a non-profit, independent, nonsectarian, coeducational elementary day school, is for children K–8. It stresses "emotional as well as academic support," with a child-centered curriculum adaptable to the child's level of readiness. The SACS-accredited school places strong emphasis on language arts (beginning with kindergarten creative writing programs) and a strong foundation of mastery of skills at each level. The academy also has a challenging middle school program that helps students prepare for high school.

Classes in art, music, computer skills, and physical education are taught in all grades. Reading enrichment programs, with small groups of six to eight students, are offered from kindergarten through fourth grade. Sometimes fifth-grade "buddies" read aloud to their kindergarten "pals." Harding Academy competes with other area middle schools in cross-country, volleyball, golf, soccer, wrestling, basketball, cheerleading, tennis, track and field, and lacrosse. All middle school students participate in athletics. There is an after-school program for all grades. The program includes arts and crafts, Spanish lessons, dance, piano lessons, chess club, and tennis lessons. Enrollment is 474; average class size is 18. Tuition for the 2007–2008 academic year was $12,425.

HARPETH HALL SCHOOL
3801 Hobbs Road
(615) 297-9543
www.harpethhall.com

Harpeth Hall, Nashville's only independent, college-preparatory school for girls, claims a 100 percent rate of graduates matriculating to four-year colleges and universities since its founding in 1951. Singer Amy Grant is a graduate of the prestigious day school, which serves grades 5 through 12, and she returned to her alma mater to be honored as 1996 Distinguished Alumna. Average SAT scores are 200 points higher than the national average, and 9 of every 10 girls who take Advanced Placement exams earn college credit, many at the nation's most prestigious institutions.

The school, which has seven academic buildings on a 35-acre campus, has an enrollment of 625 and a student–teacher ratio of 8 to 1. The school's library contains 21,000 volumes and access to more than 1,000 periodicals. Harpeth Hall, a leader in the integration of technology into a traditional curriculum, also has excellent athletic and arts programs and provides a number of opportunities for service learning. Admission is competitive, based on previous school records, personal qualifications, and entrance examinations. Harpeth Hall teams have earned 43 state championships in nine varsity sports. For the past two years, 100 percent of Harpeth Hall students have participated in community service. Its faculty averages 15 years of teaching experience and 81 percent hold an advanced degree. The class of 2007 went on to attend 44 different college and universities coast to coast and internationally. Tuition for 2008–2009 was $18,795 for middle school and $19,535 for upper school.

LINDEN CORNER
3201 Hillsboro Pike (grades 1–8)
(615) 354-0270
211 North 11th Street (preschool and kindergarten)
www.lindencorner.org

Linden Corner is a Waldorf school, following the nonsectarian educational method founded in 1919 by Austrian educator, philosopher, scientist, and artist Dr. Rudolf Steiner. It is the only Waldorf school in the state. As of spring 2008, the school had an enrollment of about 135. The school believes that "the development of a child's sense of beauty, wonder, and interest in the world of nature and all humanity is key to becoming a balanced and truly healthy adult." Art, instrumental music, song, stories, dance and movement, and crafts are integrated into the comprehensive math, language, and science curriculum. Academic excellence, social responsibility, and moral integrity are strongly emphasized. Students begin learning German and Spanish, do choral singing, and begin learning to play wood recorders in first grade. They select a stringed instrument and also study farming and gardening in grade three. In grade four they study woodworking, using only nonelectric hand tools, and build their own tepee or playhouse-type shelter. In fifth grade, as part of their study of ancient Greece, they train to compete in a Multi–Waldorf School Olympics or Pentathlon, which includes competition in javelin- and discus-throwing, long jump, wrestling, and foot races. Preschool and kindergarten programs are offered at Linden Corner's east Nashville campus, at Woodland Presbyterian Church on North 11th Street. Extended care is available for Linden Corner students. The school is accredited by the Association of Waldorf Schools of North America. Tuition for the 2007–2008 year ranged from $4,650 for preschool three days a week to $8,380 for grades six through eight.

i Harpeth Hall School for Girls has several notable alumnae, including singer Amy Grant, Olympic gold medalist Tracy Caulkins, the late *Grand Ole Opry* star Sarah Cannon (Minnie Pearl), and actress Reese Witherspoon.

High School Scholarships

The Tennessee Education Lottery Scholarship Program provides HOPE Scholarships for qualifying high school students enrolling in a Tennessee public or private college/university that is accredited by the Southern Association of Colleges and Schools. The Tennessee Student Assistance Corporation administers the scholarship program. For details or to apply, visit www.tennessee.gov/tsac or call (615) 741-1346.

MONTGOMERY BELL ACADEMY
4001 Harding Road
(615) 298-5514
www.montgomerybell.com

Montgomery Bell Academy, a boys-only day school, was founded in 1867 as a separate department within the University of Nashville by a bequest from Montgomery Bell, an iron foundry magnate in Middle Tennessee. The school, originally created to provide for "deserving and needy" students, claims an illustrious legacy and enrolls many of Nashville's finest sons. Its traditionally stated goal is "challenging each young man" to attain his highest level of accomplishment as a "gentleman, scholar, and athlete."

The school, which serves grades 7 through 12, has been at its present 35-acre campus since 1915. A building campaign has added a new classroom, a renovated library, and a new science building. Enrollment in 2007–2008 was 670, with an average class size of 11 and a student-teacher ratio of 8 to 1. Eight percent of students represent minorities, and 15 percent of students receive financial aid. Eighty-three percent of the teaching faculty have master's degrees or higher. Montgomery Bell requires 21 academic credits for graduation. Honors sections are available in most courses, and 16 advanced-placement courses are offered.

Montgomery Bell has a lengthy list of accolades. The school's debate program is consistently ranked among the top 25 in the nation. The school has the highest number of National Merit Scholars in the state. SATW scores are 28 percent higher than national averages and 100 percent of the student body is college bound. An average of 400—or about 60 percent—of students are involved in the school's diverse fine arts program. The academy has more students in the Nashville Youth Symphony than any other school in Nashville. The academy's theater program was named one of the top 50 theater programs in the nation by the American High School Theater Festival.

One hundred fifty computers are available for student use. Athletically, the school fields about 32 competitive teams in at least 12 sports; the teams have won numerous state and regional championships, including state championships in baseball, football, rifle, lacrosse, and tennis over the last four years. Community service projects include Soup Kitchen, Boys and Girls Club tutoring, YMCA coaching and tutoring, and Habitat for Humanity. Montgomery Bell has one of the nation's premier international exchange programs, with affiliations with at least seven different schools, including British boarding schools Eton College and Winchester College, the Southport School in Australia, and Michaelhouse in South Africa. Admission to Montgomery Bell is highly competitive. An Independent School Entrance Exam and application are required for admission. While applications are accepted at any time, students are encouraged to apply one year in advance of anticipated entry.

OAK HILL SCHOOL
4815 Franklin Road
(615) 297-6544
www.oakhillschool.org

Oak Hill School is an independent coed elementary school serving kindergarten through grade six. The "lower school" consists of kindergarten through third grade and the "upper school" of grades four through six. Founded in 1961 as an outreach of First Presbyterian Church, Oak Hill provides "a rich and comprehensive curriculum for qualified students within a nurturing Christian environment." The curriculum emphasizes critical thinking and active problem solving in collaboration with others.

In partnership with students' families, the school also seeks "to recognize, celebrate, and develop each student's unique talents and gifts; to foster a love of learning with emphasis on academic excellence; and to prepare students to be persons of integrity with the skills necessary to meet future challenges."

Facilities at the school, which sits on a 55-acre wooded campus, include a 12,000-volume online library/media center, fully equipped playgrounds, sports playing fields, a gymnasium, a cafeteria, a music center, an art room, a fully equipped science lab, stage, a staffed clinic, monitored Internet access, a fully equipped computer lab, and computers in every classroom. Enrollment in 2008 was 499 with 53 teachers. Tuition for the 2007–2008 year for kindergarten through grade six was $11,050.

OVERBROOK SCHOOL
4210 Harding Road
(615) 292-5134
www.overbrook.edu
Overbrook, a private, Catholic coeducational school for three-year-olds through eighth-graders, was founded in 1936 and is owned and administered by the Dominican Sisters of the Congregation of St. Cecilia. The school shares its 92-acre Dominican campus in west Nashville with St. Cecilia Academy and Aquinas Junior College. A faculty of religious and lay teachers is dedicated to "high academic standards, belief in the dignity of each child and a Christ-centered approach to education." The curriculum includes daily religious instruction. The athletics program includes volleyball (girls only), basketball, soccer, cross-country, tennis, and cheerleading. Enrollment is about 338, with an average class size of 18. Annual tuition in 2007–2008 was $9,500 for kindergarten through eighth grade.

ST. CECILIA ACADEMY
4210 Harding Road
(615) 298-4525
www.stcecilia.edu
St. Cecilia Academy is a private Catholic college preparatory school for girls in grades 9 through 12. It shares a 92-acre campus with Overbrook School and Aquinas Junior College and, like those institutions, is owned and administered by the Dominican Sisters. The school, SACS-accredited, seeks to enable each student to grow "in her life of faith" and encourages academic excellence (100 percent of its graduates go on to higher education), creativity, and the development of leadership qualities within each student. St. Cecilia Academy was named one of the Top 50 best Catholic high schools in the nation in 2007 by the Catholic High School Honor Roll. This is the third time since the Honor Roll began that St. Cecilia has been given the honor and the second year in a row. St. Cecilia Academy is the only Tennessee school named on the list for 2007. An extensive physical education program and various coeducational activities promote physical and social well-being of students. The interim program suspends regular classes for two weeks each year and offers travel opportunities to study fine arts in New York, marine biology in Florida, democracy in Washington, Mayan ruins in Mexico, or world history in Europe. Enrollment in 2007–2008 was 273 with an average class size of 13. Tuition for 2008–2009 was $13,000.

i Oprah Winfrey went to high school and college in Nashville, and her dad operates a barbershop here.

UNIVERSITY SCHOOL OF NASHVILLE
2000 Edgehill Avenue
(615) 327-8158
www.usn.org
University School of Nashville, which serves K–12, traces its heritage back to the Winthrop Model School established in 1892 by the Peabody Board of Trustees (Peabody College for Teachers is now part of Vanderbilt University). Winthrop, the first

model school in the South specifically designed to demonstrate proper teaching methods and traditions, also was the first private school in the South to integrate its student body. In 1915 the school moved to the campus of George Peabody College for Teachers and became the Peabody Demonstration School. In 1974 it became a nonprofit independent institution dedicated to the school's historic legacy. That legacy continues in the school's philosophy, which holds academic excellence as its central value but also encourages the pursuit of artistic values (including the appreciation of others' artistic expressions and the development of one's own creativity).

University School, which is SACS-accredited, consciously draws students from diverse racial, religious, and cultural backgrounds and encourages them to appreciate differences while learning about aspirations and values they hold in common. The lower school (K–4) features grade-level teams. Specialists in art, music, Spanish, library, and physical education enrich the curriculum, and noncompetitive athletics are also offered. At the middle school level (grades five through eight), learning begins to separate into subjects, with continued enrichment courses and physical education. These children also benefit from extracurricular minicourses, outdoor experiential activities, and excursions to historical sites and cultural events, as well as both intramural and competitive team sports.

College preparation is essential at the high school level, where a minimum of 23 credits is required for graduation. At the same time, "a vital part of the school's mission is to produce people of personal integrity who recognize they are part of a global community." Ongoing service projects include sponsorship of a local soup kitchen. Students also take a range of studio and art history classes and enjoy performing arts such as band, chorus, drama, select choir, and jazz band. Competitive sports include junior varsity and varsity teams.

While the main campus is near Vanderbilt University, the school's 80-acre River Campus, purchased in 1998, is located off Briley Parkway

at County Hospital Road; the campus is used for track and field sports and science study.

The school had an enrollment of 999 in 2008 with an average class size of 15. New students are admitted at all grade levels, with preference to qualified siblings of enrolled students and children of faculty members. In an after-school program for K–8, "students set their own pace and choose their own fun…under supervision of an attentive staff." Annual tuition in 2008–2009 was $14,680 for lower school, $16,000 for middle school, and $16,384 for high school. About 6 percent of nonfaculty children receive financial aid.

University School also is host to evening classes for the Nashville adult community. Benefits from this program's tuition, which ranges from $15 to $40, go toward the University School Scholarship Fund. Topics range from archaeology to dog training, computers to travel, and massage to financial planning. Phone (615) 321-8019 for information about the school's evening classes.

Special-Needs Schools

CURREY INGRAM ACADEMY
6544 Murray Lane, Brentwood
(615) 507-3242
www.curreyingram.com
Currey Ingram Academy is an independent kindergarten-through-12th-grade college preparatory day school for children with learning disabilities. The school grew out of the Westminster School of Nashville, which was founded in 1968 by concerned parents and Westminster Presbyterian Church. Westminster was Nashville's first independent day school program for students with learning disabilities. The programs and enrollment grew, and in June 1999 the school purchased an 83-acre parcel of land in Williamson County, where it built a new facility; the school moved its operations to the new campus in July 2002. The school also changed its name to honor the financial contributions of Stephanie Currey Ingram and John Rivers Ingram and their family. Today, Currey Ingram Academy has an enrollment of about 300 students from 11 counties.

According to the school's mission statement, the educational program "is structured for students to achieve a high standard of academic excellence through personalized instruction within the framework of a curriculum designed for superior to average learners." The school offers a very individualized program, addressing individual needs as well as focusing on students' strengths. The student-to-teacher ratio is 5 to 1. Support staff is available for daily tutorials for each student.

Currey Ingram Academy is on the cutting edge of technology. Apple Computer designated the school as an Apple Showcase School, chosen to showcase the concept of digital video editing. Wireless Internet access is available throughout the campus. All students in grades 5 through 11 lease an Apple laptop computer, and students in lower grades have access to mobile computer labs. As for athletics, the school has a spacious gymnasium and expansive practice fields and is able to host soccer, volleyball, basketball, and cross-country tournaments. In addition to those sports, the school also offers baseball, softball, bowling, golf, and cheerleading. The campus has a Family Resource Library with materials on learning differences and parenting.

In 2007–2008 tuition was $23,620 for grades K–8 and $27,634 for grades 9–12. About 25 percent of the school's students receive financial aid.

TENNESSEE SCHOOL FOR THE BLIND
115 Stewarts Ferry Pike
(615) 231-7300
www.tsb.k12tn.net
Tennessee School for the Blind, founded in 1844, serves K–12 students and the blind and visually impaired community. In addition to the academic curriculum, in which students pursue a regular high school diploma, there are semi-academic and nonacademic programs. The school is state funded and accepts students from all across Tennessee; about two-thirds live on campus during the week in cottages.

There is an athletics program, with swimming, track and field, wrestling, and cheerleading events. A student must be legally blind and a resident of Tennessee to attend.

Colleges and Universities

Nashville/Davidson County
AMERICAN BAPTIST COLLEGE
1800 Baptist World Center Drive
(615) 256-1463
www.abcnash.edu
American Baptist College is a private, four-year, coeducational liberal arts Bible college that trains African-American ministers and persons interested in social vocations. Affiliated with the National Baptist Convention, the college is dedicated "to educating and developing Christians for worldwide leadership and service." It is the only predominately African-American college in the nation accredited by the Accrediting Association of Bible Colleges. The college was established in 1924 under the name of American Baptist Theological Seminary. Its 53-acre site along the Cumberland River in north Nashville was purchased with the assistance of the National Baptist Convention. The Southern Baptist Convention shared equally in the operation of the college from 1937 to 1996. ABC counts among its alumni civil rights champions, national leaders, and prominent clergy. ABC offers associate of arts, bachelor of arts, and bachelor of theology degrees, as well as nondegree certificate programs in Bible, Christian training, and theology. In addition to the comprehensive interdisciplinary program in biblical studies and theological education, the curriculum includes training in business, elementary education, psychology, and counseling. The college has about 100 students, nearly two-thirds of whom are male.

AQUINAS COLLEGE
4210 Harding Road
(615) 297-7545
www.aquinas.edu
Aquinas College is part of the Dominican Campus that includes Overbrook and St. Cecilia schools (see previous listings in the Private Schools section of this chapter). As a Catholic institution of higher learning, it strives to "provide an atmosphere of learning permeated with faith, directed to the intellectual, moral, and professional formation of

the student." Aquinas, with a student body of 826 in 2008, offers both four-year and two-year programs. Degrees offered are bachelor of science in interdisciplinary studies (teacher education), bachelor of science in nursing, bachelor of business administration, bachelor of science in business administration, bachelor of science in management of information systems, associate of arts in liberal arts, associate of science in nursing, and associate of business management. Aquinas is accredited by the Southern Association of Colleges and Schools. Tuition for 2008 was $486 per credit hour, $506 per credit hour for nursing.

BELMONT UNIVERSITY
1900 Belmont Boulevard
(615) 460-6000
www.belmont.edu

Belmont University is on grounds known as Adelicia Acklen's Belle Monte Estate, hence the name. The first Belmont College was established here in 1890. It joined the Ward School and became Ward-Belmont College for Women in 1931. In 1951 the Tennessee Baptist Convention founded the second Belmont College, which became a university in 1991. The college does not receive direct assistance from the state or federal government and remains affiliated with the Tennessee Baptist Convention. It is accredited by the Southern Association of Colleges and Schools and by the Association to Advance Collegiate Schools of Business.

Seven colleges and schools—Arts and Sciences, Business Administration, Entertainment and Music Business, Health Sciences, Visual and Performing Arts, Religion, and University College—offer undergraduate degrees in more than 50 major areas of study. Nine master's degrees are available: business administration, accounting, education, English, music, nursing, occupational therapy, sports administration, and physical therapy. The school of business has a unique NAFTA trade internship coordinated with U.S. Commercial Services offices in Nashville and Guadalajara, Mexico.

The nationally recognized Curb College of Entertainment and Music Business enrolls the largest number of majors, with more than 900 students. Belmont's annual enrollment is about 4,800. The student-faculty ratio is 13 to 1. The Belmont Bruins compete in NCAA Division I in men's and women's basketball, tennis, cross-country, track, soccer, and golf; men's baseball; and women's softball and volleyball. Belmont also has an extensive intramural sports program. Tuition for 2008–2009 was $77 per credit hour or $10,035 for a 12- to 16-hour schedule.

DAVID LIPSCOMB UNIVERSITY
3901 Granny White Pike
(615) 269-1000
www.lipscomb.edu

"The Bible is still at the heart of what is now a greatly expanded liberal arts and professional curriculum." So say the folks at David Lipscomb University, which has grown in size and scope since its 1891 founding as Nashville Bible School. The coeducational university, which has a 65-acre campus, five residence halls, and 2,744 graduate and undergraduate students, was renamed in 1917 to honor David Lipscomb, an influential leader in the American Restoration Movement among the Churches of Christ. It served as a junior college until 1948, when its first senior college class graduated. The school has a master plan that will see it expand north into the surrounding community, where the university currently has student rental housing.

The university has 130 programs of study in 47 majors leading to bachelor of arts and bachelor of science degrees. Master's degrees are available in biblical studies, business administration, and education. The academic program is organized into five colleges: College of Arts and Humanities, which includes the School of Fine and Performing Arts; College of Bible and Ministry; College of Business; College of Education and Professional Studies; and College of Mathematics and Sciences. Recent additions to the academic program are a school of nursing and a school of engineering. Lipscomb is also noted for its intercollegiate athletics program, which includes men's teams in cross-country, tennis, soccer, golf, baseball, and basketball; and women's teams in cross-country, volleyball, tennis, soccer, golf, basketball, and softball. Lipscomb teams have consistently competed for national NAIA championships. The university is a member of NCAA Division I in the Atlantic Sun Conference. On Nov. 13, 2007, the Lipscomb women's basketball team defeated Fisk University 123–22 in one of the most lopsided games in NCAA history. The school requires all students to attend regular Bible classes and chapel.

DRAUGHONS JUNIOR COLLEGE
340 Plus Park Boulevard
(615) 361-7555
www.draughons.edu
Draughons Junior College began in 1879 as Draughon's Practical Business College. Professor John F. Draughon would load his teaching materials in his wagon and make monthly rounds of communities in northern Middle Tennessee and southern Kentucky, teaching business skills. He opened his first permanent school in Nashville in 1884. It received its Commission for Business Schools accreditation in 1954 and in 1978 became a fully accredited junior college. Draughons has a total enrollment of about 800 students at its Nashville campus and branches in Bowling Green, Kentucky, and Clarksville and Murfreesboro, Tennessee. About half of those are at its Nashville campus. It offers one-year diploma programs as well as two-year associate degrees in accounting, business management, computer information technology, health information technology, pharmacy technology, criminal justice, legal assisting, medical assisting, e-commerce, and Microsoft support. Draughons students can take advantage of Lifetime Placement Services, job-placement assistance available to graduates at any time during their life. Likewise, graduates can audit any Draughons course at no charge for the rest of their lives.

FISK UNIVERSITY
1000 17th Avenue N.
(615) 329-8500
www.fisk.edu
If your alumni included writer and activist W. E. B. DuBois, historian and author John Hope Franklin, and U.S. Energy Secretary Hazel O'Leary, you'd probably feel like singing. Fisk can claim not only those three luminaries but also many more, as well as one out of every six of the nation's African-American doctors, dentists, and lawyers. And sing it does. Chances are you've heard, or at least heard of, the Fisk Jubilee Singers, who for more than a century have been keeping alive the beauty of the traditional spiritual. They're still going strong, and so is this school, founded in 1866. Then known as Fisk School, it was named in honor of Gen. Clinton B. Fisk of the Tennessee Freedmen's Bureau. In 1867 it was incorporated as Fisk University, with the goal of "providing students with an education that meets the highest standards, not of Negro education, but of American education at its best."

The now world-famous singers, who came along in 1871, were originally a group of traveling students who set out from Nashville to raise money for their school. They took the name Jubilee Singers after the "Old Testament's Year of Jubilee marking the deliverance of the Jews who, like all but two of themselves, had been in bondage." (Remember, this was just years after the end of the Civil War.) After a troubled beginning, the singers were endorsed by Henry Ward Beecher, and they eventually gave command performances for President Grant and the crowned heads of Europe before returning to Nashville with enough money to build Jubilee Hall.

Music isn't the only art that's alive at Fisk. The Carl Van Vechten Art Gallery includes the Alfred Stieglitz Collection of Modern Art and one of the nation's premier collections of African-American art. Fisk offers more than two dozen areas of study in business administration, humanities and fine arts, natural sciences and mathematics, and social sciences. Enrollment at the private, coeducational university is between 950 and 1,000 undergraduate students, with a student-faculty ratio of 14 to 1.

Although Fisk's enrollment has been growing in recent years, the university purposefully remains small. Admission to Fisk is selective. Entering students are typically ranked in the top 20 percent of their high school classes. All undergraduate students who are unmarried and financially dependent on parental support are required to live in university residence halls; exceptions can be made if a student meets the right requirements. Athletically, the SACS-accredited school competes in the NCAA's Division III and the College Athletic Conference.

FREE WILL BAPTIST BIBLE COLLEGE
3606 West End Avenue
(615) 383-1340, (800) 76-FWBBC
www.fwbbc.edu
This school, owned and operated by the National Association of Free Will Baptists, was founded in 1942. Its enrollment is about 400. The school's mission is "to equip men and women, through Bible-based education, to serve Christ and His Church." Free Will Baptist Bible College offers B.A. and B.S. degrees. Programs of study include pastoral training, youth ministry, music, missions, education, business, psychology, and exercise science. It is accredited by the Southern Association of Colleges and Schools and by the Accrediting Association of Bible Colleges.

JOHN A. GUPTON COLLEGE
1616 Church Street
(615) 327-3927
www.guptoncollege.com
John A. Gupton College, founded in 1946, offers an associate of arts degree in funeral service with a general education component and a professional component in funeral service arts and sciences. It is accredited by the Southern Association of Colleges and Schools. John A. Gupton has an enrollment of 70 students.

MEHARRY MEDICAL COLLEGE
1005 Dr. D. B. Todd Jr. Boulevard
(615) 327-6111
www.mmc.edu
When the Freedman's Aid Society of the Methodist Episcopal Church founded the Meharry Medical Department of Central Tennessee College in October 1876, its dream was to educate freed slaves and provide health care services to

the poor and underserved. Today their dream is known as Meharry Medical College, and it is the largest private, historically African-American institution solely dedicated to educating health care professionals and scientists in the United States. More than 700 students and residents are enrolled in the college's four schools: Medicine, Dentistry, Graduate Studies and Research, and Allied Health Professions (a joint program with Tennessee State University). It has graduated nearly 15 percent of all African-American physicians and dentists practicing in the United States. Meharry's student body comes from about 43 states and 22 foreign countries. The college, which is accredited by the Southern Association of Colleges and Schools, has 202 full-time faculty members. The university campus comprises 20 buildings on 26 acres of land. While Meharry and Vanderbilt have formed an alliance to benefit both institutions, Meharry's goal hasn't changed much, as it focuses on "providing promising African-American and other underrepresented ethnic minority students" an "excellent education in the health sciences." The school's mission statement includes a special emphasis on clinical and applied research on diseases that disproportionately affect ethnic minority populations.

NASHVILLE AUTO-DIESEL COLLEGE
1524 Gallatin Road
(615) 226-3990
www.nadcedu.com
Established in 1919, Nashville Auto-Diesel College is one of the oldest schools of its type in the country. Its more than 1,400 students attend 11-month courses of study leading to associate degrees in applied science, auto diesel technology, and auto body technology. Extra 10-week options are available in high-performance engines and in high-performance fabrication. NADC recently joined Lincoln Educational Services, which has 32 campus locations in 15 states.

NASHVILLE SCHOOL OF LAW
4013 Armory Oaks Drive
(615) 256-3684
www.nashvilleschooloflaw.net

Nashville School of Law was launched in 1911 by a group of Vanderbilt law graduates as night law classes at the YMCA for those unable to attend law classes during the day; it has been in operation ever since. It was incorporated in 1927 and authorized by the state to confer the degree of doctor of jurisprudence. The school leased space from the downtown YMCA until 1986. Admission is competitive and requires an official transcript showing a bachelor degree from an accredited college or university, three recommending letters with at least one from a member of the legal community, and the LSAT (Law School Admission Test). Unlike most law schools, it welcomes students who are employed full time.

NASHVILLE STATE COMMUNITY COLLEGE
120 White Bridge Road
(615) 353-3333
www.nscc.edu

Nashville State Community College, founded in 1970 as Nashville State Technical Institute, received its community college designation in July 2002. Since then, it has expanded its programs. The college now offers university transfer degree programs, associate of applied science degrees in more than 20 areas, and one-year technical certificates in electrical maintenance, surgical technology, computer-aided drafting, culinary, early childhood education, Web page authoring, technical communications, photography, music technology, horticulture, and industrial automation. The top three programs, based on enrollment, are university transfer programs, business management, and computer technologies (particularly computer networking and computer programming).

The college's community education programming includes more than 175 special interest courses each semester. Nashville State Community College also offers business and industry training, which can be tailored to a specific need and offered on-site at the company's convenience. In addition to the main campus, there are satellite campuses in Cookeville and Waverly. The school is accredited by the Southern Association of Colleges and Schools and has an enrollment of about 7,000.

NOSSI COLLEGE OF ART
907 Rivergate Parkway, Goodlettsville
(615) 851-1088, (877) 680-1601
www.nossi.com

Nossi College of Art, established in 1973, is a small, private, professional college that offers associate degrees in commercial art and commercial digital photography. The college also offers a bachelor of graphic arts and design degree. The instructors are practicing professionals who specialize in the areas they are teaching. Classes are held at three campuses, all within about 1 mile of one another in the Madison/Goodlettsville area. Students can choose from daytime or nighttime classes. The college has about 250 students and is accredited by the Accrediting Commission of Career Schools and Colleges of Technology.

TENNESSEE STATE UNIVERSITY
3500 John Merritt Boulevard
(615) 963-5000
www.tnstate.edu

Tennessee State was founded in 1912 as the Tennessee Agricultural and Industrial State Normal School. In 1922 it became a teachers' college capable of granting a bachelor degree. In 1951 it was granted university status. Today the school, with an enrollment of about 10,000, offers 44 bachelor degrees, 24 master's degrees, and 6 doctorates. TSU also offers a two-year associate of science degree in nursing and dental hygiene. TSU has eight colleges and schools: Agriculture and Home Economics, Health Sciences, Arts and Science, Engineering and Technology, Education, Business, Graduate Studies and Research, and Nursing. The university is accredited by the Southern Association of Colleges and Schools. About 70 percent of TSU faculty hold doctorates or terminal degrees in their fields.

In addition to the university's approximately 500-acre main campus, which is located in a residential area, TSU has the Avon Williams Campus in downtown Nashville at 330 10th Avenue N. The downtown campus is the hub for TSU's night, weekend, and distance education course offerings. A $6.5-million grant from NASA helped establish a Center for Automated Space Science, which now operates more automated telescopes at one site than any other institution in the world. TSU has two centers of excellence: the Center of Excellence for Research and Policy Basic Skills and the Center of Excellence for Information Systems Engineering and Management. It is also one of a few historically African-American colleges and universities to offer a bachelor's degree in African studies. TSU operates the Nashville Business Incubation Center, dedicated to the successful start-up of small businesses. Fledgling businesses supported by the center have achieved a 90 percent success rate.

The university competes athletically in the Ohio Valley Conference. The football team also has a long and storied legacy. More than 100 TSU football players have been drafted into the National Football League. Since 1952, track athletes from TSU have won 29 Olympic medals. Of the 40 famed Tigerbelles (members of TSU's women's track team) who have competed in the Olympics, 39 graduated from college with one or more degrees. The most famous Tigerbelle was the beloved Wilma Rudolph, who won three gold medals at the 1960 Summer Olympics in Rome.

i Tennessee Board of Regents' colleges and universities joined to offer the Regents Online Degree Programs. All the institutions are fully accredited. Courses completed in the programs are entirely online and are transferable among all the participating institutions. The program offers full certificates, diplomas, and degrees. Read more about the programs at the TBR's Web site, www.tbr.state.tn.us, or contact the TBR at (615) 366-4400.

TREVECCA NAZARENE UNIVERSITY
333 Murfreesboro Road
(615) 248-1200
www.trevecca.edu

Trevecca Nazarene was founded in 1901 by Rev. J. O. McClurkan, a Cumberland Presbyterian minister, to train Christian teachers and ministers to serve in America and foreign countries. It became a four-year college in 1910 and was officially adopted by the Church of the Nazarene in 1917. The school became a junior college in 1932 and was rechartered as Trevecca Nazarene College in 1935 after moving to its present location. In 1969 it earned accreditation from the Southern Association of Colleges and Schools and has kept it ever since. Other milestones include the creation of Tennessee's first physician assistant program in 1978, the addition of graduate degrees in 1984 with a master of education program, and achievement of university status in 1995.

Today, Trevecca has four schools—Arts and Sciences, Business and Management, Education, and Religion—and offers 51 bachelor degrees, 13 master's degrees, and 1 doctorate. The university also offers five two-year associate degrees. A record 2,300 students are enrolled at Trevecca, which has a 75-acre campus with 20 major buildings. There are about 85 full-time faculty members, 70 percent of whom have doctorates. The student–faculty ratio is 15.7 to 1.

VANDERBILT UNIVERSITY
West End Avenue
(615) 322-7311
www.vanderbilt.edu

Commodore Cornelius Vanderbilt (yes, that Vanderbilt) founded this school in 1873 with a $1 million endowment. We'd have to call it money well spent. Today Vanderbilt University is consistently ranked among the nation's best institutions of higher learning. A 2008 survey by *U.S. News & World Report* ranked Vanderbilt 19th overall among national universities. Vanderbilt's School of Medicine was ranked 18th nationally, and the Law School was ranked 16th. Peabody College was ranked 3rd among education schools, and the Owen School of Management ranked high among business schools. With some 21,500 employees (not including clerical staff), the school is the largest private employer in Middle Tennessee and the second largest private employer in the state.

Vandy, as the school is informally known, consists of 10 schools in 213 buildings situated on a beautiful, tree-filled, 330-acre campus that was designated a national arboretum in 1988. Highlights of the SACS-accredited school include the W. M. Keck Free-Electron Laser Center, which conducts experiments using the most powerful free-electron laser in the world; a public policy institute, or interdisciplinary think tank, that focuses on such issues as health care, education, social services, environment, mental health, and economic development; and the Freedom Forum First Amendment Center, a forum for discussion and debate of free expression and freedom-of-information issues.

The university's annual enrollment is about 6,500 undergraduates and about 5,300 graduate and professional students. The ratio of undergraduate students to faculty is 9 to 1, and 97 percent of faculty have terminal degrees. Vanderbilt's 10 schools are the College of Arts and Science, Blair School of Music, Divinity School, School of Engineering, Graduate School (offering master's degrees in arts, science, arts in teaching, and liberal arts and science and doctorate degree in philosophy), Law School, School of Medicine, School of Nursing, Owen Graduate School of Management, and Peabody College. (Incidentally, Peabody College is where Susan Gray, an educational researcher, in 1963 introduced a program for disadvantaged preschoolers that became the prototype for Head Start. Although Peabody College was independent at that time, it joined Vanderbilt in 1979 and remains a top teacher-training center.) The Owen Graduate School of Management offers an executive MBA program on weekends. Students can also earn a master's of liberal sciences with one or more courses a semester in the evening or with weekend classes.

Athletically, Vandy is a member of the highly competitive Southeastern Conference for most men's and women's varsity sports. Men's sports include football, basketball, baseball, soccer, tennis, golf, and cross-country. Women's sports include a nationally ranked basketball team, soccer, tennis, golf, cross-country, indoor track, outdoor track, and lacrosse. The appropriately named Commodores play their basketball games in 14,100-seat Memorial Gym and their football games in 41,000-seat Dudley Field.

WATKINS COLLEGE OF ART AND DESIGN
2298 Metro Center Boulevard
(615) 383-4848
www.watkins.edu

Watkins, which consists of the College of Art and Design and the Watkins Film School, was founded in 1885 after the state received a gift of $100,000 and land from Samuel Watkins on which to build a school "that would strengthen our city." The institute has assumed various roles through the years, including the "Americanization" of Russian and Italian immigrants in the early 1900s, preparation of women for the workplace in the 1930s and 1940s, and providing educational opportunities for returning servicemen after World War II. Today Watkins is an independent art and design college offering four-year undergraduate bachelor degrees with studio-based programs that produce practicing artists. Watkins offers bachelor degrees in film, fine arts, graphic design, interior design, and photography. Fine art is the basis for each of these challenging programs. The college offers professional certificates in film and graphic design for those who already hold a bachelor degree but want the knowledge to pursue a career in those areas. All Watkins students study basic design and liberal arts while maintaining a conceptual basis in fine arts. Watkins is also known for its comprehensive community education programs, which offer classes in a variety of fine arts and film disciplines to youth and adults.

CHILD CARE

For newcomers, finding child care in Nashville can be tough, especially if you're looking to get into one of the more popular centers. Some programs, however, set a few positions aside for people relocating to Nashville. They generally don't advertise that information, so be sure to ask.

According to the Nashville Area Association for the Education of Young Children, parents should find an out-of-home child care situation that they are secure with and their child is happy in. Talk to your friends, neighbors, and coworkers, and compare their likes and dislikes. Phone several schools, and ask to arrange a visit for both you

EDUCATION AND CHILD CARE

and your child. Observe the caregivers interacting with children. Do they, for example, speak to children on their level? Attend a school function and observe. Arrange an appointment with the school's director and have a list of questions ready regarding such issues as staff stability and training, teacher education, programs available, fees, and policies for holidays and lateness. All nurseries and day care centers must meet licensing requirements. For more information on these regulations and child care providers, or for information on providers' quality ratings, contact the Tennessee Department of Human Services Child Care Licensing, 1000 Second Avenue N., (615) 532-4410, or visit the Web site www.state.tn.us/humanserv.

Child Care Information

NASHVILLE AREA ASSOCIATION FOR THE EDUCATION OF YOUNG CHILDREN
2021 21st Avenue S., Suite 440
(615) 383-6292
www.naaeyc.org
NAAEYC was established in 1948 as an affiliate of the National Association for the Education of Young Children with two primary objectives: to promote standards of excellence in child care practices and to raise public understanding of and support for high-quality educational programs for young children. It does not certify early-childhood programs but provides information on how to identify and select high-quality child care. For educators and child care providers, the association is a resource for information, training, and support.

NASHVILLE PARENT MAGAZINE
2270 Rosa L. Parks Boulevard
(615) 256-2158
www.parentworld.com
This monthly publication is a ready source of information on parenthood, as well as educational and recreational opportunities for area children. (See our Media chapter for more details.) *Nashville Parent* is published by Day Communications, which also publishes *Rutherford Parent* and *Williamson Parent* magazines.

Child Care Providers

The Nashville metropolitan area does have a number of chain child care providers, including several KinderCares, Children's Worlds, and a couple of La Petite Academies. Check your telephone directory for these listings. There are four preschool programs frequently used by parents who usually enter their children in the more prestigious private schools in Nashville. As you might expect, they are convenient to the Vandy, Green Hills, and Belle Meade areas. Three of the four—St. George's Episcopal Day Kindergarten, Westminster Kindergarten, and Woodmont Christian Preschool—are church-affiliated (see the Insiders' tip on the next page for addresses and phone numbers).

THE CHILDREN'S HOUSE
3404 Belmont Boulevard
(615) 298-5647
www.childrenshousenashville.com
The name is the English translation of Dr. Montessori's first school, Casa dei Bambini. Montessori schools are not structured in a traditional, classroom-based manner. Dr. Montessori recommended that teachers "follow the child" and create a school that is more of a children's community—it allows the children to move about freely and select work that captures their interest. Children, for instance, learn responsibility by preparing their own snacks and drinks, going to the bathroom alone, and helping one another clean up spills. The Children's House, for three-, four-, and five-year-olds, is nonprofit and nonsectarian. All teachers have college degrees and Montessori teaching certificates.

COOPERATIVE CHILD CARE
1808 Woodmont Boulevard
(615) 297-9256
www.cooperativechildcare.org
CCC is a cooperative preschool and day care facility; parents are actively involved in this facility's programs and make up its board of directors. Parent board meetings are held every other month, and CCC encourages active parental involvement.

CCC is for two- to five-year-olds and can handle about 42 kids a day. Focusing on the "whole child," programs help meet a child's physical, cognitive, emotional, and social needs.

Other Child Care Options

FAMILY YMCAS
Various Metro locations
(615) 259-9622
www.ymcamidtn.org
Area YMCAs provide day care for children ages six weeks to six years. Most schools also have YMCA before- and after-school care for kindergartners through eighth-graders.

i Many area churches offer day care programs. Among the most popular are St. George's Episcopal Day Kindergarten (4715 Harding Road, 615-269-9712); Westminster Kindergarten (3900 West End Avenue, 615-297-0235); and Woodmont Christian Preschool (3601 Hillsboro Pike, 615-297-9962).

YMCA OF MIDDLE TENNESSEE
900 Church Street
(615) 259-9622
www.ymcamidtn.org
With about 21 centers and more than 200 program locations, the YMCA of Middle Tennessee is the area's largest child care provider. The Y provides day care for children ages six weeks to six years; Fun Company, the Y's before- and after-school child care program, is offered at about 140 sites. The program offers a variety of stimulating and educational activities for children, ranging from art to music to science. The Y's preschool programs promote productive play and incorporate fun with learning for more than 300 children.

MEDIA

Television, cable programming, radio, newspapers, magazines, hit songs, Bibles, books, music videos—when it comes to media, Nashville has it all. Nashville is a major publishing center, and printing/publishing is one of our biggest industries. Numerous cable television programs originate here and are seen by millions of viewers. Country Music Television (CMT) takes country music into the living rooms of viewers worldwide. Many of the videos you see on CMT are shot right here in Music City. As for radio, well, Nashville owes much of its heritage to that medium. In our "Radio" section, later in this chapter, we explain how radio played a role in the city's becoming known as Music City. Nashville ranks as the nation's 44th largest radio market, according to Arbitron's spring 2008 report, and is the 30th largest television market (out of 210 total markets), according to Nielsen Media Research.

PUBLISHING

Nashville's history as a publishing center dates from the late 18th century. The city's first newspaper, *Henkle's Tennessee Gazette & Mero Advertiser,* was printed in 1799, 20 years after the first settlers arrived and 7 years before the city was incorporated. In 1800 the *Tennessee Gazette* began publishing. The first book was published in 1810, and 14 years later the hymnbook *Western Harmony* was published, marking the beginnings of music publishing in Nashville.

Nashville became a center for religious publishing in the 1800s. As Tennesseans flocked to religious revivals, Protestant denominations began publishing their books, Bibles, periodicals, and other church materials in Nashville. In 1954 the Methodist Publishing House moved here from Philadelphia, where it had been based since 1789. Baptists and the Church of Christ began publishing here, too. The National Baptist Publishing Board was founded in 1896. By the early 1900s religious publishing was an important part of Nashville's economy. It remains so today, accounting for about a third of the city's total printed output. Thirty percent of all Bibles printed in the United States are produced in this area, and Thomas Nelson, the world's largest Bible publisher, is based here. Religious publishing giants

the United Methodist Publishing House and Lifeway Christian Resources are also based here.

Nashville's publishing industry isn't limited to religious materials, however. Today there are nearly 500 firms here involved in publishing and printing. These companies employ more than 14,000 and have annual revenues of more than $250 million. Nashville companies publish or print *USA Today* and the regional editions of *Parade* magazine as well as national trade and consumer publications. One of the city's interesting publishing success stories is Rutledge Hill Press, which was founded in 1982 and achieved national recognition with the 1990 publication of H. Jackson Brown Jr.'s *Life's Little Instruction Book.* The book—written, designed, typeset, printed, and published in Nashville—has sold more than seven million copies and has been translated into nearly 20 languages. Rutledge Hill Press is also known for its books on the Civil War and local history, cookbooks, regional humor and travel, and the history of quilts. Among the many other publishing companies in the area are Abingdon Press, Gideons International, and Vanderbilt University Press. Ingram Entertainment, based in nearby La Vergne, is the nation's largest distributor of videos and video games and a leading distributor of books, music, microcomputer hardware, software, and accessories. Nashville is also a center of music publishing, the backbone of the country music industry.

PUBLICATIONS

Following is a look at some of the newspapers and magazines that serve the Nashville market as well as some published here that have national and international circulations. In addition to the following publications, there are several real estate guides and apartment guides that serve the market; we list those in our Relocation chapter.

Daily Newspapers

Nashville

THE CITY PAPER
624 Grassmere Park, Suite 28
(615) 298-9833
www.nashvillecitypaper.com
The *City Paper* came on the scene in November 2000; it has a circulation of 57,000. Published Monday through Friday, the free, tabloid-size newspaper focuses on in-depth local news, with sections devoted to news, business, lifestyle, and sports, as well as occasional special inserts on topics such as gardening, sports, or social events. You can pick up a copy at newsstands around town or have it delivered free to your office.

THE TENNESSEAN
1100 Broadway
(615) 259-8000,
(615) 254-5661 (subscriptions)
www.tennessean.com
The *Tennessean* is Nashville's largest daily newspaper, with a weekday circulation of about 161,000 and a Sunday circulation of about 232,000. It dates from 1907, but the paper evolved from the *Nashville Whig,* which began publication in 1812. A newspaper with a liberal slant, the *Tennessean* is owned by Gannett Co. Inc., the country's largest newspaper publisher. Gannett bought the paper in 1979 from the family of Silliman Evans, who purchased it in the late 1930s at auction and turned the financially ailing operation into a suc-

cess. (Gannett had owned the *Nashville Banner,* which folded in 1998, but opted to sell it in order to be able to purchase the *Tennessean.*)

The newspaper's "Davidson a.m." section focuses on neighborhoods and communities throughout Davidson County and is included in the Monday, Wednesday, and Friday editions distributed in Davidson County. Similar sections are geared to residents of Williamson and Rutherford Counties. The *Tennessean* publishes more than 30 niche publications each year, including *Tennessee Homes,* a glossy color magazine on new homes in the area, and the handy *FYI,* an annual glossy reference guidebook featuring information on everything from schools to shopping. The newsstand price is 50 cents Monday through Saturday and $1.75 Sunday; a subscription is $16.52 per month or $198.24 per year.

Surrounding Counties

THE DAILY NEWS JOURNAL
224 North Walnut Street, Murfreesboro
(615) 893-5860
www.dnj.com
This afternoon newspaper is published seven days a week. Founded in 1849 and now owned by Gannett, it has a circulation of about 15,400 Monday through Saturday and about 18,300 Sunday. Subscriptions are $11 per month. The newsstand price is 50 cents ($1.25 on Sunday).

Nondaily Newspapers

THE ADVOCATE
P.O. Box 208, Kingston Springs 37082
(615) 952-5554
www.scadvocate.com
Covering the south Cheatham County areas of Pegram and Kingston Springs, the *Advocate* is a weekly newspaper with a circulation of about 3,500. A one-year subscription is $30.

THE ASHLAND CITY TIMES
202-A North Main Street, Ashland City
(615) 792-4230
www.ashlandcitytimes.com
The *Ashland City Times* was founded in 1896 and

today covers Cheatham County news and happenings on a weekly basis. It comes out each Wednesday and costs $18 for a one-year subscription for Cheatham County residents. Owned by Gannett, its circulation is 5,900.

BELLE MEADE NEWS

GREEN HILLS NEWS

WEST MEADE NEWS

WESTSIDE NEWS
GCA Publishing
2323 Crestmoor Road, Suite 219-B
(615) 298-1500
www.gcanews.com
These weekly community newspapers are published each Wednesday by GCA Publishing and cover news in their respective areas. Their combined circulation is more than 20,000. You can pick up a copy at grocery stores, libraries, and other locations in each area. Subscriptions are available for $10 a year ($25 outside Davidson County).

CHRONICLE OF MT. JULIET
11509 Lebanon Road, Mount Juliet
(615) 754-6111
www.thechronicleofmtjuliet.com
Founded in 1980, the *Chronicle* is a free weekly community newspaper with a circulation of 11,600. It is published on Wednesday and is geared to Mount Juliet, West Wilson County, and part of Hermitage.

THE DICKSON HERALD
104 Church Street, Dickson
(615) 446-2811
www.dicksonherald.com
The *Dickson Herald,* founded in 1907, is published Wednesday and Friday. Owned by Gannett, it has a circulation of 7,500. Subscriptions are $24.

FAIRVIEW OBSERVER
7101 Adams Drive, Suite 100, Fairview
(615) 799-8565
www.fairviewobserver.com

This Gannett-owned weekly newspaper is distributed on Tuesday at newsstands in Fairview. Its coverage is aimed at the Fairview community. A one-year subscription for Williamson County residents is $19.

THE HENDERSONVILLE STAR NEWS
105 Maple Row Boulevard
Hendersonville
(615) 824-8480
www.hendersonvillestarnews.com
Published since 1951, this Gannett-owned free paper comes out every Wednesday and Friday. It features local county news and has a circulation of 16,500.

LEBANON DEMOCRAT
402 North Cumberland, Lebanon
(615) 444-3952
www.lebanondemocrat.com
Published since the late 1800s, the *Lebanon Democrat* reaches about 10,000 in Wilson County. It is published Monday through Saturday. A monthly subscription is $8; one year is $77 for Wilson County residents.

THE MESSENGER
P.O. Box 626, Madison 37122
(615) 868-0475
www.themessengernewspaper.com
This free weekly newspaper has been covering community news in Madison, Goodlettsville, and Old Hickory since 1982. It is locally owned and operated and has a circulation of 8,000. It is published on Wednesday. You can pick up a copy at retail stores and libraries in those areas and at Goodlettsville City Hall.

NASHVILLE TODAY
2323 Crestmoor Road, Suite 219-B
(615) 298-1500
Published by GCA Publishing, *Nashville Today* is a weekly community paper that covers Antioch, Brentwood, Donelson, Goodlettsville, Hermitage, Inglewood, and Madison. An annual subscription is $10 ($25 outside Davidson County).

THE NEWS BEACON
2740 Old Elm Hill Pike
(615) 391-3535

With a circulation of 15,000, the *News Beacon* covers news in southeast Nashville, including the areas around Harding Mall, Hickory Hollow, and Murfreesboro Road. It is distributed on Thursday free to area homes and select businesses.

THE NEWS EXAMINER
1 Examiner Court, Sumner Hall Drive, Gallatin
(615) 452-2561
www.gallatinnewsexaminer.com

Covering news throughout Sumner County, the *News Examiner* began publishing in the mid-1800s. Owned by Gannett, it is published on Monday, Wednesday, and Friday and has a circulation of about 9,700. An annual subscription is $42 for Sumner County residents.

THE NEWS HERALD
2740 Old Elm Hill Pike
(615) 889-1860

Published since the mid-1980s, the *News Herald* is the free community newspaper for Donelson, Hermitage, and Old Hickory. It is published on Thursday.

WESTVIEW
8120 Sawyer Brown Road, Suite 107
(615) 646-6131
www.westviewonline.com

The family-owned *Westview* is a free weekly community newspaper covering Bellevue, Kingston Springs, Pegram, Belle Meade, White Bluff, the Charlotte Pike area, and West Meade. Published since 1978, its circulation is about 12,000. It is published on Wednesday.

WILSON POST
216 Hartmann Drive, Lebanon
(615) 444-6008
www.wilsonpost.com

This community newspaper began publishing in 1980. It covers Wilson County and is distributed on Wednesday and Friday. A one-year subscription is $28.

General Interest

NASHVILLE LIFESTYLES
1510 Demonbreun Street
(615) 259-3636
www.nashvillelifestyles.com

Nashville Lifestyles, published 10 times per year, is a glossy magazine featuring all that's fashionable in Nashville. The magazine contains articles on local homes, the art scene, decorating, food, and celebrities, with a positive slant. The magazine costs $3.95 per issue; a one-year subscription is $18.00. City Publications also publishes *Murfreesboro Magazine* six times per year (a single copy is $3.95 and an annual subscription is $15.00) and the free monthly newspaper *Leiper's Fork Life*, which is distributed around Williamson County.

NASHVILLE SCENE
2120 Eighth Avenue S.
(615) 244-7989
www.nashvillescene.com

Nashville Scene is Music City's leading alternative newspaper. About 55,000 of the free weekly papers are distributed at grocery stores, convenience stores, bookstores, restaurants, record stores, and other places around town. Founded in 1983, the *Scene* covers politics, business, music, and arts in an in-depth fashion and does investigative stories. The *Scene* has a comprehensive listing of local entertainment events. Special issues, such as the annual "You're So Nashville If…" and the "Best of Nashville" winners issues, get snapped up quickly. The *Annual Manual*, published at the beginning of the year, is a city guide full of information about living in Nashville. The *Scene* also publishes restaurant guide issues. The paper has won numerous awards from the National Newspaper Association and the Association of Alternative Newspapers. It is published by City Press Publishing, a subsidiary of Village Voice Media, publisher of five other alternative weeklies around the country.

THE TENNESSEE MAGAZINE
710 Spence Lane
(615) 367-9284
www.tnelectric.org

This monthly magazine is published by the Tennessee Electric Cooperative Association. It reaches about 500,000 households in rural areas across the state. The glossy, four-color magazine does human-interest stories and has regular features on food, events, people, places, and businesses in the rural electric co-op.

Business

BUSINESS TENNESSEE
2817 West End Avenue, Suite 216
(615) 843-8000
www.businesstn.com
This locally owned monthly magazine, first published in 2003, covers business news throughout the state. It is read by more than 40,000 executives, elected officials, and small-business owners in Tennessee. A single copy is $4.95; a one-year subscription is $25.

NASHVILLE BUSINESS JOURNAL
344 Fourth Avenue N.
(615) 248-2222
www.nashville.bizjournals.com
Nashville Business Journal, published since 1985, is a weekly business newspaper published on Friday. A one-year subscription is $90. Each edition has a special-emphasis section covering such issues as employee benefits, education, commercial real estate, travel, and home business. The *Nashville Business Journal* also publishes special publications each year on such topics as small business, real estate, health care, economic development, sports business, and the arts.

---

i The Metropolitan Council meets regularly on the first and third Tuesday of each month at 7:00 p.m. Regular meetings are broadcast live on the government-access channel, cable Channel 3. WNPT, Channel 8, broadcasts regular meetings tape-delayed at 10:30 p.m. Special meetings are broadcast on the government-access channel. A video archive of council meetings can be accessed at Metro's Web site, www.nashville.gov.

NASHVILLE RECORD
1100 Broadway
(615) 664-2300
This weekly legal and business newspaper, published by Gannett, has been around since 1936. It's the source for information on foreclosures, tax sales, marriage licenses, business licenses, and the like. A single copy costs 75 cents at newsstands and at the Tennessean building at 1100 Broadway; a one-year subscription is $35.

Special Interest

ACTUALIDAD HISPANA
3030 Nolensville Road
(615) 300-6080
This Spanish-language newspaper is published on the 1st and 16th of each month. It is distributed free at restaurants and stores, with an emphasis on the Nolensville Road, La Vergne, Murfreesboro, Madison, Hendersonville, and Lebanon areas. Published since the mid-1990s, the paper features news as well as articles on sports, religion, health, immigration, and social topics. Each edition averages 22 pages, with one page printed in English.

CONTEMPORA MAGAZINE
1501 Jefferson Street
(615) 321-3268
www.thetennesseetribune.com
This bimonthly, slick-stock magazine is targeted to the mid-South's middle- and upper-income African-American community. It is similar to *Ebony* in look and focus. Nearly 100 percent of the magazine's circulation of 45,000 goes to subscribers in Nashville, Memphis, Chattanooga, and Knoxville. A one-year subscription is $15.

GALLIVANT—YOUR TRAVEL RESOURCE FOR THE SOUTH
5550 Boy Scout Road, Franklin
(615) 790-0487
Launched in 2003 by Summerlin Press, this quarterly, four-color, glossy magazine covers outdoor recreation, arts, history, romantic retreats, family fun, dining, weekend and day trips, and attractions

in six Southeastern states. The 32-page publication is mailed free to 30,000 homes in the Franklin, Brentwood, and Green Hills areas. An annual subscription is $8.

HEALTH AND WELLNESS MAGAZINE
5133 Harding Road, Suite 318
(615) 356-8404
www.healthandwellnessmag.com
This free guide to health and wellness services and products is published bimonthly. Some 20,000 copies are distributed at 160 locations, including natural foods stores, area YMCAs, wellness centers, bookstores, and libraries.

THE JEWISH OBSERVER
801 Percy Warner Boulevard
(615) 356-3242
www.jewishnashville.org
Published since 1934, this twice-monthly newspaper focuses on issues of interest to Nashville's Jewish community and also covers news of Israel and other international news. It is published by the Jewish Federation of Nashville. The free newspaper is mailed to members of the local Jewish community and is also available at the Jewish Community Center. Each summer, the Federation also publishes the *Guide to Jewish Nashville*, which is mailed to regular recipients and is also available at Noshville and Goldie's delis. A one-year subscription to the *Observer* is $25.

For a list of the Tennessee Titans' radio station affiliates, visit the Titans' Web site, www.titansonline.com.

LA CAMPANA
2210 Oakleaf Drive, Franklin
(615) 791-1274
www.lacampana.us
La Campana del Sur (Spanish for "the Southern Bell") is a free Spanish-language newspaper that is published weekly. It covers local, national, and world news, with an emphasis on news that affects Hispanics. Sections include business, health, family

and fashion, sports, and entertainment. Some 7,500 to 10,000 copies are distributed to businesses, churches, restaurants, universities, medical centers, and other locations in Middle Tennessee.

LA NOTICIA
1719 West End Avenue
(615) 977-1825
http://la_noticia.tripod.com
This free Hispanic newspaper is published twice a month. It covers local news, business, entertainment, sports, immigration, and other topics. More than 5,000 copies are distributed at some 150 locations throughout Middle Tennessee.

NASHVILLE MEDICAL NEWS
5123 Virginia Way, Suite C-23
Brentwood
(615) 385-4421
www.medicalnewsinc.com
Nashville Medical News, founded in 1989, is a monthly newspaper focusing on the health care industry. Published by Medical News Inc., based in Ridgeland, Mississippi, it is direct-mailed free to more than 10,000 health care professionals in Middle Tennessee. Averaging about 40 pages, the paper is published the first of each month. The company also publishes *Mississippi Medical News* and *Memphis Medical News.* A one-year subscription is $48.

NASHVILLE PARENT
2228 Metro Center Boulevard
(615) 256-2158
www.parentworld.com
Nashville Parent is chock-full of information that every parent needs at some time or another. You'll find everything here from medical advice to kiddie video reviews. Founded in 1992, the free monthly magazine has a circulation of about 50,000; it's available at various locations around town. *Nashville Parent* also publishes a private-school directory as well as a child care and activity directory. Parent company Day Communications also publishes *Rutherford Parent* and *Williamson Parent.*

NASHVILLE PRIDE
941 44th Avenue N.
(615) 292-9150
www.prideinc.com

The African-American newspaper *Nashville Pride*, founded in 1987, is published each Friday and has a circulation of more than 30,000. It covers community news with a positive slant. It is available by subscription for $22 per year or can be picked up at newsstands near north Nashville grocery stores or at the main office. A single copy is 50 cents.

NFOCUS
City Press Publishing Inc.
210 12th Avenue, Suite 100
(615) 244-7989
www.nfocusmagazine.com

This free monthly publication covers the Nashville social scene. It is published by City Press Publishing Inc., publisher of the *Nashville Scene*. You can find it at about 50 select retail stores and restaurants in the Belle Meade, Bellevue, Brentwood, and Green Hills areas.

THE TENNESSEE CONSERVATIONIST
401 Church Street
(615) 532-0060
www.tennessee.gov/environment/tn_consv

The *Tennessee Conservationist* is a glossy, full-color magazine published since 1937 by the Tennessee Department of Environment & Conservation. It is published every other month and features articles on history, parks, the environment, and conservation. The magazine's circulation is about 40,000, and most of that is subscription. An annual subscription is $15, a two-year subscription is $22, and a three-year subscription is $30. The magazine is available at select bookstores for $3.25 per copy.

i Here are a couple of numbers to keep handy: time or temperature, (615) 259-2222; News2 Information Line, (615) 259-WKRN.

TENNESSEE REGISTER
2400 21st Avenue S.
(615) 383-6393
www.dioceseofnashville.com

Established in 1937, *Tennessee Register* is the official newspaper for the Catholic Diocese of Nashville. Published every other Friday, this newspaper has 15 pages devoted to news of importance to Middle Tennessee's Catholic community. The publication has a circulation of 18,000. A one-year subscription is $23.

TENNESSEE TRIBUNE
1501 Jefferson Street
(615) 321-3268
www.thetennesseetribune.com

Targeted to the African-American community, *Tennessee Tribune* is a weekly that focuses on consumer-oriented news and information geared to better living. It has been published since 1992 and has a circulation of 45,000. A one-year subscription is $35.

Senior Citizens

THE SENIOR SENTINEL
174 Rains Avenue
(615) 743-3430
www.scitn.org

This monthly newspaper is filled with articles on state and national issues that are of concern to seniors, as well as features on health, travel, and politics. The *Senior Sentinel* is published by Senior Citizens Inc. (see our Retirement chapter). The paper carries the monthly schedule of activities for the senior centers. You can pick up a free copy at local Kroger stores, banks, senior centers, libraries, Shoney's, and other locations. Subscriptions are free for members, $12 per year for nonmembers.

THE SENIORS RESOURCE GUIDE
207 Wynbrook Court
(615) 662-8789
www.seniorsresourceguide.com

Published twice a year, this free guidebook features comprehensive listings of senior housing, home health care agencies, care management, professional services, community resources, and other information helpful to seniors and their caregivers. Sixty thousand copies of each edition are distributed at senior centers, libraries, and other locations. Copies are available by mail for $2.

Music and Entertainment

ALL THE RAGE
1100 Broadway
(615) 664-2270
www.nashvillerage.com

This free weekly entertainment guide is distributed at restaurants, nightclubs, record stores, and other places around town. Published every Thursday by Gannett, it features articles and detailed information on music, sports, restaurants, nightclubs, theater, movies, and more.

AMERICAN SONGWRITER
1303 16th Avenue S., second floor
(615) 321-6096
www.americansongwriter.com

American Songwriter is a bimonthly magazine with a worldwide circulation of about 10,000. Published since 1984, it focuses on topics of concern to songwriters. The magazine covers all genres of music, and most issues have a cover story about an individual songwriter. Past cover stories have featured artists ranging from Jimmy Buffett to Bob Dylan to Elton John. The magazine publishes several special editions annually. You can find copies at select newsstands around town. A one-year subscription is $12.

BILLBOARD
49 Music Square W.
(615) 321-4290,
(800) 562-2706 (subscriptions)
www.billboard.com

Billboard's country music bureau is based in Nashville. *Billboard,* headquartered in New York, is the world's most recognized publication covering the music, video, and home entertainment industries. A single copy is $6.95; a one-year subscription is $299.

CCM MAGAZINE
104 Woodmont Boulevard, Suite 300
(615) 386-3011
www.ccmcom.com

CCM Magazine is a favorite among fans of contemporary Christian music. Founded in 1978, *CCM* has a worldwide circulation of about 70,000; its target audience is Christian music consumers in their 20s. A single copy is $3.50; a one-year subscription is $19.95.

CHRISTIAN ACTIVITIES
P.O. Box 210182, Nashville 37221
(615) 662-6212
www.christianactivities.com

This free magazine covers mainly Christian music concerts. It is available at Christian bookstores, churches, and other locations and is usually published monthly. The Web site has more comprehensive content.

COUNTRY AIRPLAY MONITOR
49 Music Square W.
(615) 321-4290

Country Airplay Monitor is one of *Billboard*'s four *Airplay Monitor* publications. The weekly magazine has editorial content and charts geared to country radio and country record promotion. An annual subscription is $299.00; a single copy is $6.95.

COUNTRY WEEKLY
118 16th Avenue S.
(615) 259-1111,
(877) 566-5832 (subscriptions)
www.countryweekly.com

Country Weekly, published every two weeks, has lots of features on country music artists. Widely available, with a circulation of about 400,000, it can be found in most supermarkets. A 26-issue subscription is about $19.97.

THE JOURNAL OF COUNTRY MUSIC
222 Fifth Avenue S.
(615) 416-2096
www.countrymusichalloffame.com

The Journal of Country Music is published three times a year by the Country Music Foundation.

The magazine features interpretive articles on country music history, plus articles on current artists and record and book reviews. It is available at select newsstands and bookstores. Its readership consists mainly of music industry people, collectors, and others interested in country music history. A single copy is $5.95, and a one-year subscription is $18.00.

MUSIC ROW
1231 17th Avenue S.
(615) 321-3617
www.musicrow.com
Published monthly, *Music Row* features news of interest to Nashville's music industry professionals, including new-artist profiles, articles on finance and marketing, and other topics of concern. Don't miss Bob Oermann's always entertaining "Disclaimer" column, a series of brutally honest record reviews. Published since 1981, *Music Row* has a circulation of 4,000 and a readership of 14,000. A copy at the newsstand costs $4; a yearly subscription is $159. Music Row Publications also puts out the industry guides *In Charge*, a comprehensive listing of music industry leaders, and *Artist Roster*, a list of artists, labels, and producers. Subscribers also receive the twice-weekly *@MusicRow* e-mail supplement. The publisher also produces the RowFax professional song-pitching sheet each Friday ($129 per year via e-mail, or $155 via fax).

i Billy Block's Western Beat Roots Revival, www.westernbeat.com, is a weekly club concert series showcasing alternative-country performers. Block also hosts a syndicated radio show, which can be heard on WSM-FM (95.5) Sunday from 11:00 p.m. until midnight.

NASHVILLE MUSIC GUIDE
P.O. Box 100234, Nashville 37224
(615) 244-5673
www.nashvillemusicguide.com
This free monthly publication features music news and information on events in Music City. You can pick up a copy at nightclubs, grocery stores, record stores, bookstores, and other locations.

RADIO & RECORDS
1106 16th Avenue S.
(615) 244-8822
www.radioandrecords.com
R&R, as this trade weekly is known, tracks radio airplay. The Los Angeles–based magazine is published weekly and has a circulation of about 9,000. The country and Christian divisions are compiled at the Nashville office. *R&R* has been published since 1973. A one-year subscription is $325. *R&R* also publishes daily and weekly fax/e-mail updates and two annual directories for an additional charge.

i Nashville's first local Spanish-language television station, W42CR–Channel 42, made its debut in February 2004. The station features local news briefs, Metro schools news and information, and public service announcements of interest to Nashville's large Hispanic community. Other programming includes soap operas, talk shows, game shows, movies, and sports. For more information call the station at (615) 429-6226.

TELEVISION

What's on TV? In Nashville, just about anything: all the major networks, local independent stations, and a community-access station. Cable and satellite viewers can choose from dozens more stations. There are also some cable networks in the area, such as CMT: Country Music Television and Trinity Music City USA. Here's the rundown on the TV scene.

Major Local Stations
CATV Channel 19 (community-access television)
WHTN Channel 39 (Christian), www.ctntv.org
WKRN Channel 2 (ABC), www.wkrn.com
WNAB Channel 58 (WB), www.wnab.com
WNPT Channel 8 (PBS), www.wnpt.net
WNPX Channel 28 (PAX)

WSMV Channel 4 (NBC), www.wsmv.com
WTVF Channel 5 (CBS), www.news channel5
.com
WUXP Channel 30 (UPN), www.wuxp.com
WZTV Channel 17 (FOX), www.fox17.com
W42CR Channel 42 (Telefutura—Spanish
language programming), www
.solonashville.com

Cable Programming Networks

BLUEHIGHWAYS TV
111 Shivel Drive, Hendersonville
(615) 264-3292
www.bluehighwaystv.com
Established in 2004 by TV industry veteran Stan Hitchcock, who created Country Music Television, BlueHighways TV features programming that focuses on the "people, music, stories, traditions, and cultures of America." Programs include *The Red Road*, a series celebrating Native American culture; *Reno's Old Time Music Festival*, a bluegrass music and interview series; and *Gospel*, which presents gospel music performed live at country churches around the nation.

CMT: COUNTRY MUSIC TELEVISION
330 Commerce Street
(615) 335-8400
www.cmt.com
CMT: Country Music Television shows country music videos and original programming around the clock. Among the network's original programs are *CMT Most Wanted Live*, which includes live performances and a countdown of popular country music videos in front of a live audience, and *CMT Crossroads*, which pairs a country and a well-known rock or pop performer on stage. Owned and operated by MTV Networks, CMT reaches 60 million households in the United States.

NASHVILLE COMMUNITY ACCESS TELEVISION (CATV)
120 White Bridge Road
(615) 354-0389
http://catvnashville.tripod.com

Nashville's Community Access Television can be seen 24 hours a day on Comcast cable service's Channel 19. Most of the station's programming originates here and is locally produced. CATV's studios are located at the campus of Nashville State Technical Community College. Programming includes religious, music, public affairs, self-help/motivational, comedy, ethnic, and sports presentations, among others. CATV membership is $35 a year, and you must be a member to produce a program on the station.

SHOP AT HOME INC.
5388 Hickory Hollow Parkway, Antioch
(615) 263-8000
www.shopathometv.com
Shop at Home, which sells merchandise through broadcast, cable, and satellite TV and over the Internet, produces programming at its digital facility in Nashville. The programming is transmitted by satellite to cable television systems, direct-broadcast satellite systems, and television broadcasting stations across the country. The merchandise sold on the network, which includes electronics, jewelry, and beauty and fitness products, is distributed from the company's 43,000-square-foot warehouse, located near its headquarters.

Cable Programming Providers

COMCAST HOME
660 Mainstream Drive
(615) 244-6222
www.comcast.com
Comcast's services include basic cable, digital cable, pay-per-view, and high-speed Internet access. Channel assortment varies depending on the type of cable service ordered.

TENNESSEE CABLE TELECOMMUNICATIONS ASSOCIATION
611 Commerce Street, Suite 2706
(615) 256-7037
www.tcta.net
If you live outside of Davidson County, contact the TCTA to find out what cable TV providers

serve your area. You can quickly access contact information for your local provider at the TCTA Web site.

RADIO

Radio played the key role in Nashville's history. In the 1920s, as Americans became enamored with the new technology of radio, Nashville became an important broadcasting center. Local merchants and insurance companies established their own stations. Cain-Sloan's John E. Cain Jr., for example, founded WEBX in 1924, and in following years, stations were established by several other merchants. National Life and Accident Insurance Company's WSM, which signed on the air in October 1925, and Life and Casualty's WLAC, which arrived on the dial a year later, were the city's major stations. Both are still on the air today, but it was WSM that put the spotlight on Nashville. WSM began broadcasting the *Grand Ole Opry*, originally known as the *WSM Barn Dance*, less than two months after the station went on the air (see our History chapter for more details). The station took country music into homes and businesses around the country.

Today WSM 650 AM continues to broadcast the *Grand Ole Opry* every Friday and Saturday night. WSM is one of the nation's few clear-channel stations, meaning that no other station in a 750-mile radius has the same frequency for nighttime broadcasts. This and the station's 50,000-watt transmitter ensure that the *Opry* can be heard across a large portion of the United States and parts of Canada.

In 1941 WSM launched WSM-FM, the nation's first commercially operated FM station. WSM-FM (95.5 on the dial) can be heard today in Middle Tennessee, southern Kentucky, and northern Alabama. There is no doubt that WSM has the most famous call letters in Nashville. In recent years, however, WSM-FM has taken a backseat in the ratings to rivals WSIX-FM 97.9 and WKDF-FM 103.3, the two most highly rated country stations in the market. WSIX morning air personality Gerry House has been named the top medium-market local air personality at a country station in America.

i **If you're a bluegrass fan, you'll want to tune into WRVU's (91.1 FM) popular bluegrass program, *George the Bluegrass Show*, from 2:00 to 4:00 p.m. Sunday, and to WLPN's (90.3 FM) *Bluegrass Breakdown*, on Saturday from 8:00 to 9:00 p.m.**

Popular financial advice guru Dave Ramsey, author of best-selling books *Financial Peace* and *Total Money Makeover*, and creator of the money makeover program "Financial Peace University," got his start on Nashville radio station 99.7 WTN. Tune in to the station weekdays from 1:00 to 4:00 p.m. to hear *The Dave Ramsey Show*, a talk show dedicated to answering financial questions and to helping consumers "beat debt and build wealth." The radio show is syndicated to more than 200 radio stations nationwide and heard by more than two million weekly listeners. The program can also be heard on XM Satellite Radio Channel 165 and on Sirius Satellite Radio TALK 144. You can call in questions to *The Dave Ramsey Show* at (888) 825-5225.

Anyone who questions the power of radio or radio personalities in Nashville need only take note of conservative talk-show hosts Steve Gill and Phil Valentine (WWTN-FM 99.7), who motivated Tennesseans to drive by the State Capitol and blow their horns in protest of a proposed state income tax during the 2001 and 2002 legislative sessions.

Nashville talk radio is definitely hot, but when it comes to ratings, Nashville's most popular stations in recent years have had light pop and hip-hop formats. But as you can hear with the touch of a button or a turn of the dial, all types of music are on Nashville's airwaves. Jazz, Christian, adult contemporary, gospel, urban, bluegrass, folk, and reggae, to name a few, can be heard on Nashville stations. We also have a wonderful public radio station, as well as several college stations and Spanish-language stations. The following is a listing of most of the stations your radio will pick up in the Nashville area.

Keep in mind that stations frequently change their formats, so what was a country station in the fall might be an adult contemporary or news/talk station in the spring.

i Sirius XM Radio, Inc., has moved from the County Music Hall of Fame to its new home inside the Nashville Arena Tower. The new facilities feature expanded broadcast and production studios, as well as a performance studio, full production suite, and office space.

Adult Contemporary

WCVQ 107.9 FM
WQQK 92.1 FM (adult contemporary/urban/R&B)

Christian and Gospel

WAYM 88.7 FM (contemporary Christian)
WBOZ 104.9 FM (Southern gospel)
WENO 760 AM (Christian talk)
WFCM 91.7 AM, 710 AM (inspirational, talk)
WFFH 94.1 (contemporary Christian)
WFFI 93.7 (contemporary Christian)
WFGZ 94.5 FM (contemporary Christian)
WJQI 540 AM (contemporary Christian)
WMDB 880 AM (gospel, jazz, R&B)
WNAH 1360 AM (Southern gospel)
WNAZ 89.1 FM (inspirational/Christian alternative)
WNQM 1300 AM (Christian talk/Spanish, evenings)
WNSG 1240 AM (gospel/ministries)
WVRY 105.1 FM (Southern gospel)
WYFN 980 AM (Christian)

Classical

WPLN 90.3 FM, 1430 AM (Nashville Public Radio; classical, news, and information)

College Radio

WENO 760 AM (Trevecca Nazarene University; Christian talk)
WFSK 88.1 FM (Fisk University; jazz, gospel, urban, eclectic)

WMOT 89.5 FM (Middle Tennessee State University; jazz, National Public Radio)
WMTS 88.3 FM (Middle Tennessee State University, eclectic)
WNAZ 89.1 FM (Trevecca Nazarene University; inspirational/Christian alternative)
WRVU 91.1 FM (Vanderbilt University; alternative rock, eclectic)
WVCP 88.5 FM (Volunteer State Community College; eclectic)

Contemporary Hit Radio/Top 40

WQZQ 102.5 FM
WRVW 107.5 FM

Country

WAKM 950 AM (also news, talk, sports)
WANT 98.9
WCOR 900 AM
WHIN 1010 AM
WKDF 103.3 FM
WNKX 96.7 FM, 1570 AM
WQSV 790 AM (country, Southern gospel, bluegrass)
WSIX 97.9 FM
WSM 650 AM (home of the *Grand Ole Opry*)
WSM 95.5 FM

Jazz

WFSK 88.1 FM (Fisk University; eclectic)
WMDB 880 AM (gospel, jazz, R&B)
WMOT 89.5 FM (also National Public Radio)

News/Talk/Sports

WAKM 950 AM (news, sports, country)
WGFX 104.5 FM (sports/talk)
WGNS 1450 AM
WLAC 1510 AM
WNQM 1300 AM (Christian talk)
WNSR 560 AM (sports, talk)
WPLN 90.3 FM, 1430 AM (National Public Radio; classical, news, and information)
WWTN 99.7 FM

Oldies

WAMB 98.7 FM, 1160 AM (nostalgia, Big Band)
WMAK 96.3 FM
WMRO 1560 AM (rock oldies)
WRQQ 97.1

Rock

WBUZ 102.9 FM (modern rock)
WEGI 94.3 FM (classic Southern rock)
WJXA 92.9 (light rock)
WNRQ 105.9 FM (classic rock)
WRLT 100.1 FM (adult alternative)

Spanish

WAPB 810 AM
WHEW 1380 AM
WKDA 1200 AM
WMGC 810 AM

Urban

WMDB 880 AM (gospel, jazz, R&B)
WNPL 106.7 (hip-hop)
WQQK 92.1 FM (adult contemporary, urban, R&B)
WVOL 1470 AM (R&B, classic soul)
WUBT 101.1 (hip-hop, R&B)

Online News & Information

CITYSEARCH NASHVILLE

http://nashville.citysearch.com

This Web site search service offers in-depth information on Nashville life. Searchable categories include restaurants, hotels, movies, spa and beauty, and tickets and events.

NASHVILLEDIGEST.COM

(615) 292-8642
www.nashvilledigest.com

This online service compiles news from Tennessee news sources, focusing mainly on Nashville's top media outlets. News is published on the Web site each weekday morning. You can sign up to receive personal news e-mails each morning, as well.

i **Sunday night concerts at Nashville's 3rd & Lindsley nightclub are simulcast on WRLT-FM 100.**

NASHVILLEPOST.COM

3401 West End Avenue, Suite 685
(615) 250-1540
www.nashvillepost.com

Founded in 1999, this online news service covers business news in the Nashville area. A $9.75 monthly subscription is required to access the Web site. Group rates are available.

RETIREMENT

Lots of people apparently have chosen to live their "golden years" in the Nashville area. According to the 2000 U.S. census, 10 percent of the population in the Nashville area is 65 and older. The same benefits that make Nashville such an attractive place for all ages—in a nutshell, a high quality of life combined with a relatively low cost of living (and no income tax), convenient location, and pleasant climate—make it an especially desirable place for retired people. Those who have left the rigors of the work world now have even more time to take advantage of Nashville's thousands upon thousands of acres of parks and waterways, its golf courses, swimming pools, country clubs, tennis courts, historical attractions, shopping opportunities, music, and much more.

A number of retirement communities offer a range of lifestyle options, from independent to assisted living. A fine senior citizens center, with convenient branches throughout the area, provides opportunities for recreation, travel, relaxation, and even volunteerism with friends old and new. For many retired people, the issue of health care becomes increasingly important. With such well-respected institutions as Vanderbilt University Medical Center right in town, health care access is excellent in Nashville. The central location near major interstates, along with an international airport, makes getting in and out of town—whether you're going to see the grandkids or they're coming to see you—a snap. And plenty of public transportation is available as well. Of course, being a senior means you get to enjoy many of the fine attractions detailed in this book at a reduced cost! So enjoy your stay, and stick around for a while. The Nashville area is a great place to grow old and stay young at the same time.

ACTIVITIES FOR SENIORS

EASTER SEALS TENNESSEE
2001 Woodmont Boulevard
(615) 292-6640, (615) 385-3485 (TDD)
www.tn.easter-seals.org
While Easter Seals serves people of all ages, the organization's Turner Family Center offers a variety of health and wellness programs for seniors. The Turner Center's state-of-the-art, wheelchair-accessible fitness center offers conditioning and physical therapy for all fitness levels. The center's indoor pool is open year-round. Among the programs offered are stroke support and an Arthritis Pain Center; the latter offers physical and occupational therapy, aquatics in the therapy pool, and educational classes.

55 PLUS
Baptist Hospital, 2000 Church Street
(615) 284-8255
www.baptisthospital.com
Baptist Hospital's 55 Plus program offers a variety of activities, trips, and seminars for people 55 and older. Options include group excursions to Titans football and Predators hockey games, "55 Alive" classes for older drivers, and a changing lineup of seminars on such topics as reducing heart attack risk, osteoporosis screening, and managing stress. Membership is free, as are many of the seminars. Call for a membership application.

JEWISH COMMUNITY CENTER
801 Percy Warner Boulevard
(615) 356-7170
www.nashvillejcc.org

The facilities and programs at this center are first-rate, making it popular with families and people of all ages. The center offers a variety of programs for senior citizens, many of them using the center's pool and gym. Classes targeting seniors include water aerobics, gentle yoga, and "golden age" exercise programs. The center also has a variety of classes—poker groups for men and women, bridge clubs, and Torah and Yiddish class are just a few. You don't have to be Jewish to join, but you do need to be a member; special discounts are available for seniors.

SENIOR CITIZENS INC.
174 Rains Avenue
(615) 743-3400
www.scitn.org
Senior Citizens Inc. is a private, nonprofit organization for adults 55 years and older. The organization and its centers offer more than 60 classes, including computers, exercise classes, Spanish and French, social dancing, square dancing, quilting, art, and wood carving. Activities vary from center to center.

Two of Senior Citizens Inc.'s major programs are its adult day care and Meals on Wheels. The day care (615-463-2266) is available Monday through Friday from 8:00 a.m. to 5:00 p.m. The Meals on Wheels program (615-463-2264) is one of 12 such programs in Davidson County; Senior Citizens Inc.'s program covers south and west Nashville. Residents ages 55 and older who are homebound or who live with another elderly person can have a lunchtime meal delivered to their homes Monday through Saturday for $5 per day.

Other services offered include a nonprofit travel agency, case management for homebound seniors that coordinates Meals on Wheels, referrals to various agencies, volunteer assistance, and respite care that helps them remain in their homes as long as possible.

Members also keep young through their eager participation in a number of volunteer programs. The Foster Grandparents program serves about 1,000 area children with special needs. More than 500 seniors take part in RSVP (Retired Senior Volunteer Program), serving more than 90 sites in Davidson and Williamson Counties. FLIP (Friends Learning in Pairs) provides mentors/tutors for at-risk early-elementary students in public school classrooms. Respite Caregivers provide about four hours of relief care for a frail elderly loved one being cared for at home.

Seniors Citizens Inc. has six full-time centers: Knowles Senior Services Center, 174 Rains Avenue, (615) 743-3400; Donelson Station Center, 108 Donelson Pike, (615) 883-8375; Hadley Park Center, 3700 Ashland City Highway, (615) 248-2272; College Grove Center, 8607 Horton Highway, College Grove, (615) 368-7093; Madison Station Center, 301 Madison Street, (615) 860-7180; and the Martin Center, 960 Heritage Way, Brentwood, (615) 376-0102. The Bellevue branch (615-743-3400) provides specific programs and activities for seniors in the Bellevue area.

Membership is a $50 annual donation. All members receive the monthly newspaper *Senior Sentinel* (see our Media chapter) in the mail.

> **i** The Mall at Green Hills is a popular location for mall walking. For the serious mall walker, a distance key is posted on the mall's second level near Customer Service that details how many laps equal a mile.

SENIOR SERVICES

The following local and national organizations serve as vital resource outlets and information clearinghouses for seniors.

GREATER NASHVILLE REGIONAL COUNCIL AREA AGENCY ON AGING & DISABILITY
501 Union Street, sixth floor
(615) 862-8828
www.gnrc.org
The Area Agency on Aging serves Davidson County as well as Cheatham, Dickson, Houston, Humphreys, Montgomery, Robertson, Rutherford, Stewart, Sumner, Trousdale, Williamson, and Wilson Counties. The agency plans for the provision of federal Older American Act services and state-funded services to persons 60 and older.

It performs a wide range of activities related to advocacy, planning, coordination, interagency linkages, information sharing, brokering, monitoring, technical assistance, training, and evaluation. The agency funds services related to such areas as health promotion and disease prevention, homemaking, information and assistance, legal assistance, nutrition services, ombudsmen, public guardianship, respite care, retired senior volunteers, senior centers, and transportation.

MID-CUMBERLAND HUMAN RESOURCE AGENCY

301 South Perimeter Park Drive,
Suite 210
(615) 331-6033
www.mchra.com

The Mid-Cumberland Human Resource Agency is a nonprofit organization whose mission is "to help people help themselves by providing knowledge and resources to improve the quality of life." Founded in 1974, the agency serves the counties of Davidson, Cheatham, Dickson, Houston, Humphreys, Montgomery, Robertson, Rutherford, Stewart, Sumner, Trousdale, Williamson, and Wilson, and has offices in each county. The agency's extensive list of services available include homemaking assistance, nutrition/home-delivered meals, home health care, transportation services, and representative payee services for those who are unable to handle their own finances due to disabilities.

SENIOR PATHWAYS

113 Seaboard Lane, Suite B200, Franklin
(615) 742-0011
www.senior-pathways.com

Senior Pathways provides free care management and referral services for seniors and their families in Middle Tennessee. It's a sort of one-stop service for a variety of senior care needs. The company specializes in helping seniors find appropriate housing but also provides other helpful services. The staff of social workers and geriatric care specialists provides immediate in-home or in-hospital consultations. Those looking for a new home can get advice on independent living, assisted living, and nursing homes in the area, matched to their particular health care, budget, location, and amenity needs. Senior Pathways also can help seniors stay in their homes by matching them with qualified sitters/companions, housekeepers, transportation services, and other resources. The organization also provides information and advice on Medicare, Medicaid, long-term care insurance, legal services, estate and financial planning, real estate sales, and moving services. The company earns its fees from nursing homes, home health agencies, and other service providers.

SENIOR SOLUTIONS

501 Union Street
(615) 255-1010, (877) 973-6467
(toll-free from outside the Metro calling area)
www.askseniorsolutions.org

Senior Solutions, a sort of "one-stop shopping" for senior needs, is an information referral and assistance program for seniors and those who love and care for them. Using an extensive, nationally used software program, workers assess callers' needs and then connect them to community resources that can meet those needs. Sometimes the answer can be provided with one call; in other instances follow-up is necessary. Senior Solutions often does the legwork for social workers, calling multiple agencies to find who can provide the needed assistance. Help covers a wide range: anything from finances and health care to depression, residential facilities, and housecleaning. Senior Solutions, a service of the Greater Nashville Regional Council Area on Aging and Disability, is funded by the Tennessee Commission on Aging and Disability and United Way of Metropolitan Nashville.

211 SOCIAL SERVICES HELP LINE

www.uwnashville.org

This social services hotline established by the United Way of Metropolitan Nashville connects residents to some 2,800 health and human services programs in Middle Tennessee. Residents

Senior Services Information

These organizations may be able to answer questions or help determine which organization can provide you with the senior services information you need. For more information on some of these organizations, see our separate write-ups in this chapter.

Eldercare Locator
(800) 677-1116
www.eldercare.gov

Legal Aid Society of Middle Tennessee and the Cumberlands
(800) 342-3317

Metro Action Commission
(615) 862-8860
www.nashville.gov/mac

Mid-Cumberland Human Resource Agency
(615) 331-6033
www.mchra.com

National Council on the Aging
(202) 479-1200
www.ncoa.org

National Institute on Aging
(301) 496-1752
www.nia.nih.gov

Senior Solutions
(615) 255-1010
www.askseniorsolutions.org

Tennessee Commission on Aging & Disability
(615) 741-2056
www.state.tn.us/comaging

United Way Help Line, Nashville
(615) 269-4357
www.uwnashville.org

who need social services information or assistance simply pick up the phone and dail 211. Services range from food and shelter to health care and counseling. The system serves Metro Nashville–Davidson County as well as Cheatham, Cannon, Dickson, Maury, Robertson, Rutherford, Sumner, Trousdale, Williamson, and Wilson Counties.

Metro Nashville/Davidson County Social Services

The social-services agency for Metro Nashville–Davidson County provides a variety of services for senior citizens. The office is headquartered at 25 Middleton Street, and their main phone number is (615) 862-6400. A comprehensive list of services is available on their Web site at www.nashville.gov.

ADULT DAY CARE
1010 Camilla Caldwell Lane
(615) 862-6450
Services of the Adult Day Care program include nutrition, transportation, and adult day care assisted living. Field trips to area parks and museums, activities such as games and crafts, and special events are organized. Clients run the gamut of physical and mental abilities, with some needing more care than others. The program is open weekdays, and clients receive breakfast and lunch. Cost is based on a sliding-fee scale based on income.

ADULT HOMEMAKER PROGRAM
25 Middleton Street
(615) 862-6480
This agency provides homemaker services involving light housekeeping to low-income seniors 60 and older and to mentally and physically challenged adults who live alone. Services are intended to help program participants remain in their homes, avoiding more costly nursing home placement. Homemaker Services also runs essential errands, such as grocery shopping and picking up medication, and performs laundry services. Eligibility requirements are based on financial need.

NUTRITION PROGRAM FOR SENIOR ADULTS
25 Middleton Street
(615) 880-2292

Nutrition Program for Senior Adults serves about 1,400 lunches daily Monday through Friday to Davidson County residents 60 and older. Meals are served at about 16 managed sites, such as high-rise apartment buildings and community centers, throughout the county. In addition to each day's set menu of low-sodium food, the Nutrition Program provides activities such as arts and crafts, field trips, games, and classes to keep seniors active and involved. A home-delivered meals program serving homebound residents also is available. The Nutrition Program is partly funded by the federal government under the Older Americans Act; while there is no charge, donations are encouraged and make up a necessary part of the funding.

TRANSPORTATION SERVICES
25 Middleton Street
(615) 880-2296

This Metro service provides transportation to medical appointments on weekdays only. Transportation for shopping and other nonmedical purposes is also available, provided it's for a group of seniors, not just one individual. The service is provided on a donation basis. Those needing transportation should call two to three days ahead.

i Interested in buying organic produce and natural groceries but worried about the expense? Seniors get a 10 percent discount at Wild Oats grocery stores every Tuesday.

National Organizations

AARP
601 East Street NW
Washington, DC 20049
(888) OUR-AARP
www.aarp.org

AARP is the nation's leading organization for people 50 and older. It serves their needs and interests through legislative advocacy, research, informative programs, and community services provided by a network of local chapters and volunteers throughout the country. The organization also offers members a wide range of benefits, including a monthly magazine and the monthly *Bulletin*.

NATIONAL INSTITUTE ON AGING
Building 31, Room 5C27, 31 Center Drive,
MSC 2292, Bethesda, MD 20892
(301) 496-1752, (800) 222-2225
www.nih.gov/nia

The National Institute on Aging is responsible for the "conduct and support of biomedical, social, and behavioral research, training, health-information dissemination, and other programs with respect to the aging process and the diseases and other special problems and needs of the aged." It offers a wide variety of publications, both general and specific, about such issues as incontinence, menopause, medications, arthritis, Alzheimer's disease, depression, forgetfulness, stroke, nutrition, hearing, sexuality, accident prevention, and much more.

Area Social Security Offices

District Office: 4527 Nolensville Pike, (615) 781-5800, (800) 772-1213

Gallatin branch: 450 West Main Street, Oakland Park Building, Gallatin, (615) 451-9341

Madison branch: 104 Cude Lane, Madison, (615) 736-2514

Murfreesboro branch: 245 Heritage Park Drive, Murfreesboro, (615) 895-5790

RETIREMENT COMMUNITIES

Nashville has many housing options for seniors, including luxury retirement communities, independent-living and assisted-living communities, nursing homes, Alzheimer's assisted living, licensed residential homes, and government subsidized housing. We are profiling just a few of the retirement communities in the area. For a more complete listing, see the Nashville Chamber of Commerce's Senior Citizen Resource Directory (call 615-743-3070 to purchase, or order online at www.nashvillechamber.com). Other publications, such as the free *Seniors Resource Guide* (www.seniorsresourceguide.com), also have up-to-date listings of senior communities, including information on rates and amenities. Many of the agencies listed in this chapter can provide information on housing as well.

BLAKEFORD AT GREEN HILLS
11 Burton Hills Boulevard
(615) 665-9505
www.blakeford.com
Blakeford, with a prime location in Green Hills, is an upscale not-for-profit senior-living community. It is a continuing-care senior community, which means it offers lifetime assisted living and unlimited nursing care for those who need it. Blakeford at Green Hills occupies a 10-acre site, with four acres dedicated to green areas and walking paths adjoining Lake Burton. Inside the community buildings are a library, beauty salon/barbershop, exercise room, and creative arts center. Guest accommodations are available for visitors, and a private dining room can accommodate private gatherings. Included in the monthly fee, which ranges from $1,900 to $4,399 are one daily meal, weekly housekeeping, and scheduled transportation. Restaurant-style dining is available for two meals daily in the main dining room.

LAKESHORE ESTATES
8044 Coley Davis Road
(615) 646-4466
www.lakeshoreestates.org
Founded in 1952, the nonprofit Lakeshore is

actually three different facilities, each offering differing levels of care depending on one's needs. Lakeshore/Heartland is located at 3025 Fernbrook Lane, in the Donelson area (615-885-2320). Independent living, at the Heartland Pointe community, and nursing home care are both available.

The Heartland Pointe community has two- and three-bedroom homes designed with seniors in mind—no elevated steps and extra-wide hallways to accommodate a wheelchair. The homes also feature grip bars in all bathrooms and emergency call buttons. Other services include social outings, home maintenance, and landscaping and lawn care.

Lakeshore Wedgewood, located at 832 Wedgewood Avenue off Eighth Avenue (615-383-4006), was actually the first Lakeshore facility. Today it is a 155-plus-bed home for assisted living and nursing home residents. Wedgewood residents can choose between private or semiprivate suites with private or shared baths.

The Meadows, located at the Coley Davis Road address in Bellevue, provides full-service nursing care for about 120 residents. There is a specially designed unit for residents with memory impairment, two dining rooms, and several activity rooms offering everything from music to art classes. Staffed by LPNs and RNs, the Meadows makes a variety of physical, occupational, and speech therapies available to residents.

MCKENDREE VILLAGE
4343 Lebanon Road, Hermitage
(615) 889-6990
www.mckendree.com
McKendree Village, a nonprofit continuing-care retirement community, has been serving the area since 1963. Offerings range from total independent living in the Cottages and the Towers to varying levels of assisted living in the Manor and the Health Center. Residents, who must be 55 or older, can choose from a variety of programs. The 42-acre complex includes an indoor swimming pool and whirlpool, an exercise room, a woodworking shop, an activities/crafts room, and a chapel with a full-time chaplain and various Bible study classes throughout the week. McKendree

Village is affiliated with Vanderbilt University Medical Center and has a "covenant relationship" with the Tennessee Annual Conference of the United Methodist Church, which essentially means that the church provides money through offerings but is not involved in daily management or operations. Residents do not need to be church members.

The Village has various residential options from which to choose. Residents can lease a studio apartment or deluxe unit in the Manor, purchase cottages ranging from 1,100 to 3,000 square feet, or lease an apartment in the Towers. The Manor is designed to bridge the gap between total independent living and nursing care, providing such services as help with medication and assistance with bathing and dressing. The Cottages and the Tower are designed for more active, independent living; residents must be able to care for their own personal needs. Residents of the Village can either lease their apartments or take advantage of a refundable use fee agreement, which allows them to pay a specific amount upon entering the Village and have a discounted monthly service charge. Charges for the Manor (supportive living) and the Health Center are on a monthly basis. The Rehabilitation/Subacute Unit of the Health Center has daily rates. Rates start at around $1,600 for independent living and at $2,000 for assisted living.

MORNINGSIDE OF BELMONT
1710 Magnolia Boulevard
(615) 383-2557
Morningside of Belmont, which has been in operation since 1980, offers a variety of floor plans for independent living in the Belmont/Hillsboro area. Services and amenities include housekeeping, laundry facilities, two or three meals a day, a library, and a beauty salon. Residents also may audit classes at Belmont University. Apartments are furnished with residents' own furnishings. All have accessible bathrooms, kitchens, and large picture windows overlooking Belmont or the city. Many also have balconies. No long-term leases, entrance fees, or endowments are required. An assisted-living program is available 24 hours a day, and a resident assistant can be reached by activating a call button in each apartment. Weekly shopping trips

and a variety of social and community activities are available for residents who wish to participate. Monthly rents for independent living, for instance, begin at $1,800. Rates include three meals daily, complete dietary services, and housekeeping.

i The Tennessee Bar Association's Elder Law Section has prepared an online *Legal Handbook for Tennessee Seniors* that describes U.S. and Tennessee laws, as well as several programs of interest to seniors, including Social Security, Medicaid, and Medicare. The guide also gives an overview of housing options, health care, long-term care, wills and probate, powers of attorney, conservatorship, elder abuse, and other topics. The information is available online at www.tba.org/seniorhandbook. You may call the TBA at (615) 383-7421.

Nursing Home Comparison Guide

If you are looking for a nursing home, you may find Medicare's online nursing home comparison guide helpful. You can find the guide on Medicare's Web site, www.medicare.gov. The guide provides detailed information about the past performance of the nation's 17,000 Medicare- and Medicaid-certified nursing homes. The site allows you to search for nursing homes by state, county, city, ZIP code, or name of the facility. Once you have located the list of homes in your desired area, you can find detailed statistics on quality, deficiency, and staffing, and compare the results to national and state averages. It's a good idea to consider other sources of information as well before making a final decision about a nursing home.

PARK MANOR
115 Woodmont Boulevard
(615) 383-7303
www.parkmanorapts.com
This nonprofit independent living community is located in the prestigious Belle Meade area of west Nashville. Built in 1962, Park Manor offers efficiencies and one- and two-bedroom apartments—all with fire- and sound-resistant construction, smoke detectors, and 24-hour intercom systems—within a country-style environment on seven acres. Prices are in the $1,300 to $2,600 range. The monthly fee includes housekeeping services twice a month, all utilities except telephone and cable, and lunch and dinner every day in an elegant dining room. Private dining rooms are available for entertaining family and friends. Organized activities and seminars are offered, and transportation is also available.

PENNINGTON PLACE
202 Walton Ferry Road, Hendersonville
(615) 822-7520
Pennington Place is an all-ground-floor retirement community that offers both independent and assisted living. The one- and two-bedroom apartments feature private patios and gardens and private outside entrances. Residents pay a $500 nonrefundable community-service entrance fee. The monthly fee for independent living—starting at $1,100—includes weekly housekeeping, maintenance, 24-hour emergency response system, all utilities, and three meals daily in the community dining room. The complex contains a beauty/barbershop, free laundry facilities, and an activity room with exercise equipment, whirlpool, scheduled transportation, on-site therapy, and minimal supervision.

RICHLAND PLACE
500 Elmington Avenue
(615) 269-4200
www.richlandplace.com
Richland Place Inc. is a Tennessee not-for-profit corporation that consists of a 136-apartment continuing-care retirement community attached to a licensed, 131-bed long-term health care center. It is on the site of the former Richland Country Club near Interstate 440 at West End Avenue. The community bills itself as "a distinctive luxury retirement community designed for successful, active seniors over the age of 55." Entry fees start around $175,000 depending upon the unit square footage; this fee is entirely refundable within the first four months and 90 percent refundable after 10 months. Monthly service fees include one chef-prepared meal a day, weekly housekeeping, and flat linen service; apartment, building, and grounds maintenance; scheduled transportation; apartment insurance; property taxes; all utilities except phone and cable TV; additional storage space; and a medical-alert system. The fees also cover such activities as fitness programs in the fitness center and long-term health care services, which are provided in a semiprivate accommodation in the project's health care center for up to 180 days a year with a lifetime maximum of 360 days at no additional charge.

Richland Place also has walking paths that meander through seven acres; an investment center with real-time price quotations and computers for stock trading; an indoor swimming pool designed like a Roman spa with marble columns and floor; a restaurant, deli, soda fountain, and sundries shop; on-site banking; a pharmacy; a laundry; dry-cleaning pickup; postal facilities; and storage. Apartments feature recessed fixtures, crown moldings, state-of-the-art appliances, carpeting throughout, decorator wallpaper, brass bathroom fixtures, dining room chandeliers, and 9-foot ceilings. Entry gates are monitored by closed-circuit TV.

i **The Greater Nashville Regional Council Area Agency on Aging & Disability and the Council on Aging publish the *Directory of Services for Senior Citizens*, which provides information on services for older persons in Middle Tennessee. The directory is available free to seniors and can be found in senior centers throughout the area.**

TREVECCA TOWERS RETIREMENT COMMUNITY

60 Lester Avenue

(615) 244-6911

www.treveccatowers.com

More than 600 senior citizens live at Trevecca Towers: three 15-story buildings with apartments for retirees capable of independent apartment living "at prices senior citizens can afford to pay." No fee or endowment is required. On-site amenities include lounges and solariums, hobby and crafts rooms, a computer lounge, library, grocery store, beauty shop, private gardening spaces, heated indoor swimming pool, sauna, and exercise equipment. No meals are included, but all maintenance is provided except housekeeping inside the apartments. The towers' location beside the 55-acre campus of Trevecca Nazarene University gives residents access to many university activities, and residents can audit courses free of charge. Organized programs, tours, shopping trips, and activities are also available. Residents must be at least 62 years of age; those with a physical disability are exempt from the age requirement.

WORSHIP

Religion has always played an important role in the lives of Nashvillians. Since the first settlers walked across the frozen Cumberland River on a cold December day in 1779, bringing with them their Bibles, hymns, spirituals, and religious traditions, religion has become an increasingly prominent fixture in Nashville. Today, with some 800 churches, synagogues, temples, mosques, and other houses of worship representing more than 60 denominations and religions as well as numerous Bible schools, religious publishing houses, and several denominational headquarters, Nashville continues to grow as a center of religious activity. In this chapter we offer a brief look at some of the history of religion in Nashville. Unlike most of our other chapters, we do not break out separate write-ups on individual locations here. There are far too many houses of worship to list them all, and in an effort to be fair, we will not attempt to do so. We do want to provide useful information, so we will give you a brief overview of some of the churches, temples, and synagogues that are popular in Nashville as well as some of the locations, faiths, and organizations that are not as widely known. You might use this information as a starting point in your search for a house of worship that suits you.

OVERVIEW

Nashville is known as "the buckle of the Bible Belt" and has even been called the "Protestant Vatican." While the city is indeed dominated by Protestantism, particularly Southern Baptist and Church of Christ denominations, Nashville embraces people of many faiths. Dozens of different faiths have houses of worship here, including African Methodist Episcopal, Buddhist, Hindu, Roman Catholic, Judaic (Orthodox, Conservative, and Reform), Greek Orthodox, Quaker, and Muslim.

You've probably heard it said that Nashville has "a church on every street corner." Well, that's pretty close to the truth. In Bellevue, for example, at the corner of Colice Jeanne Road and U.S. Highway 70 S., you'll find Bellevue Baptist Church, Bellevue Church of Christ, and Bellevue Presbyterian Church. In a short stretch along Hillsboro Road in Green Hills, you'll find Woodmont Baptist, Woodmont Christian, Calvary United Methodist, and several others nearby. The busy intersection of West End and Bowling Avenues has two synagogues, a Church of Christ, and a Methodist church—and more are nearby.

In addition to the many places of worship, Nashville is home to religious publishers, denominational headquarters, various associations, and service organizations, and it's the center of the Christian music industry. The huge Southern Baptist Convention has offices downtown. Also here are LifeWay Christian Resources of the Southern Baptist Convention (formerly known as the Baptist Sunday School Board), the Gideons International (who make sure hotel and motel rooms have Bibles), Gospel Music Association (presenter of the annual Dove Awards), National Association of Free Will Baptists, National Baptist Convention USA, National Baptist Publishing Board, Thomas Nelson Publishers (the world's largest Bible publisher), United Methodist Publishing House, and World Convention of Churches of Christ. And that's just for starters.

The list of religious organizations in the yellow pages includes dozens of groups, including the African Christian Schools Foundation, the Disciples of Christ Historical Society, Kentucky-Tennessee Conference of Seventh Day Adventists, the Tennessee Baptist Convention, and the Tennessee Baptist Missionary & Educational

Convention. This is a media age, and Nashville is an entertainment city. So it's no surprise to learn that Nashville is home to Trinity Music City U.S.A., a Christian tourist attraction owned by TBN, the world's largest Christian television network. (Locals remember when Trinity Music City was Twitty City—the home of country star Conway Twitty and a tourist destination in its own right. TBN purchased the property after Twitty's death.)

Visitors can attend live Praise the Lord broadcasts, experience a re-creation of the Via Dolorosa (a street in ancient Jerusalem), and attend live concerts, theatrical productions, and seminars at its 2,000-seat auditorium (see our Music City chapter for details).

Nashville is also known as a center of religious education. Some of the city's educational institutions are devoted to preparing clergy, while others offer religious study as part of a general curriculum. There are several institutions of higher learning tied to denominations: Belmont University and the Southern Baptist Convention, David Lipscomb University and Church of Christ, Trevecca Nazarene University and Church of the Nazarene. American Baptist College and Free Will Baptist Bible College are here, too. (See our Education and Child Care chapter for information on some of these schools.) Vanderbilt University was affiliated with Southern Methodists until 1914, when the denomination founded Southern Methodist University in Dallas and Emory University in Atlanta. Vanderbilt has been nonsectarian since, and today the nationally prominent Vanderbilt University Divinity School is part of a small league of nondenominational divinity schools that includes Harvard, Yale, Chicago, and Union in New York.

HISTORICAL HIGHLIGHTS

Methodists and Presbyterians were the first two religious groups to enter the Middle Tennessee area, according to Eugene Teselle, retired professor of church history and theology at Vanderbilt's Divinity School. Scots-Irish Presbyterians came to America from Britain in the 1700s to escape drought, religious persecution, and British domination. They first settled in Pennsylvania and South Carolina but eventually pushed westward.

Thomas Craighead, a graduate of Princeton, preached the first Presbyterian sermon ever heard in Middle Tennessee. That same year he established Davidson Academy, Nashville's first school, which later became the University of Nashville. Another early Middle Tennessee preacher prepared his sermons while doing manual labor. As he plowed, he would have a pen and paper on a stump at the end of the field so he could write down his thoughts.

By 1796 Presbyterians had established 27 congregations from east Tennessee to Nashville. While the Presbyterians were largely upper and middle class, Methodists were a bit more broad-based. Both groups were financially able to send traveling ministers into the area that became Middle Tennessee. One of the area's earliest Methodist leaders was a Revolutionary War veteran named Benjamin Ogden, who preached regularly in Nashville, Clarksville, and Gallatin. Methodist societies eventually began springing up in the area, and Nashville followers built a stone meetinghouse in 1790.

According to the Metropolitan Nashville Historical Commission, Nashville's first house of worship was a Methodist church built in 1796, 17 years after the first settlers arrived. The church was on the public square, near the courthouse, jail, and stocks. In 1796, the year Tennessee became a state, Nashville's Methodist community numbered about 550 and included the city's founder, James Robertson. Traveling preachers pastored

i The Nashville Area Chamber of Commerce publishes the *Nashville Religious Resource Guide,* a comprehensive guide to local congregations. The booklet lists addresses, phone numbers, names of clergy, and some membership figures. It costs $35, or $19 for members of the chamber. For more information call (615) 743-3070 or visit www.nashville chamber.com.

ℹ **Music publishing began in Nashville in 1824 with the publication of *Western Harmony,* a book of hymns and instructions for singing.**

the Nashville group. One of Nashville's oldest churches, McKendree United Methodist Church—formerly known as Spring Street Church—at 523 Church Street, was organized in 1787.

The movement of Baptists into Tennessee differed from that of Presbyterians, who dominated both early religious life and education. Baptists did not require an educated clergy and didn't follow strict hierarchies. Their style had great appeal to Middle Tennessee's early settlers, and their numbers quickly multiplied.

Tennessee Baptists organized their first convention at the Mill Creek Church in Nashville in 1835. In 1842 the group changed to a general association, resulting in three organizations in each of the main divisions of the state. The present convention was formed at Murfreesboro in 1874, uniting the three groups.

In the 1800s religious denominations underwent a period of tremendous growth in Tennessee as revivals swept through the state, drawing hundreds of new converts into their folds. Denominations began forming state organizations, and numerous other denominations and churches were established. In 1820 Nashville's first Sunday school class was begun. Nashville's first public Mass was celebrated that year; the city's Catholics for a time shared a church with Protestants and were visited twice a year by priests. A decade later, a parish was formed, and in 1847 the state's first permanent Roman Catholic church was completed.

The Greek Revival–style St. Mary's Catholic Church, at 330 Fifth Avenue N., is the oldest remaining church in downtown Nashville. It was built with the support of numerous denominations by mechanics who had come to Nashville to build a bridge over the Cumberland River. During the Civil War, the church was used as a military hospital. Masses are scheduled at 12:10 p.m. Monday, Tuesday, Thursday, and Friday; 5:00 p.m. Saturday; and 9:00 a.m. Sunday.

Judaism arrived in Nashville as early as 1790. The census of 1840 counted 160 Jewish families in Davidson County. According to "Seven Early Churches of Nashville," a series of lectures presented at the Nashville public library, the first Jewish religious organization, a benevolent society that also met for religious services, dates from 1851. The first rabbi arrived in fall 1852. The state granted a charter for the Nashville congregation, known as Kahl Kodesh Mogen David, in March 1852. A Reform congregation was established in 1864. Construction began on the Vine Street Temple, on the east side of Seventh Avenue, in 1874, and the building was dedicated in 1876. It moved to its present location at 5015 Harding Road in 1955 and today is known as Temple Congregation Ohabai Sholom (615-352-7620).

The historic Downtown Presbyterian Church (615-254-7584), at the corner of Fifth Avenue and Church Street, was completed in 1851. The Egyptian Revival–style building was designed by William Strickland, architect of the State Capitol. The church was originally organized in 1814 as First Presbyterian Church, but it was later reorganized as the Downtown Presbyterian Church. The building served as a hospital during the Civil War. The 4,013-pound church bell was the gift of Adelicia Acklen (see the Belmont Mansion entry in the Attractions chapter). The church is a National Historic Landmark; call (615) 254-7584 to arrange a guided tour. Another historic church, Vine Street Christian Church, 104 Seventh Avenue N., was founded in 1890 but had beginnings in 1820.

As the number of houses of worship grew, and as religion became more organized, religious-based business, especially religious publishing, was beginning to take shape in Nashville. In 1854 the United Methodist Publishing House was established. Its publications include the *Upper Room,* which has a circulation in the millions. The *United Methodist Hymnal* has been the group's

ℹ **First Church Unity's Dial-A-Prayer offers uplifting daily messages of encouragement. The number is (615) 832-1885.**

most successful publication; more than four million are distributed. UMPH produces more than 1,000 new products each year under the Abingdon Press, Cokesbury, Kingswood Books, and Dimensions for Living imprints. Cokesbury Books, 301 Eighth Avenue S. (615-749-6123 or 800-672-1789), carries most of UMPH's publications. The 70-store Cokesbury chain is UMPH's retail arm and is also an official distributor for various other denominations.

LifeWay Christian Resources of the Southern Baptist Convention, today among the world's largest religious publishers, was established in 1891. Formerly known as the Baptist Sunday School Board, it employs some 1,200 people and produces 180 quarterly and monthly publications and 500 to 600 undated products annually. The board is self-supporting through the sale of church literature, books, music, films, recordings, videotapes, Bibles, and church supplies. Any income above operating expenses is returned to the denominations to help fund missions. Baptist Bookstores and LifeWay Christian Stores handle more than three million transactions a year.

THE CIVIL WAR AND POSTWAR TIMES

The issue of slavery had a great impact on Nashville churches in the 1800s. Rifts over abolition and related issues had occurred as early as the 1820s. Presbyterians and Baptists each split over the issues; eventually, so did Methodists, who early on had been firm in their opposition to slavery. Among Baptists, those in the North were against slavery, while Southern Baptists took a different view. There was a falling-out over the national foreign missions board's refusal to appoint a slaveholder as a missionary, and Baptists from the South organized the Southern Baptist Convention in 1845, gathering in Augusta, Georgia. The convention met in Nashville in 1851.

During these times, African Americans had considerable influence in religious matters. In Nashville Rev. Nelson Merry, the city's first ordained African-American minister and pastor

i During Gospel Music Week in April, Nashville clubs are filled with contemporary Christian and gospel music; many of the performances are open to the public and feature name entertainers such as Michael W. Smith and Steven Curtis Chapman. For information check local entertainment listings in the *Rage* or *Nashville Scene.*

of the First Colored Baptist Church, was Tennessee's most prominent African-American minister before the Civil War. After the war, northern denominations assisted in the establishment of churches and schools for newly freed African Americans.

In 1896, 31 years after the Civil War had ended, Rev. Richard Henry Boyd, who had been born a slave in Mississippi, moved to Nashville and established a religious publishing house to publish materials for the African-American community. His business later became known as the National Baptist Publishing Board. He contracted with a white man to bid for printing presses because the law prohibited African Americans from taking part in such business activities. His business, originally at 523 Second Avenue N., quickly became one of the largest African-American–owned businesses in the United States. Now at 6717 Centennial Boulevard, the National Baptist Publishing Board is still operated by family members and today publishes more than 14 million books and periodicals annually. Boyd also cofounded the One-Cent Savings Bank, the first minority-owned bank in Tennessee, and established the *Nashville Globe,* a newspaper that served the local African-American community until 1960.

i Nashville's walking labyrinth, an ancient tool for prayer and meditation, is located at the Scarritt-Bennett Center near Vanderbilt University. It is open to the public at scheduled times. For information call (615) 340-7543 or visit www.scarrittbennett.org.

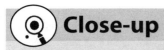 **Close-up**

Nashville Cowboy Church

The Nashville Cowboy Church (2416 Music Valley Drive, 615-859-1001, www.nashville cowboychurch.org) is not something you would find just anywhere. A country band, T-shirts for sale, and a bit of an old-time revival-style atmosphere set this nondenominational church apart from the crowd.

Founding pastor Dr. Harry Yates arrives clad in jeans, cowboy boots and hat, and Western shirt. His wife, Joanne Cash Yates, is Johnny Cash's sister. The couple married, December 27, 1971, and were regular vocalists for *Grand Ole Gospel Time* on the *Grand Ole Opry* stage from 1971 to 1975. They toured internationally from 1975 until 1990. Concluding a musical tour in 1990, the Yates family returned to settle in Nashville.

Desiring to begin a church, the couple secured a bar on Sunday mornings to hold church services. From humble beginnings of only six people to a congregation of more than 500, the church is going strong. Joanne continues to headline the musical portion of the service, in addition to other local artists who appear weekly. Services are fast moving, with local songwriters often attending to sing their favorite gospel songs. Sunday-morning meetings take place at the Texas Troubadour Theater near Opryland and are broadcast on the radio (WSM and satellite radio). Sunday-night and Wednesday-night services are held at 410 Brick Church Pike in Goodlettsville. This is a Christian church that goes by the book—the Good Book, that is—in its beliefs. The mixed congregation of regulars and tourists passes a Stetson hat for donations at the upbeat, joyous services.

After the war, one of the important events in Nashville's religious history was the arrival of revivalist Sam Jones, who was invited by the city's clergy to preach here. One of his converts was Capt. Thomas Ryman, owner of 35 steamboats. Ryman built a venue that could accommodate the large crowds Jones drew. In 1892 the building, called the Union Gospel Tabernacle, was completed. It was eventually renamed the Ryman Auditorium and earned its place in history as the "Mother Church of Country Music," serving as home of the *Grand Ole Opry* for many years. (See our History and Music City chapters for more about that.)

In the early 1900s religious diversity increased, as new opinions and movements, such as Unitarianism and transcendentalism, found followers. The Darwinian theory of the latter half of the 1800s spawned the evolution-creation debate, and Tennessee was right in the thick of it. In 1923 thousands of Nashvillians cheered as political leader William Jennings Bryan bashed Darwin's theory of evolution in his speech "Is the Bible True?" Two years later Bryan was the prosecutor of Dayton, Tennessee, teacher John T. Scopes, who was under fire for talking about evolution in a classroom, an act that was prohibited by state law.

During the Great Depression of the 1930s, overall church membership throughout the state declined about 10 percent. Church of Christ memberships declined 31 percent, while that of Baptists and Methodists declined by 16 percent each. The Presbyterian Church actually gained 11 percent during this period.

In 1960 the civil rights movement provided the backdrop for an interesting story in Nashville's religious history.

During that year, a young African American named James Lawson was attending Vanderbilt Divinity School when sit-ins started taking place in protest of segregation. Before the sit-ins began, training sessions took place, and Lawson, who had studied principles of nonviolent demonstration with Mahatma Gandhi, was one of the trainers.

When Vanderbilt chancellor Harvie Branscomb learned of Lawson's involvement in the protests, Lawson was expelled. The Divinity School faculty then threatened to resign, and the board of trustees threatened to close the school. Professors from other schools at Vanderbilt also threatened to resign. Eventually, a compromise was reached, and the school stayed open. Lawson didn't graduate from Vandy, however. He was reinstated but took his degree from Boston University. Lawson, who had been one of the first African Americans to come to Vanderbilt, became a nationally known pacifist and promoter of reconciliation. Years later, the story took a triumphant twist: Ironically, in October 1996, Lawson, then 68, met with the 101-year-old former chancellor Branscomb, the man who had expelled him 36 years previously. The occasion? Lawson was presented Vanderbilt Divinity School's first Distinguished Alumnus Award—a dignified, if long-overdue, happy ending to a chapter in the city's race relations.

WELL ESTABLISHED AND GROWING

Today, Nashville's hundreds of houses of worship include about 270 Baptist, more than 90 Church of Christ, more than 60 Methodist, more than 40 Presbyterian, and about 18 Catholic churches. There are more than 40 interdenominational or nondenominational churches, as well as 5 Jewish and 4 Islamic houses of worship and a Hindu temple. And that's just for starters. Some churches have memberships in the thousands, while others are small groups comprising just a few people.

INDEX

ABOUT THE AUTHOR

An award-winning journalist, Jackie Sheckler Finch has covered a wide array of topics—from birth to death with all the joy and sorrow in between. She has written for many publications and has been named the Mark Twain Travel Writer of the Year by Midwest Travel Writers a record four times—in 1998, 2001, 2003, and 2007. She shares her home with her grandson, Logan Peters, and his dog, Pepper. One of her greatest joys is taking to the road to find the fascinating people and places that wait over the hill and around the next bend.